Auditing
Alan Millichamp & John Taylor
Eleventh Edition

United States

Auditing, 11th Edition
Alan Millichamp & John Taylor

Publisher: Annabel Ainscow

List Manager: Jenny Grene

Editorial Assistant: Lauren Cartridge

Content Project Manager: Sue Povey

Manufacturing Manager: Eyvett Davis

Marketing Manager: Sophie Clarke

Typesetter: SPi Global

Cover Designer: Cyan Design

Cover Image: Created by Kraphix
- Freepik.com

For product information and technology assistance, contact us at
emea.info@cengage.com

For permission to use material from this text or product and for permission queries, email **emea.permissions@cengage.com**

British Library Cataloguing-in-Publication Data

A catalogue record for this book is available from the British Library.

ISBN: 978-1-4737-4930-6

Cengage Learning EMEA
Cheriton House, North Way
Andover, Hampshire, SP10 5BE
United Kingdom

Cengage Learning is a leading provider of customized learning solutions with employees residing in nearly 40 different countries and sales in more than 125 countries around the world. Find your local representative at: **www.cengage.co.uk.**

Cengage Learning products are represented in Canada by Nelson Education, Ltd.

For your course and learning solutions, visit **www.cengage.co.uk.**

Purchase any of our products at your local college store or at our preferred online store **www.cengagebrain.com.**

Printed in China by RR Donnelley
Print Number 01   Print Year 2017

John R. Taylor
MSc, FCA

John Taylor has taught accounting and auditing at Leeds Beckett University and before this was a professional auditor for many years. He is the author of various successful auditing, accounting and finance books and currently works as a freelance writer and lecturer in auditing, accounting and management.

The late A H Millichamp
BA, MSocSc, FCA, FCCA, ATII

Alan Millichamp taught at the Universities of Wolverhampton and Birmingham, at the Open University Business School and in the private sector. He was a former examiner and assessor in auditing to the Association of Chartered Certified Accountants and was also a member of the examining panel of the ACCA.

BRIEF CONTENTS

CONTENTS

ACKNOWLEDGEMENTS

EXAMINATION QUESTIONS

We are grateful to the Association of Chartered Certified Accountants (ACCA) for permission to reproduce past examination questions. The suggested solutions in the exam answer bank have been prepared by us, unless otherwise stated.

The authors would also like to thank the Institute of Chartered Accountants in England and Wales (ICAEW).

REVIEWERS

Particular thanks are due to those reviewers who gave their thoughtful comments on the strengths and weaknesses of the previous editions and the proposals for the eleventh edition:

- Carol Masters, University of Southampton
- Sue Hardman, Brunel University London
- Dr Maria Mina Rosero, Edinburgh Napier University

IFRS STANDARDS

INTERNATIONAL FEDERATION OF ACCOUNTANTS (IFAC) STANDARDS

This text is an extract from the *Handbook of International Quality Control, Auditing, Review, Other Assurance, and Related Services Pronouncements 2016–2017 Edition* of the International Auditing and Assurance Standards Board, published by the International Federation of Accountants (IFAC) in December 2016 and is used with permission of IFAC. Such use of IFAC's copyrighted material in no way represents an endorsement or promotion by IFAC. Any views or opinions that may be included in *Auditing 11e* are solely those of Cengage EMEA and do not express the views and opinions of IFAC or any independent standard setting board associated with IFAC.

PREFACE – AIMS OF THE BOOK

The primary aim of this book is to provide a simplified but thorough approach to the understanding of auditing theory and practice. It is intended for those with little or no knowledge of the subject, however, some knowledge of financial accounting, company law and information technology would be an advantage.

Students who will find this book useful will include those studying Auditing as part of an accounting or business course in a University or HE College as well as students studying for the professional examinations of the accountancy bodies such as the ACCA or the Institutes of Chartered Accountants.

This book will provide the student with a clear and succinct exposition of the subject and will, hopefully, be sufficiently interesting to encourage even the least conscientious student to proceed in easily digestible stages!

STRUCTURE OF THE BOOK

The book has been designed with several uses in mind:

- as a textbook, on its own, for specific examinations
- for use with a lecture
- as a revision text for those who are taking or retaking examinations

The case studies, student self-testing questions and exam questions are particularly useful for those taking exams.

At the end of each chapter is found:

- Summary of the chapter.
- Points to note. These are used for emphasis and clarification of points which students often misunderstand.
- Short case studies. The objective of the case studies is to illuminate the material in the chapter. Readers may find it helpful to ponder on the case study while reading the chapter.
- Questions. These are a mixture of:
  - short questions to test comprehension and learning of the material of the chapter and as an aide-memoire;
  - exercises; and
  - examination standard questions where appropriate.

In addition, the case studies can be seen as questions. Answers to the exam questions are available on the digital support resources for the book.

DIGITAL SUPPORT RESOURCES

The digital support resources contain:

- Additional questions and case studies.
- Answers to the exam questions and some discussion on the case studies.
- Mock exam questions and answers.

NOTES TO THE 11TH EDITION

The eleventh edition now takes account of:

- The revised International Auditing Standards issued by the Financial Reporting Council and applying to all audits on or after 17 June 2016. The text also includes up-to-date references to other official pronouncements, practice notes, bulletins and other practice statements extant at the time of writing.
- The relevant Financial Reporting Standards and other accounting standards issued by the Financial Reporting Council.

In addition, the opportunity has been taken to revise the text, rewrite some chapters completely and introduce new material. The final chapter considers current issues which the audit profession is currently debating and which are likely to have a significant impact on auditing practice in the future.

The test questions have also been updated and revised.

Words or phrases in **bold type** have been highlighted because their meaning has been included in the Glossary at the back of the book.

CHAPTER ORDER

The chapter order follows a logical sequence. The chapters are self-contained and can be read in any order, although some chapters do take account of what has gone before. If this is the case previous chapters have been referred to in the text.

HOW TO PASS AUDITING EXAMINATIONS

Many students have difficulty in passing auditing exams. Often this is simply due to a lack of preparation, but it can also be due to a lack of exam technique. We have begun the book with suggestions on how to pass auditing exams. This has been written from our experience as teachers and examiners in auditing. We hope it will be helpful!

There is no simple formula for success. If there was then everybody would be successful! However, there are many ways in which you can increase your chances of success.

These include:

- *Being well prepared*-there is no real substitute for hard work and application. However, reading is not enough. You must practice exam questions. At the end of each chapter there are student self-testing questions, exam questions and the case studies. The best way to learn is to write out answers to these in full. It is only by being faced with having to write things down, that you discover the gaps in your knowledge and understanding.
- *Knowing the syllabus and what you should know*-guidance on this is obtained by reading the relevant course content syllabus and any other information available from the examiners. This book is intended to be comprehensive so there may be aspects of it which will not be included in the syllabus for a particular course. It is as helpful to know what you do not need to study as it is what you do.

- *Time in the exam room*-the time in the exam room should be used efficiently and profitably. Specific points here are:
  - Answer all the questions that you are asked to answer. Given a choice, never spend time finishing a question when there is still a question unanswered. The first few marks on a question are always easy but the last few are always hard to earn.
  - Give proper weight to each question and part of a question. There is no point in filling two sides of A4 on a part of a question which earns you 2 marks. Similarly writing two lines on a 20 mark question is clearly not enough. It is a good idea to consider how much time you can allocate to each task. For example, in a three-hour, 100 mark exam, you should not spend any more than *nine* minutes per *five* marks so a 25 mark question requires you to think and write for 45 minutes. That will provide you with some indication of the size and detail of the answers required. Anyone who finishes the examination in under two hours has probably failed it!
  - Never omit parts of a question. Even if you do not know the answer, guess and write something-you never know it may get you a mark or two!

Reading through the paper

Many students have a moment of panic when they first see the paper. This will pass when you realize how easy the paper really is! Most students read through all the questions briefly first, concentrating on the requirements of each question. As you do this note down any thoughts that occur to you as soon as you can, otherwise, if you find yourself under time pressure, you may spend fruitless time trying to remember a fact you had remembered but have now forgotten.

Tackling a question

Here are some general points:

- *Plan the answer briefly.*
- *Answer the question asked*. This is a vital point. It is no good answering the question you would have preferred. Many examiners report that weak candidates simply write down everything they know about a topic rather than *relating what they know to the question being asked.* You do not get any marks for irrelevant detail. This means reading the question carefully and noting exactly what is required. A good way of doing this is to underline significant words in the question.
- *Don't waffle*. Questions are not marked by weight, so droning on with irrelevant detail will not get you any marks even if it fills up the page.
- *Make points*. This is the most important thing of all. Some questions say '*List four procedures . . .*'. Obviously four points are wanted. Some say '*State the audit tests that you . . .*'. What is wanted in such questions is as many tests as you can think of. It does not want long descriptions of two tests or a general answer. Relate the requirements of the answer to the marking scheme-if the question asks for four key points and the value of that answer is 12 points it does not take a genius to work out that each point is worth three marks so requires some detail but not pages.
- *Use all the data given in the question*. Many auditing questions have long scenarios before the requirement. This information is not just for idle reading. The examiner expects you to use it in your answer. It probably contains lots of clues to the answer required.
- *Auditing examiners expect intelligent answers*. Try to see the implications in a question. For example, a question about audit risk may want a general answer, and if so that is what it will ask for. Specific points about particular audit risks in the particular case will be in the scenario and these are what the examiner is looking for so don't waffle on about matters which are not included in the scenario.
- *Keep the answers as short and succinct as possible*. When you have made a point using one sentence consider whether you really need more sentences. Write legibly and use short sentences and paragraphs. Tabulating and listing is usually acceptable, using bullet points, and this helps the marker see what you have said.
- *Label each part of your answer*. If a question has four parts, a, b, etc., make sure each part is clearly labelled as such.

- *Explain your terms*. Suppose you are faced with a question like '*Explain why external auditors seek to rely on the proper operation of internal controls wherever possible.*' First, briefly define 'external auditor' and 'internal controls'. You may get marks for it but in any case it will give you clues to how to answer it.
- *Apply lateral thinking*. In the internal controls example think about what an external auditor is trying to do or the context in which internal controls are designed or what they are designed to prevent or ensure-don't just drone on about what internal controls are and why they are really really important-relate it to the work the auditors do and explain why internal controls are relevant to that work.

How to answer a question

It all depends on the question but here are some general ideas:

- Read the question.
- Read it again.
- Underline important words in the question.
- Make sure you know *exactly* what the examiner requires you to do.
- Note down the points you want to make, add to these points others as you think of them even while writing the answer out.
- Stop and think for a moment.
- Draft an outline plan of your answer with the key points.
- Write your answer referring back continually to the requirements of the question. Take plenty of room, use short sentences and paragraphs. Number your points if you think it appropriate.

Tackling a question-specific ideas

With many questions, you may be faced with making points but not being able to think of many. Here are a few ideas which may trigger points you can make:

- What Auditing Standards are involved?
- What Accounting Standards are involved?
- What Companies Act accounting or auditing requirements are involved?
- Is business or audit risk relevant?
- Does the question have any relevance for the letter of engagement?
- Does the question have any relevance for the auditor's report?
- What assertions about a figure in the financial statements are implied?
- Does the question have any relevance to the idea of misstatements in the financial statements?
- Is materiality worth mentioning?
- Do ethics have any relevance?
- What types of audit tests may be applied?
- What working papers may be needed?
- What errors or frauds could occur?
- Is going concern an issue?
- Is internal audit involved?

Reviewing your answer

Some students like to finish early and then proof read their answer. This is unlikely to add many marks unless:

- you think of new points or
- realize you haven't answered the question properly

mainly because you have probably put down everything you know already.

Polishing the grammar, spelling and punctuation is very unlikely to add many marks to your score and can waste time. If you finish very early either you are extremely able or you've not answered all the questions properly.

Many examinations are deliberately designed to put candidates under time pressure.

Common faults in auditing answers

Here are some common faults:

- Not obeying the questioner's requirements.

    If it says *set out, list, tabulate, to what extent, examine the truth of, state, state concisely, what are the principal matters, discuss, comment on, describe, write a short essay,* then do what it says!

- Not reading the question carefully.

    For example, students on being asked to audit a partnership will refer to company-based information such as the Memorandum and Articles.

- Not making enough points.

    This is very hard to overcome but one good technique is to try to break the question down into sections and list specific points relevant to each part of the question.

- Not being specific.

    An audit test stating '*check sample transactions in the cash book*' will not often do; '*check a sample of the entries in the cash book with available supporting documents such as . . .*' might do.

- Being irrelevant.

    Tied up with not obeying instructions and not reading the question carefully.

- Lack of planning, coherence and logic.

    Planning an answer should cure this.

- Lack of balance.

    If the examiner asks for five points they do not want four pages on point one and one line each on the others.

- Handwriting, grammar, spelling, punctuation.

    Do not waste your time and opportunities by presenting your work badly or with avoidable errors.

- Confusing the role of auditor with that of accountant, tax consultant, etc.

    If asked what the auditor should do in certain circumstances, never say, for example, 'Alter the accounts' because producing accounts is not the auditor's function. Neither should you advise an action which would save your client tax; you must say what you would do as *auditor*.

Layout and wording of answer

- Use the wording of the question wherever you can.
- Answer the question in the sequence requested.
- Obey instructions on layout, e.g. tabulate.
- State any assumptions you make in answering the question. However, do not make assumptions which change the question to suit your knowledge.

End of exam procedure

- Have a very quick look at each answer, checking for repetitions, irrelevancies, grammatical errors and badly formed letters. Add any new points if you can think of them.
- Ensure each answer sheet has your number on it. Do not leave anything lying on the table.

Conclusion

Good technique plays a large part in examination success; this is a fact. Refuse to be panicked, keep your head, and with reasonable preparation you should make it.

Finally-remember-you don't have to score 100 per cent to pass.

USEFUL ABBREVIATIONS

Auditors, like most professionals, use a lot of abbreviations as a kind of shorthand. Here is a list of the most common abbreviations-there are others but these are the ones you may come across most frequently. We refer to these in the text and explain them fully and, for quick reference, further details of many of them are contained in the Glossary at the end of the book.

ACCA-Association of Chartered Certified Accountants
AGM-Annual General Meeting
CA 2006-Companies Act, 2006
FRC-Financial Reporting Council
FSA-Financial Services Authority
GAAP-Generally Accepted Accounting Practice
HMRC-HM Revenue & Customs
IAASB-International Auditing and Assurance Standards Board
IAS-International Accounting Standard
ICAEW-Institute of Chartered Accountants in England & Wales
IFAC-International Federation of Accountants
ISA-International Standard on Auditing
NED-Non-executive director

LIST OF USEFUL WEBSITES

Details of sources and additional reading are set out at the end of each chapter. However, there are some websites which contain lots of useful information and technical updates. Here is a list of the most useful and ones which can be referred to for technical updates and research:

www.accaglobal.com
www.accountancyage.com
www.accountancymagazine.com
www.econimia,icaew.com
www.frc.org.uk/apb
www.ft.com
www.icaew.com
www.icaew.com/en/technical/audit-and-assurance
www.ifac.org
www.ifac.org/iaasb
www.iia.org,uk
www.legislation.gov.uk/ukpga/2006
www.soca.gov.uk

 CENGAGE

Teaching & Learning Support Resources

Cengage's peer reviewed content for higher and further education courses is accompanied by a range of digital teaching and learning support resources. The resources are carefully tailored to the specific needs of the instructor, student and the course. Examples of the kind of resources provided include:

- A password protected area for instructors with, for example, a testbank, PowerPoint slides and an instructor's manual.

- An open-access area for students including, for example, useful weblinks and glossary terms.

Lecturers: to discover the dedicated lecturer digital support resources accompanying this textbook please register here for access: login.cengage.com.

Students: to discover the dedicated student digital support resources accompanying this textbook, please search for **Auditing** on: cengagebrain.co.uk.

BE UNSTOPPABLE

 Learn more at cengage.co.uk/education

CHAPTER 1
INTRODUCTION TO AUDITING – THE WHY OF AUDITING

Learning Objectives

After studying the material in this chapter you should be able to:

- understand the difference between ownership and control

- understand the principles of agency theory

- understand why auditing plays a key role in equalizing the information imbalance between directors and shareholders

- understand the advantages and disadvantages of having an audit

- explain the conceptual frameworks of auditing theory

- understand what is meant by the 'expectation gap'

INTRODUCTION

In this chapter we will introduce the basic concepts and theories on which the profession of auditing is based. We will look at some of them in more detail in later chapters but for now we will concentrate on an overview of the auditing profession, what governs it and why it is needed.

One of the most far-reaching consequences of the Industrial Revolution was the introduction of the limited liability company. The first such was registered at Companies House in 1856 and this, in essence, signalled the final, formal, split between ownership and control. Whilst the modern company can be said to have come into being in 1856, the audit profession came somewhat later as it was not until the Companies Act 1900 that an obligation to produce annual accounts was placed on the directors of companies.

Once the corporation had finally developed as a legal entity in its own right, resulting in the mass ownership of shares becoming firmly separated from the management and control of the organization's activities on a day-to-day basis, the stage was set for the role of the auditor as arbitrator and judge.

To understand the position of the auditor more fully it is important to appreciate the distinction between owners and managers and the difference between them in terms of their approach to the company and the rewards of ownership and control.

This is set out in a model which has come to be known as **Agency Theory**.

AGENCY THEORY

Agency is the name given to the practice by which productive resources owned by one person or group are managed by another person or group of persons. In this case the agents are the directors or managers of the company and the principals are the shareholders or owners of the company.

The problem of owners delegating their interests to an agent or manager had been pondered as early as the eighteenth century by Adam Smith in his book *The Wealth of Nations*:

'The directors of [joint-stock] companies, however, being the managers rather of other people's money than of their own, it cannot well be expected, that they should watch over it with the same anxious vigilance with which the partners in a private co-partner frequently watch over their own. Like the stewards of a rich man, they are apt to consider attention to small matters as not for their master's honour, and very easily give themselves a dispensation from having it. Negligence and profusion, therefore, must always prevail, more or less, in the management of the affairs of such a company.'

There had been academic writings on Agency Theory in the early 1970s in different social contexts but the classic paper on Agency Theory, for those academically inclined, was that of Jensen and Meckling in 1976 in a paper called *'Theory of the Firm: Managerial Behaviour, Agency Costs and Ownership Structure.'*

In that paper they looked at agency theory and the costs of agency and stated:

'We define an agency relationship as a contract under which one or more persons (the principal(s)) engage another person (the agent) to perform some service on their behalf which involves delegating some decision making authority to the agent. If both parties to the relationship are utility maximizers there is good reason to believe that the agent will not always act in the best interests of the principal. The principal can limit divergences from his interest by establishing appropriate incentives for the agent and by incurring monitoring costs designed to limit the aberrant activities, of the agent. In addition, in some situations it will pay the agent to expend resources (bonding costs) to guarantee that he will not take certain actions which would harm the principal or to ensure that the principal will be compensated if he does take such actions. However, it is generally impossible for the principal or the agent at zero cost to ensure that the agent will make optimal decisions from the principal's viewpoint.'

This paper helped move academic writing on organizational theory away from the idea of managerial capitalism and the theories that the firm always sought to maximize value to a recognition that shareholders are the principal stakeholders with managers as their agents, and that the principal concern of these agents was empire building with a general disregard for shareholder interest – what Jensen, in 1989, called *'the systematic fleecing of shareholders and bondholders'*. Since then there have been innumerable papers written expanding on the original work and extending it to other fields of human endeavour, but we will leave it to individual students to track these down and study what are, after all, variants on this original theme and speculations as to the causes of the behaviour of agents, none of which are directly relevant to auditing.

So, at its simplest, Agency Theory is the recognition that the inclination of agents is to act rather more in their own interests than those of their employers. What this means to us in practice is that Agency Theory recognizes the tendency of company managers, or directors, to make decisions which are more favourable to their own objectives than to those of their principals, the owners or shareholders, of the business.

Agency theory is a relatively simple principle to grasp but its ramifications are extensive and it has important implications for how organizations conduct themselves and for their operational culture. It also has importance for auditors, as we shall see.

The differing objectives can be summarized in Figure 1.1.

FIGURE 1.1 **Agency theory**

Party	Objective
Principal	• Safe investment • Regular dividends • Long term capital growth • Maintenance of value
Agent	• Salary and benefits • Maximum bonus • Share options • Personal success of successful business measured by share price

The Institute of Chartered Accountants in England & Wales put it this way:

'In principle the agency model assumes that no agents are trustworthy and if they can make themselves richer at the expense of their principals they will. The poor principal, so the argument goes, has no alternative but to compensate the agent well for their endeavours so that they will not be tempted to go into business for themselves using the principal's assets to do so.

The origin of auditing goes back to times scarcely less remote than that of accounting . . . Whenever the advance of civilization brought about the necessity of one man being entrusted to some extent with the property of another the advisability of some kind of check upon the fidelity of the former would become apparent. 'Reference ICAEW (2005)'

Clearly this is not universally true, but the extent to which principals don't trust their agents will tend to determine the level of the monitoring mechanisms created for the overview of agents' activities and the extent to which agents' compensation levels are determined to be acceptable. This is where auditing comes in.

In both the UK and the USA, the growth in share ownership has been a trend towards both institutional ownership of large blocks of shares and widely dispersed ownership by large numbers of individual shareholders, which has been called *ownership without power*. Institutions which hold shares as investments are coming under increasing pressure to adopt some of the rights of ownership, particularly in curbing what has been seen, in some cases, as excessive remuneration voted to directors.

This has reinforced calls for improved transparency in reporting to correct the imbalance in financial reporting – directors have lots of information, shareholders relatively little – which will, in the longer term, enable shareholders to assume more of the responsibilities of ownership and make boards of directors more accountable.

Upon this principle rests the foundation of not only the auditing profession, but ultimately, in the latter part of the twentieth century and the early part of the twenty-first, the establishment of modern corporate governance which we will look at in Chapter 2.

The role of the auditor becomes increasingly significant when standards of corporate morality are, or are seen to be, declining. Corporate scandals in the USA and Europe in recent years involving misrepresentation of financial information, corruption and theft on a huge scale and the banking crisis of 2007/8 have increased the demand from both investors and regulators for auditors to be more efficient and more demanding of their clients. Auditors, it is suggested, should be more insistent on their client's adherence to ethical principles and improved standards of governance.

We look at this later but students should be aware from the beginning that the influence of globalization and the increasing power of corporations are placing increasing demands on the auditing profession.

WHY IS THERE A NEED FOR AN AUDIT?

As mentioned above, the problem which emerged when owners began delegating the running of an entity in which they had invested to managers, and thus sacrificed their involvement in the day-to-day control of the organization, is whether or not they could fully trust the financial report prepared by their managers?

As time went on, and organizations grew larger, the management became increasingly more powerful with the result that nowadays when managers control huge multinational corporations, they have a direct effect on the ordinary lives of thousands of individuals through their economic decisions. They can relocate or close down factories, change working conditions and terms, decide where to pay tax through transfer pricing agreements – they have a huge amount of power (Figure 1.2).

FIGURE 1.2   The Modern Corporation—Berle and Means

Adolf Berle and Gardiner Means published their seminal work *The Modern Corporation and Private Property* in 1939. In it they stated that, as corporations grew, the financing requirements made it increasingly difficult for individuals to maintain majority shareholdings so shareholding became divided and fragmented among larger and larger numbers of individuals and other investing bodies.

As shareholding became more diverse and diffuse the one constant in the company was the management and *de facto* power thereby devolved upon them.

As companies grew in size and power a relatively large amount of total corporate wealth became concentrated into relatively few huge corporations. Managers in these corporations were able to disburse company resources in the way that primarily suited them, such as through reinvestment or even enhanced pay, rather than as dividends.

These companies had an impact on society as they were able to open or close factories and branches thus influencing the lives of millions of people without any real form of democratic accountability.

Reference: Berle and Means (1932)

Even in the modern era, despite the developments and expansion of disclosure in the financial statements and the growth of accounting standards, practical access to detailed financial information by shareholders remains limited. Shareholders, or potential shareholders, may come to believe that they are not getting all the information, or the right information to enable them to make investment decisions. Financial analysts working for major institutional investors may have rather more access to the directors of major corporations than the small investor, but even they have made mistakes and many of them have still lost their employers' money despite their abilities and the access to information granted to them.

Consequently, the role of the auditor, as agent for the shareholder, becomes crucial and the costs of the audit are nothing compared with the comfort and reassurance the audit affords the shareholders. The auditor's report on the financial statements also becomes crucial to the managers of the business as a favourable opinion from the independent auditor confirms their actions and reinforces their credibility and reputation as agents for the shareholders.

Owners who appoint managers to look after their property will be concerned to know what has happened to it. In the case of companies, reporting and accounting for their actions is by means of the annual financial statements which the managers must prepare, and it is through these that, ultimately, the owners of the business monitor the activities of their agents. The independent audit is a crucial part of this process to ensure that the financial statements faithfully represent the activities of the managers during the financial period.

Parties to financial statements

Historically, annual reports and accounts of companies were produced by the directors (as managers) to the shareholders (as owners), and other people were not expected to be interested in them. However, today, a much wider range of people are interested in the annual report and accounts of companies and other organizations.

The following people or groups of people are likely to want to see and use financial statements. These are often described as **stakeholders** and comprise actual or potential:

- owners or shareholders
- lenders or debenture holders
- employees
- customers
- suppliers
- people who advise the above – e.g. accountants, stockbrokers, credit rating agencies, financial journalists, trade unions and financial analysts
- competitors and people interested in mergers, amalgamations and takeovers
- the government, including the tax authorities and government bodies concerned with consumer protection and the control and regulation of business
- the public, including those who are interested in consumer protection, environmental protection, political and other pressure groups
- regulatory organizations, for example those set up under the Financial Services and Markets Act 2000, principally the Financial Services Authority (**FSA**)

All these individuals or bodies must be sure that the financial statements can be relied upon.

What's in the Financial Statements?

Financial statements can take many forms. The best known are the **Statement of Comprehensive Income** (formerly the Profit & Loss Account) and **Statement of Financial Position** (Balance Sheet) of the business. In the specific case of limited companies, financial statements are produced annually and take the form of an Annual Report and Accounts which includes a Statement of Comprehensive Income and Statement of Financial Position and also other statements including the Directors' Report, a cash flow statement and ancillary reports.

The financial statements may:

- contain errors
- not disclose fraud
- be inadvertently misleading
- be deliberately misleading
- fail to disclose relevant information
- fail to conform to regulations

Further, owners of companies must be protected from unscrupulous management who would use the owner's investment for their own benefit and not that of the owner.

Potential investors must guard against investing in abuse of limited liability where companies are deliberately set up for speculative or high-risk ventures. In this case the initial investors have very little to lose, and the managers perhaps nothing at all apart from their employment. If later investors are not aware of company activity they could be induced to invest in a project which carries a much greater level of risk than the rewards they might achieve would warrant.

The solution to this problem of credibility in reports and accounts lies in appointing independent professionals to investigate the report and feedback on their findings. An audit helps to reduce these so-called agency costs as it helps to protect investors from the actions of predatory managers.

THE AUDIT PROCESS

The audit process is described in Figure 1.3. If the process continues down the YES route the financial statements will ultimately represent a true and fair view of the company's financial position.

If, at any point, the processes fail – indicated by a NO response – errors and misstatements will creep in and result in the financial statements becoming incorrect.

FIGURE 1.3 The Financial Audit Process

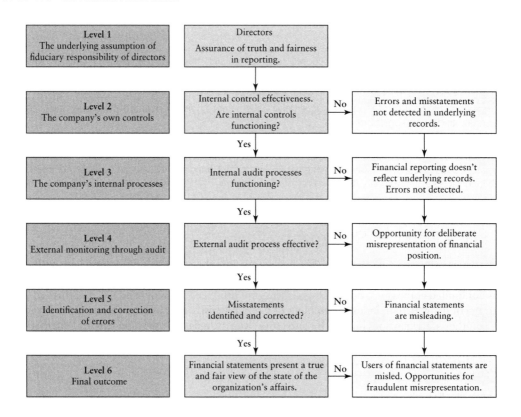

INTERNATIONAL PRESSURES AND GLOBALIZATION

Companies or groups can be very large with multinational activities and comprising many subsidiaries and related activities. The preparation of the accounts of such entities is a very complex operation perhaps involving the bringing together and summarizing of accounts of subsidiaries with differing conventions, legal systems and accounting and control systems. The examination of such accounts by independent experts trained in the assessment of financial information is of benefit to those who control and operate such organizations as well as to owners and outsiders.

The existence of a strong auditing profession is important to global markets because reliable financial reporting promotes confidence and stability in the market. Markets need the confidence and the assurance a strong audit function can bring in order to enable participants in the market, including the entities themselves, investors and potential investors, to make informed decisions.

This involves reducing risk to potential investors by providing them with 'sound' information.

Corporate failures, particularly those involving fraud by senior management, reduce confidence and create instability. They also tend to encourage increased regulation which may restrict market operations or encourage further deception.

The concepts of agency highlighted above require an auditing profession which is able to enforce standards of accountability on company managers through the mechanism of the Auditor's Report (Chapter 26).

We look at this in more detail in Chapter 28 where we look at the audit of group accounts. Students should, however, be aware that the developments in technology which have made possible increasing global trading and the expansion of capital markets have resulted in regulators requiring an improved standard of information, in terms of accuracy and timeliness, in order to protect investors. This applies particularly to banks.

It is being recognized that greater accountability and control is needed over corporate executives running companies which may have revenues considerably greater than some countries; consequently, particularly in the West, increased Corporate Governance requirements have led to increased accountability and disclosure (Chapter 2).

As we will see in Chapter 2, there is a conflict between the USA's rules-based approach to control audit firms, based on the Sarbanes–Oxley legislation, and the UK and other countries which have adopted a non-legal audit framework based on self-regulation. This has caused problems where the US jurisdiction and compliance requirements clash with non-statutory approaches to audit regulation.

The regulatory demands for lots of additional information in the financial statements and the rise of global companies has driven the requirement for auditors to increasingly use technology and develop new approaches to the audit of large, multinational businesses.

There are problems faced by auditors and accountants in producing consolidated financial information for groups of companies in common ownership in compliance with an appropriate accounting framework where financial information from international subsidiary companies may be prepared under a range of differing standards of quality and disclosure (Chapter 28). This has always been difficult but increased global trading means that audit firms have experienced an increase in the range and significance of group subsidiary companies trading in low-cost economies where standards of corporate governance are low and which produce information that has not been prepared under recognized accounting or auditing standards.

The International Federation of Accountants (IFAC) has gone a long way towards developing standards in both accounting and auditing which are being adopted across the world. This harmonization of approach is gradually reducing information asymmetry between regions.

The growth of internet-based online trading has challenged conventional audit approaches. Companies may trade globally and, apart from huge technical problems in auditing computer-based entities (Chapter 17), it may be difficult to establish which legal jurisdiction applies to such businesses and which set of standards and rules applies to them.

Audit firms are being increasingly required to carry out assurance type assignments (Chapter 31). These require a lower standard of evidence than an audit. There are moves among international regulators to separate the audit function from other types of audit work in order to reduce the inherent conflict of interest this creates in audit firms – i.e. that of acting both as auditor and advisor.

As the size of multinational companies increases, and their sphere of operations expands around the globe, the audit profession has seen the development of auditing mega-firms who, they claim, are the only firms which have the resources to audit modern corporate behemoths. The audit profession is thus dominated by the 'Big 4' (PricewaterhouseCoopers, KPMG, Ernst & Young and Deloitte). Smaller firms, with a lower level of global reach, and those which have developed international networks claim that this reduces competition in the audit market for the biggest clients. Conversely the 'Big 4' claim that they compete ferociously between themselves so market competition is limited but undiminished.

We look at all of these points in more detail in the relevant chapters.

OBJECTIVES OF AUDITING

An audit has to be carried out in accordance with a set of standards issued by the Financial Reporting Council, which is the regulator for the auditing and accounting profession. These are known as International Standards on Auditing and we will look at these in more detail in Chapter 5. Essentially they are the rules of auditing.

In one of its **International Standards on Auditing** (ISAs) (Chapter 5) namely ISA 200: '*Overall objectives of the independent auditor and the conduct of an audit in accordance with international standards on auditing*' the **Financial Reporting Council (FRC)**, which is the regulatory body responsible for issuing auditing standards and guidelines in the UK and Ireland, states:

> '*The purpose of an audit is to enhance the degree of confidence of intended users in the financial statements. This is achieved by the expression of an opinion by the auditor on whether the financial statements are prepared, in all material respects, in accordance with an applicable financial reporting framework.*
>
> *In the case of most general purpose frameworks, that opinion is on whether the financial statements are presented fairly, in all material respects, or give a true and fair view in accordance with the framework.*'

Here are some definitions and fundamental concepts that you need to know:

- In the UK the financial reporting framework is the Companies Act 2006 together with all the associated accounting standards, etc. which comprise **UK Generally Accepted Accounting Practice (UK GAAP)**.
- '**Entity**' is a general term embracing all types of business, enterprise or undertaking including companies, charities, local authorities, government agencies, etc. Some are profit oriented and some are not.
- 'Presented fairly' instead of 'true and fair' applies mainly to public sector bodies such as local authorities. In the commercial world, and for the purpose of this book, we will generally take the view that the auditor's report will use the words 'true and fair'.
- It is important to understand that responsibility for the *preparation* of the financial statements and the presentation of the information included therein rests with the *management* of the enterprise (in the case of a company, the directors). The auditor's responsibility is to *report* on the financial statements as presented by management.
- In the UK financial statements must conform to statutory or other requirements. All company accounts have to conform to the requirements of the Companies Act 2006 but many other bodies (e.g. charities, building societies, financial services businesses, etc.) also have detailed accounting requirements. In addition, all accounts should conform to the requirements of Financial Reporting Standards. We do not cover the various financial reporting standards in this book in detail except where they are relevant to the audit, for example in the valuation of inventories or the provisions relating to the treatment of research and development expenditure. Students should make themselves aware of the relevant financial reporting requirements.

In addition to carrying out the audit, accountancy firms also assist their clients with accounting and financial reporting systems, taxation, financial risk management, takeovers and mergers and even advice on such matters as recruitment and environmental issues. This type of consultancy activity can, however, give rise to ethical conflicts and we will discuss this further in Chapter 6.

DIRECTORS' RESPONSIBILITIES

It is the directors who are responsible for producing 'true and fair' accounts; the auditors simply express their opinion on them. The directors are the individuals who, collectively, have to struggle with presenting an accounting of their dealings with the shareholders' assets in as balanced and impartial a way as possible. It is their task to explain themselves in a way which can be understood and which represents what actually happened in the financial period.

Remember that the directors (as managers) are accounting to the shareholders (the owners of the business) for their actions during the financial year.

As with many seemingly simple tasks this can be quite complicated, hence the plethora of accounting standards, bulletins and guidelines!

AUDITOR RESPONSIBILITIES

The auditors should be an independent firm appointed to carry out what is, effectively, an investigation of the organization, its records and the financial statements for which the directors are responsible. The auditors must gather sufficient reliable evidence so to form an opinion on the financial statements as to whether or not they are free from significant error or misstatement and thus represent fairly (or not) what has transpired during the financial period.

Under ISA 200, referred to above, the audit objective is not simply the expression of an opinion on a set of financial statements. What ISA 200 requires is that the auditor's report is designed to enhance the confidence of a reader of the report and this requires more than a simple expression of opinion. In fact, what ISA 200 goes on to say is that the auditor must achieve the objectives of *all* the relevant ISAs. Failure to achieve the objectives of any of the auditing standards may mean that the auditor has failed to achieve their overall objective, which could have ramifications for their auditor's report.

The problems the auditors face are different from those of the directors. Their problems lie outside the area of simple bookkeeping and arise when the financial statements incorporate judgements, estimates and opinions.

For example, the accounts might contain an estimate – made by the directors to the best of their ability – of the potential loss on a contract – but is it:

- too much?
- too little?
- or shouldn't be there at all?

The auditors have to decide what they think, based on the evidence they can gather.

It is straightforward enough for a company to ensure that all the transactions in the books are properly processed (and, as we will see later in this book, there is an audit approach which doesn't even bother checking that this is so), but how do the auditors know that:

- all the transactions that should be included have been included; and
- that all the transactions that are included are bona fide ones and not transactions invented by the directors to make the results look good?

They have to check the underlying financial records, together with all the adjustments the directors have made, such as provisions and accruals, and form their opinion.

So, because the auditors are expressing an opinion, they use a term of art – *'true and fair'*. This carries with it implications of honesty, integrity, impartiality and objectivity in the telling of a story, which is what the accounts do, in as understandable a way as possible for the benefit of the people who, after all, own the business or have a significant vested interest in it.

In practical terms, and taking into consideration both the requirements of ISA 200 and the relevant provisions of the Companies Act 2006, the primary and secondary tasks of the auditors are as follows.

Primary

The primary audit objective is to gather sufficient reliable evidence so as to be able to express an opinion, in the form of a report to the shareholders, of the truth and fairness of a set of financial statements prepared by the directors so that any person reading and using them can have confidence in them.

Secondary

In addition to expressing an opinion on the financial statements the auditors also have to report:

- that the financial statements are in accordance with the underlying financial records
- that they comply with the relevant financial reporting framework
- that all information and explanations they require have been made available to them

In addition, they may also advise management of any defects or problems with the controls within their accounting systems and suggest ways of improving them.

TYPES OF ASSIGNMENT

There are three types of reporting assignment that accountants carry out, of which an audit is the most common. These are:

Statutory audits

These are audits carried out because the law requires them. Statutes which require audits to be done include the Companies Act 2006 and the Financial Services and Markets Act 2000.

Internal audits

Internal audits are conducted by employees of a business or by external auditors acting as subcontractors. They are becoming increasingly important because of the development of Corporate Governance (Chapter 2). These differ from statutory audits because the priorities are set by the management who, to some extent, control the work of internal auditors.

Other assurance assignments

These are enquiries into specific aspects of an enterprise – management, value for money, environmental matters, etc. In recent years auditors have become involved with areas which take them away from their role as reporters on financial results. Two of the areas of emerging significance are Value for Money auditing and audits relating to Environmental and Social matters. We will discuss these further in Chapter 31.

In addition, auditors are asked to carry out specific 'one-off' assignments such as:

- reporting on a prospectus for a share issue
- carrying out a fraud investigation
- reviewing systems and procedures

We will look at these in Chapter 30.

This book is principally about the statutory audit, but we will look specifically at internal auditing in Chapter 19 and we will also review the auditor's duties with regard to assurance assignments other than the statutory audit in later chapters.

ADVANTAGES AND DISADVANTAGES OF AN AUDIT

Whilst companies that are required by statute to have an audit (Chapter 3) will naturally do so, smaller companies and organizations below the **statutory audit threshold** do not need to have one, but, in practice many do. Why is this?

There are advantages and disadvantages for organizations in having an audit of their financial statements. The main advantages are:

- The provider of finance, e.g. a bank usually requires audited accounts. If they were to ask for their own independent audits this might increase costs to the entity.
- Audits can help protect creditors, which is important because of limited liability, i.e. owner/managers of failing companies could simply abandon the business, and their investment, leaving it to collapse owing money to suppliers. Whilst this undoubtedly happens from time to time, an audit can reinforce financial discipline and act as an early warning for suppliers. Again, if no statutory audit is performed major suppliers might ask for their own independent audit.

- An audit helps establish the credibility of the company at a time when fraudsters are committing so-called 'long-firm' frauds – i.e. building up trust over a period of time and then disappearing with a substantial amount of money or goods having created a false picture of the activities of the company.
- There may be shareholders who are not involved in the business and their interests need to be protected by an independent audit.
- It provides reassurance for directors that the figures they are using are reliable.
- It improves credibility of the profits or losses with **HMRC** and assists in settling tax and **VAT** liabilities.

However, there are disadvantages:

- There is an argument that an audit is only for compliance and doesn't assist management in running the business – it is simply 'red tape'.
- The costs of the audit represent a non-productive expense and the money could be better used elsewhere.
- Banks and other lenders, including suppliers, can make their own conditions for lending and don't really need historical audited accounts. For example:
  - banks will lend on security and personal guarantees;
  - they will monitor performance of the bank accounts;
  - they may require regular monthly management information;
  - suppliers will deal on a pro-forma basis (i.e. cash before supply) until a depth of trust has been established.
- Historical accounts, taking advantage of limited disclosure requirements, are of little value as they can be up to nine months old when they become publicly available.

In reality all but the smallest companies generally feel that the audit process itself adds value and that it's not all about the financial statements. Examinations of the company's internal processes and procedures and considerations of risk are felt to be of benefit and outweigh the costs and temporary inconvenience involved.

AUDITING THEORY, POSTULATES AND CONCEPTS

As with most topics in business, auditing has been the subject of a good deal of academic discussion in an attempt to divine a 'theory of auditing' and to fit auditing into the context of the business world. These theories consider the social purpose of auditing and attempt to establish some fundamental theories or truths.

There are three basic academic writings which are considered fundamental to this area.

Theory of Rational Expectations

In 1932 Professor Theodore Limperg of the University of Amsterdam published a theory, known as the Theory of Inspired Confidence, which, eventually, became known as the **Theory of Rational Expectations**. The theory holds that the value of the auditor's report derives from the expert nature of the auditor as an independent, competent professional. The theory considered both the demand and the supply for audit services. It postulated that the demand for audit services is the direct consequence of the participation of third parties (interested parties of a company) in the company. These parties demand accountability from the management, in return for their investment in the company.

Accountability is achieved through the audited financial statements. However, since this information provided by the management may be biased, and outside parties have no direct means of monitoring, an audit is required to assure the reliability of this information. With regard to the supply of audit assurance, Limperg suggests that the auditor should always strive to meet the public expectations – this leads us on to the Expectation Gap – of which more later in this chapter.

Broadly, this is a dynamic theory which holds that as the business community changes so the expectations it has of the auditor's function also changes.

Limperg held that the work carried out by the auditor should be governed by the rational expectations of those who use their reports so auditors should not disappoint those expectations. Further, auditors should not seek to raise those expectations by any more than the work they do justifies.

Limperg's theory states that the usefulness of the auditor's opinion is based on the general understanding society has about the usefulness of audit. Legal considerations aside, the necessity and cost of an audit is borne by companies because of the need of investors and lenders for reliable information to aid their decision making. If the audit process changes so that it ceases to inspire a uniform level of confidence in society, but instead inspires different levels of confidence in different users, society's confidence in the audit process will decline as the social usefulness of the audit is diminished.

Limperg emphasized the social usefulness of auditors in meeting society's expectations for reliable financial information. The auditor must meet the expectations of the reasonably well informed layman but should not create any greater expectations than can be justified by the work carried out. The auditor thus has a wider responsibility to society and is not simply a watchdog for the shareholders.

Students would do well to consider this theory in the light of the criticisms of the auditing profession following the banking crises of 2007–8. As successive financial institutions, both in the UK and the USA, either crashed or had to be rescued by the government, serious questions were raised as to why auditors did not foresee the possibility of such a crash happening. It was pointed out that as auditors considered the various institutions' exposure to risk it would have been prudent to inform shareholders and investors of the risks the organizations they were invested in were running.

Questions were raised in the media as to the purpose and relevance of the audit process and whether the accounting profession was merely talking to itself and had no relevance in the modern world.

The fact that neither the management of these institutions nor the regulators had foreseen the crash tended to ameliorate some of this criticism, but the reputation of the audit profession suffered a blow which had a profound effect on it.

The Philosophy of Auditing

The key text in this particular field is probably that of R. K. Mautz and H. A. Sharaf who in 1961 published a monograph called *The Philosophy of Auditing* in the USA. This was the beginning of attempts to codify a coherent theory of auditing and included discussion on the philosophy of auditing, methodology and auditing **postulates** or assumptions. They attempted to create order out of a somewhat chaotic mix of practices and ideas.

They held that auditing is based on scientific logic where the auditing process is a rational process of examination, observation and evaluation of evidence. A full discussion of these ideas is not appropriate for this book but the essence of Mautz and Sharaf's approach is that auditing practice should be built on a sound philosophy of auditing because basing actions on an underpinning philosophy means:

- going back to first principles of what an audit is, what purpose it serves and what usefulness it has for society
- that knowledge has to be ordered in a systematic way
- it defines auditing's place in and usefulness to society

Broadly, Mautz and Sharaf adopted a scientific approach to auditing claiming that auditing practice, with its heavy emphasis on probability and a scientific approach to evidence, has much in common with the scientific method. They developed eight tentative postulates or factors necessary for audits to achieve the desired result. These will be familiar to any student who has studied auditing or will become familiar to students who study this book:

These postulates or assumptions are:

1 Financial statements and financial data are verifiable.
2 There is no necessary conflict of interest between the auditor and the management of the enterprise under audit.
3 The financial statements and other information submitted for verification are free from collusive and other unusual irregularities.
4 The existence of a satisfactory system of **internal control** eliminates the *probability* of irregularities.
5 Consistent application of generally accepted principles of accounting result in fair presentation of the financial position and the results of operations.
6 In the absence of clear evidence to the contrary, what has held true in the past for the enterprise under examination will hold true in the future.

7 When examining financial data for the purpose of expressing an opinion thereon, the auditor acts exclusively in the capacity of an auditor.

8 The professional status of the independent auditor imposes commensurate professional obligations.

Whilst practitioners may disagree with these assumptions remember they are the basis of a theory, they are not definitive statements defining an audit. In practice they are proposals for a foundation or basis for inference and discussion. They are not intended as statements of universal truth.

Whilst these postulates or factors are useful in many ways, there are several key factors which Mautz and Sharaf did not consider which are of fundamental importance today. These are:

- The questions of risk and control which were not considered to be as important in the 1960s as we consider them to be today.
- Mautz and Sharaf do not pay much attention to the concept of accountability between parties – e.g. the accountability of the entity to the public or to investors. This was considered more by Flint (see below).
- The basis of Mautz and Sharaf's approach is founded in scientific method which refers to evidence gathering processes, the testing of hypotheses and probability theory. There are problems with this, particularly in the exercise of an auditor's judgement in the absence of conclusive evidence. As we will see later in this book the exercise of professional judgement based on the knowledge and experience of the auditor is a key part of the audit process and one which cannot be validated by a purely science based approach. Scientists are often able to repeat experiments when trying to validate a hypothesis, whereas auditors only get one opportunity to gather the evidence they need.
- The relationships between auditing concepts in order to develop a general framework of auditing.

Whilst Mautz and Sharaf undoubtedly contributed greatly to the philosophy of auditing, they were very much grounded in the idea of scientific method and paid less attention to the idea of auditing as a social phenomenon, i.e. that it had a value to society generally and not just to those involved in the commercial entity. It was Professor Flint who added this dimension.

Flint – Philosophy and Principles of Auditing

In 1988 Professor David Flint published *Philosophy and Principles of Auditing: An Introduction* which built on and updated the work of Mautz and Sharaf. He also developed a series of postulates as a basis for the development of a theory of auditing. Flint postulated that the fundamental condition for the existence of an audit is accountability, either private (e.g. between management and shareholders), or public accountability and, further, that the subject matter of accountability is too remote, too complex and/or of too great a significance for the discharge of the duty (to be accountable) to be demonstrated without the process of an audit.

Flint stated that the essential distinguishing characteristics of audit are the independence of its status and its freedom from investigatory and reporting constraint and that all aspects of an audit, its conduct, the work carried out and its conclusions must be capable of being evidenced.

Flint was of the view that there have to be standards of accountability for those who carry out audits which form the standard by which actual performance can be measured. This means:

- that there are standards of accountability for conduct, performance, achievement and quality of information
- actual conduct, performance, achievement, quality and so on can be measured and compared with these standards by reference to known criteria and
- that the process of measurement and comparison requires skill and the exercise of judgement.

The meaning, significance and intention of financial and other statements and data which are audited must be sufficiently clear that the credibility which is given to it as a result of audit can be clearly expressed and communicated. An audit thereby produces an economic or social benefit to society.

Flint's postulates are based on the fundamental idea that auditing has a social benefit and is not simply a technical exercise for the purposes of regulation for example.

In addition to the work of Limperg, Mautz and Sharaf, and Flint outlined above, there have been other academic writings on this topic. Interested students could, perhaps, consult the work of Professor Tom Lee in his book *Corporate Audit Theory* (1993) but this appears to be aimed largely at the American market and, whilst of interest, is too complex and academic for this work. He has expanded the number of postulates to 14 quite wordy ones which occupy too much space to detail here.

It has to be said that, in practice, the major professional auditing bodies which are:

- the Institute of Chartered Accountants in England and Wales (ICAEW)
- the Institute of Chartered Accountants in Scotland (ICAS)
- the Institute of Chartered Accountants Irelandn (ICAI)
- the Association of Chartered Certified Accountants (ACCA)

have not shown great interest in academic auditing theories and there is still no real universally agreed conceptual framework for auditing beyond some rather vague statements broadly drawn from the postulates and theories outlined above.

It is not the place of this book to expand on these ideas but perhaps learners could consider the value of reliable financial information to stakeholders in companies, for example:

- to potential and actual investors
- to regulators
- to employees
- to suppliers and customers
- to the taxation authorities

The FRC stated in their report *Developments in Audit: An Overview 2015/16* that confidence in audit had grown, but more needed to be done in terms of market competition and improving good practice in the profession.

One final point to note in this chapter is to explain the difference between what auditors actually do and what the public think they do. This gap in understanding is more generally known as the '**expectation gap**'.

THE EXPECTATION GAP

What auditors call the Expectation Gap is summarized as:

'the difference between what the auditors actually do and what the public think they do.'

The general public and the uninformed, which often, sadly, includes financial journalists who should know better, often labour under the delusion that one of the primary functions of auditors is, for example, to detect fraud or to discover when a bank is about to go under. For example, research has shown that ordinary members of the public, when questioned, think that auditors check all the transactions in the books, or prepare the accounts; they have little understanding of risk-based audit techniques or systems-based approaches to auditing – and who can blame them?

Typically, public perceptions of the auditor's role are that they:

- prepare the financial statements
- check every entry in the books
- find fraud
- take responsibility for financial statements
- ensure financial statements are 'accurate'
- give early warning of business failure

The audit profession is attempting to reduce the expectation gap but each financial crash or failing always brings questions as to '*why didn't the auditors tell us?*'

Professor Limperg, whose theories of auditing we met above, stated:

'The audit function is rooted in the confidence that society places in the effectiveness of the audit and in the opinion of the accountant (i.e. the auditor) . . . If the confidence is betrayed the function too is destroyed since it becomes useless.'

As we saw above, the auditors should not arouse more expectations in the lay person than can be fulfilled by the work carried out – and this is the core of the problem. In recent years the Auditor's Report, which you will meet in Chapter 26, has expanded to include details of what the directors are responsible for, what the auditors do, how far the audit goes (known as scope) and how the audit is performed in terms of sample tests rather than tests of everything. This growth in the length of the audit report can be attributed to the need of the audit profession to explain to the investing public what they actually do, rather than what the public think they do.

A Commission on Auditors'Responsibilities in 1978 looked at the Expectation Gap with a remit to consider *'whether a gap may exist between what the public expects or needs and what auditors can and should reasonably expect to accomplish'* but many academic theorists considered this definition to be too narrow and should be widened to include the wider expectations of society. Thus Liggio (1974), who first defined the term 'expectation gap', suggested it should be defined as the gap between society's expectations of auditors and its perceptions of the services auditors deliver.

Since then successive commentators have attempted to redefine what this gap is and what it means to audit. Porter, in 1993, for example, contended that it should be split between:

(a) a reasonableness gap – the gap between the responsibilities society expects auditors to meet and what can be reasonably expected of them and
(b) a performance gap – the gap between the responsibilities society reasonably expects of auditors and those it perceives they deliver – or don't deliver.

This is not an academic textbook so further academic discussion of what, in essence is a fairly simple concept we will leave to other publications. Suffice to say that a lot of what went before is now superseded as audit disclosure increases and the public becomes increasingly informed of the role of the auditors in corporate governance.

The profession has, clearly, still some way to go and this is exercising the minds of the great and good in the profession who are endeavouring to educate the public and undermine these entrenched perceptions.

SUMMARY

- The creation of limited liability for investors has resulted in the separation of ownership from control and has created the requirement for an independent objective report of financial performance.

- Agency Theory holds that agents (management) which supposedly acts in the best interests of their principals (shareholders) will, in fact, tend to make short-term decisions which may benefit them at the expense of their principals and will generally act primarily in their own best interests.

- Over the decades, managers of large companies have been able to exercise a level of power and influence which extends not simply to business but to the lives of thousands of people including their employees and businesses which depend on them as suppliers. They can influence tax policy by governments and even affect the economies of small nations. The importance of the audit in validating the financial record is therefore of significance in making managers accountable.

- Academic writers have developed a series of auditing assumptions, or postulates, which contribute to auditing theory but so far no overriding theory of auditing has been formed.

- Financial accounting is the means by which those who have day-to-day control of an entity report to the owners. The reports produced are used by many other people such as investors and other stakeholders. All those who use the reports need to be able to have confidence in them.

- The audit is one of the means by which this confidence is obtained.

- The auditing process is more than just a visit by a firm of external accountants to check the books. It encompasses all of the controls and checks carried out by the company and relies on the financial probity of the directors.

- The increasing size of multinational firms has increased the use of technology and promoted different approaches to audit. Audit firms have been forced to respond to the demands of timeliness of information and cost control of the audit process.
- Increased globalization and increased regulation has placed bigger demands on audit firms.
- There is a gap in perception between what the public think auditors do and what they actually do. This is known as the expectation gap. The increase in disclosures and additional information included in financial statements means that this gap is narrowing.
- Auditing is concerned also with improving accounting systems and the detection and prevention of error and fraud.
- Auditors form independent firms and carry out numerous other services for their clients.
- There are statutory and internal audits and other types of assignment.

POINTS TO NOTE

- The individual auditor must be independent, a person of integrity and competent to carry out their work.
- Auditors give an opinion in their report. They do not certify or guarantee.
- It would benefit students to read some of the academic literature on audit theory as it will aid an understanding of the role and function of auditors and their relationship to society.
- Auditing is a global profession and developments in the business world have a direct effect on auditors and their actions and processes.
- A number of auditing issues are becoming subjects of debate and controversy. These include increased regulation of enterprises and the effect on auditors, increased regulation of auditors, the extent of auditors' responsibilities for the detection and prevention of fraud, auditors' responsibilities for environmental reporting, the gap between the public's expectations of auditing and the legal position of auditors, risk management, corporate governance, auditor independence and the whole future of auditing as a professional activity. The accounting press has many articles on these and other auditing issues and students should read as much as possible about them.

CASE STUDY

Wren, Gibbs and Angelo are brothers who own 75 per cent of a firm of builders with a turnover of £7m, specializing in house alteration and improvements. The remaining 25 per cent of the business is owned by their sister Bertha who lives abroad and only comes over once a year. The books have been kept by Wren who has an HNC in Business Studies as well as in building and Wren has also prepared the accounts.

The company is profitable and the accounts have been filed regularly at Companies House. Although they have never had a proper audit the accounts prepared by Wren are reviewed by their financial advisor, Gibbons, a golfing friend of Angelo's who prepares and submits the tax computations. Gibbons does not give any form of opinion on the accounts.

The brothers now want to borrow a lot of money from the bank to acquire another local building company which is in financial difficulties. Bertha has also been told that the brothers seem to have a very affluent lifestyle, but she only receives a very small dividend each year.

Discussion

– What benefits would the company get from employing an independent auditor?
– Where would they find a suitable auditor?
– Would it benefit Bertha to insist on a proper audit?

STUDENT SELF-TESTING QUESTIONS

Questions with answers apparent from the text

a) List the people and groups of people who are likely to be interested in financial statements.

b) What other services do accountants provide in addition to auditing?

c) State the relationship between the Financial Statements of a company, the shareholders, the directors and the auditors.

d) From the point of view of shareholders, what may be the problems associated with only receiving detailed financial statements annually?

e) What is the primary objective of an audit?

f) What other benefits are obtained through the audit process?

g) What are the objectives of an audit report?

h) What qualities are required in an auditor?

i) Distinguish statutory and internal audits and other assignments.

j) Define an audit.

EXAMINATION QUESTIONS

1 Growbig plc used to be a medium-sized company trading in agricultural supplies and chemicals such as fertilizers and pesticides. It was owned by a consortium of farmers and growers and on flotation as a public company they each received shares and these still form the majority of shareholders even though individual shareholdings are relatively small.

On flotation Growbig also issued shares which were taken up by institutional investors and there are now four major shareholders who together own about 35 per cent of the company, the remaining shareholders being the original farmers and growers. It used the funds to buy out rival businesses and to expand production of fertilizers and pesticides under its own brand to sell to the general public.

Growbig complies with all the legal disclosure requirements but does not provide shareholders with any other information. Recently there has been adverse publicity with regard to 'dumping' products which are not allowed to be sold in the UK under environmental legislation on to the market in various developing countries using a different brand name and also the lack of health and safety provision in one of their factories overseas which manufactures fertilizer.

Required:

(a) Identify the stakeholders in this company.

(b) What information would they require?

(c) How should the auditors respond to the adverse publicity? Should they go beyond statutory reporting duties and investigate the accusations against the company?

SOURCES AND ADDITIONAL READING

Audit Quality Forum (2005) Agency Theory and the Role of Audit London: ICAEW.

Audit Quality Forum (2006) *Fundamentals: Audit Purpose*, London: ICAEW.

Audit Quality Forum (2007) *Perspectives on Assurance: Engaging Business*, London: ICAEW.

Audit Quality Forum (2008) *Stakeholder Expectations of Audit*, London: ICAEW.

Bazerman, M. H., Loewenstein, G. and Moore, D. A. (2002) 'Why good accountants do bad audits', *Harvard Business Review*, 80(11), pp. 96–102, 134.

Berle, A. and Means, G. (1932) *The Modern Corporation and Private Property (Revised edition 1991)*, Piscataway, NJ: Transaction Publishers.

Commission on Auditors' Responsibilities (1978) *Report, Conclusions and Recommendations*, New York: American Institute of Certified Public Accountants.

Financial Reporting Council (2009) *ISA 200 Objective and General Principles Governing an Audit of Financial Statements*. London: Financial Reporting Council.

Financial Reporting Council (2010) *UK Corporate Governance Code*, London: Financial Reporting Council.

Flint, D. (1988) *Philosophy and Principles of Auditing: An Introduction*. Basingstoke: Palgrave Macmillan.

ICSA (2007) *Companies Act 2006 Handbook*. London: ICSA.

Jensen, M. C. and Meckling, W. H. (1976) 'Theory of the firm: managerial behaviour, agency costs and ownership structure', *Journal of Financial Economics*, 3(4), pp. 305–60.

Jensen, M. (1989) 'Eclipse of the public corporation', *Harvard Business Review*, 67(5), pp. 61–74.

Koh H.C & Woo E.S (1998) *The Expectation Gap in Auditing*, Managerial auditing Journal, 13-3:147–154.

Liggio, C. D. (1974) 'The expectation gap – the accountant's legal Waterloo', *Journal of Contemporary Business*, 3, pp. 27–44.

Limperg, T. (1932) *The Function of the Accountant and the Theory of Inspired Confidence*. Limperg Instituut, Amsterdam.

Limperg Institute, 1932 (1985) *The Social Responsibility of the Auditor. A Basic Theory on the Auditor's Function, by Professor Theodore Limperg (1879–1961) of the University of Amsterdam*. Amsterdam: Limperg Institute.

Mautz, R. K. and Sharaf, H. A. (1961) *The Philosophy of Auditing*. New York: American Accounting Association.

Parkinson, J. E. (1994) *Corporate Power and Responsibility*. Oxford: Oxford University Press.

Porter, B., Simon, J. and Hatherley, D. (2008) *Principles of External Auditing*. Chichester: Wiley.

Smith, A (1776) *The Wealth of Nations*. London: Penguin.

CHAPTER 2
CORPORATE
GOVERNANCE

Learning Objectives

After studying the material in this chapter you should be able to:

- understand the basic principles of corporate governance

- discuss the framework approach to corporate governance versus a legal basis

- understand the principles of 'substance over form' and 'comply or explain'

- explain the value of good corporate governance

- discuss the advantages and disadvantages of audit committees

INTRODUCTION

As soon as the directors were required by law to prepare annual financial statements shareholders were able to access some financial information about the company they owned. The question investors were faced with was this – is the information the directors supply to them reliable, given the basic tenets of Agency Theory (Chapter 1)? This highlights the conflict between the short-term objectives of the directors (agents) and the longer-term objectives of the shareholders (principals) – in other words, can the directors be trusted to tell the shareholders the truth, and the whole truth, about what they have done with the money the shareholders have given them?

The directors act in a *fiduciary capacity* towards the shareholders. This means that they are in a special position of trust charged with preserving the assets of the business and running it for the benefit of the shareholders so that it increases shareholder value and pays them some dividend. The fiduciary relationship between the parties places the onus firmly on the directors to be accountable for their actions and to be transparent in their reporting.

As we saw in Chapter 1 the audit is part of this process, but it is necessary to ensure that the underlying information the auditors are dealing with has been prepared properly by the directors in their fiduciary capacity as they report on their activities to the shareholders. Nowadays it is generally accepted that the financial statements are used by a wide variety of stakeholders (Chapter 1), albeit that the directors are legally only required to report to the shareholders.

WHAT IS CORPORATE GOVERNANCE?

The definition of **Corporate Governance** most often quoted is the one contained in the 1992 report prepared by the Committee on the Financial Aspects of Corporate Governance chaired by Sir Adrian Cadbury, usually simply called the **Cadbury Report**:

> '..the system by which companies are directed and controlled'.

This definition was all very well for the time but as the various reports post-Cadbury have refined and enhanced his initial concepts, so the definition of what corporate governance actually is has also been refined. In research carried out in 2000 among UK institutional investors the definition which found the most favour was:

> 'the process of supervision and control intended to ensure that the company's management acts in accordance with the interests of shareholders.' (Parkinson, 1995)

This, as you see, goes right to the heart of the problems of Agency Theory which we looked at in Chapter 1. Agency Theory is fundamental to an understanding of corporate governance and students should be sure to understand the conceptual framework and the rationale which underpins good corporate governance.

PRINCIPLES OF CORPORATE GOVERNANCE

The underlying principles of good Corporate Governance are based around the actions of the board of directors, how it is constituted, how it operates, how it sets the values for the organization and how it governs itself. The fundamental principles of good governance, which underpin all the detailed rules contained in the UK Corporate Governance Code and in many others around the world are:

- **accountability** – this principle requires a board to take responsibility for actions with the obligation to report the outcome of those actions;
- **transparency** – this encompasses ideas of openness, willingness to communicate and is an accompaniment to accountability. Thus a board should respond positively to requests for information and disseminate more than an annual set of accounts;
- **probity** – which goes beyond the strict legal definition of compliance with laws and regulations and incorporates ideals of honesty, truthfulness and ethical behaviour in compliance with some form of moral code; and

- **focus** on the sustainable success of an entity over the longer term – which denies the Agency Theory tendency for managers to take short-term decisions which benefit themselves instead of their principals, the shareholders. This principle acknowledges the rights of shareholders, both large and small, to be treated equally and to have their interests recognized.

There are many Corporate Governance codes around the world. One of the international codes which set out some basic principles is the Organization for Economic Co-operation and Development (OECD) code, which is a model for many of the international codes, particularly those adopted by developing countries. This code is also supported by the **International Federation of Accountants** (IFAC) and can be adopted as a suitable alternative to the UK Code when students are thinking internationally. As most of these codes are broadly similar we will concentrate on the principles contained in the UK Corporate Governance Code for our purposes.

First, however, we must deal with a fundamental difference in the approach to Corporate Governance. The difference, which is an important one for auditors, is between the conceptual framework approach used in the UK, and the legislative approach adopted by other countries, principally the USA.

'COMPLY OR EXPLAIN' – FRAMEWORK VERSUS LEGISLATIVE APPROACHES

The approach to corporate governance adopted in the UK is what has become known as a **framework approach.** The principles of Cadbury and its successors have not been enforced by legislation on either companies listed on the London Stock Exchange or on any entities. Instead listed companies are required to abide by the UK Corporate Governance Code or to state in their accounts why they don't comply – the so-called **'comply or explain'** basis.

This leaves open the door to non-compliance by listed companies, which may only have to suffer a note in the Auditor's Report and perhaps a stern word from the Stock Exchange for a first offence, and, of course, it has no effect at all, other than a persuasive one, on unlisted companies.

Students should contrast this principles-based approach with the purely legalistic approach adopted by the USA in the wake of the Enron and other corporate scandals there. The USA passed the Sarbanes–Oxley legislation (see later) which sets out detailed prohibitions and rules for both companies and audit firms to follow.

The advantages and disadvantages of both approaches are set out in Figure 2.1.

FIGURE 2.1   Corporate governance – principles-based versus legal approach

Principles-based	Legal approach
Lawyers spend time trying to get around the legal rules	Everyone knows where they are and should be able to apply the rules
The legal approach leads to a 'tick box' approach to corporate governance	Principles are hard to explain so can be vague and difficult to interpret
Principles-based approaches can be applied to any jurisdiction and any legal system	Principles-based approaches are difficult to enforce in any meaningful way without legislation or sanctions

Most countries have preferred to adopt a principles-based approach because of its flexibility but this requires a commitment on the part of company directors to abide by the spirit of the Code and, in particular, to those principles outlined above, of accountability, transparency and probity.

Shareholders have no practical sanctions against a Board which fails to explain breaches of the Code – other than voting to remove directors which seems extreme – but can exert pressure on a Board which consistently flouts the recommendations – particularly when the Board might need shareholder support.

A code which is largely voluntary in nature can only be policed by consensus, and if organizations are determined to flout the principles there are few practical sanctions. However, in most cases the advantages of good governance have proved to outweigh the disadvantages and so principles-based codes are proving to be effective around the world. The case of Morrisons is a good example of this (Figure 2.2).

FIGURE 2.2 Corporate governance – the case of Morrisons

When it became a FTSE 100 company in 2001 Morrisons was still fundamentally failing to comply with the key principles of corporate governance in that it had no non-executive directors and no audit or remuneration committees. Morrisons was a successful company so there was little institutional investors could do.

Their 2004 accounts explained their approach to the question of non-executive directors.

'The company does not have any non-executive directors on the board (A.2.1, A.3.1, A.3.2, A.6.1). The directors are mindful of the provisions of the [then] Combined Code in this regard and regularly review the situation'

Morrisons decided to buy supermarket chain Safeway and it needed shareholder support. Following pressure from institutional investors a couple of non-executive directors appeared on the board – although one did not last long.

The integration of Safeway and Morrisons did not go well, profit warnings were issued and the governance of the company called into question after the board admitted failings in internal controls. Gradually formal systems were introduced and the governance structure of the company was revised to bring it into line with the Code.

Cadbury's report was followed by several others. Students need to be aware of the basic principles of these reports:

- Greenbury (1995), which looked at the question of directors pay, in particular the role of the Remuneration Committee in setting remuneration levels, guidelines on remuneration policy, the level of disclosure in financial statements and the question of terms in service contracts allowing firms to pay compensation when directors are dismissed for poor performance.
- Hampel (1998), which reinforced points made in the original Cadbury Report, in particular the separation of the roles of Chairman and Managing Director and the balance of the composition of the Board between executive and non-executive directors.
- Turnbull (1999), which offered guidance on how directors should comply with corporate governance, focusing on internal controls and risk management. This report emphasized the importance of good internal and external reporting: 'This requires the maintenance of proper records and processes that generate a flow of timely, relevant and reliable information from within and outside the organization,' it stated. The report also noted the key role that IT plays in creating internal controls and in assessing accurately the risks faced by an organization.
- Higgs (2003), which set out measures designed to improve the structure and accountability of boardrooms in the UK. It argued that boards should be free to criticize company management, and suggested limiting the number of directors that hold managerial positions to no more than half the board – the remainder being non-executive directors. This proved controversial and Higgs has since admitted that his recommendations were too harsh.

UK CORPORATE GOVERNANCE CODE

The **UK Corporate Governance Code** ('the Code'), formerly known as the Combined Code, was, as we have seen, derived originally from the Cadbury Report and sets out good practice for directors in the areas of leadership, remuneration, performance monitoring and relationships with shareholders.

The FRC (Financial Reporting Council) is the body responsible for promoting high-quality corporate governance and reporting in order to encourage investment. It promotes high standards of corporate governance through the UK Corporate Governance Code, and encourages engagement between investors and Boards. It sets standards for corporate reporting, and audit practice and monitors and enforces accounting and auditing standards. It also oversees the regulatory activities of the professional accountancy bodies and operates independent enforcement arrangements for public interest cases involving accountants.

The Code is underpinned by an FRC rule that requires companies listed on the London Stock Exchange to state, in their annual report, how they have complied with its provisions or to explain why they have not done so. This is the *'comply or explain'* basis outlined above.

The headings set out below are the key requirements of the Code. This is not a book on Corporate Governance so they are not expanded upon here but each of the headings is underpinned by guidelines and suggestions as to how boards should interpret the particular requirement of the Code.

Directors' duties

The Code sets out the key principles of good Corporate Governance. Listed companies are supposed to abide by this, but it is good practice for all companies to abide by as many of these principles as are practicable.

The main provisions, as set out in the Code, are listed below.

Directors

- Every company should be headed by an effective board, which is *collectively* responsible for the long-term success of the company.
- There should be a clear division of responsibilities at the head of the company between the running of the board and the executive responsibility for the running of the company's business. No one individual should have unfettered powers of decision. (What this means, in practice, is that the Board Chair should not be the same individual as the Managing Director or Chief Executive Officer.)
- The Chairperson is responsible for leadership of the board and ensuring its effectiveness on all aspects of its role.
- As part of their role as members of a board, non-executive directors should constructively challenge and help develop proposals on strategy.
- The board and its committees should have the appropriate balance of skills, experience, independence and knowledge of the company to enable them to discharge their respective duties and responsibilities effectively.
- There should be a formal, rigorous and transparent procedure for the appointment of new directors to the board.
- All directors should be able to allocate sufficient time to the company to discharge their responsibilities effectively.
- The board should be supplied in a timely manner with information in a form and of a quality appropriate to enable it to discharge its duties. (This is a requirement to produce good-quality management information, both financial and non-financial, in a form the directors can understand and in a timely manner.)
- All directors should receive induction on joining the board and should regularly update and refresh their skills and knowledge.
- The board should undertake a formal and rigorous annual evaluation of its own performance and that of its committees and individual directors.
- All directors should be submitted for re-election at regular intervals, subject to continued satisfactory performance. (The board should ensure planned and progressive refreshing of the board.)

Accountability and audit

- The board should present a balanced and understandable assessment of the company's position and prospects.
- The board is responsible for determining the nature and extent of the significant risks it is willing to take in achieving its strategic objectives. The board should maintain sound risk management and internal control systems.
- The board should establish formal and transparent arrangements for considering how they should apply the corporate reporting and risk management and internal control principles and for maintaining an appropriate relationship with the company's auditor.

Remuneration

- Levels of remuneration should be sufficient to attract, retain and motivate directors of the quality required to run the company successfully, but a company should avoid paying more than is necessary for this purpose.
- A significant proportion of executive directors' remuneration should be structured so as to link rewards to corporate and individual performance.

- There should be a formal and transparent procedure for developing policy on executive remuneration and for fixing the remuneration packages of individual directors.
- No director should be involved in deciding his or her own remuneration. In practice this usually takes the form of a Remuneration Committee of non-executive directors as recommended by Greenbury (see above).

Relations with shareholders

- There should be a dialogue with shareholders based on the mutual understanding of objectives. The board as a whole has responsibility for ensuring that a satisfactory dialogue with shareholders takes place.
- The board should use the **Annual General Meeting** (AGM) to communicate with investors and to encourage their participation.

The key point about good corporate governance is that its requirements should be met in the spirit of good governance and not just by observing the letter of the Code. 'Box ticking' should not be a substitute for clear thought and fair exposition.

This leads us into the fundamental doctrine of **substance over form** (see below) which students need to understand so they can appreciate the theoretical framework on which corporate governance in the UK is built.

VALUE OF GOOD CORPORATE GOVERNANCE

One of the problems auditors may initially face when dealing with companies where corporate governance is not enforced through something like the Stock Exchange listing agreement (see later), is to convince management of the value of good corporate governance. Smaller organizations, in particular, may not accept the conditions around the structure of the board and may baulk at appointing non-executive directors.

They will see the visible expense and, to some extent, the bureaucracy involved in corporate governance compliance and not be able to see the benefits which are, perhaps, rather more intangible.

However, the benefits of increased accountability and transparency have been demonstrated by academic research which has shown that companies who adopt best practice corporate governance find it much easier to raise finance and are generally more profitable and less prone to fluctuations in trading patterns than those run by small groups of owner managers.

The benefits of appointing experienced non-executives for example can bring a wealth of experience and knowledge to the board, which benefits the business in the longer term and the general improvements in internal control and relationships with external audit increases the trust investors have in the financial statements.

SUBSTANCE OVER FORM

The approach to regulating the activities of companies has been, at least in the UK, largely principles-based; that is legislation is kept to a minimum and directors, managers and auditors are expected to conform to a standard of ethical behaviour rather than be dominated by detailed regulations.

In the USA the approach is quite the opposite. They tend to adopt a stringent regulatory approach, which has, in the past, encouraged accountants and lawyers in the USA to devote a lot of time to trying to circumvent the rules.

As the UK does not have that many rules, other than those considered necessary, such as the Companies Act, the Corporate Governance Code and the various accounting and auditing standards, accountants, and in particular auditors, tend to concentrate on the nature of each type of transaction or activity rather than how it is described. This is known as substance over form.

For example: the directors may have found a way to describe a small flightless bird with a beak and feathers as a chicken despite the noise it makes and the way it walks.

The auditor will look past the directors' description and say 'if it walks like a duck and it quacks like a duck – it's a duck!' In other words, the auditors look past the *form* of the transaction, i.e. what it appears to be or what it has been described as (chicken) to its *substance*, i.e. what it really is (duck).

This doctrine of substance over form is fundamental to corporate reporting but is also a fundamental aspect of corporate governance – it requires the directors to tell the truth about what has happened and not to attempt to present or disguise financial information, for whatever reason.

COMPANIES ACT 2006

The **Companies Act 2006** incorporates within it specific duties of directors. Among other things Section 172 lays down a specific duty on a company director to:

- Act in the way he considers, in good faith, would be most likely to promote the success of the company for the benefit of its members as a whole and to have regard to:
  - *the interests of the company's employees*
  - *the need to foster the company's business relationships with suppliers, customers and others*
  - *the desirability of the company maintaining a reputation for high standards of business conduct*

For the first time there is a specific provision, in law, for the directors to have regard to the interests, not only of those who have invested in the company over which they have day-to-day control but also of others, employees, customers, suppliers and indeed – in its injunction to maintain a high standard of conduct – anyone the business comes into contact with in the course of its activities.

AUDIT COMMITTEES

The UK Corporate Governance Code requires that all listed companies set up an **Audit Committee**. Ideally:

- It should comprise at least three non-executive directors (two in the case of smaller companies) which are independent of management. The Chair of the board of directors could be a member of the Audit Committee but should not chair it.
- The members should have a wide range of business and professional skills.
- The members should have a good understanding of the business yet should have had no recent involvement with direct management of the business.
- The committee should have clear written terms of reference setting out its authority and its duties.
- The members should be prepared to devote significant time and effort to the work of the committee.

Clearly this can sometimes be difficult to achieve. However, the object is to create a committee which is competent to carry out its role, is independent and is free from bias.

The key objectives associated with the setting up of Audit Committees, from the point of view of corporate governance generally, is:

- To increase public confidence in the credibility and objectivity of published financial information.
- To assist the directors in carrying out their responsibilities for financial reporting.
- To strengthen the position of the external auditors by providing a channel of communication at board level without the constraint of any executive bias.

There are advantages to having an Audit Committee. These are:

- It can improve the quality of management accounting as it is able to criticize internal reporting, which is not necessarily the responsibility of the external auditors.
- It can facilitate communication between the directors, internal and external auditors and management.
- It can help minimize any conflicts between management and the auditors.
- It can facilitate the independence of the internal audit role if the internal auditors report to the Audit Committee directly.

The role of the Audit Committee, specifically, is:

- To monitor the integrity of the financial statements of the company and any formal announcements relating to the company's financial performance, reviewing significant financial reporting judgements contained in them.
- To review the company's internal financial controls and, unless expressly addressed by a separate board risk committee composed of independent directors or by the board itself, the company's internal control and risk management systems.
- To monitor and review the effectiveness of the company's internal audit function.
- To make recommendations to the board, for it to put to the shareholders for their approval in general meeting, in relation to the appointment of the external auditor and to approve the remuneration and terms of engagement of the external auditors.
- To review and monitor the external auditor's independence and objectivity and the effectiveness of the audit process, taking into consideration relevant professional and regulatory requirements.
- To develop and implement policy on the engagement of the external auditor to supply non-audit services, taking into account relevant ethical guidance regarding the provision of non-audit services by the external audit firm.
- To report to the board, identifying any matters in respect of which it considers that action or improvement is needed, and making recommendations as to the steps to be taken.

However, there are some disadvantages which the members of the Audit Committee have to avoid:

- It can be perceived that their purpose is to criticize or 'catch out' executive management.
- This can result in the perception, if not the reality, of a two-tier board.
- The non-executives can become too embroiled in detail and start to act like executive directors thus losing their independence.

In essence, the Audit Committee is designed to act as an independent voice on the board of directors with regard to audit and corporate governance issues and can be a valuable asset, particularly with respect to maintaining the independence and integrity of the internal audit function. Students need to be familiar with the composition and role of audit committees as it is a popular topic for examiners.

SARBANES–OXLEY (2002)

The whole question of corporate governance was dominated by the financial scandals of the early part of the twenty-first century in the USA surrounding, in particular, Enron and the lesser, but no less shocking, scandals involving WorldCom, Tyco International, Global Crossing and many others. All of the major accounting firms had clients who were caught up in these scandals, the apotheosis being the destruction of the worldwide accounting firm of Arthur Andersen.

In 2002 this resulted in the USA publishing legislation known as the **Sarbanes–Oxley Act** (often shortened to 'Sarbox').

It does not affect UK companies unless they are subsidiaries of US firms or are listed on US stock exchanges.

The Act is designed to enforce corporate accountability through new requirements, backed by stiff penalties. Under the Act, chief executives and chief financial officers must personally certify the accuracy of financial statements, with a maximum penalty of 20 years in jail and a $5m fine for false statements. In addition, and of great significance to auditors, under Section 404 of the Act, executives have to certify and demonstrate that they have established and are maintaining an adequate internal control structure and procedures for financial reporting. This requires them to ensure that all the financial reporting systems, including the ancillary systems such as procurement and HR, are functioning in such a way as to prevent material misstatements appearing in the financial accounts – and it is a personal liability.

It should be pointed out that this legislation, passed in haste is, in the current climate, slowly being reassessed as being too prescriptive and too inhibiting of US business freedoms, so there may be further changes to come!

SUMMARY

- Corporate governance has become an important issue and is a regular subject for examination questions.
- The UK Corporate Governance Code must be complied with by all listed companies and represents good practice for nonlisted ones.
- Directors of UK listed companies have specific duties under the Code which sets out the form, composition and behaviour of Boards and the requirements for establishing independent committees such as Audit and Remuneration Committees.
- In order to ensure that the directors place due reliance on the requirements of investors and wider society the Code places responsibilities on boards of directors to promote competence, communication with shareholders and openness in reporting.
- Auditors have some duties connected with the reports by the directors on their compliance with the requirements of the Code.
- These duties include reporting in true and fair terms about extensions to directors' remuneration disclosures, reviewing certain items and reading for consistency and misstatement all other corporate governance disclosures in the annual report.
- Auditors may need to report departures from the Code by means of a statement in the auditor's report.
- Audit Committees have a role to play in maintaining the standard of corporate governance within the company.

POINTS TO NOTE

- If the Audit Committee does its job properly the auditors will not be so close to executive management that their independence is compromised.
- It is advisable for students to read one or more complete annual reports of listed companies to see how these things work out in practice.
- In some circumstances there may be a departure from a Code provision specified for auditor review but there is a proper disclosure of this fact and the reasons for it. In such cases the auditors may not need to report the departure in their report.

CASE STUDY

Bolington Ltd is a rapidly growing company presently owned by the Bolington family. It sells designer clothing and accessories which it sources from around the world and trading results are exceeding expectations.

The family is looking to cash in on the success of the business and also provide some capital for expansion so they have decided to float the company on the Stock Exchange.

At present the board of directors consists of Mark Bolington, who is Chairman and Managing Director, and his two sons Dave and Phil who are Sales and Buying Directors respectively. They are going to appoint Bill Sticker, who is presently the Chief Accountant, as Financial Director just before the flotation.

The auditors, Tickitt & Run are a little concerned that the Stock Exchange will find the level of corporate governance unacceptably low, if not actually non-existent, and they think they should tell Mark Bolington, who is fairly dogmatic and not a man who like others interfering in his business, what he needs to do to comply with aspects of the listing agreement.

Discussion

– What will Bolington Ltd need to do in order to start complying with some of the key aspects of corporate governance?

STUDENT SELF-TESTING QUESTIONS

Questions with answers apparent from the text

a) What was the principal report from which most corporate governance requirements originate?

b) What are the duties of directors with regard to corporate governance?

c) How does the UK approach differ from that of the USA?

d) What is 'substance over form'?

e) What are the functions of the audit committee?

f) What are the roles of non-executive directors in connection with corporate governance?

EXAMINATION QUESTIONS

1 Extract from the financial statements of Megablast Ltd regarding corporate governance:

'Mr Tidyman is the Chief Executive Officer and board chairman of Megablast. He appoints and maintains a board of six executive and two non-executive directors, one of which is his father, the former Chairman of Megablast, Sir Roger Tidyman.

The board sets performance targets for the senior managers in the company but there are no formal targets for directors and the company does not have a remuneration committee. Mr Tidyman carries out a review of board policies annually in conjunction with the non-executive directors. Salaries for executive directors are set and paid by Mr Tidyman based on his assessment of all the board members, including himself. There is no formal measure of actual performance of individual directors.

Internal controls in the company are monitored by the senior accountant, although detailed review is assumed to be carried out by the external auditors; Megablast does not have an internal audit department.

Annual financial statements are produced, providing detailed information on past performance.
Required:
Write a report for Mr Tidyman to:

(a) Explain why Megablast does not meet international codes of corporate governance.
(b) Explain why not meeting the international codes may cause a problem for Megablast.
(c) Recommend any changes necessary to implement those codes in the company.

2 If there is a need for a uniform set of international accounting standards and international auditing standards, there is also a need for global corporate governance standards.

Required:

Discuss and reach a conclusion. (*ACCA*)

SOURCES AND ADDITIONAL READING

Audit Quality Forum (2005) *Fundamentals: Agency Theory and the Role of Audit*. London: ICAEW.

Cadbury, Sir A. (1992) *Financial Aspects of Corporate Governance*. London: Gee & Co.

Financial Reporting Council (2009) *ISA 720 Section A – The Auditor's Responsibilities Relating to Other Information in Documents Containing Audited Financial Information* and *ISA 720 Section B – The Auditor's Statutory Reporting Responsibility in Relation to Directors' Reports*. London: Financial Reporting Council.

Financial Reporting Council (2009) *Bulletin 2009/4: Developments in Corporate Governance Affecting the Responsibilities of Auditors of UK Companies*. London: Financial Reporting Council.

Financial Reporting Council (2010) *UK Corporate Governance Code*. London: Financial Reporting Council.

ICSA (2007) *Companies Act 2006 Handbook*. London: ICSA.

Organization for Economic Co-operation and Development (2004) *OECD Principles of Corporate Governance*. Paris: OECD.

Parkinson, J. E. (1995) *Corporate Power and Responsibility*. Oxford: Oxford University Press.

Razaee, Z. (2008) *Corporate Governance and Ethics*. Chichester: Wiley.

Solomon, J. (2007) *Corporate Governance and Accountability.* Chichester: Wiley.

Simpson, J. and Taylor, J. (2013) *Corporate Governance, Ethics and CSR*. London: Kogan Page.

TSO (2006) *Companies Act 2006*. London: The Stationery Office.

CHAPTER 3
THE STATUTORY
FRAMEWORK FOR
AUDITING

Learning Objectives

After studying the material in this chapter you should be able to:

- understand the statutory framework within which audits are performed

- know the statutory limits for company audits

- explain who can be or can't be an auditor and the requirements to be met to become a registered auditor

- understand the requirements of a recognized supervisory body and a qualifying body

- explain the process of appointment and removal or resignation of auditors

- discuss the rights and duties of auditors and their powers

- understand the basis of auditors' remuneration and appreciate the conflict between the appointment of auditors by the shareholders and their remuneration by the company

- understand the purpose and procedures of the annual general meeting

INTRODUCTION

The majority of audits performed in the UK are of companies which are regulated by the Companies Act 2006. As we have seen, there are other bodies (charities, financial service companies, etc.) where other regulations may apply but these are generally outside the scope of this book.

In this chapter we will concentrate on the legal foundation behind the audit of companies under the provisions of the Companies Act 2006, which is the statutory financial reporting framework for the UK.

We will look at the law as it applies to auditors, who is eligible to be an auditor, their professional bodies, the appointment and removal of the auditors and their rights and duties.

We haven't followed the sequence of sections in the Companies Act as we feel it is more useful to put the legislation in the context of the auditors and not simply follow a sequence devised for legal purposes.

Later chapters of this book return to these topics in detail and outline *how* directors and auditors carry out their duties and what form of words are used in reports, etc. This chapter explains the legal reasons *why* directors and auditors have to report in the way they do. Much of this is technical and at first can appear quite daunting.

Examiners rarely expect students to be able to quote the law but they will expect students to have a good understanding of the legal framework which underpins the financial roles of auditors and directors in terms of corporate reporting. We have put it all in one chapter so that students can get a good grasp of the legal background before becoming embroiled in the detail of how to actually carry out an audit.

THE COMPANIES ACT 2006

The Companies Act 2006 contains detailed regulations on the conduct of an audit, the accounting records on which the auditor will work, the financial statements on which they will report and on the auditor's relations with the company. The next sections summarize the Companies Act rules in these areas.

The Companies Act 2006 has been described as 'gargantuan' as it is said to be the largest piece of legislation ever passed by Parliament, with 1300 sections and 16 schedules. We will deal only with the provisions that affect auditors and the financial statements of the entities they audit, so many other parts of the legislation will not be covered by this book. Students wishing to immerse themselves in the detail should consult a specialized Company Law textbook.

All references are to the Companies Act 2006 unless otherwise stated.

REQUIREMENT TO HAVE AUDITORS

The basis of the audit requirement is set out in Section 485 and Section 489 which state that every company shall appoint an auditor if it is required to produce audited accounts, i.e. if it is not dormant and is above a certain size.

Some organizations don't need an audit and this is, generally, defined by size. The official definitions for entities which don't require an audit are:

- *Small companies* – private limited companies, which are not part of a larger group, and are not banking or insurance companies. Their turnover must be £10.2m or less, their Statement of Financial Position totals £5.1m or less and they should employ fewer than 50 people. Small companies who fulfil two of these criteria do not need what is known as a **statutory audit**. Companies who have been or are a public company or one involved in banking, insurance or certain financial services cannot qualify for exemption. These criteria must be met for, generally, two consecutive financial years.
- *Small groups* – the same limits apply to small groups as to small companies except that reference can be made to net or gross amounts. The equivalent figures are – turnover £10.2m (£12.2m gross), Statement of Financial Position totals £5.1m (£6.1m gross), the aggregate number of employees to be not more than 50. Groups cannot be eligible for exemption if any member of the group falls within one of the criteria listed above i.e. unless it is a banking or insurance company or one engaged in certain financial services.
- *Small charities that are companies* – these are charities which are companies with a gross annual income of £1m or less unless their Statement of Financial Position totals £3.26m or more with an income of £250 000 per annum or more.

- *Dormant companies* (i.e. companies which have not carried out any transactions in the financial period).
- The organization is not a public company or a banking or insurance company.
- The organization is not an authorized person or an appointed representative under the Financial Services and Markets Act 2000.

However, members of the company holding not less than 10 per cent of the share capital can require an audit and press the company to hold one.

Small companies are permitted to file, at Companies House, abbreviated financial statements. Students should be aware of the form and content of such accounts.

The auditor's report need not be filed but the auditors have some duties where **abbreviated accounts** are filed. They have to attach a special report stating that in their opinion:

- The company is entitled to deliver abbreviated accounts.
- The abbreviated accounts to be delivered are properly prepared.

If the auditor's report is qualified in any way (Chapter 26) then the special report must include the full auditor's report together with any further information necessary to understand the qualification.

Dormant companies do not need an auditor as they have had no significant accounting transactions in the relevant period.

Companies which do not require a statutory audit by law may still choose to have one. The main reasons for this are:

- Protection of shareholders in owner-managed (family) companies where some of the shareholders are not involved in the day-to-day management.
- To add credibility to the figure for the benefit of lenders who otherwise might commission their own audit.
- To provide audited and thus credible figures for tax authorities or regulators.

From this it can be seen that an audit adds *credibility* and *reassurance* to the financial statements and goes some way to providing protection for investors in the company.

WHO CAN BE AN AUDITOR?

Anyone can check a set of books, and anyone can write a report, but to be a statutory auditor signing a report on a set of financial statements under the provisions of the Companies Act requires a specific accreditation. Anyone who does not have these specific qualifications and signs an Auditor's Report, leaves themselves open to disciplinary proceedings if they are a qualified accountant, or possible legal proceedings if they are not.

The definition of who can be an auditor is set out in Section 1212 of the Companies Act 2006. Note that, under the Act, auditors are referred to as 'statutory auditors'. This is to confirm their legal status as properly qualified auditors eligible to audit a range of different organizations in addition to both quoted and unquoted companies.

Section 1212 says:

(1) *An individual or firm is eligible for appointment as a statutory auditor if the individual or firm –*
   (a) is a member of a recognized supervisory body; and
   (b) is eligible for the appointment under the rules of that body.

Note that the legislation refers to 'individual or firm' though, generally, it is an audit firm who is appointed, not a named individual.

Section 1222 concerns auditors who are not members of professional bodies recognized by the Companies Act 1967. These individuals retain rights to audit individual unquoted companies as a consequence of being in office when the Companies Act 1967 came into force. There are still some of these accountants around and many are now members of the Association of Authorized Public Accountants which is a recognized supervisory body (see below).

Note that there is no prohibition on corporate bodies (e.g. companies) being auditors. This has enabled many firms to incorporate as limited liability partnerships (LLPs). This protects the firm, as a whole, from being damaged by claims arising, for example due to the negligence of one partner. We will look at this further in Chapter 29.

The Companies Act 2006 (on the subject of supervisory bodies) requires that any firm appointed as auditors must be controlled by qualified persons. This means that firms of accountants may have unqualified members or differently qualified partners, but a majority of the individuals which form the controlling board or committee of the firm must be individuals qualified to act as statutory auditors. The Supervisory Bodies have complex rules to cover this point.

Ineligible persons who can't act as auditors

As well as knowing who can be an auditor students should be aware of those who can't. These individuals are specifically excluded from being auditors under Section 1214. Mostly the prohibitions are obvious ones to exclude anyone who might have a conflict of interest, so they are:

- officers and employees of the company
- partners or employees of such persons or a partnership of which such a person is a partner
- persons who have a connection with the company or where the company has a connection with an associate of his of any description specified in regulations made by the Secretary of State

Note that persons who are ineligible to act as auditor of a particular company are also ineligible to act as auditor of a parent, subsidiary, or fellow subsidiary of that company.

The whole purpose of this section is to secure the **independence** of the auditor from the company.

It is an offence for a statutory auditor to be a company auditor if their independence is lost because of the sorts of connections mentioned above. If the statutory auditor becomes compromised in that way, they must resign immediately and notify the company that they are unable to continue because of their lack of independence.

THE RIGHTS AND DUTIES OF AN AUDITOR UNDER THE COMPANIES ACT 2006

The law on the rights and duties of an auditor under the Companies Act is principally laid down in Section 475(1) and in Sections 495–507.

We will consider the relevant parts of each section as they affect the conduct of the audit and the duties, rights and powers of auditors.

Remember that you do not have to be able to quote the law, nor is it a general requirement that you remember section numbers of the various provisions of the Companies Act. However, it is useful for students, and practitioners, to read the actual law rather than just seeing an interpretation of it in a textbook so, for this reason, we quote it rather extensively in this chapter.

We set out the law for the whole process, ending with the auditor's report. The reason for this is to show the legal basis on which auditors carry out all their work. Without the legal requirement for an auditor to make a report, it could be argued that the rest of this book, which deals with how they go about doing that, would be rather pointless!

APPOINTMENT OF AUDITORS

Public companies

Section 489 details how auditors of public companies are to be appointed:

- The company shall, at each general meeting at which Accounts are presented (usually at each AGM), appoint an auditor or auditors. Note that it is the company (i.e. the shareholders) who appoint the auditor.

- The appointment is for the period of time known as the tenure of office and that is from the conclusion of the meeting to the conclusion of the following annual general meeting at which accounts are laid (i.e. presented at the meeting) (Section 491). The auditors hold office from the end of one meeting (say, 19 July 2X10) until the end of the following AGM (say, 17 July 2X11). That is their tenure of office. They report on the financial statements presented at the AGM of 2X11, which is within their tenure of office.

- On the commencement of a new company the directors may appoint the auditor at any time before the first AGM and the appointment has to be approved by the shareholders at the next AGM after appointment.

Private companies

Private companies no longer have to hold an AGM the tenure of office of the auditor is slightly different for them.

Basically, auditors must be appointed *before* the end of a 28-day period which starts either:

- nine months from the year end, the date accounts are sent to the shareholders; or
- the date the accounts are filed with the Registrar, whichever is earlier.

The term of office technically ends at the end of the equivalent period for the following year.

Where a private company does not hold an AGM, generally the auditor is deemed to be automatically reappointed, unless there is a provision in the company's Articles of Association that they must be physically re-elected by a vote at a meeting or unless disgruntled shareholders, holding at least 5 per cent of the shares, object to automatic reappointment.

In the event of a company, either public or private, not appointing an auditor, Section 486 states that the company must inform the Secretary of State within one week of the end of the period allowed for appointing auditors. The Secretary of State may then make an appointment.

The directors have the power to appoint the first auditors of a company and to appoint auditors to fill a casual vacancy, perhaps caused by resignation of the existing auditors. In both these cases the appointment must be approved by the shareholders at the next opportunity, e.g. at the next AGM.

REMUNERATION OF AUDITORS

Under Section 492 the remuneration of the auditors is fixed by the person/persons appointing. If this is the company in General Meeting the company AGM agenda might include something like:

> 'To re-appoint the auditors Tickett & Run. as the company's auditors until the conclusion of the next AGM of the Company, and to authorize the Board to fix the auditors' remuneration.'

You will notice that the independence of the auditors is made by them being appointed by the shareholders in general meeting. If you refer back to Chapter 2 on Agency Theory you may think that the auditor's independence is then compromised by the delegation of the fixing of their remuneration to the directors. This is a problem which has bedevilled the auditing profession almost since its inception but there is no mechanism whereby shareholders are able to pay audit fees. Consequently, this is one of the reasons why such emphasis is placed in the Ethical Code (Chapter 6) on auditor independence and why auditors must not only be independent of their client, but must be seen to be independent and not influenced by the size of any fees.

Section 493 requires that the remuneration of the auditors shall be stated in a note in the company's accounts.

Disclosure in the accounts must be made of all amounts (including benefits in kind) paid to the auditor for both audit and non-audit work (preparing accounts, tax, consultancy, etc.). Inclusion must be made of the remuneration from non-audit work paid to associates of the audit firm (e.g. management consultancy firms which are connected with the auditors) and for work done for subsidiaries of the client. The auditors must supply the necessary information to the company.

Thus auditors' remuneration must be disclosed to members and other users of the accounts and cannot be hidden by including it in a global figure such as administration expenses.

THE REMOVAL OF AN AUDITOR

The Companies Act takes a serious view of the removal of an auditor and there are a number of special procedures and rules to go through in order to effect a change of auditor.

Suppose that the directors prepare the accounts with the inclusion of some unusual accounting policy in order to increase profits in a particular year. The auditors, Tickett & Run, being honourable people may feel that the unusual policy is not acceptable and inform the directors that they will qualify their report if the policy is not changed. The directors may decide to abandon the policy for this year and change the auditors to Flexible & Co. in order that, in future years, the unusual policy may be adopted. Flexible & Co. may privately indicate that the unusual policy is acceptable to them.

Company law takes the view that company auditors must be capable of being changed if the *members* wish it, but it is designed:

- To ensure that the reality of the usual company situation, where the appointment of the auditors is by the members, cannot be manipulated by the directors to change auditors who are doing their duty, but who do not please the directors.
- To ensure that maximum publicity is given to any proposed change of auditors so that members are aware of the matter and can make informed choices.
- To give the auditors, who the directors would like to remove, every opportunity to state their case.

The relevant Companies Act legislation is:

- Section 510 – which states that a company may remove its auditors by ordinary resolution (a simple majority) notwithstanding anything in any agreement between it and them.
- Section 511 – which requires that special notice (28 days) must be given to the company of intention to move a resolution to remove an auditor or appoint some person other than the retiring auditor; most such resolutions are moved by the directors but occasionally shareholders may band together to remove an auditor who they may consider has become too complacent or pliable.

On receipt of such an intended resolution the company must immediately send a copy to the auditors who are to be removed. At least the removal cannot be done behind the auditor's back.

The auditors proposed to be removed, may make representations in writing to the company and request their notification to members. Thus the auditors who do not wish to be removed can state their case and require it to be sent to the members. Note that representations may not exceed a reasonable length.

The company must do two things (unless the representations are received too late):

- state the fact of representations being received in any notice of the resolution; and
- send a copy to every member of the company to whom notice of the meeting has been or will be sent.

The auditors have a general right to speak at the meeting on the subject of their intended removal and, if the representations have *not* been sent to the members, they have the right to have them read out at the meeting.

Note:

- The object of these rules is not to prevent the auditors being removed, if the members wish to remove them, but to ensure that they have adequate opportunity to put their case to the members before they vote on the resolution.
- Section 511(6) allows the company to seek an injunction against the auditor to restrain him or her from using his or her representations as a vehicle for needless publicity for defamatory matter.
- Where a motion to remove the auditors from office is passed the company must give notice to the Registrar within 14 days.

RESIGNATION OF AUDITORS

Auditors can resign. There are two main reasons why they may wish to do so. These are:

- Operational reasons – for example the company has grown too large for a small audit firm, the fee is inadequate, there is a conflict of interest where the auditor is representing both parties in a dispute, the client may have been taken over by a larger firm with its own auditors, etc.

- Ethical reasons – where the auditors conclude that because of fraud or other irregularity the accounts do not show a true and fair view and there is no immediate opportunity to report to members. They would be unable to report to members if the company refused to issue its financial statements, or if, at another stage in the year, the auditor has considerable doubts about management's integrity.

The procedures are set out in the Act. Section 516 states that an auditor may resign by depositing a notice in writing to that effect at the registered office. This is not effective unless accompanied by a statement of circumstances. This basically sets out the reasons for the auditor's resignation.

The statement of circumstances should contain a statement of any matters which they consider should be brought to the attention of members or creditors or if they consider that there are no such matters then a statement that there are none (Section 519).

The company must send a copy of the notice of resignation to the **Registrar of Companies** within 14 days on pain of a fine (Section 517). Thus any person searching the company's file will have notice of the resignation.

The auditors can cease to be auditors by simply not seeking re-election. However, in that case they must still deposit a statement of circumstances and there are time limits for this.

Statement of circumstances

If the statement of circumstances contains matters which the auditor considers should be brought to the attention of members or creditors then the company must, within 14 days of receipt of it, send a copy to all persons entitled to receive copies of the accounts (i.e. the shareholders) or must apply to the court.

The court may order that the statement may not be sent out if it thinks the statement is seeking needless publicity for defamatory matter but otherwise the statement must be sent out.

The auditors must send their statement to the Registrar.

Rights and duties of the resigning auditor

Section 518 gives specific rights and duties to the resigning auditor:

- The auditors may deposit, with their notice of resignation and statement of circumstances, a notice calling on the company to convene a general meeting for the purpose of receiving and considering the statement of circumstances and other explanations which the auditors wish to place before the meeting.
- The directors must call such a meeting within 21 days, or pay a fine, and they must send out copies of the statement and if they fail to do so the auditors can require that the statement be read at the meeting.

There are the usual caveats regarding the court and defamatory matters.

These provisions do give the auditors power to explain the circumstances of their resignation. Remember that the auditors are acting on behalf of the members who own the company.

If they are being forced out by the directors, for example, they have the right to call upon the shareholders to listen to their case.

This gives the auditors a very powerful tool in situations where they are in conflict with the directors and they feel that the rights of the shareholders are at risk, for example, in the case of a major fraud perpetrated by senior management.

AUDITOR'S DUTIES

Section 498 reads:

(1) *A company's auditor, in preparing their report, must carry out such investigations as will enable them to form an opinion as to–*
(a) *whether adequate accounting records have been kept by the company and returns adequate for their audit have been received from branches not visited by them, and*

    (b)   *whether the company's individual accounts are in agreement with the accounting records and returns, and*

    (c)   *in the case of a quoted company, whether the auditable part of the company's directors' remuneration report is in agreement with the accounting records and returns.*

  (2) *If the auditor is of the opinion–*

    (a)   *that adequate accounting records have not been kept, or that returns adequate for their audit have not been received from branches not visited by them,*

    (b)   *that the company's individual accounts are not in agreement with the accounting records and returns, or*

    (c)   *in the case of a quoted company, that the auditable part of its directors' remuneration report is not in agreement with the accounting records and returns, the auditor shall state that fact in their report.*

  (3) *If the auditor fails to obtain all the information and explanations which, to the best of their knowledge and belief are necessary for the purposes of their audit, they shall state that fact in their report.*

Subsection 1 requires the auditors to carry out investigations to determine if **proper accounting records** have been kept and proper returns from branches (at least branches not visited by the auditors) have been received.

What 'proper accounting records' comprise is considered later. The subsection also requires the auditors to investigate whether the accounts are in agreement with the accounting records and with returns from branches.

Subsection 2 requires that if the investigations required by subsection 1 lead the auditors to decide that proper accounting records have *not* been kept or if the financial statements *do not* agree to the underlying records then the auditors have to state the fact of their negative opinion in their Auditor's Report. If they form a positive opinion they need say nothing on the matter in their report. We will look at the wording of Auditor's Reports in more detail in Chapter 26.

Subsection 3 is another duty. If the auditors fail to get all the information and explanations which are necessary for the purposes of the audit they have to say so in their report. For example:

- if the auditors feel they need to know if the repairs expense account includes any capital expenditure and the invoices have been lost they have to say so in their report or
- if the auditors ask the directors if they have received any benefits in kind from the firm and they refuse to answer the auditors have to disclose that refusal in their report.

Auditors also have to report on disclosure in the financial statements in respect of director's remuneration and benefits. We will deal with this in detail in Chapter 26.

Subsection (5) of Section 498 requires the auditor to report adversely if the directors have prepared accounts as if the company was a small company when it is not.

AUDITOR'S RIGHTS

Section 499 states:

  (1) *The auditor of a company–has a right of access at all times to the company's books, accounts and vouchers (in whatever form they are held), and*

    (a)   *may require any of the following persons to provide them with such information and explanations as they think necessary for the performance of their duties as auditor.*

  (2) *Those persons are–*

    (a)   *any officer or employee of the company;*

    (b)   *any person holding or accountable for any of the company's books, accounts or vouchers;*

    (c)   *any subsidiary undertaking of the company which is a body corporate incorporated in the United Kingdom;*

(d) *any officer, employee or auditor of any such subsidiary undertaking or any person holding or accountable for any books, accounts or vouchers of any such subsidiary undertaking;*

(e) *any person who fell within any of paragraphs (a) to (d) at a time to which the information or explanations required by the auditor relates or relate.*

This section gives the auditors some very powerful rights. They have a right of access at all times to the company's books, accounts and vouchers in whatever format they are retained by the company. This recognizes the fact that many companies maintain their books and records in electronic formats.

A whole range of people are put under an obligation by subsection (2) to provide the auditors with information and explanations. These range from officers and employees of the company itself through officers and employees working for subsidiary companies, who either still work there or who have left the company but who worked there during the period for which the auditors are asking for information. This duty to disclose information also extends to anybody who doesn't work for the company directly but is concerned in maintaining the books and records.

This would cover a situation where, for example, a company has outsourced part of its accounting. The most common aspect of outsourcing is payroll and, in such a situation, the company which prepares the payroll is covered by this section and has to disclose information to the auditors.

In the same way Section 500 gives the auditors similar rights to information from overseas subsidiaries, (i.e. a subsidiary company not incorporated in the United Kingdom), and persons connected with it as defined in subsection (2) above.

Section 501 states (in part):

'*A person commits an offence who knowingly or recklessly makes to an auditor of a company a statement (oral or written) that–*

(a) *conveys or purports to convey any information or explanations which the auditor requires, or is entitled to require, under section 499, and*

(b) *is misleading, false or deceptive in a material particular*'.

This section is designed to punish individuals who deliberately set out to mislead the auditors and knowingly supply them with false information.

The penalties for doing so are set out in subsection (2) and include a term of imprisonment and/or a substantial fine.

THE AUDITOR'S REPORT

A public company must hold an AGM of its members (i.e. shareholders) in each calendar year. Private companies can decide whether or not to hold an AGM, unless their Articles of Association (essentially the rules of company procedure) require them to do so, (see above.)

When an AGM is held, the annual accounts, including the Statement of Financial Position and Statement of Comprehensive Income (and, in the case of holding companies, **group accounts**), which together comprise the financial statements, are presented to the meeting for approval by the members. Chapter 4 deals with this in more detail.

Included in the annual accounts must be a report by the auditors. The auditor's report has very specific content. In particular:

- The Act requires, in Section 396, that the financial statements must give a **true and fair** view of the state of affairs of the Company (i.e. by the Statement of Financial Position and of its profit or loss (i.e. by the Statement of Comprehensive Income) so the auditors must specifically state in their report whether or not, in their opinion, the financial statements give a '*true and fair*' view.

  The concept of true and fair is a difficult one and we will consider it in a later chapter. At this stage assume that it means that the accounts are free from any significant errors or misstatements.

- The Act contains very detailed requirements on the form and contents of accounts. The auditor has to say whether in his opinion the financial statements have been prepared in accordance with the Act.

- The auditors must examine whether or not there is any inconsistency between the information given in financial statements and that given in the rest of the annual accounts including the statutory **Directors' Report** and any other nonstatutory reports such as a trading review or a Chairman's Report.

We will deal with all this in more detail later in the book but for the moment you should understand that auditors are not being asked to give an opinion on the Directors' Report as a whole; they are only asked to review the Directors' Report and to consider whether the statutory disclosures, which the directors have to make, are properly stated and whether, taken as a whole, the report is consistent with the financial statements. If the auditors form an opinion that there is an inconsistency they have to say so in their audit report. As we stated in Chapter 2, the auditors are required by International Standard on Auditing 720 to review the non-statutory information contained in the financial statements for material misstatements and inconsistencies.

For example, suppose the Directors' Report contains a statement that '*production at the Bilston Factory has ceased and the plant there will be sold for scrap*', but the financial statements include the Bilston plant at full cost. There is an inconsistency in that the Directors' Report shows the Bilston plant to have no further use and the accounts assume further use. If the matter was material (i.e. of significant size) then the auditors would have to detail this inconsistency in their report.

Publication of the auditor's report

The Companies Act has a number of rules for publicising the Auditor's Report. However, the Companies Act treats small companies and large quoted companies rather differently. These are a summary of the regulations designed to set out the basic principles. A lot of the detailed provisions have been left out in the interests of clarity and brevity.

Students should be aware from their studies in Financial Accounting of the form and content of company accounts and the various dates for filing these with the Registrar of Companies, so much of that detail is omitted from the following paragraphs.

These are the main provisions:

(a) Firstly, Section 423:

> (1) *Every company must send a copy of its annual accounts and reports for each financial year to–*
> (a) *every member of the company,*
> (b) *every holder of the company's debentures, and*
> (c) *every person who is entitled to receive notice of general meetings.*

(b) Secondly, Section 430, which only applies to quoted companies:

> (1) *A quoted company must ensure that its annual accounts and reports–*
> (a) *are made available on a website, and*
> (b) *remain so available until the annual accounts and reports for the company's next financial year are made available in accordance with this section.*
> (2) *The annual accounts and reports must be made available on a website that–*
> (a) *is maintained by or on behalf of the company, and*
> (b) *identifies the company in question.*

Sections 431 and 432 are also relevant. Section 431 states:

> (1) *A member of or a holder of debentures of an unquoted company is entitled to be provided, on demand and without charge, with a copy of–*
> (a) *the company's last annual accounts,*
> (b) *the last directors' report, and*
> (c) *the auditor's report on those accounts.*

Section 432 says the same thing in respect of quoted companies. The auditor's reports must include any additional reports the auditors make, including those in respect of the Directors' Remuneration Report and the Directors' Report. We will discuss these in more detail in Chapter 26.

And Section 434:

(1) *If a company publishes any of its statutory accounts, they must be accompanied by the auditor's report on those accounts (unless the company is exempt from audit and the directors have taken advantage of that exemption).*

Finally, Section 437:

(1) *The directors of a public company must lay before the company in general meeting copies of its annual accounts and reports.*

Remember that this section applies only to public companies.

The reason for this is that private companies no longer have to hold Annual General Meetings unless they wish to do so. However, Section 424 requires a private company to send a copy of its annual report and accounts to its shareholders within nine months of the year end (Section 442) or the date it files its accounts with the Registrar of Companies, if earlier.

Section 441 requires each company to deliver to the Registrar each year a set of reports and accounts in the prescribed format within a set period after the financial year end. There are various requirements dependent upon the size of the company and whether it is quoted or unquoted. These are too detailed to be set out here but interested students should refer to Sections 442–7 of the Act.

Thus, whenever the full or summary financial statements are sent to members and other entitled persons, published, put onto a website, laid before the company in general meeting, or delivered to the Registrar of Companies then the Auditor's Report has to be included.

Every company has a file at **Companies House** and the accounts sent to the Registrar are included in the file. The file is open to inspection by members of the public. Thus, any interested person has access to the file without the company being aware of the enquiry.

AUDITOR'S RIGHTS TO ATTEND MEETINGS

Section 502 establishes the right of an auditor to receive notice of and to attend at meetings:

(2) *A company's auditor is entitled–*
 (a) *to receive all notices of, and other communications relating to, any general meeting which a member of the company is entitled to receive;*
 (b) *to attend any general meeting of the company; and*
 (c) *to be heard at any general meeting which they attend on any part of the business of the meeting which concerns him as auditor.*

In the case of private companies which are no longer required to hold Annual General Meetings, unless they wish to, Section 502(1) requires a private company to send to the auditors a copy of any written resolution to which a member is entitled. Written resolutions can be used by private companies and circulated to members instead of having meetings.

POWERS OF AN AUDITOR

Auditors of limited companies are given extensive duties by the Companies Act so, because of these responsibilities, the Act has also given the auditors extensive rights and powers. In practice, however, whilst the Act lays down provisions requiring directors and employees of a company to provide the auditor with information and insists that that information is true and correct, this is something which cannot really be enforced. The main power the auditors have lies in the reports the auditors write and we will discuss this further in Chapter 26.

RECOGNIZED SUPERVISORY BODIES

We noted above that for an individual to become a statutory auditor they must be a member of a **Recognized Supervisory Body (RSB)**. These are bodies recognized by the Financial Reporting Council as being suitable to control and monitor the actions of auditors.

A RSB is a body established in the UK which maintains and enforces rules both as to the eligibility of persons seeking appointments as statutory auditors and of the conduct of audit work. These rules are binding on members because they are members of these supervisory bodies or subject to its control.

Recognition will only be given to a Supervisory Body if it has rules on:

- holding of appropriate qualifications
- professional integrity and independence
- technical standards
- investigation of complaints and meeting of claims arising out of audit work

There are currently four RSBs:

- the three Institutes of Chartered Accountants, in England and Wales, Scotland and Ireland (ICAEW, ICAS, ICAI)
- the Association of Chartered Certified Accountants (ACCA)

The Association of Authorised Public Accountants which was a subsidiary of the ACCA and which represented individuals qualified to act as statutory auditors ceased to be an RSB from 31 December 2016.

RSBs have to maintain a register of persons and firms which are eligible to be company auditors and to make the register available to the public.

RECOGNIZED QUALIFYING BODIES

In addition to RSBs there are also Recognized Qualifying Bodies. The Act recognizes a distinction between supervisory bodies and qualifying bodies but in practice all bodies, are both, so the currently recognized qualifying bodies are the three Institutes of Chartered Accountants (England and Wales, Scotland and Ireland) and the Association of Chartered Certified Accountants.

A qualifying body means a body established in the UK which offers a professional qualification in accountancy. The body must have enforceable rules on:

- admission to or expulsion from a course of study leading to a qualification
- the award or deprivation of a qualification
- the approval of a person for the purposes of giving practical training or the withdrawal of such approval
- entry requirements
- courses of instruction
- professional experience
- examination and practical training

Appropriate qualifications

Essentially, the only persons so qualified are members of one of the three Institutes of Chartered Accountants or the ACCA.

There are also some provisions regarding qualified accountants from EC countries who wish to conduct audits in the UK. The rules are set out in Section 1221 which deals with overseas qualifications generally.

What this means, in practice, is that to be an auditor you have to be a member of a qualifying body and accredited by that qualifying body, in its capacity as a RSB, to carry out statutory audits.

PROFESSIONAL BODY RULES

All the professional bodies have strict rules on granting a licence to practise as a professional accountant, known as a Practising Certificate.

Members of the professional bodies cannot practise, i.e. sell their services to the public, unless they have a Practising Certificate. Obtaining a Practising Certificate is difficult and the rules about experience are strictly enforced. The precise rules change regularly and can be obtained by enquiry of the relevant professional body.

Professional bodies also require auditors to carry Professional Indemnity Insurance (PII). This is to indemnify clients from loss in the case of any errors, mistakes or, indeed, negligent behaviour by members so that, hopefully, the client is not made worse off.

In addition, all members of professional bodies have to keep themselves up to date with a programme of continuing professional education, to ensure that their skills remain up to date and relevant.

Disciplinary rules

Supervisory bodies must have a code of conduct and a disciplinary procedure to punish firms or individuals who have transgressed. Firms or individuals signing audit reports when not accredited to do so, breaches of independence requirements, failure to deal satisfactorily with clients, criminal convictions, etc. will all result in the member or firm having to explain themselves to some form of disciplinary committee of the Supervisory Body.

The result could be fines, reprimands and, in extreme cases, expulsion from the professional body.

Investigations into members or audit firms which are considered to be 'in the public interest' are conducted by the independent regulator through the Codes and Standards Committee and the Conduct Committee of the FRC. This is to reassure the public that high profile cases which might raise issues of real concern are not 'swept under the carpet' but are properly investigated. It has the power not only to have cases referred to it but also to intervene in cases which it decides are in the public interest. Figure 3.1 shows how the profession is regulated by the independent regulator the Financial Reporting Council.

FIGURE 3.1 Regulation of the auditing profession

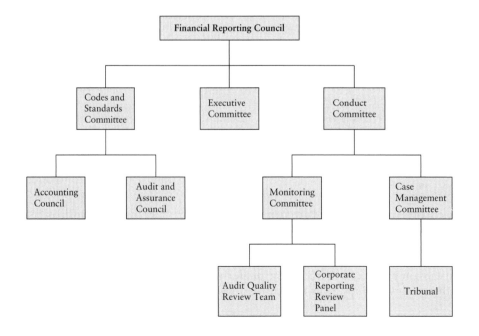

In addition, another part of the Financial Reporting Council, called the Monitoring Committee, which is an advisory committee of the FRC's Conduct Committee, and which includes the Audit Quality Review Team (AQR) provides independent oversight of the regulation of the auditing profession by the Recognized Supervisory and Qualifying bodies. Overall their functions include:

- monitoring of the quality of the auditing function in relation to economically significant entities (very large companies)
- independent oversight of the regulation of the accountancy profession by the professional accountancy bodies

Similar rules also apply to many other bodies. These include bodies registered under other Acts of Parliament, e.g. Building Societies, Financial Services Companies, Clubs and Societies registered under the Friendly Societies Act, Associations registered under the Industrial and Provident Societies Act 1965, Solicitors, etc. Special rules apply to Charities under the Charities Act 2006.

The object of all these rules and regulations is to:

- ensure all company auditors are fit and proper persons
- ensure professional integrity and independence
- maintain technical standards
- have procedures to maintain competence
- ensure practitioners have professional indemnity insurance
- investigate complaints
- maintain a register of eligible auditors
- monitor and enforce the rules on individual members

SUMMARY

- The statutory framework is the Companies Act 2006.
- There are limits below which smaller entities do not have to have audits.
- The law lays down restrictions as to who can act as an auditor. These are to ensure the auditor is independent from the company.
- Auditors have rights and duties under the Companies Act. Students should be aware of these. Their primary right is that the accessibility to information. Explanations cannot be restricted and their primary duty is to report to shareholders.
- There are some specific rules for private companies.
- Auditors can only be appointed and removed by shareholders.
- If auditors resign they must explain why. This explanation is a public document.
- Auditors must report and their report must be published with the financial statements.
- Most small entities need not have a statutory audit.
- The audit profession is regulated by Recognized Supervisory Bodies who control admissions, qualification, ethical compliance and training.
- An important issue is whether a small company's financial statements should be audited – there are advantages and disadvantages.
- Small and medium-sized companies may file abbreviated accounts.
- Dormant companies do not need an auditor.

POINTS TO NOTE

- Audits of all companies and enterprises are governed by the same audit principles and need for evidence irrespective of size.
- Students must be aware of the rights and duties of auditors contained in the Companies Act 2006.
- The appointment and removal of auditors and the legal requirements should also be studied.
- The whole issue of excessive laws, rules, regulation and bureaucracy as they affect small and medium-sized businesses is always a current issue, despite extensive deregulation. Changes need to be monitored.

CASE STUDY 1

Mainbrace Ltd is a book publisher and retailer which trades via the internet. The company was formed using a kit bought from a legal stationer, start-up capital was provided by the major shareholder, Bertie Bracewell's father, another friend and co-owner Angela Main also provided some capital. Bertie's father owns 10 per cent of the company but doesn't take any part in its activities.

When it was set up Angela and Bertie didn't want to get too 'tied up in paperwork' so they put on the forms that Bertie's father and Angela's mother, who just signed the form because she was asked to, were the first directors.

Since it started the company has done exceptionally well and, some 18 months after it started up it is now turning over approximately a million pounds per month, employs 60 people in three offices and has recently entered into a contract to buy a huge distribution warehouse valued at over £5m.

The company has Angela and Bertie to run the business and make all the decisions between them, with occasional advice from the company accountant Ron Whistler. He produces monthly management accounts but the company has never had an audit and has never filed any accounts with the Registrar of Companies.

Ron is getting a little concerned, particularly as he has just received an envelope from 'Companies House'. He daren't open it because he thinks it will be bad news.

Discussion

– What provisions of the Companies Act are Bertie, Angela and Mainbrace Ltd not complying with?

– What should they do as a matter of urgency to correct the situation?

CASE STUDY 2

Winfred Metal Reclamation Ltd, a small company, buys scrap metal residues from local companies and treats the residues to recover the metal which is then sold to other local companies.

The company is 75 per cent owned equally by Joe Winfred and his brother Eric, with their mother owning the remaining 25 per cent. The directors are Joe and Fred. The bank has advanced the company £0.5m for a new smelter. They have an audit at the insistence of the Bank but Eric is always complaining about the cost of it and thinks they don't need one now they have the bank loan.

Some purchases are made from itinerant scrap merchants. No evidence is available for the purchase of this scrap which totalled £160 000 in the year ending 30 November 2X16. However, there is no evidence that it is incorrect and Joe has had to give the auditors a letter giving them assurances over the completeness and validity of the transactions. The auditors find all other matters to be satisfactory and records are reasonable.

Office staff consists of Mary and Susan, who deal with all accounting matters including wages between them. There is no formal split of responsibilities, they just do what needs doing when it needs doing. Mary is living with Fred.

Some figures in the year ending 30.11.2X16 are:

	£
Sales	4 176 000
Net profit	124 000
Statement of Financial Position total	2 981 000
Employees	20

Discussion

- Is it possible for this company to dispense with an audit? Is this a good idea?
- Can the company file abbreviated accounts? What should the auditor do if they do?

STUDENT SELF-TESTING QUESTIONS

Questions with answers apparent from the text

a) What is the main piece of legislation regulating companies?

b) What are the limits for the statutory audit to apply to a company?

c) Who can be an auditor?

d) List the main rights of auditors.

e) How are auditors appointed?

f) What should auditors do on resigning their office?

g) What exemptions apply to smaller organizations?

h) What is the role of a Recognized Supervisory Body?

i) Which are the Recognized Supervisory Bodies in the UK?

EXAMINATION QUESTIONS

1   All professions have standards to which members of that profession are expected to adhere. These may encompass standards of both professional practice and personal conduct.

   Auditing in the UK is subject to a regulatory framework which includes a process for setting audit standards impacting directly upon the scope and powers of both external and internal auditors.

   Auditors are further required to exercise due care in the context of relevant case law and auditor liability.

   Required:

   (a)   Document the current regulatory framework for UK auditing.
   (b)   Describe the key roles of the Financial Reporting Council (FRC) and the Audit Quality Review Team.
   (c)   Detail the objectives by which the FRC intends to achieve its aims.

SOURCES AND ADDITIONAL READING

Financial Reporting Council (2009) *ISA 700 The Auditor's Report on Financial Statements*. London: Financial Reporting Council.

Financial Reporting Council (2009) *ISA 720 Section A – The Auditor's Responsibilities Relating to Other Information in Documents Containing Audited Financial Information* and *ISA 720 Section B – The Auditor's Statutory Reporting Responsibility in Relation to Directors' Reports*. London: Financial Reporting Council.

HMSO (2006) *Companies Act 2006*. London: HMSO.

ICAEW (2009) *Companies Act 2006 – Audit-Related Requirements and Regulations*. London: ICAEW.

ICSA (2007) *Companies Act 2006 Handbook*. London: ICSA.

TSO (2006) *Companies Act 2006*. London: The Stationery Office.

CHAPTER 4 ACCOUNTING REQUIREMENTS OF THE COMPANIES ACT 2006

Learning Objectives

After studying the material in this chapter you should be able to:

- understand the accounting requirements of the Companies Act 2006

- explain what is meant by accounting records

- understand the difference between statutory books and accounting records

- explain the fundamental accounting principles

- understand the concept of the true and fair override

INTRODUCTION

This section details the requirements on the keeping of accounting records by companies. The basis for this is, as might be anticipated, set out in the Companies Act 2006 ('the Act'). This lays down the minimum requirements for the books and records a company has to keep.

Auditors must know these rules because, as you will remember from Chapter 1, one of the duties of the auditors is to carry out investigations to enable them to form an opinion on whether the company has kept proper accounting records and has received proper returns from any branches not visited by the auditors.

Further, if the auditors form an opinion that the company has not kept proper accounting records, they have to say so in their report. The word 'proper' here means in accordance with custom or appropriate to the circumstances.

Particular problems that may cause the auditor to reflect on whether proper accounting records generally have been kept include:

- delays in writing up the records
- frequent alterations in records
- exceptionally large numbers of errors found by the auditor
- audit trail difficulties (the audit trail is the ability to follow a transaction through the records and documentation)
- computer problems including failure of software, chaos, hardware breakdowns, changes of computer staff, viruses, loss of data, etc.

We will look at these in more detail as we look at the process whereby the auditors gather their evidence by probing the company's books and records in their search for the truth but before that we must consider the accounting requirements of the Act.

ACCOUNTING AND ACCOUNTING RECORDS

It is important to understand the responsibility for keeping proper accounting records lies *wholly* with the directors.

The Companies Act 2006 sets out the company's responsibilities towards maintaining proper accounting records. Once again we must quote extracts from the Act but we think it important that students understand the legal framework within which they have to operate as auditors.

Section 386 states:

    (**1**)   *Every company must keep adequate accounting records.*

    (**2**)   *Adequate accounting records means records that are sufficient–*

        (a)   *to show and explain the company's transactions,*

        (b)   *to disclose with reasonable accuracy, at any time, the financial position of the company at that time, and*

        (c)   *to enable the directors to ensure that any accounts required to be prepared comply with the requirements of this Act.*

    (**3**)   *The accounting records must in particular contain–*

        (a)   *entries from day-to-day of all sums of money received and expended by the company, and the matters in respect of which the receipt and expenditure takes place, and*

        (b)   *a record of the assets and liabilities of the company.*

    (**4**)   *If the company's business involves dealing in goods, the accounting records must contain–*

        (a)   *statements of stock held by the company at the end of each financial year of the company,*

        (b)   *all statements of stocktakings from which any statement of stock as is mentioned in paragraph (a) has been or is to be prepared, and*

    (c)   *except in the case of goods sold by way of ordinary retail trade, statements of all goods sold and purchased, showing the goods and the buyers and sellers in sufficient detail to enable all these to be identified.*

  (5) *A parent company which has a subsidiary undertaking in relation to which the above requirements do not apply must take reasonable steps to secure that the undertaking keeps such accounting records as to enable the directors of the parent company to ensure that any accounts required to be prepared under this Part comply with the requirements of this Act.*

Section 387 deals with the failure of a company to comply with these requirements. It states:

  (1) *If a company fails to comply with any provision of Section 386 (duty to keep accounting records), an offence is committed by every officer of the company who is in default.*

  (2) *It is a defence for a person charged with such an offence to show that he acted honestly and that in the circumstances in which the company's business was carried on the default was excusable.*

A person guilty of an offence under this section is liable to a term of imprisonment or a fine, or both.

What are accounting records?

The Act says that the accounting records must be sufficient to disclose the financial position of the company:

- with reasonable accuracy
- at any time

In practice, with computerized accounting systems, this should not present any difficulty.

The company's accounting records must also record all the information the directors need in order to ensure that any financial accounts they prepare for presentation to the shareholders comply with the Act.

Note that most companies of any size produce detailed financial information regularly as part of their management processes. These management accounts will not be in a statutory format but do provide, as we will see in a later chapter, a good source of information for the auditor.

In detail, *as a minimum*, the accounting records have to include:

- a cash book to record sums of money received and expended and the matters about which the receipts or payments took place
- a record of assets and liabilities – which includes sales and purchase ledgers recording receivables (debtors) and payables (creditors) balances
- except for ordinary retail sales (i.e. cash sales over the counter), statements of all goods purchased and sold, showing the buyers and sellers and identifying them which means retention, in some form, of invoices, or copy invoices
- sales and purchase day books
- where the company deals in goods then:
  - statements of inventory (stock) held at each year
  - (where perhaps the company carries out a rolling inventory or perpetual inventory count) statements of inventory counts from which the yearend inventories figure is to be calculated

Subsection (5) is concerned with subsidiary undertakings abroad. The directors must ensure that they can obtain the information they need from the accounting records of subsidiary companies. This may present a difficulty in the case of companies incorporated in countries where the accounting regime is not as strict as it is in the UK, and don't forget these will be in a foreign currency and a foreign language so will require translation.

The company's accounting records can be kept wherever the directors think fit.

There are some special rules relating to accounting records kept outside the UK. Accounts and returns in respect of such business must be sent to the UK.

These accounts and returns sent to the UK must be such as to disclose with reasonable accuracy the financial position of the overseas business at intervals not exceeding six months and enable the directors to ensure that accounts comply with the Act as to form and content.

STATUTORY BOOKS

The Companies Act requires a company to keep the following **statutory books,** in addition to the accounting records as described above:

- a register of directors (Section 162)
- a register of charges (fixed and floating) (Section 876)
- minute books of meetings of the company, including meetings of its directors and meetings of its managers (Section 248)
- a register of members (Section 113); if it has more than 50 members the register must be indexed (Section 115)
- public companies must keep a register of information received from any person to whom they have sent a notice requiring them to disclose whether or not they have an interest in the company's voting shares (Section 808)

The auditor is interested in the statutory books being properly maintained because they are directly concerned with the accounts. The Statutory Books are audit evidence to be used in verifying detailed items in the accounts; for example, the total share capital shown by the sum of the individual share holdings in the register of members must agree with the share capital recorded in the books of account.

ACCOUNTING REQUIREMENTS

This section deals with the Companies Act requirements for accounts prepared in the UK on:

- the **accounting reference date**
- the form and content of company accounts
- the procedure on the completion of the accounts
- modified or abbreviated accounts and
- the publication of full and abridged accounts

An auditor must know these rules because the majority of audits are company audits (others may be, for example, public sector bodies which have different rules). The principal objective of the audit is to report on the truth and fairness of the financial statements. Section 495 requires the auditors to state in their report whether, in their opinion, the accounts have been properly prepared in accordance with the Act.

Some of this you will know from your studies into Financial Accounting and Financial Reporting, nevertheless we include them here because it is a part of the auditor's role to ensure that all the financial rules have been complied with. It is outside the scope of this book to detail all the various disclosure requirements for a set of financial statements, but knowledge of the fundamental accounting principles is vital to sound understanding of audit work.

Remember also that the responsibility for preparing financial statements, laying them before the company (i.e. presenting them to shareholders) and delivering them to Companies House lies wholly with the management.

Accounting reference date

Every company has to have a period end and the Statement of Comprehensive Income is for the period ending on that date and the Statement of Financial Position is made up as at that date. A company's period end is known as the Accounting Reference Date and the financial statements are made up for the accounting reference periods ending on that date.

Sections 390 to 392 give the law on this matter in unbelievable length. In short:

- the company can give notice to the Registrar of its chosen date
- if this is not done then the Accounting Reference Date is either
  - the last day of the month in which the anniversary of its incorporation falls
  - if the company was formed before 1 April 1990, it is automatically 31 March

The date can be changed by going through the prescribed procedures. The company must prepare accounts for each and every accounting reference period. The actual date used may be up to seven days either side of the accounting reference date.

Financial statements required

For information, students should note that some familiar terms describing the individual financial statements have been amended by International Accounting Standard 1 *'Presentation of Financial Statements'*. We use the new terminology but have included the old one in brackets for clarity. Note these notes apply to accounts prepared under UK accounting rules.

The following financial statements must be prepared:

- a Statement of Comprehensive Income (Profit & Loss Account) for each accounting reference period (Section 396)
- a Statement of Financial Position (Balance Sheet) as at the accounting reference date (Section 396)
- if the company is a holding company, then group accounts must also be prepared (Section 399); it is permissible and is the common practice not to publish the company's own Statement of Comprehensive Income but to publish a consolidated Statement of Comprehensive Income which shows how much of the consolidated profit or loss for the financial year is dealt with in the company's individual accounts (Section 408)
- notes attached to and forming part of the Accounts:
  - giving the detailed information required by the Act and various accounting standards without cluttering the financial statements
  - giving certain required additional information (Sections 409–413)
- a Directors' Report (Sections 415–418)
- a Directors' Remuneration Report (Section 420)

This is the minimum required by law. Most public companies, particularly those listed on the Stock Exchange, include a lot more in their annual accounts. These may take the form of a chair's statement, a review of operations, a five-year summary of accounts, etc.

The auditors are not responsible for auditing these as they are not part of the statutory minimum accounts but, as we will see in more detail in a later chapter, under ISA 720 the auditors must make sure that these extraneous pages are consistent with the statutory accounts.

Form of company accounts

The financial statements must follow the formats specified by the Act. In addition to the Companies Act requirements there are Financial Reporting Standards (FRSs) which is part of what is known in the UK as Generally Accepted Accounting Practice (GAAP). These includes the various rules relating to disclosure and reporting in company accounts in the UK. Listed UK groups of companies are required to report using International Financial Reporting Standards (IFRSs) but in this book we have made reference to UK GAAP and Companies Act reporting. The new financial reporting standard FRS 102 is applicable to unlisted groups and by individual listed or unlisted entities, so could be adopted by a parent or subsidiary of a listed group of companies, and thus has a possible wider application in the UK for auditors.

Section 395 allows a company to prepare individual accounts either in accordance with the Companies Act or in accordance with international accounting standards. It does not specify which standards could be applied where.

Auditors must be familiar with the principles which lie behind the preparation of, and disclosures required in, company accounts.

In practice, checklists will be used to ensure that nothing vital has been missed. However, many examination bodies set questions which require some knowledge of accounting disclosures so students must have in mind their studies in financial accounting when answering auditing questions. We will include an outline of the financial reporting requirements where these are relevant to the auditor's work.

ACCOUNTING PRINCIPLES

Accounts are prepared under four fundamental accounting principles. These constitute the underlying framework for all the items to be included in the accounts and all the specific disclosures required either by the Act or the various accounting standards.

The fundamental accounting principles are listed here.

Going concern

The company is presumed to be carrying on business as a going concern. What this means, in practice, is that the company will have the ability to continue to trade in substantially the same way as it does in the financial period being reported on for the foreseeable future. This has been defined elsewhere as being a period of 12 months from the accounting date. This particular principle is very important to the auditors and we will look at it in more detail in Chapter 23.

Consistency

Accounting policies must be applied consistently within the same financial statements and from one financial year to the next.

Prudence

The amount of any item reported on the financial statements has to be determined on a prudent basis for example, what this means is:

(a) Only profits actually realized at the period end date should be included in the Statement of Comprehensive Income – so profits should not be anticipated in the financial statements in case they eventually do not materialize.

(b) All liabilities and losses which have arisen or are likely to arise in respect of the financial year to which the accounts relate or a previous financial year shall be taken into account, including those which only become apparent between the period end date and the date on which it is signed on behalf of the board of directors.

What this means in practice is that profits or earnings should only be included in the accounts if they are certain to be achieved but known or anticipated losses and liabilities should be included to be on the safe side. This is to safeguard against too much optimism on the part of the directors in accounting for profits which haven't been earned and ignoring possible costs and liabilities.

Accruals basis

All income and charges relating to the financial year to which the accounts relate will be taken into account, irrespective of the actual date of receipt or payment. The alternative to this is known as the *Cash Basis* where only actual receipts and payments are accounted for. This is now only used by the very smallest businesses.

Departure from the accounting principles

If it appears to the directors of a company that there are special reasons for departing from any of the principles stated above in preparing the company's accounts in respect of any financial period they may do so but particulars of the departure, the reasons for it and its effect must be given in a note to the accounts.

CONTENT – DISCLOSURE REQUIREMENTS

The Act and associated financial reporting standards give extensive detailed rules on the *minimum* information which must be given in the financial statements or in notes attached to them.

There is no objection to the financial statements giving *more* information than the minimum, but in practice most accounts, particularly of private companies, just disclose the minimum required by the law.

Companies are required to state, with their statement of accounting policies, whether the accounts have been prepared in accordance with applicable accounting standards and give particulars of any material departure from those standards and the reasons for any such departure.

TRUE AND FAIR OVERRIDE

The Act requires that the accounts show a true and fair view. This means that when they are prepared they must be prepared giving full recognition to all the relevant accounting principles and the requirements of the statutory reporting framework. This is the responsibility of the directors.

In the event that compliance with the law meant that the accounts did not show a true and fair view, Section 396 has the answer:

1. *If compliance with the regulations, and any other provisions made by or under this Act as to the matters to be included in a company's individual accounts or in notes to those accounts, would not be sufficient to give a true and fair view, the necessary additional information must be given in the accounts or in a note to them.*
2. *If in special circumstances compliance with any of those provisions is inconsistent with the requirement to give a true and fair view, the directors must depart from that provision to the extent necessary to give a true and fair view. Particulars of any such departure, the reasons for it and its effect must be given in a note to the accounts.*

In other words, this, admittedly somewhat nebulous concept of a 'true and fair view', takes precedence over the strict legal requirements of the reporting rules. This is closely tied to the doctrine of substance over form which we looked at in Chapter 2 and students should be familiar with these ideas. It has to be stressed that application of the **true and fair override** is quite rare and only used in exceptional circumstances. If it is applied, it has to be fully explained and justified in the financial statements. It is not a licence for noncompliance.

PROCEDURE ON COMPLETION OF THE FINANCIAL STATEMENTS

The financial statements comprising:

- the Statement of Financial Position
- the Statement of Comprehensive Income
- the Directors' Report
- the Directors' Remuneration Report
- the Auditor's Report
- group accounts, where required

must be approved by the board of directors and then the Statement of Financial Position must be signed by at least one director of the company on behalf of the board (Section 414).

For a public company required to hold an AGM:

- A copy of the Accounts must be sent to all persons entitled at least 21 days before the AGM (Section 424).
- Copies of the Accounts must be laid before the company in general meeting (usually the AGM) (Section 437).
- A copy of the Accounts must be delivered to the Registrar of Companies (Section 441).

For a private company not holding an AGM the shareholders must be sent the accounts not later than nine months from the year end, or the date the company files them with the Registrar if earlier (Section 424).

PERIOD ALLOWED FOR FILING ACCOUNTS

The directors of a company are required by the Act (Section 441) to file the accounts with the Registrar of Companies in accordance with a timescale as:

- Private companies – within *nine months* after the end of the accounting reference period.
- Public companies – within *six months* after the end of the accounting reference period.

ABBREVIATED ACCOUNTS

Sections 444 and 445 gives a number of exemptions to small and medium-sized companies. These are, broadly:

- Small companies are exempt from some filing requirements.
- They need only file an abbreviated Statement of Financial Position and need not include many of the notes to the accounts. They do not need to file a Statement of Comprehensive Income or a Directors' Report.
- Medium-sized companies can file a set of financial statements which can include a slightly abbreviated Statement of Comprehensive Income and exemption from certain disclosures of information.

Small and medium-sized companies are defined as companies which satisfy *two or more* of the following:

	Small-sized	**Medium-sized**
Turnover does not exceed	£10.2m or gross turnover of £12.2m	£36m or gross turnover of £43.2m
Balance Sheet total does not exceed	£5.1m or gross turnover of £6.1m	£18m or gross turnover of £21.6m
Average number of employees does not exceed	50	250

These exemptions apply to groups of companies where the *whole group* falls within either the net or gross limits. The exemptions do not apply to a company if, in the year, it is:

- a public company
- an insurance company
- a company carrying on a regulated activity under the Financial Services and Markets Act 2000, which, basically, includes banks, building societies, investment and pension advisors, friendly societies, credit unions, etc.
- a group where one of its members is also a public company or regulated under the Financial Services and Markets Act 2000

Auditors have to give special reports where small and medium-sized companies file abbreviated accounts. We will deal with this in Chapter 26 when we discuss forms of audit report.

PUBLICATION OF ACCOUNTS

Sections 434–6 contain some rules on the publication of accounts.

A company may publish its statutory accounts and if it does so, it must also publish its Auditor's Report. Statutory accounts mean the full accounts or the reduced accounts allowed to small or medium-sized companies described above.

A company may also publish nonstatutory accounts, i.e. accounts containing more than the statutory minimum or extracts (Section 435). If it does, then it must also publish a statement:

- that the accounts are not statutory accounts
- whether statutory accounts have been delivered to the Registrar of Companies
- whether the auditors have made a report
- whether any such report has been qualified or modified

In addition, the Companies Act brought in a new provision. Listed companies must publish accounts on a website and must maintain them on that website until accounts for the next period are available (Section 430). The directors are responsible for maintaining the website and for ensuring that any financial information published on it which purports to be from the financial report is in accordance with it.

These must be freely available to anyone logging on and not restricted unless there is a legal requirement to do so. The website must clearly identify the company and be maintained by it.

This gives auditors some special problems insofar as they have to ensure that the financial statements on the website remain as originally posted there and are not subsequently amended in any way.

SUMMARY ACCOUNTS

Section 426 contains the option for a company to provide its shareholders with summary accounts if the shareholders so wish. This is to reduce the burden of sending full accounts to shareholders who may only be interested in certain parts of them. The company's shareholders can pass a resolution allowing the company to send summary accounts to all shareholders except those who insist on having the full accounts.

Sections 427 and 428 contain detailed rules as to the form and content of these summary accounts for both quoted and unquoted companies. Insofar as these rules affect auditors the key aspect is that they must contain a statement from the auditors that:

- the summary accounts are consistent with the full accounts;
- the information in the summary accounts is derived from the full accounts, including the Directors' Report;
- the summary accounts comply with the Act;
- whether or not their report on the full accounts was qualified and, if it was,
- details of the qualification.

DORMANT COMPANIES

Section 1169 has some rules on dormant companies:

A company is dormant in a period if during the period no significant accounting transaction occurred. Such companies need not appoint an auditor but must still file accounts.

SUMMARY

- The Companies Act lays down rules for keeping of proper accounting records and for proper returns from branches including those overseas.
- The Companies Act also requires a company to keep a range of additional records called the statutory books.
- The directors are wholly responsible for the maintenance of accounting records and statutory books.
- The auditor has a duty to investigate and form an opinion on whether proper accounting records have been kept.
- The Companies Act lays down rules for the keeping of proper accounting records and proper returns from branches overseas and the directors have the responsibility for seeing that the company obeys the rules.
- Failure to obey the rules may mean that:
    - proper books of account have not been kept
    - proper returns have not been received
- Sufficient information has to be available for the proper disclosure of matters of which the Companies Act requires detailed disclosure.
- The Companies Act lays down very detailed rules on:

- - what financial statements are required
  - the form of the financial statements
  - the accounting principles to be followed
  - detailed information to be disclosed
- Auditors must know the rules because their duties laid down by the Act include a requirement to report on the true and fair view and compliance with statute of the Financial Statements.
- There are accounting period and time limits for laying and delivering financial statements to the shareholders and to the Registrar of Companies.
- Specified exemptions from these rules are given to small and medium-sized companies.
- Listed companies may send out summary financial statements.
- Quoted companies must publish accounts on a website.

POINTS TO NOTE

- Returns in the context of this chapter are of two types:
  - Those from branches in the UK. The auditors must see that proper returns have been received by head office when they have not visited the branches. Some companies have numerous branches, e.g. Tesco. The auditors cannot be expected to visit them all.
  - Those from branches overseas. These are subject to special statutory requirements but the auditors have the same duty to satisfy themselves on overseas branch matters as they do for UK branches.
- There are penalties for failing to keep proper accounting records or statutory books.
- Organizations other than companies may have specific statutory requirements with regard to accounting records (e.g. financial service companies) and the auditor needs to ensure that these have been complied with.
- Note the requirement in Section 386 to be able to prepare financial statements 'at any time'.
- In addition to the Companies Act requirements on financial statements, there are also two other sets of requirements to be fulfilled. These are:
  - Financial Reporting Standards
  - Stock Exchange requirements for listed companies
- Shareholders are entitled to a full set of accounts which contains all the disclosures required by the Companies Act and various accounting standards.

CASE STUDY

Cicero Ltd has now realized that it needs to improve its financial records and send some accounts to Companies House. So far it has managed with a series of spreadsheets devised by the company accountant, Eric Chopper, who is not a qualified accountant, which records incoming cash and cheques, payments and outstanding invoices. There are no ledgers and no double entry system. Eric does, however, reconcile his bank spreadsheets with the bank statements each month. He claims that all the company needs to know to run the business is how much money is in the bank.

The business consists of four small supermarkets and two clothes shops. The company has never prepared audited accounts, even though it has traded for three years. Inventory counts are held annually at each of the shops, and when the total figure is calculated the inventory count sheets are thrown away as they are only rough counts.

Discussion

– What does Cicero Ltd need to do to rectify the situation?

– Who is responsible for ensuring this is properly dealt with?

– By improving the position of Cicero Ltd, what advantages will this bring?

– Why might Eric Chopper not be keen to rectify the position?

STUDENT SELF-TESTING QUESTIONS

Questions with answers apparent from the text

a) What must appear in books of account?

b) List the statutory books.

c) Who are responsible for maintaining the books of account and the statutory books?

d) What is the auditor's interest in these documents?

e) What financial statements must be prepared?

f) What are the time limits for laying and delivery of accounts?

g) Define small and medium-sized companies.

h) What exemptions are available to them?

i) What is the true and fair override?

j) What are the rules on publishing accounts in abridged form?

k) What are the rules on sending out accounts in summary form?

l) What additional reports are required from an auditor?

SOURCES AND ADDITIONAL READING

Charlesworth's Company Law (2010), 18th Edition. London: Sweet & Maxwell.

Financial Reporting Council (2009) *ISA 700 The Auditor's Report on Financial Statements*. London: Financial Reporting Council.

Financial Reporting Council (2009) *ISA 720 Section A – The Auditor's Responsibilities Relating to Other Information in Documents Containing Audited Financial Information* and *ISA 720 Section B – The Auditor's Statutory Reporting Responsibility in Relation to Directors' Reports*. London: Financial Reporting Council.

International Accounting Standards Board (2007) *IAS1 Presentation of Financial Statements*. London: IASB.

ICSA (2007) *Companies Act 2006 Handbook*. London: ICSA.

TSO (2006) *Companies Act 2006*. London: The Stationery Office.

Wood, F. (2008) *Business Accounting I and II*, Harlow: Pearson Education.

CHAPTER 5
AUDITING AND ACCOUNTING STANDARDS AND GUIDELINES

Learning Objectives

After studying the material in this chapter you should be able to:

- understand the development of International Standards on Auditing and the role of the international bodies

- explain the role of the Financial Reporting Council

- appreciate the structure of financial reporting in the UK

- understand the form and content of an ISA

- appreciate the publications of the Financial Reporting Council and what they are for

- explain the relevance of Accounting Standards to auditing

INTRODUCTION

The increase in globalization and cross-border trading has driven the need for international standards for auditors to ensure that audits are carried out with the same levels of quality and with the same evidence requirements across the world. Accordingly, the **International Auditing and Assurance Standards Board (IAASB)**, which is a subcommittee of the International Federation of Accountants (IFAC), was tasked with developing generic international standards which can be adapted for local conditions but which, essentially, provide a common standard for audit work across the globe. This is intended to provide assurance to both regulators and investors that financial information is audited to a common standard.

IFAC is the global organization for the accountancy profession with 164 members in 125 countries. It comprises most of the world's major accountancy bodies. In the UK both the ACCA and the ICAEW are members of IFAC, for example. Its global role is to protect the public interest by developing high-quality international standards, promoting strong ethical values, encouraging quality practice and supporting the development of all sectors of the profession around the world.

It is important to realize that IFAC is financed and run by accountancy bodies, it is not any form of government sponsored organization and has to balance various competing national interests. Critics of IFAC point out that, through the medium of the accountancy bodies which are its members, the very large accounting firms, the so-called Big 4, may have a lot of influence on the activities of these bodies.

The generic international auditing standards are produced by the IAASB. It defines its role as:

'to improve auditing and assurance standards and the quality and uniformity of practice throughout the world, thereby strengthening public confidence in the global auditing profession and serving the public interest'.

Not all countries, including the UK, have adopted all of the ISAs developed by the IAASB in full, and there are some standards issued by the IAASB which have not been adopted by the Financial Reporting Council (FRC) and which are not fully dealt with in this book.

The conduct of audits in the UK is regulated by International Standards on Auditing (ISAs), shown in Figure 5.1, which are issued in the UK and Ireland by the FRC. These used to be issued by the Auditing Practices Board (**APB**) but in 2012 a reorganization renamed the APB the 'Audit and Assurance Council' and made it an advisory component of the Codes and Standards Committee of the FRC.

FIGURE 5.1 International Standards on Auditing

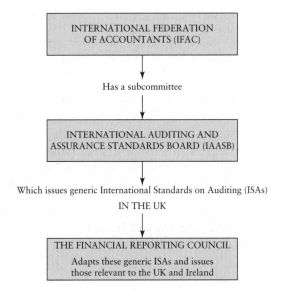

For convenience we will refer to the regulator as the FRC throughout, as it simplifies the relationship.

The FRC uses those generic standards issued by the IAASB to produce the UK and Ireland versions which are used by auditors registered in the UK.

ROLE OF THE FINANCIAL REPORTING COUNCIL ('FRC')

The FRC's role is to lead the development of auditing practice in the United Kingdom and the Republic of Ireland, so as to:

- establish high standards of auditing
- meet the developing needs of users of financial information; and
- ensure public confidence in the auditing process.

To achieve these objectives, it issues:

- International Standards on Auditing (ISAs) which are mandatory and which we will be dealing with at length in this book
- Practice Notes which are helpful and indicative of good practice; and
- Bulletins which comment on items of current interest.

The professional bodies are particularly concerned about the maintenance of auditing standards and the **Monitoring Committee** (Chapter 3) will look at any cases where very large audits of major organizations ('economically significant entities') are involved to ensure that standards are maintained in even the largest audit firms.

INTERNATIONAL STANDARDS ON AUDITING ('ISAs')

Each ISA contains two types of material:

- *basic principles and essential procedures* with which auditors are required to comply with
- *explanatory and other material* which is designed to assist auditors in interpreting and applying auditing standards

ISAs are structured consistently and each one has five sections:

1   Introduction – this explains the scope of the ISA (i.e. what it covers) and any explanatory material relevant to an understanding of the particular requirements of the ISA.
2   Overall Objectives of the Auditor – this is repeated in each ISA and confirms the objectives of a financial audit.
3   Definitions – relevant terms are explained for the avoidance of doubt.
4   Requirements – the actions to be taken by the audit and the specific considerations that must be borne in mind when dealing with the issue which is the subject of the ISA.
5   Application and other explanatory material – this section is a more detailed explanation of the requirements of the ISA and contains explanatory material to assist the auditor in carrying out their duties.

Auditors <u>must</u> comply with the International Standards on Auditing. The wording of the ISAs themselves is framed in a positive way using words like 'should' and 'shall' rather than, say, 'could', which is less prescriptive. This leaves the auditor very little room for manoeuvre when trying to argue that the ISA should not be applied in a particular situation. An example of this is contained in ISA 501 *Audit evidence – specific considerations for selected items.*

Previous versions of the standard suggested that attendance at the inventory count was good audit practice and was generally a good idea so they 'recommended' that auditors attend. ISA 501 leaves no room for doubt and states auditors 'shall' attend or explain why they did not.

Failure to comply with ISAs can lead to disciplinary or regulatory action against the auditor by their accrediting RSB (Chapter 3). In addition, the courts may take into account any noncompliance with ISAs when considering if audit work was adequate in negligence cases.

Appendix 1 summarizes the key aspects of all the ISAs currently published by the Financial Reporting Council. The details are necessarily brief, however all of these will be dealt with in more detail in the relevant sections of the book.

PRACTICE NOTES

The FRC also issues Practice Notes which are designed to assist auditors in applying Auditing Standards of general application to particular circumstances and industries. Clearly some of these Practice Notes are quite specialized, such as PN 14 (Housing Associations) or PN 21 (Investment Businesses) but this is what distinguishes a Practice Note from an ISA. Details of these are shown in Appendix 2.

They are persuasive rather than prescriptive and have similar status to the explanatory material in the ISAs. Practice Notes may later be developed into or be included in ISAs. The IAASB also issues *International Auditing Practice Statements* which provide practical assistance to auditors on implementing the ISAs.

In addition, the IAASB is also responsible for issuing the International Standards on Quality Control (ISQCs), ISQC 1 having been adopted by the FRC, and also the International Framework for Assurance Engagements (IFAE). We will refer to these in later chapters.

The FRC also issues bulletins which provide auditors with timely advice on new or emerging issues which, like Practice Notes, are persuasive rather than prescriptive.

Other FRC documents include '*The Scope and Authority of FRC pronouncements*' and the FRC Ethical Standards which we will deal with in Chapter 6. In addition, the FRC also issues Press Notices from time to time which refers to new guidance in specific areas. For example, they have stressed the importance of professional scepticism when carrying out audits and have also issued revised guidance on attendance at inventory counts. We will mention these in the relevant chapters but students should be aware of contemporary pronouncements by the FRC.

ACCOUNTING STANDARDS

In general, published accounts are required to conform to the relevant financial reporting standards. This book is concerned with those accounting standards issued by the FRC and which are collectively known as UK GAAP – Generally Accepted Accounting Practice.

Students may also refer to accounting standards issued by the International Accounting Standards Board (IASB) known as International Financial Reporting Standards (IFRS).

In either case the point is the same – part of the auditor's duty is to assess whether or not the financial statements they are auditing do comply in general and in detail with the relevant financial standards. This book is about auditing and cannot include a detailed description of all the accounting standards. For a detailed understanding readers will need to consult an accounting textbook.

The financial reporting standards relevant to UK GAAP are issued by the FRC. The FRC has greatly simplified the number of standards in issue and there are now only five relevant accounting standards.

The five standards are:

● FRS 100 – Application of Financial Reporting Requirements
● FRS 102 – The Financial Reporting Standard Applicable in the UK and Republic of Ireland
● FRS 103 – Insurance Contracts
● FRS 104 – Interim Financial Reporting
● FRS 105 – The Financial Reporting Standard Applicable to the Micro-entities Regime

Of these only FRS 102 need concern us at it is this standard which governs the form and content of company accounts. Basically it incorporates all the other accounting standards previously in issue and adds some new features of its own.

Auditors should be aware of FRS 102 and its provisions. Most audit firms have now developed checklists to ensure nothing is missed as the provisions of FRS 102 are detailed and complex.

Some areas, particularly charities and public sector bodies, have Statements of Recommended Practice (SORPs), which are also approved by the ASB. The financial statements of organizations within the relevant sectors would normally comply with the appropriate SORP. The best known of these is probably the SORP which relates to the accounts of charities.

FRS 105 The Financial Reporting Standard Applicable to the Micro-Entities Regime is applicable to small companies (i.e. those that are classed as small under the Companies Act 2006 – see Chapter 3).

THE RELEVANCE OF ACCOUNTING STANDARDS TO AUDITING

As we have seen from the previous chapter auditors must include, in their reports, their opinion on whether the financial statements they report on give a true and fair view.

Accounts, to show a true and fair view, must comply with these financial reporting standards, unless circumstances are exceptional. The Companies Act 2006 formally recognized a financial reporting framework and requires that accounts should include a statement confirming that the accounts have been prepared in accordance with applicable accounting standards to comply with the relevant framework.

Thus auditors are, in effect, being asked to give an opinion on whether all accounting standards have been complied with in the preparation of the accounts they are auditing – which means that auditors must know and understand the accounting standards in detail.

Auditing students are expected to know the key provisions of the main accounting standards. Many auditing questions in examinations require this knowledge and examinees are advised to quote from the accounting standards and state which of the accounting standards are relevant to their answer.

Students will be reassured to note, however that, in certain key areas, particularly those relating to non-current assets, this book will explain the significance of the relevant accounting treatment and the provisions of an appropriate standard.

SUMMARY

- The Financial Reporting Council issues ISAs, Practice Notes, Bulletins and other pronouncements.
- The professional auditing bodies have undertaken to adopt all ISAs issued by the FRC.
- Apparent failures by auditors in the UK to comply with the Auditing Standards contained in the ISAs may be investigated and may lead to penalties. The penalties may ultimately include withdrawal of registration in the worst cases.
- The Auditing Standards are likely to be taken into account in a court of law where the adequacy of an auditor's work is being considered, for example, if auditors are being proceeded against for the recovery of damages caused by their alleged negligence. All the FRC pronouncements are in practice likely to be taken into account in this way.
- The ISAs contain numbered Auditing Standards which are mandatory and also explanatory and other material which is persuasive.
- The main principles included in Financial Reporting Standards are essential knowledge for auditing students.
- Amongst the requirements for a true and fair view is compliance with the relevant financial reporting standard whether it be UK GAAP or an IFRS.
- The ISAs which apply to the audit of larger companies also apply to the audit of smaller entities, although the documentation requirements may be reduced.

POINTS TO NOTE

- Departures from the accounting standards are rare and have to be fully explained.

- SORPs (Statements of Recommended Practice) are normally issued with regard to the accounts of specialized bodies (e.g. universities, pension schemes, charities). SORPs are not mandatory but accounts for a body where a relevant SORP exists are unlikely to show a true and fair view if the SORP is not followed. Examiners do not normally expect students to know the SORPs.

- Financial Reporting Standards are mandatory except where a true and fair view would not be given which is very unlikely.

CASE STUDY

Both Cicero Ltd (from Chapter 4) and Mainbrace Ltd (from Chapter 3) have realized that things cannot go on as they are. They have approached audit firm Tickitt & Run who have agreed to act and are currently setting up a meeting with each company to explain the legal and audit situation.

Discussion

– What will be the key points Tickitt & Run will have to explain to them about auditing standards?

– How will Financial Reporting Standards, broadly, affect these businesses?

– How would you go about explaining to entrepreneurial management the need for all these auditing and accounting rules?

STUDENT SELF-TESTING QUESTIONS

Questions with answers apparent from the text

a) What documents are issued by the FRC?

b) What material is contained in an International Standard on Auditing?

c) What is a SORP?

d) In the audit of small companies which Financial Reporting Standard is particularly important?

e) Why are financial reporting standards important to auditors?

EXAMINATION QUESTIONS

1 The profession has been criticized by politicians for its role in monitoring potential corporate failure. Radical reforms have been called for in the way the audit is regulated. For example, politicians have stated there should be a change of legislation in the following ways:

- *Auditing standards*

    Auditing standards should be set and enforced independently from the accounting profession by an external regulator.

- *Fraud*

Auditing firms should have a duty to detect and report fraud.

- *Non-audit services*

Non-auditing services supplied to a client should be stopped.

- *The duration of the appointment of auditors*

The appointment of auditors should be for a maximum period of seven years.
Required:
Discuss the reasons why you feel that the audit profession might be open to criticism in the above areas.

2   International Standards on Auditing (ISAs) apply equally to the audit of all entities, whatever their size. However, the manner in which ISAs are applied differs from entity to entity and depends on the use of the auditor's judgement. The characteristics of smaller entities may include:

- Common ownership and management – so the owners run the business.
- A dominant individual in charge who makes most of the decisions.
- Limited controls over the processing of transactions with few administrative staff taking on a variety of duties.
- The use of standardized computer packages.
- Reliance on the auditor for accounting expertise.

These characteristics have an effect on the way the audits of smaller entities are approached, how the audit is conducted and the relationship between auditor and client.
Required:
Describe how the audit might be affected by the circumstances shown above and the nature of the relationship between auditor and client in this case as opposed to, say, carrying out the audit of a much larger company.

SOURCES AND ADDITIONAL READING

Audit Quality Forum (2006) *Fundamentals: Principles-Based Auditing Standards, Fatal Flaw Review*. London: ICAEW.

Financial Reporting Council (2015) *FRS 102 – The Financial Reporting Standard Applicable in the UK and Republic of Ireland*. London: Financial Reporting Council.

Financial Reporting Council (2009) *Summary of the Main Changes in the New ISAs (UK and Ireland)*. London: Financial Reporting Council.

Financial Reporting Council (2009) *All International Standards on Auditing*. London: Financial Reporting Council.

ICAEW (2009) *Right First Time with the Clarified ISAs*. London: ICAEW.

Wood, F. (2008) *Business Accounting I and II*. Harlow: Pearson Education.

CHAPTER 6
ETHICAL STANDARDS AND RULES OF PROFESSIONAL CONDUCT

Learning Objectives

After studying the material in this chapter you should be able to:

- understand the importance of an auditor being independent from their client

- discuss the difference between a principles-based approach and a rules-based approach

- understand the ethical principles

- understand the threats which might compromise ethical behaviour

- explain the role of the ethics partner

- explain the various prohibitions which serve to maintain auditor independence

- understand contingency fee arrangements and the provision of non-audit services to audit clients

- understand the rules relating to insider trading and money laundering

- appreciate the principles surrounding whistleblowing and the public interest

INTRODUCTION

Auditing, as we have seen, is carried out by accountants in public practice. A vital feature of auditing, for obvious reasons, is that the auditors must be *independent* from the management who are responsible for the financial statements and the owners who receive them.

This creates an instant dilemma as it is of course that very management which pays the auditors' fees, (Figure 6.1). There is always pressure on the auditors to retain the goodwill of their client but this makes it all the more important that no one client can exert such pressure that the firm becomes tame auditors who will sign off whatever numbers are put in front of them.

The consequences of being thought of as so financially irresponsible that the standards of the profession are compromised or betrayed are likely, in practice, to amount to financial penalties which often the large firms may be able to well afford, but the greater loss is that of reputation. Ultimately the transgressing individual may have sanctions against them, have their audit licence taken away, maybe even their professional qualification if their crimes are serious enough, but the cost of the loss of reputation to the firm as a whole can be immense.

The loss of clients, the scorn of the financial press, even the opprobrium of the public can be far more damaging than mere loss of money. The whole firm can be damaged by the actions of a few so, generally, it pays off for firms to maintain the standards of the profession and maintain a clear objective independent line with their client no matter what the temptation.

FIGURE 6.1   The auditor's conflict

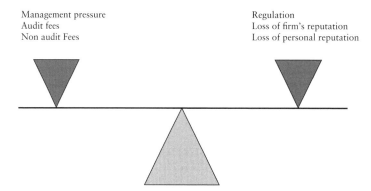

Management pressure
Audit fees
Non audit Fees

Regulation
Loss of firm's reputation
Loss of personal reputation

In the case of companies, the auditors must not be connected with either the directors or the shareholders. They must also be independent of government agencies or other groups who have contact with the business.

For these reasons external auditors form themselves into independent firms willing to perform audits for a fee for whoever is able and willing to employ them. Some of these firms are very large, with worldwide connections and employ thousands of people. Others are very small with sometimes only one or two principals and a low number of staff.

Auditors have to conduct their audits, not only taking into account the relevant sections of the Companies Act 2006, or any appropriate legislation, but also as instructed by Auditing Standards, Practice Notes and Bulletins issued by, in the United Kingdom, the Financial Reporting Council (Chapter 5).

Accountancy is a profession and all professions have certain distinguishing characteristics which include an ethical code and rules of conduct. This chapter is concerned with the rules of conduct prescribed by the Financial Reporting Council and reinforced by the relevant professional bodies.

For the reasons set out in Chapter 1 in respect of Agency Theory, if for no other reasons, it is imperative that auditors retain their professional credibility and respect in the eyes of the investing public. Loss of trust would be devastating to the financial world and it is for this reason that the Recognized Supervisory Bodies

(Chapter 3) place such a great emphasis on ethical behaviour by their members and infractions of the rules are heavily punished.

Accounting trainees wishing to join any of the professional auditing bodies should be aware of the Ethical Code of the professional body they are trying to join as it applies to registered students as well as qualified members. In any case there are some generic ethical standards which are included in the ethical codes of all the professional accountancy bodies.

Professional ethics for accountants come from The International Ethics Standards Board for Accountants (IESBA). This is one of the Standards Setting Boards located within the International Federation of Accountants (IFAC).

The IESBA Code of Ethics for Professional Accountants is arranged in three parts:

- Part A – General Application of the Code
- Part B – Professional Accountants in Public Practice
- Part C – Professional Accountants in Business

Part A contains over-arching principles that should be considered paramount.

The existing Ethical Codes of the ACCA and the chartered bodies (ICAEW, ICAS and ICAI) are derived from this.

However, the FRC has issued Revised Ethical Standard 2016, which all of the RSBs have to conform to and which contains new restrictions on the activities of audit firms which are designed to further strengthen auditor independence. Broadly these are mainly confined to what is known as a **Public Interest Entity** (PIE). A PIE is defined as, in this case, a UK entity with securities traded on an EU regulated exchange, credit institutions (banks) or insurance companies.

The new FRC standard bans the provision of certain types of non-audit services, and subjects others to a fee cap of no more than 70 per cent of the audit fee calculated on a rolling three-year basis. This has been seen as being overly prescriptive by accountancy bodies many of whom take the view that their existing framework approach is a sufficient safeguard of auditor independence which does not need a detailed listing of prohibitions of services an audit firm may or may not offer a client.

In this chapter we will look at the fundamental ethical principles which underpin the auditor's day-to-day work. Ethical behaviour in connection with certain specific circumstances, principally fraud, changes in professional appointments (professional etiquette) and professional liability will be dealt with in separate chapters.

PRINCIPLES-BASED OR RULES-BASED APPROACH?

Before we consider the ethical code in detail it is instructive to consider the approach taken by the FRC and the accountancy bodies. As we saw in Chapter 2 when looking at Corporate Governance the approach taken by the regulatory bodies is very much a framework approach, i.e. to adopt a series of guiding principles and then require companies to either comply with them or explain why they have not done so. This has been preferred to a prescriptive rules-based approach which tries to regulate for every possible combination of situations.

So it is with professional ethics. The FRC has set out a standard which sets out 'rules' of professional conduct to be observed by auditors. Whilst these are rules in the sense that they set out a series of Do's and Don'ts for practising auditors they are not a prescriptive set of requirements which attempt to cover every situation. Rather they form a **conceptual framework** based on fundamental principles. What this means in practice is that there are five fundamental principles which, taken together as a code of conduct, will enable the auditor to retain the required level of independence from their client and observe appropriate standards of competence and behaviour.

For example, one of the fundamental principles is **integrity**. The ethical code defines it and says auditors must have it and behave in an appropriate way. For example, the rules point out one obvious problem, that of **conflicts of interest,** defines what they are and requires auditors to avoid them and that is about it. They do not seek to list a prescriptive set of circumstances where a conflict of interest might arise – audit firms are left to exercise their skill and judgement in evaluating situations in the light of ethical principles and taking appropriate action to ensure their independence is not compromised.

A rules-based approach would attempt to define for the auditor how to behave in specific situations or when dealing with specific types of client. The accountancy bodies in the USA have adopted this approach, principally with the Sarbanes–Oxley legislation. Such rules-based codes tend to be much bigger and contain pages and pages of prescriptive requirements. There are advantages and disadvantages on both sides of course which can be summed up in Figure 6.2.

As can be seen from Figure 6.2 rules-based codes are generally seen as inflexible and encouraging of legalistic style quibbling and 'bending' of the rules. Principles-based approaches are seen as flexible and place the onus on the auditor to demonstrate compliance, rather than simply ticking a box, but their very imprecision may lead to misinterpretation or rule bending without there being much in the way of possible sanctions. It is difficult to discipline an auditor when the rules they are supposed to observe are ambiguous or imprecise and use words such as 'appropriate'.

FIGURE 6.2 Approaches to ethical codes – principles- or rules-based?

Conceptual framework – principles-based	Rules-based
Advantages	**Advantages**
• Flexible – capable of fitting changing situations and circumstances	• Provides certainty – auditors are told what to do
• Can be applied across boundaries	• Contains definite prohibitions which reduces ambiguity and the scope for personal 'interpretations' of the requirements
• Onus is on the auditor to prove they have considered everything and comply	
• Can include specific prohibitions	
Disadvantages	**Disadvantages**
• Lack of precision may lead to 'interpretations' of rules	• Encourages a legalistic approach to redefining or reinterpreting the rules to fit a situation where there are no rules
• Requires judgement on the part of the auditor which can lead to differing interpretations.	• Can't deal with every situation
	• Inflexible

For example, what might be considered to be an 'appropriate' level of corporate hospitality from a client? Is it none at all (which is the rule in the public sector), lunch in the pub, a box at the opera, tickets to the Cup Final, a holiday in the Maldives – clearly that last one would be inappropriate but what about the others? If you are the senior partner of a multinational accountancy firm dealing with a huge client, Cup Final tickets may not be classed as inappropriate, but if you are a partner in a small auditing firm dealing with a small client with financing issues it might well be totally inappropriate to accept an expensive gift from them.

The auditor is always required to exercise judgement and discretion in such matters. Whether a code is based on a conceptual framework or contains a prescriptive set of rules they both require the auditor to maintain their independence from their client and any action which might possibly compromise that must be resisted whether it is technically permitted by the rules or not.

FUNDAMENTAL ETHICAL PRINCIPLES

These fundamental principles apply to all members of the professional bodies in some form and are the basis for the way auditors carry out their work and in their dealings with other people. Students must have a full understanding of these principles and should conduct their work in accordance with them.

It is important to bear in mind that auditors cannot give unbiased opinions unless they are independent from all the parties involved, in particular their client. There is a dilemma, which we referred to briefly in

Chapter 3 and which we will discuss in more detail later, in that auditors receive their fees from their client, i.e. the entity they are auditing, and not from the shareholders to whom they report. Nonetheless, independence from the client is critical to the carrying out of an audit and not only must auditors be independent in fact and in attitude of mind but they must also be *seen* to be independent.

The ethical principles taken together are designed to ensure that auditors become and remain independent enough to be able to give a clear and unbiased opinion.

A key principle is that auditors should consider their independence from the perspective of an objective, reasonable and informed third party. If such a party would conclude that an action would compromise the auditor's independence, the auditor will need to ensure that the action is not taken or they would no longer be able to undertake the audit engagement. The revised standard makes clearer the risks to independence posed by situations where the auditor acts as an advocate, and emphasises the prohibition which applies in all but immaterial situations.

The FRC standard requires firms to comply with what it calls **Overarching Principles**. These are fundamental to any ethical standard and are basically:

- integrity
- objectivity and
- independence.

These principles together form a framework of ethical outcomes required to be met by the auditor.

Integrity

Auditors should behave with integrity in all professional, business and personal financial relationships. Integrity includes not merely honesty but fair dealing, truthfulness, courage and confidentiality. One of the issues which might compromise integrity is the question of a conflict of interest. This can arise when:

- The duty of an auditor to be impartial conflicts with some personal interest they may have in the client. This conflict may arise in the context of both business and personal relationships. For example, auditors of family companies may develop a personal relationship with director/shareholders over time which may compromise the auditor's ability or willingness to challenge their client's actions and speak honestly to them.
- Auditors or accountants find themselves advising both sides in a dispute. Clearly they cannot act impartially for both parties and must take steps to extricate themselves from that situation.

Objectivity

Auditors should strive for **objectivity** in all professional and business judgements. Objectivity is the state of mind which has regard to all considerations relevant to the task in hand but no other. It presupposes intellectual honesty and excludes bias, prejudice and compromise. Auditors must give fair and impartial consideration to all matters relevant to their task and disregard all those that are not. Objectivity must not be impaired by conflicts of interest (see above).

Independence

Independence is defined as freedom from conditions or relationships which, in the context of an engagement would compromise the integrity or objectivity of the auditor. As Regulator the FRC has laid heavy emphasis on auditor independence and consequently it is seen as an overarching principle in itself.

The FRC standard then goes on to prescribe the approach to independence in some detail and what firms must do, or not do, to ensure compliance with it. We will deal with these in more detail later.

In addition to these Overarching Principles professional bodies set out their own. For example, the ACCA has a code which includes Objectivity and Integrity – but not Independence as a separate item – and in addition three other ethical principles which are worth including here: confidentiality, competency and professional behaviour.

Confidentiality

The auditor must treat all information gathered during the course of their audit as confidential and should not disclose any information to third parties without their client's permission or unless there is a legal or professional duty to disclose. It is important that directors and management of an audit client can rely on the auditors to treat the information obtained during the audit as confidential, unless they have authorized its disclosure or it is already known to a third party or the auditors have a legal right to disclose it.

Accountants should not use any information gathered during the course of their professional work for their own personal gain.

Competency

Auditors should not accept or perform work which they are not competent to undertake unless they obtain such advice and assistance to enable them to carry out the work competently. Auditors should carry out their professional work with due skill, care, diligence and expedition and with proper regard for the technical and professional standards expected of them.

Professional behaviour

Auditors should behave with courtesy and consideration to all with whom they come into contact during the course of performing their work. They should also comply with relevant laws and regulations and avoid any behaviour which might bring their profession into disrepute.

ETHICS – GENERAL RULES

Professional accountants are required to observe proper standards of professional conduct whether or not the standards required are written in the requirements or are effectively unwritten rules of implied standards of behaviour and conduct.

Clearly, auditors are specifically required to refrain from misconduct, which is difficult to define precisely, but which includes any act or default which is likely to bring discredit on themselves, their professional body or the profession generally.

Several general points can be made:

- As we have already said professional independence is exceedingly important. This is very much an attitude of mind rather than a set of rules but there are many specific requirements which we will describe later. Auditors who observe the general principles outlined above will be able to act independently without any further prompting from their professional body.
- Integrity is vital. Synonyms for integrity include honesty, uprightness, probity, moral soundness and rectitude. Auditors are required to have the intellectual honesty to come to their own conclusions and the courage to defend their opinions in the case of any dispute. An important aspect of integrity is confidentiality.
- Accountants must not only be people of integrity and independence; they must also be seen to be so. Any interest (e.g. owning shares in a client company) which might diminish an accountant's objectivity of approach, or which might appear to, must be avoided.
- When auditors have ethical difficulties or are unsure of what course of conduct to follow, they should consult their professional body or take legal advice. If in doubt always seek advice.

Ethics partner

Audit firms should appoint an Ethics Partner, whose role is:

- to ensure that standards of professional conduct are maintained
- to organize training for staff and partners or directors on ethical matters

- to ensure client review procedures are properly carried out
- to review matters such as contingency fee arrangements or threats to independence caused by involvement with clients

GENERAL ETHICAL THREATS

Compliance with these fundamental principles may potentially be threatened by a broad range of circumstances. Most threats fall into the following categories:

- *Self-interest threats*, which may occur as a result of the financial or other interests of a professional accountant or of an immediate or close family member.
- *Self-review threats*, which may occur when a previous judgement needs to be re-evaluated by the accountant originally responsible for that judgement.
- *Advocacy threats*, which may occur when an accountant promotes a position or opinion to the point that subsequent objectivity may be compromised.
- *Management threat*, the professional auditor must not take any part in the management of an entity nor influence any management decisions that the entity makes. This is particularly relevant in the case of the provision of non-audit services and auditors must ensure that their objectivity and independence are not compromised by being drawn into the decision-making process.
- *Familiarity threats*, which may occur when, because of a close relationship, a professional accountant becomes too sympathetic to the interests of others.
- *Intimidation threats*, which may occur when a professional accountant may be deterred from acting objectively by threats, actual or perceived.

Safeguards that may eliminate or reduce these sorts of threats to an acceptable level fall into two broad categories:

- safeguards created by the profession, legislation or regulation and
- safeguards in the work environment.

Safeguards created by the profession, legislation or regulation include, but are not restricted to:

- educational, training and experience requirements for entry into the profession
- continuing professional development
- corporate governance regulations
- professional standards
- professional or regulatory monitoring and disciplinary procedures by the Regulator (FRC) and the relevant RSB

Safeguards in the work environment include generally avoiding or minimizing threats to auditor objectivity and independence. We discuss these in more detail below.

THREATS TO INDEPENDENCE

As we have seen, the auditor's independence and objectivity must be beyond question when conducting an audit. Auditors must always approach their work with their integrity and objectivity unimpaired by any of the threats to their independence outlined above. There are a number of matters which may threaten or appear to threaten the independence of an auditor.

Undue dependence on an audit client

Public perception of independence may be put in jeopardy if the fees from any one client or group of connected clients dominate the auditor's practice. To avoid this happening the FRC Ethical Standard states that the income from any one client should not exceed 15 per cent of gross practice income or 10 per cent in the case of listed or other public interest companies. This is generally known as *the 15 per cent rule*.

This general observation needs modifying in the cases of new practices. Clearly this is a guideline and a certain amount of flexibility is permissible in practice, but audit firms must be prepared to resign from a client's audit where the fee income from that client starts to exceed this 15 per cent (or 10 per cent) limit. Firms would be wise not to have one client which dominates their practice as the consequences of this, the intimidation threat detailed above, could lead the individual auditor on to some very unsavoury, unethical paths.

It is this 15 per cent rule which is seen as a cornerstone of independence and enables auditors, in some circumstances, to offer additional, non-audit services to non-PIE clients (i.e. non listed clients) without compromising their objectivity as they are not financially dependent on any one client.

Care should also be taken by individual audit partners within firms where their portfolio of work is dominated by one or two clients. It is for this reason, if for no other, that regular rotation of audit partners after a period of time, suggested to be five years, is a recommended practice.

Family or other personal relationships

It is essential to avoid professional relationships where personal relationships exist. Examples of personal relationships include mutual business interests between members of the group comprising the client, the audit firm, officers or employees of the client, partners or members of staff of the audit firm. In addition, family or personal relationships must be avoided. For example, it would be extremely unethical for an auditor to audit a company where:

- Members of their family had a major interest even if they did not.
- A close relative or the auditor's spouse was a senior officer or director of the company.
- The auditor had worked for the company prior to joining the audit firm or a member of the audit team had joined the client in a senior capacity. We look at this situation in more detail below.

Involvement in the audit in these circumstances could give rise to the familiarity or intimidation threats outlined above so this must be avoided.

Beneficial interests in shares and other investments

Partners, their spouses and minor children should not hold shares in or have other investments in client companies. This extends to investments in pension funds or family trusts as well as individual holdings by themselves or by a close relative.

An audit staff member should not be employed on an audit if that staff member or some person connected with him or her has a beneficial interest in the audit client. In most firms the rules which apply to partners are extended to all staff and audit firms will take steps to ensure that none of their staff or families have any interest in audit clients.

Loans to and from clients

An auditing practice or anyone closely connected with it should not make loans to its clients. Firms or individuals within audit firms should not receive loans from clients, unless they are on the same commercial terms as an ordinary member of the public would receive, i.e. on an arm's-length commercial basis. The same applies to guarantees.

Note that not collecting fees for an unrealistic amount of time could be interpreted as a loan to a client so fees should be collected under normal trade terms.

Acceptance of goods and services

Goods and services should not be accepted by an audit practice or by anyone closely connected with it unless the value of any benefit is modest. Acceptance of undue corporate hospitality poses a similar threat; a box of chocolates as a gift is probably acceptable, but a weekend in Paris would not be. Acceptance of continuing or excessive corporate hospitality, for example regular attendance at football matches with a client, may well lead to the perception that the auditor's objectivity has been compromised.

Actual or threatened litigation

Litigation or threatened litigation (e.g. on auditor negligence) between a client company and an audit firm would mean the parties being placed in an adversarial situation which clearly undermines the auditor's objectivity.

Influences outside the practice

There is a risk of loss of objectivity due to pressures from associated practices, bankers, solicitors, government or those introducing business.

PROVISION OF NON-AUDIT SERVICES

One of the major problems which the audit profession is wrestling with is the question of true independence from the audit client where an audit firm supplies additional consultancy type services.

This topic is continually under review by the professional bodies. It was a contributory factor in several financial scandals where the audit firms in question seemed to lose their objectivity and become unnecessarily involved in the affairs of their clients. The most shocking example of this was the demise of audit mega firm Arthur Andersen following the collapse of Enron and WorldCom in the USA.

The provision of non-audit services to clients who are not PIEs is acceptable in principle, but care must be taken to ensure that the quality of audit work is not compromised because of the urge to cross-sell other, more lucrative, services to the client.

In previous years the urge to cross-sell advisory services to clients led to the practice of 'lowballing' where audit firms would quote unfeasibly low fees to a potential audit client so they could sell additional services at a later date. This is, generally, prohibited by the regulatory bodies and auditors must be prepared to justify the fees charged to the client in terms of work done, hours spent and rates at which staff are charged out.

In the case of audit fees there is a specific requirement, in Ethical Standard ES4, that the size of the audit fee should *not* be influenced by fees charged to the client for other services.

There is no evidence that 'lowballing' compromises audit quality as the regulations and the fear of litigation generally ensures that auditors try and deliver a quality service to their client irrespective of the size of the fee charged. The problem is one of independence. Firms must ensure that advisory and other services supplied to clients:

- are separate and distinct from audit services, i.e. that there are no common personnel involved in both activities
- do not include any form of management decision making
- do not include the design of any systems which might later be audited by the same firm

We look at this in more detail below.

The FRC has set out in some detail prohibitions on services which audit firms may not supply to PIE's and similar bodies and these prohibitions may prove valuable guidance to Ethics Partners in respect of non-PIE clients. These prohibitions include:

- certain tax services, in particular where the audit firm may be acting as an advocate for their client
- management and decision making
- bookkeeping and accountancy services
- design and implementation of internal control or risk management procedures for one year before they begin to perform the audit
- payroll
- valuation or litigation support services

- services related to Internal Audit
- HR services including sourcing management staff
- services related to financing, capital structure and investment strategy

Where the client is not a PIE and therefore is not absolutely covered by the FRC prohibition firms must be careful to ensure their independence is not compromised through the provision of substantial non-audit-related services.

Generally, the rules clearly require a separation of the staff providing advisory services from those carrying out the audit. There should be a system of what have become known as 'Chinese walls' within the accounting firm to ensure that information disclosed in an advisory capacity is not revealed to audit staff and vice versa.

This may seem perverse, but it retains the independence of each set of staff to carry out their defined roles as if they were from separate firms and not merely different departments of the same firm.

This does pose difficulties to very small firms, but they have to find a way of abiding by these principles and retaining their objectivity and independence. In most cases small firms carry out little or no statutory audit work because of the size limits on firms which no longer have to have a statutory audit, so much of their work is advisory rather than audit based.

It is understood that the nature of preparing complex accounts must necessarily require that some services (e.g. finalizing the financial statements) should be performed by the auditors. However, any such assistance should be solely of a technical or mechanical nature and any advice given must be of an informative nature only.

The auditor can advise on issues but must not take part in making any management decisions. The overriding rule is that the auditor should not be involved in decision-making and, where there is a threat to independence, the risk has to be reduced to an acceptable level.

COMMISSIONS AND FEES

Auditors should not allow their judgement to be swayed by the receipt of a commission, fee or other reward from a third party as a result of advising a client to pursue one course rather than another.

IAS 220 'Quality control for an audit of financial statements' requires audit firms to review their relationship with every client on an annual basis to determine if it is proper to accept or continue an audit engagement, bearing in mind actual or apparent threats to audit objectivity.

Warnings are included in the ethical guides of the professional bodies of the risks to objectivity in performing non-audit services, but these all fall a long way short of prohibition.

Fees

The normal basis for charging for professional work is on the time spent on the work calculated at appropriate hourly rates for principals, senior and other staff. The hourly rate may vary according to the difficulty or complexity of the work involved. It is up to the accountants to decide upon their hourly rates depending on cost structures, the complexity of the work, the timetable for completion, market conditions, etc.

It is not permissible to charge on a percentage basis except where statute or custom allows, e.g. in liquidation and receivership work, nor should audits be carried out on a contingency fee basis.

Accountants who receive commissions from stockbrokers, insurance brokers, etc. for transactions effected for clients or for trusts of which the accountant is a trustee should either:

- pass on the commissions to the client or trust by deducting the amounts received from their fees and showing the deduction on the invoice or
- keep the commissions if specifically authorized to do so by the client.

Contingency fees

A contingency fee is one based on the achievement of some goal or target, for example, a fee based on the successful raising of finance. Audit work cannot be carried out on a contingency fee basis.

It is permitted for accountants to charge for non-audit services on a contingency fee basis, however, the basis of charging such fees must be notified to the client in writing and agreed by the client. This practice is, however, discouraged by the RSBs.

Where non-audit work is taken on a contingency fee basis the audit firm should consider the effect on the firm and should notify an Ethics Partner that such an arrangement is contemplated. The audit firm should not undertake an engagement to provide non-audit services in respect of an audited entity on a contingency fee basis where:

- the contingency fee is significant to the audit firm, or that part of the firm by reference to which the audit engagement partner's profit share is calculated or
- the outcome of those non-audit services (and, therefore, the amount of the fee) is dependent on a future or contemporary audit judgement relating to a significant matter in the financial statements of an audited entity.

These two prohibitions are designed to ensure that the audit partner is not tempted to make a favourable decision in order to collect a contingency fee and thus enhance their profit share or make a favourable decision in order to collect the fee and increase the profits of the audit firm both of which instances would probably be classed as corrupt acts by any disciplinary tribunal.

CONFLICTS OF INTEREST

Conflicts of interest can arise between accountants and their client. Conflicts of interest can also arise between a client and another client, and accountants should not act for both parties if the parties are in dispute.

Conflicts can arise where auditors have some kind of personal or business involvement with their client. The specific prohibitions outlined above will prevent financial involvement in the client's affairs but the development of personal relationships is more problematic. Auditors should be aware of the familiarity threat shown above which can create conflicts and compromise independence.

For example, the accountants may be called upon to advise two clients who are tendering for the same contract; or they may be advising a company and also one of its directors who are in dispute. In all such cases the accountants should not accept assignments where they are put in a position where they are being asked to advise both sides. On the other hand, they may well be able to put forward proposals to settle the dispute.

Specific examples of conflict of interest include:

- Provision of other services to audit clients. It is customary for auditors in many cases to provide other services as well as the audit, for example preparing tax computations. This is perfectly acceptable providing the service does not involve performing executive functions or making executive decisions. For example, discussing the annual dividend decision with the board would be an executive action and hence unacceptable.
- Preparation of accounting records. Care should be taken that the client takes responsibility for the work done and that objectivity in auditing is not impaired. The accounting records of public company clients should not be prepared by the auditor.
- A practice should not report on a company if a company associated with the practice is the company secretary to the client. However, it is acceptable to provide assistance to the company secretary.
- As we have seen, no person in an accounting firm should take part in the audit of a company if he or she has, in the accounting period or, it is recommended, in the previous *two years* been an officer or employee of that company. This may cause a conflict of some description so the position is best avoided.
- There is no similar rule regarding a senior member of the audit staff or a partner joining an audit client, however, where an individual is indicating an intention to join a client they should be taken away from any involvement with that client's affairs as soon as practicable. Again it is recommended that a 'cooling-off' period be instituted where the individual who proposes to join an audit client is taken away both from the audit and from any possibility of influencing the course of the audit or the audit firm's approach to the audit. The more senior the individual the more problematic this becomes.
- If it is not possible to have any sort of cooling-off period, the audit team should be changed and, if possible, a new audit approach instituted with a different team. The involvement of the former employee should be monitored to ensure there is no question of undue influence being brought to bear on the audit work.

- Receivership, liquidation and audits. In general, auditors should not accept receiverships or appointment as a liquidator of client companies without a three-year gap between the assignments. Clearly a liquidator of a company would be inhibited from taking a negligence action against the audit firm if he or she had been the statutory auditor.

ADVERTISING AND PUBLICITY

There are still considerable restrictions on advertising. Any advertisement should not:

- bring into disrepute themselves, any member of the professional body, the firm or the accountancy profession generally
- discredit the services of others by, for example, claiming superiority
- contain comparisons with other members or firms
- be misleading, either directly or by implication
- fall short of the Advertising Standards Authority as to legality, decency, honesty and truthfulness; adverts may refer to the basis on which fees are calculated, but this is often best avoided

Firms must be careful about comparisons with other audit firms to avoid being misleading. Under certain circumstances they may offer free consultations and possibly discounts, but this has to be handled very carefully. Audits may not be carried out free of charge or at a discount!

None of this means that accountants' advertisements need to be dull or unimaginative; many firms have put out exciting adverts but whether they are also 'attractive' is a different matter.

Accountants may advertise for work and engage in other forms of publicity, for example, by posters or hoardings or on motor vehicles, on sportswear or by sports sponsorship providing that the advertising itself is considered concomitant with the dignity of the profession. Accountants may not make any unflattering references to, or comparisons with, competitors or other professional service providers.

Accountants may pay an introductory commission, fee or reward to a third party for introducing clients, however, it is advisable that such payments are declared to the client.

ETHICS AND QUALITY ISSUES

The professional bodies require strict adherence to the ethical codes and have considerable enforcement mechanisms. Of course ethical codes should be obeyed in the spirit as well as the letter but this intention sometimes crumbles in the face of commercial pressures. The use of aggressive accounting practices in order to maintain profits (and often, coincidentally, bonus payments), can put auditors under severe pressure. No firm is willing to lose a large client and the temptation must be to bend and stretch the rules as far as possible to accommodate the client.

This is not to say that audit firms succumb to pressure, but the reality is that the audit world is very competitive and results have to be maintained. The increased use of risk management approaches must not change ethical behaviour such that the truth stops being truth and starts becoming the fact that no one found out you lied.

There are three key issues:

- The profession had a severe shock following the destruction of the giant auditing firm of Arthur Andersen, post-Enron closely followed by the banking crises of 2007–8 which claimed several large financial institutions around the world and forced governments to bail out several banks, and it is these crises which prompted the regulators to look closely at quality control and to ensure that lapses in ethical behaviour are punished.
- The regulation of the profession has moved away from the RSBs towards government-based regulators such as the FRC who now determine how the profession is regulated. Whether this will result in the public's having any greater perception of the independence of the profession remains to be seen.
- Research indicates that the 'expectation gap' (Chapter 1) is still a real issue. The question of trust remains vital. A major loss of trust by the investing public could result in a severe shock to the financial world and the role of the independent, ethically sound, technically competent auditor remains central to that trust. Whilst companies are undoubtedly responding to the rise in Corporate Social Responsibility their primary function is to create wealth and increase shareholder value, so their ethical progress may well be corralled within financial realities.

ETHICAL STANDARDS – SMALLER COMPANIES

The Financial Reporting Council has included in its Ethical Standard a section entitled *Provisions Available for audits of Small Companies.*

The standard recognizes that there are particular circumstances applicable to the auditing of smaller entities. 'Smaller entities' are defined in the standard and include not only small companies and groups as defined above but also such organizations as small pension funds (less than 100 members) and registered social landlords with less than 250 units. The standard attempts to take account of the close relationships which often exist between auditors of small companies and their clients, in particular where the auditor may well provide some of the financial information such as tax liabilities or a limited amount of accountancy services.

The standard exempts auditors of smaller entities from some of the ethical provisions of the standard – subject to certain conditions.

These are:

- The auditor is not required to carry out an external independent quality control review of the kind detailed in Chapter 7. However, the Ethics Partner must be informed that the client's fee represents only between 10 and 15 per cent of the audit firm's fee income.

- The firm must be aware of the '*self-review*' threat where the audit firm is providing services in addition to carrying out an audit. Auditors of small businesses often contribute to the preparation of the accounts and usually perform other tasks for the business (tax matters, IT advice, etc.) and this close acquaintance with the business can constitute good audit evidence in some circumstances. The danger is obviously that the auditor can be auditing their own work and that there is a lack of independence and no objective overview of the figures. The auditor should discuss the situation with management and include a review of the client in a cycle of internal quality control reviews to ensure that independence is not being compromised.

- There is the danger that, in the absence of capable management, the audit firm will make what are, effectively, management decisions. This is the 'management threat'. The ethical rules state that audit firms should attempt to avoid any situation where it has to become involved in the decision-making process, but the FRC recognizes that this may not always be possible. This standard creates an exemption from the ethical requirement providing the firm explains to the management the need for it to retain its objectivity and independence. This can be difficult as smaller organizations, lacking financial expertise, may well see the auditor as some form of quasi financial director and ask the auditor for their opinion on the merits of particular strategies or commercial activities. The auditor must decline to give such an opinion as this would severely compromise their independence, even if this results in some cooling of the relationship with their client.

- The FRC Ethical Standards require that the audit firm should not act as an advocate for its client in any tribunal or court – this is the 'advocacy' threat. The danger is for example, where the audit firm provides, say, tax services, that it will be drawn into an appeals procedure which will result in the firm appearing in the tribunal on behalf of the client. This will, again, reduce independence and objectivity. Again the standard creates an exemption from this requirement for the small client providing the ethical position is discussed with them.

There are provisions in the FRC Ethical Standards regarding an audit partner leaving an audit firm and joining a client where at any time in the previous two years they have been a lead audit partner, an independent review partner or in the chain of command of the firm. It states that in these situations the firm should resign as auditors and not accept reappointment for a two-year period.

This provision is relaxed in the case of smaller entities providing the audit team can demonstrate that the employment of the former partner does not present any threat to the integrity, independence and objectivity of the audit team.

If the auditors take advantage of any of these exemptions, they must disclose the fact in their Auditor's Report.

INSIDER DEALING

In addition to being totally contrary to the ethical rules, insider dealing is illegal under various statutes, principally Part V of the Criminal Justice Act 1993 and The Financial Services and Markets Act 2000 which defines market abuse. The fundamental rule is that individuals who, during the course of their work, come across 'unpublished price-sensitive information' are prohibited from dealing in securities to which that information relates.

Unpublished price-sensitive information covers specific matters not generally known to those who normally deal on the Stock Exchange but which, if it were known to them, would alter the prices of those securities to which the information relates.

The prohibition applies to anyone who has a connection at present or had one at any time in the previous six months and to any third person whom the insider may wish to instruct.

Auditors with their close connection with the accounts of a public company client are often in possession of insider information. For example, they may know that the profit is £12 million when the market is expecting only £10 million. They must not take advantage of this information by buying shares in the company on the expectation of a rise in the price when the accounts are published.

MONEY LAUNDERING

Money laundering is the process by which criminals try to conceal the true nature of proceeds of illegal activities. The term includes possessing, in any way dealing with or concealing the proceeds of any crime.

This includes monies generated through tax evasion, bribery and corruption or the operation of gangs involved in more conventional criminal activities, such as drug or people smuggling, illegal arms trading, theft and robbery, etc. The relevant legislation is contained in:

- The Proceeds of Crime Act 2002
- The Money Laundering Regulations 2007
- Terrorism Act 2000

The broad provisions are that firms must appoint a Money Laundering Reporting Officer (MLRO) to deal with the whole matter. The job of the MLRO is to receive and assess reports about suspicious transactions from partners and staff and to make reports to the National Crime Agency (NCA). The reports must give full details of the suspicious transactions and the identities of the persons involved.

In addition, firms must put in place systems and procedures which fundamentally ensure that staff are aware of their responsibilities under the legislation and that the firm itself has procedures and internal controls which will enable suspicious transactions to be identified and reported in accordance with the regulations.

In particular, these should include procedures which ensure that:

- Before accepting an assignment, they take all necessary steps to establish that their potential new client is who it claims to be. This can include proof of identity for individual clients and inspecting the company certificate of incorporation.
- If they handle clients' money accountants have controls which ensure that the identity of the client, the commercial purpose of the transaction, the source of the funds and their destination are known and verifiable.
- Staff have training in the regulations and how to identify suspicious transactions.
- The firm has procedures to review client's activities on an ongoing basis.
- 'Suspicious transaction reports' are made to the MLRO should they be identified.
- The MLRO reports these to the NCA.

Generally, firms commit an offence under the regulations if they fail to implement these procedures.

In addition, there are some other offences which can be committed under the regulations, which students should be aware of. These are:

- attempting, conspiring with or inciting someone to commit an offence
- aiding or abetting an offence or advising on the commission of an offence
- obtaining, concealing or investing funds or property knowing or suspecting that they are the proceeds of crime or funds for terrorist activity
- doing or disclosing anything that might prejudice an investigation into money laundering activities – this is known as **Tipping off**
- proceeding with a transaction without the consent of the relevant authority after having submitted a Suspicious Transaction Report

Suspicious transactions

Whilst carrying out their work auditors are expected to be on the alert for suspicious transactions (see Chapter 20). Risk factors which can be associated with such transactions are:

- 'secret' or 'confidential' transactions which are dealt with outside the main accounting systems, possibly by one individual or a small group; be aware, however, that secrecy can be associated with commercial confidentiality and be perfectly innocent
- routeing transactions through tax havens or countries with lax fiscal rules
- routeing transactions through several countries or institutions
- routeing transactions through a country different from the one from which the underlying transaction is sourced, e.g. services are purported to be bought from Country A but payment is made to a bank in Country B; note that there may be underlying commercial reasons for this such as foreign currency hedging or even tax evasion by the supplier, but it is suspicious and should be investigated
- frequent use of wire transfers or money transfers which do not disclose details of the ultimate recipients of the funds, e.g. transfers to overseas lawyers or nominee bank accounts
- transactions which involve the use of large amounts of currency or 'bearer' financial instruments (financial instruments which can be cashed by the person who has physical possession of them)
- large movements of funds in and out of an account on the same day without any apparent commercial reason
- high-value deposits or withdrawals which don't fit the normal patterns of the movement of funds through an account, especially in cash
- movement of funds 'through' (i.e. in and straight out again) an account by electronic transfer

There are two important things for auditors to bear in mind:

- Reporting suspicious transactions to the authorities does not breach the auditor's duty of confidentiality to their client. Auditors will have a statutory defence under these circumstances.
- Auditors encountering what they think might be suspicious transactions are in a difficult position. Having knowledge of a transaction may include:
  - actual knowledge
  - refraining from making enquiries
  - deterring someone else from making enquiries
  - closing one's mind to what is obvious and ignoring it

So auditors should make the sort of reasonable enquiries about a transaction which might be expected of a careful and conscientious professional auditor and carefully note the client's response to their questions.

Having said that auditors must be careful when making enquiries not to 'tip off' their client that they have detected what they think is a suspicious transaction and are going to report it to the MLRO and thus, ultimately, to NCA, as they could be charged with an offence.

As noted in Chapter 5, the FRC revised their practice note PN12 *'Money laundering – Guidance for auditors on UK legislation'* in September 2010 and this is a useful source of further advice and information on this topic.

WHISTLEBLOWING

Whistleblowing means informing the proper authorities of some significant breach of law or regulation. It is an issue for employees who feel compelled to tell the proper authorities of some wrong doing by their employers, but fears being dismissed if they do. In this case employees are protected under the Enterprise and Regulatory Reform Act 2013.

Employees of companies, who are also members of professional accountancy bodies, may be required by their ethical code, particularly the aspects of it relating to integrity and objectivity, to make reports.

Protections are available if reports are made:

- in the public interest
- to the proper authority
- without malice

The key issue here is the 'public interest' test – the whistleblower must 'reasonably believe that their disclosure is in the public interest.' What constitutes the public interest is not defined in the legislation, however it would encompass things like:

- criminal offences
- threats to public safety
- environmental threats
- terrorist activity

Reports to an outside body, such as a regulatory authority, by professional accountants, be they auditors or employees, can be defended against any accusation of breaching client confidentiality as the matter would be in the public interest.

There are additional issues for auditors:

- If auditors become aware of a significant noncompliance they should report it to the directors in the first instance with a recommendation that it be disclosed to the proper authority.
- If the directors don't do that then the auditors should report it, relying on the public interest defence to guard them against accusations of breach of client confidence.
- Breaches of law or regulation may have an impact on the financial statements and the auditors should assess what this effect might be and the disclosures which might be required. This may have an influence on their audit report if suitable disclosures are not made in the financial statements. We will look at this sort of issue later in Chapter 26.

SUMMARY

- The professional bodies require their members and students to behave in an ethical manner.
- There are significant threats to auditor independence. These can be countered by adherence to professional standards and the regulatory regimes of the professional bodies.
- Codes of ethics and conduct are spelt out in detail both by professional bodies and the Financial Reporting Council.
- Independence is of particular importance and detailed guidance is issued to members.
- Auditors become privy to all sorts of information in the course of their work, about both the organizations they audit and the individuals who work for it. Audit staff must regard all such information as totally privileged and not disclose it to third parties except in circumstances where there is a legal right or duty to disclose it. They may not also use such information for personal gain, e.g. by insider trading.
- Partners and staff of audit firms can become so familiar with the management or staff of a client company that they lose their objectivity. This must be avoided, perhaps by rotating the partners and staff involved.
- There are particular ethical threats associated with the audit of smaller organizations and auditors should be aware of the risks.
- Disclosing unpublished price sensitive information in order to make a gain is a criminal offence under the insider trading rules.
- Auditors should be aware of the Money Laundering Regulations and are allowed to make disclosures of suspicious transactions without breaching their duty of confidentiality.

POINTS TO NOTE

- The ethical codes are mandatory, particularly in the area of dealing with clients and the designatory letters accountants may use to describe the services they offer.
- In some areas they give guidance only. For example, in the independence ethical guide, the 15 per cent fees rule is for guidance only, a client giving 10 per cent of gross fees may influence auditors who fear the loss of income if they lose the client.
- In all these ethical matters, accountants must not only behave correctly, they must be seen to be behaving correctly.
- Ethics is taken very seriously by professional accountants.
- Small companies are often owned and run by entrepreneurs who are not interested in obeying bureaucratic rules and see the company as an extension of themselves.
- This can make life difficult for the auditor. As a result, audit risk can be higher in small companies. The need for evidence is still paramount but the type of evidence available may be different from that available in larger enterprises.
- Professional accountants are not allowed to give investment advice or conduct investment business unless they are authorized to do so by their professional body under the Financial Services Act.
- Independence is a big issue and the practice of accounting firms performing other services for their audit clients is constantly under review.

CASE STUDY

Tickitt & Run are auditors of McColl Holdings plc, a chemical manufacturer. The financial director has left the company recently to take up another post and McColl have so far been unable to find a suitable replacement. They have therefore asked Tickitt & Run to be responsible for the preparation of the financial statements for the year ending 31 December 2X16 as part of the audit.

McColl have also asked Tickitt & Run to:

- help in designing and selecting a new computerized management accounting system
- assist in finding a new financial director and
- discuss at a board meeting the dividend to be paid

The company is also subject to a probable takeover bid and wants Tickitt & Run to act for them in rebutting statements made by the takeover bidder.

During the audit, the audit team find that the company are systematically breaching safety guidelines on chemicals shipped to a developing country and they suspect some bank transactions with an offshore-based bank.

Discussion

– What are the ethical implications for Tickitt & Run?
– How far can they ethically go in assisting their client?

STUDENT SELF-TESTING QUESTIONS

a) List the fundamental principles.

b) What general ethical rules are there?

c) What should an accountant do if faced with an ethical dilemma?

d) Enumerate the guidelines to independence.

e) What should an accountant do about commissions?

f) Give examples of areas where conflicts of interest may occur.

g) What restrictions are there on advertising?

h) How can an accountant obtain publicity in an ethical manner?

i) What are the rules on auditors' remuneration?

j) What are the implications for auditor's independence and objectivity in connection with small company audits?

k) What is insider dealing? What does an audit team member do when they know their mother has shares in Risky plc and that, whilst on the audit of Risky, they discover that the company's new pharmaceutical product of which the market expects much, has been banned as unsafe? An announcement of the ban will be made next week.

l) What is money laundering?

m) What is whistleblowing? When may an auditor inform the proper authorities of a breach of the law?

n) What criteria apply to the decision of auditors as to whether they can assist their client in non-audit ways?

EXAMINATION QUESTIONS

1 The objectivity of the external auditor may be threatened or appear to be threatened where:

   i) There is undue dependence on any audit client or group of clients.

   ii) The firm, its partners or staff have any financial interest in an audit client.

   iii) There are family or other close personal or business relationships between the firm, its partners or staff and the audit client.

   iv) The firm provides other services to audit clients.
     Required:

     (a) For each of the four examples given above, explain why the objectivity of the external auditor may be threatened, or appear to be threatened, and why the threat is important.

     (b) Describe the ethical requirements that reduce the threats to auditor objectivity for each of the four examples given above.
     (ACCA)

2 A waste disposal company has breached tax regulations, environmental regulations and health and safety regulations. The auditor has been approached by the tax authorities, the government body supervizing the award of licences to such companies and a trade union representative. All of them have asked the auditor to provide them with information about the company. The auditor has also been approached by the police. They are investigating a suspected fraud perpetrated by the managing director of the company and they wish to ask the auditor certain questions about him.
   Required:
   Describe how the auditor should respond to these types of request.
   (ACCA)

SOURCES AND ADDITIONAL READING

ACCA (2011) *ACCA Rule Book Section 3 Code of Ethics and Conduct*. London: ACCA.

Crown Prosecution Service (2007) *Proceeds of Crime Guidance*. London: CPS.

Financial Reporting Council (2016) *Revised Ethical Standard*. London: Financial Reporting Council.

Financial Reporting Council (2010) *Practice Note 12 Money Laundering – Guidance for Auditors on UK Legislation*. London: Financial Reporting Council.

International Ethical Standards Board for Accountants (2015) *Code of Ethics for Professional Accountants*. New York: IFAC.

TSO (2002) *Proceeds of Crime Act 2002*. London: The Stationery Office.

CHAPTER 7
QUALITY CONTROL IN AUDIT FIRMS

Learning Objectives

After studying the material in this chapter you should be able to:

- understand the quality control requirements of the various standards

- understand the importance of quality control procedures in audit firms

- explain how audit firms maintain a system of quality control

- understand the principles of 'hot' and 'cold' reviews

- understand the importance of audit documentation

INTRODUCTION

It is of primary importance to the business world in general and to the auditing profession in particular that the question of audit quality is addressed by practitioners to ensure that:

- the firm and its staff comply with professional standards and legal and regulatory requirements; and
- reports issued by the firm are appropriate.

It is important to distinguish between procedures designed to ensure that the firm, as a whole, provides a high standard product in all professional engagements and procedures to ensure that each individual engagement is properly carried out. A review of an audit may be to sample the effectiveness of the overall procedures or may be to ensure that a particular audit was performed effectively. In both cases it forms part of the Quality System of the audit firm.

Drivers of quality include individual responsibilities, collective responsibilities, a quality culture, the collective wisdom of the audit team in resolving difficult or contentious matters, building quality into processes and monitoring the results.

ISA 220 'Quality control for an audit of financial statements' requires that, in all firms, quality control procedures should be introduced that are applicable to the individual audit engagement. ISA 220 places the responsibility specifically on the audit or **engagement partner**, who is in charge of the audit, to ensure that all matters in respect of the audit are dealt with properly.

In addition to ISA 220 there is the snappily titled International Standard on Quality Control (ISQC 1) 'Quality control for firms that perform audits and reviews of historical financial information and other assurance and related services engagements' issued by the IAASB. This creates an obligation for the firm to establish a system of quality control to provide reasonable assurance that professional standards and legal requirements are complied with and that any reports issued are appropriate in the circumstances.

All firms issuing reports to clients, whether they are audit reports or reports on other types of assurance engagements, are exposed to risk, i.e. the risk of giving an incorrect or inappropriate opinion in the report. The result of that could be legal action against the firm for damages, adverse publicity and loss of reputation and certainly the loss of the client.

Consequently, it is in the interest of the firm to ensure that there are the highest standards of ethical behaviour and full compliance with reporting standards within it.

This chapter deals with quality control under three headings:

- audit firm organization
- planning, controlling and recording individual audits
- reviews of audit firms' procedures in general and of particular audits

AUDIT FIRM ORGANIZATION

Audit firms are, generally, organized on hierarchical lines with a partner or director at the top and audit trainees at the bottom. Individual firms may vary with some having more levels and some firms have different ways of describing roles but broadly they are structured as shown in Figure 7.1.

FIGURE 7.1 Structure of an audit firm

Job title	Responsible for
Audit partner /director* (*if the firm is a Limited Liability Partnership – see Chapter 29)	The final overview of the audit and signing the Audit Report
Senior manager	Review of audit procedures, ethical considerations and approving audit planning. Will bring key issues to the attention of the Audit Partner
Manager	Audit planning and general overview of the audit process as it takes place. File reviews and quality control of the audit
Assistant manager	Assisting with planning the audit, and day to day management of the audit process including monitoring and reviewing audit progress, signing off audit tests and carrying out file reviews
Audit senior	Carrying out audit work at the client in accordance with the audit programme and monitoring the work of audit trainees
Audit trainees and associates	Carrying out audit tests under the supervision of the audit senior and the assistant manager

There many seem to be a lot of levels and, of course, not all firms have that many levels in their hierarchy but there is designed to be a steady progression from audit trainees to audit partner as qualifications are achieved and experience gained. Each level in the hierarchy will review the work of the one below it to ensure that the chances of errors or mistakes in the audit process are minimized.

It is recognized that each firm has its own needs depending on size, geographical spread, special expertise, etc., but all firms must organize quality control policy and procedures.

These procedures should include:

- Clear designation of leadership responsibilities – to ensure that quality is part of the culture of the firm. This should be the managing or senior partner's responsibility and partners should give clear leadership in this area.
- Ethical requirements – to ensure that the firm complies with relevant ethical requirements particularly those involving audit independence and involvement with clients. Firms may appoint an Ethics Partner to this effect.
- Acceptance and continuation of relationships with clients – considering the integrity of individual clients and whether the firm can continue to supply services at the appropriate level.
- Human resource policies – to ensure that the firm has sufficient staff, of the right levels of competence and commitment to ethical principles, to carry out the work required and also to ensure a continuing programme of training and development. These policies should also include performance evaluation, promotion and training needs for individual staff members at all levels.
- Assigned engagement partners – engagement partners should be assigned to each client. They are responsible for quality at the audit or engagement level. Their job is to ensure that there is a system of written procedures for engagements and that these are complied with, that each engagement or audit is supervised, all audit work is reviewed and that quality control reviews for each assignment are carried out as appropriate.
- Monitoring of procedures – a monitoring system to ensure that quality procedures within the firm are reviewed and that there is a process for recommending improvements. This will include such things as evaluation of standard procedures and reviews of completed assignments (known as 'cold' reviews). All procedures must be documented.

Every firm should establish and monitor control policies and procedures and communicate these to all partners and staff. Larger firms employ printed manuals but smaller firms may have to rely on verbal instructions and handouts.

There should be a procedure for evaluating prospective clients with consideration of the firm's ability to meet the client's needs and for making the decision on acceptance which may be made by an individual partner, or by a committee.

Procedures should exist to ensure all partners and staff are aware of, and adhere to, the principles of objectivity, integrity, confidentiality and professional competence. It is important to instruct staff who are not members of professional bodies in ethical principles and to monitor the observance of ethical standards on a firm-wide basis. For example, staff might not be aware of the prohibition on ownership of shares in client companies or may be unwilling to sell them if they are so aware.

Capability and competence of staff should be monitored – the objective is to have a fully competent and skilled set of partners and staff. Procedures include:

- Recruitment – only of suitably qualified and expert staff. Staffing needs should be planned ahead.
- Technical training and updating – all partners and staff should be encouraged to learn and to keep up-to-date with technical matters. The firm could provide literature, maintain a technical library, send people on courses and hold courses themselves. Some firms produce a special newsletter at intervals to update staff with technical developments. All qualified staff should be up-to-date with Continuing Professional Development (CPD) requirements.
- On-the-job training and professional development – planning, controlling and recording emphasizes the importance of relating staff abilities to client needs but opportunities should also be provided for staff to have adequate experience on a range of clients as on-the-job training. Performance of staff should be evaluated and discussed with staff concerned.

Individual members of the firm, including engagement partners, should not take decisions on problem areas without consultation with others. Problem areas might be technical (e.g. IT issues where expert members of staff should be consulted) or matters of risk evaluation. Sole practitioners are advised to consult with other firms or with professional advisory services.

Finally, suitable procedures should be introduced to ensure that all procedures are working adequately. This is dealt with in the review section.

PLANNING, CONTROLLING AND RECORDING INDIVIDUAL AUDITS

ISA 220 deals with quality issues in respect of individual audits. Its purpose is to ensure audit procedures take into account many of the firm-wide points mentioned above.

The engagement partner is responsible for quality at the audit level and for ensuring that the audit engagement is subject to a form of quality control review. All audits should be led from the top.

It is important that procedures are in place to ensure that the audit firm does not breach any ethical requirements by acting for the client and audit firms should accept only those clients where it can be sure it can deliver a service to the required standard. Existing client relationships should be reviewed to ensure their continuing integrity.

The Engagement Partner must ensure that the audit has been planned and performed properly, all procedures documented, all work reviewed, staff properly supervised, etc. and that sufficient appropriate evidence has been obtained to support the audit opinion.

Client disputes should be resolved and all discussions with the client must be properly documented and any decisions or conclusions reached must be explained and justified.

The Engagement partner must have made sure that consultation on technical issues has been carried out and that any 'hot' reviews needed have been undertaken (see below).

The control procedures to be applied to individual audits or assignments include:

- *Allocation of staff* – staff should have appropriate training, experience, proficiency and, if required, special skills (e.g. in computing).

- *Proper briefing of staff* – before the assignment commences staff should be properly informed on:
  - the nature of the client, its industry and the client's place in it
  - objectives of the audit
  - timing
  - the overall plan of the audit
  - significant accounting and auditing risk areas, including fraud risk areas
  - related parties (see Chapter 21)
  - the need to bring problems and enquiry situations to more experienced staff, the audit manager or audit partner.
- *Audit completion checklists* – with sections for completion by staff and reporting partner. It is a common experience that, in the rush to complete an audit on time, matters of importance can be overlooked.
- *Contentious matters* – all problems, special difficulties and potential Audit Report qualifications must be identified, recorded and discussed by the reporting partner with colleagues or even another practitioner.
- *Documentation* – all audit work and conclusions reached must be fully recorded in the working papers – the rule is always *'if it's not documented it doesn't exist'*. Recording can be either by paper-based records or computer-based audit software (see Chapter 18).
- *Reviews* – all audit work must be fully reviewed. This is dealt with in the next section.
- *Signed off* – all audit work and review action should be acknowledged in writing by the performer by initialling or signing the working paper, or recording the sign off on the audit worksheet in the computerized file.
- *Supervision* – personnel with supervisory responsibilities should monitor the progress of the audit to consider whether:
  - assistants have the necessary skills and competence to carry out their assigned tasks
  - assistants understand the audit directions and
  - the work is carried out in accordance with the overall audit plan and the audit programme.

REVIEWS OF AUDIT FIRMS' PROCEDURES IN GENERAL AND OF PARTICULAR AUDITS

We have already mentioned above the cold review, which is a post audit completion review of processes and procedures but more pertinently there is another form of review, a hot review, which is conducted whilst the audit in progress.

Hot reviews

Firms should ensure that an independent review is undertaken for all listed company audits and where the audit is particularly large or complex. This type of review is known as a **hot review**. A hot review should be carried out *during the course of the engagement or audit* (hence the use of 'hot') by a partner not connected with the audit or assignment and should be applied to all audits of listed companies and a selection of other assignments.

In addition, firms should establish policies setting out the circumstances in which an independent review should be performed for other audits or assignments, whether on the grounds of the public interest or particular audit risk.

The independent review should take place before the audit report is signed so as to provide an objective, independent assessment of the quality of the audit. The policies should set out in detail the manner in which the review is to be performed.

The independent review involves consideration of the following matters in order to assess the quality of the audit:

- the objectivity of the audit engagement partner and key audit staff and the independence of the audit firm
- the rigour of the planning process including the analysis of the key components of audit risk identified by the audit team and the adequacy of the planned responses to those risks

- the results of audit work and the appropriateness of the key judgements made, particularly in high-risk areas
- the significance of any potential changes to the financial statements that the firm is aware of but which the management of the audited entity has declined to make
- whether all matters which may reasonably be judged by the auditors to be important and relevant to the directors, identified during the course of the audit, have been considered for reporting to the board of directors and/or the audit committee (or their equivalents)
- the appropriateness of the draft auditor's report

Monitoring

Firms should appoint a senior audit partner to take responsibility for monitoring the quality of audits carried out by the firm by means of **cold reviews**. These take place after the audit work has been completed and are primarily designed to ensure that the firm's policies and procedures have been complied with. Of particular relevance will be the issue of continuing independence from the client and the quality of decision making in connection with audit issues.

These independent reviews by persons unconnected with the detail of an audit can lead to the discovery that:

- The firm's procedures are not always followed.
- There are gaps in the procedures.
- There are technical matters of general interest which need investigation.
- There are deficiencies in the quality of the staff or in their training.

Findings from both hot and cold reviews may well result in changes to firms' procedures and the identification of training requirements for staff and thus form an important part of the quality process within the firm.

Documentation

It is an important principle that all processes and procedures carried out are properly documented and auditors use a variety of checklists and programmes which we will refer to in the relevant chapters. As stated above the rule is always *'if it's not documented it doesn't exist'*.

However, it is important to emphasize that one of the most important facets of auditing, the exercise of judgement, must also be documented and in sufficient detail that succeeding auditors, including those carrying out cold reviews, clearly understand the rationale and methodology of why judgements were made and the process of arriving at a decision.

In particular, routine decisions about the level of audit work, the audit strategy, **materiality** levels, etc. must be properly documented. Clearly, where there have been discussions with management or disputes about particular audit items this too must be recorded.

In addition to audit matters the standards stress the importance of communication within the audit team itself. Team briefings and discussions should also be documented or minuted so that there is evidence in the audit working papers that attention was paid to key audit matters such as the need for **professional scepticism** or the likelihood of significant misstatements or fraud.

In the case of Public Interest Entities (basically listed entities, banks and insurance companies) there has to be a more detailed independent review.

The reviewer must consider such factors as:

- the independence of the firm from the client
- the evaluation of audit risk (see Chapter 10) the rationale for the materiality level and significant decision making regarding risks
- the nature and materiality of corrected and uncorrected errors
- subjects discussed with the Audit Committee and management

This follows fairly closely the processes for evaluating the quality of non PIE audits but has to be applied in every case and with some rigour.

SUMMARY

- Quality control is a major issue for audit firms.
- The partners or directors of an audit firm should take a lead in quality issues.
- Procedures must be in place to ensure continuing independence from the client and that ethical considerations have been reviewed. These must be fully documented.
- Clients should be assessed to ensure they retain their integrity and are suitable clients of the firm.
- All staff must be aware of quality procedures and those not members of an RSB must receive suitable training.
- Each engagement should be headed by an engagement partner who is responsible for the conduct of the audit.
- The firm should recruit, employ and train capable and competent staff.
- All audit work should be carried out ethically.
- All audit work and decisions made must be properly documented.
- Quality control should be implicit in an audit firm's systems and procedures for carrying out audits.
- Audit work must be subject to review before the report is signed where the audit is large or complex and in the case of listed clients.
- Hot reviews are carried out by partners not connected with the audit client.
- Reviewers must be independent and objective.
- Cold reviews are aiming to ensure consistency of practice and the maintenance of quality standards.
- All matters relevant to the audit including decisions and team briefings should be documented.

POINTS TO NOTE

- Auditors are under pressure to ensure that audit standards are high because:
  - Publicly aired failure is bad for business.
  - Failure to live up to standards can lead to expensive litigation.
  - Inefficiency is unprofitable.
- Quality control can be seen in several stages:
  - proper organization of the firm and its procedures
  - planning for each audit
  - control of each audit
  - working papers
  - review of work done
  - review of organization and procedures
- In order to ensure that all that needed to be done on an audit was done, any review should be conducted on the basis of a checklist.

CASE STUDY

In Newtown there are three small firms of qualified accountants and registered auditors who, between them, have most of the large businesses, farmers and landowners and other service providers as clients.

They have heard a rumour that one of the 'Big 4' firms want to set up an office in the town with a view to taking over all their best clients and expanding into the adjacent area.

As a defensive measure they decide to amalgamate their practices and set up as one firm under the name of Rocke & Rolls. This will mean merging their offices into one new building and rationalizing all their administrative staff and systems, but this can be done relatively painlessly.

Angela Goodbody is one of the senior partners and has been asked to look at the quality standards in the new firm. Previously, as they had all been small firms, they hadn't bothered with formal systems and if they had an ethical dilemma they had contacted their institute.

Now they feel they have to introduce a new regime.

Discussion

- How should Angela convince her fellow partners this is a good idea and will not just be a costly waste of time?
- What procedures should Angela introduce:
  - in the short term?
  - over a longer period?

STUDENT SELF-TESTING QUESTIONS

Questions with answers apparent from the text

a) What are the key aspects of good organization in an audit firm to ensure quality?

b) What are the responsibilities of the audit partner?

c) What is the difference between a hot review and a cold review and when is each one carried out?

d) What control procedures should be applied to individual audits?

EXAMINATION QUESTIONS

1 Quality control policies and procedures should be implemented at both the level of the audit firm and on individual audits states ISA 220 *'Quality control for an audit of financial statements'*.

   Required:

   Describe the nature and explain the purpose of quality control procedures appropriate to the individual audit.

   (ACCA)

2 You are an audit manager in Fayre & Even, a firm of Chartered Certified Accountants. Your specific responsibilities include planning the allocation of professional staff to audit assignments. The following matters have arisen in connection with the audits of three client companies:

   (a) The Finance Director of Almond, a private limited company, has requested that only certain staff are to be included on the audit team to prevent unnecessary disruption to Almond's accounting department during the conduct of the audit. In particular, he has requested that Xavier be assigned as manager of the audit and that no new trainees be included in the audit team. Xavier has been the manager for this client for the last two years.

(b) Alex was one of the audit trainees assigned to the audit of Phantom, a private limited company, for the year ended 31 March 2X16. Alex resigned from Fayre & Even with effect from 30 November 2X16 to pursue a career in medicine. Kurt, another audit manager, has just told you that on the day Alex left he told Kurt that he had ticked schedules of audit work as having been performed when he had not actually carried out the tests.

(c) During the recent interim audit of Magenta, a private limited company, the audit manager, Jamie, has discovered a material error in the prior year financial statements for the year ended 31 December 2X16. These financial statements had disclosed an unquantifiable contingent liability for pending litigation. However, the matter was settled out of court for £45 million on 14 March 2X17. The auditor's report on the financial statements for the year ended 31 December 2X16 was signed on 19 March 2X17. Jamie believes that Magenta's management is not aware of the error and has not drawn it to their attention.

Required:

Comment on the ethical, quality control and other professional issues raised by each of the above matters and their implications, if any, for Fayre & Even's staff planning.

(ACCA)

SOURCES AND ADDITIONAL READING

Financial Reporting Council (2009) *ISA 220 Quality Control for an Audit of Financial Statements*. London: Financial Reporting Council.

IAASB (2008) *ISQC 1, Quality Control for Firms that Perform Audits and Reviews of Financial Statements, and Other Assurance and Related Services Engagements*. New York: IFAC.

ICAEW (2010) *Quality Control in the Audit Environment*. London: ICAEW.

CHAPTER 8
ACCEPTING
APPOINTMENT
AS AUDITORS

Learning Objectives

After studying the material in this chapter you should be able to:

- understand the process and importance of client screening

- understand the preconditions for audit acceptance

- understand the process of accepting an engagement

- explain the contents of a Letter of Engagement

- discuss the ethical considerations in connection with new client acceptance

- explain what is meant by professional etiquette in the context of client acceptance

INTRODUCTION

The relevant requirements are set out in ISA 210 '*Agreeing the terms of audit engagements*'. There are several practical considerations but overriding these is the principle that, before accepting an audit engagement, accountants should first consider two things:

1   whether the preconditions for an audit are present; and
2   whether or not they can take on the work from an ethical, legal and practical point of view.

The intention is to reduce **Engagement Risk,** the risk of agreeing to accept an engagement which either the firm cannot fulfil properly to the required standard or with a client which might prove to be unacceptable or untrustworthy to a minimum. We will look at these matters separately but first there have to be some preliminary considerations.

CLIENT SCREENING

When a firm is approached to take over an existing audit from another firm, or is to be appointed as the first auditors they must make some investigations before they even consider accepting the appointment. As we saw from Chapter 7, audit firms must monitor the integrity of their clients so no firm wishes to take on a new client they either do not have the resources to handle or whose sense of ethics might be rather more flexible than could be desired.

The ISA 315 '*Identifying and assessing risks of material misstatement through understanding the entity and its environment*' requires the auditors to obtain a thorough understanding of the client, its industry and its business environment. We look at this in more detail in Chapter 10. This process begins *before* the client is accepted.

It is incumbent on the incoming auditor to discover all they can about their potential client. This will include:

- Establishing the potential client's business, its products and customer base – what does it actually do?
- Consideration of the potential client's position in its industry and its reputation – is it a reputable company or is it seen as being a bit dubious?
- Consideration of the potential client's management and their ability – is it a new company with inexperienced, perhaps unqualified management or does the senior management have long experience in the industry – do they have a successful track record?
- Consideration of the strength of the finance function – does the company have a qualified financial director, is the finance function a part of the business or is it seen as a necessary evil by the operational directors?
- Reviewing the client's financing and capital structure – how is it financed, are there any potential problem areas looming involving repayment of loans or debentures?
- Consideration of any particular legal or special reporting requirements – is it in a highly regulated industry where additional certificates may be required or special reports prepared?

Sources of information will include:

- previously published accounts
- trade literature and brochures
- press and magazine articles
- the internet
- local knowledge
- discussions with the potential client and any detailed information provided by the client in response to enquiries, e.g. management information

OTHER CONSIDERATIONS

Ethical considerations have been dealt with in Chapter 6 and students should be familiar with these. For example, an audit firm should not accept a client where the total value of fees would significantly exceed 15% of the firm's total fee income or where a partner in the firm is closely related to a director of the proposed audit client.

Assuming there are no ethical problems around independence and objectivity there are practical considerations to take into account.

The auditors have to consider:

- Whether or not they have the physical resources to carry out the audit satisfactorily. This includes not only physical locations and availability of staff, but also whether or not any specific expertise, e.g. computer auditing is required.
- Any potential conflicts of interest – for example, does the firm represent any other client connected with the potential new one?
- If there are any considerations which must be taken into account in connection with possibilities of money laundering, insider dealing or any other dubious activities.

PRECONDITIONS FOR AN AUDIT

The preconditions for an audit are:

- the use by management of an acceptable financial reporting framework, e.g. UK GAAP, in the preparation of the financial statements
- the agreement of management to the premise on which an audit is conducted, i.e. their responsibilities for accounts preparation, etc.

It would be rare to find management using an unacceptable framework and basically it is only likely where auditors find themselves auditing an entity which is incorporated outside the UK. In this case the audit report may have to be modified in order to mitigate a possible loss of understanding relating to relevant auditing standards.

The premise on which an audit is conducted requires the directors to understand and acknowledge their responsibilities for preparation of the financial statements and for making an audit possible. This, as we will see, requires the directors to:

- prepare 'true and fair' financial statements
- maintain an adequate accounting system with appropriate internal controls
- allow the auditors access to the records and to all the information, explanations and unrestricted access to individuals that they require

Audit firms may also wish to consider the provisions of ISA 260 *'Communication with those charged with governance'* which requires auditors to monitor the two-way communication process between auditor and client and ISA 580 *'Written Representations'* concerning Management Letters (Chapter 27). Both of these processes might need to be discussed with the directors at an early stage.

Clearly, if the preconditions for an audit are not met the auditor should decline the appointment.

PROFESSIONAL ETIQUETTE

If the organization already has an auditor who is ceasing to act, i.e. one firm is replacing another, the professional bodies require the new auditor to communicate with the previous auditor.

The professional bodies have specific rules which their members must follow. A member (of a professional body) on being asked to act as auditor should request the client's permission to communicate with the previous auditor (if there is one). If this permission is refused, the firm must refuse the appointment as auditor.

If permission is given the firm should request from the outgoing auditor, in writing:

- confirmation that there is no professional reason why the appointment may not be accepted
- any information required to enable them to decide whether or not they are prepared to accept the appointment

Members receiving such a request should, in turn, request the client's permission to discuss the client's affairs with the proposed new auditor. If this permission is refused, the outgoing auditor will inform the new auditor who will then refuse the appointment.

If permission is given, then the old auditor:

- confirms that there is no professional reason why the appointment cannot be accepted
- discloses to the proposed auditor all information which they will need to decide whether or not to accept the appointment
- discusses freely with the new auditor all matters relevant to the appointment which the new auditor will need to know

This is a matter of courtesy between professionals. It enables the proposed auditors to know if it is proper for them to accept the appointment. If, for example, the outgoing auditors are in dispute with the client over unpaid fees or they feel they are being dumped in favour of a new firm which might be more amenable to signing an audit report and asking fewer questions, this is the opportunity for the outgoing auditors to say so. It also safeguards the position of the retiring auditors who can express any reservations they may have.

This procedure also protects the shareholders and others interested in the final accounts.

The next step, assuming all the formalities are completed and there are no problems regarding the appointment, is to agree a **Letter of Engagement** with the client. This sets out the agreement between the auditor and the client. We look at these in a later section of this chapter.

The new auditors must also confirm that they have been properly and legally appointed. They do this by examining the minute books of meetings at which they were appointed and placing a copy of the appropriate minute on a new **Permanent File** (Chapter 18). In companies these minutes will be of the company in general meeting, if they were appointed at the Annual General Meeting (AGM), or meetings of the directors if the appointment is to fill a casual vacancy or is between AGMs – see Chapter 3.

LETTERS OF ENGAGEMENT

Before commencing any professional work, an accountant should agree, in writing, the precise scope and nature of the work to be undertaken. This is done through the medium of an Engagement Letter. The Engagement Letter forms the basis of a legally binding contract between the auditors and their client. If the auditors carry out their work in a negligent manner it is on the basis of this letter that the client may well sue them.

ISA 210 '*Agreeing the terms of audit engagements*' governs the form and content of such letters. This states:

> '*The auditor shall agree the terms of the audit engagement with management or those charged with governance, as appropriate.*
>
> *The agreed terms of the audit engagement shall be recorded in an audit engagement letter or other suitable form of written agreement and shall include:*
>
> *(a) the objective and scope of the audit of the financial statements;*
> *(b) the responsibilities of the auditor;*
> *(c) the responsibilities of management;*
> *(d) identification of the applicable financial reporting framework for the preparation of the financial statements; and*
> *(e) reference to the expected form and content of any reports to be issued by the auditor and a statement that there may be circumstances in which a report may differ from its expected form and content.*'

The principles behind the use of Engagement Letters are designed to ensure that the preconditions for the audit are satisfied (see above) and that management understands and accepts its responsibilities:

- for the preparation of the financial statements in accordance with the applicable financial reporting framework, including, where relevant, their fair presentation
- for such internal control as management determines is necessary to enable the preparation of financial statements that are free from material misstatement, whether due to fraud or error

- to provide the auditor with:
  - access to all information of which management is aware that is relevant to the preparation of the financial statements such as records, documentation and other matters
  - additional information that the auditor may request from management for the purpose of the audit and
  - unrestricted access to persons within the entity from whom the auditor determines it necessary to obtain audit evidence.

The Engagement Letter serves to ensure that the work of the auditor and the basis on which the audit will be conducted are explained and understood. It forms the contract between the parties and includes reference to the facts that:

- the audit will be conducted in accordance with the ISAs
- the audit work will be planned
- tests will be conducted on a sample basis
- there is a possibility that material errors may go undiscovered because of this

The letter should also explain that the auditors may require written representations from management in certain circumstances about key aspects of the audit.

It should also confirm that the auditors will provide management with details of any weaknesses in their accounting systems detected during the audit and any errors, material or otherwise which the audit has uncovered.

The letter may also include any special factors. These might include:

- relations with the internal auditors, if any
- audit of divisions or branches
- any overseas location problems
- relationships with other auditors, if any

The letter will also indicate whether or not the auditors intend to include in their Auditor's Report details of Key Audit Matters which have been a feature of the audit process.

We deal with these in Chapter 26 but for now they can be summarized as technically complex areas of accounting or issues which require an exercise of judgement where the outcome is significant in relation to the financial statements. Disclosure of these is mandatory for listed companies but there may be audits of unlisted companies with a significant number of outside shareholders where such disclosure would be of relevance to their understanding of the financial statements.

It will include details of any other services the audit firm is to carry out, e.g. preparation of tax computations and the basis on which fees will be charged, i.e. based on an hourly rate.

An example of an Engagement Letter is shown on the digital support resources.

Once agreed the letter will be signed by representatives of the management as a confirmation of acceptance of the terms. The signing process should be evidenced by a directors' board meeting minute. This will confirm acceptance by both the client and the auditor of the terms of the engagement and thus constitutes the legal contract between the parties.

When to send an Engagement Letter

Engagement Letters should be sent:

- to all new clients *before* any professional work has been started
- to all existing clients who have not previously had such a letter
- whenever there is a change of circumstances (e.g. extra duties to be performed or a major change in ownership or management of the client) or any change in the audit firm (e.g. merger, change of name); the engagement letter should be reviewed every year to see if there is a need for a revized letter

In the case of groups of companies where group accounts are to be prepared, an Engagement Letter should be sent to each member company of the group that is to be audited by the firm. If a standard letter is satisfactory, then, in practice, a letter can be sent to the group board requesting that it be copied to all group members to be audited by the firm and that acknowledgement be received from all of them.

This should be carried out before any audit work is commenced in the case of a new client or before the current audit starts in the case of an existing client.

On or before acceptance of a new client auditors must discuss the precise terms with the directors and review the draft of the letter with the client. If the client is an existing one, they should review the terms of the letter to ensure they are still current and applicable.

The letter should be signed before commencing any part of the assignment and two copies sent to the client. One copy has an acceptance confirmation which the client is required to sign and return to the auditors.

When the signed letter is returned by the client a copy of it should be placed on the Permanent File.

SUMMARY

- Apart from ethical considerations auditors must ensure they have the resources to carry out the work for the proposed client and there are no ethical considerations which might be relevant.
- Potential auditors should attempt to find out all they can about their client before accepting the assignment.
- The importance of communication between directors and auditors must be stressed as auditors must monitor that communications are effective and must also communicate any deficiencies they may encounter.
- There is a procedure involving communication with any outgoing auditors which must be followed.
- The auditors must ensure that the preconditions for accepting an audit are present.
- The letter sets out the respective duties of directors and auditors in connection with the preparation and audit of the financial statements.
- It will also cover any ancillary matters which are relevant.
- All assignments given to accountants should be subject to an Engagement Letter agreeing the terms of the assignment with the client.

POINTS TO NOTE

- The Letter of Engagement is central to agreeing the basis on which audit firms act for their clients and all services which auditors perform for clients should be on the basis of detailed, written instructions.
- Students should have a knowledge of the form and content of such letters.
- The ISAs stress the importance of communication during the audit process and the Letter of Engagement is important in agreeing the basis on which the relationship between the auditors and their client is to be conducted.
- Students should look for opportunities to put 'agree a Letter of Engagement' in many answers.

CASE STUDY

Juliet B a partner in Stamp & Hoppit, Registered Auditors, receives a telephone call from the Managing Director of Chateaubriand Ltd which runs a chain of restaurants and bars. They wish to appoint Stamp & Hoppit as auditors as they have a disagreement with the existing auditors. The audit would be due to commence in about two months' time.

The Managing Director tells her that Chateaubriand runs a chain of 12 restaurants and 10 bars situated in the Northern region. It also sells ready meals under the 'Chateaubriand' name which are manufactured by another independent company; Chateaubriand buys them in, adds a margin and sells them on through supermarkets and smaller food retailers. This is becoming an increasingly significant part of the business.

Juliet B carries out some further research and discovers that Chateaubriand is a private company wholly owned by the Staples family. The managing director is R. A. Staples, his son is the sales director and his wife is responsible for 'Product Design'. The finance director has been with the company for eighteen months and there have been three other finance director appointments in the last five years.

The company turns over some £15m and made a profit of some £800 000 before tax in the last financial year.

Discussion

– What should Juliet B consider before accepting the appointment?

– What matters should be discussed at the meeting?

– In the light of the first question, draft an Engagement Letter.

– What might be the consequences of omissions from the letter?

STUDENT SELF-TESTING QUESTIONS

Questions with answers apparent from the text

a) List the purposes of an Engagement Letter.

b) What are the preconditions for an audit?

c) What happens if they are not met?

d) What is an acceptable reporting framework?

e) What are the procedures connected with Engagement Letters?

f) List the principal contents of an Engagement Letter.

g) What other forms of communication might it be wise to discuss when agreeing the Engagement Letter?

h) How are Engagement Letters dealt with in a group situation?

EXAMINATION QUESTION

1 Viswa is a company that provides call centre services for a variety of organizations. It operates in a medium-sized city and your firm is the largest audit firm in the city. Viswa is owned and run by two entrepreneurs with experience in this sector and has been in existence for five years. It is expanding rapidly in terms of its client base, the number of staff it employs and its profits. It is now 15 June 2X16 and you have been approached to perform the audit for the year ending 30 June 2X16. Your firm has not audited this company before. Viswa has had three different firms of auditors since its incorporation.

Viswa's directors have indicated to you informally that the reason they wish to change auditors is because of a disagreement about certain disclosures in the financial statements in the previous year. The directors consider that the disagreement is a trivial matter and have indicated that the company accountant will be able to provide you with the details once the audit has commenced. Your firm has explained that before accepting the appointment, there are various matters to be considered within the firm and other procedures to be undertaken, some of which will require the cooperation of the directors.

Your firm has other clients that operate call centres. The directors have asked your firm to commence the audit immediately because audited accounts are needed by the bank by 30 July 2X16. Your firm is very busy at this time of year.

Required:

(a) Describe the matters to consider within your firm and the other procedures that must be undertaken before accepting the appointment as auditor to Viswa.

(b) Explain why it would be inappropriate to commence the audit before consideration of the matters and the procedures referred to in (a) above have been completed.

(c) Explain the purpose of an Engagement Letter and list its contents. *(ACCA)*

SOURCES AND ADDITIONAL READING

Financial Reporting Council (2009) *ISA 210 Agreeing the Terms of Audit Engagements*. London: Financial Reporting Council.

Financial Reporting Council (2009) *ISA 315 Identifying and Assessing Risks of Material Misstatement through Understanding the Entity and its Environment*. London: Financial Reporting Council.

CHAPTER 9 ACCOUNTING SYSTEMS AND INTERNAL CONTROLS

Learning Objectives

After studying the material in this chapter you should be able to:

- explain the need for accounting record keeping

- explain the components of an internal control system

- understand the basic principles of internal controls

- define and list internal controls within an accounting system

- explain detailed control procedures using SOAPSPAM

- understand the components of accounting systems for purchases, revenues and wages

- understand the control objectives of different aspects of a business comprising:

    - purchases and payables

    - payroll

    - revenues and receivables

    - cash

- the limitations of internal control

- the danger of management override of controls

INTRODUCTION

The management of an enterprise needs to maintain complete and accurate **accounting records** because it is impossible to control the business without them.

For example, day-to-day records of receivables and payables are indispensable so the business knows who owes it money and who it owes money to. Assets can only be safeguarded if a proper record of them is made and financial statements which are required for numerous purposes, not least keeping the bank happy, can only be prepared if adequate accounting records exist.

There are legal requirements to keep financial records in particular for **PAYE**, National Insurance, **VAT**, statutory sick pay and statutory maternity pay. For companies the Companies Act, 2006 and other relevant legislation have specific requirements on record keeping for specific types of business.

What constitutes an adequate system of accounting depends on the circumstances. A small company may use a bespoke accounting package from one of the many suppliers of accounting software but a large international company clearly needs rather more sophisticated records.

The basic needs of a system are that it provides for the orderly assembly of accounting information to enable the financial statements to be prepared but all the other requirements of an accounting system, set out above, must be borne in mind.

For auditing purposes, we tend to concentrate on the financial accounting systems, the cash book, sales, purchase and nominal ledgers, etc. and the supporting documentation, but auditors should be aware that organizations often combine their basic financial accounting with more sophisticated and analytical management accounting, which includes budget and costing information, etc.

This enables auditors to obtain much more detailed information about the business, its financial performance, its weak areas and its strong, than the financial accounts alone may be able to provide. In addition, cost information and management accounts will assist not simply with audit tasks such as inventory valuation but also in the carrying out of analytical procedures (Chapter 12).

The need for controls over the system

No system of accounting and record keeping will succeed in completely and accurately processing all transactions unless controls, known as internal controls, are built into the system.

The purposes of internal controls are:

- To ensure transactions are executed in accordance with proper general or specific authorization.
- To ensure all transactions are promptly recorded at the correct amount, in the appropriate accounts and in the proper accounting period so as to permit preparation of financial statements in accordance with relevant legislation and accounting standards.
- To ensure access to assets is permitted only in accordance with proper authorization.
- To ensure recorded assets are compared with the existing assets at reasonable intervals and appropriate action is taken with regard to any differences.
- To ensure errors and irregularities are avoided or made apparent.

INTERNAL CONTROL

Introduction

This part considers the auditor's approach to **internal control** systems as outlined in ISA 315 '*Identifying and assessing risks of material misstatement through understanding the entity and its environment*' and then considers what internal control is and gives a detailed review of internal controls in specific areas. At the end we take a look at the ideas on control environment and control procedures and consider the limitations of internal control.

In 1999 the Turnbull Report entitled 'Internal Control: Guidance for Directors on the Combined Code' was published. This aimed to persuade directors of listed companies of the benefits of sound internal controls. It was superseded in 2014 by the FRC's Risk Guidance but an extract from the original report is still illustrative of the need for strong internal controls (Figure 9.1)

FIGURE 9.1   Internal Control – The Turnbull Report

A company's system of internal control has a key role in the management of risks that are significant to the fulfillment of its business objectives. A sound system of internal control contributes to safeguarding the shareholders' investment and the company's assets.

Internal control facilitates the effectiveness and efficiency of operations, helps ensure the reliability of internal and external reporting and assists compliance with laws and regulations.

Effective financial controls, including the maintenance of proper accounting records, are an important element of internal control. They help ensure that the company is not unnecessarily exposed to avoidable financial risks and that financial information used within the business and for publication is reliable. They also contribute to the safeguarding of assets, including the prevention and detection of fraud.

Source: The Turnbull Report

The auditor and internal control

ISA 315 requires auditors to obtain an understanding of the internal control sufficient to plan the audit and develop an effective audit approach.

This includes:

- using the understanding of internal control to identify types of potential misstatements
- considering factors that affect the risks of potential misstatements; and
- designing the nature, timing and extent of audit procedures.

ISA 315 is based on the idea that internal control is not simply a set of procedures and checks but instead includes a whole range of activities and attitudes. Internal control consists of the following:

- the control environment
- the risk assessment and risk management processes
- control activities
- monitoring of controls

This is contained within the information system, including the related business processes relevant to financial reporting and communication, and is governed by:

- the culture of the organization; and
- the attitude of those charged with governance towards risk management and internal control.

We will look at these, individually, in more detail later.

Clearly, smaller and less complex organizations will have less complex systems but this lack of complexity may also create problems for the auditor. They may not, for example, have detailed written procedures, or formal risk assessment policies; in owner-managed businesses the owner/manager may well be directly involved in internal control matters which, in larger organizations, would be the responsibility of accountants, managers or internal auditors. This, in turn, can lead to the dangers of management override of controls.

Within the organization there will be many and various controls of many and various aspects of the organization's activities. It is important to understand that the ones the auditor is interested in are the ones which relate to the objective of preparing financial statements which are true and fair. This will, primarily, centre on financial system and the control of assets and liabilities as well as some of the controls involved in the risk management processes of the organization.

Some internal controls used for management control purposes are not immediately relevant to the audit. For example, a company may have controls designed to prevent excessive use of materials in production, or controls designed to make operations efficient, such as an airline's automated controls to maintain flight schedules. These are not directly relevant to a financial statement audit.

The auditor must exercise professional judgement in deciding whether a control, or series of controls, is relevant and should be tested. Included in that decision-making process will be judgements which involve:

- the size of the business
- its nature, including its ownership and how it is organized
- how diverse and complex its operations are
- the legal and regulatory framework it operates within
- the nature and complexity of the financial and management systems
- the level of materiality or significance of the transactions being controlled (Chapter 10) – which the auditor will have set at the planning stage

What the auditors are trying to do is to make judgements about the efficiency and reliability of the internal control systems and the risks involved should it fail, so that the audit effort can be concentrated in areas of highest risk and where the systems are most vulnerable.

The auditor has to obtain a full understanding of how the controls work and how effective they are in preventing misstatements and detecting errors. They do this by asking questions of managers and staff, observing controls in operation, inspecting documents and reports and by tracing transactions thorough the system.

We deal with this in detail in Chapter 10. However, one important thing for the student to understand is that *understanding* the controls is *not* the same as *testing* the controls. Auditors use their knowledge of the systems and controls to design their audit procedures for the testing of the system and its controls. Students need to understand the integrated nature of the accounting system and the internal controls which are built into it.

LIMITATIONS OF INTERNAL CONTROLS

Before we look at the controls applicable to specific parts of an accounting system it is important for learners to realize that the whole system of controls is not infallible and can have within them certain limitations. This is why auditors must ensure that the controls which they have documented on lovely flow charts and which look totally secure on paper are actually working in practice by testing the systems.

Internal controls are essential features of any organization that is run efficiently. However, internal controls have inherent limitations which include:

- A requirement that the cost of an internal control is not disproportionate to the potential loss which may result from its absence. This may mean management dispense with controls in which case auditors must consider the implications for the financial statements. Hopefully there won't be any but it pays to check.
- Internal controls tend to be directed at routine transactions. The one-off or unusual transaction tends not to be the subject of internal control.
- Controls often fail through human error caused by stress, excessive workload, alcohol, carelessness, distraction, mistakes of judgement, apathy and the misunderstanding of instructions.
- The possibility of circumvention of controls either alone or through collusion with parties outside or inside the entity.
- Deliberate fraud committed either by directors in misrepresenting the financial statements or by employees.
- Changes in environment making controls inadequate or incomplete.

One of the dangers auditors face, particularly in smaller companies, is the danger of **management override** of controls. Managers or senior managers instruct subordinates to disregard internal control procedures or managers process transactions themselves without going through proper procedures. This invariably increases audit risk and is frequently an indicator of dysfunctional activity in the organization.

ISA 240 '*The auditor's responsibilities relating to fraud in an audit of financial statements*' requires that this be treated as a significant risk and the risk of management override of controls must be evaluated by the auditor.

The IAS 315 requires that, because of the inherent limitations of internal controls auditors must always perform some **substantive**, that is detailed, tests of material, i.e. significant items as well as relying on internal controls.

INTERNAL CONTROL SYSTEMS

As shown in Figure 9.2, there are five key aspects to internal control.

FIGURE 9.2 Internal Control

The control environment

This includes the attitudes, awareness and actions of the directors and senior managers of the organization. It is, in effect, the culture of the organization insofar as it relates to internal control and is part of the Corporate Governance framework (Chapter 2). It includes:

- the fostering and communication of a culture of honesty and ethical behaviour throughout the organization
- a commitment to competence – to training and maintaining the appropriate levels of skill and knowledge
- management's philosophy and operating style, their approach to risk and attitudes toward correct financial reporting
- the organizational structure including levels of supervision and authority
- the involvement of non-executive directors in the audit process – discussed in Chapter 2
- the human resource policies – recruitment, training, evaluation, promotion and rewarding of staff

The auditor must assess the control environment, and ensure that the policies and procedures which are part of it are actively being implemented. This will form part of the routine audit tests which we will look at later.

The risk assessment process

We look at this in more detail in Chapter 14 when we discuss business risk and the business risk approach to auditing. Suffice to say now that the auditor should review the organization's approach to business risks, or at least those relevant to financial reporting, and assess what impact, if any, these are likely to have on the financial accounts.

The auditor will look at how management identifies business risks relevant to financial reporting, how it estimates the significance of those risks, assesses the likelihood of their occurrence and what actions they decide to take in respect of the risks they have identified.

Once again we are only concerned with the risks which affect financial reporting. Operational risks, for example, the risk of loss of customers due to competition or risks posed by the potential loss of a key supplier, are not directly relevant to the audit of the financial statements; however, the risk of fraud or the risk of noncompliance with laws and regulations is directly relevant so how management identifies and deals with these types of risk is something the auditors have to review.

There is one important point to make here which must be emphasized. Business risk is the risk to the *business* – it is not the same as **audit risk** which is something completely different insofar as it is the risk to the *auditors*. Students must learn to distinguish the two. We will return to this topic later.

The information system

The auditor has to obtain a full understanding of the information system and the related business processes. This includes:

- the classes of transaction in the organization's operations which are significant to the financial systems
- the procedures, both IT and manual, which are used to record those transactions
- the related accounting records, whether electronic or manual and the supporting information used to initiate, record, process and report transactions
- how the systems work
- the process by which the organization prepares its financial statements

We look at auditing using IT in more detail in Chapter 17.

Control activities

These are the detailed policies and procedures that help ensure that management directives are carried out, for example, that necessary actions are taken to address the risks that threaten achievement of the organization's objectives.

Control procedures

These are the controls built into the accounting systems which regulate the day-day processing activities of financial information. We look at these in more detail below.

Monitoring of controls

It is important to understand that the management should not be using the external auditors as the vehicle for monitoring the effectiveness or otherwise of their system of internal control.

They should have their own procedures which might take the form of:

- internal audit – carried out by specialist internal auditors
- senior management review – where senior managers perform audit-type tests on selected parts of the system
- analysis of the results by applying analytical procedures to, say, monthly management accounts and detecting anomalies or areas for investigation

CONTROL PROCEDURES

This is a critical part of auditing which the student must fully understand. These are frequently the basis of examination questions and a failure to understand what constitutes good control procedures will undermine your work in the rest of this book.

Control procedures determine both the structure of accounting departments and the flows of information which pass through them. The objectives of internal control are:

- that no one person has complete control of a transaction from start to finish
- that the work of each person involved in accounting for transactions is supervized or checked by someone else

In this way no one individual should have the opportunity to manipulate accounting information and the risk of a material error or misstatement going undetected is reduced. Control procedures are designed to ensure that the internal control objectives are achieved.

Examples of specific control procedures are:

- **S**egregation of duties
- **O**rganizational controls
- **A**uthorization and approval
- **P**hysical controls
- **S**upervision
- **P**ersonnel
- **A**rithmetical procedures
- **M**anagement

You can remember these through the mnemonic **SOAPSPAM**.

Let's look at these in more detail.

Segregation of duties

This is the most important single control activity and is the key to good system and procedure design. What it means is that *no one person should be responsible for the recording and processing of a complete transaction.*

The involvement of several people reduces the risk of intentional manipulation or accidental error and increases the element of checking of work. An example of how a given transaction, in this case for the purchase of lubricating oil, could be separated is:

- Initiation – the works foreman decides the firm needs more lubricating oil and raises a purchase requisition.
- Authorization – the works manager approves the purchase.
- Execution – the buying department order the oil using a purchase order form.
- Receipt – on arrival the oil is taken in by the goods-inwards section and passed with appropriate goods-inwards documentation (e.g. a Goods Received Note ('GRN')) to the stores department.
- Recording – the arrival is documented by the goods inward section. The resultant purchase invoice is compared with a copy of the original order and the GRN by the accounts department and recorded by them in the books.
- Payment – at an appropriate time the invoice will be paid by the cashier's department.

Another example is the area of sales of goods where initiation is by a sales executive, authorization by credit control and the sales manager, execution is by the finished goods warehouse staff who physically send the goods, custody is transferred from the warehouse staff to the transport department and the transaction is recorded by the goods outward section, the invoicing section and the accounts department.

Organizational controls

An enterprise should have a plan of organization which should:

- Define and allocate responsibilities – every function should be in the charge of a specified person who might be called the responsible official; thus, the administration of the accounts department should be entrusted to a particular person who is then responsible (and hence answerable) for that function.
- Identify lines of reporting both upwards and downward through the organization, and where appropriate, across it as well.

In all cases, the delegation of authority and responsibility should be clearly specified. Employees should always know the precise powers delegated to them, the extent of their authority and to whom they should report. Two examples:

- The works manager may be permitted to buy items of plant and equipment up to a certain value e.g. £X each or within a total budget amount for the year. Above these limits the responsibility would revert to directors or more senior managers.
- Responsibility for the correct operation of internal controls may be delegated by the board to specific management personnel and to the internal audit department.

Authorization and approval

All transactions should require authorization or approval by an appropriate person. The limits to these authorizations should be specified.

Examples of such procedures are:

- All credit sales must be approved by the credit control department.
- All overtime must be approved by the factory manager.
- All individual office stationery purchases may be approved by the office manager up to a limit of £X. Higher levels of purchasing must be approved by the chief accountant.

Remembering the principle of segregation of duties outlined earlier it should not, for example, be the case that the individual who has authority to say, set up a new supplier's account in the purchase ledger, is also responsible for authorizing invoices from that supplier and approving payment to them. That opens the door to a particular kind of fraud – the creation of a fictitious supplier. Auditors should always, when reviewing use of authorizations and authorities as system controls, also look at what else those individuals are allowed to do and how they do it.

Physical controls

These are such things as physical custody of assets and involve procedures designed to limit access to assets and systems to authorized personnel only.

These controls are especially important in the case of valuable, portable, exchangeable or desirable assets. Examples of physical controls are:

- use of passes to restrict access to a warehouse
- locks or keypads on doors
- use of passwords to restrict access to particular computer files
- hierarchical menus for computer operators

Supervision

All actions by all levels of staff should be supervized. The responsibility for supervision should be clearly laid down and communicated to the person being supervized.

Personnel

Procedures should be designed to ensure that personnel operating a system are competent and motivated to carry out the tasks assigned to them, as the proper functioning of a system depends upon the competence and integrity of the operating personnel.

Measures include appropriate remuneration and promotion and career development prospects, selection of people with appropriate personal characteristics and training, and assignment to tasks of the right level.

Arithmetical procedures

These are the controls in the recording function which check that the transactions are all included and that they are correctly recorded and accurately processed.

Procedures include checking the arithmetical accuracy of the records, the maintenance and checking of totals, reconciliations, control accounts, trial balances, accounting for documents (sometimes known as sequence checks or continuity checks). Examples include:

- bank reconciliations
- control accounts
- reconciliations of suppliers statements with payables ledger accounts
- checking the calculations on purchase invoices

Management controls

These are controls, exercised by management, which are outside and over and above the day-to-day routine of the system. They include overall supervisory controls, review of management accounts, comparisons with budgets, internal audit and any other special review procedures.

Examples are:

- Senior management must be aware of day-to-day activities and be seen by staff to be so. Glaring failures of control (inventory thefts, excess inventory, unnecessary overtime) will become apparent and staff will be motivated to perform well.
- Management accounts should be designed to summarize performance in detail. Any anomalies (cost overruns, higher than budgeted wastage levels) should become apparent.
- Budgeting and variance analysis is a management tool which should prevent or at least detect departure from management's intended plans.

Individuals performing control activities should acknowledge their checking by means of signatures, initials, rubber stamps, etc. For example, if invoice authorizations have to be checked, the checker should initial some kind of posting slip attached to the invoice to indicate that this check has been carried out. In modern accounting systems all the evidence of checking and authorization may be done within the IT system, but the principles are the same whether the system is exclusively IT based or is wholly or partly paper based.

If a control procedure is not evidenced, it cannot be proved to have been performed. The rule is:

'If it's not evidenced it didn't happen'

Auditors will look for this evidence of performance as part of their audit procedures.

CONTROL ACTIVITIES IN SPECIFIC AREAS OF A BUSINESS

This section is divided up into the areas of activity usually found in a business.

It does consist of a lot of lists which the learner is not expected to memorize of course but this really is the only way to describe what happens.

The key to understanding is to follow the flow of the processes rather than worrying about every single step. However, this is a regular topic for examiners and learners should be familiar with the key aspects of these systems, the key control objectives and the controls which enable their achievement.

We will look at the **control objectives** in each area and give some examples of control procedures which will enable the organization to achieve those objectives.

Students should be familiar with the term 'control objectives' which is fairly self explanatory and simply refers to what the control procedure is designed to do. In this section we will look at general control objectives for the whole accounting system and individual parts of an accounting system, favoured by examiners, relating to:

- purchases and payables
- payroll
- revenues and receivables
- cash transactions

Internal control generally

The overall control objectives of any internal control system are primarily:

- to carry on the business in an orderly and efficient manner
- to ensure adherence to management policies
- safeguard its assets and
- secure the accuracy and reliability of the records.

Accordingly control procedures have to be devised which produce:

- an appropriate and integrated system of accounts and records including internal controls over those accounts and records
- financial supervision and control by management, including budgetary control, management accounting reports and interim accounts
- backup and security of data
- engaging, training, allocating to specific duties staff who are capable of fulfilling their responsibilities; rotation of duties and cover for absences

Purchases and payables system

Figure 9.3 shows the layout of a basic purchases system.

Control objectives

- To ensure that goods and services are only ordered in the quantity, of the quality and at the best terms available after appropriate requisition and approval.
- To ensure that goods and services received are inspected and only acceptable items are accepted.
- To ensure that all invoices are checked against authorized orders and receipt of the goods and services in good condition.
- To ensure that all goods and services invoiced are properly recorded in the books.

Control procedures

- There should be procedures established so that the requisitioning of goods and services can be carried out only by specified personnel up to pre-determined limits. So for example a supervisor could order goods to a value of say £1000, a manager to the value of, £5000 and a director up to, £25 000 with anything above this having to go to the Board of Directors. Obviously the limits will depend on the size of the business.
- If ordering from suppliers is carried out on a computer-based system or online there must be a hierarchy of amounts any one individual is able to order and orders should be authorized separately before being sent to the supplier e.g. a foreman in a factory could order up to, £1000 worth of inventory at any one time so they could enter the order into the order system but it has to be authorized by a procurement purchaser before being transmitted to the supplier. The procedure is there to stop individuals accidentally entering £10 000 of goods when they meant to order £100.00.
- Orders should only be sent to approved suppliers and there should be a procedure for approving new suppliers.
- Individuals who can approve suppliers should not generally be involved in processing and authorizing invoices from those suppliers. This is to stop individuals setting up their own companies to supply goods and services to their employer at inflated prices.

FIGURE 9.3 **Purchases System**

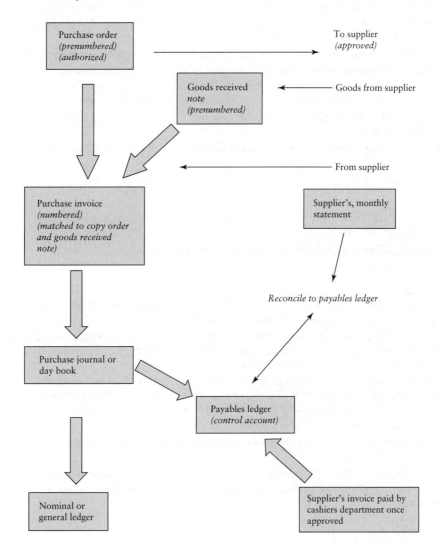

- Order procedures should include requirements for obtaining tenders, estimates or competitive bids.
- Sequence checks of orders should be performed regularly and missing items investigated.
- All goods received should be recorded on goods received notes (preferably pre-numbered) or in a delivery system which will then match with the order and invoice.
- All goods should be inspected for condition and agreement with order and counted on receipt. The inspection should be acknowledged. Procedures for dealing with rejected goods or services should include the creation of debit notes (pre-numbered) with subsequent sequence checks and follow-up of receipt of suppliers' credit notes.
- At intervals, a listing of unfulfilled orders should be made and investigated. This would also form the basis of a month end accrual for any management accounts.
- Invoices should be checked for arithmetical accuracy, pricing, correct treatment of VAT and trade discount and agreement with order and goods-in records.
- These checks should be acknowledged by the performer in some way to prove the activity has been carried out.
- Invoices should have consecutive numbers put on them and batches should be pre-listed.

- Purchase invoices should be pre-listed before entry into the accounting system and the pre-list total compared independently with the total of the invoices entered into the system.
- Totals of entries in the invoice register or day book should be regularly checked with the pre-lists.
- Responsibility for Payables Ledger entries should be vested in personnel separate from personnel responsible for ordering, receipt of goods and the invoice register.
- Payables Ledger account balances should be regularly compared with suppliers' statements of account.
- All goods and service procurement should be controlled through budgetary techniques.
- The system should be designed such that orders can only be placed that are within budget limits. There should be frequent comparisons of actual purchases with budgets and investigation into variances.
- Cut-off procedures at the period end are essential to ensure that Inventories and the cost of Inventories are in the same accounting period.
- A proper coding system is required for purchase of goods and services so that the correct nominal accounts are debited.

Payments

Control objective

To prevent unauthorized payments being made from bank accounts.

Control activities

- Individuals responsible for the preparation of cheques or credit transfers should be different to the individuals who process invoices and enter them into the purchases system.
- Rules should be established for the presentation of supporting documents before cheques, cheque requisitions or payment lists are to be signed. Such supporting documents may include invoices, a copy of the payroll, purchase account reconciliations, aged payables listings, etc.
- Establishment of who can sign cheques or authorize credit transfers. All cheques should be signed by at least two persons, with no person being permitted to sign if they are a payee. Credit transfers might be processed by one person up to a pre-set limit then authorization may have to be by a more senior member of staff.
- The signing of blank cheques must be prohibited.
- Special safeguards should be implemented where cheques have pre-printed signatures including controls over unused and spoilt cheques.
- Rules to ensure prompt despatch of payments to prevent interception or misappropriation.
- There should be a regular review of direct debits and standing orders including a review of suppliers who are paid by direct debit.

Payroll

Figure 9.4 shows the outline of a basic payroll system.

Objectives

- To ensure that wages and salaries are paid only to actual employees at authorized rates of pay.
- To ensure that all wages and salaries are computed in accordance with records of work performed whether in respect of time, output, sales made or other criteria.
- To ensure that payrolls are correctly calculated.
- To ensure that payments are made only to the correct employees.
- To ensure that payroll deductions are correctly accounted for and paid over to the appropriate third parties.
- To ensure that all transactions are correctly recorded in the books of account.

FIGURE 9.4 **Payroll System**

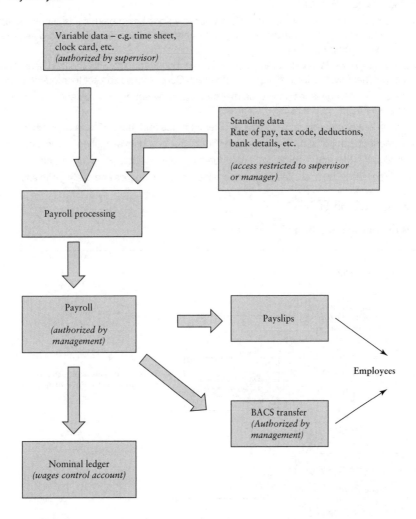

Control procedures

- There should be separate records kept for each employee. The records should contain such matters as date of employment, age, next of kin, agreed deductions, skills, department and specimen signature. Ideally these records should be maintained by a separate HR department.

- Procedures for employment, retirements, dismissals, fixing and changing rates of pay. Procedures should be laid down for notification of these matters to the personnel and payroll preparation departments.

- Time records should be kept for hourly paid staff or staff on time-based payments (e.g. part-time staff) as opposed to a regular monthly salary. These can take the form of clock cards or electronic data from a Time & Attendance System. There should be supervision of any time recording system to ensure that staff do not abuse the system by getting other staff to clock them in or out.

- Time records should be approved before preparation of salaries and wages. All overtime should be authorized.

- Output or piecework records should be properly controlled and authorized and procedures should exist for reconciling output or piecework records with production records.

- Procedures should be established for dealing with advances, holiday pay, lay-off pay, new employees, employees leaving, sickness and other absences and bonuses.

- Starters and leavers should be dealt with by the HR department and details passed to payroll separately. These should be followed up to ensure that leavers have been removed from the payroll and starters brought on at the correct time for the correct amount.
- The payroll should be approved by a senior official prior to wages being paid. If this is not practical arrangements should be made for managers to confirm the employees entered on the payroll at fixed dates to ensure only bona fide employees are being paid.
- Deductions such as PAYE, National Insurance, pension contributions and other authorized deductions should be subject to prompt payment over to the institutions concerned. Control totals subject to frequent review should be kept.
- Regular independent comparisons should be made between personnel records and wages records, in particular direct bank transfer (such as BACS payments) lists.
- Regular independent comparisons of payrolls at different dates and reconciliation of numbers.
- Regular independent comparisons of wages paid with budgets and investigation of variances.
- Surprise investigation of wage records and procedures by internal audit or senior officials.
- A wages supervisor should be appointed to be responsible for settling queries and dealing with some control procedures.

Revenues and receivables

Figure 9.5 shows the outline of a basic Revenues system.

FIGURE 9.5 **Revenues System**

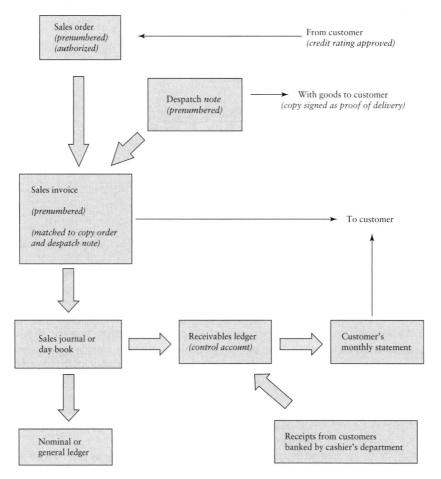

Control objectives

- To ensure that all customers orders are promptly executed.
- To ensure that sales on credit are made only to bona fide good credit risks.
- To ensure that all sales on credit are invoiced, that authorized prices are charged and that before issue all invoices are completed and checked as regards price, trade discounts and VAT.
- To ensure that all invoices raised are entered in the books.
- To ensure that all customers' claims are fully investigated before credit notes are issued.
- To ensure that every effort is made to collect all debts.
- To ensure that no unauthorized credits are made to receivables accounts.

Control procedures

- Incoming orders should be recorded and, if necessary, acknowledged on pre-numbered order forms. Orders which come in online must be recorded into the financial system to ensure that they are ultimately fulfilled at the agreed price.
- Orders should be matched with invoices and lists prepared at intervals of outstanding unfilled orders for management action.
- Credit control. There should be procedures laid down for verifying the credit worthiness of all persons or institutions requesting goods on credit. For existing customers, credit worthiness data should be kept up-to-date and checks made that outstanding balances plus a new sale does not cause the pre-set credit limit to be exceeded. For new customers, investigative techniques should be applied including enquiry of trade protection organizations, credit rating agencies, referees, the company's file with the Registrar of Companies, etc. A credit limit should be established based on a judgement of the customer's ability to pay. This might be based on a trading history where previous transactions were carried out on pro-forma (cash before goods) basis. This may be fixed at two levels, a higher one such that further sales are not made and a lower one such that management are informed and a judgement made on granting credit.
- Selling prices should be clearly stated. Policies on credit terms, trade and cash discounts and special prices should be established and communicated to all the relevant staff in writing.
- Despatch of goods should only be on properly evidenced authority. Goods out should be recorded by using pre-numbered despatch notes or a bar coded system identifying the goods which have to be signed for on delivery.
- Unissued sets of despatch notes should be safeguarded and issues of sets recorded.
- Sequence checks of despatch notes should be made regularly by a senior official.
- Acknowledgement of receipt of goods should be made by customers on copy despatch notes or by some other form of acknowledgement such as signing a handheld terminal and the records should be retained as proof of delivery.
- Invoicing should be carried out by a department or staff separate from the department processing invoices and collecting sales receipts.
- Invoices should be pre-numbered and the custody and issue of unused invoices controlled and recorded unless these are computer generated in which case they should be sequenced automatically. Sequence checks should be regularly made and missing or spoiled invoices investigated.
- All invoices should be independently checked for agreement with customer order, with the goods despatched record, for pricing, discounts, VAT and other details.
- Accounting for sales and receivables should be segregated by employing different staff for sales receipts, from those responsible for invoices, sales ledger entries and statement preparation.
- Sales invoices should be pre-listed before entry into the accounting system and the pre-list total independently compared with the total of the invoices entered into the system.
- Customer claims should be recorded and investigated. Similar controls (e.g. pre-numbering) should be applied to credit notes. At the year end, uncleared claims should be carefully investigated and assessed. All credit notes should be subject to acknowledged approval by a senior official.
- A control account should be regularly and independently prepared.
- Procedures must exist for identifying and chasing slow payers. This is normally done via an aged receivables listing. Very overdue balances should be brought to the attention of management for legal or other action to be taken.

- All balances must be reviewed regularly to identify and investigate overdue accounts, receivables paying by instalments or round sums and accounts where payments do not match invoices.
- Bad debts should only be written off after due investigation and acknowledged authorization by senior management. This is to prevent sales staff from misappropriating sales receipts then writing off the debt to Bad Debts in the Nominal Ledger to hide the fraud.
- Also at the year end, cut off procedures will be required. Particular attention will be paid to orders despatched but not invoiced.

Cash sales and collections

Control objectives

- To ensure that all cash, to which the enterprise is entitled, is received.
- To ensure that all such cash is properly accounted for and entered in the records.
- To ensure that all such cash is deposited promptly and intact in the bank.

Control activities

- Prescribe and limit the number of persons who are authorized to receive cash, e.g. sales assistants, cashiers, collectors, sales representatives, etc.
- Establish a means of evidencing cash receipts, e.g. pre-numbered duplicate receipt forms, cash registers with sealed till rolls. Any duplicate receipt form books should be securely held and issue controlled.
- Ensure that customers are aware that they must receive a receipt form or ensure that the amount rung up on the cash register is clearly visible to the customer.
- Appoint persons with responsibility for emptying cash registers at prescribed intervals and agreeing the amount present with till roll totals or internal registers. Such collections should be evidenced in writing and be initialled by the assistant and the supervisor.
- Immediate and intact banking. Payments out should be from funds drawn from the bank using an **imprest** system.
- Investigation of 'shorts' and 'overs' in excess of an agreed limit should be carried out promptly.
- Independent comparison of agreed till roll totals with subsequent banking records.
- Persons handling cash should not have access to other cash funds or to purchase or sales ledger records.
- Rotation of duties and cover for holidays (which should be compulsory) and sickness.
- Collections by collectors and sales representatives should be banked intact daily. There should be independent comparison of the amounts banked with records (e.g. duplicate receipt books) of the collectors and sales staff.

Payments into bank

Control objectives

- To ensure that all cash and cheques received are banked intact.
- To ensure that all cash and cheques received are banked without delay at prescribed intervals, preferably daily.
- To ensure that all cash and cheques received are accounted for and recorded accurately.

Control procedures

- Cash and cheques should be banked intact.
- Cash and cheques should be banked without undue delay.
- The bank paying-in slip should be prepared by an individual with no access to cash collection points, purchase or sales ledgers.
- Bankings should be made with security in mind, e.g. for large cash sums, security guards should be used.
- There should be independent comparison of paying-in slips with collection records, post lists and sales ledger records.

Cash and cheques received by post

Control objectives

- To ensure that all cash and cheques received by post are accounted for and accurately recorded in the books.
- To ensure all such receipts are deposited in the bank promptly and intact.

Control procedures

- Measures to prevent interception of mail between receipt and opening.
- Two persons to be present at the opening of the post.
- Immediate entry of the details of the receipts (date, payer, amount, cash, cheque, or other) in a 'rough cash book' or post list of money received. The list should be signed by both parties present.
- Regular independent comparison of the post list with banking records. The tests should be of total, detail and dating to detect **teeming and lading** at a later stage in the processing.

SUMMARY

- The control environment means the overall attitude, awareness and actions of directors and management regarding internal controls and their importance in the entity. The control environment encompasses the management style, corporate culture and values shared by all employees.
- Control activities are those policies and procedures in addition to the control environment which are established to achieve the entity's specific objectives. They include in particular procedures designed to prevent or detect and correct errors.
- Specific control procedures can be recognized by the mnemonic SOAPSPAM.
- Auditors are expected to make an assessment of the control environment in a client. A good control environment may well mean that the commitment to internal control is strong, but nonetheless actual control procedures may be weak or ineffective. It is generally felt that a poor control environment will mean unreliable control procedures.
- Internal control procedures have limitations insofar as, for example, they may not be operated properly but by inadequately trained or demotivated staff, they may be overridden by management or be evaded by deliberate fraud.

POINTS TO NOTE

- You must be able to define 'Control Environment' and 'Control Procedures' clearly so as to explain the difference between them.
- All entities have some sort of accounting system with some internal controls over the transactions. Indeed, listed companies are required to have systems and report on them in accordance with the UK Corporate Governance Code (see Chapter 2). Auditors may rely on these controls as evidence of prevention or detection and correction of errors and irregularities, but whether or not they do so depend on their assessment of the risks attached. In any event some substantive tests must be performed on all material balances and classes of transaction.

CASE STUDY

Skye Antiques Ltd operates a large shop in the centre of North Bromwich and two smaller shops in adjacent towns. They sell expensive reproduction antique furniture. Normally customers see the furniture in the shop and place an order for delivery in the company van within four weeks. The delay occurs because each sale results in a purchase order for one of the suppliers. On placing the order, the customer pays by cash, cheque, credit card or signs a hire purchase agreement. There are four sales assistants, a van driver and a cashier in the shop.

The smaller shops have a shop manager who deals with all the paperwork and part-time staff who assist at busy times. Customer orders are sent through to the main shop for sending to suppliers. Receipts from customers are banked daily – weekend receipts being banked on the Monday – and duplicate sales invoices are also sent to head office. Tills for any cash sales are cashed up daily and cash sheets agreed to till rolls. Managers have to sign the record of receipts.

Accounting and purchasing is done centrally by the manager and a part-time bookkeeper.

The three directors all have other businesses and review the company operations once a month at an all-day board meeting.

Discussion

– Devise an internal control system for the shops.
– Relate your system to the definition of internal control.
– Identify the types of internal controls in your system.

STUDENT SELF-TESTING QUESTIONS

Questions with answers apparent from the text

a) Define internal control and control risk and tests of control.

b) List the types of internal controls.

c) What categories of internal controls are comprised in the term 'organization'?

d) What functions should be segregated so that no two are under the control of one person?

e) What types of arithmetical and accounting controls are possible?

f) What are the internal control objectives of personnel policies?

g) What personnel policies achieve these ends?

h) List two management controls.

i) What budgeting benefits have internal control implications?

j) When are physical controls especially important?

k) List four physical controls.

l) List three controls over a petty cash system.

m) How can the issue of fraudulent cheques be prevented?

n) List four possible wages frauds.

o) What is a control environment?

p) List four limitations of internal control.

EXAMINATION QUESTIONS

1 You are the audit manager in charge of the audit of Millipede Ltd a manufacturer of children's furniture. Their products are made of wood and consist mainly of small versions of adult sized furniture principally children's chairs, small tables, beds, cots and nursery furniture often painted in bright colours, have jolly images attached and are generally designed to be cheerful and enjoyable for children to use. Their customers are mainly large retail chains and the Revenues for the year ended 31 December 2X16 were £11.4m.

To assist you in your audit planning, one of the audit team has provided the following description of the purchasing system. No other controls exist apart from those described.

1. The company has no buying department so employees place orders in their own area of responsibility. These orders can be considerable as the company generally buys in bulk wherever possible. These departments are *Cutting* where wood is cut to shape based on a standard pattern for each product before being passed to *Assembly* which makes up the product and passes it to *Painting* which completes it and sends it to *Dispatch* who wrap the products and hold in finished inventory.

2. A three-part order form is used. The top copy 1 is sent to the supplier, copy 2 is sent to the goods inward department and copy 3 is retained by the originator.

Goods are received and checked against the order by the goods inwards department who are responsible for putting items into stores. Once received the advice note from the supplier and their copy, (Copy 2) of the purchase order for those goods, are sent to the finance department.

3. When the supplier's invoice is received the purchase ledger clerk checks the calculations on it, initials it and staples the advice note and purchase order to it.

She then enters the invoice on to the purchase ledger.

4. The invoice is sent to the manager responsible for the employee who ordered the goods. The manager codes the invoice and returns it to the purchase ledger clerk. Purchase invoices are coded, entered on an analysis sheet and posted to the nominal ledger monthly.

5. The cashier pays suppliers monthly on instructions from the purchase ledger clerk.

6. The purchase ledger control account is reconciled monthly by the purchase ledger clerk who also reconciles suppliers' statements.

Required:

i. Set out the control objectives of a purchasing system.

ii. Identify four significant weaknesses in the internal controls in the above system and explain their significance in terms of potential loss to the business.

2 A proper understanding of internal controls is essential to auditors in order that they understand the business and are able to effectively plan and execute tests of controls and an appropriate level of substantive procedures.

You are the auditor of a small manufacturing company, Dinko, that pays its staff in cash and by bank transfer and maintains its payroll on a small stand-alone computer.

Required:

(a) For the payroll department at Dinko, describe the:

(i) internal control *objectives* that should be in place

(ii) internal control *environment* and internal control *procedures* that should be in place to achieve the internal control objectives

(b) For the payroll charges and payroll balances (including cash) in the financial statements of Dinko:

(i) describe the external auditor *audit objectives;*

(ii) list the *tests of control* and *substantive procedures* that will be applied in order to achieve the audit objectives identified in (b) (i) above.

(ACCA)

SOURCES AND ADDITIONAL READING

Financial Reporting Council (2009) *ISA 240 The Auditor's Responsibilities Relating to Fraud in an Audit of Financial Statements*. London: Financial Reporting Council.

Financial Reporting Council (2009) *ISA 315 Identifying and Assessing Risks of Material Misstatement through Understanding the Entity and its Environment*. London: Financial Reporting Council.

Jones, M. (2006) *Financial Accounting*. Chichester: Wiley.

Turnbull (2005) *Internal Control – Revised Guidance for Directors on the Combined Code*. London: FRC.

Wood, F. (2008) *Business Accounting I and II*. Harlow: Pearson Education.

CHAPTER 10
AUDIT PLANNING, AUDIT RISK AND MATERIALITY

Learning Objectives

After studying the material in this chapter you should be able to:

- understand audit objectives and how they must be met

- understand the meanings attributed to specific phrases in an audit context

- discuss the importance of **professional scepticism** in applying audit procedures

- understand the components of audit risk

- explain what is meant by **materiality** and **performance materiality**

- discuss the influences affecting audit planning

- understand the client risk evaluation process

- explain how to document a client's system as part of audit planning including the use of flow charts and questionnaires

- understand the three main audit strategies

- understand the planning process

- explain how analytical procedures are used in planning

- understand the timing of audit visits

INTRODUCTION

Before delving into the technical details of how to plan, conduct and report on an audit it is useful to consider the objective of an audit and the general principles which underlie the auditor's work. Unless this is fully understood the planning process may become a mere mechanical exercise perhaps based on previous period's audit without much consideration of what may have changed, or indeed whether the previous audit was effective. Instead, if the objective and role of auditors is fully appreciated, the planning process can be directed and unnecessary or ill-directed work avoided.

This section is based on ISA 200 *'Overall objectives of the independent auditor and the conduct of an audit in accordance with International Standards on Auditing'*.

OBJECTIVES

ISA 200 begins with a statement of the objectives of an audit. The primary objective of an audit of financial statements is to:

'enhance the degree of confidence of intended users in the financial statements. This is achieved by the expression of an opinion by the auditor on whether the financial statements are prepared, in all material respects, in accordance with an applicable financial reporting framework.'

Let us first clarify three key phrases used in the ISA 200 objective quoted above:

- *An opinion* – is not a guarantee or a certificate, just an opinion – see Chapter 26. Although the auditor's opinion enhances the credibility of the financial statements the user of the accounts cannot assume that the audit opinion is an assurance as to the future viability of the entity nor of the efficiency or effectiveness with which management have conducted its affairs. The phrases used to express the auditor's opinion are *'give a true and fair view'* or *'present fairly in all material respects'* which are equivalent terms.
- *In all material respects* – this is a difficult point. We have not yet considered the concept of materiality so for this purpose the reader can substitute the word 'significant'. Essentially there is a degree of imprecision in all but the very simplest of financial statements because they contain accounting estimates about uncertainties and unresolved transactions. There may even be some nonmaterial, or insignificant, misstatements in some of the individual items. However, the objective is that the auditor's work will provide evidence to support an opinion that the overall view given by the financial statements is a true and fair one (or that it is not).
- *True and fair* – this too is a difficult concept which we discuss in more detail in Chapter 26. Broadly, it means that the financial statements show the financial position of the entity in as fair and reasonable a way as is possible in the circumstances.

The auditor is thus required to express an opinion on a set of financial statements and, in order to do that, the auditor has to gather evidence in order to ensure that the opinion given is capable of being substantiated.

MEETING AUDIT OBJECTIVES

In order to achieve this objective ISA 200 makes it a requirement that not only must the auditor gather sufficient reliable evidence in order to substantiate their opinion on the financial statements, thus meeting the objective of ISA 200, but the auditor must also meet the objectives of *all* of the other underlying ISAs relevant to the particular audit.

Each ISA now has one or more objectives which clarifies the purpose of the ISA itself and forms a link with the overriding objective in ISA 200. Failing to meet the objectives of any of the underlying ISAs may mean that the auditor has failed to achieve the primary objective. Thus, as part of the planning process the auditors must identify whether or not the requirements of any particular ISA are pertinent to the audit to be conducted.

The achievement of these ISA objectives does not have to be separately documented as it will become apparent during the course of the audit work, but any non-achievement would have to be highlighted and considered. Clearly it is incumbent on auditors to comply with all the requirements of each relevant ISA, so in order to fulfil the objectives of a particular ISA and thus fulfil the objectives of ISA 200, all the requirements of an ISA must be complied with unless there are exceptional circumstances.

REQUIRED PROCEDURES

ISA 200 requires that, in undertaking an audit of financial statements, auditors should:

- Conduct their audit in accordance with ISAs.
- Plan and perform the audit with an attitude of professional scepticism recognizing that circumstances may exist that cause the financial statements to be materially misstated; this requires the auditor to make a critical assessment with a questioning mind as to the validity of the audit evidence obtained, and to be alert to any audit evidence that contradicts or brings into question the reliability of documents or management information.

This is a critical component of the way that auditors are expected to conduct themselves during the course of the audit and is designed to:

- Reduce the likelihood of auditors ignoring or turning away from suspicious circumstances.
- Prevent auditors from drawing *general* conclusions from *specific* events.
- Minimize the possibility of auditors using faulty assumptions when carrying out audit procedures.

This is not to say that auditors should assume that management is intrinsically dishonest, or indeed that they are totally honest. Accordingly, representations from management are not a substitute for auditors obtaining sufficient reliable evidence on which to base their conclusions.

Auditors must:

- Carry out procedures designed to obtain sufficient appropriate audit *evidence*, in accordance with Auditing Standards, to determine, with **reasonable assurance**, whether the financial statements are free from material misstatement.
- Plan and perform the audit so as to reduce audit risk to an acceptably low level. We will examine the concept of audit risk in more detail later. It is the risk that the auditor will give an inappropriate opinion on the financial statements, i.e. by saying they are 'true and fair' when they are not.
- ISA 200 also makes the important point, which the student must fully appreciate, that the responsibility for preparing and presenting the financial statements rests with the management of the entity and that the audit does not relieve them of that responsibility.

It is appropriate to make some comment about phrases which you will find repeated throughout this book. It is important you become familiar with them and fully understand what they mean.

'Sufficient, appropriate audit evidence'

This is a phrase to be committed to memory. Audit evidence is the subject of Chapter 11. The gathering of evidence is a matter of judgement in deciding on the nature, timing and extent of audit procedures. Even when evidence has been gathered it is a matter of judgement as to what conclusions are drawn from the evidence. For example, the auditors may gather much evidence on the future useful life of some plant and machinery – its natural life, the possibility of obsolescence, the cost of repairs versus replacement, etc. but still have to determine whether they think the life selected by the directors is reasonable in the circumstances.

'Reasonable assurance'

This is a difficult concept and, to some extent, can be rather subjective. It relates to the accumulation of evidence throughout the audit process which allows the auditor to conclude that the financial statements, taken as a whole, are free from material misstatements. The level of assurance required is that of 'reasonable' rather than 'absolute'.

Absolute assurance is not possible because:

- auditors carry out their work based on sampling of transactions
- internal controls can be overridden by management or defeated by collusion; and
- most audit evidence is persuasive rather than conclusive.

For example, the auditors might test a sample of 200 sales invoices out of a total population of 100 000 in order to verify the operation of an internal control in the sales system. If they find no errors, or even an acceptable number of errors, they may reasonably conclude that the remaining 99 800 invoices contain the same level of errors – but they don't know for sure that they do. They come to a conclusion, based on a balance of probabilities, which persuades them that it is more likely to be true than not true.

This test of reasonableness is based on the notion that a trained professional auditor, looking at the evidence objectively, would conclude that it was of sufficient quantity and quality as to provide evidence that the conclusion that had been drawn based on the evidence was justifiable, even if it was not conclusively proven.

'Free of material misstatement'

Materiality is discussed in detail later in this chapter. It relates to the significance, or otherwise, of errors or misstatements in the context of either the accounts as a whole or in the context of individual transactions and balances. Misstatement is usually in terms of fact, for example, if Payables does not include a significant accrual or the valuation of inventory does not comply with FRS 102, or the requirements of the Companies Act in respect of noncurrent tangible assets have not been fully complied with. In those cases, the auditor has to consider the effect of the error or omission on the accounts and to recommend appropriate action.

INFLUENCES ON AN AUDIT

There are many influences on how an actual audit is conducted. These include:

- International Standards on Auditing. These have to be complied with – see Chapter 5.
- Professional body rules. These are now very extensive – see Chapter 6.
- Legislation – for companies this is the Companies Act 2006 but most enterprises seem to be affected by some legislation or other.
- The terms of the engagement – see Chapter 8.
- Codes of practice – some audits are influenced by codes of practice; local authorities are an example, where the accountancy body CIPFA (Chartered Institute of Public Finance and Accountancy) issues Statements of Professional Practice relating to such public sector bodies.
- The level of audit risk. Risk permeates all auditing. Risk arises due the nature of the organization and its management, the quality of the **internal controls** within the organization and the ability of the auditor to perform the audit in such a way that any material errors or misstatements which evade the company's procedures will be detected by the audit work performed. We explore this in more detail later.
- The possibility of fraud or misrepresentation which is committed with **collusion** by staff or management. Communication between members of the audit team is seen as a critical factor in audits and this helps reduce the possibility of a fraud where collusion is present passing unnoticed by the audit team.
- The quality and quantity of audit evidence available to the auditor.
- Fear of litigation – Actions under the law of tort to recover losses alleged to be caused by the negligence of auditors, if successful can be very expensive for auditors in terms of cost, time and loss of clients and reputation, (Chapter 29).
- Ethics – ISA 200 requires that in the conduct of any audit of financial statements auditors should comply with the ethical guidance issued by their relevant professional bodies. These guides are now fairly extensive – see Chapter 6. Relevant matters include integrity, objectivity, professional competence, due care, professional behaviour and confidentiality.
- The individual auditing manuals of the firm of auditors. These will reflect the quality control standards of the individual firm (Chapter 7) and the requirements of the relevant ISAs and legislation.

However, before we look at the detailed processes of deciding an audit strategy and planning the work to be done we need to look at two important concepts of auditing: audit risk and materiality.

Audit risk

Audit risk is the risk that the auditor might give an incorrect or inappropriate opinion on the financial statements. What this means, in practice, is that the auditor has certified that the financial statements show a true and fair view when, in fact, they do not.

This can result in damage to the audit firm for giving a negligent opinion if the audit has not been performed properly so the objective of the auditor is to reduce audit risk to a minimum. Damage to the audit firm may be in the form of monetary damages paid to a client or third party as compensation for loss caused by the conduct (e.g. negligence) of the audit firm or simply loss of reputation with the client and the business community. We look at this in more detail in Chapter 29.

It is important for the student to appreciate that audit risk is *not* the same as business risk, although there are some common features. Audit risk is the risk *auditors* have to assess, business risks are the totality of risks faced by a *business* or organization carrying on its everyday activities.

Audit risk is not the same as business risk. Nor should it be necessarily confined to areas of audit difficulty, such as those which may require a lot of subjective judgement, say perhaps where there needs to be provisions for future losses on long term contracts or where there may have to be a judgement as to whether an entity is a going concern or not (Chapter 23). Areas of audit difficulty and the inherent and control risks contribute to the auditor's overall assessment of audit risk, but as part of a much wider consideration of the possibility that they may combine in some way with the result that the auditor will give the wrong opinion i.e. state that the financial statements are true and fair when they are not.

Audit risk is defined in ISA 200 '*Overall objectives of the independent auditor and the conduct of an audit in accordance with International Standards on Auditing*' and comprises two things:

1 the risks of a material misstatement in the financial statements as a whole or in the disclosure of individual transactions and balances
2 detection risk – the risk that the auditor's own procedures will fail to detect a material error or misstatement

We look at materiality later, for the moment the word 'significant' is an acceptable substitute. We can thus define audit risk as the risk of a significant error or mistake not being detected either by the organization's systems of control or the auditor's own procedures.

The assessment of audit risk is a matter of professional judgement and is a key part of the planning process. The risks of a material misstatement are split into two components:

- inherent risk
- control risk

Audit risk must be assessed at both the organizational level, i.e. looking at the financial statements as a whole, and at the transaction level where the auditor is seeking to verify disclosure of individual components of the financial statements, e.g. the value of Inventory and Work in Progress or the Revenue figure. However, the general approach to assessing audit risk is the same whether it is being considered at the organizational level or at the transaction level.

Inherent risk

Inherent risk is the risks which derive from the nature of the entity itself, its business and from the business and commercial environment in which it operates, or, at the transaction level, it is the susceptibility of the transactions to possible misstatement due to their nature or complexity.

Factors influencing inherent risk at the organization level are:

- the nature of the entity's business, e.g. a construction company is a more volatile business than a fruit importing business
- the quality and experience of the management

- the level of competition in its market
- the complexity of its operations
- the cash situation of the business
- the trading history of the business

At the transaction level inherent risk is affected by:

- the susceptibility to misappropriation
- the complexity of the transactions
- the degree of judgement involved

Control risk

Control risk is the risk that the client's internal control procedures will fail to detect a material error or misstatement. Control risk is influenced by:

- the attitude of the directors and management towards internal control – what is known as the **control environment**
- the internal controls present in the system (Chapter 9) and the capabilities of the staff in maintaining and operating them
- the level of supervision in the business
- the integrity of the staff and management

The ICQs, flow charts and ICEQs (see below) will all influence the assessment of control risk, as will some of the areas of audit difficulty such as those described in the Metalbash example below, for example:

- new and inexperienced staff
- changes in accounting systems
- additional locations or branches
- new products

Evaluating inherent and control risk

The auditor will make a preliminary assessment of the levels of inherent and control risk.

This can be done either by a simple subjective judgement, assessing risk as 'high', 'medium' or 'low' or by applying a value weighting or a statistical technique.

Auditors generally aim to have no more than a 5 per cent risk that the financial statements are materially incorrect – in other words they would be 95 per cent certain that their opinion is the correct one. This is known as the *confidence level*.

Detection risk

Detection risk is the risk that the auditor's own procedures and review of the financial statements will not detect material errors or misstatements.

The important thing for the student to appreciate is that detection risk is the variable in the equation. The higher the level of inherent and control risk, the more checking work the auditor has to do as the objective is to reduce audit risk overall to as low a level as possible.

They do this by carrying out more audit work. So the level of audit risk has a direct bearing on how much and what type of audit work is carried out.

Care must be taken to weigh the risk from each source of evidence as it is gathered and then to avoid over auditing in the remaining evidence gathering. For example, if adequate weight is given to inherent factors and analytical review it may be that minimal internal control evaluation and/or detailed testing will be required.

In order to properly evaluate the levels of inherent and control risk auditors need to carry out the investigatory procedures set out below, namely:

- Get to know their client – as part of their planning procedures and the procedures described in Chapter 8 above and related to ISA 315 – *'Identifying and assessing the risks of material misstatement through understanding the entity and its environment'.*
- Review the client's internal control systems by documenting them thoroughly and by the use of questionnaires.

It cannot be stressed enough that without this preliminary review of the client's business and thorough documentation and evaluation of its financial systems the audit may be seriously flawed.

Auditors base all of their checking work, indeed their whole audit strategy, on their opinion of the client's financial capabilities and the business risks involved in the client's activities. All the auditor's subsequent activity stems from this preliminary investigation and discovery work which, if it is incomplete or flawed, may well lead to:

- inadequate testing of key areas
- being misled by managers because of incomplete knowledge of the business
- failing to identify areas where frauds could be committed

Materiality

Materiality is a matter of professional judgement and can be a particularly difficult matter in practice but is of great importance. Great care should be taken before coming to a conclusion on matters of materiality.

ISA 320 *'Materiality in planning and performing an audit'* states:

'Misstatements, including omissions, are considered to be material if they, individually or in the aggregate, could reasonably be expected to influence the economic decisions of users taken on the basis of the financial statements.'

In addition to that, the Companies Act is full of references to materiality. For example, there must be shown separately in the Income Statement the amount, *if material*, charged to revenue in respect of sums payable for the hire of plant and machinery.

Performance materiality

Performance materiality is an estimate of materiality which is set lower than the estimate for the financial statements as a whole and is used by the auditors to reduce to an appropriately low level the probability that the aggregate of uncorrected and undetected misstatements exceeds materiality for the financial statements as a whole.

Performance materiality is linked to the estimates of the levels of audit risk (see above) and the amount of audit testing. Students will recall that the risk is that a material error or misstatement will go undetected either by the organization or by the audit procedures. The lower the level of materiality the more audit work has to be done. To illustrate the point, for example, if performance materiality was set at £1 the auditors would have to check a huge number of transactions as every transaction of £1 or over not properly recorded or omitted from the records entirely would be a material error. Conversely, if performance materiality was set at too high a level errors or mistakes might not be detected because of reduced levels of audit testing, with the result that there would be an increased likelihood that a genuinely material error or misstatement world go undetected.

Performance materiality is set at a lower level than materiality for the financial statements as a whole to take account of undetected errors or misstatements. It gives the audit team a little 'headroom' as it were. They will collect all the errors they have detected during the course of their audit work and decide if they constitute errors which exceed the level of performance materiality. Auditors are always conscious that, because they carry out audit testing on a sample basis, there is the risk of material errors going undetected by their audit work, even though they have carried out their testing conscientiously. They can consider the level of detected errors within their performance materiality limit, and decide how close the level of detected errors plus an allowance for undetected errors is to the overall materiality limit.

The estimates of both materiality and performance materiality are a matter of professional judgement and they have both quantitative (amount) and qualitative (nature) dimensions.

Quantitative estimates

A figure might be material purely because of its size relative to other amounts in the accounts. Auditors often set some form of percentage values on errors which will decide if they are material or not, for example:

- 5–10 per cent of pre-tax profits
- 1 per cent of revenue
- 5 per cent of net asset value

For organizations, which are profit driven, materiality levels may be set in terms of net profit or loss. However, where this measure might be volatile other measures such as revenue or gross profit might be more appropriate. In any case it is a matter of professional judgement – the percentages quoted above should not be taken as being prescriptive.

For example, an error detected might be quite small but is sufficient to turn a pre-tax profit into a pre-tax loss. This would almost certainly be material as it would be likely to influence the economic decisions of a reader of the accounts. There are some methods by which auditors can assess whether or not items are material:

- Compare the magnitude of the item with the overall view presented by the financial statements.
- Compare the magnitude of the item with the magnitude of the same item in previous years.
- Compare the magnitude of the item with the total of which it forms a part (e.g. 'Receivables' may include employee loans but if employee loans become large, i.e. material, then the description 'Receivables' may be inadequate).
- Some items are always material irrespective of size, e.g. disclosure of directors' remuneration because it is a statutory disclosure under the Companies Act 2006.

The information which the auditor uses to decide on materiality levels must be reliable, so if preliminary materiality levels are being set on the basis of, say, management accounts the auditors must be reasonably sure that these accounts are broadly representative of the financial position of the business before using them to decide on materiality levels.

Qualitative estimates

Materiality also has qualitative aspects and these relate to the nature of the error or misstatement detected, regardless of its financial value. For example, errors which are material by virtue of their nature would include:

- omission of a disclosure required by the Companies Act or accounting standards
- an item which is misstated in the accounts – e.g. a short-term loan classified as a long-term loan
- an item which might affect the accounts but which has been omitted because it cannot be quantified with a reasonable degree of certainty, e.g. the outcome of a court case

In these cases, the auditors should remind the directors of their duty to comply with the Companies Act and the accounting standards and rectify omissions or misstatements.

Materiality and audit procedures

Auditors should take materiality, in particular performance materiality, into account when considering the nature, timing and extent of audit procedures.

Materiality should be estimated at the planning stage but must be reviewed as the audit progresses and reconsidered if the outcome of tests, enquiries or examinations differs from expectation. This is particularly true of performance materiality which the auditors may be using as a basis for deciding the levels of audit testing.

In evaluating whether the financial statements give a true and fair view, auditors should assess the materiality of the *aggregate* or total of uncorrected errors. These may be those identified during the audit and the best estimate of others which the auditors have not quantified specifically. Examples might be numerous small errors in the sales ledger or in coding expense invoices. If the directors adjust the financial statements for these all may be well, but if not the aggregate misstatement may be material when each individual misstatement is not.

PLANNING THE AUDIT

There are three key ISAs which relate directly or indirectly to the planning process. These are:

- ISA 200 *'Overall objectives of the independent auditor and the conduct of an audit in accordance with International Standards on Auditing'*
- ISA 300 *'Planning an Audit of Financial Statements'*
- ISA 315 *'Identifying and assessing the risks of material misstatement through understanding the entity and its environment'*

These ISAs, and of course particularly ISA 200, require the auditor to carry out a process of planning to ensure:

- Professional ethics issues, particularly independence, are considered and evaluated so that the client continues to be one the auditor can audit.
- The terms of the engagement, as set out in the letter or engagement (Chapter 8) are understood and planned for.
- An appropriate audit strategy is adopted in order to achieve all audit objectives as set out in the appropriate ISAs.
- The audit work can be controlled, supervised and reviewed.
- Attention can be focused on critical and high-risk areas.
- Any potential problem areas can be identified as early as possible.
- The work can then be completed economically and to timescale requirements.

An audit can be carried out on enterprises both large and small, and both new and well established. The ISAs do not distinguish between large and small organizations, except in particular circumstances, so that any audit must be carried out to the same standard regardless of the size of the organization.

This chapter describes the stages in the audit of an established client enterprise which is big enough to have a comprehensive system of accounting and record keeping and a system of controls over those records.

Know your client

ISA 315 *'Identifying and assessing risks of material misstatement through understanding the entity and its environment'* sets out the matters the auditor should consider before commencing the audit planning process and certainly before starting work.

Fundamentally it requires the auditor to carry out a form of **risk assessment** to assess the risk of a serious misstatement arising either at the level of the financial statements as a whole or in any component of them. The auditor must do this by obtaining a thorough understanding of their client's business, its management, the environment in which it operates and the quality of its internal financial procedures.

ISA 315 requires the auditors to:

- obtain a knowledge of the business which is sufficient to enable them to identify and understand the events, transactions and practices that may have a significant effect on the financial statements and the audit of them
- use the knowledge gained to understand the client's own risk assessment processes sufficient to form conclusions as to their effectiveness in identifying and evaluating:
  - factors affecting the business which might affect financial reporting
  - the risks of fraud and error (Chapter 20)
  - risks arising through transactions with related parties (Chapter 21)
  - risks associated with complex transactions – particularly relevant to banks and financial institutions but could also apply to, for example, complex construction contracts
  - the degree of subjectivity which might be involved in deriving information included in the financial statements
  - transactions which arise other than in the normal course of business or which appear to be unusual
  - risks associated with unrecorded liabilities (Chapter 16)

As we saw in Chapter 8, if the client is a new one, before commencing the audit proper, the auditor must get to know their prospective client. If the client is an existing one the auditor must nevertheless undertake some research in order to establish the extent and nature of any significant changes since the last audit.

This involves ensuring the auditors have comprehensive knowledge of:

- the present condition and future prospects of the industry of which the client is a part, including the competition
- the past history and the present condition and future prospects of the client itself
- the client's:
  - products and services
  - important customers
  - key suppliers and
  - details of significant contracts
- the management and key personnel of the client and any recent changes
- the products and manufacturing and trading processes of the client and any recent changes
- the locations of all the client's operations
- any difficulties encountered by the client in:
  - manufacturing
  - trading
  - expanding or contracting the business
  - labour relations
  - financing the continuing operations
- the accounting and internal control systems, in particular:
  - the information systems and the related business processes relevant to financial reporting
  - the types of transactions and business activities which are significant to the financial statements
  - the financial procedures, including both IT and paper based, through which transactions are initiated, recorded, processed and authorized
  - the accounting systems and financial records, including procedures for correcting errors and misstatements, and all the supporting documentation
  - the operation of the financial systems, both IT and manual, including the internal control activities and procedures within those systems which are designed to detect errors
  - the process by which the financial statements are produced
  - the controls over journals designed to record nonstandard or unusual transactions including the correction of errors
  - the structure and communications within the organization, in particular the reporting between management and directors and between the organization and the outside world, including any regulators

The auditor must also gain an understanding of some specific control issues including:

- risks relating to the use of IT including external threats such as hacking and malware and the risks associated with operating an IT system such as data corruption or loss (Chapter 17)
- particular problems arising from the estimation of values, particularly those which increase audit risk, e.g. the value of long term work in progress
- practical problems which might be encountered when carrying out the audit, for example a client with operations in widely spread geographical locations or overseas or ones requiring specific skills such as computer audit, or those with very tight timescales
- any recent changes in the law or regulations which may affect the client's operations or the conduct of the audit

In order to obtain the information they require the auditor will have to carry out a good deal of background research. This will include consulting or reading previous years' audit files, any published material concerning the client company and the industry, including articles in trade magazines or the financial press carrying out Internet searches and reviewing the company's interim, internal and management accounts, if these can be obtained.

Holding discussions with the management and audit staff who have been previously engaged on the audit will also provide a good deal of information, both anecdotal and factual.

In order to carry out a comprehensive and effective audit which is nevertheless efficient in terms of time spent, the auditor must focus the audit on areas of particular difficulty and risk. In addition, the evaluation of many areas in the financial statements must entail a consideration of the whole circumstances of a client.

As simple examples, the evaluation of the life of noncurrent tangible assets liable to obsolescence or estimating the value of an investment in a subsidiary company can only be effected by having knowledge of all factors having a bearing on the matter and many of these factors are external to the company.

CASE STUDY 1

Metalbash Pressings Ltd

Jane is the audit manager of Knight & Shade and is about to start to plan the audit of Metalbash Pressings Ltd, a company which manufactures parts for UK commercial vehicle manufacturers. She will need to research the background of:

- **The industry**

She finds that UK commercial vehicle output is 75 per cent of normal levels. This reduces the market demand for components and stimulates greater competition between component manufacturers, resulting in lower prices for component suppliers. Companies with high manufacturing costs could find their market share declining rapidly.

- **The company**

The company is suffering from price and cost squeezes, plant closures and redundancies. She finds that a factory has closed and 50 workers have been made redundant. However, the company has purchased for cash (with a bank loan) the business of another company in receivership which is in a related industry. This new company will require a cash injection, some new plant and new management before it can start trading profitably. It has a factory in a neighbouring town and Jane has to plan visits there and interviews with management and personnel. Metalbash itself has gone through an administrative reorganization during the year and some experienced office staff have left. Any significant changes to operations may weaken controls, change policies or worsen accounting records. Jane finds that there is now a new chief accountant who is not familiar with the components business.

- **Products and processes**

New production processes have been introduced and some new machinery installed. Jane does not know what has happened to the old machines. Changes in costs of manufacture may have possible consequences to Inventory values and there is the value of redundant equipment to consider.

- **Locations**

Closures may involve closure costs with possible disclosure problems under FRS102.

- **Client's difficulties**

Difficulties experienced by the client (e.g. on labour relations or cost and quality control) may impact on internal controls. Jane finds that the new accountant has streamlined several accounting processes and controls may have changed and be weaker.

- **Systems changes**

Accounting systems change frequently as a consequence of improved technology and the need to improve management information systems. The accounting records of the new business have been incorporated into new systems and some teething problems have occurred. A new computer system has been installed.

- **Accounting issues**

Accounting measurement problems may arise in product costs, redundant Inventories, closure costs, redundancy costs, lives of fixed assets, etc.

- **Key risk areas**

Some commercial vehicle manufacturers have gone into receivership and there is a risk of Metalbash losing its business or incurring potentially fatal bad debts. Jane will need to concentrate consequently upon the value of receivables and whether or not the business is going to survive the next few years. In addition, any changes to systems and personnel all have to be evaluated.

- **Key audit issues**

  New systems will need to be documented, the audit programmes amended for the new business and additional audit procedures thought through to take account of the changed circumstances of the business.

- **Planning**

  In planning the audit, Jane will need to consider locations, timing problems, staff requirements and the quality of audit staff needed for some of the risky areas including a possible need to look into and assess new systems.

- **Sources of information**

  Jane will do all this by:
  - reading the previous years' files
  - talking to the staff member responsible for last year's audit
  - discussing the impact of all the changes with the management
  - discussing audit timings and the access to records with the new chief accountant
  - reading the minutes of directors' and senior management meetings
  - reviewing the management accounts
  - reading any newspaper and magazine articles
  - looking at the company's website and surfing the net for information about the industry generally and any comments about her client from third party sources

INTERNAL CONTROL SYSTEM REVIEW

Internal controls are the client's procedures which ensure that all transactions, assets and liabilities are recorded correctly in the accounting records.

In essence, what auditors need to do when faced with a new system or a system that has changed significantly is:

- ascertain the system
- record it
- corroborate that record with the client
- review the overall system for reliability
- test the system with some sample checks
- evaluate its reliability
- form a conclusion on the adequacy of the client's system of internal control

The objectives of investigations and recording of the accounting and internal control systems are to enable the auditor to have evidence that the client maintains adequate books and records – don't forget this is a secondary objective of the audit.

It must also be established that the client has a system of internal controls over the processing and recording of transactions such that all transactions are recorded correctly both numerically and in principle and that the books of account can be relied on to form a reliable basis for the preparation of the financial statements.

The auditors are primarily looking to rely upon the financial systems. If the systems are satisfactory then they can substitute an investigation and tests of the systems for a lot of detailed tests of individual transactions and balances.

Only by examining the systems can they gather evidence to prove that all the transactions are recorded correctly and in the right accounting period.

If, in some areas of the business, internal controls do not exist or are weak the auditors cannot rely on the controls and other evidence needs to be sought so that the auditors can form an opinion as to the completeness and accuracy of the records.

There are three basic techniques used when documenting client's systems. These are:

- use of **Internal Control Questionnaires** (ICQs)
- flow charting and documenting the system
- use of **Internal Control Evaluation Questionnaires** (ICEQs)

Internal control questionnaires (ICQs)

These are often standardized checklists established by the audit firm, which may be adapted to individual clients. The use of standardized lists means that questions are less likely to be omitted or go unanswered. These documents can have several functions:

- as a method of ascertaining of the system
- to enable the auditors to review and assess the adequacy of the system
- to enable the auditors to identify areas of weakness
- assisting the auditors to design a series of tests; in effect this means enabling the auditors to draw up their audit programme
- enabling audit staff to familiarize themselves with the system quickly and comprehensively

Figure 10.1 is an example of part of an ICQ relating to a purchase ordering system. Each component of each system within the organization will have an ICQ devoted to it so the auditor can make inquiries and evaluate the answers. Note the separate columns for:

- questions
- answers – yes/no
- reviewer's comment which can identify systems weaknesses

Note also the fact that the individual completing the questionnaire must initial and date it to evidence completing, and the finished questionnaire must be reviewed. Evidence of the review must also be noted on the form.

The auditor is looking for '**NO**' answers as these indicate a possible systems weakness which must be followed up and evaluated.

Flow charts

Flow charts are a method of recording internal control systems from the auditor's standpoint. There are two methods of flowcharting – charting of processes and charting of document flows. Auditors find it more useful to chart document flows as documents form the basis of their checking work.

The *advantages* of flow charts are as follows:

- Narrative notes can be lengthy and confusing. Changes in the system usually require the whole of the notes to be re-written. Flow charts provide a visual representation of a system which is much more easily appreciated than a lengthy written note.
- Flow charts enable the system to be recorded in such a way that it can be understood by:
  - new staff coming to the audit
  - supervisors, managers and partners
  - client's staff responsible for the system and for implementing changes to deal with identified weaknesses
- The overall picture of a firm's financial systems can be seen which may enable the auditor to improve the design of audit tests.
- Flow charting is a consistent system of recording.

FIGURE 10.1 Internal control questionnaire (extract)

Client name: **METALBASH LTD** Period to **31 December 2X16** Subject area: PURCHASE ORDERING	Prepared by **JT** Reviewed by **DB**		Date **19/7/2X16** Date **22/8/2X16**

Process	Yes	No	Comments
Are all purchases made as a result of written orders?	✓		
Are all orders sequentially numbered?	✓		
Are all numbers accounted for?		✓	**Spoiled orders destroyed**
Do orders have to be authorized by a senior manager?	✓		**CEO or purchasing manager**
Are orders only sent to approved suppliers?	✓		
If there are no approved suppliers, is the procedure for approving a supplier carried out before the order is placed?	✓		**Only approved suppliers used**
Do all purchase orders show quantities? Prices? Terms? Initials of authorizer? Date?	✓ ✓ ✓ ✓ ✓		
Is there a limit to individual order values?	✓		**CEO – no limit Purchasing Manager – limit £50 000**
Are copies of the purchase order sent to Purchase ledger department?	✓		
Stores?	✓		
Are purchase orders matched to invoices?	✓		
Are copies of all orders retained in the purchasing department?	✓		

- Flow charting requires a full understanding of the financial systems to be able to draw them.
- Flow charting highlights the relationships between different parts of a system. By linking charts together even complex systems can be described easily.
- Weaknesses are easier to spot.
- Superfluous forms and bottlenecks are easily spotted. Auditors can help their clients improve document flows and to increase efficiencies in processing.
- Flow charts are a permanent record but can be updated where parts of a system change.
- In complex systems flow charting is the only way to gain an understanding of the interactions between the various parts of the accounting function.

There are computerized flow charting packages available to simplify the process. The *disadvantages* of flow charting are:

- They can become overcomplicated or confusing if badly drawn.
- They have to be redrawn if the system changes significantly.
- They are fine for describing accounting processes where documents are moving through a system, but once documents stop moving they cannot describe controls, e.g. flow charts can describe procedures for controlling goods inward and outward but not the controls over Inventory in the stores.

When preparing flow charts the following points should be borne in mind:

- Systems flow charts should be accompanied by an organization chart showing the relevant personnel and their relative place in the organization.

- Simplicity and clarity are fundamental.
- Flow charts must not be congested. Use separate charts for sub-procedures, exceptional procedures, etc. Small congested charts can be misleading.
- Use only horizontal and vertical lines and standard flow charting symbols.
- Start at the top left and finish at the bottom right.

Charts must show:

- initiation of each document and operation
- the sequence of all operations on documents and all copies of documents, especially operations of control, inspecting, checking, comparing and approving
- the sections or individuals who perform operations
- the ultimate destination, i.e. where is it filed?
- explanatory narrative notes should be included where required

Specimens of documents could be attached and cross-referenced.

The objective of a flow chart is that it is complete in itself and can be read and understood quickly and comprehensibly. However, this takes practice.

CASE STUDY 2

Metalbash Ltd sales order and invoicing system

A narrative description of the system might be:

- The company has a number of separate departments (e.g. sales, credit control). This is important for segregation of duties.
- Orders are received from customers in various forms including telephone, online or through customer visits.
- All orders are transcribed onto pre-numbered official 'sales order forms'. Pre-numbering ensures all orders will be fulfilled or discovered as unfulfilled.
- The blank order forms are kept locked in the manager's safe. Order forms are important as they initiate the release of goods.
- The sales order forms are in duplicate. One copy is attached to the original customer order and filed in a temporary file.
- The second copy is sent to credit control. Credit control check that the customer is credit worthy by reference to their records and the customer's ledger account printout (to see the customer is not overdue or has not exceeded their credit limit).
- If credit is not approved, then a credit approval sub-routine applies. (The sub-routine is on another flow chart which is not included).
- The order is then sent to the warehouse. There, the goods on the order are checked for availability. If the goods are not available, then a routine is operated (to order more from the supplier).
- A despatch note with four copies is made out from the details in the sales order form. This despatch note is pre-numbered.
- One copy of the despatch note is put with the goods (which are picked off the shelves and packed) and signed by the goods-out foreman who compares the goods with the despatch note.
- This copy is then attached to the sales order form and filed in despatch note number order in the warehouse.

(Continues)

- The second and third copies of the despatch note are checked against the goods and sent with the goods to the customer. One copy will be returned, signed, as proof of delivery.
- The fourth copy is used to make out the invoice. It is subsequently attached to a copy of the invoice and filed in invoice number order in the invoice section. But before being attached it is checked for sequence (to see none are missing, meaning goods were despatched but not invoiced) by the invoice section manager.
- The invoice has three copies. The top copy is sent to the customer.
- The second copy has been dealt with (see above).
- This copy is checked for accuracy and initialled by the checker. The second copy is batched daily. From the batch a prelist is made out in duplicate. The top copy of the prelist is filed in numerical sequence in the invoice department.
- The second copy of the prelist is sent with the batch of copy invoices daily to computer input (this is yet another flow chart, not included).
- The third copy of the sales invoice is sent to the sales department.
- From the order forms and the invoice copies, a schedule of outstanding orders is made out weekly in duplicate.
- The matched order forms and invoices are attached to each other and filed monthly in alphabetical order of customer.
- The top copy of the schedule is filed. The second copy is sent to the managing director.

As you can see from the Case Study above, narrative notes describing a system can be long and tedious. It is often difficult to mentally track where all the copies of a document go and it would be easy for the reader to miss the fact that a significant internal control procedure may be missing as they wade through the mass of detail.

The same system can be described in a flow chart (Figure 10.2). From this it can be seen that the key aspects of the system are much more easily recognized and if any internal control process has been omitted it is much more likely to be spotted. The flow chart has been simplified a little for clarity.

The symbols used are explained below and the internal control features listed. Note the incidence of:

- separation of duties between departments and individuals:
  - initiation (by customer)
  - authorization (credit control)
  - custody (warehouse)
  - documentation and recording
- a specified organization structure
- arithmetic controls (prelist)
- acknowledgement of performance (invoice checking)
- physical controls (blank sales order forms kept in safe)
- formal transfer of goods (warehouse to goods out)
- pre-review (by credit control)
- post-review (sequence checks)

FIGURE 10.2 **Flow chart for audit purposes**

Metalbash Ltd – Flow chart of sales orders and invoicing procedures

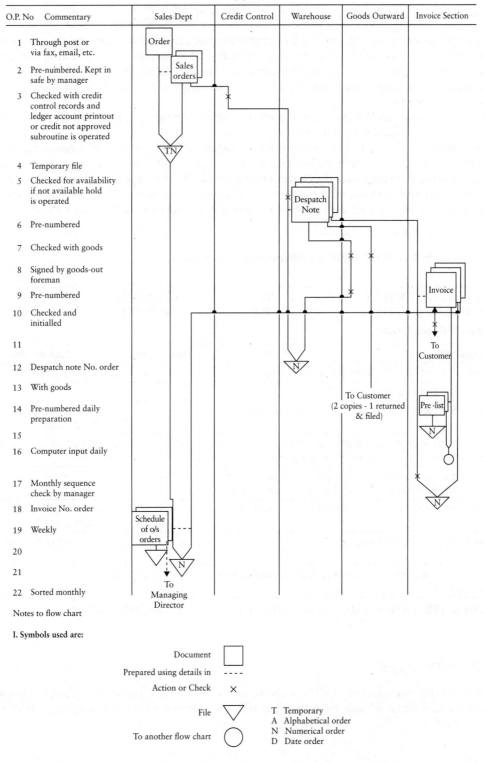

I. Symbols used are:

Document	□
Prepared using details in	----
Action or Check	×
File	▽
To another flow chart	○

T Temporary
A Alphabetical order
N Numerical order
D Date order

Notes to students:

1   This is, of course, incomplete. The warehouse, goods-out section, etc., have not been included.
2   Further detail could be included if desired, e.g. actual names of officials, their location, etc.

Internal control evaluation questionnaires (ICEQs)

Internal control questionnaires (ICQs) and flow charts are used to ascertain and record the system. However, it is also necessary to evaluate the system's strengths and weaknesses. An ideal method of doing this is by means of an Internal Control Evaluation Questionnaire. This is a standardized set of questions which has the advantage, like the ICQ, of ensuring all the right questions are asked and the strengths and weaknesses of a system are brought out.

The basic questions in an ICEQ are called control questions. An example from the sales area is '*Can sales be invoiced but not recorded in the books?*'

You will recall that for an ICQ the auditors were looking for 'YES' answers because they were trying to confirm that controls were operating. Here they are looking for 'NO' answers as the purpose of the ICEQ is to see if it is possible to get round the controls in the system. A 'NO' answer confirms it is not possible.

Note that the same quality control procedures of evidencing work done and review that we saw with the ICQ also apply here. Figure 10.3 is an example of an ICEQ relating to a goods inward system.

FIGURE 10.3   Example internal control evaluation questionnaire – extract

Client name: **METALBASH LTD** Prepared by **JT** Date **19/7/2X16** Period to **31 December 2X16** Reviewed by **DB** Date **22/8/2X16** *Subject area: Goods Inward*			
Control Question	**Yes**	**No**	**Comments**
Can goods be accepted without being inspected for damage?		✓	Damaged goods report
Can goods be delivered without being signed for?		✓	
Can goods be delivered without a goods received note being prepared?		✓	Invoices not paid without copy GRN attached
Are the individuals who deal with goods inward the same as those who deal with the security and recording of Inventory?	✓		Stores staff deal with goods inward
Are the individuals who deal with goods inward the same as those who deal with the security and recording of purchase ordering?		✓	
Is it possible for invoices to be paid without goods having been received?		✓	Invoices not paid without copy GRN attached
Is it possible for goods to be accepted without having been ordered?		✓	Copy order sent to stores
Are damaged goods stored in the same part of the warehouse as accepted goods?		✓	Quarantine area

In this case the '**YES**' answer should be followed up to see if it has any internal control implications.

Walk-through tests

Once the system has been documented, flow charts and notes prepared and reviewed and ICQs and ICEQs completed, the final step is to 'walk-through' the system to ensure that what is noted on the audit files actually happens in practice.

The auditor will take a small number, say three or four, of transactions and trace them through the system following the system notes as they go. This is called a '**walk-through test**' and ties the system notes to the actual live system. These tests will be documented on the audit files as they form part of the auditor's understanding of the systems in place and how they operate in practice.

AUDIT STRATEGIES

Basically there are three approaches when deciding an audit strategy:

1 **Substantive approach**

   This is usually adopted for the audit of small organizations where the internal systems are weak and there is a limited number of staff. For example, a small charity or perhaps a small family company requiring an audit might have a simple proprietary computer-based bookkeeping system and a part-time bookkeeper who does all the accounting work.

   There are no real controls within the system and the auditor has little choice but to test a large number of transactions. Clearly this approach is not practicable in any but the smallest organizations. We look at special features of the audit of small organizations in Chapter 20.

2 **Systems-based auditing**

   This approach is used on larger organizations where there is a proper accounting system and sufficient staff to constitute a proper system of internal control. We look at this in detail in Chapter 13.

   This is an approach to auditing which relies on the controls contained within the client's financial systems to validate the accounting records. The auditors must make an evaluation of audit risk and determine whether or not controls can be relied upon, based on their preliminary review work. There is an element of risk involved as limited numbers of transactions are being tested based on samples. The auditors test the controls (a process known as **compliance testing**) by means of testing a sample of transactions and extrapolating the results of those sample tests to the population as a whole. In this way they can draw conclusions as to the reliability of the accounting records.

   Note that the individual transactions are only chosen because they are representative of the types of transaction checked by the particular control or set of controls the auditors are testing.

   The auditors will carry out detailed testing (known as **substantive testing**) on items in the Statement of Financial Position or unusual transactions which haven't gone through the normal accounting system.

3 **Business risk-based auditing**

   The development of strong IT systems has made this an increasingly effective form of auditing and the days of lots of detailed testing are definitely numbered as computerized accounting procedures and increasing use of technology make some of the old forms of audit testing obsolete or unnecessary. We will look at this specifically in Chapter 14. Basically this is used to audit larger organizations or those with excellent internal control systems. The auditors carry out a limited amount of testing of transactions and balances and concentrate their efforts on analysing the business risks faced by the organization. These then become the subject of the auditor's attention. The audit logic is that errors or misstatements will not arise from wrongly recorded day-to-day transactions – because the underlying systems and controls are so good, but will have their source in an identified area of risk. The risks can be either actual operational risks arising from the nature of the business (e.g. oil exploration) or from the complexity of the accounting required (e.g. derivatives trading).

   This approach requires the auditors to use experienced and competent staff and to have faith in the client's underlying systems. It is, however, an efficient way of auditing very large organizations where errors or misstatements have to be fairly huge to have any impact on the financial statements.

   It is also a good way to audit efficient organizations with strong internal controls and lots of management supervision. It saves a good deal of time, thus reducing audit costs and enables the audit team to focus on risks and key issues rather than the minutiae of transaction reporting.

ISA 200 states that a decision must be made as to the audit strategy to be adopted and the rationale for that decision must be documented. There should be an overall audit plan, which will be documented set out in the **Audit Planning Memorandum,** which outlines the general strategy which will underpin the detailed programme of audit work specified in the **Audit Programme.**

CASE STUDY 3

Metalbash Pressings Ltd – deciding the audit strategy

We will use the information set out in Case Study 1 to illustrate the process.

Before the detailed audit planning work commences Jane must ensure that she has a good understanding of the client, the industry in which it operates and its products and processes. Before deciding on an audit strategy she must go through the following steps:

1 *Understand the client and its background* – history, products, locations, especially noting factors like the new directors and chief accountant, a new computer system, new products and the new subsidiary. In particular, she must review and update the records on:

- the management structure
- the products and processes
- the financial accounting system
- the abilities of the management to control the business
- the operating style (e.g. direction from the top or disseminated decision-making)
- the attitude of directors and management towards internal control

2 *Select an audit strategy*

The audit strategy will take into account the following:

- The terms of the engagement with the client, i.e. what work is to be done? This will obviously include the audit but will also include any accounting work to be done for the client (i.e. drafting the final accounts, tax computations, etc.) and preparing any reports to third parties, e.g. The Lorry Parts Manufacturers Association.
- Important figures and ratios – from previous years and, if available, from relevant management and draft accounts. This will form the basis of a preliminary analytical review which may highlight audit problem areas.
- Identification and consideration of key risk areas to the financial statements as a whole – these might include Inventory and asset valuations, work in progress, or liquidity. We look at these further in later chapters.
- The extent of reliance on internal controls and systems. There is no internal audit so no help there!
- Possibilities of material error, misstatement or fraud. This will involve evaluation of the systems notes and consideration of previous experience with this client.
- Any going concerns issues (see Chapter 23).
- Any specific regulatory requirements (especially important in some types of company, e.g. those in financial services).

Once all these factors have been evaluated the general audit strategy will have to be decided upon.

PLANNING THE AUDIT WORK

The planning process is the basis of good auditing. Without proper planning the audit will be more likely to be inefficient and incomplete. We have seen that the auditor must gather sufficient reliable evidence to substantiate their audit opinion. This process must be planned and moreover the auditor must be able to demonstrate that they have planned their work.

Poor or inadequate planning can mean:

- Areas of risk are not clearly identified and addressed.
- Insufficient audit work may be devoted to areas where errors or misstatements are likely to occur.

- Conversely some areas which are, in fact, quite well controlled or of low importance may be over audited.
- The risk of fraud may not be identified.
- Staff may be carrying out audit work without the relevant skills or experience.
- Resources may be wasted or misused, deadlines missed or costs escalate.
- Audit work may not be properly supervised.
- Where other auditors, e.g. auditors or overseas subsidiaries, or experts are involved their engagement may not be properly co-ordinated.

The planning process

Planning is not a single process but is a continual and iterative process which continues until the audit is completed.

The process includes the preliminary and ongoing review of the client detailed above and it also includes the possibility that plans may be changed if the outcome of audit testing so dictates. However, at a point before the actual audit work begins, a detailed plan of the assignment should be drawn up in order to enable the audit team to be briefed and to direct and control the work.

The plan will normally be contained in a document known as an Audit Planning Memorandum. It is important that auditors document the planning process and this memorandum is the evidence for that process. The memorandum should be signed off by the audit partner after discussions with the audit team and included on the current audit file (Chapter 18).

The planning process will normally involve:

- Reviewing last year's working papers for key issues and problem areas. Carrying out a form of risk assessment process in order to identify areas for attention.
- Considering the impact of any changes in legislation, regulatory issues or auditing and accounting standards.
- Considering the background of the client and the nature of any changes in its industry or business environment resulting in issues which may affect the level of audit work. This would include considerations of, for example, changes in technology or fashion.
- Considering the impact of changes in the business itself or its management or ownership.
- Reviewing the effect on the audit of changes in systems or accounting procedures.
- Carrying out an analytical review of management accounts.
- Setting of preliminary materiality and performance materiality levels.
- Consulting with management on any key issues which have arisen in the financial period.
- Deciding on how much reliance could be placed on the client's own internal controls so a systems-based approach could be adopted, which areas may need detailed substantive testing or whether a risk-based audit strategy could be used (see Chapters 13 and 14).
- Deciding on the degree of reliance to be placed on any internal audit reports and whether this will reduce the amount of audit work carried out by the external auditors.
- The effect of information technology on the audit, in particular the new systems.
- Any requirement for involvement of specialists. These may be from within the audit firm, e.g. computer audit or external specialists such as valuers.
- Agreeing the timing and extent of client responsibilities. The responsibilities of the client to provide draft accounts, supporting schedules and analyses, and to provide computer time, arranging visits to branches, etc. If the deadline is to be met the client has to fulfil its part of the arrangement.
- Agreeing the timing of the audit work, for example the number and timing of audit visits, and such matters as attending inventory counts and requesting confirmations from third parties.
- Liaising with joint auditors, if any, and, in the case of group audits, liaison with any auditors of subsidiary companies.
- Planning the rotational testing where there are multiple locations or branches so the ones to be visited this year can be agreed and visits scheduled. Care must be taken however not to compromise the audit work by disclosing too much information about the checking work to the client.
- Working out the time budget.

- Planning and arranging staffing requirements.
- Considering the budget in the light of the likely fee to be charged.
- Organizing liaison with the company's Audit Committee, if any.

The planning process should involve the engagement partner who is ultimately responsible for the audit work and the engagement partner should review and agree the final plan before any audit work is actually carried out.

Metalbash Pressings Ltd

Steps in planning the audit

In order to illustrate the process of audit planning we will use an example in order to illustrate the process. We looked at this in Case Studies 1 and 3 and can now continue the story.

Let us consider the case of Metalbash again, and the auditors who are Knight & Shade. The December 2X16 audit plan is to be prepared by audit manager Jane. She has to consider all the matters mentioned above and finds the following matters require attention:

- A special report has to be prepared for the Lorry Part Manufacturers' Association on the cost structures in the company.
- As Jane is new to the audit she needs to read previous years' papers especially carefully as her predecessor has left Knight & Shade and the audit partner, to whom she reports, has also changed as old Mr Tick has retired and gone to live in the Bahamas.
- The 2X15 audit was completed in May 2X16 when the AGM was held and the date is now August 2X16.
- There are several new FRSs and ISAs and some new relevant legislation. Happily, all these are summarized in Knight & Shade's internal updating and Jane is sent on courses regularly.
- The client produces monthly accounts internally and Jane finds that Revenue increased substantially after March 2X16 as a new branch was opened in Wigan and two major new products began manufacture. These two products are new technology and the company have taken a risk in introducing them at this time. Substantial capital expenditure throughout the first part of the year has already led to liquidity problems and this has been added to by increases in inventory and receivables and the acquisition of the new company.
- A structural review of the company consequent on the items mentioned above has led to three senior directors and managers being retired early and new appointments made in June. There is a new Chief Accountant and new Sales and Production Directors.
- A completely new networked computer system was installed in April 2X16 and is working well.
- The directors have expressed a wish for the audit to be completed by March and they promise to have the accounts ready by mid-February 2X17. Jane feels this is very rushed compared to last year and is doubtful that the company can fulfil its promise.
- Every conceivable schedule is available from the computer system. Jane feels she should think up analyses which will help her prepare her analytical review procedures.
- The company has no internal audit function.
- The company relies heavily on internal controls to control its day-to-day transaction processing. Jane thinks that once the controls have been properly documented it may well be possible to rely on them to a significant extent.
- There are no joint auditors.
- Metalbash is based in one location except for the branch in Wigan and the new company which is based in Essex.

Jane will have to choose one of the audit strategies.

Clearly for a company such as Metalbash a **systems-based auditing approach** is likely to be the most appropriate. She could consider moving to a more business risk based approach once she is confident the new systems are working properly and the new financial controller is competent and understands the business.

The overall plan which Jane needs to prepare takes into account:

- An amendment of the Letter of Engagement to include the report to the Lorry Parts Manufacturers' Association and the visit to Wigan and the new company.
- Assessment of the impact of new directors, staff and managers and the need for Jane to meet all the relevant staff and tour the works.
- Extra time needed to audit capital expenditure and consider the impact of all the changes on the organization as a whole.
- Identification of audit risk areas. These include:
  - going concern
  - capital/revenue identification on new plant
  - the branch in Wigan
  - new company in Essex, formerly insolvent
  - increased inventories and receivables
  - identification of all payables especially as payment is likely to be slower because of the liquidity problems; Jane will have to consider the possibility that key suppliers might withdraw from the business and the effect that this might have
  - the new computer system even though this is apparently going well
  - the viability of the new products
- Need to plan year-end presence at the inventory count at all locations.
- Need to spend time evaluating the new computer system and the changes in internal controls which have been introduced.
- Identification of areas which are not material and setting preliminary materiality levels.
- The making of a list of all assets and liabilities, revenues and expenses so that detailed schedules of these can be requested from the client. For example, she may request a breakdown of sales by product in order to examine the success/failure of the new products.
- Need to identify and test, at the interim audit, an audit visit made during the financial year, internal controls which she may wish to rely on.
- Need to audit assets and liabilities as much as possible before the year end in view of the short time available after the year end.
- Jane will need staff for the interim (which is flexibly dated), at the year-end inventory count (at an awkward time and in widely separated locations), and at the final audit which will be rapid and therefore may need extra staff.
- Extra work is required this year (capital expenditure, new computer system, faster audit, Wigan, new company in Essex, liquidity problems) and the fee will need to reflect this.

Jane will need to discuss the specific audit areas, the timing and the work the client will undertake in terms of providing draft accounts and supporting schedules.

ANALYTICAL REVIEW PROCEDURES

Auditors are expected to be able to analyse sets of accounts and students who lack this skill should learn at least the basics of ratio analysis. We discuss analytical review procedures in more detail in Chapter 12. For now, it is sufficient to say that, as part of the initial planning process, it is important that the planner obtains a reasonable idea of what has happened in the period so far and obtains a preliminary view of any possible problem areas at which audit work can be directed.

Apart from discussions with management, etc., one way of doing this is by carrying out a preliminary analytical review of the latest management accounts.

Analysis of certain key ratios, for example:

- gross profit per cent
- net profit per cent
- inventory turnover
- receivables days
- payables days
- liquidity and quick ratios

can give an indication of possible problem areas, which can be discussed further with management and investigated. It also aids the planner's understanding of the client and its activities.

THE TIMING OF AUDIT WORK

Audit work on the records and financial statements relating to a financial year are carried out at various times during, at the end and after the end of the financial period. The timing of audit work depends upon many factors including:

- Deadlines fixed by the client. For example, the client may arrange an AGM for three months after the year end.
- The organization of the accountant's office. For example, bunching of client year ends around certain dates (e.g. 31 December) can create severe problems.
- The extent to and the time in which the client can provide schedules and analyses. If these are not available more time is required on the final audit.
- The extent to which the client has very strong systems in routine areas such as Receivables, Payables, Inventory control and tangible asset registers.

Audit visits

Audit work will be carried on at the client's premises. Where the client has branches, this can create problems of travelling for the auditor but in such cases some branches are visited as samples or all the branches are visited by rotation.

In the majority of cases, three extended visits are made by the auditor to the client's premises to carry out audit work:

- during the year – the interim audit
- at the year-end for inventory counts and any other procedures where observation is to be the form of evidence gathering (Chapter 11)
- after the year end – the final audit

Clearly, on audits of very large organizations, there may be almost a permanent audit presence at the client. For example, the audit of a very large multinational may warrant almost a full-time presence on site.

If this is the case it is important that the staff be rotated regularly. The reason for this is that it is very easy for audit staff who are almost permanently in contact with their client to lose their objectivity and to begin to feel that they are, in fact, part of the client and not its auditors. The most notorious case of this was the audit of Enron in the USA by Arthur Andersen, where it was noted that visitors to Enron could not tell the difference between Arthur Andersen staff and Enron personnel.

Interim audit

The interim audit will be carried out during the financial year. Very often the interim audit will be about two-thirds of the way through the year, e.g. September or October for a December year end.

The work done includes:

- Ascertain the system of accounting and internal control or review any changes from the previous year.
- Record the system or update systems records using flow charts or other methods.
- Evaluate the systems for adequacy and the presence of apparent weaknesses.
- Design and carry out compliance tests to determine if the system is operated at all times in accordance with the description of the system evaluated by the auditor.
- Design and carry out tests to determine if, in areas where controls are weak or nonexistent, the records can be relied upon.
- Draw conclusions on the adequacy of the systems and hence of the reliability of the books of account and other records.
- Seek evidence, by substantive tests, that unusual or one-off transactions have been fully and correctly recorded.
- Where possible carry out tests on assets and liabilities. Tests on assets and liabilities should be carried out after the year end but with clients with strong systems, some verification can be done at the interim stage. Examples are physical verification of Inventory records and a Receivables circularization.

Year-end work

On the last day of the client's year end it will be possible to verify some year-end assets and liabilities in a way impossible at any other time. Thus attendance will be required for:

- observation and testing of any Inventory count; this is now mandatory under ISA 501 *Audit Evidence –Specific considerations for selected items*
- observation and testing of cut-off procedures
- counting of cash balances where these are a material figure on the Statement of Financial Position

Final audit

The final audit will take place after the year end and is designed to seek evidence that financial statements give a true and fair view and comply with statutory and other requirements.

The timing of the final audit varies from client to client. Some final audits are commenced within days of the year end and the financial statements are published within as short a period as two months after the year end. Others are commenced many months after the year end. The advantage of an early audit and early publication of the accounts is that the information given to members and other stakeholders is up to date.

From the audit point of view, however, certain transactions in progress at the year-end are often not resolved and estimates of their outcome have to be made and evaluated. The advantage of a later audit is that transactions in progress at the year-end are often resolved and fewer estimates need to be made. For example, after a few months it will have become clear whether or not a doubtful debt is in fact bad. The disadvantage of a late audit is that information reaching members and others can be somewhat out of date. The accounts will have become truly historical.

The work carried out after the year end will be:

- Updating of the auditor's review of the systems of accounting and internal control. This will involve:
  - determining if the systems have changed between the interim audit and the year end by interviewing officials and carrying out a few 'walk-through' tests
  - thoroughly testing new systems
  - compliance tests of the unchanged systems from the interim audit to the year end
  - drafting a report for management regarding any weaknesses found in the control systems (Chapter 27)
- Drawing conclusions on:
  - the adequacy of the accounting system and the system of internal controls
  - whether proper books of account have been kept

- whether the book of account and other records form a reliable base for the preparation of the financial statements
- comparing the financial statements with the underlying records and books of account to see that they correspond
- performing substantive tests on assets and liabilities
- performing the final analytical review
- preparing and signing the auditor's report

The Audit Planning Memorandum

This records, in a standard format, all the decisions taken and the reasons for the decision. In our Case Studies, above, audit manager Jane will have to complete this and it will have to be agreed with and signed off by the audit engagement partner.

An example of an Audit Planning Memorandum is included on the digital support resources.

SUMMARY

- The audit can be seen as having several stages, key to which is planning.
- Evaluation of audit risk can determine the audit approach and influence the amount of audit work carried out.
- Audit risk involves consideration of the levels of inherent and control risk. The higher these are the more audit work has to be done to reduce detection risk.
- Materiality has both quantitative and qualitative aspects and is a matter of judgement.
- Performance materiality is set lower than the level of materiality for the financial statements as a whole and is used by the auditors to take into consideration the levels of detected and undetected errors.
- Auditors must approach their work with an attitude of professional scepticism.
- Planning work and audit risk assessments should be properly documented.
- The work is usually distributed between an interim audit during the financial year, year-end attendance and things like the inventory count with a final audit visit after the year end.
- The interim audit is principally for the investigation and testing of the systems of recording and internal control.
- The year-end work is mainly for the observation and testing of the Inventory count but also the examination of cash balances where these are material.
- The final audit is all the rest of the work and includes:
  - testing systems for the period from the interim audit to the year end
  - substantive testing of transactions and balances
  - final analytical review
  - preparation and signing of the report

POINTS TO NOTE

- The auditors are not concerned with individual routine transactions but with the systems for documenting and recording them. They are still concerned with material nonroutine transactions.
- It is important to remember that the system of accounting is not separate from the system of internal controls over the books and records.

- Professional scepticism is an important part of audit work. There have been many documented cases where auditors have accepted explanations at face value or taken copy documents as originals without corroboration thus enabling fraudsters to escape detection or errors to go undetected.
- Students should not confuse business risk with audit risk. This causes students to fail case study type questions where they identify business risks which might adversely affect the business and not risks which might prevent the auditor from achieving their primary objective.
- Audit firms have sought greater effectiveness in their audit procedures together with greater efficiency. This has led to:
  - Greater use of risk-based techniques
  - Greater reliance on analytical review
- When an audit is carried out for the first time on a new client, additional visits may be necessary, in order that the auditor may obtain knowledge of the client, its background, personnel, accounting problems, audit risk areas, etc. Following the visits, the audit plan can be prepared.
- In some large audits with very highly computerized records, audit evidence is sometimes available on a temporary basis only. For example, where internal control (say over the creditworthiness of customers) is operated by a computer program which is changed at intervals. Then the auditor needs to be present at fairly frequent intervals to test the functioning of the controls on which they wish to rely.

CASE STUDY 5

You are working on the audit of your client Sweetie Ltd for the year ended 31 March 2X16.

The company employs one hundred workers in a doughnut manufacturing plant. Wages are paid weekly. The following procedures are carried out:

- Employees clock cards are signed by supervisors and brought to the wages office every Monday morning.
- Hours are taken from the cards. Overtime hours are calculated and entered on an overtime sheet which is then used to calculate overtime payments.
- The overtime sheet is authorized by the production manager.
- Wages are prepared using a standard computerized wages software package.
- Standard hours and overtime hours are entered into the payroll using the input screen.
- Any amendments to employees' details, e.g. changes of address or tax code, are entered on each employee's computer file by any of the wages clerks.
- Details of any new starters are entered into the system by any of the wages clerks.
- Leavers are removed from the system once their final week's wages have been calculated.
- The payroll is processed and then authorized by the production manager.
- It is then passed to the accounts department who prepare BACs payments for each employee.
- Wages are paid on Friday so the payroll has to be prepared in time to ensure employees are paid promptly.

Discussion

- The audit manager has asked you to complete the ICQ below (Figure 10.4) based on the payroll system details set out above.

FIGURE 10.4 Internal control questionnaire

Client name ___				Prepared by ___
				Date ___
Period to ___				Reviewed by ___
				Date ___

WAGES SYSTEM
Control procedures

Process	Yes	No	N/A	Comments
Is there an individual file recording each employees details?				
Are rates of pay authorized by a responsible official?				
Are there procedures to remove leavers from the payroll as soon as they have been paid their final wages?				
Are there procedures to ensure new starters are included on the payroll correctly?				
Is access to the payroll master file restricted?				
Are there procedures to ensure that changes in employees' details are properly recorded?				
Is the payroll software a standard package? (Record details)				
Is there a wages preparation timetable?				
Do employees have to record start and finish times?				
Are overtime rates approved by a responsible official?				
Are hours worked authorized by a responsible official of the company? (record details)				
Is the payroll approved by a responsible official before wages are paid?				
Are employees paid by bank transfer?				
Are the people involved in making the payments different to those who prepare the payroll?				

CASE STUDY 6

One of your junior staff has prepared some slides for a presentation to a client on the practical procedures involved in auditing. The slides contain the following statements:

a) Materiality is generally defined as being about 5 per cent of gross profit or 10 per cent of net profit.

b) Audit sampling depends on the level of materiality – the higher the level the less work you need to do.

c) Audit risk and business risk are more or less the same.

d) Analytical procedures should only be used as a final procedure at the end of the audit just to check the figures look OK.

e) Auditors need to select samples which represent the population as a whole.

f) Providing the financial statements comply with the law auditors have to accept them.

Discussion

– Which of these should you remove from the slides before the presentation is given and why?

STUDENT SELF-TESTING QUESTIONS

Questions with answers apparent from the text

a) Outline the key stages of the audit.

b) What is the difference between an ICQ and an ICEQ?

c) Give three advantages of flow charting a client's system.

d) What is a walk-through test?

e) What are the components of audit risk?

f) Define materiality.

g) What is inherent risk?

h) What are the three main audit strategies?

i) What is performance materiality?

j) What sort of work can be carried out at an interim audit?

k) What would be the main components of an audit plan?

l) How would an audit plan be recorded?

EXAMINATION QUESTIONS

1 You have been presented with the following draft financial information about Hivex, a very successful company that develops and licenses specialist computer software and hardware. Its fixed assets mainly consist of property, computer hardware and investments, and there have been additions to these during the year. The company is experiencing increasing competition from rival companies, most of which specialize in hardware or software, but not both. There is pressure to advertize and to cut prices.

You are the audit manager. You are planning the audit and you are conducting a preliminary analytical review and associated risk analysis for this client for the year ended 31 May 2X16. You have been provided with a summarized draft profit and loss account (Figure 10.5), which has been produced very quickly, and certain accounting ratios and percentages.

You have been informed that the company accounts for research and development costs in accordance with IAS 38 *Intangible Assets*.

FIGURE 10.5 Statement of comprehensive income year ended 31 May

	2X16	2X15
	£ 000s	£ 000s
Sales	15 206	13 524
Cost of sales	3 009	3 007
Gross profit	12 197	10 517

Distribution costs	3 006	1 996
Administrative expenses	994	1 768
Selling expenses	3 002	274
Profit from operations	5 195	6 479
Net interest receivable	995	395
Profit before tax	6 190	6 874
Corporation tax	3 104	1 452
Net profit	3 086	5 422
Dividends paid	1 469	1 439
Retained profits	1 617	3 983
Accounting ratios and percentages		
Earnings per share	0.43	1.04
Performance ratios include the following:		
Gross margin	0.80	0.78
Expenses as a percentage of sales:		
Distribution costs	0.20	0.15
Administrative expenses	0.07	0.13
Selling expenses	0.20	0.02
Operating profit	0.34	0.48

Required:

(a) Using the information above, comment briefly on the performance of the company for the two years.

(b) Use your answer to part (a) to identify the areas that are subject to increased audit risk and describe the further audit work you would perform in response to those risks.

(ACCA)

SOURCES AND ADDITIONAL READING

Financial Reporting Council (2009) *ISA 200 Overall Objectives of the Independent Auditor and the Conduct of an Audit in Accordance with International Standards on Auditing*. London: Financial Reporting Council.

Financial Reporting Council (2009) *ISA 315 Identifying and Assessing Risks of Material Misstatement through Understanding the Entity and its Environment*. London: Financial Reporting Council.

Financial Reporting Council (2009) *ISA 300 Planning an Audit of Financial Statements*. London: Financial Reporting Council.

Financial Reporting Council (2009) *ISA 320 Materiality in Planning and Performing an Audit*. London: Financial Reporting Council.

Financial Reporting Council (2009) *ISA 450 Evaluation of Misstatements Identified during the Audit*. London: Financial Reporting Council.

IAASB (2009) *Materiality in Planning and Performing an Audit*. New York: IFAC.

Jones, M. (2009) 'Audit risk', *Student Accountant*, November, London: ACCA.

Ryan, B. (2008) *Finance and Accounting for Business*. London: Cengage.

- Financial statements are subject to much regulation (by the Companies Act or other Acts and by various accounting standards). Audits are regulated by the professional bodies acting as supervisory bodies. It is essential that auditors perform all the tests and reviews that are necessary to ensure that financial statements comply with the regulations, that the audit is comprehensive and that nothing has been overlooked. All actions must be fully recorded. One way of ensuring that all is done is to have checklists which must be completed, signed and reviewed by staff, managers and partners.

- Working papers can be stored in a choice of media – paper, film, electronic or other. If stored in the cloud they should be encrypted.

CHAPTER 11
AUDIT EVIDENCE AND USING THE WORK OF AN EXPERT

Learning Objectives

After studying the material in this chapter you should be able to:

- explain what is meant by assertions and describe them

- understand what is meant by 'professional scepticism'

- understand the concepts of sufficiency and appropriateness of evidence

- understand that evidence is often persuasive and not absolute

- explain the various sources of audit evidence and what does and does not constitute good audit evidence

- outline the advantages and disadvantages of using an auditor's expert and the conditions under which one may be used

- understand the responsibility of the auditor towards evidence and opinions provided by specialists

INTRODUCTION

The requirement to gather audit evidence is set out in ISA 200 *Overall objectives of the independent auditor and the conduct of an audit in accordance with international standards on auditing* which, as we saw in Chapter 5, requires the auditor to express an opinion on the financial statements and, in doing so, to reduce audit risk to an acceptably low level by gathering evidence to support their opinion. The evidence requirement is defined in ISA 330 *The auditor's responses to assessed risk*.
This states that:

> 'The objective of the auditor is to obtain sufficient appropriate audit evidence regarding the assessed risks of material misstatement, through designing and implementing appropriate responses to those risks.'

It goes on to describe the types of audit testing, comprising tests of control and substantive testing, which the auditor can use to do this. We will return to these concepts in Chapter 12.

ISA 500 *Audit evidence* sets out the standards and guidelines as to what constitutes suitable audit evidence. It will be apparent by now that the purpose of all of the auditor's planning and testing work is towards the gathering of *sufficient appropriate* evidence which can be used to substantiate their audit opinion.

ISA 500 says:

> 'The objective of the auditor is to design and perform audit procedures in such a way as to enable the auditor to obtain sufficient appropriate audit evidence to be able to draw reasonable conclusions on which to base the auditor's opinion.'

This extract from the International Standard tells us two things:

- evidence has to be 'sufficient' and 'appropriate'
- that auditors do not have to audit everything because their conclusions have only to be 'reasonable' not absolute

These key words are highlighted because the student must be aware of their importance. They are not merely descriptive adjectives they are, effectively, the standard the auditor has to achieve:

- *Sufficiency* is the measure of the *amount* of evidence gathered.
- *Appropriateness* is a measure of its *quality*, its fitness for purpose.

For example, an auditor looking at tangible assets verification may go and inspect the relevant assets. This may be sufficient evidence if the auditor can inspect a significant number of the relevant assets and it may be appropriate—but only as far as existence of the assets are concerned. The amount of audit evidence which is *sufficient* to verify their existence is also *appropriate* for validating their existence but is *not* appropriate as evidence of their ownership.

This question of the sufficiency and appropriateness of audit evidence is directly linked to the concept of audit risk which we looked at in Chapter 10. Before we look at how auditors go about gathering evidence, however, we must examine some underlying concepts which, collectively, are classed as **assertions.**

PROFESSIONAL SCEPTICISM

The audit approach sets great store by the auditors approaching their work with an attitude of **professional scepticism.**

This is defined as 'a questioning mind' and this was amplified by Lord Denning in the case of *Fomento (Sterling Area) Ltd. v Selsdon Fountain Pen Co. Ltd. 1958)*. In that case Lord Denning stated about an auditor that:

> 'to perform his task properly he must come to it with an enquiring mind—not suspicious of dishonesty— but suspecting that someone may have made a mistake somewhere and that a check must be made to ensure that there has been none.'

However, auditors have always borne in mind the dicta of Lord Justice Lopes in the Kingston Cotton Mill case in 1896 that an auditor *'is not bound to be a detective, he is a watchdog not a bloodhound.'* (Chapter 29)

(Auditors, of course, may be female – it is just a legal convention that individuals are always referred to as 'he' – this is clearly an antiquated throwback.)

What this means is that auditors must adopt this 'questioning mind' and not accept easy explanations or assurances in the absence of corroborating evidence. There have been several instances of fraud where the perpetrators have managed to bluff the external auditors only to be derailed by internal auditors who are more familiar with day-to-day systems and procedures, as shown in Figure 11.1.

Where possible, auditors must, like good detectives, obtain corroborative evidence for statements made to them and obtain sufficient reliable evidence to support their conclusions. They must follow up anomalies or unusual transactions uncovered during the audit and, if necessary, carry out some additional procedures in order to verify explanations given to them. This is actually known as the 'loose thread' theory of fraud detection.

This latter point can be difficult where audit teams are under time pressures but could, perhaps, avoid the audit firm being considered negligent for missing a fraud. Audit firms rely, even today, on the idea that an auditor is a *'watchdog not a bloodhound'*, but this is not to be used as an excuse for failing to follow up a suspicious transaction. It may be that scepticism comes with age and experience and, if that is the case, it behoves the young and inexperienced to communicate with the old and wizened so that they can take a decision as to whether to expend time following up curiosities.

This is another reason why communication between audit team members is important and audit managers should ensure that all members of the team are encouraged to report their suspicions however odd they may be.

Figure 11.1 **The importance of professional scepticism**

Eric

Eric was the owner/manager of a property development company who defrauded the business of which he was the majority shareholder. When questioned about his activities and the risk of being detected by the audit he said

'Accountants can only work on the figures they have got, audit the same. Auditors came to see me and I just lied to them and gave them false pieces of paper and that was that. The checking process was abysmal I was not worried because I have twenty years experience of auditors. . . . the lack of attention to detail, the lack of knowledge in auditing and accounting . . . there was no interrogation from audit and that was good for me.'

Gill, 2007

Purpose of audit tests

Remember that auditors are testing two things:

- the functioning of the internal control procedures and activities; and
- that the company's financial procedures have been complied with.

Learners should remember that the testing of control objectives is carried out in order to validate the assertions regarding the transactions in a particular part of the financial systems. It is possible to relate control objectives for each of the components of the accounting system to the assertions shown below. We look at this in Chapter 13 looking at systems based auditing and there we link the component parts of a typical, generic system to the assertions described below so the relationships can be clearly understood.

Some of the tests which are carried out are not simply about whether transactions have been accurately recorded in the books; they are about discovering whether the staff involved are obeying company rules and procedures. For example, there may be a company rule that goods can only be ordered from approved suppliers. This rule has got nothing to do with the accuracy of the underlying records but has everything to do with the business's approach to risk and the operation of its control environment.

Therefore, when designing an audit test or carrying out the work, auditors should be aware of the purpose for which the test has been designed and the implications for the organizations if they discover errors or misstatements.

ASSERTIONS

The Directors produce, or cause to be produced, financial statements and in doing so they are *asserting* that:

- the individual items are:
  - correctly described
  - properly classified
  - show figures which are arithmetically correct or fairly estimated
- the accounts, as a whole, show a true and fair view

Implicit in the production of the financial statements is a series of assumptions which are defined in ISA 315 '*Identifying and assessing risks of material misstatement through understanding the entity and its environment*' as assertions.

These are similar, in principle, to the fundamental accounting concepts which also underlie accounts preparation such as the historical cost convention and the prudence concept, which students learn about when they first start to study accounting.

The assertions in ISA 315 are a series of statements which deal with the underlying bases on which the financial statements are prepared and deal with the measurement, presentation and disclosure of the various elements of financial statements and related disclosures.

ISA 315 splits the assertions into three categories, as follows:

1 Assertions about classes of transactions and events for the period under review

Occurrence	Transactions and events that have been recorded relate to the company being audited and not to another organization.
Completeness	All transactions and events that should have been recorded have been recorded.
Accuracy	Amounts and all other data relating to recorded transactions have been recorded appropriately.
Cut-off	Transactions and events have been recorded in the correct accounting period.
Classification	Transactions and events have been recorded in the proper accounts (in the books and records).

2 Assertions about account balances at the period end

Existence	Assets, liabilities and equity interests (shareholdings) exist.
Rights and obligations	The company holds or controls the rights to assets, and all liabilities are those of the company.
Completeness	All assets, liabilities and equity interests that should have been recorded have been recorded.
Valuation and allocation	Assets, liabilities and equity interests are included in the financial statements at appropriate amounts and any resulting valuation or allocation adjustments are properly recorded.

3 Assertions about presentation and disclosure

Occurrence and rights and obligations	Disclosed events, transactions and other matters have occurred and pertain to the company.
Completeness	All disclosures that should have been included in the financial statements have been included.
Classification and understandability	Financial information is appropriately presented and described and disclosures are clearly expressed.
Accuracy and valuation	Financial and other information is disclosed fairly and at appropriate amounts.

The assertions are set down in this way but, as you can see, some of them are the same in each category. Note that assertions can be at the transaction level and at the level of the financial statements, or parts of the financial statements, as a whole.

Auditors are allowed to combine them together for audit purposes so, for example, tests which provide evidence validating assertions about transactions in (1) can also be used to validate assertions about balances in (2).

Providing auditors gather sufficient evidence of the right type to validate these assertions they will have enough to support their audit opinion.

The auditor's attitude to each item in the accounts will be as follows:

- Identify the express and implied assertions made by the directors in including (or excluding) the item in the accounts.
- Evaluate each assertion for relative importance to assess the quality and quantity of evidence required.
- Collect information and supporting evidence.
- Assess the evidence for:
  - appropriateness – appropriateness subsumes the ideas of quality and reliability of a particular piece of audit evidence and its relevance to a particular assertion.
  - sufficiency – more of this in a later paragraph.

It is important to note that audit evidence tends to be persuasive rather than absolute. Consequently, like a good detective, auditors tend to seek evidence from several different sources or of a different nature to support the same assertion.

Note also that auditors only have to provide reasonable assurance that the financial statements are free from a material misstatement, they don't have to prove the assertions beyond doubt – although if they can do it is very reassuring!

Having formulated judgements on each individual item in (or omitted from) the accounts, the auditors must formulate a judgement on the truth and fairness of accounts as a whole.

To do this they will need other evidence in addition to the judgements they have made on the individual items. As an extreme example, they may need evidence of the directors' implied assertion that the accounts should be drawn up on the going concern principle (Chapter 23).

RELIABILITY OF AUDIT EVIDENCE

The evidence an auditor collects can be from many different sources, not all of which can be relied upon to the same extent. The reliability of audit evidence falls into three categories:

1 **Auditor-derived evidence**

   The best evidence is evidence derived by the auditors as a result of their own tests and procedures. These can include:
   - **compliance testing** of controls
   - **substantive testing** of transactions and balances
   - observation of company procedures, e.g. inventory counts
   - inspection of documents, assets, etc. — these include:
     - authoritative documents prepared *outside* the firm, e.g. title deeds, share and loan certificates, leases, contracts, franchises, invoices
     - authoritative documents prepared *inside* the firm, e.g. minutes, copy invoices

2 **Independent third-party evidence**

   The next most reliable form of evidence is that provided by independent third parties. Examples of this include:
   - bank letters
   - receivables circularization
   - supplier's statements

3   Representations made by directors and officers of the company

In many ways this is the least reliable form of evidence. Auditors should not accept the unsupported testimony of directors or staff without any other form of corroboration unless there is absolutely no other evidence available. We discuss this in Chapter 24 in connection with the Letter of Representation.

This type of evidence may be formal, for example, the Letter of Representation, or informal, for example, in replies to ICQ questions (Chapter 10).

Auditors must also consider the form the evidence takes. For example:

- Written evidence is always more reliable than oral evidence, even if oral evidence takes the form of a taped interview, as the process of committing something to paper has a finality about it which oral evidence simply doesn't have. Remember the auditing rule – '*if it's not in writing, it doesn't exist!*'
- Original documentation is more reliable than copy documents. Auditors should always inspect original documents and if they must copy them they should do it themselves. Reliance on copy documents can mean that auditors are relying on a forgery. The same school of auditing mentioned above has a second rule which is '*never, ever, ever, accept a copy document as audit evidence, unless you've copied it from the original and you can validate the original*'.

BASIC TECHNIQUES FOR COLLECTING EVIDENCE

There are several ways the auditors can gather sufficient appropriate evidence. The main methodologies are:

- *Inspection* of documents, procedures and tangible assets.
- *Observation*. Seeing for oneself is the best possible confirmation, especially in connection with internal control systems.
- *Inquiry*. Asking questions. This is a necessary and valid technique. The reliability of the evidence depends on the qualification and integrity of its source. A good example is the review of internal controls through the use of ICQs and ICEQs.
- *Confirmations*. These should be in writing, external sources being preferable to internal sources; for example, a supplier's statement can be used to confirm a payables (purchase) ledger balance.
- *Computation*—additions, calculations, reconciliations, etc.
- *Re-performance*—testing controls by re-performing them, for example, checking the bank reconciliation. Auditors do much of their compliance testing, testing of controls, based on samples. We look at this further in Chapter 12 but it needs some consideration here.

Auditors obtain evidence about each type of transaction by examining a representative sample of each type. This sample testing is applied as much to assets and liabilities as to routine transactions.

The size of the sample to be tested depends on:

- the strength of the internal control system
- the materiality of the items
- the number of items involved
- the nature of the item
- the level of audit risk at the level of the transaction

Sources of audit evidence

Sources of audit evidence include that derived from within the organization's:

- accounting systems
- accounting records
- documents
- management and staff

and from without through:

- customers
- suppliers
- lenders
- professional advisers, etc.

The sources and amount of evidence required by the auditors will depend on the materiality, relevance and reliability of the evidence available from a source.

Remember that auditors have to provide evidence that is *appropriate* to the assertion being validated, it must be *reliable* evidence, i.e. not flawed by a wrongly performed or invalid test or evidenced by a copy document rather than an original and there must be enough of it to make a valid test, so it must be *sufficient*.

Sufficiency

Sufficiency is the great problem. The auditor's judgement will be influenced by their knowledge of the business and its industry and the degree of audit risk.

Assessment of this is helped by considering:

- The nature and materiality of items of account (e.g. provisions for liabilities may be material but may be difficult to measure accurately because of the assumptions involved).
- The auditor's experience of the reliability of the management and staff and the records.
- The financial position of the enterprise (in a failing enterprise, directors may wish to bolster profits by over-valuing assets or suppressing liabilities).
- Possible management bias (as above) but also the management may wish to 'even out' profits for stock market image or taxation reasons.
- The persuasiveness of the evidence.
- The nature of the accounting and internal control systems and the control environment.

Appropriateness

The appropriateness of audit evidence depends upon whether it assists the auditors in forming an opinion on some aspect of the assertions on which the financial statements are based. For example, attendance at an inventory count provides evidence that indicates that the inventory exists and also, by inspecting the inventory, evidence as to its condition and therefore its value. This test is relevant and appropriate for validating some of the assertions underlying both the Statement of Comprehensive Income and the Statement of Financial Position.

Reliability

We have seen that some types of evidence are more reliable than others. Returning to our analogy of the inventory count evidence which comprises a simple statement from the directors that the entire inventory exists and is correctly valued, would not constitute reliable evidence for audit purposes whereas a certificate of value from an independent third party valuer might.

USING THE WORK OF AN AUDITOR'S EXPERT

Introduction

ISA 620 *Using the work of an auditor's expert* states:

> 'The auditor has sole responsibility for the audit opinion expressed, and that responsibility is not reduced by the auditor's use of the work of an auditor's expert. Nonetheless, if the auditor using the work of an auditor's expert . . . concludes that the work of that expert is adequate for the auditor's purposes, the auditor may accept that expert's findings or conclusions in the expert's field as appropriate audit evidence.'

In other words, it is up to the auditors to confirm whether or not the work performed by the expert is 'adequate' for the audit – the responsibility remains, as always, with them.

Remember that the work of an expert is subject to the audit quality control procedures we looked at in Chapter 7, based on the provisions contained in ISA 220 *'Quality control for an audit of financial statements'*, as their work has to be of use to the audit team as evidence.

In general, the auditor's programme of work will provide them with sufficient reliable relevant evidence to enable them to substantiate their opinion. However, there can be circumstances where the auditor's knowledge is insufficient and they may then need to rely on the opinions of experts or specialists to help them form an opinion.

What is an expert?

What is an expert, in this context? IAS 620 defines an expert as:

'An individual or organization possessing expertise in a field other than accounting or auditing, whose work in that field is used by the auditor to assist the auditor in obtaining sufficient appropriate audit evidence. An auditor's expert may be either an auditor's internal expert (who is a partner or staff, including temporary staff, of the auditor's firm or a network firm), or an auditor's external expert.'

Examples of specialists whose work may be relied upon by auditors include:

- valuers – on the value of fixed assets such as freehold and leasehold property or more rarely plant and machinery and on the value of specialist stock in trade such as beers, wines and spirits or specialist stock such as jewellery
- quantity surveyors – on the value of work done on long-term contracts
- actuaries – on the liability to be included for pension scheme liabilities
- geologists – on the quantity and quality of mineral reserves
- stockbrokers – on the value of stock exchanges securities
- lawyers – on the legal interpretation of contracts and agreements, or the outcome of disputes and litigation

The expert may come from within the auditor's own firm. For example, a member of staff who has practical experience of a particularly complex business, or is an expert on a particular type of transaction, may also be used; clearly also auditors are used to dealing with experts such as tax accountants or lawyers.

Points to consider

In general, in deciding whether the auditors need to have specialist opinions they will consider:

- The knowledge and abilities of the audit team – does it have the expertise to deal with the issue itself? If not an expert may have to be called in.
- The risk of a material misstatement based on the nature, complexity and materiality of the material being considered.
- The quantity and quality of other audit evidence which can be obtained.

Often auditors have little other evidence on which to base their opinion on such values. Property companies incorporate values of properties in their accounts, the source of such valuations being specialist commercial valuers. The auditors may have little other reliable evidence except the specialist valuer's opinion.

The expert can be hired either by the auditor or the client – either way the client is likely to end up paying – so cost considerations are important. The auditor should involve experts *only* when no other sufficient appropriate evidence is available.

Factors which may influence the auditor to rely upon or not to rely upon the work of a specialist include:

- *The competence of the specialist* – This may be indicated by technical qualifications, certification and licensing or membership of professional bodies. The expert also should have some level of reputation or standing in the area of their expertise.
- *The experience of the specialist* – The expert should have the appropriate experience to carry out the work. For example, if the matter involves a valuation of commercial property it would not be appropriate to engage an expert whose experience was only that of valuing domestic property, however well-qualified technically that person was.

- *The independence of the specialist* – The degree of relationship with the client may be the key factor. Any specialist who is related to the directors or employees of the client or who has financial interest (other than their fee) with the client is clearly less than wholly independent. Apparent dependence may be mitigated by professional body disciplinary and ethical codes.

Process

If it is the intention of the auditor to place reliance on the work of a specialist, it is important to hold a consultation between auditor, client and specialist, at the time the specialist is appointed, to reach agreement on the work to be performed. The agreement should cover:

- Objectives, scope and subject matter of the specialist's work.
- Assumptions upon which the specialist's report depends and their compatibility with the accounts. For example, are going concern or market values to be taken?
- A statement of the bases used in previous years and any change to be made.
- The use to be made of the specialist's findings (they may need this for professional indemnity insurance purposes).
- The form and content of the specialist's report or opinion.
- The sources of information to be provided to the specialist.
- The identification of any relationship which may affect the specialist's objectivity.

An example of this may be the case of an architect who, though in private practice, obtains most of his commissions from the client who is subject to audit.

It is possible to use a specialist's opinion without this process but it is desirable to go through this procedure.

Evaluation of the specialist evidence

As we have seen the sufficiency and appropriateness of such evidence will depend upon:

- The nature of the evidence required.
- The materiality of the items being evidenced.
- The auditor's assessment of the competence of the specialist.
- Their independence from the client.

The auditors have to review the findings of the experts and draw their own conclusions. In particular, they will look at:

- The source data used, i.e. what has the expert based their opinion on?
- The assumptions and methods used – and their consistency with previous periods.
- When the expert's work was carried out – i.e. were valuations carried out at the end of the financial period or at some other date and does it matter?
- An overall evaluation of the expert's work in the light of the auditor's overall knowledge of the business and the industry and the results of other audit procedures which may go some way towards corroborating the expert's opinion.

The auditors may well want to:

- Review the sources themselves to ascertain whether or not they are reliable.
- Review the specialist's procedures.
- Review any data used by the expert for themselves.

in order to satisfy themselves that the work the expert has done can be relied on.

Clearly the auditor does not have the same level of expertise and experience as an expert and the expert's opinion can be difficult to challenge.

The key point is this:

- The expert's opinion is their responsibility – they have to carry out the work they do to the best of their ability.
- Whether that work provides sufficient appropriate evidence for the auditor is the *auditor's* responsibility – and that is what they alone can decide.

If the auditors are not happy with the expert's work, they have some options:

- Try again with another expert – cost considerations are important and there is no guarantee the outcome will be any different.
- Discuss the situation with the client and the expert together to see if difficulties can be resolved.
- Apply additional audit procedures.
- As a last resort it may be necessary to modify (qualify) the auditor's report on the grounds of lack of evidence.

SUMMARY

- Auditors must gather sufficient reliable evidence with which to support their opinion.
- The evidence has to be relevant to the item or assertion being tested.
- When the directors prepare accounts they are making assertions about the items in the accounts, items omitted from the accounts and the accounts as a whole.
- Assertions underpin the financial statements. They are divided into three parts: assertions about transactions, assertions about balances and assertions about presentation and disclosure which are broadly analogous to the Statement of Comprehensive Income, The Statement of Financial Position and the Financial Statements as a whole.
- The auditor conducts an audit by:
  - identifying the assertions made
  - considering the information and evidence needed to validate those assertions
  - collecting sufficient, reliable evidence relevant to validating audit objectives
  - evaluating the evidence
  - formulating a judgement
- There are many different varieties of evidence. Some varieties are of more value to the auditor than others.
- An established method of collecting evidence is based on the auditor's own tests. Other forms of evidence include representations from third parties and confirmations from those charged with governance or the directors.
- Not all evidence has the same degree of reliability. Evidence from the auditor's tests and confirmations from independent third parties is much more reliable than representations from directors. Written evidence is more reliable than oral evidence.
- Auditors should endeavour to collect evidence from a variety of different sources.
- Some legal decisions have appeared to guide the auditor in assessing what evidence is needed. We will look at this in Chapter 29.
- IAS 500 'Audit evidence' discusses relevance, reliability and sufficiency and gives some criteria for assessing these qualities in audit evidence.
- An expert should be suitably qualified and appropriately experienced for the task.
- The expert should have their terms of agreement drawn up after consultation with the auditors.
- It is up to the auditors whether or not to accept that the evidence produced by the expert is sufficient and appropriate for their purposes.
- The opinion of an expert could be essential evidence to the auditors so they should review the bases on which the expert's opinion is founded.

POINTS TO NOTE

- It is a very good idea both in practice and in examinations to identify what express and implied assertions are being made when an item appears in accounts or does not appear. Students should get into the habit of doing this as often as possible.
- A mental review of the varieties of evidence and the techniques of evidence collection as shown above will often suggest a comprehensive answer to practical and examination problems of verification.
- There is a distinction made in the more theoretical books on auditing between evidential matter and audit evidence. The auditor gathers immense quantities of evidential matter from the business records and management and staff and from third parties. This evidential matter is evaluated by the auditor. If it is relevant to the audit objectives (e.g. ownership of an asset or completeness of a revenue total) and it is reliable to any extent, it becomes audit evidence.
- An expert may be engaged by or employed by the entity or the auditor. When the expert is employed by the auditor then ISA 220 *Quality control for an audit of financial statements* will apply to the work.
- Auditors should never uncritically accept the opinion of a specialist. Corroborative evidence should always be sought.
- In all cases, the auditors have to consider whether they have relevant and reliable audit evidence which is sufficient to enable them to draw reasonable conclusions.

CASE STUDY 1

Down Market Department Stores plc sell a high proportion of their merchandise on hire purchase (HP) credit. The system for dealing with HP sales is highly organized and well controlled. The HP receivables ledger is kept on a specially designed computer system. The HP receivables of the company at 30 September 2X16 appear in the accounts at £4.6 million out of gross assets of £19.3 million.

Discussion

- What assertions are the directors implying in stating the HP receivables at £4.6 million?
- What possible misstatements could occur?
- What varieties of evidence may be collected about this current asset?
- What basic techniques for collecting evidence can be applied to the item?

CASE STUDY 2

Archaic Manufacturing plc has a freehold factory which has been used to make the company's heavy metal products for generations. The factory was revalued ten years ago and is being depreciated over 50 years from that value. The company made a product for many years which has now been shown to be toxic and legal actions against the company have been expected. No mention occurs in the financial statements of these possible actions.

Discussion

- What are the assertions relevant to these matters?
- What kind of evidence might be collected?

CASE STUDY 3

Hermit Galleries plc are international art dealers with a turnover of £30 million a year.

They specialize in Impressionist paintings and have an inventory valued at £20 million. Recently it has been rumoured that some £9 million worth of their inventory may be the work of a particularly brilliant forger.

Towards the end of the financial year the company have agreed with the auditor to commission a report on the authenticity of the inventory from a well-known academic expert.

Discussion

– Draw up the terms of reference for the expert.
– Draft a checklist to examine the expert's report as audit evidence.
– The actual expert's opinion was certainty on the authenticity of £5.1 million worth, certainty on the forged nature of £2.2 million worth and doubt about the remainder.
– What should the auditor do?

STUDENT SELF-TESTING QUESTIONS

Questions with answers apparent from the text

a) What are the main classes of assertions about items in accounts?

b) What varieties of audit evidence are there?

c) What basic techniques for obtaining audit evidence are there?

d) What criteria are there for assessing reliability of audit evidence?

e) What criteria are there for assessing sufficiency?

f) List sources of audit evidence.

g) What might influence an auditor's judgement on sufficiency of audit evidence?

h) Give examples of reliance by auditors on the evidence supplied by specialists.

i) In what conditions may such reliance be required?

j) What factors indicate the reliability of the specialist?

k) What terms should appear in the agreement?

l) How should the auditor evaluate the evidence?

EXAMINATION QUESTIONS

1 You have recently been appointed auditor of DonkeyAid, a small registered charity which raises funds to rescue distressed donkeys. The charity makes payments to individuals who adopt rescued donkeys so they can provide suitable accommodation and to meet initial vet's fees, etc.

The charity is run by a voluntary management committee, which has monthly meetings and employs the following full-time staff:

(a) a director, Mrs Wimble, who is responsible for fund raising and who makes payments to individuals and implements policies adopted by the management committee and

(b) a secretary (and book-keeper), Ms Khan, who deals with correspondence and keeps the accounting records.

You are planning the audit of the charity for the year ended 5 April 2X16 and are considering the evidence you will need to verify income and expenditure.

The draft accounts show the following income and expenditure:

Income Statement for the year ended 5 April 2X16 (extract)

Gift Aid Declarations (by standing order)		1 258 740
Postal donations	452 436	
Fundraising activities	5 687	
Legacies	8 300	
Bank deposit account interest	3 714	470 137
		1 728 877
Expenditure		
Grants to Donkey Adopters		£901 452
Trustees Expenses		£ 2 431
Vets fees		£ 53 208

Notes:

(a) Gift Aid Declarations are completed by each person who intends to make contributions during the year. These are paid directly into the charity's bank account on a monthly basis by standing order. Gift Aid Declaration forms are kept by Ms Khan. (Gift Aid Declarations are used in the UK. Tax on these payments can be reclaimed but this should be ignored for the purposes of this question.)

(b) Postal donations, which can be cash or cheques, are dealt with by Ms Khan who prepares a daily list of donations. She also updates the cash book and prepares the bank paying-in slip.

(c) Fundraising activities include street collections and an Autumn Fair. This is a major event and takes place every year on a Saturday in October. Supporters of the charity provide items to sell or auction, a charge is made for entrance and refreshments are sold. Mrs Wimble collects the takings, prepares a summary of receipts and banks them the following Monday.

(d) Legacies are received irregularly, are usually sent to the director of the charity, who gives them to Ms Khan for banking.

(e) Bank deposit interest is paid gross by the bank, as the DonkeyAid is a charity.

Required:

You are required to gather sufficient, reliable evidence to validate that the income or expense shown above is fairly stated.

For each individual item of income and expense shown above list the type of evidence you would consider could provide the evidence you need.

SOURCES AND ADDITIONAL READING

Financial Reporting Council (2009) *ISA 200 Overall Objectives of the Independent Auditor and the Conduct of an Audit in Accordance with International Standards on Auditing*. London: Financial Reporting Council.

Financial Reporting Council (2009) *ISA 220 Quality Control for an Audit of Financial Statements*. London: Financial Reporting Council.

Financial Reporting Council (2009) *ISA 315 Identifying and Assessing Risks Of Material Misstatement Through Understanding the Entity and its Environment*. London: Financial Reporting Council.

Financial Reporting Council (2009) *ISA 330 The Auditor's Responses to Assessed Risk*. London: Financial Reporting Council.

Financial Reporting Council (2009) *ISA 500 Audit Evidence*. London: Financial Reporting Council.

Financial Reporting Council (2009) *ISA 620 Using the Work of an Auditor's Expert*. London: Financial Reporting Council.

Fomento (Sterling Area) Ltd. v Selsdon Fountain Pen Co. Ltd. (1958).

Gill.M, (2005) Learning from Fraudsters, London: Protoviti.

In Re: Kingston Cotton Mill Co. (1896).

CHAPTER 12
AUDIT TESTING, SAMPLING AND ANALYTICAL REVIEW PROCEDURES

Learning Objectives

After studying the material in this chapter you should be able to:

- understand the principle of evaluation of the risk of material error or misstatement going undetected

- explain the relationship between audit sampling, audit risk and materiality

- understand the nature of compliance and substantive testing

- understand the various techniques of audit sampling

- discuss the use of sampling as a valid audit technique including its limitations

- understand the use and application of analytical procedures

INTRODUCTION

In order to gather the evidence they need, auditors carry out audit testing on the transactions and balances which are represented in the financial statements presented to them.

The approach to audit testing will be dependent on several issues, in particular:

- The **risk assessments** carried out both by the client as assessments of **business risk**. ISA 315 *Identifying and assessing the risks of material misstatement through understanding the entity and its environment* requires auditors to evaluate business risks insofar as they may be likely to influence the probability of a material misstatement occurring (Chapter 14).
- The auditor's own assessment of **audit risk** (Chapter 10).
- The nature and complexity of the client's activities and associated financial systems. The more complex the transaction the auditor is asked to consider; the more evidence the auditor is likely to want in respect of the assertions (Chapter 11) made about it by the directors.
- The availability of corroboration of evidence. If evidence about transactions is available from more than one source the auditor is more likely to place reliance on the validity of the assertions at the transaction level. For example, the auditor could carry out sample tests on the client's sales system. As part of the testing of Receivables the auditor may carry out a circularization of individual receivables balances (Chapter 15).
- The confirmations from customers which validate the receivables balance at the period end also support the testing of the sales system insofar as they show (assuming all is well) that the client's receivables ledger is being written up properly.

RELATIONSHIP TO AUDIT RISK AND MATERIALITY

The *amount* of testing carried out and the *emphasis* of the tests is very much geared to the assessment of audit risk (Chapter 10).

If the risk of a material misstatement is considered to be high, it follows logically that the auditors will have to do more audit work than if it was considered to be low. In this case samples for testing will be larger and the audit will focus on testing a larger number of transactions and balances than if the risk assessment was low and the audit approach could be one based on the successful operation of the company's internal control procedures (Chapter 9).

Broadly, the greater the level of audit risk the more work the auditor will be likely to do in order to reduce **detection risk** to an acceptable level. This is an important determinant of audit strategy and is, of course, largely determined by such factors as:

- the auditor's assessment of the management
- the auditor's assessment of the client's internal control procedures; and
- previous experience with the client.

The level of materiality (Chapter 10) also has a bearing on the amount of audit work carried out. Learners should understand that materiality levels affect the amount of testing carried out; the higher the level of materiality (including performance materiality) the lower the level of testing. This is logically because the lower the level of materiality the greater the number of transactions which are likely to be material. If materiality is set at £100, for example, every transaction or combination of transactions of £100 or over is material so more testing would have to be done, depending again on the auditor's assessment of controls etc. outlined above.

FORMS OF AUDIT TESTING

The form of testing the auditors carry out is divided into compliance tests of the system of controls and substantive testing of transactions and balances. The level of audit testing is very much related to the assessment of audit risk (Chapter 10) – the greater the level of Audit Risk identified at the planning stage the more work must be done to give the auditors the reassurance they need.

Testing takes many forms but modern auditing relies on compliance testing and risk-based techniques such as sampling to provide the evidence the auditor needs.

Compliance tests

Compliance tests are tests to obtain audit evidence about the effective operation of the control environment, in particular the operation of **control procedures.**

The auditor will review:

- systems notes and flowcharts describing the systems noting any areas in which controls may appear to be weak or which have proved to be weak in prior years (assuming this is not the first year of audit testing)
- answers to internal control questionnaires (ICQs) (Chapter 10) which may indicate areas of weakness
- any changes to systems or operating procedures since the previous audit; this would include any changes to computer systems, in particular any changes to accounting processes and procedures as a result of new technology

Note that if systems have changed markedly since the last systems review the audit team may well have to amend their systems documentation significantly and carry out a new **walkthrough test,** etc. (Chapter 10). The auditor will also review the answers from:

- the internal control evaluation questionnaires (ICEQs) which will highlight any potential areas of weakness
- previous period's audit files to identify any problem areas encountered in previous years
- the **Management Letter** (Chapter 27) sent to management at the conclusion of the previous period's audit identifying any areas of weakness in the control environment which management was being asked to address

In areas where the system appears to be particularly defective or weak then the auditor may need to abandon a systems-based approach and apply more detailed substantive tests. These would normally be applied more at the period end than at the **interim audit.**

Two points must be made about compliance testing. Firstly, it is very important for the student to understand that it is the application of the *control procedure* that is being tested, *not* the transaction itself, although the testing is through the medium of the transactions. When designing audit tests emphasis must be placed on designing tests which check the operation of the *control*. The actual transaction is, to this extent, not relevant as long as it is representative of the entire population being tested.

Secondly if the auditors discover that the control procedures were not functioning correctly in a particular way then:

- they may need to revise the system description and re-appraise its effectiveness
- they will need to determine if the failure of compliance was an isolated instance or was symptomatic of a larger failure
- it may be that a larger sample needs to be taken

As an example of a test of control procedures, suppose that a system provided that all credit notes issued by the client had to be approved by the sales manager and that a space was provided on each credit note for his initials. The auditor would inspect a sample of the credit notes to determine if all of them had been initialled. This is testing that the *control* is operating – and the details of the credit note aren't relevant to the test being performed.

Substantive testing

Substantive procedures are detailed tests of transactions and balances. They are designed to obtain audit evidence to detect material misstatements in the financial statements and are required to be used in testing the Statement of Financial Position in particular.

They are generally of two types:

- substantive procedures, such as tests of details of transactions and balances, reviews of minutes of directors' meetings and enquiries. We look at these in later chapters
- **analytical review procedures** – see later in this chapter

From this definition, you may deduce that *all* audit work comes within the definition of substantive procedures. However, the term 'substantive testing' is usually used to mean all tests other than tests of controls. A substantive test is any test which seeks *direct evidence* of the correct treatment of a transaction, a balance, an asset, a liability, or any item in the books or the accounts. Analytical review is also seen as a separate type of substantive test.

Some examples of audit testing:

- Of a transaction – the sale of a piece of plant will require the auditor to examine the copy invoice, the authorization, the entry in the plant register and other books, the accounting treatment and some evidence that the price obtained was reasonable.
- Of a balance – direct confirmation of the balance in a deposit account is obtained by means of a confirmation letter from the bank.
- Analytical procedures – evidence of the correctness of **cut-off** is obtained by examining the gross profit ratio.

When considering audit testing auditors must also consider:

- Completeness of information – e.g. obtaining confirmation from a client's legal adviser that all potential consequences arising from any litigation in which the organization is involved have been considered.
- Accuracy of information – e.g. obtaining from each director a signed confirmation that an accurate statement of their remuneration and expenses has been obtained.
- Validity of information – e.g. validity means based on evidence that can be supported. For example, a provision for future warranty claims may be extremely difficult to estimate in precise monetary terms. If such a provision is made in the Financial Statements, the auditor would need to apply substantive tests to determine its validity, i.e. that it was supported by adequate evidence.

Auditors must use both substantive and compliance testing in order to gather the evidence they need to validate the assertions on which the financial statements are based, which in turn then serves to support their audit opinion.

The tests set out below comprise a mixture of compliance and substantive approaches, as it is really not necessary when designing audit tests to decide which test falls into which category.

We looked at the sources of audit evidence in Chapter 11 and students should be familiar with these. Remember that audit tests, broadly, comprise a combination of:

- inspecting for evidence that a control has been operated
- re-performing the accounting procedures on a sample of transactions, in either direction, to demonstrate that they have been carried out correctly
- carrying out substantive tests on balances and reconciliations including obtaining independent third party evidence and analytical review procedures
- inspection tests to validate assertions for existence

Tests of control, compliance tests, are invariably based on samples as it is usually not feasible to test an entire population of transactions except in the smallest of organizations, or where there is a very small number of very large transactions. Auditors can carry out substantive tests based on samples as well so a sampling approach is simply a way of identifying transactions or balances to test – it is not evidence of a particular audit strategy.

Directional testing

It is important to understand, when carrying out audit testing, that the direction in which the test is carried out can provide evidence – but only up to a point. To illustrate the concept of **directional testing**, consider a basic Revenues transaction, very much simplified:

Order from customer → goods dispatched and signed for → invoice sent → revenues nominal ledger listing → customer account in Sales Ledger

The auditors might be testing that:

- a valid customer order has been received
- the goods have been sent to the customer and signed for
- that the transactions have been properly entered into the revenues nominal ledger listing with the right codes for the right customer and nominal ledger account, and from there, logically, into the Receivables ledger

The obvious thing to do to this is to select a sample of invoices either from the revenues nominal ledger listing or from customer accounts and check them against the source documents – a test known as **vouching**. So the direction of the test is:

Revenues listing recording invoice → Approved customer order → Despatch note signed by customer i.e. from the books of account towards the originating documentation.

This is a valid test and will confirm, or otherwise, that the controls within the system are operating i.e. that for Sales Invoices sent to customers there has been a valid customer order and that the goods have been delivered and paid for.

However, the test fails as a test for the Assertion of Completeness. How do we know that all the customer orders resulted in a supply of goods to the customer which were actually delivered and paid for? How do we know that goods haven't been sent without an invoice being prepared so the customer got free goods? In other words, how do the auditors confirm that all the transactions are entered in the books?

The only way to do this is to take a sample of source documents – goods despatched notes or revenues orders and test them *in the other direction* thus:

Despatch note signed by customer → Sales invoice issued → Recorded in nominal ledger revenues listing → Entered in customer account in Revenues Ledger

i.e. from the originating source documents towards the books of account.

This will help validate the assertion for Completeness *and* the other Assertions tested.

CASE STUDY 1

Bobo Ltd – directional testing

You are the audit senior of Bobo Ltd, a manufacturer of electrical goods. You have been asked to design audit tests for part of the purchases system.

Key aspects of the system you are reviewing are:

1   All purchases are ordered by means of an official order signed by the purchasing manager.
2   All goods received are evidenced by a goods received note raised by the stores.
3   Purchase invoices are matched with purchase orders and goods received notes before being entered in the purchase ledger.

Required:

Design audit tests to evidence the relevant assertions in the most efficient way.

Solution:

There are two ways of carrying out these tests:

(a)   Select a sample of purchase invoices and test to the relevant purchase orders and goods received notes. This will help to validate the assertions of:

Occurrence – the fact that Bobo ordered the goods means that the purchases and the liability to pay for them belong to them.

Accuracy (part) – the goods ordered have been delivered and, combined with other audit tests on prices and a test to trace them into the purchase ledger, the auditors could use this to validate the accuracy of the suppliers account. Or the auditors could do it the other way round.

(b)   Select a sample of goods received notes including the goods received notes at the year end and compare them with purchase orders and invoices.

By testing in this direction they can evidence:

Occurrence – they can evidence that Bobo both ordered and received the goods so they and the liability to pay for them belong to Bobo.

Accuracy – as in test (a).

Completeness – by selecting a sample of goods received notes the auditors can evidence whether Bobo has received any goods which haven't been invoiced yet.

Cut-off – including in this test the goods received notes around the year end means the auditors can evidence that the transactions are included in the correct accounting period.

AUDIT SAMPLING

Introduction

Clearly it is impossible, in all but the very smallest organizations, for auditors to check every transaction. In the case of the largest companies there may be millions of items of data which the auditor would have to consider. Oddly, the general public often has the perception that auditors check all the transactions in a financial period, which is why, when some form of financial scandal surfaces, uninformed speculation often tries to attach blame to the auditors because they are supposed to have checked everything.

The sheer impossibility of this, not to mention the prohibitive cost if it were to be even attempted, is why auditors adopt either a systems-based approach to auditing or a risk-based approach (Chapters 13 and 14) both of which require the auditors to select samples of transactions for testing.

Note, however, that the auditors expect to gain audit evidence about a population from sampling it but wise auditors will use sampling tests only in conjunction with other available evidence, in addition to the evidence from the sample.

Sampling is only one method of gathering evidence by audit testing and students should be familiar with other methods of evidence gathering, as discussed in Chapter 11.

Basis of sampling

The objective in all sampling is to draw conclusions about a large volume of data, known as the **population,** based on examination of a sample taken from that population. The population, for this purpose, is defined as a specific category of transactions, e.g. all the sales invoices or all the PAYE calculations or all the goods received notes. A population is not a mixed category so attempting to use sampling techniques on a population which includes several different documents, say purchase invoices and purchase credit notes would not be valid.

There is an auditing standard ISA 530 *Audit Sampling* which states:

> 'The objective of the auditor, when using audit sampling, is to provide a reasonable basis for the auditor to draw conclusions about the population from which the sample is selected.'

What this means is that the application of audit procedures to less than 100% of items within a population enables the auditors to draw conclusions, based on the results of those tests, about the population as a whole. There are two key issues fundamental to all sampling techniques:

1   The population has to be homogeneous – i.e. each item in the population has to be the same as the next one.
       For example, sampling test on sales invoices cannot include credit notes; a sampling test on finished goods inventory items cannot include raw material inventories. Each class of transaction has to be sampled separately, which may mean lots of tests.

2   Every item in the population must have an equal chance of selection.
       This means that, for example, a technique known as **block sampling**, where auditors pick a block of transactions to test, e.g. all Goods Returned Notes in May, is not actually a very good basis for testing as, in this case, the Goods Returned Notes for January to April and June to December have no chance of being selected.

When sampling is not appropriate

Note that sampling may *not* be appropriate in certain circumstances. These are primarily:

- when the auditor has already been advised of a high level of errors or systems failures or in connection with a possible fraud
- where populations are too small for a valid conclusion – it may be quicker to check them all!
- where all the transactions in a population are material, e.g. a manufacturer of aeroplanes – they may only sell 20 in a year but each contract is worth several hundred million pounds
- where data is required to be fully disclosed in the financial statements, e.g. directors' emoluments
- where the population is not homogeneous

Points to consider before sampling

Auditors should consider:

The objective of the test

Why is this test being carried out? What contribution does it make to the overall assessment of a true and fair view?

What is the population from which the sample will be taken?

The population has to be defined precisely. This may be, for example, all Finished Goods Inventory.

The sampling unit

Note that in compliance testing it is the operation of the *control* on a transaction which is being tested, not the transaction itself. It is the transaction which is the sampling unit used to test the control and, in a way, isn't relevant – it is only selected to check the control is working and has no other significance so it doesn't matter if it is a large transaction or a small one.

The definition of error

The auditors have to define what constitutes an error. Some 'errors' may not be material or not considered to be significant. Auditors have to decide what it is they are looking for.

What level of errors will we expect to find and what level will we be prepared to tolerate as not material?

We look at this in more detail later but auditors will have to expect to find some errors and will have to evaluate the significance of those errors in the light of performance materiality levels (Chapter 10) and, ultimately, their effect on the financial statements.

Sampling risk

As they do not check the entire population there is a risk that the sample, however well chosen, will not be representative of the population as a whole. This is called **sampling risk**.

Auditors have to deal with sampling risk both in compliance and substantive testing. The risks to the auditors are:

- In the case of compliance testing, that controls are either more or less effective than they actually are, because the rate of errors in the sample is not the same as the actual rate of errors in the population.
- In the case of substantive testing, that a material misstatement does not exist, when in fact it does, because no indication of such an error has appeared in the sample selected.

If the basis for choosing the sample is a rational one and the planning, testing and evaluation procedures are properly carried out then sampling risk can be reduced to an acceptable level. However, the use of sampling does emphasize the importance of corroborative evidence from other sources in order to eliminate the possibility of a material error or misstatement not being detected because of the sampling approach used by the auditors.

Designing the sample

There are a number of factors that the auditors need to consider.

Population

As already stated, the population is the data set from which the sample will be chosen. The essential feature of the population is that it be homogeneous. Care has to be taken to ensure this is the case. For example, suppose the population to be tested is all credit sales invoices, but that, part way through the year, the company replaced its old invoice recording system with a new one. In this case there are, in fact, *two* populations, the old system and the new system and both have to be tested.

Note also that testing the sample of a population does not test that population for the assertion of completeness – it only tests what is actually there. To test for completeness tests, have to be performed from source documents into the population. What this means in practice is that, for example, when testing a sales system as well as testing the population of sales invoices recoded in the accounting records, it is necessary to test a sample of delivery notes or sales orders to ensure that there are no transactions where, for example, goods were despatched but never invoiced.

Testing the population

A key point to remember here is that, whilst sampling is the best way to statistically validate the Assertions relevant to a large population by taking a statistically valid sample from that population and testing it, this does not mean that one test will do. Auditors have to bear in mind all the Assertions they need to test for, which might mean carrying out more than one test on, essentially, the same population of transactions.

In practice what the auditors will do is set up a sampling test which takes into account all the elements of the system. So, for example suppose a simple purchasing system includes the following elements:

- purchase order to supplier
- despatch note from supplier to confirm goods received signed by warehouse staff
- purchase invoice from supplier
- purchase credit notes from supplier to correct errors in invoicing
- purchase invoice coded to nominal ledger
- approval of purchase invoice
- electronic payment of supplier

The auditors might take as their sample a selection of the population of purchase invoices and design a sample test to include all the elements of the system relevant to those transactions (Figure 12.1)

FIGURE 12.1 Extract from working paper – sample test of purchase invoices

BLOGGINS LTD							Prepared by	JT			
							Checked by	RB			
							Date	07.09.2X17			
Sample test – Purchase Invoices											
Purchase invoice number	Purchase order number	Purchase order approved by authorized signatory	Purchase order date	Delivery note number	Delivery note signed by goods inwards	Invoice approved by authorized signatory	Invoice coded to correct nominal ledger account	Invoice posted to correct supplier account	Date posted to correct Nominal ledger account	Invoice paid	Date paid
1234	871	√ (PG)*	23.03.17	9123	04.04.17	√ (AL)*	√	√	10.04.17	√	15.05.17

* Initial of approver

Obviously in real life the sample size would be greater than one!

But this is only one element of the overall population. How do the auditors know, for example, that all items delivered have been invoiced and paid for? So a second sample test must be performed but this time the sample will be based on a selection of Delivery Notes rather than Purchase Invoices (Figure 12.2)

FIGURE 12.2 Extract from working paper – sample test of delivery notes

BLOGGINS LTD									Prepared by	JT		
									Checked by	RB		
									Date	07.09.2X17		
Sample test – Purchase Invoices												
Delivery note number	Delivery note date	Delivery note signed by goods inwards	Purchase order number	Purchase order approved by authorized signatory	Purchase order date	Purchase invoice number	Invoice approved by authorized signatory	Invoice coded to correct nominal ledger account	Invoice posted to supplier account	Date posted to correct Nominal ledger	Invoice paid	Date paid
7496	22.06.17	√	942	√ (PG)*	06.06.17	1792	√ (AL)*	√	√	02.07.17	√	03.08.17

* Initial of approver

This is actually a form of Directional Testing, which we looked at above.

This second test is a test for the Assertion of Completeness and by undertaking two tests the auditors have tested that:

1   Goods invoiced and paid for were originally ordered and delivered and properly authorized.

2   Goods delivered were originally ordered and have been invoiced and paid for and properly authorized.

A third test could be performed if considered appropriate based on a sample of customer orders to show that all orders received have been delivered and invoiced.

Sample size

The size of the sample has to be sufficiently large to constitute a meaningful test but not so large that the audit team are wasting time carrying out tests which do not add to the validity of the evidence already gathered. When a non-statistical basis is adopted (see below) this can present problems as the auditor has no valid basis for selecting a sample size, merely experience, intuition or blind faith that the sample size is big enough.

When statistics are involved and decisions are made about confidence levels and degrees of precision it is possible to establish a sample size using a mathematical approach which is statistically significant. In this way the audit team can be employed usefully in gathering sufficient reliable evidence based on one of the statistically valid sampling approaches described below.

Level of confidence

Auditors work to levels of confidence which can be expressed precisely. For example, a 5 per cent confidence level means that there are 19 chances out of 20 that the sample is representative of the population as a whole. The converse view is that there is one chance in 20 that the sample, on which the auditor draws conclusions, is nonrepresentative of the population as a whole.

Precision

From a sample it is not possible to say that the auditors are 95 per cent certain that, for example, the error rate in a population of inventory calculations is x per cent, but only that the error rate is x per cent $\pm$ y per cent where $\pm$ y per cent is the precision interval. Clearly the level of confidence and the precision interval are related, in that for a given sample size higher confidence can be expressed in a wider precision interval and vice versa.

Tolerable misstatement

Tolerable misstatement is, broadly, the same as performance materiality (Chapter 10). It may be set at the same level or may be set lower depending on circumstances. It cannot be set higher than performance materiality. The auditor sets a level of tolerable misstatement to deal with the risk that the total of detected errors or deviations which are individually immaterial and possible undetected errors are not sufficiently high as to result in a material misstatement of the accounts.

In essence this is the maximum level of error in the population that auditors are willing to accept and still conclude that their audit objectives have been achieved.

The tolerable misstatement level in a population is usually determined in the planning stage.

Tolerable rate of deviation

This is a rate of deviation from prescribed internal control procedures which is set by the auditor. The auditor is then trying to obtain an appropriate level of assurance that the rate of deviation set by the auditor is not exceeded by the actual rate of deviation in the population.

SAMPLING APPROACHES

To be effective a sample should be:

- Random – a random sample is one where each item of the population has an equal (or specified) chance of being selected. Statistical inferences may not be valid unless the sample is truly random.
- Representative – the sample should be representative of the items in the whole population. For example, it should contain a similar proportion of high- and low-value items to the population.
- Protective – protective, that is, of the auditor. More intensive auditing should occur on high-value items known to be high risk.
- Unpredictable – client should not be able to know or guess which items will be examined.

Bases of sampling

There are two approaches to selecting samples:

- non-statistical or 'judgement' sampling
- statistical sampling

Non-statistical sampling

This means selecting a sample of appropriate size on the basis of the auditor's judgement of what is desirable. This approach has some advantages:

- The approach has been used for many years. It is well understood and refined by experience.
- The auditors can bring their judgement and expertise into play.
- No special knowledge of statistics is required.
- No time is spent on struggling with mathematics.

There are, however, some serious disadvantages:

- It is unscientific.
- Often sample sizes are too large, which can be wasteful, or too small, which renders the test invalid.
- There is no consistency of results – two different auditors will produce two different samples.
- No quantitative results are obtained.
- Personal bias in the selection of samples is unavoidable.
- There is no real logic to the selection of the sample or its size.
- The sample selection can be slanted to the auditor's needs, e.g. selection of items near the year end to help with cut-off evaluation, may invalidate the test if it is also to be used to validate transactions for the entire period.

Overall, judgement sampling is considered difficult to defend in court and far too subjective to have any real validity so is rarely used.

Statistical sampling

Statistical sampling requires the use of mathematical procedures, but it still requires the exercise of judgement, for example, in deciding what constitutes a misstatement or deviation and what the performance materiality level is.

Drawing inferences about a large volume of data by an examination of a sample is a highly developed part of the discipline of statistics. It seems only common sense for the auditors to draw upon this body of knowledge in their own work. In practice, a certain level of mathematical competence is required if valid conclusions are to be drawn from sample evidence.

The advantages of using statistical sampling are:

- It is scientific.
- It is defensible.
- It provides precise mathematical statements about probabilities of being correct.
- It can be used by all levels of staff.
- It is efficient – overlarge sample sizes are not taken.
- It tends to result in a uniform standard of testing.

Its primary disadvantages are:

- that it is a mathematical process, which needs to be understood; and
- the principles of testing have to be applied properly in order for the tests to be valid.

SAMPLING METHODS

Auditors can adopt a variety of approaches to selecting samples for testing. Some are statistically valid, as discussed above, others are more subjective and may not be entirely appropriate as a method of gathering audit evidence. However, all approaches are included here and the student may evaluate their merits or otherwise as appropriate.

Random sampling

This is simply choosing items subjectively but trying to avoid bias. Bias might come in by tendency to favour items in a particular location or in an accessible file, or conversely in picking items because they appear unusual. This method is acceptable for non-statistical sampling but is insufficiently rigorous for statistical sampling.

Simple random

All items in the population have (or are given) a number. Numbers are selected by a means which gives every number an equal chance of being selected. This is done using random number tables or computer-generated random numbers.

Random systematic selection

This method involves making a random start and then taking every '*nth*' item thereafter. The sampling interval is decided by dividing the population size by the sample size, i.e. if the population is 1000 and the number to be sampled is 100 the sampling interval will be every tenth transaction. The starting point can be determined randomly.

This method is useful when sampling nonmonetary items, e.g. despatch notes.

However, the sample may not be representative as the population may have some serial properties, for example, there may be a pattern in the way documents are filed so that say, every tenth despatch note is for Hull. If this is the case the sample will be distorted and the test will be invalid.

Value-weighted selection

This method uses the currency unit value rather than the items as the sampling population and is sometimes called **Monetary Unit Sampling** (MUS).

- Its application is appropriate with large variance populations. Large variance populations are those like receivables balances or inventories where the individual members of the population are of widely different sizes.
- The method is suited to populations where errors are not expected.
- It implicitly takes into account the auditor's concept of materiality.

Procedures are:

1   Determine sample size. This will take into account:
    - the size of the population;
    - the level of tolerable misstatement (related to performance materiality – see above);
    - the assurance level required.

2   List the items in the population (we will use receivables); e.g. here is a selection from a list of receivables balances:

Customer name	Balance £	Cumulative £	Selected
Jones	**6 201**	6 201	**yes**
Brown & Co	474	6 675	no
XY Co Ltd	**1 320**	7 995	**yes**
JB	1 220	9 215	no
RS Acne	**4 197**	13 412	**yes**
and so on . . .	. . .	. . .	. . .
	384 200	384 200	

If the sample size were 100 items the sampling interval will be every 3842nd pound (£384,200/100) thereafter.

If we start from £0:

- the first balance, Jones, has within it the first sampling interval of £3842
- the next, £7684 (£3842 + £3842), arrives in the balance belonging to XY & Co; and
- finally (in our list) the interval having reached £11 526 (£3842 + £3842 + £3842) in the balance belonging to RS Acne . . . and so on.

The sample is random as the starting point can be selected at random – it does not have to be £0.

Note that, using this method, the larger balances have a greater chance of being selected which is protective for the auditor.

MUS has some disadvantages:

- It does not cope easily with errors of understatement. A receivables balance which is underestimated will have a smaller chance of being selected than if it was correctly valued. Hence there is a reduced chance of selecting that balance and discovering the error.
- It can be difficult to select samples if a computer cannot be used, as manual selection will involve adding cumulatively through the population.
- It is not possible to extend a sample if the error rate turns out to be higher than expected. In such cases an entirely new sample must be selected and evaluated.

MUS is especially useful in testing for overstatement where significant understatements are not expected. Examples of applications include receivables, noncurrent assets and inventories. It may not be suitable for testing payables balances where understatement is a primary characteristic to be tested for.

At the end of the process, auditors should evaluate the results, which might be a conclusion that the auditor is 95 per cent confident that the receivables are not overstated by more than £x, £x being the materiality factor chosen.

If the conclusion is that the auditors find that receivables appear to be overstated by more than £x then they may take a larger sample and/or investigate the balances more fully.

Stratified sampling

Stratified sampling means dividing the population into subpopulations (strata = layers) and is useful when parts of the population have higher than normal risk (e.g. high-value items, overseas receivables). Frequently, high-value items form a small part of the population and are 100 per cent checked and the remainder are sampled.

The information can be produced by a report generator from the management information system and used by the auditor to design the test.

For example:

	Number of items in stratum	Value of stratum	Test size
Above £1m	10	£38m	10
£750 000–£1m	30	£28m	20
£500 000–£750 000	50	£42m	20
£250 000–£500 000	100	£28m	15
£50 000–£250 000	1000	£93m	50
£10 000–£50 000	4000	£65m	40
Under £10 000	8000	£12m	15

As can be seen, the sample chosen is weighted towards the high-value transactions because they are the most material. If one of the transactions in excess of £1m is in error it may be material to the accounts, an error in a transaction totalling £50 000 may not be.

Multi-stage sampling

This method is appropriate when data is stored in two or more levels. For example, inventory in a retail chain of shops. The first stage is to randomly select a sample of shops and the second stage is to randomly select inventory items from the chosen shops.

Block sampling

This is carried out by choosing at random one block of items, e.g. all June invoices.

This common sampling method has none of the desired characteristics and is not recommended. Analogous to this is Cluster Sampling where data is maintained in clusters (i.e. groups or bunches), as wage records are kept in weeks or sales invoices in months. The idea is to select a cluster randomly and then to examine all the items in the cluster chosen. The problem with this method is that the sample may not be representative of the whole accounting period as the month or cluster chosen may have unique characteristics.

Additional aspects of sampling

These include the following:

Estimation sampling for variables

This method seeks to estimate (with a chosen level of confidence and precision interval) the total value of some population. For example, the auditor might be 95 per cent confident that the total value of receivables, inventories or loose tools, might lie between £58.3m and £59.4m and the best estimate is £59m.

The procedure is to extrapolate from a sample to an estimate of the total value. However, the calculations involved in carrying this out scientifically are complex and can only be performed easily using a computer application.

Attribute sampling

This provides results based on two possible attributes, i.e. correct/not correct and is used primarily in connection with the testing of internal controls, i.e. nonmonetary testing.

It is generally used in compliance testing where the extent of application of a control is to be determined, i.e. the test is 'complies/does not comply'. Each deviation from a control procedure is given an equal weight in the final evaluation of results.

MUS is an attribute sampling technique as it measures monetary deviations.

Projecting the error into the population

When testing controls, the rate of errors detected through sample testing is the rate of error in the population as a whole. Thus, for example, if a sample test reveals that 20 per cent of transactions are not authorized when they should be then the rate of error in the whole population is that 20 per cent of all the transactions are unauthorized, unless there are extenuating circumstances which can be applied to the deviations found in the sample.

For substantive tests the auditors will have to project the level of misstatement found in the sample to the whole population and determine if the consequent level of misstatement for the whole population is within tolerable limits. For example, if the auditors test 20 per cent of a population of balances and aggregate errors of £10 000 the error in the population can be projected to be at least £50,000 i.e. £10,000 / 20 × 100 = £50,000. The auditors will have to decide if this is likely to be material and refer to their performance materiality and tolerable misstatement levels set at the planning stage.

Working papers

As in all audit work, the work done in audit sampling situations should be fully documented in the working papers. In particular, the documentation in the working papers should evidence:

- planning the sample:
  - stating the audit objectives
  - definition of error or deviation
  - the means of determining the sample size
  - the tolerable error rate
- selecting the items to be tested:
  - the selection method used
  - details of the items selected
- testing the items:
  - the tests carried out
  - the errors or deviations noted
- evaluating the results of the tests:
  - explanations of the causes of the errors or deviations
  - the projection of errors or deviations
  - the auditor's assessment of the assurance obtained as to the possible size of actual error or deviation rate
  - the nature and details of the conclusions drawn from the sample results
  - details of further action taken where required (e.g. a larger sample or other forms of evidence gathering)

Review of sampling results

Whichever method is considered appropriate the auditor must constantly be aware of the key issues in sampling, principally:

- homogeneity of the population from which the sample is chosen; and
- the possibility of bias in selecting the sample.

In modern auditing it would be almost unheard of for an auditor to choose a non-statistical basis for selecting their sample, but it would be foolish to state it never happens! The key point is to evaluate the results of the tests taking into account the possibility of sampling risk i.e. that the sample is not truly representative of the population.

Statistical techniques will give the auditor a confidence level within which they can safely base a conclusion but this should be corroborated by other audit evidence wherever possible. Sampling is not something to be performed in isolation. For example, a sample check on a Revenues and Receivables system may validate processing controls which might satisfy the auditor that the Revenues figure is correctly stated but it will take another type of audit test to validate the Receivables number in the Statement of Financial Position. As Revenues and Receivables are part of one system two different types of audit test will serve to validate the system as a whole.

In modern computerized accounting systems, the incidence of transaction errors is quite low and overall errors found may not be material. However the auditor should not lose sight of the fact that it is the efficient working of internal controls which is being tested and this is the starting point the auditor has to work from – that the transactions in the records are valid and are a true record of what has happened in the year. As we will see there are many other aspects to auditing which cannot be evaluated by sampling. This is just one tool in the auditor's toolbox but it is powerful if used correctly.

ANALYTICAL REVIEW PROCEDURES

As we have seen, auditors are required to carry out procedures designed to obtain sufficient appropriate audit evidence to determine with reasonable confidence whether the financial statements are free of material misstatement. They are also required to evaluate the overall presentation of the financial statements, in order to ascertain whether they have been prepared in accordance with relevant legislation and accounting standards. The auditors have to give an opinion on whether the accounts give a true and fair view and comply with regulations.

One of the key ways of gathering such evidence is the use of analytical procedures at each stage of the audit.

The purpose of analytical procedures is to help in telling the story of the financial statements, prepared by the directors, to gather evidence to show that the relationships between the numbers in the accounts are reasonable and logical and bear out what is known from other sources about the events of the accounting period.

There is an auditing standard ISA 520 *'Analytical procedures'*. This standard requires that auditors should apply analytical procedures:

- at the planning stage;
- as a substantive procedure during the course of the audit work; and
- at the final overall review stage of the audit.

Definition

Analytical procedures can be defined as:

'evaluations of financial information through analysis of plausible relationships among both financial and non-financial data. Analytical procedures also encompass such investigation as is necessary of identified fluctuations or relationships that are inconsistent with other relevant information or that differ from expected values by a significant amount.'

This can involve:

- investigating unexpected variations identified by the use of analytical procedures
- obtaining and substantiating explanations for such variations
- evaluating the results of an analytical review with other audit evidence obtained

Analytical procedures involve:

- recognizing increases in magnitude corresponding to inflation or in excess of inflation
- evaluating changes in amounts arising from changes in output levels
- comparisons with previous periods
- trends and ratio analysis
- comparisons with budgets and forecasts
- comparisons with other, similar, organizations, e.g. by inter-firm comparison

Auditors are looking for deviations from what might be predicted. For example, a noticeable increase in credit sales might indicate a similar increase in receivables. Analysis of receivables days would indicate whether or not the level shown by the Statement of Financial Position is reasonable or not. Where ratios diverge from previous levels or comparisons of budget figures with actual results show major variations, these may be highlighted at the planning stage and can be investigated by the auditor as part of substantive testing.

Similar techniques are also applied by management, investment analysts and internal auditors to provide information on the performance of an entity, the efficiency of its operations or the quality of its management. Remember that, in performing these procedures, an auditor has a quite different purpose.

Analytical procedures can be simple tests comparing absolute magnitudes of different years, comparing ratios with earlier years, budgets and industry averages but also using computer audit software or using advanced statistical techniques, e.g. multiple regression analysis.

These are outside the scope of this book.

Problem areas

A word of warning; there are three critical aspects to the use of analytical procedures which should be observed.

1   All the information used must be reliable. Analytical procedures are the analysis of relationships and are commonly used to indicate trends over time. The results for one period in isolation, in themselves, are meaningless until they are compared with other periods or benchmark numbers from a reliable source.

The point is that the comparison numbers have to be reliable; if all the numbers used are false the test will reveal nothing specific except perhaps a series of confusing variances. For example, if accounts for Year 4 are considered to be dubious they can be compared with accounts for Years 1–3 and variances noted. However, if the directors have manipulated the figures for each of the Years 1–4 the tests have no validity.

There is a form of analytical review known as Beneish Ratios which are used in fraud detection to identify manipulation of financial statements and which highlight anomalies such as these. These are outside the scope of this book but students may well find them of interest.

2   Analytical procedures raise questions, but they rarely provide answers. Indicators thrown up using these techniques must be followed through and investigated in detail and, where possible, explanations received for the apparent anomalies.

3   Disaggregating the numbers into divisions, subsidiaries or regions may be much more successful than looking at the entity as a whole as anomalies may be confined to one area of the business under local control. Meaningful discoveries could be masked if analysis was carried out on an organization-wide basis.

Timing

Analytical procedures will be applied throughout the audit but specific occasions include:

- *At the planning stage*. The auditors will hope to identify areas of potential risk or new developments so that they can plan their other audit procedures in these areas. As a simple example, the auditors might discover that the gross profit ratio in a retail organization had changed from the 28 per cent to 30 per cent in previous years to 24 per cent in the current year; or they might discover that a sales analysis revealed that exports had increased from 3 per cent to 26 per cent of Revenue. This will lead to a direction of the emphasis of audit testing in order to investigate these apparent anomalies.
- *During the audit* as a form of gathering audit evidence. Audits with their emphasis on efficiency and economy depend heavily on analytical procedures as a valid audit technique either used alone or in conjunction with internal control reliance and other types of substantive testing.

It can be as reasonable to obtain assurance of the completeness, accuracy and validity of the transactions and balances by analytical procedures as by other types of audit evidence. For example, if the relative amounts under different expense headings repeat the pattern of previous years the auditor has evidence of the accuracy of expense invoice coding.

- *At the final review stage* of the audit. Analytical procedures can provide support for the conclusions arrived at as a result of other work. The techniques are also used to assess the overall reasonableness of the financial statements as a whole.

Extent of use of analytical procedures

Analytical review procedures can best be carried out on particular segments of the organization, e.g. the branch at Walsall or the paint division or the subsidiary in France rather than on the organization as a whole. For example, a motor dealership derives income from various sources, selling cars, repair work, petrol and oil sales, etc. each of which can be analyzed separately if the financial records are sufficiently detailed. They can also be used on individual account areas such as payables or fixed asset depreciation.

The procedures involve a breaking down of data into subdivisions for analysis over time, by product, by location, by management responsibility, etc., but analytical procedures are not effective in reviewing an entity as a whole unless it is very small or only has one activity. The greater the disaggregation the better.

One approach is to identify the factors likely to have an effect on items in the accounts; to ascertain or assess the probable relationship with these factors and items and then to *predict* the value of the items in the light of the factors. The predicted value of the items can then be compared with the actual recorded amounts.

For example, production level is related to materials usage. If the auditors are aware of the profile of production levels, e.g. lower in summer than in winter, the profile of materials purchasing can be matched to it and any anomalies identified. The auditors should consider the implications of:

- significant fluctuations
- unusual items
- relationships that are unexpected or inconsistent

with evidence from other sources. Similarly, they should consider the implications of predicted fluctuations that fail to occur.

Any significant variations should be discussed with management. Independent evidence must then be sought to validate management's explanations. The auditor's reactions to significant fluctuations or unexpected values will vary according to the stage of the audit:

- at the planning stage, the auditor will plan suitable tests
- at the testing stage of the audit, further tests and other techniques will be indicated
- at the final stage the unexpected should not happen

All fluctuations and unexpected values must be fully investigated and sufficient appropriate audit evidence obtained.

Key analytical review procedures

These procedures may well be familiar to students through their accounting studies. The main ratios are shown in Appendix 3, analysis of which should tell the story of the financial statements.

In addition to these ratios auditors can attempt analyses of all items of revenue and expense showing increases /decreases year on year (horizontal analysis) and expenses as a percentage of sales revenue (vertical analysis). Again comparisons with previous period may prove interesting.

An example of horizontal analysis of results is shown in Figure 12.3.

FIGURE 12.3 Horizontal analysis

	2X15 £	2X16 £	% Change	2X17 £	% Change
Income statement					
Revenue	257 000	286 000	11.3	294 000	2.8
Cost of sales	(224 000)	(255 000)	13.8	(258 000)	1.2
Gross profit	**33 000**	**31 000**	-6.1	**36 000**	16.1
Administration costs	(9000)	(8000)	-11.1	(10 000)	25.0
Selling and marketing costs	(11 000)	(12 000)	9.1	(15 000)	25.0
Interest	(3000)	(2000)	-33.3	(1500)	-25.0
Taxation	(2000)	(3000)	50.0	–	-100.0
Net profit	**8000**	**6000**	-25.0	**9500**	
Statement of Financial Position					
Cash and bank	7000	4000	-42.9	1500	-62.5
Inventories	12 000	14 000	16.7	18 000	28.6
Receivables	9000	11 000	22.2	15 000	36.4
Total current assets	**28 000**	**29 000**	3.6	**34 500**	19.0
Non current assets	167 000	172 000	3.0	168 000	-2.3
Total assets	**195 000**	**201 000**		**202 500**	0.7

Payables	22 000	24 000	9.1	29 000	20.8
Other current liabilities	2000	2000	0.0	1100	-45.0
Loans	15 000	13 000	-13.3	9000	-30.8
Share capital and reserves	156 000	162 000	3.8	163 400	0.9
Total liabilities and share capital	**195 000**	**201 000**	3.1	**202 500**	0.7

This analysis shows at a glance key changes that have occurred over a three-year period. Clearly there will be good and sufficient reasons for many of them but it also highlights areas of interest for the auditor such as increases in Administration and Selling costs, decline of cash and bank balances and changes to the levels of Receivables and Inventories. This is a quick and easy way to highlight key areas for audit focus.

Vertical analysis shows costs as a percentage of Revenue and, on the Statement of Financial Position, individual assets and liabilities as a percentage of total assets. This is another way to highlight changes which may indicate areas of concern to the auditor and somewhere where they could focus audit work.

	2X17 £	%	2X16 £	%	2X15 £	%
Income statement						
Revenue	294 000	100.0	286 000	100.0	257 000	100.0
Cost of sales	(258 000)	87.8	(255 000)	89.2	(224 000)	87.2
Gross profit	**36 000**	12.2	**31 000**	10.8	**33 000**	12.8
Administration costs	(10 000)	3.4	(8000)	2.8	(9000)	3.5
Selling and marketing costs	(15 000)	5.1	(12 000)	4.2	(11 000)	4.3
Interest	(1500)	0.5	(2000)	0.7	(3000)	1.2
Taxation	-	0.0	(3000)	1.0	(2000)	0.8
Net profit	**9500**	**3.2**	**6000**	**2.1**	**8000**	**3.1**
Statement of Financial Position						
Cash and bank	1500	0.7	4000	2.0	7000	3.6
Inventories	18 000	8.9	14 000	7.0	12 000	6.2
Receivables	15 000	7.4	11 000	5.5	9000	4.6
Total current assets	34 500		29 000		28 000	
Non current assets	168 000	83.0	172 000	85.6	167 000	84.6
Total assets	**202 500**	100.0	**201 000**	100.0	**195 000**	100.0
Payables	29 000	14.3	24 000	11.9	22 000	11.3
Other current liabilities	1100	0.5	2000	1.0	2000	1.0
Loans	9000	4.4	13 000	6.5	15 000	7.7
Share capital and reserves	163 400	80.7	162 000	80.6	156 000	80.0
Total liabilities and share capital	**202 500**	100.0	**201 000**	100.0	**195 000**	100.0

In this case the analysis shows a fair degree of consistency over the period and, of course, some fluctuations in the calculations may be easily explained. Any large variances in the percentages year on year would give rise to audit investigations with a view to identifying the underlying cause.

Documentation

As with all audit work, analytical procedures should be fully documented in the working papers. The files should include:

- the information examined, the sources of that information and the factors considered in establishing the reliability of the information
- the extent and nature of material variations found
- the sources and level of management from which explanations were sought and obtained
- the verification of those explanations
- any further action taken, e.g. further audit testing
- the conclusions drawn by the auditor

CASE STUDY 1

Example of use of analytical techniques

Zilpha Fashion Shops plc own a chain of high fashion shops in major towns. Each shop is operated by a separate subsidiary company. All subsidiaries buy from the parent. The auditors of the Covhampton shop are reviewing the accounts for the year ending 31.1.2X16 before starting the audit.

These reveal (in extract):

	Actual 2X15 £000s	Actual 2X16 £000s	Budget 2X16 £000s
Revenue	600	638	640
Cost of sales	(400)	(459)	(425)
Gross profit	200	179	215
Wages	(78)	(71)	(70)
Overheads	(70)	(75)	(74)
Net profit	52	33	71
Inventory	58	53	62
Payables	71	79	74

External data known to the auditors includes:

- Rate of inflation – 5%.
- A university survey, found on the internet, of the traders in the precinct in which the shop is situated indicates a 5% growth in real terms.
- The rate of gross profit achieved by other shops in the group was 34% and average inventory was 45 days' worth.
- Payables days in three other shops averaged 65 days.
- Wages in the other shops averaged 13% of Revenue.

From all this data:

- The auditors could compute estimated Revenue as $600 \times 1.05 \times 1.05 = 661$. The actual Revenue is significantly less. The difference must be investigated.
- Both the budget figures and the 2X15 numbers showed the gross profit per cent at about 34 per cent. For 2X16 gross profit based on Revenue could be estimated as $638 \times 0.34 = 217$. The actual rate of gross profit is only 28 per cent, resulting in a profit of only 179. This might be explained by the drop in Revenue if selling prices have been reduced.
- Inventory should be about 53 days' worth based on previous and budgeted figures – Actual is $53 \times 365/459 = 42$ days. Actual is lower and requires investigating.
- Payables should be around 65 days. In 2X16 they should therefore be about $79 \times 365/459 = 63$. This confirms the figure as the actual level of payables is not materially different.
- Wages perhaps ought to be $638 \times 0.13 = 83$. Wages are in line with budget and should be confirmable by considering the numbers on the staff.
- Other expenses should perhaps have risen by 5 per cent but they should be reviewed after disaggregation.

Conclusions:

- Revenue and Inventory are not in line with expectations.
- Globally other overheads are out of line and disaggregation is required.
- Sales are lower than expected. Causes may be misappropriation of inventory or cash or a reduction in selling price which might explain the reduced gross profit also. Investigation is required.
- Gross profit is anomalous. This might be as a result of cut off errors but payables seem to be about right, or could be connected to the lower than expected inventory valuation. The lower level of sales could be due to an erosion of margin caused by discounting selling prices. Receivables are negligible in this type of retail business.
- If customers pay by cash, cheque or credit card it might be that misappropriation of inventory or cash has occurred. Further investigation is required. It may be of course that the management have other explanations – burglary losses, excessive shoplifting, price competition, sales of old inventory at low prices, etc.

SUMMARY

- The level of audit testing is related to the audit risk assessment and the auditor's judgements concerning the level of materiality.
- Compliance tests are tests of controls, substantive tests are detailed tests of transactions and balances.
- Traditionally, auditors have relied upon test checks or samples in forming conclusions about populations of data.
- The size and composition of samples can be determined by the judgement of the auditor but this is considered too subjective and unreliable.
- Statistical methods are more reliable and more easily justified. These have the advantage of enabling the auditor to draw conclusions like '*I am 95 per cent certain that the error rate in the wage calculations is 1.4 per cent* $\times$ *0.3 per cent*'.
- Samples should be random, representative, protective and unpredictable.
- Sample selection methods include random, stratified, random systematic, block and value weighted or monetary unit sampling (MUS).
- Sample sizes are a function of population size, confidence levels and precision limits.

- Confidence levels and precision limits are a function of risk assessment, performance materiality and other subjective factors relating to other forms of audit evidence (internal control, analytical review, knowledge of the business, correlative factors).
- Statistical sampling can be used in all areas of an audit and with both compliance and substantive tests.
- Sampling methods include estimation sampling for variables and attribute sampling.
- Amongst the methods for obtaining audit evidence available to an auditor are analytical review procedures.
- Analytical review can be and should be carried out at all stages of the audit from planning to final review.
- The extent of use of analytical review depends on many factors but must be capable of generating sufficient reliable evidence relevant to the assertion being validated.
- Procedures include:
  - disaggregation
  - concentration on segments or single areas
  - identifying influences, assessing mathematical relationships, predicting values, comparing predictions with actual
  - examining unexpected values and seeking explanations which must be fully verified

POINTS TO NOTE

- The design of the sampling techniques is a technical matter and needs an understanding of statistics.
- Materiality is very important in auditing. In sampling materiality manifests itself in the terms 'tolerable misstatement' which can be the same as performance materiality. The term 'tolerable rate of deviation' indicates the efficiency or otherwise of internal controls.
- Risk is important. In statistical sampling this is related to the level of confidence required.
- The nature of analytical procedures includes a comparison over time and the use of past experience on the audit. Therefore, it is desirable to build up a picture of the organization and the relationship between numbers by including five- or seven-year summaries in the permanent file.
- There is a relationship between the use of analytical review and the reliability of the information being reviewed. Information which is subject to good control procedures is clearly more susceptible to analytical review techniques than other information.
- Analytical review is especially useful in obtaining evidence of completeness of accounting information.
- If anomalies are found and inadequate explanations are received, then further audit work will be necessary.

CASE STUDY 2

Hoopoe plc is an old established large food processing company mainly buying poultry from local farmers, freezing them and selling them to retailers on credit terms.

Assets employed total £6 million, revenue £15 million, profits are £1.8 million and receivables are £3 million. The company has excellent internal controls which the auditors have evaluated at the interim audit. The auditors are examining the receivables schedule. They find that there are 3900 items upon it. Four balances are over £100 000, being to large supermarket chains; 162 balances totalling £114 000 are for customers overseas.

Discussion

- Discuss the tolerable misstatement level that might be acceptable in the case of receivables.
- What audit risk factors are relevant? What substantive tests and analytical review techniques will enable the audit to reduce the detection risk?
- Outline the stages of a suitable audit sampling approach to the receivables in this case, determining the audit objectives, the population, the sampling unit, the definition of error, the sample selection method and the sampling method. In each area, discuss the difficulties which might be encountered.

CASE STUDY 3

Sheek Clothing plc is a retailer with 200 branches throughout the UK. Most of the branches are small. The inventory is a very significant item in the financial statements.

Inventory is counted physically at all branches on the nearest Sunday to 31 March and that Sunday becomes the year end. Each branch buys some inventory on its own initiative and some from the company's central buying department in Birmingham.

Discussion

- The auditors, Tickitt & Run, are planning the audit of inventory in March 2X16. How might they use statistical or other sampling methods?

CASE STUDY 4

Tickitt & Run are about to embark on the audit of Hosiah Wholesale Health Foods Ltd. The company have been established for five years and have been modestly successful. The auditors have not encountered many problems in the past except for debt collection problems and bad debts. A feature of the accounts each year has been the large amount of inventory. The management is good and monthly accounts are prepared by Hortensia Goodbody FCCA who was headhunted from the auditors. The accounts are disaggregated for management purposes into dried goods, tinned goods and specialty imports.

Discussion

- To what extent can Tickitt & Run engage in analytical techniques?
- Devise analytical techniques using financial and nonfinancial data for verifying the expense 'motor van running expenses'. The company have 20 vans.
- Devise analytical techniques for verifying sales figures. The auditors are particularly worried that they have no systems assurance that all sales have been invoiced.

STUDENT SELF-TESTING QUESTIONS

Questions with answers apparent from the text

a) Why is a 100% check not usual in auditing?

b) How does the level of sampling relate to audit risk?

c) Where is a 100% check likely to be applied?

d) What is the difference between a compliance test and a substantive test?

e) What is meant by: representative population; sampling units?

f) What is 'tolerable misstatement' and how is it related to performance materiality?

g) What factors are relevant in considering whether to sample?

h) List the stages in sampling.

i) Auditors are looking at purchases. Should they see the population to be sampled as all goods entered in the goods received book or all purchase invoices?

j) Auditors are sampling (statistically) purchase invoices to ensure that all are checked against goods inwards notes. Such checks are evidenced by the signature of a member of staff in a grid. Given the population size (25,000), the sample size (500) and that 24 items carried no signature, what should the auditors do? What conclusions can be drawn?

k) List the sampling methods available.

l) List the advantages and disadvantages of judgement sampling and of statistical sampling.

m) List some sample selection methods.

n) Distinguish level of confidence from precision interval.

o) List some statistical sampling techniques.

p) Explain monetary unit sampling.

q) Why is MUS not good for testing understatement?

r) What is tolerable rate of deviation?

s) Define analytical procedures.

t) When should analytical procedures be used?

u) What factors influence the extent of use of analytical procedures?

v) List some analytical review procedures.

w) What actions can auditors take if they find fluctuations or unexpected variations?

EXAMINATION QUESTIONS

1 There are a number of different methods of obtaining audit evidence. Methods include:
   (i)   analytical procedures;
   (ii) audit sampling;
   (iii) tests of controls;
   (iv) detailed testing of transactions and balances.
   These methods overlap and may be used for different purposes during an audit of financial statements.
   Required:

   (a) Explain the advantages and disadvantages of each of the methods of evidence-gathering listed above. *NB: You are not required to describe the methods listed above.*
   (b) Describe the relationship between the four methods of evidence-gathering described above.
   (ACCA)

   (a) Explain how analytical review procedures can contribute to an audit.
   (b) Explain how the results of analytical review can influence the nature and extent of other audit work.
   (c) Give THREE specific examples of analytical review procedures that might be carried out as part of the audit of a company that operates a chain of department stores.
   (ICAEW)

SOURCES AND ADDITIONAL READING

Financial Reporting Council (2009) *ISA 315 Identifying and Assessing the Risks of Material Misstatement through Understanding the Entity and its Environment*. London: Financial Reporting Council.

Financial Reporting Council (2009) *ISA 520 Analytical Procedures*. London: Financial Reporting Council.

Financial Reporting Council (2009) *ISA 530 Audit Sampling*. London: Financial Reporting Council.

Taylor, J. (2011) *Forensic Accounting*. Harlow: Prentice-Hall.

Upton, G. (1997) *Understanding Statistics*. Oxford: Oxford University Press.

CHAPTER 13 SYSTEMS-BASED AUDITING

Learning Objectives

After studying the material in this chapter you should be able to:

- understand the principles of a systems-based auditing approach

- emphasize the importance of communication between members of the audit team

- be able to link audit and control objectives to assertions

- understand the audit objectives, control procedures and audit tests for three components of the accounting system:

  - purchases and expenses

  - revenues

  - wages and salaries

- explain what is meant by 'significant deficiency'

- appreciate the problems faced by auditors in auditing smaller entities

INTRODUCTION

Systems-based auditing is a technique whereby the auditors review, through testing, the operation of internal control procedures within the client's accounting system.

The objective is to gather sufficient appropriate audit evidence to demonstrate that the controls are functioning well enough to give the auditors reasonable assurance that they will discover any material error or misstatement which might affect the financial statements.

Systems-based auditing was, at one time, the universally accepted method of carrying out audit work, except for the audits of the largest companies and organizations, but auditors are increasingly adopting a business-risk-based approach and moving away from detailed forms of testing where systems are considered to be reliable. This is particularly relevant as modern computer-based systems lead to improvements in internal controls, the reduction or elimination of processing errors and the ability to produce management and statistical information readily. We will look at this in the next chapter.

Students should familiarize themselves with the principles of systems-based auditing because:

- It is still tested in examinations and is likely to be for the foreseeable future.
- At some point – even using risk-based techniques – some investigation of the reliability of internal controls has to be carried out, whether this is carried out by external auditors or by evaluating the work of internal audit.
- Auditors should develop the skills of understanding financial systems in order to identify areas of potential problems and studying systems-based auditing is a good way to develop that understanding.

In this chapter we look at the systems-based approach to the most common processing cycles which are tested by examiners.

These are:

- purchases and payables
- revenues and receivables
- wages

This chapter will pull together the internal controls outlined in Chapter 9 and the assertions detailed in Chapter 11 and will also provide a list of tests whereby internal controls can be evaluated.

It is important for the learner to relate the audit tests described to the internal controls and the assertions so that a proper understanding of systems-based auditing can be obtained.

Students will, however, also need to refer to later chapters where we look specifically at testing items included in the Statement of Financial Position because, whether the audit approach is systems- or business-risk-based, the Statement of Financial Position still needs to be verified by substantive testing at some level.

TESTING SYSTEM COMPONENTS

Every system can be broken down into a series of component parts which, when linked together, form the entire system. For example, in the case of the purchases system the system can be subdivided into:

- ordering
- goods received
- invoice processing
- accounting

Auditors need to test every part of the system. They need to provide evidence that the assertions (see Chapter 11), which apply to the purchases system, have been properly tested and that there is evidence to justify the audit conclusions.

However, you will be reassured to know that, in order to do this, audit tests can be combined so that one test will provide evidence for more than one assertion in more than one part of the system. This means that auditors don't have to create a single test for every assertion for every part of the system, thus repeating work unnecessarily.

You will need to be familiar with the principles of audit sampling explained in Chapter 12 when designing audit tests.

The reasons for this are:

- You will need to be able to justify the sizes of the samples and the method chosen for selecting the sample in order to conclude that the work done meets the audit objectives.
- By selecting the direction of testing more than one assertion can be tested at the same time.

Obviously there are more tests to do to evidence these assertions, for example, the auditors might want to support a test of completeness by selecting a sample of purchase orders but this example shows how a good deal of audit time can be saved by intelligent design of audit tests.

Bearing all these aspects of audit testing in mind, let us look at specific approaches to the testing of the purchases, revenues and payroll systems.

THE PURCHASES AND EXPENSES SYSTEM

The first point to consider is the objectives of the audit of the purchases and expenses system. At this point the student should refer to the systems diagram and the description of the internal controls found in a purchasing system shown in Chapter 10. The objectives are based on the assertions set out in Chapter 11 which are shown in italics.

Audit objectives – purchases and expenses system

The audit objective is to carry out audit work so as to gather sufficient appropriate evidence to validate the assertions about the purchases system. These can be summarized as:

- Purchases of goods and services relate to the company being audited (*occurrence*).
- All purchases of goods and services that should have been recorded have been recorded (*completeness*).
- Purchases of goods and services have been recorded at the correct amounts (*accuracy*).
- All the relevant transactions have been recorded in the correct accounting period (*cut-off*).
- Purchases of goods and services have been recorded in the correct accounts in the nominal and purchase ledgers and any other related records, e.g. inventories or costing records (*classification*).

System objectives – purchases and expenses system

The purchases and expenses system has objectives which are the basis for the internal controls designed into the system.

We can consider the purchases system in three sections:

- ordering
- receipt of goods and invoicing
- accounting

These objectives, together with the assertions they relate to, can be summarized as follows.

Ordering

- All orders for goods and services are properly authorized, are for goods and services that are actually received and are for the company (*occurrence*).
- Orders are made only to authorized suppliers (*accuracy*).

Receipt of goods and invoicing

- All goods and services received are for the purposes of the business and not for the private purposes of any individual (*occurrence*).
- Goods and services are accepted only if they have been ordered (*completeness*).
- All receipts of goods and services are accurately recorded (*accuracy*).
- Liabilities are recognized for all goods and services received (*accuracy*).
- Any credits due to the business for faulty goods and services have been claimed (*completeness*).
- It is not possible to record a liability for goods or services which haven't been received (*completeness*).

Accounting

- All payments have been properly authorized (*occurrence*).
- All payments are for goods and services which have been received *(completeness).*
- All expenditure has been recorded correctly in the books and records of the business in the right accounting period (*cut-off*).
- All credit notes have been properly recorded in the books and records of the business in the right accounting period (*cut-off*).
- All entries in the purchase ledger are to the correct supplier's accounts (*classification*).
- All entries in the nominal ledger are to the correct account (*classification*).
- Cut-off procedures have been applied correctly (*cut-off*).

System controls – purchases and expenses system

The purchases and expenses system will have within controls and procedures which are designed to achieve the system objectives and minimize the possibility of fraud and error.

Learners should be familiar with the principles of internal control, i.e. SOAPSPAM, from Chapter 9, but if not you should review them before reading further.

Ordering

Segregation of duties	• separation of staff responsible for approving suppliers from those who authorize purchases orders or approve invoices
	• separation of staff responsible for raising orders from those involved in processing and paying invoices
Organizational controls	• written procedures
	• policy on ordering from approved suppliers
	• authority levels for order limits
	• defined structure of who can order what
Arithmetical and accounting checks	• pre-numbered order forms
	• review of orders placed but not delivered or invoiced
Physical controls authorization	• safeguarding blank order forms
	• all orders to be authorized by a responsible person

Delivery of goods and invoicing

Segregation of duties	• separation of staff responsible for checking goods received from those responsible for checking purchase and posting invoices

Organizational controls	• written procedures • authority limits for approving invoices • procedures for obtaining credit notes from suppliers
Physical controls	• monitoring quantity and condition of goods received • recording arrival and acceptance of goods (pre-numbered goods received notes) • recording return of goods (pre-numbered goods returned)
Authorization and approval	• matching of invoices with orders and goods received notes • matching suppliers' credit notes with goods returned notes • confirmation that invoices have been checked with orders and goods received notes

Accounting

Segregation of duties	• separation of staff responsible for checking and posting invoices from those responsible for payment
Organizational controls	• written procedures • authority limits for making payments • cheque signatories (usually minimum two)
Physical controls	• numbering supplier invoices consecutively • controls on processing invoices, e.g. batch totals • control over blank cheques • restriction of access to parts of accounting system not relating to purchases
Authorization and approval	• authorization of invoices for payment

Arithmetical and accounting checks	• checking of invoices for
	  – prices
	  – calculations
	  – quantities

	• invoices and credit notes entered into accounting records promptly • regular reconciliations of suppliers' statements with purchase ledger balances • reconciliation of purchase ledger control account with purchase ledger balances • cut off checks and accrual of goods received notes not matched by purchase invoices at the year end

Audit testing – purchases and expenses system

The auditor's objective is to test that the controls are functioning properly.

Audit work to be carried out

The key areas of audit testing for the purchases and expenses system are:

- Match invoices with:
  - goods received notes
  - purchase orders
- Check evidence that invoices are:
  - checked for arithmetic, prices and calculations by staff

- correctly coded with supplier and nominal codes
- entered in day books, ledgers and inventories records
- Test numerical sequences and enquire into missing numbers (including unused copies) of:
  - invoices
  - purchase orders
  - goods received notes
  - goods returned notes
- Obtain explanations for items outstanding for a long time – e.g. unmatched orders and goods received notes or unprocessed invoices.
- Confirm authorization of invoices approved for payment either by confirmation with authorized order or by direct authorization of invoice.
- Confirm more than one approved supplier for purchases of goods and services where possible and that orders are not sent always to the same suppliers.
- Check goods returned:
  - supported by goods returned note
  - evidence of correspondence with supplier
  - credit note entered in ledgers
  - invoices for faulty or defective goods or services cancelled
- If the records are not computer-based check a sample of postings between day books, cash book and ledger.
- Check that a sample of payments to suppliers are debited in full to correct account in purchase ledger.
- Match entries in inventories records with purchases records to ensure Inventory purchased is correctly identified in Inventory records.
- Review cut-off procedures at period end – see Chapter 15 for a detailed explanation of how to do this.
- Confirm purchase ledger control account reconciliations are carried out.
- Check evidence of reconciliation of purchase ledger balances with suppliers' statements and review the actions taken where there are disagreements unresolved.
- Check explanations for contra and journal entries in purchase ledgers.
- Examine all records for particularly large or unusual entries or transactions.

These tests can be used in different combinations and different ways to audit virtually any kind of purchases and expenses system. It is the skill of the auditor in using combinations of these tests to provide the sufficient appropriate evidence needed.

THE REVENUES (SALES) SYSTEM

Audit testing – the revenues system

The first point to consider is the objectives of the audit of the revenues system. The objectives are, again, based on the assertions. At this point the student should refer to the systems diagram and the description of the internal controls found in such a system and shown in Chapter 10. The objectives are based on the assertions set out in Chapter 11.

Audit objectives – revenues system

The audit objective is to carry out audit work so as to gather sufficient appropriate evidence to validate the assertions about the revenues system. These can be summarized as:

- Revenues from sales of goods and services relate to the company being audited (*occurrence*).
- All revenues from sales of goods and services that should have been recorded have been recorded (*completeness*).
- Revenues from sales of goods and services have been recorded at the correct amounts (*accuracy*).

- All the relevant transactions have been recorded in the correct accounting period (*cut-off*).
- Revenues from sales of goods and services have been recorded in the correct accounts in the nominal and revenues ledgers and any other related records, e.g. inventories records (*classification*).

System objectives – revenues system

The revenues systems can be considered in three sections:

- ordering and granting of credit
- despatch and invoicing
- accounting

Ordering and granting of credit

- Goods and services are supplied to customers with good credit ratings (*occurrence*).
- Orders are recorded correctly (*accuracy*).
- Customer orders are fulfilled (*occurrence*).
- Goods and services returned by customers are recorded (on goods returned notes) and the reasons investigated (*completeness*).

Despatch and invoicing

- All invoices raised relate to goods and services supplied by the business (*occurrence*).
- All despatches of goods and services are accurately recorded (*accuracy*).
- All despatches of goods or provision of services are invoiced correctly (*completeness* and *accuracy*).
- Any credit notes are only given for a valid reason (*completeness*).
- Cut off procedures are correctly applied to the recording of despatch of goods inventories records (*cut-off*).

Accounting

- All invoices and credit notes are properly recorded in the books and records in the right accounting period (*completeness*, *accuracy* and *cut-off*).
- All receipts from customers have been properly recorded (*accuracy*).
- All payments are for goods and services which have been supplied (*completeness*).
- All credit notes given have been properly recorded in the books and records of the business (*accuracy*).
- All entries in the receivables ledger are to the correct customer's accounts (*accuracy*).
- Potential or actual bad debts are identified (*accuracy*).
- All entries in the nominal ledger are to the correct account (*classification*).
- Cut-off procedures have been applied correctly (*cut-off*).

System controls – revenues system

As with the purchases and expenses system, the revenues system will have within it controls and procedures which are designed to:

- achieve the system objectives
- minimize the possibility of fraud and error

This second objective is considered to be of increasing significance to auditors who are required to approach audits with an attitude of professional scepticism.

In businesses where revenues income may be vulnerable, e.g. businesses which involve a lot of cash transactions, there is an increased risk of fraud and auditors have to be very much aware of this when they are designing their procedures.

The controls built into each part of the system will include:

Ordering and granting of credit

Organizational controls	• written procedures • authority for approving new customers • procedures to be adopted for credit checking customers
Segregation of duties	• separation of staff responsible for despatching goods or supplying services from those involved in processing invoices or collecting monies
Physical controls	• pre-numbered sales order forms • safeguarding blank sales order forms
Authorization	• authorization for changes in customer data (e.g. discount allowed) • authorization for customer credit limits
Arithmetical and accounting checks	• correct prices quoted to customers' discounts calculated correctly • VAT correctly calculated • matching of customer orders to despatch notes and queries over orders not matched

Despatches and invoicing

Organizational controls	• written procedures • authority levels for selling prices and discount arrangements • authority for issuing credit notes to customers
Segregation of duties	• separation of staff responsible for despatching goods received from those responsible for processing sales invoices
Physical controls	• monitoring quantity and condition of goods and services supplied • pre-numbering of: – delivery notes – sales invoices – goods returned notes • safeguarding blank forms • recording delivery of goods to customer (signed delivery notes) • recording return of goods by customer (pre-numbered goods returned notes)
Authorization and approval	• authorization of selling prices • authorization of discounts • special authorization of goods on special terms or free of charge • matching of sales invoices with despatch and delivery notes • matching credit notes with goods returned notes

Accounting

Organizational controls	• written procedures • authority to write-off debts
Segregation of duties	• separation of staff responsible for posting invoices and maintaining customer accounts from those responsible for receipts from customers

Physical controls	<ul><li>numbering sales invoices consecutively</li><li>controls on processing invoices, e.g. batch totals</li><li>control over unused invoice sets</li><li>control over spoilt invoices</li><li>restriction of access to parts of accounting system not relating to revenues</li></ul>
Authorization and approval	<ul><li>authorization to implement credit control procedures</li></ul>
Arithmetical and accounting checks	<ul><li>checking of invoices for: – prices – calculations</li><li>invoices and credit notes entered into accounting records promptly</li><li>sending statements to customers</li><li>production of aged receivables reports and credit control procedures</li><li>reconciliation of receivables ledger control account with receivables ledger balances</li><li>cut off checks to ensure goods despatched but not invoiced are dealt with in the correct period</li><li>analytical review of receivables ledger and profit margins</li></ul>

Audit testing – revenues system

As we've already outlined in the section above on purchases and expenses, auditors must use a mixture of compliance and substantive procedures in order to obtain the evidence they need.

The key areas of audit testing are procedures to:

- check new customer credit procedures are operating
- check new accounts and credit limits are properly authorized
- check orders only accepted from customers within credit limits
- check evidence that sales invoices are supported by customer orders:
    - signed delivery note or evidence of supply of goods or services
- check evidence that invoices are:
    - checked for arithmetic, prices and calculations, particularly of VAT
    - correctly coded with customer and nominal codes
    - entered in day books, ledgers and inventories records
- test numerical sequences and enquire into missing numbers (including unused or cancelled copies) of:
    - invoices
    - sales orders
    - delivery notes
    - goods returned notes
- check goods returned:
    - supported by goods returned note
    - evidence of correspondence with customer
    - credit note authorized
- check nonroutine revenues, e.g. scrap, sales of fixed assets
- check authorization for sale
- check evidence of arrangements for sale
- check assets removed from plant register
- check postings between day books, cash book and ledgers
- ensure receipts from customers posted to correct accounts

- investigate payments on account or round sum amounts
- investigate sums received where no invoice has been issued
- check analysis in day books
- check additions where appropriate
- check entries in inventories records for despatches of goods
- check cut-off procedures at period end
- check receivables ledger control account reconciliations
- check remittances from customers are credited in full to the correct account in receivables ledger
- check aged receivables analysis and evidence of credit control procedures such as follow-up of overdue debts
- check explanations for contra and journal entries in receivables ledgers
- examine records for particularly large or unusual receipts or transactions

These tests can be used in different combinations and different ways to audit virtually any kind of revenues system. It is the skill of the auditor in using combinations of these tests to provide the sufficient appropriate evidence needed.

Special procedures – cash revenues

There are some types of business where a significant proportion of trading activity is carried out in cash. Examples of such types of business are:

- shops and supermarkets
- bars, cafés and restaurants
- taxi firms

Auditors therefore have not only to be aware of the correct procedures for verifying that sales revenue has been recorded correctly but of the increased likelihood of fraud.
Audit procedures will also include:

- review of procedures for recording cash revenues – e.g. tills, cash sheets, etc.
- review and sample testing of reconciliations of cash taken with an independent record, e.g. a till roll
- review and sample testing of banking procedures:
  - ensure cash takings banked intact, i.e. money is not taken from cash revenues to pay small bills or top up petty cash floats
  - ensure reconciliation and banking of cash receipts is carried out by persons not responsible for revenues
  - ensure takings banked the same day to reduce cash retained on client's premises by checking paying in slip dates
  - check entries in cash book with bankings and till receipts or cash sheets

It is often very difficult to obtain conclusive proof that all cash revenues have been recorded and auditors should be alert to opportunities for recommending improvements to the client's systems wherever possible.

THE PAYROLL SYSTEM

Audit testing – the payroll system

The objectives of the payroll system are similar to those of the purchases and expenses system insofar as the business only wants to pay for work done and at the correct rate. At this point the student should refer to the systems diagram and the description of the internal controls found in such a system and shown in Chapter 10.
The objectives are based on the assertions set out in Chapter 11.

Although wages and salaries are often mentioned separately there are many common features from an audit point of view. The principal differences are that wages tend to be paid weekly and often vary from week to week with overtime or piecework payments. Piecework is based on the amount of work an employee completes rather than the length of time they spend at work. Salaries on the other hand tend to be paid monthly, be the same amount each month and only vary with, say, commission payments or bonuses.

In some businesses wages are paid weekly in cash. Nowadays this tends to be quite rare in all but the smallest businesses, mainly for reasons of security, but we will mention a few points relating to wages paid in cash so you can understand the special issues involved in that situation. It can, of course, still apply where casual labour is paid in cash where individuals such as refugees or asylum seekers are employed and have no bank account or where employees are paid through Gangmasters.

The common features when considering both wages and salaries are:

- All employees have to have a contract of employment setting out terms and conditions of employment.
- Rates of pay have to be agreed.
- All deductions either have to be statutory (e.g. PAYE and NI) or authorized by the employee (e.g. pension contributions).
- Calculations of tax and NI are basically the same for monthly paid and weekly paid workers.
- They have to be paid on time.

Where businesses have a mixture of weekly and monthly paid employees there may be two payrolls. The weekly payroll may be prepared by specialized staff in a separate department whereas the monthly payroll may be prepared by a senior official of the company, particularly if it includes salary payments for senior managers and directors. It may be outsourced to an independent body in which case the auditors will have to adopt some separate procedures as outlined in Chapter 22.

In that case the auditor will have to carry out separate tests on each payroll to ensure both are being operated correctly.

It is possible that some of the work that auditors do can be used to validate both types of payment. For convenience we will cover both wages and salaries together and highlight areas which relate only to one type of payment.

Confidentiality – payroll

As discussed in Chapter 6, auditors have to treat all the information they gather from dealing with a client's affairs as confidential. This is very much the case when dealing with payroll as matters such as the rate of pay between individuals can be a very sensitive subject.

The payroll system contains a lot of personal data about employees including:

- rate of pay
- deductions
- home address
- bank details
- birth date
- National Insurance number

all of which is confidential information and can be used by unscrupulous individuals as raw material for 'identity theft'.

The auditor should be very much aware of this and it is quite often the case that only the more senior members of the audit team are allowed access to payroll data.

Care also has to be taken when documenting tests on the audit files so confidential information about individual employees should be kept to a minimum. The important thing is to meet the audit objectives from a company-wide point of view so employees can be identified by a work number, payroll number or clock number rather than by name in audit documentation.

Audit objectives – payroll system

The audit objective is to carry out audit work so as to gather sufficient appropriate evidence to validate the assertions about the payroll system. These can be summarized as:

- Payment for wages and salaries relate to work done for the company being audited (*occurrence*).
- All payments of wages and salaries that should have been recorded have been recorded (*completeness*).
- Wages and salaries and any deductions relating to them have been calculated and recorded at the correct amounts (*accuracy*).
- All the relevant payments and liabilities have been recorded in the correct accounting period (*cut-off*).
- Payments of wages and salaries have been recorded in the correct accounts in the nominal ledger and any other related records, e.g. costing records (*classification*).

There are businesses where payroll can be a particularly difficult area such as those involving a lot of casual workers where sums are paid in cash often with little documentation. Where there is a risk of fraud it is the practice that auditors have to be very much aware of this when they are designing their procedures.

System controls – payroll

As with the purchases and revenues systems the payroll system will have within it controls and procedures which are designed to:

- achieve the system objectives
- minimize the possibility of fraud and error

The payroll system can be subdivided into two parts:

- basis of payroll calculation
- payment of wages and salaries and accounting

Basis of payroll calculation

Organizational controls	• written procedures
	• approved wage and salary rate lists
	• procedures to be adopted for starters and leavers
Segregation of duties	• separation of staff responsible for preparing payroll from those involved in payment
	• separation of staff involved in personnel administration from staff involved with payroll
Physical controls	• restriction of access to payroll office
	• restriction of access to parts of accounting/computer system not relating to relevant payroll
Authorization	• authorization for changes in rates
	• employee authorization for non-statutory deduction
	• authorization of hours worked
	• authorization of bonuses
	• authorization of commission payments
	• authorization of piece work payments
Arithmetical and accounting checks	• correct basic rates set as basis for calculation of gross pay
	• correct overtime rates applied
	• piecework payments reconciled to completed quantities

- tax codes applied for correct tax years as notified by HM Revenue & Customs
- computerized payroll upgrades received and applied following tax rate changes

Calculation and payment of wages

Organizational controls	• written procedures • separate payroll department from personnel department • individual personnel file for each employee
Segregation of duties	• separation of staff responsible for preparation of wages from those authorizing payment
Physical controls	• filling of pay packets by staff not involved with preparing payroll • general security of cash in transit and on premises • distribution of wage packets by staff not involved with preparing payroll • controls for security of unclaimed cash wages
Authorization	• payroll authorized by responsible official before payment • wages cheques signed by two senior officers of the company not connected with payroll preparation • BACS transfer signed by two senior officers of the company not involved in wages preparation
Arithmetical and accounting checks	• wages control account • reconciliation of payroll between dates • payment of PAYE and NI to HM Revenue and Customs • comparison and reconciliation with budget figures

Audit testing – payroll

The tests performed on payroll are basically designed to ensure that:

- internal controls are working
- the scope for fraud is limited

Payroll has often been a vulnerable area to fraud but the decline in the payment of cash wages has limited the opportunities open to the fraudster and the use of reliable payroll software has further eroded the possibility of falsifying payroll details in order to defraud the business. However, this does not reduce the auditor's responsibility to ensure that the systems are functioning correctly.

The key areas of audit testing are designed to test that:

- all employees exist
- all employees are paid at the correct rate
- all deductions from wages are properly calculated
- net pay and deductions are accounted for correctly

Again the audit work will consist of a mixture of compliance and substantive tests.

The main procedures are:

- check authorized rates of pay are being used
- confirm authorization procedures operating with regard to:
  - clock cards, job cards, time sheets or other evidence of time worked
  - production records for payments based on productivity
  - signed lists for bonuses

- approved lists for commission payments to sales staff
- check calculations of gross to net pay for a sample of employees verifying authorization for and calculation of:
  - gross pay
  - overtime payments
  - piecework payments
  - PAYE and NI using HM Revenue and Customs documents, e.g. coding notices
  - holiday pay
- inspect authorized payment lists for BACS transfers
- obtain cancelled cheques from bank and compare to payroll
- test non-statutory deductions from payroll authorized by employee
- test holiday pay calculations
- observe delivery of pay advice to employees
- ascertain reason for any pay advice not delivered
- check additions and calculations on payroll
- reconcile movements in payroll for two different periods
- test starters and leavers procedures applied to payroll, i.e. ensure leavers removed at correct date and starters started on correct date
- check payroll summary to payroll
- check payroll summary to nominal ledger
- check any cost analysis reconciles to payroll
- check salary payments are in accordance with contracts of employment
- ensure payments made to HM Revenue and Customs within permitted period to clear tax and NI creditor

For payment of cash wages:

- check the packets to the payroll to ensure each employee has a packet
- attend wages payout and observe procedures
- check procedures are secure from point of view of staff paying out
- ensure all wage packets signed for by recipients
- check no employee receives more than one packet
- check unclaimed wages entered in unclaimed wages book
- check unclaimed wages details with payroll
- ascertain reason for unclaimed wages

Most payroll systems operate on broadly the same principles, although there are frequently special arrangements for calculating such things as overtime or commission. Auditors can apply the principles outlined above to their audit of both weekly and monthly payrolls, adapting them to suit the particular circumstances of each client.

SIGNIFICANT DEFICIENCIES

During the course of their work the auditors may well encounter:

- errors or mistakes; and
- areas where the internal controls (Chapter 9) are not functioning as well as management might like them to.

Where the errors are minor the auditors should simply record them and, initially, do nothing. However, an accumulation of minor errors may become a major error once the level of performance materiality (Chapter 10) threshold has been passed.

In addition to processing or recording errors, audit staff may discover that an internal control check or process is not being carried out properly, or indeed does not exist at all.

Errors above a **threshold amount**, below which they are clearly trivial, and failures or weaknesses in internal control may, in the judgement of the auditors, be of such importance as to constitute a **significant deficiency**. Significant deficiencies must be reported to management by the auditors and they use a Letter of Weakness or Management Letter to do this. There is no legal requirement on the auditors to do this but ISA 265 '*Communicating deficiencies in internal control to those charged with governance and management*' requires them to do so. We look at this in more detail in Chapter 27.

THE AUDIT OF SMALL ENTITIES

The ISAs we have been considering throughout this book contain provisions for small companies so, apart from the ethical provisions detailed in Chapter 6, audits of smaller entities should, within reason, be conducted with the same considerations as the audit of a larger entity. There is no difference, as far as the standard and quality of audit work and the evidence gathering requirements are concerned, between a small entity and the largest audit. The differences are based around:

- Ethical considerations – smaller entities present different threats to audit independence than larger ones.
- Audit strategy – the emphasis is likely to be much more orientated towards substantive testing approaches than it would be for a larger entity.
- Documentation – some of the rules on documenting audit processes are relaxed for smaller entities, basically because they are evident from the audit work carried out.
- The limitations smaller entities have in respect of such factors as risk evaluation, internal control and the involvement of and representations from management.

Most ISAs have a separate paragraph '*Considerations Specific to Smaller Entities*' which deals with any points relevant to them. For our purposes we will deal with the full audit requirements according to the standards but the special problems presented by smaller entities should be borne in mind.

Small organizations, however, present problems because of their intrinsic characteristics, in particular:

- The somewhat closer relationship auditors of smaller organizations have with owner/managers or trustees and the dangers of blurring ethical boundaries (Chapter 6).
- Auditors are often seen as advisors, particularly in the case of owner/managers or trustees who may have limited financial experience and they tend to become involved with their clients at a much deeper level than would the auditors of a larger business so there is a danger of them becoming inadvertently involved in management decisions.

Smallness and uncomplicated activities, and the close personal relationship with auditors, make a thorough knowledge of the business much easier but can make it difficult for the auditors to raise contentious issues with the management. This can, however, help in reducing 'know your client' documentation (Chapter 8) as the smaller entity is generally simpler and the internal financial systems less complex than those of a larger organization.

Internal control

The auditor faces particular problems with internal control in smaller entities. These are:

- Internal control, or more likely the lack of it, is the biggest problem the auditors face. Small businesses tend to have:
  - a concentration of ownership and management
  - few sources of income and uncomplicated activities
  - relatively uncomplicated record keeping and limited management information
- Segregation of duties is often a major problem as there are usually limited numbers of staff.
- Bookkeeping might be fairly informal without much in the way of systems. Whilst some level of basic controls might be instituted, e.g. pre-printed, consecutively numbered sales invoices, wages preparation done independently, etc. the auditor is often not able to rely on them for audit purposes to any significant extent.
- Owner-managers generally have unlimited opportunities for overriding what controls there are.

Failure to separate corporate and private activities

One of the biggest problems facing the auditors is the lack of distinction owner-managers often have between assets and income which belong to the company and assets and income which belong to them as individuals. Similarly, costs may be charged to the company which are, in fact, personal expenditure.

As a result, errors may be overlooked, assets may be misappropriated and fraudulent transactions take place and the auditors can be put under pressure to 'turn a blind eye'. This can become difficult for the auditors if they have developed a good personal relationship with their client.

Conversely, owner-managers can exercise much personal control over transactions so auditors should neither assume that management is dishonest nor assume unquestioned honesty.

Problems arise when businesses are expanding rapidly. Owner-managers give their time to the expansion of the business and do not worry about bookkeeping procedures. They may also lose some of the day-to-day contact with aspects of the business which creates opportunities for fraud and error.

Specific audit considerations

As always, the first duty is for the auditors to consider the suitability of the firm to accept the assignment. This will involve not only the usual procedures centred on finding out about the suitability of the client (Chapter 8) but also consideration of the level of costs which the client might incur and the relative size of the client and the audit firm.

It may be that the auditors are familiar with the client's business and management due to the close nature of the relationship, but the important thing to remember is that the appointment would be that of *auditor* which carries with it specific ethical considerations, particularly those of independence and integrity.

Specific audit considerations and procedures include:

- Agree an Engagement Letter. This is essential as it will set out, for the benefit of both the auditors and the client, the precise nature of the relationship between them. Whilst the relationship may be somewhat less formal than with a larger client it will remove any misunderstandings as to the role the auditors will play.
- Where there is to be a significant level of accountancy work it may not be possible to accept the appointment as auditor because of the threat of self review.
- Plan the work to be done, including the materiality level.
- With small company clients the emphasis is likely to be on a high level of substantive checking work because of the inadequacies of the internal control environment.
- In particular, key items such as inventories and trade receivables will be significant. Other audit areas to consider include verification that all income has been received and that costs are all bona fide business expenses and do not include any element of private expenses.
- The important consideration for the auditor is that, if internal controls are weak, no amount of substantive testing will give the auditors the assurance they need. The particular problem is likely to be completeness – especially if the business deals with a lot in cash.
- If the auditors cannot gather sufficient appropriate audit evidence they should decline to express an opinion. Completeness is a major problem for small audits due to the lack of internal controls and the possible danger of owner-managers manipulating the business for their own purposes. It is not always possible for auditors to ensure that all the transactions are reflected in the records.
- Included in the checking work should be an in-depth analytical review of the financial statements. It is not easy to determine the depth of this but it will include comparing ratios against previous years, budgets and industry averages. Other matters may include inspecting an aged list of receivables for anomalies and reviewing items that require particular management judgement. Problems may arise if the amount of management information is limited or rather simplistic and, of course, if internal controls are weak the underlying information may not be totally reliable.
- The auditor may be faced with some problems concerning comparability if the business is expanding.
- Obtain management representations (Chapter 24). Whilst these are not a substitute for audit evidence they may be supportive where other audit evidence exists. **Letters of Representation** may be relied on to a greater extent

than in the audit of larger businesses and should be used to focus management's attention on particular issues, supported by analytical review and substantive procedures.

- Consider subsequent events, i.e. events after the performance of the audit up to the date the financial statements are approved. Particular attention needs to be paid to **going concern** issues (see Chapter 23).
- The audit report should contain either a disclaimer or an 'except for' opinion on the grounds of, effectively, limitation of audit evidence if the records or explanations are not considered adequate (see Chapter 26).
- Occasionally the uncertainty surrounding small businesses can be so pervasive that the business is unauditable. In such cases it may be better to decline to accept or to resign the post of auditor. There is no point in a **disclaimer of opinion** as this really negates the purpose of carrying out any audit work and incurs costs the client will be reluctant to pay!

SUMMARY

- A system can be broken down into its component parts and each part tested separately.
- Directional tests should be used especially for testing completeness.
- It is necessary to link audit testing to control objectives and assertions.
- Tests can be combined to validate more than one assertion simultaneously.
- Tests must be relevant to the assertion being evidenced.
- Tests are designed to ensure control objectives are being achieved.
- Significant deficiencies must be reported to management.
- Audit issues centre on the degree of control the owner-manager may have and the lack of proper internal controls.
- Auditors need to ensure they maintain their independence, particularly where they are advising their client or assisting in the raising of finance.
- Lack of segregation of duties and override of controls by owner-managers are the biggest problems the auditor faces when reviewing the effectiveness of internal controls in smaller organizations.
- Auditors cannot rely on management representations for the audit of smaller organizations – they must still gather evidence to support their opinion.
- Going concern and completeness are key audit issues for small entities.

POINTS TO NOTE

- Fraud is an issue in auditing and auditors must be aware of the possibilities of fraud or the potential for misstatement, particularly where cash is concerned.
- Systems-based auditing is often tested in examinations as it is still the basis for many audits.

CASE STUDY 2

Tickitt & Run are in the process of completing the audit of their client Fredbare Ltd, a manufacturer of swimwear and sports clothing.

They have just carried out the interim audit and have discovered the following:

1   The audit team have discovered that the purchases system has changed. They have provided the following description of the purchasing system. No other controls exist apart from those described.

- Fredbare has no specific buying department so employees can place orders with suppliers in their own area of responsibility. A three-part order form is used; copy 1 is retained by the originator, copy 2 is sent to the goods inward department and copy 3 is sent to the supplier.

- Goods are received, but not checked, by the warehouse personnel who also deal with inventories control and dispatches. Once received, the advice notes and purchase order for those goods are sent to the purchase ledger clerk.

- When the supplier's invoice is received the purchase ledger clerk checks the calculations on it, initials it and staples the advice note and purchase order to it. The purchase ledger clerk enters the invoice on to the purchase ledger.

- The invoice is then sent to the manager responsible for the employee who ordered the goods. The manager codes the invoice and returns it to the purchase ledger clerk. Purchase invoices are coded, entered on an analysis sheet and posted to the nominal ledger monthly by journal entry.

- The cashier pays suppliers monthly on instructions from the purchase ledger clerk. The purchase ledger control account is reconciled monthly by the purchase ledger clerk who also reconciles suppliers' statements.

- On a number of occasions goods have been delivered to customers but no invoice raised.

2   In the wages department the wages for staff are based on clock cards for factory staff which are passed to the wages department on Monday morning by the night watchman whose job it is to put new cards out ready for the staff. Weekly paid office staff are paid the same every week so don't need to complete any form of time sheet.

Wages are made up by Mrs Bobbin with assistance from one part-time member of staff and occasional secondment from the office. Mrs Bobbin calculates the wages, adjusts for any starters, leavers and any other changes, and produces the payroll.

You are required

To list any weaknesses, you can identify in the above systems. You should amplify the weakness as appropriate, explain its implications and suggest recommendations for improvement.

STUDENT SELF-TESTING QUESTIONS

Questions with answers apparent from the text

a)   What is the basis of systems-based auditing?

b)   What are control objectives?

c)   List control objectives for a purchasing system.

d)   What types of control would there be in a revenues credit system?

e)   What types of control would there be in a wages system?

f)   What audit tests would be performed on purchase invoices?

g)   When would cash balances not be audited?

h) What is the main principle of segregation of duties?

i) Why is it important?

j) List other forms of internal controls.

k) How would you verify the existence of an arithmetical control?

l) What are the key audit considerations when auditing small businesses?

EXAMINATION QUESTIONS

1 Your firm is the external auditor of Bestwood Engineering Ltd which manufactures components for motor vehicles and sells them to motor vehicle manufacturers and wholesalers. It has Revenues of around £20m and a profit before tax of £800 000.

  The company has a new financial director who has asked you for advice on controls in the company's purchasing system.

  Bestwood Engineering has separate accounts, purchasing and goods received departments. Most purchases are required by the production department but other departments are able to raise requisitions for goods and services. The purchasing department is responsible for obtaining goods and services at the lowest price which is consistent with the required delivery date and quality and for ensuring their prompt delivery.

  The accounts department is responsible for obtaining authorization of purchase invoices before they input to the computer which posts them to the purchase ledger and the nominal ledger. The accounting records are kept on a computer and the standard accounting software was obtained from an independent supplier. The accounting software maintains the revenues ledger, the purchase ledger, nominal ledger and payroll. The company does not maintain inventories records as it believes the cost of maintaining these records outweighs the benefits.

  The financial director has explained that services include gas, electricity, telephone repairs and short-term hire of equipment and vehicles.

  Required:

  (a) Describe the procedures which should be in operation in the purchasing department to control the purchase and receipt of goods.

  (b) Describe the controls the accounts department should exercise over obtaining authorization of purchase invoices before posting them to the purchase ledger.

  (c) Explain how controls over the purchase of services, from raising the purchase requisition to posting the invoice to the purchase ledger, might differ from the procedures for the purchase of goods described in your answers to parts (a) and (b).

  (ACCA)

2 You are responsible for the statutory audit of Servit Ltd (Servit) for the year ended 30 November 2X16. Servit provides industrial maintenance services to companies operating in the engineering sector. Customers sign a standard contract for each job which can last between 1 and 15 days. The company charges for its services hourly and all claims for work done have to be submitted to customers for approval before invoicing.

  Historically only the receivables ledger was computerized and the company experienced a number of invoicing errors, including failure to invoice, which had a detrimental effect on the cash collection. In order to reduce errors and speed up the invoicing and cash collection process the company has upgraded its computer system.

  A new system which integrates job costing, payroll, invoicing and ledger processing was implemented during the year ended 30 November 2X16.

  Under the new system each job is logged on the computer and the software automatically allocates a sequential job number and produces time logs to be completed by each contract manager. Each contract manager inputs daily the hours worked by each employee and the system generates a copy of the time log to be approved by the customer. At the end of each week, or on completion of a job if less than a week, an invoice is generated from the information stored on the system and details are automatically posted to the receivables ledger and revenues account in the nominal ledger. Customers are required to pay within 30 days of invoice date.

  In addition to the time logs and invoices, the system routinely produces statements of customer balances and reports detailing:

  ● standing data amendments
  ● age analysis of receivables and
  ● list of customer balances

Required:

(a) State the responsibilities of external auditors and directors in relation to the design and operation of internal control systems.

(b) Describe the control procedures that should be in place in the receivables system to:
   (i) reduce the risk of invoicing errors, including failure to invoice promptly or at all; and
   (ii) speed up the cash collection process.

(c) Outline the audit procedures you would undertake in order to ensure that receivables are fairly stated in the financial statements of Servit for the year ended 30 November 2X16.

(ICAEW)

SOURCES AND ADDITIONAL READING

Financial Reporting Council (2009) *ISA 265 Communicating Deficiencies in Internal Control to Those Charged with Governance and Management*. London: Financial Reporting Council.

Financial Reporting Council (2009) *ISA 315 Identifying and Assessing Risks of Material Misstatement through Understanding the Entity and its Environment*. London: Financial Reporting Council.

Financial Reporting Council (2009) *ISA 402 Audit Considerations Relating to an Entity Using a Service Organization*. London: Financial Reporting Council.

Financial Reporting Council (2009) *ISA 450 Evaluation of Misstatements Identified during the Audit*. London: Financial Reporting Council.

Financial Reporting Council (2009) *ISA 500 Audit Evidence*. London: Financial Reporting Council.

CHAPTER 14
RISK-BASED AUDITING

Learning Objectives

After studying the material in this chapter you should be able to:

- understand the definition of business risk

- differentiate it from audit risk

- understand the difference in the purpose of the risk assessment between the two approaches

- understand the various types of external and internal risk which can affect a business' performance

- explain the importance of understanding the client's approach to risk

- explain the process of risk assessment

- explain the formal processes involved in COSO (the Committee of Sponsoring Organizations of the Treadway Commission) and CRSA (Control and Risk Self Assessment)

- understand what is meant by the 'top down approach'

- understand the audit planning implications of risk-based auditing

- discuss the need for substantive testing of the statement of financial position

INTRODUCTION

The definition of *business risk* contained in ISA 315 *'Identifying and assessing the risks of material misstatement through understanding the entity and its environment'* is:

> *'A risk resulting from significant conditions, events, circumstances, actions or inactions that could adversely affect an entity's ability to achieve its objectives and execute its strategies, or from the setting of inappropriate objectives and strategies.'*

It can be split between both external and internal factors which affect the organization both by virtue of the environment in which it operates and through its own internal structures, policies and processes.

The auditor is not simply required to certify that a set of accounts are 'true and fair' the auditor is required to express an opinion. Clearly this implies that auditors will not achieve that level of certainty that the financial statements are totally free from error or misstatement. If they could do so they could give a 'certificate' to that effect, rather they are expected to state that in their opinion the financial statements are true and fair.

Clearly therefore there is always some element of doubt caused by the fact that, under normal circumstances, the auditor cannot achieve a level of absolute assurance. Rather they will attempt to obtain 'reasonable assurance and this means that there is always a risk that something has been missed, that they have been misled or that the work that they have done has been somehow inadequate. Performing a failed audit often leads to legal action against the auditor.

Auditors strive to perform audits in an efficient and economical manner and constantly strive to reduce the level of audit work that they carry out as audit fees are time based and carrying out audit testing involves a time commitment. Consequently, auditors walk the tightrope between reducing the amount of work they do and still getting the level of assurance they need.

This involves risk.

Auditors seek to evaluate the risks of them not being able to achieve the right level. In Chapter 10 we looked at the topic of audit risk – the risk that the auditor will give an incorrect audit opinion and we looked at the relationship between:

- inherent and control risk, which together can be classed as business risk; and
- audit risk

and we saw that the more audit work that is performed, the more checking work is done, the lower the level of audit risk.

Tied into this is the question of materiality, which we also looked at in Chapter 10 – the auditor is only looking to ensure that any errors or mistakes are not material – i.e. they would not affect the economic decisions of a user of the accounts.

In previous chapters we established that the stronger the control environment within the client entity the less substantive testing work the auditors have to do and the more they could rely on the internal controls and the checks and balances within the entity's own systems. Where the control environment is strong auditors may be more likely to be of the view that material errors or mistakes will not come from the processing of routine transactions. Instead they may prefer to look at the risks the business faces, the problems it may have in running its business and the factors which influence the course of its activities – in other words the business risks it faces every day.

The business risk approach to auditing involves:

- looking at the business in its entirety
- evaluating the various risks the business faces
- considering the impact, if any, that those risks might have on the financial statements

The concept behind this approach is that as all businesses face risks in their normal course of activity. An understanding of these risks requires the auditor to have a thorough understanding of the client's business, which will tend to suggest where misstatements are most likely to occur in the financial statements.

Relevant auditing standards here are ISA 315 'Obtaining an Understanding of the Entity and its Environment and Assessing the Risks of a Material Misstatement' and ISA 330 'The Auditor's Procedures in Response to Assessed Risk.'

Students must clearly understand that this approach is not the same as the systems-based approach to auditing we covered in Chapter 13. Systems-based auditing also involves a risk assessment process but this is part of the process of evaluating the client's systems and of identifying areas where audit attention could be focused – in other words, that risk assessment is protective of audit risk. The business risk approach covered in this chapter has some similarities, insofar as there is a risk assessment process in both approaches which might cover a lot of the same ground, but the business risk approach is all about risk and not about systems so it is a lot more intense.

Auditors, as part of their risk assessment processes when evaluating audit risk (Chapter 10), should evaluate the organization's risk assessment processes based on their knowledge of it and its trading environment and come to their own conclusions as to its effectiveness. Sound risk assessment processes by management are an integral part of the control environment and, consequently, auditors should be very much aware of the effectiveness of these management processes.

They should review the management's assessments of risk as an integral part of their audit planning.

EXTERNAL RISKS

It is an obvious statement but needs to be made at the outset. There is no such thing as a foolproof risk assessment process and, however well thought out and operated, organizations will continue to be surprised by the unexpected or by events which, with hindsight, might have been anticipated. However, the organization must do what it can to reduce the likelihood of unexpected events and to minimize the damage caused if one materializes.

There are several types of risk arising from outside the organization.

Political risk

These are risks arising from changes in government policy and also risks arising from changes in the political climate. This may be particularly relevant to companies operating globally where, in some countries, the political situation may suffer sudden and often violent change. This may bring with it, for example, the threat of nationalization of assets or actions against foreign ownership. In more stable countries a change in the political climate may have an effect on economic policy which, in turn, could affect such things as increased regulation, inflation and interest rates.

EXAMPLE 1

The effect of the referendum on leaving the EU and any consequent knock-on effects on the business.

Economic risk

This is the risk caused by changes in the economic situation of the country which might result in changes in anticipated levels of inflation, higher or lower unemployment, interest rate movements, etc. It may also result in increased competition from low-cost producers from abroad. Again, auditors have to consider the risks applicable in all the countries in which the business operates.

EXAMPLE 2

The effect on UK manufacturing of increasing competition from low-cost producers in Eastern Europe, India and China.

Legislative risk

Changes in legislation may result in restrictions to operations or increased costs of compliance. Environmental legislation has increased 'clean up' costs and businesses increasingly have to provide information to government bodies.

EXAMPLE 3

Clean up costs and damages paid arising from asbestos-related claims. Claims against oil companies in connection with oil spills.

Compliance risk

This is the risk arising from non-compliance with laws and regulations. Most organizations are capable of ensuring compliance with tax or VAT rules but many still have, judging by the number of cases still coming before the courts and tribunals, inadequate procedures for complying with employment law or health and safety legislation.

It is particularly relevant in the area where the law and finance interact, in particular with reference to such matters as money laundering, insider dealing and tax or VAT fraud.

EXAMPLE 4

Damages for constructive dismissal arising from sexual harassment awarded against financial institutions in the City of London.

Physical risk

Evaluation of physical risk includes consideration of natural hazards such as floods, fires, tornados and the effects of global warming. It includes problems caused to organizations because of loss of power or water supplies, deliberate damage to machinery or equipment often by disgruntled employees, key component failures, etc. It also includes the risk of problems caused to the business or its employees because of direct or implied terrorist action, particularly where companies operate in some of the more volatile parts of the world.

EXAMPLE 5

The damage caused to businesses as a result of arson by disaffected employees.

Technological risk

Many businesses, and not only those involved in so-called 'hi-tech' operations, face risks from new and developing technologies. Businesses which fail to spot the potential or the risks to their existing operations presented by new and emerging technologies may well find themselves overtaken by competition or find their markets so radically changed they are no longer able to compete in them.

Developments in computing are an obvious area for most businesses but more scientific advances such as developments in biotechnologies may well lead to changes which will have a major impact on current businesses.

EXAMPLE 6

Electronic books such as the Kindle and the E-reader affecting the business models for conventional booksellers.

Market risk

Risks arising from sudden or unexpected changes in the company's market e.g. increased competition, price wars, new products, etc.

EXAMPLE 7

The development of internet-based music downloads threatens the high street record retailer.

Financial risk

This is probably the biggest single area affecting businesses and is very wide ranging. It includes:

- Credit risk – the risks arising from nonpayment of debts due either to insolvency of customers, fraud or unresolved disputes.
- Foreign exchange risk – risks caused by trading in foreign currencies or the translation risk on the conversion of assets held in foreign currencies in overseas subsidiaries to UK £.
- Interest rate risks – risks to business financing caused by unexpected movements in interest rates.

Many businesses have examples of losses arising from unpaid debts – insolvency causes many defaults in payments and several high profile insolvency cases also involve some element of fraud. Problems caused by trading in complex financial instruments, coupled with some element of failure of internal systems, caused the collapse or near collapse of several banks in the UK, USA and Iceland with predictable knock-on effects in the economic situation.

EXAMPLE 8

Lehman Brothers (USA), Royal Bank of Scotland (UK), Setanta (Ireland), Landsbanki (Iceland).

Note that organizations often face a combination of risks so auditors should avoid the temptation of adopting a 'tick list' approach and consider the possibility of what might be perceived to be a number of low-level risks combining to produce a very serious problem.

An understanding of the risks facing a client adds to an auditor's understanding of the client. The auditors also need to extrapolate their risk analysis into a consideration of how some of these may affect the financial statements. Some may affect the value of assets and some may affect the going concern concept for all or part of the enterprise.

INTERNAL RISKS

These are risks arising from inside the company and include the following.

Strategic risk

This involves management making a set of bad strategic decisions which define the company's objectives wrongly and result in trading losses and, in the worse cases, insolvency.

Strategic risk includes:

- emphasis on outdated or outmoded products
- attempting to break in to unfamiliar markets without adequate expertise
- inappropriate or expensive acquisitions
- poor planning processes
- lack of focus on key objectives by senior management
- lack of key performance indicators
- poor monitoring procedures
- inadequate management information systems

Operational risk

These are risks caused by underlying flaws in the way the business is carried on, its processes and systems. These are not confined to manufacturing industry: the failure to correct poor processes affecting customer service has adversely affected many service-based organizations.

Operational risk includes:

- failure to modernize products and processes
- diversification into business areas where the organization has no expertise
- poor quality products or customer service
- increased competition from low cost suppliers
- increased use of electronic media to trade
- poor labour relations
- weak marketing
- loss of key employees
- breakdown of relationships with key suppliers or customers
- reliance on a few products, customers, suppliers
- lack of research and development of new products

Governance risk

Risks to the organization can be created by poor or inadequate Corporate Governance (see Chapter 2). This includes problems arising from inappropriate board structures, poor communications within the business and no support for a strong internal control environment.

Governance risk includes:

- excessive reliance on a dominant chief executive
- weak or non-existent non-executive directors
- weak or incompetent executives
- lack of board review and performance evaluation
- ineffective decision making processes
- poor monitoring of operational decisions
- poor internal control environment
- failure to communicate goals and objectives
- inefficient feedback mechanisms and poor corporate communications
- lack of, or ineffective, internal audit function

Financial risks

These include risks arising both from the structure and financing of the business and the operation of financial systems. Auditors have to consider not only the detail of the financial processes within the business but the appropriateness of its structure and the ability to finance its operations so as to achieve its objectives for the **foreseeable future**.

Financial risks include:

- inadequate finance for future operations or development of new products and markets
- high levels of gearing at a time of rising interest rates
- overtrading resulting in cash flow difficulties
- related parties involved in the business with no obvious commercial motive or inappropriate terms of trading
- systems failures and loss of records

- internal control weaknesses
- fraud

Any of these risks can damage a company and may impact on the financial statements.

The auditor thus has to consider two things before embarking on audit planning. These are how well do I know my client and all aspects of its operations and will my audit procedures identify all the potential risks my client faces? The auditor must decide whether they can, from what they have discovered about their client, anticipate the key risks which may result in a serious error or misstatement in the financial statements.

THE CLIENT'S APPROACH TO RISK

Many smaller companies do not have a formal risk assessment process and their goals and objectives may not be incorporated into detailed plans. Such companies though are often very flexible, know their markets and can respond quickly to threats and changes.

Larger organizations often have a hierarchy of plans involving:

- *Strategic planning* – longer-term planning (often incorporating a Mission Statement or Statement of Goals). This may include Key Performance Indicators (KPIs) which indicate progress towards stated objectives.
- *Detailed tactical planning* – shorter-term operational planning in order to achieve milestones or goals as part of the achievement of the wider strategic plan.
- *Budgets and forecasts* – in detail for shorter-term tactical plans and sometimes on a wider scale to consider financing implications as part of strategy planning.

Auditors need to be familiar with the plans and the processes which are used to derive the plans. In other words, they need to be assured that both strategic and operational planning, and the financial information derived from it, is based on an ordered and systematic consideration of the business' future carried out by experienced and competent senior management.

Where the management use KPIs to evaluate achievement the auditor must reassure themselves that the KPIs are valid indicators and that they have been properly evaluated and calculated.

As part of the development of these plans the organization should carry out risk assessments from which the auditors can begin to derive their audit planning.

Risk assessment

This has two components:

- risk identification
- risk evaluation

Risk identification requires the organization to carry out a systematic review of itself its place in its industry and its industry's place in the wider economic context.

This encompasses consideration of all the forms of risk highlighted above. It is not appropriate for the company simply to identify all its internal risks; it must look at the factors affecting its own industry and the wider economic and social factors which might have an impact on its industry.

Often organizations are surprised by events which do them harm. Frequently a post-disaster review reveals that the organization could have foreseen the catastrophe coming had it been alert to danger signs. Of course this will not help predict a sudden catastrophic event such as a fire or explosion (although good safety practice may minimize damage) but it may help anticipate commercial difficulties if the organization is able to read the signs of impending doom.

EXAMPLE 9

A good example of this need for wider considerations is retail banking in the UK.

As late as the 1980s retail banking was very much the same as it had been for a hundred years. Banks dealt with retail customers on the High Street and maintained a network of branches to service the public. Some of these were relatively small and serviced a local community. Building societies were mutual organizations (i.e. owned by their members), which were lenders in the home buying market.

The development of the Internet and deregulation by government meant that competition for banking services increased, consumer credit expanded and customers had new and, to them, better ways of contacting their bank, i.e. after hours and on weekends when traditional bank branches were shut. Building societies demutualized in order to raise cash for expansion and moved into retail banking at the same time as banks moved into the home loans market.

The result of this was a wave of mergers, of bank branch closures, the loss of thousands of jobs from the banking sector, adoption of electronic banking (once customers could be persuaded to trust it), amalgamation of banks in order to meet the threats from overseas banking giants seeking to enter the lucrative UK market and banks and building societies competing to sell a range of financial products including insurance, credit cards and pensions.

In the present century the operation of retail banking has became completely different to what it was less than 30 years previously, i.e. in less than a working lifetime. Not only have individual banking companies either expanded hugely or disappeared completely, but legislative changes have created new opportunities, and risks, for those organizations which have survived and prospered. Now commercial retail organizations such as supermarket groups, who previously had no connection with banking, are offering credit card and banking services by starting their own banks. The very fact they are in the retail credit market is an indicator of the increasing levels of competition in this area and how far modern practice has come from traditional banking.

Risk evaluation

Once risks are identified they should be evaluated. There are many ways of doing this but the least complicated is a simple matrix.

Here is an example based on a company selling specialist skateboarding clothing over the Internet.

	High likelihood	Low likelihood
High impact	• Distribution difficulties with parcel delivery based on present supplier	• Loss of computer systems due to software failure
	• Small parcels and low order quantities are expensive	• Loss of consumer trust due to breakdown in security of payments system
Low impact	• Competition from new entrants into market. We have dominant position at this time and are well known to customers	• Loss of popularity of skateboarding – clothing may not suffer

As can be seen, risks can be categorized into:

- high impact/ high likelihood
- high impact/low likelihood
- low impact/high likelihood
- low impact/low likelihood

Organizations can use some form of analysis to attribute probabilities of identified risks occurring and also evaluate the impact in financial terms. They can thus calculate the possible risk impact to their organization by:

Financial cost of risk occurring $\times$ probability it will occur = possible impact of risk.

Clearly a lot of this is subjective, particularly the estimate of the likelihood, or probability, of the risk crystallizing which is why it requires involvement of senior, experienced management and staff.

ACTIONS TO MITIGATE RISK

Once risks are identified and evaluated the organization is faced with a range of actions. This approach is known as the **TARA** (Transfer, Accept, Reduce, Avoid) approach to risk management but there are others, mostly dealing with risk in the same way:

- *Transfer the risk* – by insuring the risk, subcontracting or outsourcing.
- *Accept the risk* – do nothing and hope for the best – not really recommended except for low-impact/low-likelihood risks. The level of risk which the organization will be prepared to accept and meet the consequences of should the events materialize is known as **residual risk** or sometimes Acceptable Risk.
- *Reduce the risk* – reduce the risk – by, for example:
  - raising staff awareness of risk
  - establishing physical measures such as improved security
  - diversifying computer systems instead of having one complex one
  - active development of new products and markets
  - strengthening internal controls
  - developing quality controls over production of goods, production of services
  - good staff recruitment and training policies
- *Avoid the risk* – don't allow the organization to engage in high-risk activities. For example, if trading in a volatile country where there is a risk of government interference, instead of funding the operation from say the UK or the USA use local finance and local management and suppliers wherever possible, thus mitigating the effects of possible nationalization, import controls, etc.

Formal approaches to risk management

One of the ways organizations can deal with risks and the risk assessment process is by adopting a formalized structure. The Committee of Sponsoring Organizations of the Treadway Commission (COSO) in the USA has developed guidance on what they call integrated control frameworks.

COSO defines internal control to include processes which will provide management with reasonable assurances regarding the achievement of objectives in:

- the effectiveness and efficiency of operations – addressing the organization's business activities and goals
- the reliability of financial reporting – including the preparation of financial statements
- compliance with applicable laws and regulations

COSO takes the view that the components of an internal control system are interrelated. We looked at these in Chapter 9 but to remind you they include:

- the control environment
- the risk management processes
- the information system, including the related business processes, relevant to financial reporting and communication
- control activities
- the monitoring of controls

As discussed in Chapter 2, the principles of sound corporate governance require the directors to institute a proper system of internal control. Directors also have a statutory duty to act in the way they consider best promotes the success of the company for the benefit of the members as a whole (Companies Act 2006, Section 172) and this statutory duty places on them the duty to preserve the assets of the company which reinforces the requirement for them to establish and maintain a positive internal control environment, which, of course includes sound internal control activities and procedures and a risk assessment process.

Good systems reinforce good behaviour, however COSO is at pains to point out:

- internal control is not a panacea
- internal control cannot ensure success
- internal control will not turn an inherently poor manager or department into a good one
- it cannot, by itself, respond to changing factors that are beyond management's control, e.g. increased competition
- there is no such thing as 100 per cent effective internal control

Without going into too much detail, which is not appropriate here, the COSO principles outlined above can be implemented into an organization using a system known as Control and Risk Self Assessment (CRSA).

CRSA takes a similar approach to risk-based issues, including fraud, as management initiatives such a Total Quality Management (TQM) insofar as it requires all employees to become involved in the process.

There are basically five approaches to CRSA:

- improve auditee participation to build upon and enhance the 'normal' audit process
- audit initiated control awareness seminars
- use of control questionnaires by management as a framework for evaluating risk and controls
- self-certification by managers of the effectiveness of controls
- systematic and open-minded evaluation of risk and controls through workshops and focus meetings

The formal processes are documented and circulated so that everyone in the organization becomes part of the risk assessment process and is able to contribute to it. This of course requires commitment on the part of senior management and a willingness to communicate throughout the organization at all levels.

WHY USE A BUSINESS RISK APPROACH TO AUDITING?

By evaluating the organization's risk management processes and studying the outcomes of the risk identification and evaluation the auditors can reduce their workload considerably and, it is argued, carry out an audit which is more directly relevant to the client's day-today activities and more likely to identify the possibility of significant errors or misstatements arising.

Consider the formula we mentioned earlier:

$$\text{Audit risk} = \text{Inherent risk} \times \text{Control risk} \times \text{Detection risk}.$$

By evaluating inherent and control risk the auditor can use the audit work that has to be done to minimize detection risk far more effectively than by simply carrying out lots of tests to confirm what they already know. There is little point in carrying out lots of testing of controls if the auditor is confident that the systems work well – this is simply over-auditing to little effective purpose. Far better to spend that time evaluating the entity's response to assessed business risks which may, if not identified and acted on, cause far more problems to the business than a failed control.

There are, as might be expected, both advantages and disadvantages to adopting a business risk approach. Research shows that major audit problems are rarely caused by accounts processing errors. Major audit problems (e.g. companies failing shortly after receiving an unqualified audit report) arise out of issues such as going concern, major fraud by top management, larger-scale systems breakdown, failure to modernize products, lack of response to market forces, etc.

The pace of change in business and in computing and communications means that companies are much more at risk of failure than ever before. The global economy is more competitive and more unforgiving than the national economy. The business, environmental, corporate governance issues and the nature of management control are all now more significant for businesses. They also translate more quickly into the financial statements.

Audit firms wish to be in the forefront of innovation in order to attract clients.

The business risk evaluation may show up areas where the audit firm can suggest other services that can be offered to the client. Investigation of business risk enables the auditor to have a profound knowledge of the business (as required by ISA 315) and focuses the audit on the high-risk areas. This risk-based approach tends to involve partners and senior managers much more in the planning stages of an audit.

Consequently, risk-based auditing can add value to the audit and can enable the auditor to offer some commercial benefits to the client in improving business processes or reducing potential risk areas. As we have seen, using a systems-based audit approach is impractical, expensive and uneconomic in large company audits where the internal control environment is strong, so focusing on risk is more likely to bring auditor/client benefits and a better audit than simply confirming that internal checks and controls are working.

There are , however, some important disadvantages which also have to be considered.

The risk-based approach increases the level of risk to the audit firm. This requires the firm to have strong quality control procedures and to document all its processes thoroughly. In order to make it work effectively the process requires highly qualified and competent staff both at the planning stage and during the audit itself which negates some of the efficiency gains as these are more expensive.

Throughout the audit process firms must be careful to maintain their **objectivity** and independence. The assessment of risk will undoubtedly require a close relationship with senior management and the development of mutual trust. Auditors may come to discover facts which the management may not wish to disclose and auditors may have to take hard decisions which may cause a rift in that relationship. However, the destruction of Arthur Andersen following the collapse of Enron is a salutary lesson in what happens to audit firms who get too close to their client.

UNDERSTANDING THE BUSINESS RISK APPROACH

Students need to obtain a clear understanding of the business risk approach and of the difference between *business risk* and *audit risk*.

There is still a lack of clarity in the articulation between business risk and audit risk, however the ideas of inherent risk and control risk have tended to merge into the larger idea of business risk. To simplify the position:

- Audit risk (see Chapter 10) is the risk the *audit firm* has to consider.
- Business risks are the risks facing the *client*.

The interaction between the two is that audit risk includes assessment of inherent and control risk, which include some of the components of business risk.

Looking at the business risk approach it is important to realize that the direction of the audit is from the evaluation of external and internal risks towards the financial statements. Earlier approaches to auditing tended to start with the financial statements and work backwards into the organization.

The approach is very much a strategic one – much less of the '*can wages be paid to non-employees?*' and much more of '*the client has closed its Bristol factory and now manufactures in China so what are the consequences for the company and its financial statements?*'

Some aspects of auditing are made easier or are simplified. In practice because of the better understanding of the client's business it is possible to use analytical review more frequently as a verification of assertions procedure and going concern considerations (see Chapter 23), because they are a natural by-product of business risk investigation and separate consideration of going concern may be unnecessary. However, auditors should realize that the audit needs to be tailor-made and a generalized approach to audits is neither productive nor economical.

The concept implies a continuing relationship with the client rather than a one-off, each year separate, view. It is an aid to the client acceptance and continuation procedures ('*Do we want this client?*').

Top-down approach

Auditors can adopt what has become known as the **top-down approach**. In this the general risks are assessed first and then specific risks are evaluated. The auditor must gain an understanding of the business' strategies, both current and future, as well as the risks associated with business operations and the controls in place to deal with them.

The auditor can then assess the expectations developed from this assessment of the business with what is shown by the accounts. The approach is known as a 'top-down' approach because it begins with management discussions and evaluations of controls at the highest level in the business and then cascades down as specific issues are addressed. It attempts to look at the accounts holistically, as a part of the ongoing business and its processes, tackling say, materiality on the basis of the financial statements as a whole and looking at the control environment from the point of view of the highest level of control, i.e. senior management level, downwards through the organization.

THE IMPLICATIONS OF THE BUSINESS RISK APPROACH FOR THE AUDIT

Planning

The auditor needs to plan the audit (ISA 300) and needs to develop a thorough understanding of the business. The planning process still needs an assessment of audit risk (Chapter 10).

The effects on planning may include:

- A consideration of the control environment. Is the control environment strong, including the assessment of the internal audit function? If it is not, the business risk approach may not be appropriate.
- Does the management manage risk effectively? Do they have in place procedures which can identify and evaluate the business risks faced by the organization? This should be evaluated at all levels of management.
- Is the Management Information System (MIS) adequate to provide the information needed to manage the business effectively?
- Do any risks threaten the going concern status of the company?
- Do any of the risks have implications for cash flow?
- Is there a high risk of fraud? For example, poor controls, management override, egotistical ambition and arrogance in the chief executive?
- Are there related parties with different agendas?
- Is the business under threat of being taken over with the risk of management misstating financial statements?
- Is there a risk of litigation against the company?
- Is there any risk of withdrawal of support by loan or trade creditors?

Audit procedures

Although detailed systems-based audit checking work may be eliminated altogether because the auditor is relying on the strength of the company's own internal controls this does not mean that the auditor does not have to carry out any detailed checking. The auditors must be sure that the internal control processes are strong. This will require them to validate that assumption, perhaps by considering the internal audit function and the effectiveness of corporate governance within the organization. These tests need to be carried out and documented.

Inevitably auditors cannot escape some level of substantive testing of items comprising the Statement of Financial Position. Whilst they may consider issues such as non-current asset recording, receivables and purchase ledger balances and possibly even inventories to be within the internal control system and therefore not subject to detailed testing, such matters as provisions, contingent liabilities and analytical review cannot be overlooked. Audit firms must ensure that they have gathered sufficient appropriate evidence to validate their audit opinion so cannot abrogate detailed testing completely.

The amount of testing carried out will depend on the risk of each item in the Statement of Financial Position being likely to be seriously misstated and of the financial statements as a whole not showing a true and fair view. This assessment will be carried out in the context of the business risks identified and evaluated by the auditors.

In the end many of the audit risks come down to:

- possible misstatements due to inadequate controls or weak corporate governance; company failures have been caused as much by overvaluations of inventories, or underprovisions for bad debts or situations where senior management have overridden controls and procedures, as they have by simply running out of cash
- working capital shortage leading to cash flow difficulties and technical insolvency (inability to pay debts as they fall due), often due to too rapid expansion
- inappropriate accounting policies; these can often lead to overstatement of assets or understatement of liabilities which can delude management into thinking a business is worth more or is financially sounder than it actually is; compliance with accounting standards is essential
- deliberate suppression or concealment of liabilities
- fraud by management
- activities of related parties
- computer systems failures
- litigation and regulatory issues and attempts by management to subvert disclosures

Audit firms must be able to demonstrate that they have considered and dealt with all of these possibilities and considered their implications for the financial statements. A thorough evaluation of business risks and a level of substantive testing of assets and liabilities can provide an effective audit framework.

SUMMARY

- Business risk is the threat that an event or action will adversely affect a business's ability to achieve its ongoing objectives.
- Business risk relates to all risks faced by the business, including both internal and external risks.
- Businesses should have procedures for identifying risks and evaluating their impact on the business. These can include formal approaches such as COSO and CRSA.
- Auditors need to develop a thorough understanding of their client and the risk management process.
- Auditors can considerably reduce the amount of checking work they carry out by auditing the risks rather than carrying out systems audits.
- Business risk and audit risk are not the same, however the evaluation of both types of risk includes some common components.
- Auditors need to carry out substantive tests on high-risk items in the financial statements.

POINTS TO NOTE

- This area is becoming increasingly popular with examiners and students must be clear on how this works and the advantages and disadvantages of the business risk approach.
- Don't make the mistake of confusing audit risk and business risk.
- Remember that this approach is only really appropriate for the best run companies. Any problems with internal controls will make this approach far too risky for the auditor.

CASE STUDY

You are the manager responsible for prospective new clients and you have visited Bolington Publishing plc which publishes a small range of fiction paperbacks. The chief executive is Daniel Dunbar and he has asked your firm to make a proposal for the company's audit and other services.

During the initial meeting you have ascertained the following:

- The company's turnover has increased by about 20 per cent a year for the last three years.
- Daniel is a dominating personality who is very ambitious.
- The company has recently paid very large sums to two relatively unknown authors for new books which Daniel thinks will be highly successful.
- Bolington has borrowed heavily from its bank and a major repayment of the loan is due shortly. The company is already on its overdraft limit as a result of the advances to the new authors. Daniel is in negotiation with a foreign bank for further finance.
- Many of the company's books are printed in a country with an exchange rate which is very favourable to the UK. The financial press has lately suggested that this rate may change in the near future.
- The company recently purchased a very large and very complex computer system to control all its affairs. The IT manager has just left and gone to Australia.
- The company has agreed to sponsor a sailor who is racing around the world single-handedly and the cost of this is not yet clear. The company has a racing yacht which Daniel sails.
- The company has received a writ from a person who alleges he has been wronged by a book published by the company. The company has large stocks of this book and is contesting the issue.
- The company has no formal management accounting system but the new IT system, when it is working, will supply this.
- Daniel wishes to maintain the company's high share price so that he can use the shares to take over a competitor.
- The company recently took over an ailing printing firm. Daniel reckons he can turn it round.

Discussion

– Identify and describe the principal business risks relating to Bolington.

– Justify an appropriate audit strategy for the first audit of Bolington.

– Suggest some procedures that Bolington could implement immediately to manage the risks.

– What effect might these risks have on the financial statements?

STUDENT SELF-TESTING QUESTIONS

Questions with answers apparent from the text

a) Define business risk.

b) List some external risks facing companies.

c) List some internal risks facing companies.

d) Why do auditors use a business risk approach?

e) What are the consequences of the approach?

f) What is COSO and how does it assist risk management?

g) What can a company do about risk?

h) Explain the difference between business risk and audit risk.

i) Explain the common features between business risk and audit risk.

j) What are the implications of business risk for the audit?

EXAMINATION QUESTIONS

1 You are a manager in Costello, a firm of Chartered Certified Accountants, which has recently adopted a business risk methodology. You have been involved in briefing clients about this 'top-down approach' and promoting the risk management assurance services which Costello offers.

The following information concerns one of your clients, Ferry, a limited liability company:

In July 2X16, Ferry purchased exclusive rights to operate a car and passenger ferry route until December 2X26. This offers an alternative to driving an additional 150 kilometres via the nearest bridge crossing.

There have been several ambitious plans to build another crossing but they have failed through lack of public support and government funds.

Ferry refurbished two 20-year-old roll-on, roll-off ('Ro-Ro') boats to service the route. The boats do not yet meet the emission standards of Environmental Protection Regulations which come into force in early 2X17. Each boat makes three return crossings every day of the year, subject to weather conditions, and has the capacity to carry approximately 250 passengers and 40 vehicles. The ferry service carried just 70 000 vehicles in the year to 31 December 2X17 (2X16: 58 000; 2X15: 47 000).

Hot and cold refreshments and travel booking facilities are offered on the one-hour crossing. These services are provided by independent businesses on a franchise basis.

Ferry currently receives a subsidy from the local transport authority as an incentive to increase market awareness of the ferry service and its efficient and timely operation. The subsidy increases as the number of vehicles carried increases and is based on quarterly returns submitted to the authority.

Ferry employs 20 full-time crew members who are trained in daily operations and customer service, as well as passenger safety in the event of personal accident, collision or breakdown.

The management of Ferry is planning to apply for a recognized Safety Management Certificate (SMC) in 2X18.

This will require a ship audit including the review of safety documents and evidence that activities are performed in accordance with documented procedures. An SMC valid for five years will be issued if no major non-conformities have been found.

Your firm has been asked to provide Ferry with a business risk assessment (BRA) as a management assurance service.

Required:

(a) Identify and explain the business risks facing Ferry which should be assessed.

(b) Describe the processes by which the risks identified in (a) could be managed and maintained at an acceptable level by Ferry.

(ACCA)

2 The principal activity of Bateleur Zoo Gardens (BZG) is the conservation of animals.

Approximately 80 per cent of the zoo's income comes from admission fees, money spent in the food and retail outlets and animal sponsorship. The remainder comprises donations and investment income.

Admission fees include day visitor entrance fees and annual membership fees. Day tickets may be prebooked by credit card using a telephone booking 'hotline' and via the zoo's website. Reduced fees are available (e.g. to students, senior citizens and families).

Animal sponsorships, which last for one year, make a significant contribution to the cost of specialist diets, enclosure maintenance and veterinary care. Animal sponsors benefit from the advertisement of their names at the sponsored animal's enclosure.

BZG's management has identified the following applicable risks that require further consideration and are to be actively managed:

(i) Reduction in admission income through failure to invest in new exhibits and breeding programmes to attract visitors.

(ii) Animal sponsorships may not be invoiced due to incomplete data transfer between the sponsoring and invoicing departments.

(iii) Corporate sponsorships may not be charged for at approved rates – either in error or due to arrangements with the companies. In particular, the sponsoring department may not notify the invoicing department of reciprocal arrangements, whereby sponsoring companies provide BZG with advertising (e.g. in company magazines and annual reports).

(iv) Cash received at the entrance gate ticket offices ('kiosks') may not be passed to cashiers in the accounts department (e.g. through theft).

(v) The ticket booking and issuing system may not be available.

(vi) Donations of animals to the collection (e.g. from Customs and Excise seizures and rare breeds enthusiasts) may not be recorded.

Required:

(a) Describe suitable internal controls to manage each of the applicable risks identified.

(b) Explain the financial statement risks arising from the applicable risks.

(c) Comment on the factors to be considered when planning the extent of substantive analytical procedures to be performed on BZG's income.

(ACCA)

SOURCES AND ADDITIONAL READING

Clark, F., Dean, G. and Oliver, K. (2003) *Corporate Collapse*. Cambridge: Cambridge University Press.

Financial Reporting Council (2009) *ISA 300 Planning an Audit of Financial Statements*. London: Financial Reporting Council.

Financial Reporting Council (2009) *ISA 315 Identifying and Assessing the Risks of Material Misstatement through Understanding the Entity and its Environment*. London: Financial Reporting Council.

Financial Reporting Council (2009) *ISA 330 The Auditor's Procedures in Response to Assessed Risk*. London: Financial Reporting Council.

Geiger, M. A. and Rama, D. V. (2006) 'Audit firm size and going concern reporting accuracy', *Accounting Horizons* 20(1):1–17.

CHAPTER 15
THE AUDIT OF ASSETS

Learning Objectives

After studying the material in this chapter you should be able to:

- understand the basis of auditing tangible and intangible assets including:
    - property plant and equipment
    - leased assets
    - intangible assets such as patents, trademarks and goodwill
    - inventories and work in progress
    - receivables
    - bank and cash balances

- explain cut-off procedures and their relevance to the financial statements

- appreciate the legal consequences of failing to audit assets properly

INTRODUCTION

A large part of the final audit stage will be taken up with the verification of the assets and liabilities appearing in the Statement of Financial Position. There are well-established techniques for verifying specific assets and liabilities.

One of the problems the auditor has to deal with in connection with assets is the problem of *overstatement*. This is when directors inflate the values of assets or fail to provide for diminutions in value in order to show a stronger financial position than is, in fact, the case.

The auditor has a duty to verify all the assertions relating to assets appearing on the Statement of Financial Position and also a duty to verify that there are no other assets which ought to appear on the Statement of Financial Position but don't.

Assets are normally divided into categories as shown in like this:

ASSETS
Noncurrent
Tangible
> *e.g.*
> *Land and buildings*
> *Plant and equipment*
> *Motor vehicles*

Intangible
> *e.g.*
> *Patents*
> *Development expenditure*
> *Goodwill*

Investments
> *e.g.*
> *Loans*
> *Shares in other companies*

Current
> *Inventories*
> *Work in progress*
> *Receivables*
> *Bank and cash*

We will look at the audit implications of each category in turn. This is not an accounting book so it does not include detailed explanations of how these categories of assets have to be disclosed in the financial statements. We will refer to them in the text where the elements of disclosure are significant from an audit perspective, e.g. disclosures relating to intangible assets, but students should be aware of the detailed disclosure requirements contained in the Companies Act 2006 and the relevant Financial Reporting Standards.

ASPECTS TO BE VERIFIED

When we are looking to audit assets, whether they are current or noncurrent we have to bear in mind the requirements of the assertions set out in Chapter 11. In particular, we are concerned with the second section of those assertions – '*Assertions about account balances at the period end*' but, of course, the other assertions, particularly those relating to transactions, also apply.

The assertions set out the following matters about which the auditor has to gather sufficient appropriate evidence so as to verify their truth – or otherwise:

> *Assertions about account balances at the period end*

Existence	• Assets, liabilities and equity interests (shareholdings) exist.
Rights and obligations	• The company holds or controls the rights to assets and all liabilities are those of the company.
Completeness	• All assets, liabilities and equity interests that should have been recorded.
Valuation and allocation	• Assets, liabilities and equity interests (shareholdings) are included in the financial statements at appropriate amounts and any resulting valuation or allocation adjustments are properly recorded.

One mnemonic often used by students in connection with the audit of Statement of Financial Position items is:

- **C**ost
- **A**uthorization
- **V**alue
- **E**xistence
- **B**eneficial **O**wnership
- **P**resentation in the Accounts

CAVEBOP

CAVEBOP covers all aspects of the assertions and might be easier to remember.

The audit approach to dealing with gathering sufficient reliable evidence is to consider each of these assertions and to obtain such information as is necessary to validate them. You will also appreciate that the amount of evidence required will depend partly on the risk of a material misstatement in the accounts (Chapter 10).

Older auditing textbooks tended to stress *existence, ownership* and *value* only. The addition of *presentation* reflects the relatively greater importance attached now to the 'fair' as well as the 'true' view given by the financial statements and the importance of the appropriate selection and disclosure of accounting policies.

For assets held at the beginning of the year, the acquisition will have been dealt with in a previous year. The presentation will, of course, need to be consistent with the presentation adopted in previous years. You will appreciate that this distinction does not arise with current assets.

VERIFICATION OF NONCURRENT ASSETS

Tangible assets

Tangible assets are so called because you can see them and touch them. They primarily consist of such assets as:

- land and buildings
- plant and equipment
- furniture and fittings
- motor vehicles

FRS 102 *The Financial Reporting Standard applicable in the UK and Republic of Ireland* defines these as:

assets that: (a) are held for use in the production or supply of goods or services, for rental to others, or for administrative purposes; and (b) are expected to be used during more than one period.

There are three key aspects to consider before we look in detail at audit procedures to verify tangible assets:

- It is permitted to include these assets at valuation rather than original cost. There are extensive disclosure requirements where assets are shown at valuation – we will look at the audit aspects of valuing tangible assets separately. This has become a key area of auditing, particularly where asset values are falling.

- Auditors should carefully consider the depreciation policy – the amount to be written off these assets (cost less residual value) should be allocated on a systematic basis over the asset's useful economic life. Auditors should look for consistency in applying depreciation policies and be alert where policies are changed. Rates of depreciation, residual values and economic lives of assets should be reviewed regularly to ensure they are still applicable.

- Auditors should look at the question of **impairment**. Where the value of assets becomes impaired, in other words they are not worth the value at which they are shown in the accounting records, they should be written down to a realistic or market value. This is particularly true of intangible assets such as brands or goodwill, which we will look at later, but can also apply to tangible assets due to obsolescence or changes in regulations.

Leased assets

Assets which are leased cause a problem as the auditor has to determine whether assets are financed through operating or finance leases. Finance leases are defined as those which '*transfer substantially all the risks and rewards incidental to ownership of an asset*'.

It is important that auditors fully understand the accounting requirement applicable to finance leases as these values could be significant in the financial statements and the rules are far from straightforward. Detailed calculations are necessary in respect of each lease so auditors have to:

- Review each lease for its main terms and conditions, establishing that it is a finance lease, and noting the applicable values, rates and payment terms.

- Check a sample of the calculations prepared by management in respect of these leases to provide sufficient appropriate evidence that management has calculated the appropriate values correctly and that the accounting treatment is correct.

FRS 102 classifies leases into finance leases and operating leases based on whether the lessee or the lessor holds the risks and rewards of ownership. This is the same principle as current UK GAAP; however current UK GAAP also includes a presumption that where the present value of the minimum lease payments is 90 per cent or more of the fair value of the asset, then the lease is a finance lease. FRS 102 does not include this '90 per cent test' so the classification of some leases may change. The key aspects of the lease agreement which would normally lead to a lease being classified as a finance lease are:

- The lease transfers ownership of the asset to the lessee by the end of the lease term.
- The lessee has the option to purchase the asset at a price that is expected to be sufficiently lower than the fair value at the date the option becomes exercisable for it to be reasonably certain, at the inception of the lease, that the option will be exercised.
- The lease term is for the major part of the economic life of the asset even if the title is not transferred.
- At the inception of the lease the present value of the minimum lease payments amounts to at least substantially all of the fair value of the leased asset.
- The leased assets are of such a specialized nature that only the lessee can use them without major modifications.

The reason why this is important is that costs incurred under operating leases should be expensed through the Statement of Comprehensive Income whilst assets acquired under finance leases can be capitalized. It is not beyond the realms of possibility that unscrupulous managers will try and capitalize operating lease costs thus increasing asset values and profits incorrectly, so the auditors should activate their professional scepticism whenever they are confronted with leased assets. It is necessary to read the lease agreements carefully to ensure the costs are treated correctly.

The same rules of valuation and impairment which apply to owned assets apply to assets leased under finance leases. Auditors also have to ensure that liabilities under finance leases are properly stated.

Looking ahead, the IASB has issued a new standard IFRS 16 *Leases* which has a mandatory date of 1 January 2019. This standard is based on the premise that all leases result in a company (the lessee) obtaining the right to use an asset at the start of the lease and, if lease payments are made over time, also obtaining financing. UK companies under UK GAAP currently are not affected by this as the provisions of FRS 102, with some exceptions, reflect the position of the old Statement of Standard Accounting Practice 21 (which was superseded by FRS 102) and distinguish between operating and finance leases. However, this may change if IFRS 16 is seen to be effective in corporate reporting.

Accordingly, IFRS 16 eliminates the classification of leases as either operating leases or finance leases as is required by IAS 17 and, instead, introduces a single lessee accounting model. Applying that model, a lessee is required to recognize:

- assets and liabilities for all leases with a term of more than 12 months, unless the underlying asset is of low value; and
- depreciation of leased assets separately from interest on leased liabilities in the income statement.

The present operating cost of the lease is replaced by a depreciation charge and a finance charge based on the net present value of the lease payments.

IFRS 16 eliminates the classification of leases as either operating leases or finance leases for a lessee. Instead all leases are treated in a similar way to finance leases applying IAS 17. Leases are 'capitalized' by recognizing the present value of the lease payments and showing them either as lease assets (right-of-use assets) or together with property, plant and equipment. If lease payments are made over time, a company also recognizes a financial liability representing its obligation to make future lease payments. The most significant effect of the new requirements in IFRS 16 will be an increase in lease assets and financial liabilities. Accordingly, for companies with material off balance sheet leases, there will be a change to key financial metrics derived from the company's assets and liabilities (for example, leverage ratios). This may well have a significant effect on certain types of company where there is a preponderance of leased assets such as telecoms companies or banking and retail chains, who may have a considerable part of their operation involving operating leases, where the transition from operating to finance leases will increase assets but also liabilities.

This will ease the auditor's position somewhat as companies adopting IFRS 16 will have to justify keeping off balance sheet operating leases as there will be a de facto presumption that all leases are finance leases. However, auditors will have to carefully check the calculations of asset values and liabilities as these will change over the period of the lease.

Control objectives

The **control objectives** in relation to all tangible fixed assets are:

- To ensure that all tangible fixed assets exist, are owned by the company and are in use.
- To ensure that tangible fixed assets are recorded in the books, at the correct valuation, are adequately secured and properly maintained.
- That acquisitions and disposals are properly authorized.
- That assets are properly depreciated and the depreciation is properly accounted for.

Audit procedures

We will look at the audit procedures applicable to different categories of asset and, at the same time, identify which assertions these procedures will provide evidence for – these are shown in italics.

Land and buildings

- Physically inspect a sample of land and buildings. Individual assets must be clearly identifiable for this purpose, particularly where buildings are contiguous (*existence*).
- Inspect all documents of title, lease agreements, invoices, etc. relating to the purchase or disposal of land and buildings. If title deeds or other such documents are held by a third party, for example, a lender as security for a loan, the lender should be asked to certify possession in writing (*ownership*, *rights* and *obligations*).

- Inspect minutes of directors' meetings to ensure all agreements for the purchase or sale of assets are properly authorized and signatures on documents such as title deeds, leases, conveyances and tenancy agreements are properly minuted and approved (*occurrence*, *rights* and *obligations*).
- Check a sample of entries in the asset register or asset accounts in the nominal ledger and trace back to source documentation (*valuation*).
- Review the depreciation policy and check sample calculations. Consider in relation to expected useful lives of assets (*valuation*).
- Review assets for any permanent impairment in value (*valuation*).
- If assets are stated at valuation, if a valuation has been performed in the year, ensure name or qualification of valuer and basis of valuation is appropriate and that proper disclosure is made in the accounts (*valuation*).
- Ensure the asset register reconciles to the nominal ledger (*completeness* and *accuracy*).
- Ensure tangible noncurrent assets are properly disclosed in financial statements in accordance with FRS 102 (*completeness*, *valuation* and *allocation*).

Showing land and buildings at cost is often the norm, particularly in smaller entities, and creates no real problems for the auditor. However, many companies will show land and property at valuation and this can give rise to particular problems in establishing the valuation, which must be reviewed annually. Undoubtedly the auditor will require the services of an expert commercial property valuer for this purpose and we looked at this in Chapter 11.

Land shown at below cost will be unusual and the auditor will need to:

- Examine the reason for the write down.
- Examine the director's minute authorizing it.
- Appraise the adequacy of the write down.
- Ensure that there is adequate disclosure of the facts in the financial statements.

Buildings can be under construction and can be being constructed by the client. In this case care has to be taken to ensure that only costs, including overheads, which directly relate to the construction of the asset are included. These will include:

- material and labour costs;
- the costs of borrowing to finance the construction; and
- direct overheads relevant to constructing the building.

Indirect overheads such as administration costs are not allowable for this purpose.

Auditors should be aware that capitalizing expenses is a way of unscrupulous management 'improving' the reported profits and asset values.

The building should not really cost more than it can be valued at – excessive costs allocated to the construction of a building should be investigated, in case this represents a misallocation of costs more properly charged to revenue. If the costs are bona fide, the question of impairment of value has to be considered. It is likely that the auditors will have to take specialist advice in this area.

Intangible assets

Intangible assets include:

- development costs
- patents, trademarks, licences, concessions, etc.
- goodwill – if purchased on an acquisition

These can be areas of some difficulty for the auditors, the principal one being in the area of valuation. It is, generally, reasonably easy to evidence the fact that intangible assets exist and that the business owns them, it is less easy to decide what they are worth. Again there are accounting rules set out in FRS 102 which the student should be familiar with.

There are some key issues which relate to intangible assets generally.

Research and development

You need to know the difference between research and development.

- *Research* is original investigation work often undertaken with a view to developing a commercial project but often only with a view to extending knowledge. This is not an asset and the costs of research should be *written off* in the financial period.
- *Development* is the application of research into a commercial product or service. This is preliminary cost incurred before the product or service goes into commercial production.

Development costs may be capitalized as an asset, subject to some key considerations:

- Is the project technically feasible – i.e. will it be completed and result in a commercial product or service? This may require the auditors consulting an expert to determine the answer.
- Is the ultimate product going to be used or sold? – consult minutes of meetings and discussion papers.
- Can the product be sold – i.e. does the business have the capability to deliver the product to the market place? Again meeting minutes and discussion papers will provide evidence of the company's thinking on this.
- Will the product or service provide an income stream – is there a market for the product, what sort of volumes will be sold and at what price? If it is to be used internally in the organization what sort of transfer price will be available? Market research reports will give guidance on this.
- Are resources available to complete the project, how much longer will it take and how much more will it cost? Budgets, plans and forecasts will evidence this as well as evidence of costs charged to date.

Whilst there is evidence to be gained from several sources, as suggested above, at the end of the day the auditors are left with having to make a judgement based on the available evidence. An important part of coming to that judgement is the discussion with management. Management needs to demonstrate why it has the confidence in the project and its ultimate benefits, and why therefore the expenditure can properly be capitalized. If necessary, they should put it in writing in the Letter of Representation (Chapter 24). The auditors may need specialized help in some cases, but the ultimate decision lies with them.

Development costs should be amortized (depreciated) over their expected useful lives, which is either the length of time the resulting product or service is in production and being sold or, if this is an inordinately long period, the value should be reviewed annually for impairment.

Trademarks, patents, etc.

These should be capitalized and written off over their expected useful lives. The auditors should consider the value each year – it may be that because of technical changes or changes in rules and regulations the value of a patent or trade mark becomes impaired, in which case it must be written down as the income stream from it will reduce or cease.

The auditor should check that any renewal fees have been paid, and written off, so the patents and trademarks are still current and the auditors should also inspect the agreements to make sure they are still current in the name of the company.

If the company uses a patent agent it may be possible to obtain a third party confirmation from them as to the ownership and currency of the patent.

Goodwill

This is purchased goodwill, i.e. goodwill arising on the acquisition of a business or part of a business. It represents the difference between the price paid and the value of the underlying assets.

This can be capitalized and written off over its useful life – which may, in some circumstances, be quite short.

Auditors must look at the value of goodwill and, assuming they can satisfy themselves over the value at which it was capitalized, their main consideration is the expected useful life.

EXAMPLE 1

Suppose Company A takes over Company B for an amount in excess of the value of the assets of Company B. This creates an intangible asset – goodwill – which the auditors can evidence through the takeover agreement. However, suppose, in the course of its business, Company A assimilates company B to such an extent that Company B's name disappears and all its products and services are marketed under the name of Company A – how then can the Statement of Financial Position of Company A continue to carry goodwill as an asset in its Statement of Financial Position if the business to which it originally referred has effectively ceased to exist?

The short answer, in reality, is that it cannot justify upholding such goodwill so that it should be written off through the Statement of Comprehensive Income, in much the same way as if the value of the goodwill had become tainted in some way.

It is a matter of judgement. Remember though that it is for management to decide on the value it intends to include in the Statement of Financial Position – the auditor has to form a judgement, based on as much evidence as can be found, as to whether that value is true and fair.

Investments

Investments are assets held to generate income or to create a profit from simply holding them for a period of time. These can comprise, amongst other things:

- loans
- money market deposits
- shares in other companies either quoted or unquoted
- properties
- gilts (UK Government stocks)

Note that investments in shares for this purpose exclude investments in **subsidiary companies** (holding of more than 50 per cent of the voting shares) or **associated companies** (holding of more than 20 per cent, i.e. having a 'significant' influence).

Students should be familiar with the provisions of FRS 102 which relate to Financial Instruments. These can often be complex and difficult to understand. However auditors should bear in mind the principle of 'substance over form' discussed in Chapter 2 – in other words they should look at what the instrument actually is not what it purports to be.

For example many of the complex instruments which brought down Lehman Brothers, although being described in complex terms were, in effect, loans – loans which in reality had no prospect of ever being repaid which made them worthless.

So the basic audit principles apply regarding evidencing existence and ownership and value:

- understand the nature of the asset
- physical inspection of loan notes, share certificates, title deeds
- third-party verification from banks, brokers or agents
- inspection of income streams from dividends, rents, etc.
- inspection of transaction evidence
- minutes of directors' meetings

One important point is that where investments are described as 'long term' by the company the auditors must consider whether the company has the capability of holding the investments for the long term, i.e. will the cash flow be sufficient to meet the company's needs, or will the investment have to be sold to meet liabilities or fund trading ventures in the short term? This is done by discussing the matter with management and obtaining written representations from them (Chapter 24).

The reason for this is obvious – if the company cannot hold the investment for the long term, because, say, it is running out of money and will have to sell them to raise cash, then they are incorrectly disclosed in the accounts.

Valuation can be more difficult. FRS 102 requires investments to be stated at cost and then for their value to be re-measured at each Statement of Financial Position date to a 'fair value' except for:

- loans, held to maturity investments and other receivables which should be measured at amortized cost
- equity investments whose fair value cannot be measured – this is most likely to apply to investments in unquoted companies

For quoted investments this is relatively straightforward as a share price can be obtained at the period end from published sources, but the valuation of unquoted investments is considerably more problematic and may require some discussion with the directors. The valuation of unlisted investments is notoriously difficult. Much depends on the size of the holding and the influence wielded by the company. For example, the company may, on paper, own less than 50 per cent of the unlisted shares in an entity but exert such dominance over its affairs that the company has de facto control over it.

Care must be taken by auditors looking at unlisted entities, partnerships and ventures which the company may claim to be holding purely as an investment but which may, in fact, be being used as a vehicle to disguise losses or to hide trading activities so they are not disclosed. Chapter 21 deals with this in more detail.

Properties held as investment properties can be valued by a competent valuer.

At each Statement of Financial Position, date the question of impairment arises and the value must be assessed individually.

CURRENT ASSETS

Introduction

Here we consider some standard verification techniques for current assets including:

- inventory and work in progress
- receivables
- cash at bank and loans

The basic asset verification techniques described above (CAVEBOP, etc.) apply to current assets as much as to Tangible and Intangible assets.

However, there are some specific techniques which relate to the audit of current assets, particularly inventory and work in progress, so it is necessary to describe these particular techniques separately.

The audit of current assets is often the subject of examination questions so students must become familiar with the procedures relevant to each category of asset.

INVENTORY AND WORK IN PROGRESS

Inventory and work in progress is often a key item in the financial statements and its verification is a common examination question.

It cannot be stressed too much that it is the directors' responsibility to ensure that:

- inventory and work in progress are correctly identified
- physical quantities are correctly ascertained and recorded and condition assessed

- valuation on proper bases is correctly made
- proper disclosure is made in the financial statements

There is an auditing guideline which has a specific relevance to inventories and that is ISA 501 *Audit evidence – specific considerations for selected items.*

Students should also be aware of the disclosure requirements of FRS 102.

A categorization, which follows the broad disclosure requirements in the financial statements, is into:

- finished goods and goods purchased for resale
- raw materials and components purchased for incorporation into products for sale and consumable stores (oils, fuels, spare parts, etc.)
- work in progress
- payments on account of work in progress

Inventories may be:

- recorded in book inventory records and checked by periodic complete physical counts, particularly at the period end; or
- recorded on a rolling or **continuous inventory** system and checked by regular partial counts such that the whole of the inventory is checked to financial records at least once in the financial period.

Cost and net realizable value

The accounting standards require that inventory and work in progress should be valued at the lower of cost and net realizable value.

- Cost – includes cost of the actual item plus any costs related to bringing it to its present location and condition, so can include import duties, transport costs, handling costs, etc. and net of any rebates or discounts.
- Net realizable value – is the estimated selling price of those goods in the ordinary course of business, less any costs to complete and sell. This can be calculated after deduction of a proportion to cover selling and distribution costs if this is appropriate. Auditors need to review the actual selling prices of a sample of inventory items after the year end in order to establish whether or not the items have been sold at more than cost.

Note this really only applies to finished goods – it may often be the case that raw materials and consumables have a selling price less than cost but this wouldn't justify writing down inventory values.

Valuation

Cost has to be based on:

- For individual items, i.e. 'one-off' items, e.g. a car in a motor dealership – the actual cost for the individual item.
- For interchangeable items – e.g. boxes of welding rods in a store cost calculated on a **First In First Out** (FIFO) or on an Average Cost basis. The same method must be used for similar items of inventory. The FIFO basis requires that inventory is valued at the cost at which it was purchased so that, generally, the oldest inventory is carried at the lowest cost – inventory items are not revalued as costs per item increase.

Production overheads

One of the problems in valuing inventory and work in progress is the allocation of overheads as part of the cost. These are overheads incurred in the manufacture of the items – obviously this does not include any element of selling or distribution overhead.

Production overheads can be either fixed or variable. The calculation of the level of overheads to be apportioned should be based on the normal level of activity. The 'normal' level of activity is a question to be decided based on management accounting actual and budgeted forecast performance levels. Where overheads are allocated using an **absorption costing** basis which includes some element of nonproduction overheads, it is necessary to attempt to exclude these from the valuation.

This might require either recalculating the absorption basis or making an estimate of the nonproduction overheads and excluding this proportion from the inventory valuation. This may mean some substantial recalculation so auditors should estimate the effect of any proposed revision of overhead allocation on the financial statements as a whole with an eye to materiality before beginning what might become a very tortuous process.

Inventory count procedures

In small companies' inventory counting may occur on only one day a year, other companies have more regular counts and yet others carry out regular inventory checks on a continuous or rolling count basis. Inventory counting is essentially a part of the internal control system.

A good set of procedures will have the following characteristics:

- Good planning so that the work is carried out carefully and systematically – early issue of inventory count instructions with consideration of feedback from staff.
- Division of the inventory count into manageable areas for control purposes.
- Identification of inventories and especially of high value items.
- Nomination of people responsible for each aspect of the count. These should, ideally, be persons independent of those normally responsible for the control over inventory items. This is based on the internal control principle of segregation of duties – separating those responsible for control of inventory from those responsible for counting it.
- Written instructions to counters for counting, weighing, measuring and checking should be issued and all counters must ensure they are familiar with them.
- Controls to ensure all inventory is counted and once only.
- Proper control over the issue of blank inventory count sheets by numbering them and the control over the return of completed and unused inventory count sheets. This ensures none are mislaid or lost.
- Control of inventory movements during the count – no goods in or out.
- **Cut-off** arrangements – we look at this in more detail later.
- Arrangements for identification of defective, damaged, obsolete and slow-moving inventory.
- Identification of inventory on the premises owned by third parties and of client's inventory held by outside parties.
- Appropriate treatment for sealed containers, dangerous goods and goods with special problems.

Inventory count – the auditor's duties

As mentioned above, ISA 501 *Audit evidence – specific considerations for selected items* requires the auditors to attend inventory taking.

It says:

'If *inventory is material to the financial statements, the auditor shall obtain sufficient appropriate audit evidence regarding the existence and condition of inventory by:*

(a) *Attendance at physical inventory counting, unless impracticable, to*
  (i) *evaluate management's instructions and procedures for recording and controlling the results of the entity's physical inventory counting;*
  (ii) *observe the performance of management's count procedures;*
  (iii) *inspect the inventory;*
  (iv) *perform test counts; and*
(b) *Performing audit procedures over the entity's final inventory records to determine whether they accurately reflect actual inventory count results. The purpose of attendance is not only to gather evidence to support the audit opinion but also as part of the auditor's work on the internal controls of the business. In particular:*
  - *the physical count will validate (or otherwise of course) the book inventory records.*
  - *it will provide evidence of the operation of internal controls over inventories, including the client's inventory count procedures.*

- *it provides substantive evidence for the auditors of a material Statement of Financial Position and Statement of Comprehensive Income figure. The auditors must satisfy themselves as to the validity of the amounts attributed to inventory and work in progress in the financial statements. They do this by first considering the client's system of internal control. This applies to inventory count as it does to all areas of audit enquiry.*

It is essential for students to understand that inventory count procedures are part of the system. The auditor's duties are usually divided into three parts – before, during and after the inventory count.

Before the inventory count – planning

- Review the previous year's working papers and discuss with management any significant changes from the previous year.
- Discuss inventory count arrangements with management.
- Familiarize themselves with the nature and volume of inventories and especially with high value items.
- Consider the location of inventories (e.g. at branches) and the problems thus caused for the client and the auditors.
- Consider likely points of difficulty, e.g. cut-off.
- Consider internal audit involvement and if reliance can be placed upon it.
- Arrange to obtain from third parties confirmation of inventory held by them.
- Establish whether expert help may be needed from a third party (e.g. pubs, clubs and restaurants in the licensing trade use specialist valuers, advice may be required with regard to the valuation of specialized inventory, e.g. gems, contract work in progress).
- Evaluate the client's inventory count instructions, especially that they:
  - include inventory held in all locations
  - plan to use staff separate from those concerned with the inventory on a day-to-day basis
  - make arrangements for suspending the delivery of goods into the stores and the taking of goods out of inventory – there should be no movement of goods during the count
  - are discussed with, and adequately communicated to, inventory count staff
  - include arrangements for marking inventory counted so it isn't counted twice
  - include arrangements for inventory takers to count in pairs so counts can be verified as they go around
  - include arrangements for identifying old, obsolete or damaged inventory
  - ensure that all audit teams have a copy of the client's instructions (and have read and understood them!)
  - review surrounding systems of internal control to identify areas of potential difficulty and
  - plan usage of audit staff as to availability to cover all required locations, etc.

During the inventory count

Remember that the purpose of the attendance is not to take inventory or to supervise the inventory take but to *observe* the client's internal control system in action.

The actual work to be done is:

- Observe the inventory count to ascertain that the client's employees are carrying out their instructions.
- Check the count of a selected number of lines. This must be done by selecting some items found to be present in the stores and some items recorded on the inventory sheets.
- Note for follow-up:
  - details of items selected by the auditors to compare with final inventory sheets
  - list of items counted by client's staff in the auditor's presence
  - details of defective, damaged, obsolete or slow-moving items identified during the count
  - instances of inventory count instructions not being followed
- Details of items for cut-off purposes (see below). These will consist of recording the details of the last delivery note number for goods inwards and the last goods outward note number for deliveries to customers.
- Enquire into, observe and discuss with store-keeping staff the procedures for identifying damaged, obsolete and slow-moving inventory.

- Form an impression of the magnitude of inventory held for comparison with the accounts.
- Record fully the work done and impressions of the inventory count in the working papers.
- If any aspects prove unsatisfactory, inform the management and request a recount.
- High-value items should be given special attention.
- Photocopies of rough inventory sheets should be taken if possible.
- Details of the sequence of inventory sheets should be verified.

After the inventory count

- Check the cut-off with details of the last numbers of goods inward and goods outwards notes during the year and after the year end (see below).
- Test that the final inventory sheets have been properly prepared from the count records. In particular, the record of inventory count sheets issued and returned must be checked.
- Follow up any notes made at the attendance.
- Check final inventory sheets for pricing, extensions, additions, summarizing and officials' signatures.
- Inform management of any problems encountered in the inventory count for action in subsequent counts.

If it is not practicable to attend the inventory count, for example, if the client has inventory at remote or overseas locations, the auditors must still attempt to gather evidence concerning the physical existence, ownership and value of inventories.

This can be done by:

- Arranging for the inventory count to be at an earlier date and reconciling the count with the year-end inventory figure.
- Appointing agents, e.g. for overseas locations.
- Examining continuous inventory count records and carrying out sample testing.

None of these solutions is wholly satisfactory and the auditors must make very extensive enquiries before they give a clean report.

Continuous inventory

Many organizations, and supermarkets are perhaps the most accessible example, cannot close their operations down for inventory count or find it impracticable to do so. Instead they practice a continual inventory count procedure where every item of inventory is checked to the book inventory records at least once in the year, and probably more than once, in a systematic and orderly manner.

The records of such checking should demonstrate concurrence between the actual inventory and the records.

In this case what the auditor has to do is:

- Attend physical inventory counts when they are being carried out by client's staff on more than one occasion.
- Examine the book inventory listing at the year end and examine records of counts near the year-end date.
- Examine reconciliations between counts and the book inventory records and ensure the client has procedures in place to follow up any discrepancies during counts and adjust book inventory records as appropriate.

This last point is probably the most important because, in the absence of an independent physical count at the year end, the auditor has to ensure that the client has sufficient controls in place to maintain the book inventory records accurately.

Inventory counts other than at the year end

ISA 501 states that inventory counts carried out before or after the year end may be acceptable for audit purposes provided records of inventory movements in the intervening period are such that the movements can be examined and substantiated. The greater the interval the more difficult this will be. Acceptability depends also on the auditors being satisfied that there is a good system of internal control and satisfactory inventory records.

CUT-OFF

This subject has been mentioned already and it is extremely important. Consider a basic trading account:

	£000s	**£000s**
Revenues		1000
Opening inventory	100	
Purchases	(750)	
	850	
Closing inventory	(150)	
Cost of sales		(700)
Gross profit		300

Consider two scenarios:

1 Supposing goods valued at £50 000 were:

  (a) dispatched and invoiced by the supplier *before* the Statement of Financial Position date; but
  (b) received *after* the Statement of Financial Position date owing to delays in transit.

   The invoice could be included in purchases, as a payable, as a consequence of (a) but the goods might be excluded from closing inventory as a consequence of (b).
   In this case either the inventory has to be included as inventory in transit (and the auditors would have to verify the existence, ownership and value of that inventory) or the invoice should be deleted from payables and purchases and the whole transaction included in the next accounting period. This is a matter of judgement by management and the auditors would have to consider whether or not the approach adopted is consistent with previous periods and does not represent an attempt by management to distort the financial statements.

2 Suppose goods in the stores valued at £50 000 were invoiced as a sale the day before the inventory count but not actually despatched to the customer until the day after.
   In this case the goods could be included in both Inventory – because they had been counted unless they had been particularly set aside – and Receivables (and also Revenues) so the financial statements would, again, be distorted. Again, the auditor has to check that only goods actually despatched to customers are included in sales.

Avoiding this possibility is a vital part of the system of internal control as applied to inventory and consequently is of prime concern to the auditor.

A famous case on the subject of cut-off was *Re, Thomas Gerrard & Son Ltd* (1967). This was a cotton spinning and manufacturing company. The manager and principal shareholder:

  (a) post-dated purchases invoices received before the year end thus moving costs into the next accounting period; and
  (b) ante-dated sales invoice copies in the new year to dates prior to the year-end thus moving income into the accounting period.

He did this quite openly for five half-year periods for bigger sums each time, thus turning losses into profits and causing the company to pay tax and dividends. The auditors discovered the alterations, asked questions about them but were satisfied by answers such as '*these were year-end adjustments*' or '*it is more convenient*'.

The judge awarded damages against the auditors on the grounds that once their suspicions were aroused they had a duty to probe the matter to the bottom and they were negligent in not doing so. This highlights the importance of inspecting transactions around the year end as part of cut-off procedures.

Auditors have a duty to satisfy themselves as to the validity of inventory and work in progress and this cannot arise solely out of the assurances from management, however trustworthy in appearance.

How do auditors go about ensuring that the cut-off procedures are properly applied?
There are three key aspects to validating the cut-off:

1) The audit work on the accounting systems for sales and purchases should have established whether or not the systems are reliable and that dates, etc. can be trusted. If the system is not reliable then a great deal more detailed checking work would have to be performed on sales and purchase transactions around the cut-off point but, assuming all is well, the dates of numbers of invoices, delivery notes, goods received notes, etc. can be relied upon.

2) For purchases into inventory the auditors should take a note of the <u>last goods inwards or delivery note number at the close of the cut-off period</u> so that all deliveries before that number are included in inventory and all deliveries with a number after that are not – they fall into the following period. Reference then has to be made to the purchasing system to ensure that no invoices for goods with a delivery note number <u>after</u> the closing one have been included in liabilities. In short the auditors have to ensure that the assets match the liabilities and both are in the same account period.

3) Similarly for sales – the auditors should take a note of the <u>last despatch note number recording items delivered to customers before the close of the cut-off period</u> and match this to the relevant sales invoices checking that no sales invoices have been included in Revenues for goods which are also included in Inventories.

CASE STUDY

Twinkle plc manufactures lighting and lighting equipment for the home and commercial premises. The audit team are looking to test the year end cut-off procedures for Purchases and Inventory as at 31 March 2X17.
  The auditors attended the Inventory count and noted that the last Goods Received Note number was 3487. They then reviewed the listing of purchase invoices received after the year end and included in Accruals. This showed the following:
Which invoices should be included in Accruals and thus as Liabilities?

Invoice number	Supplier	Invoice date	Goods received note number	Amount £
73567	Queen Ltd	30 March	3485	11 345.62
58392	Wires plc	30 March	3489	82 367.00
15683	Betta Bulbs	31 March	3486	17 395.95
2303	Phillament	31 March	3488	92 393.00
82965	Lighty Light	1 April	3487	22 583.00

1) The invoice from Lighty Light is dated 1 April but the goods were actually received in the period as this delivery is the last one in – with GRN number 3487 – before the Inventory count. Despite the invoice date being after the year end the fact the goods were delivered at the year-end means that the liability related to that financial year (2X17) – not the next one (2X18). Consequently, this invoice should be included as a Liability and the goods included in Inventory.

2) The invoices from Wires plc (£82 367) and Phillament (£92 393) related to deliveries made *after* the cut-off date as they had GRN numbers 3488 and 3489 respectively – so after the year end. Consequently, those goods were not included in Inventory so the invoices should be excluded from Liabilities.

Work in progress

All that has been said about inventory applies equally to work in progress but this item presents even greater problems of ascertainment and valuation to the directors and to the auditors.

This category relates primarily to *long-term work in progress*, i.e. work which will cover more than one, and sometimes several, accounting periods.

With short-term work in progress it is relatively easy to value the work done as the contract may well be completed before the audit is signed off and the auditors can evaluate its outcome, but for longer-term contracts the future may be more uncertain. This requires an exercise of judgement and, sometimes, the involvement or opinion of an expert valuer, such as a quantity surveyor.

The auditor's investigations will include:

- Examination of contracts to ensure that salient features such as timescales and penalty clauses are known.
- Enquiry into the costing system from which work in progress is ascertained.
- Enquiry into the reliability of the costing system. In particular, a costing system integrated with the financial accounting system will, *prima facie*, be more reliable because of the discipline of double entry and the inherent checks imposed by external data such as creditors' statements.
- Enquiry into statistical data concerning inputs of materials and outputs of products and expectations, e.g. for given tonnages of materials purchased there should be some identifiable outcome in the contract. Actual progress can be matched with theoretical models.
- Enquiry into the system of inspection and reporting to enable due allowance to be made for scrapping and rectification work.
- Enquiry into the basis on which overheads are included in costs.
- Enquiry into the qualifications and experience of any valuers (e.g. quantity surveyors) who are certifying valuations of completed work.
- Enquiry into the basis on which any element of profit is dealt with. Profit should be eliminated from work in progress. However, it is legitimate to include an element of profit in long-term contract work in progress in accordance with FRS 102. The calculation of the amount of profit to be taken should be treated with extreme caution.
- Any losses identified on contracts in progress must be recognized immediately in the valuation. This is to reduce the valuation of work in progress to its estimated realizable value. Auditors have to review not only the costs already included in the calculation of work in progress but also the costs to complete the particular contract. This requires them to form a judgement on the assumptions used by management to calculate such costs.
- Where items such as buildings and plant are constructed internally, it is important for the auditor to make sure that, if such items are under construction at the year end, they are not included twice, i.e. in fixed assets and work in progress.

Auditors should, where possible, inspect the works in progress in order to familiarize themselves with the scale and nature of the projects and to provide basic evidence that the project exists.

They may also have to consider the use of experts in connection with the valuation of work in progress and legal advice in connection with any dispute which may be taking place over the contract.

Analytical review

While detailed work on inventory and work in progress is imperative in an audit, there are a number of analytical review procedures which the auditors should carry out in order to provide additional, substantive evidence. See Chapter 12 for more detailed explanations.

These could include:

- Reconciliation of changes in inventories at successive year ends with records of movements, e.g. purchases and sales.
- Comparison of quantities of each kind of inventory held at year end with those held at previous year ends and with purchases and sales.
- Consideration of **gross profit ratio** (Appendix 3) with that of previous years, other companies and budgeted expectations.
- Consideration of rate of inventory turn (Chapter 12) with previous years, etc.
- Comparison of inventory figures with budgets for inventory, revenues and purchases.
- Consideration of standard costing records and the application of variances in the valuation of inventory and work in progress.

Valuation of inventory and work in progress

Remember that inventory and work in progress should be valued in accordance with the provisions of FRS 102 which state that they must be valued at the lower of cost or net realizable value.

Net realizable value is the value the inventory would achieve in the open market in its present condition. The audit tests could include detailed substantive tests such as:

- Ascertain accounting policies adopted for valuing inventory and ensure they have been consistently applied.
- Test the inventory sheets or continuous inventory records with relevant documents such as invoices and costing records to determine if 'cost' has been correctly arrived at.
- Examine and test the inclusion of overheads, as outlined above.
- Test the treatment and examine evidence for items valued at net realizable value.
- Test the arithmetical accuracy of calculations.
- Test the consistency with which the amounts have been computed.
- Consider the calculation of any profits included as part of the valuation of work in progress and the valuation of any losses. This requires the auditor to be familiar with the provisions of the contracts and take a view on management's calculations.
- Consider the adequacy of the description used in the accounts and disclosure of the accounting policies adopted.

Independent inventory counts

In some trades it is found that the inventory is counted and valued by an independent firm of inventory counters. Examples include the jewellery, licensed and retail pharmacy trades.

The question arises as to whether this influences the extent of the auditor's examination. The answer is that the auditors have a duty to form an opinion on the amount at which inventory is stated. We looked at the use of an auditor's expert in Chapter 11.

Auditors cannot simply accept an outside inventory counter's valuation but it is usual to do so if:

- They are satisfied of the inventory counter's independence.
- The inventory counter is suitably qualified.
- The inventory counter has a suitable level of experience in the trade carried on by the company.
- The auditor is satisfied:
    - that the basis of valuation used is appropriate and
    - proper cut-off procedures were employed

Remember that the auditors have final responsibility for their audit opinion and cannot blame the inventory counter if things go wrong.

Historical note

There are some lessons for auditors to learn from past cases and the three that follow are among the most famous.

Re, the Kingston Cotton Mill Co. Ltd (1896)

The auditors failed to detect overstatements of the amounts of inventory. They accepted a certificate from the manager on the amount of inventory after comparing it with the inventory journal which contained accounts for each item or class of items purporting to be in inventory and a summary. The summary was agreed by the auditors to be in agreement with the detailed accounts. In fact, the entries were falsified to show more inventory than was actually in existence. The auditors were exonerated on the grounds that it is no part of the auditor's duty to take inventory and that they were entitled to rely upon other people for the details of inventory in trade. This, of course, would not be the case today!

The judge's remarks contained the famous phrase, '*He is a watchdog, not a bloodhound*'. This means that if the auditors discover something which is suspicious they should probe it to the bottom but in the absence of suspicious circumstances they are only bound to be reasonably cautious and careful.

Today the judgment in this case would undoubtedly be against the auditor, but the comfortable words of the judge have been used by auditors as a defence against charges of negligence in relation to frauds – a subject we look at more closely in Chapter 29.

McKesson and Robbins Inc., USA (1939)

In this almost unbelievable case, the directors of the company created fictitious records of trading, sales, purchases, bank accounts, receivables and inventory so that the assets were overstated by over $20m. This extraordinary state of affairs was not detected by the auditors. In particular, they did not attend the inventory count. Had they done so they would have rapidly realized that no inventory existed!

Allied Crude Vegetable Oil Refining Corporation of New Jersey (1963)

In this scandal, methods were used to fool auditors who were present at the inventory count.

Three methods, at least, were used:

- The quantity of vegetable oil in a tank was checked and before the quantity was checked in a second tank, the contents of the first tank were pumped through to the second tank.
- The counters used a dip stick to measure the quantity of oil in a tank. In reality the tank was empty and oil was contained only in a thin drainpipe down which the dipstick was dropped.
- The fraudsters filled the tanks with mostly water and a small quantity of oil – the oil floated on the top and it looked like a full tank.

The oil 'inventories' were certified by the auditors and were used as collateral for millions of dollars' worth of loans which were used fraudulently. The auditor's procedures were found to be totally inadequate and they had signed the certificates of value on the basis of very flimsy audit evidence.

RECEIVABLES

Receivables form a significant item amongst the assets of most companies and its verification is a key part of the audit work. A description of a Receivables system is contained in Chapter 9.

Receivables generally comprise two main components:

- trade receivables, i.e. receivables (sales) ledger balances; and
- prepayments.

The auditor will be gathering sufficient appropriate evidence to verify the assertions that:

- The receivables represent bona fide customers (*existence*).
- The amounts are due to the business (*rights* and *obligations*).
- The amounts due are correctly stated at the appropriate value (*valuation* and *allocation*).
- All amounts due have been recorded (*completeness*).

One point to remember is that auditors are only interested in validating the figure for receivables as a *total*, they are not interested in individual receivables accounts except:

- if there is a suspicion of fraud;
- as part of compliance tests of the sales system; or
- to validate any provision for unrecoverable debts or amounts written off.

Trade receivables – compliance testing of internal control procedures

Students should refer to the relevant section of Chapter 13 wherein we outlined the process of auditing the Revenues system.

As part of their audit of Statement of Financial Position items auditors will have regard to the internal controls incorporated into the system in which the receivables are recorded. For example, the figure for trade receivables is largely derived from the receivables ledger which is part of the sales or revenues system, so controls within the revenues system are relevant to the auditor's evidence-gathering procedures for trade receivables verification.

The auditor will consider controls designed to ensure that the control objectives for the revenues and receivables systems are achieved, i.e.:

- All goods and services despatched are invoiced.
- Invoices are raised for the correct prices.
- All discounts are authorized.
- Goods on credit are only despatched to approved, credit-worthy customers.
- All invoices for sales are properly recorded in the books.
- Amounts received from customers are properly recorded and the persons responsible for dealing with these are separate from those responsible for processing sales transactions.
- Outstanding balances are reviewed and possible bad debts pursued.
- All credit notes are authorized.
- All balances written off are authorized.

Compliance tests

The first task is to determine the system of internal control over sales and receivables. The system for receivables should ensure that:

- Only bona fide sales bring receivables into being.
- All such sales are to approved customers.
- All such sales are recorded.
- Once recorded the debts are only eliminated by receipt of cash or on the authority of a responsible official.
- Debts are collected promptly.
- Balances are regularly reviewed and aged, a proper system for follow-up exists and, if necessary, adequate provision for bad and doubtful debts is made.

Substantive testing procedures

- Obtain an aged schedule of receivables and agree the total to the control account. Note that with computerized accounting systems the balances will undoubtedly agree.
- Test a sample of balances on ledger accounts to the schedule and vice versa where this has not been produced directly from the sales ledger system.
- Examine the make-up of balances. They should be composed of specific items.
- Ensure each account is settled from time to time.
- Enquire into the reason for any credit balances – this may lead to omitted sales.
- Enquire into the reasons for any transfers between accounts or any amounts recorded in the cash book as a receipt for one amount but split into two or more when being recorded in the sales ledger – this could be evidence of fraud (Chapter 20).
- Consider the valuation of receivables. This is dealt with in the next paragraph.

Provision for bad and doubtful debts

The valuation of receivables is really a consideration of the adequacy of the provision for bad and doubtful debts. The auditors should consider the following:

- The adequacy of the system of internal control relating to the approval of credit and following up of poor payers.
- The period of credit allowed and taken.
- Whether balances have been settled after the year end.
- Whether an account is made up of specific items or not, i.e. if the debtor is paying amounts 'on account' this could be indicative of cash flow difficulties and might be the prelude to a bad debt.
- Whether an account is within the maximum credit approved.
- Reports on major receivables from collectors, trade associations, etc.
- Present value and reliability of any security lodged as collateral.
- The state of legal proceedings and the legal status of the debtor, e.g. in liquidation or bankruptcy.

Analytical review

Auditors should carry out analytical review procedures as part of substantive testing. These should include one particular ratio, the Receivables days:

$$\frac{Receivables \times 365}{Creditsales}$$

which can be compared with previous periods. Any pronounced fluctuation in the ratio could indicate changes to credit control procedures or, in extreme cases where the ratio has increased dramatically, fictitious sales which, of course, will never be paid.

Additional procedures include:

- Comparisons with budgets or prior years.
- Comparison of aged receivables bands (i.e. 30 days, 30–60 days, etc.) with prior years to identify increased receivables ageing.

Note that:

- Debts which are considered irrecoverable should be written off to the Statement of Comprehensive Income.
- Specific provisions for doubtful debts should be set up against debts which are considered doubtful.
- Some companies make round-sum or percentage provisions against doubtful debts. This practice is generally unacceptable as it may be a way of hiding profits with a 'fictitious' provision. Any such provision would have to be justified and be based on statistical evidence which may come from past experience or from data about other similar undertakings which is obtainable from trade associations or which is publicly available.

Receivables circularization

Good independent audit evidence can be obtained from circularizing the receivables (or some of them) for direct confirmation. The approach to this is set out in ISA 505 *External confirmations*.

The advantages of this technique are:

- Direct external evidence is available for the existence and ownership and value of the amount due.
- It provides confirmation of the effectiveness of the system of internal control. If the sales ledger is recording the receivables correctly it follows that the system that leads up to it, i.e. the sales system, is also functioning properly.
- It assists in the auditor's evaluation of cut-off procedures as it can identify invoices in transit over the year end.
- It provides evidence of items in dispute.

The methodology to be adopted is known as *positive circularization*. The customer is asked to reply whether they agree the balance or not, or is asked to supply the balance themselves. The approach is as follows:

- Obtain the co-operation of the client – only they can ask third parties to divulge information.
- Select a sample. All customers can be circularized but this is unusual.
- Do *not* omit –
  - nil balances
  - credit balances
  - accounts written off in the period
- Give weight to overdue or disputed balances.
- Use stratified samples, e.g. all large balances and only some small ones.
- The letter should:
  - be from the client
  - request a reply *directly to the auditor*
  - contain a stamped, addressed, envelope or a pre-paid reply envelope addressed to the auditor
  - be despatched by the auditor – do not let the client post the letters as this will devalue the independence of the test
- Receive and evaluate replies.
- Follow up when replies are not received. This is the major problem – it is usual to get less than a 5 per cent response.
- Circularization is sometimes carried out at dates other than the year end. This can provide evidence about the operation of the sales and receivables system but will not, of course, validate the year-end figure.

EXAMPLE 2

Example of receivables circularization letter

FROM:
HEDONITE MANUFACTURING LTD
CLOGHAMPTON

TO:
ECSTATIC MINING LTD
WIMPTON

Dear Sir,

As part of their normal audit procedures, we have been requested by our auditors Tickitt & Run to ask you to confirm direct to them your indebtedness to us as shown on the enclosed statement as at 31 December 2X16.

If the statement is in agreement with your records, please sign in the space provided below and return this letter directly to our auditors using the pre-paid envelope provided.

If the statement is not in agreement with your records, please notify our auditors directly of the amount shown by your records and if possible send them full particulars of the difference.

It will be of assistance to us if you will give this request your early attention.

This is not a request for payment and no remittance should be sent to our auditors.

Yours faithfully,
J. Brown,

Chief Accountant

Name of account   *Ecstatic Mining Ltd*

The balance shown on the statement at 31.12.2X16 of £1432.00 due from us is/is not *(delete as appropriate)* in agreement with our records at 31.12.2X16.

If it does not agree the reason for the difference is

_____ Signature   _____ Date
_____ Position
_____ Company Stamp

If the client refuses permission for the auditor to carry out such a circulation the auditors should:

- Enquire as to why permission has been denied – often the excuse is that it might upset the customers.
- Evaluate the implications of this refusal on the auditor's estimate of the risk of a material misstatement and carry out alternative verification procedures as necessary.

They should communicate this refusal to those charged with governance, unless the refusal has, of course, come from them. Ultimately they will have to consider the implications of management's refusal for their auditor's report (Chapter 26).

There is a version of this test called a *negative circulation* but it is never used because under this method the respondent is only asked to reply if they disagree with the balance shown on the letter. It is impossible therefore to distinguish between a nonreply which means that the respondent agrees with the balance or a nonreply because the respondent has thrown the letter in the bin. Accordingly, only a positive circularization is used where the respondent is asked to reply whether they agree or disagree.

Prepayments

These are amounts paid for in one period which relate to the next period. In many cases these are not material and audit testing will be minimal.

Most prepayments are verified by:

- reviewing the client's system for ensuring all prepayments are identified and properly calculated
- re-performing the calculations
- reviewing previous year's working papers for evidence that the same prepayment existed previously
- reviewing transactions after the year end

ACCOUNTING ESTIMATES

It may be that the financial statements include various estimates which, if material, the auditors have to consider and validate.

We look at this in more detail in Chapter 16 but for this purpose there are two key points:

- The responsibility for these estimates lies with the directors or other governing body and may involve special knowledge and judgement. Some are routine, e.g. depreciation and some are one-off, e.g. a potential write down in Inventory values.
- Auditors should obtain sufficient appropriate audit evidence on all material accounting estimates. The evidence should give assurance that the estimates are reasonable in the circumstances and, when required, appropriately disclosed.

Note that the estimates used in the Financial Statements have to have some validity, i.e. the directors cannot simply 'think of a number' and use that. There has to be some element of calculation, a rationale and a sense of proportion in the estimate. Generally, these are only used where a precise figure is not known but it is possible to come to some form of realistic estimate based on calculations or valid assumptions. Consequently, the underlying rationale and any calculations are capable of being audited and conclusions drawn by the auditor as to the reliability of the estimated figures.

The accounting estimates and the audit work applied to them may well be included in the Auditor's Report as a Key Audit Matter (Chapter 26) where disclosure is made of the relevant estimate, the audit work carried out to validate the estimate is described and the conclusions the auditors have drawn fully stated.

In the latter cases and if the matters are material, the auditor might consider that the uncertainty and/or the lack of objective data is so great that there are implications for the Audit Report – see Chapter 26.

BANK BALANCES

The auditor will be gathering sufficient appropriate evidence to verify the assertions that:

- The balances are in the name of the company *(existence)*.
- The balances belong to the business *(rights and obligations)*.
- The balances due are correctly stated at the appropriate value *(valuation and allocation)*.
- All balances due have been recorded *(completeness)*.

These procedures apply whether balances are in hand or overdrawn. Overdrawn balances will be included as payables (Chapter 16) unless there is a right of set off which the bank will advise.

Verification of bank balances is effected by compliance tests and substantive tests.

Compliance tests

Appraisal of the internal control system relating to payments and receipts to ensure that:

- all payments are authorized
- all payments are made in respect of bona fide liabilities
- all receipts are collected and banked intact
- all amounts are correctly recorded in the books
- persons dealing with payments and receipts differ from those who deal with sales and purchases transactions

Substantive tests

- Examination and investigation of the bank reconciliation, noting particularly:
  - That any uncleared cheques have been cleared after date. These are payments which have been issued by the organization and entered in the cash book, but which have not yet been debited to the account by the bank. They should be checked to ensure that they are cleared after the Statement of Financial Position date.
  - Lodgements credited after date, but actually paid in before date. These are deposits into the account which have been entered into the cash book as receipts but which had not been credited to the account by the bank at the year end. They should be checked to ensure that the receipts are cleared by the bank and are not subsequently reversed. If the customer has insufficient funds to meet the payment, the bank will 'bounce' their cheque or bank transfer. In this case the customers' account has to be restored to its receivables status and consideration given by the client to a possible bad or doubtful debt provision.

The auditors should look for evidence that:

- the bank reconciliation is prepared at least monthly
- it is reviewed periodically by a responsible official or checked by Internal Audit

The auditors obtain the key piece of audit evidence, which can be used to verify the assertions regarding:

- ownership
- existence
- valuation

by direct confirmation from the bank or banks.

The bank must have the permission of the client to do this which is given by asking the client to sign an authority letter to the bank authorizing them to release any information the auditors may require directly to them.

The bank letter is usually a standard format and, in addition to requesting confirmation of balances at the Statement of Financial Position date, opportunity is usually taken to ask the bank a number of questions at the same time.

These include enquiries such as:

- confirmation that all bank accounts with the bank are disclosed, including accounts with nil balances and accounts opened and closed in the period
- the company's credit limits and overdraft facilities
- the existence and terms of loans or other borrowings
- whether the bank has knowledge of other bank accounts in other banks
- details of outstanding charges and interest accrued but not applied at the Statement of Financial Position date
- any outstanding bills of exchange, guarantees, acceptances, etc.
- details of foreign currency contracts
- the existence of any asset repurchase or hire purchase/leasing agreements
- whether or not there are any items held in safe custody or as security for borrowings

This bank letter plus a validated bank reconciliation will provide the evidence the auditors need.

LOANS

Loans are not usually material assets of companies other than those whose business it is to make loans. We shall consider two types of loans:

1. Loans other than to directors.
   Verification will be:

   - Examine and evaluate internal controls. Authority to make loans is particularly important.
   - Obtain a schedule and confirm details with:
     - loan agreements
     - interest calculations
     - repayments received
   - If the loan is material, it may be thought necessary to obtain a certificate directly from the borrower.
   - Examine agreements and ensure terms are being adhered to.
   - If a loan is secured, examine the security and consider its value and whether the security is sufficient, if it has to be sold quickly, to cover the outstanding balance of the loan.
   - If a loan is guaranteed, examine the status of the guarantor.
   - Review the adequacy of any provision for bad debts. For example, a bad debt may occur when a loan to an employee is made and the employee leaves before repayment is complete.

2 Loans to directors and connected persons.

This is the subject of several Companies Act requirements. Section 197 of the Companies Act 2006 prohibits loans to a director, or for the company to act as guarantor for such a loan, unless the transaction has been approved by the members (i.e. the shareholders). For public companies this also includes what are known as 'quasi-loans' – which are situations where, for example, the directors buy goods, the company pays for them and the director reimburses the company, i.e. the company provides credit for the director. This provision can catch use of a company credit card by a director (S198, CA 2006).

However, there are some exemptions from these provisions, assuming the company doesn't make loans in the ordinary course of business, which would all be exempt anyway if they were made on commercial terms. The following are not prohibited:

- Loans and quasi-loans not exceeding £10 000 outstanding at any one time.
- Loans, quasi-loans and credit transactions to meet expenditure on company business not exceeding £50 000 outstanding at any time.
- Small credit transactions up to £15 000.
- Money lent to fund a director's defence costs in a legal action in connection with their actions as a director. There is an upper limit of £50 000 beyond which the loans require shareholders' approval.

Audit procedures

The auditor's duties in respect of these types of transactions involving directors are as follows:

- Review all transactions involving directors which were outstanding at any time during the year. Materiality does not apply; all loans must be reviewed.
- If approval of shareholders is required, ensure the relevant resolution has been approved.
- If felt necessary, obtain a certificate of confirmation from the director concerned.
- Ensure that all such loans are subject to board minute.
- Ensure that the law has been complied with.
- Ensure that full disclosure is made as required in the financial statements.
- If the requisite information is not given in the accounts, the auditors are required to give the information in their report.

CASH

In many cases cash will not be a material item in the Statement of Financial Position and auditors will, consequently, not carry out any detailed substantive checking work on cash balances at the year end. However, this does not mean that cash transactions should be ignored completely, even if they are relatively minor, as there is a high **inherent risk** of fraud in connection with cash.

Auditors should therefore consider the internal control aspects of cash transactions. Internal control objectives in dealing with cash receipts and cash payments, where these are a substantial part of the company's business, are dealt with in Chapter 9.

As far as the Statement of Financial Position audit is concerned the auditor should also carry out the following substantive checking work where the amounts are material:

- Review the operation of the cash system. For petty cash this should be an **imprest system** which should be reviewed by a responsible official periodically and the petty cash book initialled as evidence of review. For businesses which deal in substantial cash amounts there needs to be a full internal control review.
- An imprest system is a method of controlling petty cash expenditure whereby the amount spent in the previous period is refunded so that the cash float remains at a constant amount. For example, if the cash float is £100 and £57.65 is spent in period 1, the amount of £57.65 is refunded to petty cash to bring the float back up to £100. The expenditure should be supported by authorized petty cash vouchers.
- Count the cash, either at the year-end if the balance is material or at a random point during the audit as a 'surprise' count. If this is to be carried out the auditors must:

- Ensure they have control of all cash balances simultaneously to ensure funds cannot be 'swopped' from one to another.
- Count the cash in the presence of an independent member of the client's staff to ensure that any shortages cannot be attributed to the auditor.
- List the individual details of notes and coins.
- Ensure any IOUs are recorded and are collectible. Auditors should review the company's policies towards making loans (as evidenced by an IOU).
- Reconcile the count to the petty cash book and investigate any differences.
- Ask the cashier to initial the reconciliation as evidence of agreement.

SUMMARY

- The verification is of assertions about each asset. A useful mnemonic is CAVEBOP.
- Verification methods vary according to the asset but the basic principles are to verify existence and ownership by inspecting the asset, or evidence of it, and the relevant title documents.
- Most transactions in assets are evidence in the minutes of directors' meetings and these should be inspected as a matter of course.
- Valuation of both tangible and intangible assets is sometimes complex and auditors may have to exercise a degree of judgement in deciding whether the asset is properly stated in the accounts.
- Auditors should be alert to the possibility of impairment in the value of assets.
- Auditors need to be aware of the accounting requirements for accounting for leased assets and take care in distinguishing between operating and finance leases.
- There are accounting rules on disclosure of noncurrent assets and you should be familiar with them.
- Inventory on a Statement of Financial Position is subject to a correct count, a correct assessment of condition and appropriate valuation.
- Inventory can be considered under a number of separate categories.
- ISA 501 makes attendance at inventory count to observe the incidence of internal control normal audit practice.
- Detailed audit tests must be supplemented by analytical review.
- The valuation of work in progress can be difficult and care has to be taken concerning the inclusion of overheads, the taking of profit or the inclusion of losses.
- Independent inventory counters can be used by clients and within limitations be relied upon by the auditor.
- Cut-off is a key issue in identifying inventory values.
- Receivables can be verified directly by circularization and by reviewing compliance tests of controls.
- A key part of the verification process for bank balances is the bank confirmation letter.
- A bank reconciliation is a key procedure. Auditors should check it at the period end date as an evidence-gathering procedure and review other bank reconciliations carried out by the company during the financial period as evidence of internal control procedures operating in the business.
- Loans to directors are subject to company law restrictions which you should know.
- Cash balances should be audited if material, but auditors should be aware of the potential for fraud so might wish to carry out audit work as part of their work on internal control.

POINTS TO NOTE

- Students often fail to answer examination questions properly by making too few points. This chapter will provide enough ideas for students to make sufficient points in their answers.
- Questions on asset verification are sometimes on existence, ownership, value and presentation. Some are specifically on one or two aspects only.
- To answer specific questions, remember the assertions and the mnemonic CAVEBOP and apply them as required.
- Note that many syllabuses require students to have an appreciation of the accounting requirements of the Companies Act 2006 and the Financial Reporting Standards.
- The extent and manner of verification of an asset depends on the degree of risk of misstatement possible with the asset. Inherent risk depends on many factors including the complexity of the assets (e.g. work in progress), the judgement involved (e.g. inventory at net realizable value) and the susceptibility to loss or misappropriation (e.g. cash). The extent of reliance on internal control in reducing substantive tests depends on the auditor's perception of control risk.
- Inspection of work in progress by the auditor is desirable in that it gives evidence that work in progress exists and helps with determining the state of completion, especially of large contracts.

CASE STUDY 1

Osocheep Supermarkets Ltd have a main depot and five large supermarkets. Their financial year end is Thursday 31 March 2X16 and inventory is to be evaluated as at the close of business on that date. The next day is an exceptionally busy one with much business in terms of deliveries from supplier, movements of inventory and sales. The sales margins are narrow and it is very important to obtain an accurate figure for inventory. Goods in inventory in the warehouse are kept on a continuous inventory system (quantities only) on a computer with a printout of the previous day's inventory available at noon each day. The inventory at branches is not recorded continuously. The bulk of the inventory is carried in the back rooms and moved onto the supermarket shelves continuously during the day.

Discussion
– What are the problems in this case with regard to:
a) cut-off
b) inventory identification and quantity determination
c) valuation?

STUDENT SELF-TESTING QUESTIONS

Questions with answers apparent from the text

a) What are the six aspects to be covered in verifying an asset?
b) List the points that could be covered in verifying an asset.
c) How is land and buildings verified?
d) What is the key issue in the valuation of intangible assets?

e) What is the difference between research and development?

f) When should purchased goodwill be written off?

g) What are the directors' responsibilities for inventory count?

h) List the characteristics of good inventory count procedures.

i) What are the auditor's duties toward inventory count:

   (a) Before the inventory count?

   (b) During the inventory count?

   (c) After the inventory count?

j) What is the main audit issue in connection with the valuation of long-term work in progress?

k) Outline the procedures for verifying receivables.

l) What matters should be considered in reviewing the provision for bad and doubtful debts?

m) Outline the procedures for a positive circulation of receivables.

n) What audit evidence accrues from the bank letter?

o) Summarize the contents of the standard bank letter.

p) What are the Companies Act rules on loans to directors and connected persons?

q) What are the auditor's duties on such loans?

EXAMINATION QUESTIONS

1 Movit Ltd (Movit) is a company which hires out heavy plant used in the construction industry. All plant is hired out with a driver who is responsible for ensuring that the plant is immobilized and stored securely when left on customers' sites overnight. Movit operates from ten depots throughout England.

   The directors of Movit have requested that your firm provides a report on the reliability of the internal control system in respect of the acquisition, custody and recording of its plant. They have provided you with the following information.

   All plant is uniquely numbered and logged in a plant register and integrated hire management system which can indicate the location of each item of plant at any point in time. Head office staff are responsible for maintaining the register, reconciling it each month with the nominal ledger and investigating any differences. They also undertake periodic physical checks involving checking items listed in the register to the asset and checking the asset to the register. The results of such checks are reported to the operations manager who authorizes any adjustments to the register on a standard form.

   The hire management system produces performance measures of usage and downtime for each item of plant. This is used by the operations manager to determine the need for additional new plant or replacement of existing plant. All acquisitions are processed by head office. A capital expenditure form has to be completed and supported by three quotations from suppliers and authorized by the operations and finance directors.

   The finance director also undertakes an appraisal exercise to confirm whether it is appropriate to lease or buy the plant and this is evidenced on the capital expenditure form.

   New plant is delivered directly to the depot requiring the item. Each depot manager confirms, by entering on to the system via a terminal at the depot, that the items have been received, physically checked and are of the correct specification. Industry regulations require plant to be subjected to regular maintenance checks.

   These checks are carried out by engineers who complete a standard checklist evidencing such checks and each depot manager is required to submit a copy of the checklist to head office staff who log the date of each check on the plant register.

   Head office staff are responsible for monitoring that timely checks have taken place, investigating any breaches of this policy and reporting their findings to the operations director.

   Required:

   (a) Identify how Movit's internal control procedures meet the objectives of ensuring that:

      (i)   plant acquisitions are required and provide an acceptable rate of return;

      (ii) plant is recorded, safeguarded and complies with laws and regulations; and

      (iii) plant is appropriately valued.

(b) State the methods that you would use to obtain evidence that procedures established by the management are operating effectively and for each method provide two examples of how you would apply it to Movit.

(ICAEW)

2 Harrier Motors deals in motor vehicles, sells spare parts, provides after-sales servicing and undertakes car body repairs. During the financial year to 30 June 2X16, the company expanded its operations from five to eight sites.

Each site has a car showroom, service workshop and parts storage.

In May 2X16, management appointed an experienced chartered certified accountant to set up an internal audit department.

New cars are imported, on consignment, every three months from one supplier. Harrier pays the purchase price of the cars, plus 3 per cent, three months after taking delivery. Harrier does not return unsold cars, although it has a legal right to do so.

Harrier offers 'trade-ins' (i.e. part-exchange) on all sales of new and used cars. New car sales carry a three-year manufacturer's warranty and used cars carry a six-month guarantee. Many used cars are sold for cash. An extensive range of spare parts is held for which perpetual inventory records are kept. Storekeepers carry out continuous checking.

Mr Joop, the sales executive, selects a car from each consignment to use for all his business and personal travelling until the next consignment is received. Such cars are sold at a discount as ex-demonstration models. Car servicing and body repairs are carried out in workshops by employed and subcontracted service engineers. Most jobs are started and finished in a day and are invoiced immediately on completion.

In July 2X15 Harrier purchased a brand name, 'Uni-fit', which is now applied to the parts which it supplies. Management has not amortized this intangible asset as it believes its useful life to be indefinite.

Required:

(a) Using the information provided, identify and explain the audit risks to be addressed when planning the final audit of Harrier Motors for the year ending 30 June 2X16.

(b) Identify and briefly explain the principal matters to be addressed in Harrier Motors' instructions for the conduct of its physical inventory count as at 30 June 2X16.

(c) Describe the audit work to be carried out in respect of the useful life of the 'Uni-fit' brand name as at 30 June 2X16.

(ICAEW)

SOURCES AND ADDITIONAL READING

Financial Reporting Council (2015) *FRS 102 The Financial Reporting Standard Applicable in the UK and Republic of Ireland*. London: Financial Reporting Council.

Financial Reporting Council (2009) *ISA 501 Audit Evidence – Specific Considerations for Selected Items*. London: Financial Reporting Council.

Wood, F. (2008) *Business Accounting 1 and 2*. London: Prentice-Hall.

CHAPTER 16
THE AUDIT OF
LIABILITIES

Learning Objectives

After studying the material in this chapter you should be able to:

- understand the principles of the audit of liabilities in the Statement of Financial Position

- explain the difference between an accrual and a provision

- understand the audit of accounting estimates

- understand the problems of auditing contingent liabilities

- discuss the procedures to be followed to ensure that all liabilities have been included in the Statement of Financial Position

INTRODUCTION

A Statement of Financial Position will contain liabilities grouped under various headings including:

- payables – due either before or after one year comprising:
    - trade payables – e.g. amounts due to suppliers
    - accruals and deferred income
    - provisions
    - amounts owed to group and related companies
- bank loans and overdrafts
- debenture loans
- share capital and reserves
- corporation tax and deferred taxation

In addition, the financial statements will contain details of any **contingent liabilities** by way of a note to the accounts. The auditor's task is to gather sufficient, appropriate evidence to validate the assertions (Chapter 11) shown here in *italics*.

Students should refer to Chapter 15 for details of the assertions relating to the Statement of Financial Position. The problem the auditor is always trying to deal with in the audit of liabilities is the question of *understatement*. Directors seeking to make the most of their financial situation may well seek to understate liabilities so one of the auditor's areas of difficulty is not simply auditing what is there but in finding out what, if anything, is not there.

In particular, the auditor must gather sufficient appropriate evidence:

- that the liabilities exist *(existence)*
- that the company is due to pay or discharge these liabilities *(rights and obligations)*
- that all liabilities which should be included have been included *(completeness)*
- that all liabilities have been recorded at their full amounts *(valuation)*
- that liabilities have been properly disclosed in the financial statements *(classification)*

VERIFICATION PROCEDURES

Verification procedures are relatively straightforward and there is good third-party verification evidence available in the audit of trade payables. Students should refer to Chapter 9 which described the essential features of the purchases and expenses system.

Amounts falling due within one year – current liabilities

Into this category will fall:

- trade payables
- accruals
- provisions
- bank overdrafts and short-term loans (or part of loans due in the next 12 months)
- amounts due to other groups or related companies

TRADE PAYABLES

Students should refresh their memory of Chapter 13 which described the audit objectives of the purchases and expenses system.

Compliance testing of internal control procedures

As part of their audit of items in the Statement of Financial Position auditors will have regard to the internal controls incorporated into the system in which the liability is recorded. For example, the figure for trade payables is largely derived from the payables ledger which is part of the purchases system, so controls within the purchases system are relevant to the auditor's evidence-gathering procedures for trade payables verification.

The auditor will consider controls designed to ensure that:

- Purchased goods and services are properly authorized and documented.
- Purchases of goods and services are only made for the purposes of the business.
- Goods and services received are inspected for quality and condition before being accepted.
- Invoices and similar documents are properly checked before being processed.
- Only valid transactions are entered into the accounting records.

Substantive testing

In addition to testing control procedures the auditors will carry out substantive testing procedures. These include:

- Testing individual balances with third party evidence. This could consist of evidence gathered from a payables circularization but is more normally carried out by reconciling payables ledger balances with statements from suppliers.
- This is a key test as it provides independent third party evidence as to the size and composition of the balance. It is also indicative that the purchases system is processing invoices correctly and is *prima facie* evidence for the assertion of accuracy.
- Reconciling the list of trade payables with the control account – note that in most cases with computerized systems these will automatically agree.
- Reviewing year end cut-off procedures – see Chapter 15.
- A sample of balances should be subject to specific tests such as:
  - Is the balance made up of specific amounts over a reasonable period?
  - Have all the entries making up the balance been authorized?
  - Was the balance paid in full after the year end?
    This can be done as part of the suppliers' statement reconciliation process. The purpose of this is to ensure that the client is not making payments on account rather than dealing with specific liabilities. This could be indicative of cash flow and hence going concern issues (Chapter 23).
  - Carrying out an analytical procedures of the payables figure, i.e. look at payables days, comparison of payables with previous periods, etc. for reasonableness. See Chapter 12 for more details.

The payables days' analytical procedure is analogous to the day's sales in receivables calculation in Chapter 15 and is represented by the formula:

$$\frac{\text{Trade payables} \times 365}{\text{Purchases}}$$

This should be compared with previous periods.

CUT-OFF

The question of checking cut-off procedures (see Chapter 15) is important as falsifying the cut-off by, say, including items in Inventory but ignoring the associated liability by including it in the following year's transactions is a way to manipulate the financial statements favourably – so this work cannot be minimized.

ACCRUALS

Students should understand the definition of an **accrual**. An accrual is an amount set aside for a specific liability, i.e. where the expenditure has been incurred in the period but for which no invoice has been received.

Commonly these cover such expenses as gas, electricity, rent, telephone, etc. They are often relatively immaterial and analytical procedures will often provide sufficient evidence.

Key audit procedures include:

- Identifying how the client identifies all accruals required to be made – discover and test the procedures.
- Check the schedule of accruals for arithmetical accuracy.
- Check the calculations of accruals.
- Compare with previous periods to ensure consistency.
- If material include reference to accruals in the management letter. We look at this later in Chapter 24.

PROVISIONS

Provisions differ from accruals. A **provision** is a liability which exists but for which the amount or its timing is uncertain. An example of a provision is an amount set aside to meets the costs and any penalties arising from claims against the business. It may not be known when the claims will be made and how much they might amount to, particularly if the company is contesting them.

Provisions, by definition, are subject to a level of uncertainty as to timing or amount and the auditor needs to be aware of the level of uncertainty. We look at this further below in the section on auditing.

In order to establish some basis for estimating the level of uncertainty auditors should establish procedures to ensure that there is a liability of some amount – e.g. legal documents, claim letters, minutes of meetings (*existence*) and that the company may be liable and that the liability will not be met by someone else, e.g. an insurer (*rights* and *obligations*).

The auditor must establish that management have made as reasonable an estimate in the circumstances, that the assumptions they have used are valid and that the basis on which it has been calculated is acceptable and on a similar basis to that of previous years, if appropriate (*valuation*).

The auditors may have to use a certain amount of judgement in order to satisfy themselves as to the value of the liability. They may well, if the provision is material, want to receive specific assurances from management in the Letter of Representation (see Chapter 24) but these will not replace the auditor's own evidence-gathering procedures.

Finally, the auditors must ensure that provisions are properly disclosed in the financial statements, including any explanatory notes (*classification*).

FINANCE LEASE LIABILITIES

There are other liabilities incurred which are not accruals or provisions as such. One major one is liabilities under finance leases. We looked at the assets side of finance leases in Chapter 15 so reference should be made there to ensure accounting treatment is consistent.

It is important that, when verifying liabilities under finance leases, these remember being ones which '*transfer substantially all the risks and rewards incidental to ownership of an asset*', auditors understand the relevant accounting rules – which can be quite complicated.

Finance lease commitments can be a significant figure in the accounts of companies many of whom lease assets on a large scale; consider for example telecoms companies, mining and extraction companies, retail chains or fleet operators. So these liabilities could, in some instances, be considerable so the correct accounting treatment may be significant in the context of the financial statements as a whole.

FRS 102 requires a lessee to split the minimum lease payments between the capital element of the lease and the interest cost. However, the reduction in the outstanding liability is calculated using the *effective interest method*. The effective interest method is a method of calculating the amortized cost of either a financial asset or a financial liability and allocating the interest component of the lease payments over the relevant period.

Under the effective interest method:

- the amortized cost of the finance lease liability is the present value of future payments discounted at the effective interest rate; and
- the interest expense in a period is equivalent to the carrying amount of the liability at the beginning of a period multiplied by the effective interest rate for the period.

For the purposes of this calculation, the effective interest rate is the rate that exactly discounts the future payments through the expected life of the lease.

So auditors will be required to:

- check the basic terms of the finance leases to ensure that they are still current and to verify the various values, rates and terms within each lease; and
- test check the calculations management has performed in calculating the value of the liabilities under each lease.

Clearly any errors of principle or actual errors in calculation will have to be considered for materiality and brought into any evaluation as to whether an adjustment to correct the errors will have to be made.

BANK OVERDRAFTS AND SHORT-TERM LOANS

These will be disclosed separately on the Statement of Financial Position even if there are other bank balances in credit unless there is a right of set-off of accounts, which the bank will advise on in the bank confirmation letter (see Chapter 15).

Verification of these overdrawn bank balances is similar to verifying bank balances as detailed in Chapter 15 and basically requires the auditors to check the bank reconciliation and obtain independent third-party evidence from the bank in the form of a bank confirmation letter.

Verification of amounts due on loans will require the auditors to review the loan documentation and confirm any calculations.

It is necessary to review original documentation and to obtain confirmation that the company has met all its obligations to date and has not defaulted on any loan repayments. If necessary, these should be traced through the records.

AMOUNTS DUE TO GROUP AND RELATED COMPANIES

If the auditors are auditors to the other companies in the group, the balances can be reconciled with each other. We look at this in more detail in Chapter 28.

Particular attention should be paid to how the balances have arisen to ensure that only *bona fide* intercompany transactions are included such as head office charges, recharges of costs and expenses, management fees, etc. and that related companies, i.e. those that are not full subsidiaries, in particular are not being used to hide trading losses, etc. (see Chapter 21).

Again assurances from management may be required in respect of transactions with related or associated companies.

LONG-TERM LIABILITIES

These mainly comprise long-term loans and debenture loans.

Audit procedures for long-term loans are the same as for short-term loans, i.e.:

- review the loan documentation;
- confirm the company is not in default; and
- obtain a confirmation from the lender of sums outstanding.

Debenture loans are different insofar as these are, effectively, an issue of loan notes carrying a fixed rate of interest and repayable on a set date. They are part of the company's financing and as such the auditor will have to confirm that the company has the power under its constitution to issue debentures.

If it has, then it is only necessary for the auditors to confirm the amounts with:

- the issue documentation
- the sums received

and ensure that they are correctly disclosed in the financial statements.

SHARE CAPITAL AND RESERVES

This is a relatively straightforward procedure but nevertheless should be carried out. The amounts can normally be verified by recourse to:

- previous period's accounts
- minutes of directors' meetings
- documentation and sums received in respect of new issues of shares
- returns made to the Registrar of Companies

Note that the Companies Act 2006 abolishes the concept of authorized share capital. However, there are still various legal rules surrounding the issue of shares and auditors should ensure that they have been validly issued. Issues of shares still require a shareholder's resolution and auditors should ensure that the appropriate resolutions have been properly passed.

Auditors should ensure that Reserves are properly classified and disclosed in the accounts and that the provisions regarding disclosure of, in particular, non distributable reserves, such as any Share Premium Account, are complied with.

Any movements or transfers to reserves should be evidenced by Board minutes.

UNRECORDED LIABILITIES

It is not enough for the auditors to be satisfied that all the liabilities recorded in the books are correct and are incorporated in the final accounts. They must also be satisfied that no other liabilities exist which are not, for various reasons, recorded in the books and the accounts.

Examples of such unrecorded liabilities might be:

- Claims by employees for injury.
- Claims by ex-employees for unfair dismissal.
- Unfunded pension commitments. A company may have a liability to pay past or present employees a pension in respect of past service and have no funds separated out for this purpose.
- Liability to 'top-up' pension schemes. When money has been put into separate trusts to pay pensions, inflation has often meant that the amount is insufficient and the company may have to implement clauses in the scheme whereby they have to put in extra money which could run into millions of pounds. Auditors may have to obtain actuarial valuations in order to review the position regarding unfunded pension liabilities and might also have to obtain legal advice as to extent of the company's liability.
- Bonuses under profit sharing arrangements.
- Returnable packages and containers.
- Value Added Tax and other tax liabilities. The auditor's knowledge of tax may lead them to suspect a liability of which the directors are blissfully ignorant
- Claims under warranties and guarantees.
- Liabilities on debts which have been factored with recourse. To explain: A owes B £50. B sells (factors) the debt to C for £45. Thus B has no debt any more but £45 in the bank. A fails to pay C. C can claim £50 from B (C has recourse).
- Bills receivable discounted (similar to above).
- Pending law suits.
- Changes in environmental or similar legislation which renders previously acceptable products obsolete. This may result in claims against the company.

- Losses on forward contracts. Example: A Ltd makes a contract to sell a million tons of Hedonite, which it does not have, at £50 a ton in six months' time. No entry will appear in the books or accounts, but when the time comes Hedonite has risen on the commodity market to £70 a ton and A Ltd, has to buy in at that price in order to make the sale for which it has contracted, thus making a loss on the transaction of £20 a ton. Auditors will have to ascertain when the loss is incurred, how it should be reported in each financial period and look at any uncompleted contracts.

It is important that the auditors appreciate that such liabilities exist. It may be in management's interest to understate or omit liabilities for which there are no accounting records and little hard evidence but auditors have a positive obligation to take reasonable steps to unearth them.

How is this to be approached? The possibilities of unrecorded liabilities should have been considered as part of the audit risk assessment process and suitable audit procedures identified to deal with identified risks. (Chapter 10).

The actions to take include:

- Direct enquiry of the directors and senior managers.
- Obtaining a Letter of Representation from the Board of Directors – see Chapter 24.
- Examination of events post the Statement of Financial Position date. This will include a review of major transactions in the period from the year end to the date the auditor's report is signed.
- Examination of minutes of director's meetings and senior management meetings where the existence of unrecorded liabilities may be mentioned.
- A review of the working papers and previous years' working papers.
- An awareness of the possibilities at all times when conducting the audit. For example, discovery during the audit that the client deals in 'futures' will alert the auditor to the possibility of outstanding commitments.
- Carrying out a subsequent events review for matters which have a bearing on issues at the period end date. We look at this in more detail in Chapter 23.

CONTINGENT LIABILITIES

This is a very difficult area for both management and auditors as it often demands quite a high degree of judgement and often very little evidence.

A contingent liability is liability arising from a condition which exists at the date of the Statement of Financial Position where the outcome will only be confirmed by the occurrence (or non-occurrence) of some future event which is outside the control of the business. A typical example of this would be the outcome of a court case where the judgement is uncertain.

The first decision to be made is whether any provision needs to be made in the accounts, i.e. is a real liability likely to crystallize even if the precise amount or timing is uncertain? This, in itself, can be a contentious issue.

The fundamental accounting concept of Prudence, enshrined in UK GAAP states that:

- probable losses should be provided for
- possible losses should be disclosed as a note to the financial statements
- probable gains should be disclosed as a note to the financial statements
- possible gains should be ignored until they crystallize or become probable

Typical examples of contingent liabilities include:

- guarantees given to third parties, e.g. in respect of a subsidiary company's overdraft
- discounted bills of exchange
- forward contracts
- the outcome of court cases where damages or costs might result
- claims under guarantees or warranties

The amount of any liability, its nature and whether any security has been provided has to be disclosed in the accounts.

Audit evidence

The bank confirmation letter (Chapter 15) will provide independent third party evidence in respect of forward currency contracts, discounted bills and guarantees.

Legal matters

This is a particularly difficult area in practice because of the inherent uncertainty involved in estimating the outcome of legal actions. There are some audit procedures which will lead to the verification of the existence of, but not necessarily the amount of, liabilities arising out of legal actions.

These include:

- Reviewing the client's system for recording claims and disputes and the procedures for bringing these to the attention of the board.
- Reviewing the arrangements for instructing solicitors.
- Examining the minutes of the board or other responsible committees (e.g. **Audit Committee**) for references to or indications of possible claims.
- Examining invoices from solicitors and the attached Memorandum of Services.
- Obtaining a list of matters referred to solicitors from the directors or other responsible official with an estimate of the possible ultimate liabilities.
- Obtaining a written assurance from the directors that they are not aware of any matters referred to solicitors other than those disclosed. (Chapter 25).
- Where possible the auditors should obtain a direct confirmation from the company's legal advisers. The request must be sent by the client requesting the reply or that a copy of the reply is sent direct to the auditor. The letter to the solicitor should include a request for details of cases referred to the solicitor not mentioned in the letter.

Letter to a client's legal adviser to confirm contingent liabilities arising out of pending legal matters sent by client on client's headed paper.

Messrs Scrooge & Co.
New Street
Oldcastle   26th February 2017

Dear Sirs,

Joy Manufacturing Ltd

In connection with the preparation and audit of the accounts for the year ending 31 December 2016 the directors have made estimates of the amounts of the ultimate liabilities (including costs) which might be incurred, and are regarded as material, in relation to the following matters on which you have been consulted. We should be grateful if you would confirm that in your opinion these estimates are reasonable.

Matter	Estimated liability including costs
1. Claim by James Brown for wrongful dismissal	£ 20 000
2. Claim by Hedonite Manufacturing Ltd for damages in respect of faulty goods	£ 180 000
3. Action by Difur plc for damages caused by late delivery of equipment— contested	£ 105 000
4. Action by Joyful Mfg plc for breach of copyright in our Catalogue	£ 124 000

We would also request that you confirm that these are the only legal actions that you are aware of in which our client is a party. Please send a copy of your reply to our auditors Messrs High & Lowe, Flat Street, Oldcastle.

Yours faithfully,
J Jones
Financial Director
Megablast plc

Note that solicitor's opinion letters often do not satisfactorily resolve the auditor's uncertainties and it may be that the auditor may wish to take independent legal advice.

It should be stressed that the auditors are responsible for their own opinion and it is their judgement which needs to be supported by as much evidence as can be gathered.

AUDITING ACCOUNTING ESTIMATES

In this chapter we consider many liabilities which are uncertain as to existence or amount. Liabilities are sometimes certain (e.g. most trade payables) but some need to be estimated and there are many other areas of accounting where estimates are made, such as valuing stock at net realizable value, estimating provisions, etc.

At this point we can summarize the auditing processes attached to accounting for estimates in general taking into account the provisions of the auditing standard ISA 540 *'Auditing, accounting estimates, including fair value accounting estimates, and related disclosures'*.

One of the key considerations is the level of uncertainty. For example, a building has been revalued for the Statement of Financial Position at £15m. Shortly after the year end an offer of £15.5m is received for it. The uncertainty surrounding the valuation is virtually nil and the auditor can evidence the valuation with the offer received. However, take an alternative situation where the client has been held responsible for a major pollution incident and will be subject to damages claims and legal penalties when the clean-up is complete and the situation has been assessed. The client makes an estimate of £100m which is little more than educated guesswork. How is the auditor to respond to that degree of uncertainty?

All the auditor can do is to consider the management's approach and to make their own calculations and consider the level of disclosure made in the financial statements i.e. have management fully explained the position so readers of the accounts can use their own judgement and come to their own conclusions?

This requires that auditors gather sufficient, appropriate evidence in respect of accounting estimates.

The following points are relevant:

- Accounting estimates have to be made in all areas where precise means of measurement cannot be applied. We have seen several examples in this book already (losses on work in progress, lawsuits, warranty claims, etc.).
- The responsibility for these estimates lies with the directors or other governing body and may involve special knowledge and judgement.
- Any estimates used in the Financial Statements have to have some validity, i.e. the directors cannot simply 'think of a number' and use that. There has to be some element of calculation, a rationale and a sense of proportion in the estimate. Generally, these are only used where a precise figure is not known but it is possible to come to some form of realistic estimate based on calculations or valid assumptions. Consequently, the underlying rationale and any calculations are capable of being audited and conclusions drawn by the auditor as to the reliability of the estimated figures.
- Some estimates are routine, e.g. depreciation, and some are one-off, e.g. the outcome of a lawsuit. Many are capable of reasonable estimation but some might not be. In the latter cases and if the matters are material, the auditor might consider that the uncertainty and/or the lack of objective data is so great that there are implications for the Audit Report – see Chapter 26.
- Auditors should obtain sufficient appropriate audit evidence on all material accounting estimates. The evidence should give assurance that the estimates are reasonable in the circumstances and, when required, appropriately disclosed.
- Auditors should consider the requirements of the appropriate financial reporting framework (e.g. UK GAAP) and ensure that the making of any accounting estimates has been done in accordance with that framework.

Auditors need to review the procedures and methods adopted by management to identify and to make accounting estimates. These may include Internal Audit. In some cases, a formula will be used (e.g. in estimating warranty claims or in setting depreciation rates). There should be systems for continually reviewing these formulae. The fact that directors do actually consider the formulae or other methods of calculating estimates on a continuing basis is itself reassuring to the auditor, but auditors should be alert to the possibility of management bias when judging an outcome.

These procedures should be tested in connection with each estimate; auditors must evaluate the data and consider the assumptions on which the estimates have been made. For example, in looking at depreciation, what assumptions on obsolescence have been made? Has management considered all the alternative possibilities of a particular situation when making an estimate of its financial outcome? Any calculations or applications of formulae should be reviewed to see if they are logical and representative.

Auditors can make their own independent estimate on each estimate and compare it with the one made by the directors and investigate any difference. In order to test the accuracy of estimates auditors can compare estimates made in previous years with actual outcomes, where known, to judge the accuracy of previous predictions and to provide experience for current estimates.

Clearly it is important to review subsequent events, i.e. events after the year end date for additional information which might not have been available to the directors at the time.

At the final stage of the audit, the auditors should make a review of the estimates (as with all the accounting data in the financial statements) and assess them in the light of their knowledge of the business and consistency with other evidence obtained during the audit.

If the auditors consider that a material estimate is unreasonable, they should ask the directors to adjust the financial statements and if this is not done then they should consider whether or not there is a material misstatement and ponder the implications for their Auditor's Report (Chapter 26).

In the event that the auditors consider that every reasonable effort has been made to quantify the amount involved but the level of uncertainty remains high they must consider the disclosure in the financial statements. The disclosure must be sufficient to explain the full situation to users of the accounts so that they are able to draw their own conclusions, consequently these may well be disclosed in the Auditor's Report as a Key Audit Matter (Chapter 26).

This means that the auditors would give a full description of the issue, i.e. the nature and size of the estimates, detail what audit work they carried out in order to verify the figures as best as they can and the conclusions that they have drawn from their audit work. This will enable a reader of the accounts to fully understand the issue and form their own view. This is not any form of modification of the Auditor's Opinion, as there is no dispute with the management, it is a form of disclosure.

SUMMARY

- The auditor must verify the existence, amount and adequate disclosure of all liabilities. They must also be satisfied that all liabilities are included.
- Each liability is verified from whatever evidence is available but some general procedures common to most liabilities can be discerned.
- Provisions are a difficult area. The auditor must take special care in considering the adequacy of provisions.
- Auditors must be aware of the level of uncertainty involved in the making of accounting estimates however there has to be a rational basis for the estimate and reasonable calculations of its size.
- Share capital is verified like other liabilities but special procedures apply to new issues.
- Subsequent events reviews are of assistance in reviewing the accuracy of provisions and estimates.
- Contingent liabilities must be considered firstly to see if they are contingent and secondly as to size. Careful disclosure has to be made of such liabilities.
- Auditors should consider not only the liabilities which have been identified but also those which may have been omitted or not recognized.
- Pending legal matters can be verified by direct confirmation from the company's legal advisers.
- Where the financial statements include significant accounting estimates auditors may disclose the relevant details in a section of their Auditor's Report headed Key Audit Matters (Chapter 26).
- Where there is a disagreement with the directors over the size and nature of material accounting estimates used in the financial statements, or where there is a significant uncertainty with regard to them, the auditors may well seek to modify their opinion in the Auditor's Report (Chapter 26).

POINTS TO NOTE

- The liabilities section of the Statement of Financial Position is subject to numerous Companies Act rules on disclosure. These must be known.
- Be very careful to use the words 'provision' and 'accrual' correctly. They are not synonymous.
- Two important matters in connection with liabilities are contingencies and consideration of events after the date of the Statement of Financial Position.
- The letter of representation may be some form of evidence in this area, especially in the problem of inclusion of all liabilities. This is discussed in Chapter 24.
- Some companies may have enormous potential liabilities arising, for example, out of legal claims, financial transactions or unfunded pension liabilities which have not been recognized in the financial statements. Legal advice may be required in connection with such liabilities.

CASE STUDY

Song & Danse LLP is a city firm of Chartered Certified Accountants. The firm's accounts are produced by the administration partner but are subject to audit by Blanket, Mange LLP, another firm of Chartered Certified Accountants. In June 2X16, a partner in Song & Danse who was suffering from overwork failed to realize that an enormous error had occurred in the preparation and audit of the financial statements of International Maize Ltd ('IM') for the year ended 31.5.2X15. Quantities of maize in transit had been inadvertently included in the company's inventories in both the producing country and the receiving country. The company had been acquired by Universal Porage Inc. which has now discovered the mistake. They have given notice that they intend to bring an action to recover damages from Song & Danse on the grounds that they relied on the audited accounts for the year ending 31.5.2X15 and that they would not have purchased IM had they known of the error.

The stock of IM was overstated by £22.4 million as a consequence of the error. The profit of IM was reported as £14.3 million and UP paid £41 million cash for IM.

Song & Danse carry professional indemnity insurance but only in the sum of £1 million due to an administrative error.

The partners of Song & Danse dislike each other and rely heavily on Blanket, Mange. No one at Song & Danse has informed Blanket, Mange of the pending legal action.

Discussion

– What auditing procedures might allow Blanket, Mange to discover the existence of the action?
– How might the amount of the ultimate award and costs be determined by Blanket, Mange?
– What other hidden liabilities might Song & Danse have at their year-end, 31.12.2X16?

STUDENT SELF-TESTING QUESTIONS

Questions with answers apparent from the text

a) List the general procedures for verifying liabilities.

b) List some liabilities that may be omitted.

c) How can the auditor determine if all liabilities are included?

d) What is the difference between a provision and an accrual?

e) What factors about a liability must be verified by an auditor?

f) How might audit evidence of the truth and fairness of the item 'share capital' be obtained?

g) How might pending legal matters be dealt with by an auditor?

h) List audit procedures in connection with accounting estimates.

EXAMINATION QUESTIONS

1 Company A has a number of long- and short-term payables, accruals and provisions in its Statement of Financial Position.

Required:

(a) Describe the audit procedures you would apply to each of the three items listed below, including those relating to disclosure.

(i) A 10-year bank loan with a variable interest rate and an overdraft (a bank account with a debit balance on the bank statement), both from the same bank.

(ii) Expense accruals.

(iii) Trade payables and purchase accruals.

(b) Company B has a provision in its Statement of Financial Position for claims made by customers for product defects under 1-year company warranties.

Required:

Describe the matters you would consider and the audit evidence you would require for the provision.

(ACCA)

2 Curdco is a company that runs a chain of fast food restaurants. The company has a centralized operating style and managers of individual restaurants have very limited decision-making powers on day-to-day operational matters. The company's centralized administration is responsible for the buying of food, the payment of staff, the maintenance and cleaning of restaurants by staff employed by a national agency and all other matters relating to the running of the business. The company has good internal controls over purchasing. Inventory counts are conducted at each restaurant at the year-end. Your firm has recently been appointed as auditor to Curdco.

Required:

(a) List the account headings you would expect to find in Curdco's schedule of accounts payable and accrued expenditure.

(b) Describe and give reasons for the audit tests you would carry out to obtain audit evidence for Curdco's accounts payable and accrued expenditure.

(c) Explain the difficulties faced by auditors, and the decisions that auditors have to make, in conducting direct confirmations of accounts payable.

(ACCA)

SOURCES AND ADDITIONAL READING

Financial Reporting Council (2015) *FRS 102 The Financial Reporting Standard Applicable in the UK and Republic of Ireland*. London: Financial Reporting Council.

Financial Reporting Council (2016) *ISA 540 Auditing, Accounting Estimates, Including Fair Value Accounting Estimates, and Related Disclosures*. London: Financial Reporting Council.

ICSA (2007) *Companies Act 2006 Handbook*. London: ICSA.

Taylor, J. (2010) *Forensic Accounting*. Harlow: Pearson.

CHAPTER 17 AUDITING AND COMPUTERS

Learning Objectives

After studying the material in this chapter you should be able to:

- understand the aspects of computerized systems which affect the auditor's approach to risk

- explain the audit approaches of auditing around the computer and auditing the system

- understand the use of computer-assisted auditing techniques (CAATs) in the audit environment

- understand the principles of Data Analytics and the use of audit interrogation software such as IDEA

- discuss how auditors could use IT to replace paper-based files

INTRODUCTION

Even the smallest organizations have computers now and use computerized accounting packages to maintain their accounts. The availability of relatively cheap and reliable accounting software has changed the way auditors approach financial accounting systems.

Organizations are increasingly dependent on computerized systems and, indeed, most large organizations could not function without them. It is arguable that modern organizations could not grow to their present size without computer-based systems.

In earlier years' auditors tended to treat computers as extensions of manual accounting systems and, indeed, the early computers were little more than calculators and recorders of information in a pre-ordained way. Generally, the type of hardware determined the software and reports produced by the computers were produced to a preset format by a report generator.

The structure of information storage, generally hard coded into fixed locations, previously meant that the capacity to produce reports was somewhat constrained. However modern methods of data storage and advances in software mean that auditors now have at their disposal a range of tools which they can use to interrogate client's systems and to produce reports in various configurations.

AUDITORS AND MANAGEMENT INFORMATION SYSTEMS

As even the most computer illiterate accountant will realize, computer-based accounting imposes a discipline on data entry:

- The information being input into the system is controlled, for example:
  - Single entry input is impossible so the books always balance.
  - Computers enforce coding structures. Data has to be coded to a destination and information input has to be tagged in some way so that it can be retrieved later.
- Management reporting is improved and produced more quickly which aids decision making and analysis.

However, there is a strong caveat here. It is important to understand that IT-based systems can become a problem both for the auditors and the management if data entry is not properly controlled.

Once information is input and later extracted in some form it tends to be believed. The computer can confer a spurious authenticity on computerized reports, so much so that many fraudsters have realized that if they can authenticate data input into the financial system it is unlikely to be challenged and automated processes will result in successful extraction of funds. Consequently, auditors should always approach data analysis, be it management accounts or other forms of report extracted from the system with an attitude of professional scepticism. They must continue to ask themselves whether what they are presented with is supported by other evidence or, indeed, makes sense when looked at in isolation. For example, if a company produces a set of management accounts which show a big increase in turnover, improved GP and lower overheads thus producing a very favourable profit outcome, is this supported by an improvement in the bank balance?

Auditors must balance what they presented with against what they know from independent sources and their own tests to ensure consistency in reporting.

Planning

At the planning stage, auditors have to consider how the computerized aspect of the accounting system affects the tracking of information and the flow of documents.

One problem area for the auditor is that transactions can be generated by the computer and the audit trail is lost. The auditor cannot follow the flow of documents which evidence a transaction because there aren't any – all the data is electronic.

Difficulties arise within computerized systems because:

- Transactions can be generated by the computer automatically, e.g. direct debits.
- Electronic forms of trading (e.g. through websites) require validation checks and secure payments systems which the auditor must validate as controls.
- Computers perform complex calculations without demonstrating how they were carried out, e.g. interest charges, debt analysis.
- Transactions can be exchanged between systems or locations using electronic data interchange (EDI) without any paper trail, e.g. automatic ordering systems.
- The control principle of segregation of duties can be bypassed because computerized systems use relatively low numbers of staff.

AUDIT RISK AND IT SYSTEMS

The evaluation of audit risk for a **Management Information System** (MIS) follows the same basic principles, as set out in Chapter 10, for the financial system as a whole. However, there are several unique aspects of audit risk which have to be considered specifically in connection with computerized systems.

Within a computerized system, inherent risk and control risks can be summarized as follows:

Risk	Features
Inherent risk	• Management may feel they have no control over the system and that they are in the hands of IT specialists.
	• As many of the operations are automatic incorrect standing data will continue until it is detected, for example an incorrect wage rate or sales price.
	• There is the 'illusion of control' because controls exist and systems are computerized management is readily able to accept that they are functioning and that reports produced are accurate and complete.
Control risks	• If software has been tampered with or illicit software introduced it is possible to generate fraud within the computer which is hard to detect.
	• A manual system transaction can be viewed by several people in different departments. Computerized environments require fewer staff so the segregation of duties can become blurred.
	• Data can be stolen by staff without any record of the theft as it can be simply downloaded on to memory sticks or CDs. If this is done using the correct passwords identifying the culprit can be impossible.
	• It can be difficult to trace the authority for transaction processing through the computer where routines are automated, e.g. in automatic reordering systems the reorder levels may be authorized once and never be revisited. The computer does not know if an order level has subsequently been amended without authorization.
	• Internet-based trading automates transactions and creates problems for management in terms of data security.
	• Online trading requires secure payment systems and auditors must ensure that data is secure from unauthorized intrusion, i.e. hacking or data theft by employees.
	• IT systems are subject to external attacks, e.g. viruses, worms, Trojans and denial of service attacks so considerations of data security should be included in risk evaluations.

However, computerized systems also have advantages which the auditor should bear in mind when evaluating audit risk. For example, a computer will only do what it is told, consequently processing is uniform and totally accurate. This tends to reduce clerical errors and a computer will go on processing as long as it is given information to process.

With the appropriate software it is possible to generate reports and analysis and provide much more information than is feasible under a purely manual system and auditors can use **Computer-Assisted Audit Techniques** (CAATs) to interrogate the system and carry out comparative and analytical tests. Within the entity managers and internal auditors can obtain data and use analytical techniques which may enhance control.

THE CONTROL ENVIRONMENT

The principles of good internal control described in Chapter 9 apply equally in both computerized and manual environments, so the auditor will be looking for many of the same features. These are systems-based controls which apply to the operation of an IT function just as much as to, say, invoice processing and students should ensure that they are familiar with these principles which we have denominated with the mnemonic SOAPSPAM.

Auditors will review the IT systems to:

- Evaluate the efficiency and effectiveness of key controls.
- Review the actual operation of key controls in practice including the work of internal audit. They want to be sure that the controls in fact operate the way they are supposed to in theory.

Another consideration is to ask the question as to who might be in a position to take advantage of a control weakness or operate in an area without satisfactory controls. This will require a review of the position and status of senior managers and directors and will incorporate a consideration of any propensity to override controls or institute 'special arrangements'. This is to overcome the problem of computerized information appearing to be authentic when it has been falsely introduced.

Computerized systems require additional controls over unauthorized system intrusions e.g. firewalls, intrusion detection systems, etc. and over data security e.g. customer details.

Effective controls can be summarized as shown in Figure 17.1.

FIGURE 17.1 Software controls

Controls	Require
Strong control environment	• All staff should be aware of the need for internal controls and the procedures to be followed.
Documented procedures	• Staff should be made aware of the control procedures by means of documentation and training.
Systems documentation	• The suppliers of the software should provide full documentation for the programs in use.
Control of access	• Access to application software, e.g. the programs which control how data is processed, should be restricted. • Access to data should be restricted to the staff that use it in the course of their work and to no-one else. This is done by limiting the menu systems available when a member of staff logs on. • The company must protect its systems against unauthorized intrusions such as viruses, worms and Trojans.
Password controls	• Access to the system should be controlled by passwords and authorized logons. Passwords should be changed regularly and not disclosed or shared.
Application controls	These consist of controls such as: • Batch controls, e.g. prelists and manual totals to compare with computer totals when processing batches of documents. • Sequential numbering systems. • Controls over coding as incorrect coding can lead to misstatements in the financial accounts. • Manual authorization of input documentation. • Arithmetical controls such as check digits, gross to net, etc. • Range checks, i.e. automatic checking that input is within acceptable limits, e.g. hours worked are not more than 50 per week. • Logging of when and who performed document processing.

In addition to a review of systems-based controls auditors should also consider what is known as the **key fields approach**. This requires auditors to identify and evaluate:

- Who can enter, modify or delete data fields?
- Would any fraud require collusion with a data entry operator?
- Why might this be done?
- Are there key controls that would prevent this from happening?
- Does the reality of data entry invalidate the principle of segregation of duties, i.e. operators are able to access areas which enable them to bypass internal checks?

The use of a formalized system such as CRSA (Control Risk Self Assessment) (Chapter 14) greatly aids the review of internal control.

You need to be aware of controls applicable to computerized systems as questions on this often appear in examinations.

THE AUDIT APPROACH TO COMPUTERIZED SYSTEMS

Auditors will require access to the client's system so will need to be provided with the appropriate log-in details and passwords. Once in the system the advantages of IT-based audit techniques to auditors are considerable.

They can use data directly from the client's system and produce reports themselves rather than having to rely on reports filtered through the client's report generating software and can interrogate entire populations of data if necessary.

The use of computerized audit techniques increases audit productivity as tests can be performed more quickly than by using cumbersome manual techniques. Indeed some audit processes can be automated and built in to the client's software.

The emphasis on computer-based audit approaches increases the knowledge of auditors of new tools and approaches to IT.

There are two approaches:

- auditing around the computer; and
- understanding and interrogating the MIS.

Auditing around the computer

This is an approach often taken where auditors are faced with auditing smaller organizations which use industry standard, 'off the shelf' software packages where systems are likely to be based on a single PC or a small PC network. The auditor takes the view that the computer simply replaces manual records and that there are few, if any, automated routines. As it is standard software it is likely to be well tested and error free.

The approach is to:

- Examine the controls around data input to ensure that the day-to-day input of transaction information, e.g. invoices, orders, bank transactions, etc. is properly controlled.
- Examine the standing or master file data, e.g. wage rates, prices, VAT rate, interest rates, which the computer uses as a basis for making calculations, ensure it is properly authorized and is used currently by the computer.
- Examine the output and relate it to the input so that, say, a selection of sales invoices can be traced directly to the customer's account in the sales ledger.
- Examine the output with external verification, for example, the purchase ledger balances with suppliers' statements.

Understanding and interrogating the MIS

Where computerized systems are more complex, and the computer generates information internally through automated routines, the auditor needs to adopt a different approach.

There are two problems faced by the auditor in this situation:

1 In complex systems it may be that even the organization's own IT staff do not understand all the detail. They may know *what* the system will do but not *how* it does it.

2 Management may feel that they don't understand the computer system and may actively avoid becoming involved with its day-to-day operations. This can result in a loss of control or dependence on one or two experts.

Auditors will try and adopt an approach whereby they use the computer's ability to process data to interrogate its operations using computer-assisted audit techniques (CAATs).

This is specialist audit software used to interrogate the client's data files and to carry out sample audit tests on their contents. Some software may need the use of specially trained computer auditors to operate it, particularly if it is interrogating live client files.

There are various types of CAAT including:

- Dummy data (sometimes known as 'test decks') which comprises fictitious transaction data run through the client's system to test the operation of the programs.
- **Parallel simulations** where the auditor models the client's system but on their own hardware.
- Embedded audit files, known as Systems Control Audit Review or SCARF files, set up within the client's system which can be used by the auditor to obtain information on demand or continuously.
- Interrogation software to examine large volumes of data relatively easily, known as **Data Analytics**. This is particularly useful in obtaining information from files which can then be examined by audit staff.

We will look at each of these separately.

Use of dummy data

The principle behind the use of **dummy data** is that by using the client's software to process false or fictitious data, extreme transactions can be used to test the parameters of the software to ensure that such things as edit checks and application controls are working correctly.

This requires a good knowledge of the client's software and the dummy data itself needs to include every type of transaction in order to ensure that controls and checks are properly tested.

The dummy data will include exceptional transactions which the client's system ought to reject or highlight on a report as well as more normal transactions to check the operations of the controls and checks within the machine. For example, transactions might be introduced which would deliberately create a negative inventory balance for a range of items – the computer should reject transactions once the inventory level reaches zero, or an exceptionally high payment could be made to an employee which should be queried by the system as being outside pre-set data entry ranges.

There are, basically, two ways of using dummy data:

- Introduce a range of dummy transactions into the client's system as a routine processing run.
- Create a dummy department or set of accounts in the system and process dummy data through it using the client's software. This is known as an integrated test facility.

The major risk with both these approaches is to ensure that the dummy data is reversed out of the system once tests are complete otherwise the auditor runs the risk of corrupting the client's data.

Parallel simulation

This requires an understanding of how the client's system calculates and processes data so the system can be modelled. Original client data is then entered and the results compared with the data processed by the client's system. This methodology avoids the danger of corruption of the client's data and enables the auditor to compare the simulated data processing with the real thing. This will detect any tampering with the software. Using original data from the client requires their permission of course but this should be forthcoming.

Embedded software

Embedded software sits within the client's systems and monitors it either continuously or when activated. This type of software is known as **Systems Control Audit Review Files** (SCARF) and it works continuously to identify transactions which are outside pre-set data parameters or which fail reasonableness tests. It also identifies and reports on such things as irregular entries, abortive logons or signs that the software has been tampered with or that unusual transactions are being processed.

A variation on SCARF software is Sample Audit Review Files (SARF) software which works in the same way as SCARF files, but on a random basis sampling transactions.

Clearly, this type of software can only be introduced with the permission of the client and one problem with it is that, quite often, it has to be embedded at the design stage of the system, it has to be written into the program software in some way so that it is monitoring the actual processing on a real-time basis.

In both cases they are techniques which should be handled with care and usually requires the use of experts to operate them. For this reason, they can be expensive and are often only used on larger audits. Embedded software uses can be used for two types of audit test in particular – *exception reporting* and *comparative testing*. Figure 17.2 shows these details.

FIGURE 17.2 Embedded software

Test	Procedure	Example
Exception reporting	• report transactions exceeding a set parameter	• all purchases in excess of £5000 • all sales ledger balances over three months old
Comparative testing	• identical reports at two different dates • auditors identify and explain differences	• wages details at two dates in the year • the auditor could use the data as a basis for reviewing the procedures for new staff, staff leaving and changes in wage rates

Data Analytics

Data analytics is the science of examining raw data with the purpose of drawing conclusions about that information. This is probably the fastest growing aspect of modern auditing and in many ways is re-engineering the audit process.

It offers a way for auditors to manage the problems of auditing some of the huge IT systems in large companies and a way to enhance audit quality overall.

The ability to extract and interrogate large volumes of data from a corporate system enables auditors to focus on key areas and examine large quantities of data in a way that simply isn't possible using conventional means. It serves to reduce audit risk, thus improving the risk assessment process, it benefits substantive testing procedures as auditors are able to interrogate much larger volumes of data than had previously been the case and improves the testing of controls. For example, when sampling data the audit team can sample a much larger proportion, possibly up to 100 per cent, of the **population**, in order to carry out their tests.

It also enables the production of more complex models and projections in order to facilitate audit processes involving the exercise of judgement.

Generally extensive use of data analytics requires a considerable investment in time and money for audit firms to develop their own forms of data analytics tools which will work on a variety of systems. In many cases the up-front investment is not worth it and smaller and mid-tier audit firms might well not adopt bespoke solutions on the grounds of cost. The systems have to be user friendly and able to be used by non specialist audit staff on site so there is an extensive training commitment in addition to the costs of bespoke software design. Firms may be able to buy in solutions from specialist providers or work co-operatively to share the costs.

For the large multinational firms auditing huge corporations these tools are a 'must have'.

One such software in use by mid-tier and larger firms is Caseware Analytic's **IDEA** (Interactive Data Extraction and Analysis). A modern MIS uses forms of data storage which enable the auditor to extract and reformat data in many ways so as to interrogate it as a major part of audit testing. The applications are many and varied and the constraints are based on the type of data storage rather than the limitations of audit software as modern audit interrogation software is designed to accept data in many formats.

Audit software can be used to:

- Extract data to define populations for sampling e.g. block sampling of receivables balances (Chapter 12).
- Analyze expenditure or revenues in various ways such as by date, size, type, product or location.
- Analysis of trends in revenue by region, product, etc.
- Calculate aged receivables or inventory balances (Chapter 15).
- Analyze gross margin and sales by product.
- Test user codes to ascertain whether segregation of duties is working in practice and whether combinations of users have been processing transactions and bypassing controls.
- Check for duplicates, e.g. sort and compare supplier listings looking for anomalies such as:
  - same supplier, different addresses;
  - different suppliers, same address;
  - supplier data matches employee record.
- Sorting and indexing data, for example sorting by value may be looking for clusters of transactions around certain authority levels or by date may be looking for high value transactions posted just before a period end.
- Statistical analysis of data looking at highest/lowest values, average values, etc.
- Analyze data by time, date processed, etc. looking for data processed at odd or unusual times such as weekends, out of hours, etc. This could indicate the activities of a fraudster hoping to work unseen.
- Produce trend analysis in detail or in summary as required.
- Produce exception reports within parameters defined by the auditor.

Care has to be taken however in design and use of audit processes using data analytics software. For example, badly specified tests or applying them to an inappropriate population can result in thousands of exceptions or anomalies which make a nonsense of the tests.

Some of these techniques are of particular use in fraud investigations but can also be used for routine audit work. In many cases use of this type of software is replacing the use of CAATs such as parallel simulations or dummy data as more can be gained by questioning the client's data than by running artificially distorted transactions through the system.

Documentation

It can be difficult for auditors to document the use of IT-based audit tests as, by definition, interrogation of client systems is a computer-based process and it is unrealistic to print all the data off. Audit teams should record the use and circumstances of such tests by way of report and, of course, the outcomes of any tests carried out.

It is important to realize that ISA 230 '*Audit Documentation*' requires auditors to document their tests in a way that facilitates review and in a way that would enable another suitably competent auditor to duplicate the work done. Accordingly audit teams must ensure that they copy appropriate files as part of the documentation and provide full details of the work they have done without denominating every transaction.

Auditors' use of IT

In addition to the use of computerized audit software such as IDEA, audit firms are increasingly looking to computerize their own audit files. Audit teams would be equipped with laptops and portable printers and scanners so that they can operate on client's premises independently.

Use of electronic audit systems has several advantages, for example previous years' files can stored electronically and accessed easily so audit teams do not have to carry large amounts of paper with them. Computerized systems can create backups so audit files are not lost.

Where accounts are being finalized audit files can be linked to accounts production software so lead schedules can be updated automatically. Data can be rolled forward into the next year.

In terms of ensuring satisfactory audit completion the system can ensure that pre-set audit manuals and forms have to be completed properly before the audit file can be closed, which aids compliance. Partners and managers can review files remotely if they are recorded on the firm's network.

However, there are disadvantages:

- Initial set-up costs can be considerable requiring an investment in portable equipment.
- The firm's own network must be robust and of sufficient size to accept large volumes of data when audit files are loaded on to it.
- If papers are misfiled they are very difficult to trace.
- Data security is important to avoid unauthorized access to client data.

Paperless office systems are quite environmentally friendly and the growth of IT-based audit techniques, particularly audit interrogation software, is likely to mean that the whole audit process becomes automated and that, gradually, the old paper-based audit files fade away except for the smaller client.

SUMMARY

- Auditors can use two approaches to auditing computerized systems, auditing around the computer or using computer-assisted audit techniques (CAATs).
- Auditing in a computerized system environment requires the auditor to evaluate the internal controls which relate to the computer system.
- CAATs may require specialists to operate them in order to obtain information from client files and to maintain the audit trail.
- Use of dummy data can be a way of confirming whether reasonableness tests and edit checks are working.
- Parallel simulations will reveal any tampering with processing software.
- Use of audit interrogation software is increasing. It is used to derive information for the auditor from the total population and to search for anomalies such as duplications.
- Auditors are moving away from paper-based audit systems to computerized audit files.

POINTS TO NOTE

- Auditing with computers should be approached with caution, particularly if it is proposed to interfere in any way with the client's accounting system.
- This method of auditing is becoming more prevalent as the use of computers in auditing gradually supersedes written records. Many companies now scan in documents and send all paper records to deep storage.
- This method of auditing requires skills which all auditors will have to acquire.

CASE STUDY 1

Bing Properties plc is a large property developer in the north of England. It has two divisions, industrial and domestic. The industrial division builds factories and offices for various clients and also contracts on major construction projects such as schools and hospitals as one of several contractors.

Its domestic division builds houses. Bing has a substantial land bank acquired over many years but also specializes in converting 'brownfield' sites, former factory sites, into housing developments.

It has recently purchased a new computer system. All incoming documents, letters, invoices, advice notes, etc. are sent to the central processing office where they are scanned into the computer. They are then sent to a warehouse for storage. As they are scanned in they are identified by type by the operator and the computer then allocates the document a unique number which is used to track its progress through the system. Staff are able to call up images of the documents on screen.

A purchase invoice, for example, from a supplier is batched with several others and then the batch is scanned in to the computer. The supplier's name is read electronically and the operator enters the invoice details such as amount, VAT, etc. and a nominal code. The transactions are then processed by the computer.

If the invoice is queried its image can be held in a special file in the computer. Copies can be printed as required.

Sales invoices and requests for payment are generated on screen and only printed to be sent to the customer. There are no copies, but an image of the invoice can be created on screen as required.

Only cash and bank transactions are dealt with in a conventional way.

Discussion

– What approach could be taken by the auditors?
– How will this type of system affect conventional audit approaches?

STUDENT SELF-TESTING QUESTIONS

Questions with answers apparent from the text

a) What approaches to a computer audit can auditors take?

b) What types of CAATs are there?

c) How does the use of embedded software provide good audit evidence?

d) What internal controls would you expect to find in a computer environment?

e) What is test data?

EXAMINATION QUESTIONS

1 Furnistores Ltd is a wholesaler of furniture (such as chairs, tables and cupboards). Furnistores buys the furniture from six major manufacturers and sells them to over 600 different customers ranging from large retail chain stores to smaller owner-controlled businesses.

The receivables balance therefore includes customers owing up to £125 000 to smaller balances of about £5000, all with many different due dates for payments and credit limits. All information is stored on Furnistores' computer systems although previous audits have tended to adopt an 'audit around the computer' approach.

You are the audit senior in charge of the audit of the receivables balance. For the first time at this client, you have decided to use audit software to assist with the audit of the receivables balance.

Computer staff at Furnistores are happy to help the auditor, although they cannot confirm completeness of systems documentation, and warn that the systems have very old operating systems in place, limiting file compatibility with more modern programs.

The change in audit approach has been taken mainly to fully understand Furnistores' computer systems prior to new internet modules being added next year. To limit the possibility of damage to Furnistores' computer files, copy files will be provided by Furnistores' computer staff for the auditor to use with their own audit software.

Required:

(a) Explain the audit procedures that should be carried out using audit software on the receivables balance at Furnistores Ltd. For each procedure, explain the reason for that procedure.

(b) Explain the potential problems of using audit software at Furnistores Ltd. For each problem, explain how it can be resolved.

(c) Explain the concept of 'auditing around the computer' and discuss why this increases audit risk for the auditor.

SOURCES AND ADDITIONAL READING

Coderre, D. (2009) *Internal Audit: Efficiency through Automation*. Hoboken, NJ: Wiley.

Financial Reporting Council (2016) *ISA 230 Audit Documentation*. London: Financial Reporting Council.

Financial Reporting Council (2016) *ISA 300 Planning an Audit of Financial Statements*. London: Financial Reporting Council.

ICAEW (2016) *Data Analytics for External Auditors*. London: ICAEW.

Taylor, J. (2010) *Forensic Accounting*. Harlow: Pearson.

Vaassen, E., Meuwissen, R. and Schelleman, C. (2009) *Accounting Information Systems and Internal Control*. Chichester: Wiley.

CHAPTER 18
AUDIT WORKING PAPERS

Learning Objectives

After studying the material in this chapter you should be able to:

- understand the purpose of audit documentation

- understand the nature and content of audit documentation

- explain the need for documentation of areas of the application of professional judgement

- discuss the advantages and disadvantages of the use of standardized audit working papers

- explain the contents of Permanent and Current Files

- understand how to format an audit programme

- explain how the audit of smaller entities is documented differently

- understand the rules on retention of audit working papers and the auditor's lien

INTRODUCTION

An audit has been defined as a process by which the auditor amasses paper; the more paper they have collected the better the audit they have done! This view is by no means a totally frivolous one, for audits generally do involve the collection of papers in such large numbers that an orderly file structure is invariably required.

The chapter is entitled Audit Working Papers but clearly, many audits are now computerized and, as we saw in Chapter 17, the concept of paper-based audit working papers is beginning to feel like an anachronism nowadays. However, many firms still use paper to some extent and the use of computers to store audit data does not invalidate the file structures and the ordering of information contained in this chapter.

Client files may be quite voluminous and occupy a good deal of space whether this is in a storage warehouse in the case of paper records or on a server if computerized. Increasingly firms are turning to cloud-based storage systems but there are some considerations to bear in mind. In particular:

- Security of data is paramount so client data held on cloud storage files should be encrypted. Firms should know who might have access to stored files.
- It is necessary to ensure that the storage provider is financially sound and that, in the event of the provider failing, the files can still be accessed.

The principles of documenting and supervising audit work also apply whether the records of work carried out are computer-based or written in pencil.

ISA 230 *'Audit documentation'*, states:

'The objective of the auditor is to prepare documentation that provides:

(a)   *A sufficient and appropriate record of the basis for the auditor's report; and*
(b)   *Evidence that the audit was planned and performed in accordance with ISAs (UK and Ireland) and applicable legal and regulatory requirements.'*

It goes on to say that they should document:

- the nature, timing and extent of the procedures carried out;
- the results of the audit procedures and the evidence obtained; and
- significant matters arising during the audit and decisions reached.

What this means, in effect, is that auditors should prepare working papers that are sufficiently complete and detailed to provide an overall understanding of the audit process by an experienced auditor. They should document in their working papers matters which are important in supporting their audit opinion, including records of meetings with clients and third-party confirmations.

Working papers should record the auditor's planning, the nature, timing and extent of the audit procedures performed and the conclusions drawn from the audit evidence obtained. They should also record who performed the work, who reviewed it and the dates this was carried out.

Auditors should record in their working papers their reasoning on all significant matters which require the exercise of judgement and their conclusions. Where the auditor has information which is inconsistent with the auditor's final conclusions about a particular significant matter the auditor should document how they dealt with such inconsistency.

The ISA also explains that it is neither necessary nor practicable for the auditor to document every matter considered, or professional judgement made, in an audit, although clearly all significant or material judgements should be documented. Further, it is unnecessary for the auditor to document separately (as in a checklist, for example) compliance with matters for which compliance is demonstrated by documents included within the audit file, e.g. the existence of an adequately documented audit plan demonstrates that the auditor has planned the audit.

PURPOSES

Audit working papers are produced and collected for several reasons. Clearly these should evidence the planning of the audit and the design of audit procedures and include a system to control the current year's work. A record of work done is essential.

In detail they must provide a record of the detailed testing, including compliance and substantive testing and analytical review and record the conclusions drawn from the audit tests performed. The papers should record evidence of review at each stage of the audit testing so as to enable the audit team to be accountable for its work.

The working papers are there to assist the audit managers to direct and supervise the audit work and to evidence the fact of their reviews.

At the conclusion of the audit work the working papers are there in the final overall review stage of an audit. They enable audit partners to look at the scope of the work carried out, review decisions involving issues of professional judgement and to consider overall whether the financial statements show a true and fair view and comply with statutory requirements so they can sign off the audit report accordingly.

Conversely, where there is some form of dispute with management or difficulties encountered in gathering sufficient reliable audit evidence the working papers will demonstrate the nature of such dispute, the conversations with management and the outcome of any discussions.

Where, in exceptional circumstances, the auditor has to depart from the requirements of the ISAs a rationale for that departure and details of the additional testing performed must be recorded and where, unusually, the auditor has had to perform audit work after the audit report has been signed the papers should record a full explanation of why this has happened and details of the work performed.

The working papers enable an experienced auditor to conduct quality control reviews and inspections (Chapter 7) or external inspections as required by any legal or regulatory requirements.

Finally, they form a basis for the plan of the audit of the following year. Clearly a starting point for a year's audit is a review of the previous year's work however, a slavish following of the previous year's work must be avoided and new initiatives taken.

Auditors should beware of formulaic auditing, where they simply re-perform the same tests each year. Rigidly following the same audit procedures year after year can lead to:

- client staff getting to know the procedures
- client staff designing frauds which the procedures will not uncover

EVIDENCE OF WORK CARRIED OUT

Audit staff need to provide evidence that they have carried out the audit tests prescribed in the **audit programme**, that they have drawn a valid conclusion from each test and that the work carried out has been reviewed at a more senior level.

Whether it be a computer-based record or a paper schedule each audit working paper should contain, as a minimum:

- the name of the client, the accounting period and the assertion, transactions or balance being tested
- objective of the test to be carried out
- details of the work done, i.e. details of the sample transactions tested or the substantive tests undertaken
- the outcome of the tests
- the conclusions that can be drawn
- the initials or name of the person carrying out the test and the reviewer
- date of test and date of review

Figure 18.1 illustrates what a sample page from an audit programme might look like. This, of course, could be computerised with boxes to be filled in and cross referenced by audit staff. Illustrative answers have been give to key audit questions for information.

Figure 18.1 Sample Audit Programme

STATEMENT OF FINANCIAL POSITION			Tangible fixed assets	
Note here any significant risks associated with the audit of this section:				
There has been a property revaluation during the year. We have a copy of the valuation. Management have not considered any property to have diminished in value or have its value impaired.				
Assertion	**Audit procedures**	**Sample size**	**Ref/Comments**	**Initials and date**
Existence	Carry out sample physical inspection of major assets. Ensure all assets are being used in the business.	5	A24	*LD* 05/06/1X
Rights and obligations (ownership)	Inspect title deeds, invoices, contracts or information held at the Land Registry to establish title.	5	A24	*LD* 06/06/1X
Rights and obligations (ownership)	Inspect vehicle registration documents. If the documents are not in the name of the company, obtain written confirmation from the registered keeper that the vehicle is owned by the company.	8-	*A27*	*LD* 05/06/1X
Completeness	Review other expense areas, for example repairs, and ensure that there are no capital items included.	-	*Reviewed repairs and renewals nominal for year. All items below capex limit.*	*LD* 05/06/1X

NATURE AND CONTENT OF WORKING PAPERS

The form and content of working papers are affected by:

- the nature, size and complexity of the business
- the nature and complexity of the internal controls
- the need for direction, supervision and review of work performed by audit staff
- specific audit methodology and technology used in the course of the audit
- the form of the audit report – see Chapter 26

Auditors will use standardized forms and checklists to improve the efficiency of the audit and will also incorporate schedules and analyses prepared by the business, providing these have been properly prepared.

The extent of working papers is a matter of judgement. A useful way of deciding what is needed is to consider what information would be needed to provide another auditor who had no experience of the client with an understanding of the work performed and the basis of the decisions reached.

DEPARTURE FROM BASIC PRINCIPLES

Recording is particularly important if the auditors are departing, for some reason, from basic principles or essential procedures. If they do this they must record how, in their view, the alternative course they have adopted, and the evidence they have gathered, supports the audit objective.

CONTENT OF WORKING PAPERS

The auditor's working papers must contain a copy of the Engagement Letter and any relevant instructions. They will also include information and documents which are of continuing importance to each annual audit, for example the information obtained in understanding the business and its internal control, such as:

- the organizational structure
- extracts from important legal documents
- background information about the industry, etc.
- details of the management and senior staff
- extracts from company manuals if relevant

There should be evidence of the planning process (Chapter 10) and evidence of the lead audit partner's involvement in the planning process and the direction and supervision of the audit process. Evidence of the lead partner taking responsibility for key aspects of the audit might be found in records of them taking part in audit team briefings and discussions as required by ISA 315.

Clearly, the working papers should also contain details of the client's systems and records with the auditor's evaluation of them, i.e. flow charts, ICQs, ICEQs, etc. and evidence of the evaluation of the efficiency of internal audit, if applicable.

In detail, the work carried out must be evidenced such as:

- analyses of transactions and balances
- analyses of significant ratios and trends
- identified and assessed risks of material misstatements at both the financial statements and assertion level
- details of the nature, timing and extent of audit work carried out, notes of queries raised with action taken thereon and the conclusion drawn by the audit staff concerned

Of interest to the review process and forming part of the audit evidence are copies of communications with third parties, e.g. banks, legal advisors and other auditors (in the context of a group audit) as well as copies of letters or notes in respect of audit matters discussed with management and their responses.

One of the key aspects of the audit must be recorded also that is the conclusions reached by the auditor in respect of significant audit matters including any exceptional or unusual items and what impact these may or may not have on the final report.

Copies of the financial statements and auditor's report should also be included for completion.

There is a Practice Note 26 '*Guidance on Smaller Entity Audit Documentation*' which allows the auditor to reduce the amount of documentation to be included in audit files in the light of the practical realities of auditing smaller firms.

SAMPLE WORKING PAPERS

Working papers can be in any form desired by the auditor but a usual division is between a **Permanent File** and a Current File.

The Permanent File

The Permanent File usually contains documents and matters of continuing importance which will be required for more than one audit.

A sample index for a Permanent File is shown in Figure 18.2.

FIGURE 18.2   File Index – Permanent File

Section	Title	Contains
1	Constitution	• Memorandum and articles – *Note that the Companies Act 2006 changed the requirements around the company's Memorandum and Articles of Association and these are no longer as significant as they once were, however auditors should ensure they fully understand the legal position of the company and its rules* • Partnership agreements • Trust deeds
2	Background and Organization	• History of the business • Activities • Ownership • Registered office • Management structure – *organization chart* • Industry – *background, client's relative importance and position, economic factors, seasonality* • Premises and equipment – *locations, capital expenditure details, etc., owned or leased, age* • Products • Main suppliers • Main customers distribution, pricing, exports, etc. • Staff – *numbers, departments/functions, method of remuneration (monthly/ weekly), contracts, union agreements, pension liabilities*
3	Systems	• Processing method – *computerized/manual* • Records and location • Flowcharts and notes, ICQs, ICEQs, etc. • Nominal ledger code lists • Copies of relevant sections of company accounts manuals • Statistical analysis – *five year summary/benchmark data*
4	Legal documents and minutes	• Leases • Title deeds • Royalty agreements • Ongoing minutes – *directors meetings/AGM* • Stock Exchange undertakings • Funding documents
5	Group	• Structure and details
6	Other advisors	• Lawyers • Bankers • Other lenders • Stockbrokers • Insurers
7	Administration	• Copy Engagement Letter • Authority letters from client • Time budget, costings • Staff budgets
8	Audit testing	• Rotation of visits • Rotational audit testing • Examination of title documents • Review of other auditors • Management letters
9	General	• Any other relevant information

The Current File

The Current File will contain matters pertinent to the current year's audit. A copy of a Current File index is shown in Figure 18.3.

Throughout the Current File, reference should be made as to how each item is used as audit evidence. In addition, for each type of transaction and balance, the nature of the audit evidence supporting it should be demonstrated. This evidence may be from internal control reliance, substantive testing or from analytical review or from a combination of these sources.

Remember – a procedure not documented is a procedure not carried out!

FIGURE 18.3 File Index – current File

Section	Title	Contains
1	Financial statements	• Copy of draft accounts • Copy of final accounts
2	Reports	• Reports to client • Comments from client • Letter of representation • Points for next year • Management letters • Final journal entries • Companies Act Disclosure checklist • Partner review • Audit completion checklist
3	Job planning	• Planning programme • Budget and fee estimate • Time and costs • Briefing notes for staff
4	Systems audit	• Audit programme • Working papers • Queries and explanations • Letter of weakness and non-reported weaknesses
5	Accounts schedules	• Schedules for balances included in the Statement of Financial Position • Copy of accounts • Key schedules for Income Account items • Supporting schedules and evidence of audit work • Management account information • Third party confirmations including bank letter • Disclosure checklists • Queries and replies
6	Minutes	• Minutes of directors and other relevant committee meetings
7	Analytical review and statistics	• Final overview and analytical review of statistical information
8	General	• Any other relevant information

PROFESSIONAL JUDGEMENT

Auditors frequently have to exercise professional judgement during the audit and examples of this are scattered throughout the book. For example, decisions may have to be made concerning the acceptability of provisions, the disclosure of contingent liabilities and the level of testing work carried out.

One point made by IAS 200 'Overall objectives of the independent auditor and the conduct of an audit in accordance with International Standards on Auditing' is that professional judgement cannot be used as a justification for decisions which are not otherwise supported by facts or sufficient appropriate audit evidence. In other words, the auditor cannot make decisions on a hunch or an impression – there has to be evidence. The auditor must exercise judgement in a transparent and justifiable manner and, consequently, documentation becomes particularly important. The exercise of professional judgement is likely to be an area to which reviewers of the files, be they review partners, lawyers or regulators, will pay particular attention so the auditor's thought processes and logic in coming to a decision is of critical importance. The process of coming to the decision must be properly set out with the facts of the situation.

In the case of significant matters that may require the exercise of judgement, the working papers should contain details of the matter and all information available, the management's conclusions on the matter and the auditor's conclusions on the matter in a clear and logical manner so the process of reasoning is transparent.

This is because the auditor's judgement may be questioned later by someone with the benefit of hindsight; this may be a lawyer or an external regulator and not just a review partner. Consequently, it will be important to be able to tell what facts were known at the time when the auditor reached their opinion. It may be necessary to demonstrate that, based on the then known facts, the conclusions were reasonable.

For example, the matter in doubt may be the question of whether to include in the financial statements a provision for an amount expected to be paid under a guarantee given by the client company to a bank which has lent money to a related company in financial difficulty, or to include it by way of a note as a contingent liability.

The working papers should contain:

- All the facts with copies or extracts from relevant documents (the related company's financial statements, the document containing the guarantee given to the bank, budgets and forecasts for the related company, etc.).
- The management's conclusions. Perhaps the related company will survive and meet its commitments so that no payment will be required of the client company. The reasons for this conclusion should be summarized.
- The auditor's conclusions. Perhaps that a payment of £x will be required. Again reasoning should be spelt out in detail so if the audit partner has to make a final decision they will be in possession of all the facts.

Where audit decisions include an element of uncertainty the extent of that uncertainty and the basis for the auditor's decisions should be documented at the time. This is particularly important in the case of the audit of accounting estimates (Chapter 16).

The audit working papers should record all instances where the auditor has made such judgements and the rationale for them. This explains the auditor's conclusions and reinforces the quality of the auditor's decision making process. Clearly, judgement decisions made by auditors are of interest to reviewers of the files and, of course, document the decision making process for the benefit of those carrying out subsequent audits.

The ISA suggests that it may be useful for the auditor to prepare a summary of significant matters arising during the audit and how these were addressed. Clearly, where there has been doubt, for example as to the authenticity of a document, representations made by directors or staff or over a matter of professional judgement the full details should be explained including the rationale for the auditor's eventual decision as to what to do.

Some matters are difficult to document and evidence, such as the attitude of professional scepticism adopted by the audit team in carrying out the work. In this case the records of work carried out must speak for themselves.

THE AUDIT PROGRAMME

An audit programme is simply a list of the work the auditors do on the audit.

The tests are designed to check the internal control procedures or to substantiate balances or transactions rather than the authenticity of individual entries. The results of tests, particularly if based on statistical sampling, would need some evaluation and the audit programme should provide space for this.

The advantages of using audit programmes are that they provide a clear set of instructions on the work to be carried out. They provide a clear record of the work carried out and by whom so work can be reviewed by supervisors, managers, etc.

They prevent work from being duplicated and ensure no important work will be overlooked. Evidence of work done is available to reviewers.

The disadvantages of audit programmes are that work may become mechanical and that parts may be executed without regard to the whole scheme. It may be that programmes are rigidly adhered to although client personnel and systems may have changed.

When an auditor's suspicions are aroused they should probe the matter fully. A fixed audit programme and limited time tends to inhibit such probing and there is a danger that initiative may be stifled.

If work is performed to a predetermined plan, client staff may become aware of the fact and fraud is facilitated.

Example of an audit programme

This is a systems-based approach to the audit of a revenues and receivables system and the example in Figure 18.4 uses that approach. Students can refer to Chapter 13 and Chapter 9 for details if required but this is merely an illustrative programme.

Note how it is set out:

- The control objectives are identified for the sales and receivables system.
- Tests are then devised to check that control procedures exist to ensure those control objectives are achieved and the risk of a material error or misstatement is minimized.
- Substantive testing is carried out on parts of the system and on the receivables balances in order to provide sufficient, appropriate evidence.

Audit working papers will be prepared for each test carried out showing the:

- control objective
- the nature of the test
- the work done and conclusion derived from the results of the testing work

These will also carry the initials of the person carrying out the work and the reviewer. Clearly more than one objective can be tested using the same sample data.

Students should recall from their earlier reading of Chapter 13 that the testing of system components is done in order to validate the assertions regarding the transactions comprising the financial statements for the accounting period.

FIGURE 18.4 **Example of an audit programme**

Audit area:	Sales and receivables	Prepared by: JT
Client	Bodgitt Ltd	Date: 5 /4/201X
Period	31 March 201X	Reviewed by: AM
		Date: 29/4/201X

Control objectives

- Sales are made to approved, creditworthy customers in accordance with company objectives.
- Customer orders are authorized, controlled and recorded.
- Uncompleted orders are controlled and recorded so as to be filled at the earliest opportunity.

(Continues)

FIGURE 18.4 (Continued)

- Goods delivered are controlled and recorded to ensure that invoices are issued for all sales.
- Goods returned and claims by customers are controlled to ensure that claims are valid and credit notes are approved and issued as appropriate.
- Invoices and credit notes are authorized and checked before being entered in the receivables ledger.
- Procedures are in place to ensure that overdue debts are pursued and appropriate provisions made in respect of debts where recovery is doubtful.

Tests of controls	Initial and date
- Test new customer procedure to ensure credit checks and references completed. - Test allocation of credit limits. - Check sample of customer orders to ensure approved by sales department. - Check sample of delivery notes to ensure goods signed for by customer on receipt. - Check sample of sales invoices for authorization by sales department. - Check sample of sales invoices for matching against sales order and delivery note. - Check sample of sales invoices for evidence of arithmetic checks. - Check batching procedure for posting sales invoices to sales ledger. - Confirm all order forms, sales invoices and credit notes numerically sequenced. - Review selection of customer claims and check authorization of credit note or refund. - Check selection of credit notes with copy goods returned note. - Check credit notes authorized by sales manager or equivalent. - Check statements sent to customers monthly. - Confirm aged receivables printout produced monthly and confirm evidence of review by sales manager.	

Substantive procedures	

- Check sample of sales invoices for:
  - arithmetical check
  - match to sales order
  - match to delivery note
- Vouch sample of sales invoices to customer account in sales ledger.
- Check numerical sequence of:
  - customer order forms
  - sales invoices
  - credit notes
- Ensure all sequence numbers accounted for and cancelled documents retained on file.
- Test batch processing procedures and ensure cash totals agree.
- Check sample of authorized credit notes against customer claims.
- Review period end aged receivables analysis for possible doubtful debts.
- Review subsequent payment or clearance.
- Check client's provision for doubtful debts.	

Other working papers

Other audit working papers may include:

- Manuals

  Most audit firms of any size have printed audit manuals which complement internal instruction given to staff. They contain general instructions on the firm's method of auditing in each area and on the audit firm's procedures generally.

- Time sheets

  These are not strictly a part of the audit working papers but are of great importance in controlling the work of audit staff and making a proper charge to the client.

- Review checklists (if kept separate)

  These, again, are usually incorporated in the working files. They are papers which are concerned with a review of the work done by audit staff and acceptance of the work by supervisors, managers, partners and reviewing committees. In most cases evidence of review will be entered on the working paper but such sheets can be used to evidence final review prior to signing the Auditor's Report (see Chapter 26).

STANDARDIZATION OF WORKING PAPERS

Most firms adopt a system of standard working papers which can be used on all audits.

This has many efficiency advantages including the fact that staff become familiar with them, the use of checklists mean matters are not overlooked and they help to instruct staff. The use of standardized questionnaires and checklists means work can be delegated to lower level staff and work can more easily be controlled and reviewed.

However, there are disadvantages to standardization. Chiefly the main worry is that work becomes mechanical and work also becomes standard. There is a danger that client staff may become familiar with the method, initiative may be stifled and the exercise of necessary professional judgement may be reduced.

FINALIZATION

Once the audit is complete and the audit report signed the auditor should complete the file in a timely manner (defined in the ISA as being within 60 days of the date of signing the auditor's report), ensuring it is complete. The audit documentation within that file should not then be altered, removed or amended until the time comes to destroy the file.

If, in exceptional circumstances, the auditor has to carry out new or additional procedures after the audit report has been signed then:

- the circumstances of this have to be documented;
- the work done and the conclusions reached; and
- who carried out the work and when have to be included in the file.

These circumstances might arise if matters come to light which the auditors were unaware of at the time of the audit and which might have affected their auditor's report had they been aware of them at the time.

SMALLER AUDITS

Clearly for audits of smaller entities the documentation may be much reduced, particularly where audit partners are practically involved in the performance of audit testing.

However, this does not release them from documenting the planning, the work carried out and the issues encountered and dealt with. Clearly there will not be a specific requirement to demonstrate, for example, that the lead audit partner was involved because the working papers will speak for themselves, but this does not mean that significant professional judgements made should not be documented.

Audit partners dealing with smaller entities should be particularly aware of the threats to independence relevant to small clients and detailed in Chapter 6. As part of the audit documentation the files should evidence, where appropriate, how any threats to auditor's objectivity and independence have been addressed.

It should not be forgotten that a regulator may well wish to inspect the quality of audit work carried out by smaller audit firms so evidence of matters such as planning, audit risk evaluations, decisions about materiality, evidence of evaluations of internal controls, etc. should be included on the file, although the extent of the documentation may not be as elaborate as it would be for a much larger audit involving a much larger audit team.

OWNERSHIP OF BOOKS AND PAPERS

The ownership of the working papers of an accountant hinges on whether the accountant is acting as an agent for the client. The leading case is *Chantrey Martin & Co v Martin (1953)*.

The general rules are:

- Where the relationship is that of client and professional, then all documents are the property of the accountant. The only exceptions are original documents, e.g. bank statements, invoices, etc., which remain the property of the client.
- Where the relationship is that of principal and agent a relationship which will exist in situations where the accountant, say, is dealing with the HMRC to settle tax liabilities, or acting in connection with a takeover or sale of a business. In these cases, the papers may technically be the property of the client.

The ownership of working papers may not seem important, but it may be relevant in situations such as changes in professional appointments, legal proceedings for the recovery of documents, negligence actions, etc.

ACCOUNTANT'S LIEN

Accountants are considered to have a particular lien, i.e. the right to retain physical possession, over any books of account, files and papers which their clients have delivered to them and also over any documents which have come into their possession in the course of their ordinary professional work until any outstanding fees are paid.

The leading case is *Woodworth v Conroy (1976)*. That case Lord Justice Lawton (with whom the rest of the court agreed) said:

> *'I would adjudge that accountants in the course of doing their ordinary professional work of producing and auditing accounts, advising on financial problems, and carrying on negotiations with the Inland Revenue Department in relation to both taxation and rating have at least a particular lien over any books of account, files and papers which their clients delivered to them and also over any documents which have come into their possession in the course of acting as their client's agents in the course of their ordinary professional work.'*

This gives the auditor the right to retain papers and documents until any debt arising in connection with those goods, i.e. any outstanding fees, is paid.

RETENTION OF WORKING PAPERS

Auditors should retain their working papers for at least *five years* after the signing of the auditor's report. Other retention periods are dependent on a number of factors in particular:

- Prospectus requirements are for accounts for the preceding six years.
- Tax assessments can be made up to six years after the end of the chargeable period but in fraud cases, can be made at any time.
- Actions based on contract or tort (e.g. professional negligence) must be brought within six years.

In most cases detailed Current File information may probably be safely disposed of after six years, but auditors would be wise to retain information about any nonroutine or contentious issues on which they had to make a decision.

Permanent File data is what it says it is, i.e. permanent and should probably only be destroyed six years after losing the client – it should be retained for that length of time to ensure the period for bringing any legal actions is safely past.

SUMMARY

- Documentation of audit processes and decision making is an essential part of an audit. It should be carried out in such a way that an experienced auditor, having no connection with the assignment, could understand the client, the audit process and the decisions made.
- The reasons for documenting audit work include:
  - The engagement partner needs be satisfied that all audit work has been properly performed. This is done by reviewing the working papers.
  - The files must evidence involvement by the engagement partner in the audit process.
  - The files should contain a detailed explanation of professional judgements made during the course of the audit work and any material issues which have arisen and had to be resolved.
  - Working papers provide for future reference, details of work performed, problems encountered and conclusions drawn.
- The preparation of working papers encourages the audit staff to adopt a methodical approach.
- Audit working papers will typically contain:
  - Information and documents of continuing importance to the audit.
  - Audit planning information.
  - The auditor's assessment of the client's accounting systems and a review and assessment of the internal controls.
  - Details of all audit work undertaken, problems and errors met and of all conclusions drawn.
  - Evidence that all work carried out by audit staff has been reviewed by more senior staff and ultimately by the engagement partner.
  - Records of relevant balances and other financial information including summaries and analyses of all items in the financial statements.
  - A summary of significant points affecting the financial statements and the auditor's report, and how they were dealt with.
- The working papers detail what evidence has been obtained for each class of transaction and balance.
- Working papers are often divided into Permanent and Current files.
- Working papers will also include:
  - internal control questionnaires
  - internal control evaluation forms
  - flow charts
  - audit programmes

POINTS TO NOTE

- Financial statements are subject to much regulation (by the Companies Act or other Acts and by various accounting standards). Audits are regulated by the professional bodies acting as supervisory bodies. It is essential that auditors perform all the tests and reviews that are necessary to ensure that financial statements comply with the regulations, that the audit is comprehensive and that nothing has been overlooked. All actions must be fully recorded. One way of ensuring that all is done is to have checklists which must be completed, signed and reviewed by staff, managers and partners.

- Working papers can be stored in a choice of media – paper, film, electronic or other. If stored in the cloud they should be encrypted.
- Auditors use many schedules, analyses and other documentation prepared by the client. It is essential that there is adequate audit evidence that such information is properly prepared. This is especially true of computer printouts.
- ISA 230 requires that auditors should adopt appropriate procedures for maintaining the confidentiality and safe custody of their working papers.

CASE STUDY 1

Charlatan Furniture Ltd is a large company engaged in the manufacture and import of self-assembly furniture kits. Their system for the placing of purchase orders is:

(a) Requisitions are drawn up by production control, by marketing and by stores accounting who keep stores records on a micro-computer. Requisitions are not pre-numbered.

(b) All requisitions must be cost allocation coded and be signed as approved by a departmental manager. Certain codes (e.g. capital expenditure) are excluded from this process.

(c) Requisitions are passed to the purchasing department. They approve requisitions and complete purchase orders. Orders are placed with approved suppliers. There is an ongoing programme to find the optimal suppliers.

(d) The orders are in triplicate – 1 retained, 2 to requisitioner and 3 to the supplier. Orders are pre-numbered and are valued. Cost codes and total purchases for that cost code are entered on the order together with budgeted allowance for that code.

(e) The orders are checked and signed by the purchasing manager.

Discussion

– What information would you expect to see on the Permanent File in respect of this company?
– Draft and document an audit programme for the audit of the above system.
– What information would you keep on the Current File?

STUDENT SELF-TESTING QUESTIONS

Questions with answers apparent from the text

a) What are the objectives of working papers?

b) List the content of a Permanent File.

c) List the content of a Current File.

d) Who owns an accountant's working papers?

e) What is a lien and why might it be important to an accountant?

f) How long should auditors retain their working papers?

g) In the case of significant matters that require the exercise of judgement, what should working papers do?

h) List the advantages and disadvantages of standardizing working papers.

EXAMINATION QUESTIONS

1 Rapidrise Ltd is a firm of plumbers' and electricians' merchants which has expanded very rapidly to a turnover of some £13 million in five years. There are three founder director/shareholders and some 20 staff and six clerical staff including Ted who is a part qualified accountant. The system for ordering and paying for incoming goods is as follows.

Each morning Ted visits the warehouse and the foreman and his deputy tell him precisely what to order to replace existing inventories and to obtain new lines. New lines are usually suggested by the directors. Ted telephones through the orders to the regular suppliers. Some suppliers require a written order and for them he writes out an order from a duplicate pad which is not sequentially numbered.

On arrival of the goods, the goods are checked by the foreman or his deputy and the delivery note marked 'OK' and passed to Ted. Ted places the delivery notes in a file.

When the invoices arrive they are placed in a box. Jean, a clerk, compares the invoices with the delivery notes, settles queries and staples the invoices to the matching delivery notes. She then enters the details of the invoices (supplier, net, gross, VAT) into the computerized purchase ledger.

At the end of each month the file is printed out and a listing obtained of the outstanding invoices in supplier name order. When the monthly statements are received, Jean compares them with the printout and settles any queries over the phone with the supplier or with the foreman.

She then passes the statements to Ted who decides which items are to be paid (the company has cash flow difficulties caused by its rapid expansion). Ted then lists the amounts to be paid and processes the payments through an on-line banking system using his confidential password. He then passes the payments list to Jean who enters the payments in the Payables Ledger.

The computer system also:

- prints out transaction lists of invoices, credit notes and supplier payments;
- updates the cash book file which is used by Ted to control the bank overdraft; matches payments with invoice items and eliminates them where possible.

Jean journalizes entries to match and eliminate invoices where several are settled with one payment.

Jean has no other duties apart from some typing and the keeping of the petty cash.

There are no inventory control systems and the warehouse is open during the day to all staff and to customers. Good security operates at night and at weekends.

Required:

(a) Flow chart this system.

(b) Identify and list the weaknesses in this system.

(c) List the possible consequences of these weaknesses. These should include possible frauds as well as errors.

(d) Suggest a better system.

2 Alset Ltd have 12 electrical appliance shops in the Midlands. The company maintains a warehouse in Bilston and supplies goods to the branches using two lorries. There is a central accounts department at the warehouse with five staff under the chief accountant Louise.

Supplies are ordered for the central warehouse from specific suppliers (these are changed as necessary and Toby, a director, is in charge of an effective system for selecting suppliers). An inventory control system is used in the central warehouse which works well.

The 12 shops are in the charge of individual managers who have autonomy over most aspects of the shop including hiring staff. They are expected to indent for supplies from the central warehouse but are permitted to buy some supplies elsewhere if the central warehouse does not stock items and there is customer demand. Prices for items supplied from head office are fixed by head office as there is central advertising with prices given.

The accounting system is:

- Shop managers send in a weekly form of requisition for supplies to the central warehouse which orders the good from approved suppliers.
- The supplies are invoiced at cost and the invoices form input for the central warehouse inventory control system.
- Supplies bought for individual shops are paid for by head office. The cost of items supplied to each shop is recharged to it by Head Office.

- Sales are made in the shops for cash, cheque or by credit card. These are recorded on till rolls and the managers count the takings daily each morning and bank the proceeds. They agree the till rolls and retain the bank paying in counterfoils and the till rolls. Petty cash and wages are taken out of takings before banking. Each manager maintains his own wages records but payments to the HM Revenue & Customs are made centrally. A weekly return is sent to head office showing takings and payments made from takings.
- Overheads of the branches such as rent, rates and electricity are paid for centrally.
- Inventory counted half yearly by the managers and accounts prepared for each shop based on the data at head office. Action is taken if the profit margins are less than expected.
- Some sales are made on hire purchase (HP). The managers fill in the HP forms and keep the recording in the branches. They collect the instalments which are normally paid in cash. Full details are sent to head office on the weekly return. Some HP customers pay direct to head office bank account by standing order.
- Each shop manager is remunerated up to 50% by a commission on the net profit of the shop he/she manages.

Required:

(a) Document the weaknesses in this system indicating the possible frauds and errors that could occur.
(b) Prepare a flow chart of this system.
(c) Devise auditing tests for the existing system indicating whether these are compliance tests, substantive tests or analytical review.
(d) For each of the weaknesses identified in a) above set out how the systems might be changed to eliminate the weakness.

SOURCES AND ADDITIONAL READING

Chantrey Martin & Co. v Martin [1953] 2 QB 286.

Financial Reporting Council (2016), IAS 200 *Overall Objectives of the Independent Auditor and the Conduct of an Audit in Accordance with International Standards on Auditing*. London: Financial Reporting Council.

Financial Reporting Council (2016) *ISA 230 Audit Documentation*. London: Financial Reporting Council.

Financial Reporting Council (2016) *ISA 300 Planning an Audit of Financial Statements*. London: Financial Reporting Council.

Financial Reporting Council (2016) *ISA 315 Identifying and Assessing Risks of Material Misstatement through Understanding the Entity and its Environment*. London: Financial Reporting Council.

Financial Reporting Council (2016) *Practice Note 26 Guidance on Smaller Entity Audit Documentation*. London: Financial Reporting Council.

Woodworth v Conroy [1976] QB 884.

CHAPTER 19
INTERNAL AUDIT

Learning Objectives

After studying the material in this chapter you should be able to:

- understand the role and function of internal audit

- discuss the differences between internal and external auditors

- evaluate the role of the internal auditor in the public sector

- understand the criteria for external auditors to use the work of internal audit

- explain the options for outsourcing internal audit and the ethical issues involved

INTRODUCTION

The role and function of the internal auditor is defined by The Institute of Internal Auditing (IIA):

'Internal auditing is an independent, objective assurance and consulting activity designed to add value and improve an organization's operations. It helps an organization accomplish its objectives by bringing a systematic, disciplined approach to evaluate and improve the effectiveness of risk management, control and governance processes.'

Establishment of an **internal audit** function is not a legal requirement for companies in the same way that they are required to be audited by external auditors. However, the principles of good corporate governance (Chapter 2) require that an independent, objective and capable internal audit function is established with a clear mandate to review not only the accounting function, but all aspects of the organization including corporate governance itself.

For listed companies an internal audit function is a particular requirement of the UK Corporate Governance Code and good practice under the Code requires the internal audit function to be monitored by the Audit Committee (Chapter 2).

Internal audit is, however, a legal requirement in the public sector, including local authorities and the NHS as well as for government departments. The overriding reason for this is that government and public sector bodies are funded by public money and must therefore be accountable for its use. Accordingly, the public sector auditing process perhaps places a greater reliance on the effectiveness of internal audit than does the audit process in the private sector.

Internal audit differs from external audit in scope; it does not focus solely on financial statements or financial risks. Much of the work of internal audit considers operational or strategic risks and the management processes set up to address them. As can be seen from the IIA's definition, internal audit sees itself very much as part of the management function, particularly as part of the quality system.

It does *not* see itself as a corporate police force constantly checking on people's work with a view to finding fault and attaching blame. Internal auditing is intended to be proactive not reactive, its intention is to add value to the organization, not to be simply an overhead cost.

The awarding body for internal audit qualifications is the Chartered Institute of Internal Auditors, as mentioned above. They also publish the International Standards for the Professional Practice of Internal Auditing, which we don't cover in this book, together with bulletins and guidance material for internal auditors.

ROLE OF INTERNAL AUDIT

Internal auditors look at how organizations are managing their risks. They provide the Audit Committee (if there is one – see Chapter 2) and the board of directors with information about whether risks have been identified and how well they are being managed.

As we have seen, the responsibility to manage risk always resides with management. Internal Audit's role as part of that process of managing risk is:

- identifying potential problem areas, both financial and operational
- recommending ways of improving risk management and internal control systems
- monitoring corporate governance issues including ethics, performance management and accountability, communications throughout the organization in connection with risk management and internal control and with firm wide values and acceptable behaviours
- reviewing operational procedures including, for example **Value for Money** initiatives (Chapter 31), procurement and supply chain management or HR processes
- reviewing compliance with laws and regulations

Their role includes examination and evaluation of information – both financial and non-financial. This can result in what amounts to a continuous audit of the organization's operations as the internal auditors review all aspects of its activities on a rolling basis and is similar in many ways to the work of external auditors.

They are required to give an opinion on whether internal controls – including management's policies and procedures put in place to manage business risks – are actually working as intended.

The role of Internal audit also includes providing an evaluation of policies and procedures in operational areas with a view to making recommendations for improvement or cost saving and reporting on compliance issues and ethical matters which may affect the operations of the organization.

These activities will include:

- a review of the policy making/procedural process
- assessment of the adequacy of guidance given to managers and staff
- review of organizational, personnel and supervisory arrangements within the organization
- review of procedures for accounting for, and safeguarding from loss, assets, business interests and income streams
- review of controls to ensure the appropriateness, timeliness, reliability and integrity of information
- review of the economy, efficiency and effectiveness of operations. This is known as 'value for money' auditing
- review of compliance with applicable laws and regulations. internal audit can have specific responsibilities, for example, in the area of money laundering or insider trading
- review of and advice in connection with the development of information systems; note that, as auditors, they should *not* get involved in systems design – they cannot audit independently a system they helped design

DIFFERENCES BETWEEN INTERNAL AND EXTERNAL AUDIT

The best way to highlight this is by means of a table which will contrast the respective roles (Figure 19.1).

FIGURE 19.1 Internal and external audit

	Internal audit	**External audit**
objectives	to evaluate the organization's risk management processes and systems of control and to make recommendations for the achievements of organizational objectives	to provide an opinion on whether the financial statements show a true and fair view and whether proper accounting records have been maintained
responsibility	to management: part of quality system and corporate procedures on an ongoing basis	to shareholders: report on financial accounts on an annual basis
carried out by	frequently employees of organization: if outsourced the provision is largely within management's control and direction	external body independent of organization
scope	all aspects of the organization's activities, including operational considerations and compliance issues	audit programme working papers queries and explanations letter of weakness and non-reported weaknesses
approach	risk based evaluate internal control systems test systems evaluate operational efficiencies	risk based test basis on which financial accounts produced and reliability of systems verification of assets and liabilities
legal status	report to management: no specific legal requirement but UK Corporate Governance Code for listed companies requires internal audit mandatory in the public sector	report to shareholders: Companies Act 2006

PUBLIC SECTOR

It is not within the scope of this book to cover the role of internal audit in the public sector. However, within that sector, encompassing all aspects such as local and national government, the National Health Service and bodies such as housing associations, internal audit plays a much more significant role than in private sector organizations. Indeed, internal audit is mandatory in local government and the NHS.

This is due to two factors:

- **Accountability** – most public sector organizations are funded primarily through taxpayers' money – and so it has to be properly accounted for as they are accountable to the public for how the money has been spent.
- **Regularity** – this is a term used in the public sector and it means use of funds for the purpose for which they were intended, i.e. capital funds cannot be used for revenue, grants for specific activities must be spent on those activities.

To a large extent these are not issues which affect private organizations who raise their income from selling goods and services in the marketplace and are accountable, primarily, only to their shareholders.

The accountancy body responsible for training accountants with a specific role in the public sector, the Chartered Institute of Public Finance and Accountancy (CIPFA) has issued several bulletins on the role of internal auditing in the public sector and students who are interested in this should study CIPFA's pronouncements.

EXTERNAL AUDITORS AND INTERNAL AUDIT

ISA 610 '*Using the work of internal auditors*' requires that external auditors obtain a thorough understanding of the internal audit function so as to assist in the planning of the audit work and determine the degree of reliance on internal audit.

There are some specific problems the auditor has to deal with particularly how closely do the objectives of internal and external audit coincide? Are the internal auditors mostly looking at, for example, efficiency gains, or are they properly evaluating internal controls?

Remember that Internal auditors work for the entity so the auditors will need to know how independent the internal audit function actually is – in particular:

- Can it decide its own pattern of work i.e. is Internal Audit constrained by management in any way by being denied access to certain records or being told to concentrate only on specific aspects of the organization's activities?
- Does it have unrestricted access to management at the highest level, i.e. the CEO or the Audit Committee?
- Does the head of internal audit have a senior management or board level position, independent of the Financial Director?
- Is the potential scope of its work restricted in any way?
- Is it free of any operational responsibilities?
- Can it communicate freely with the external auditors?
- How competent is the internal audit function? Does the department contain sufficient numbers of trained, competent professional accountants to carry out the role effectively? Is it well enough resourced? Do they have professional qualifications and training programmes both for trainees and for continuing professional development?

The external auditors have to consider these factors and evaluate how much reliance can be placed on the work carried out in the period by the internal auditors.

This is particularly important if the external auditors are adopting a risk-based audit strategy, as a strong, independent internal audit function is a significant part of the overall internal control environment (Chapter 14).

If the external auditors decide to place a reliance on the work of internal audit they must consider the timing of the work, the approach to such matters as audit risk, sampling, materiality levels and how the work is to be documented. This should be discussed with the internal auditors prior to the work being carried out. In particular, external auditors should review:

- the materiality of the areas or items tested;
- the level of audit risk inherent in those areas;

- the level of judgement required;
- how good the corroboratory evidence for the work done by the internal auditors is.

It is important for external audit to be able to evaluate whether the internal auditors have the skills needed to carry out the work effectively, especially any specialist skills. The auditors must build this into their planning documentation, together with the rationale for using the work of the internal auditors. Communication between the two parties is important and regular meetings should be held to review significant issues.

Once the work is done it should be reviewed by the external auditors to consider whether the work has been properly supervised and reviewed when completed. External audit will consider how the work compares with work carried out by the auditor's own staff in a similar area. Ensure any issues coming to light have been properly resolved. They will read reports prepared by internal audit and management's responses and ensure working papers are up to an acceptable standard.

OUTSOURCING INTERNAL AUDIT SERVICES

It is one of the principles of good corporate governance that the internal audit function be independent. Internal audit may be provided by in-house staff, or an outsourced team. Either way, it should be independent from the management structure and report directly to the Audit Committee or the Chief Executive *not* the Financial Director or Chief Financial Officer, to maintain the independence of the internal audit function.

There are both advantages and disadvantages to outsourcing. The advantages to the organization are:

- The outsourced auditors are independent from the organization.
- There is a wide range of best practice expertise available.
- There are no staff administration or training costs.
- The facility can be 'right sourced', i.e. only used when needed.
- The resource can be used flexibly as required.
- Professional firms are responsible for the level of service and its ethical standards – it can be sued for any failures.
- External audit firms tend to have a higher level of training, numbers of professional staff and technical resources.
- Specialized skills, e.g. computer auditors may be available.

There are, however, a number of significant disadvantages:

- Costs may be high.
- There is likely to be a lack of commitment to the goals and objectives of the organization.
- Consistency of staff is not always available.
- Professional firms cannot be ordered about in the same way as your own staff.
- There is loss of control over quality of staff provided.
- Clients pay for what they have contracted for and anything else is extra.

If internal audit is provided by an outsourced team this may be provided by the external audit firm, however this has to be handled with care. It is an ethical principle of external audit firms that they remain objective (Chapter 6). In the case of Public Interest Entities external auditors are specifically forbidden from providing internal audit services.

If internal audit is provided by the external audit firms this may result in cost savings but it may also result in ethical conflicts within the audit firm. The two roles would undoubtedly have to be kept separate, with individual teams and no staff sharing to avoid the firm giving the impression that its independence as external auditor is compromised in any way because of its involvement on a day-to-day basis in a management function.

If the outsourced team is drawn from a firm other than the external audit firm, there is the issue of client confidentiality. The internal audit provider will have to obtain their client's permission to reveal the information gleaned during its audits. If it cannot make full disclosure the external auditors could be faced with a limitation of scope qualification in their auditor's report.

If both teams are from the same firm this should not be a particular problem, but the client should understand that the internal audit team will be disclosing its findings to the external audit team. If the client attempts to limit this the audit firm should consider its position regarding the trustworthiness of their client.

SUMMARY

- Internal auditors see themselves as part of the management function and try to operate more as consultants than corporate police officers.
- The aim of internal audit is to add value to the company's operations, to safeguard its assets and to review the operations of internal procedures and controls.
- Internal auditors are part of the management of the business, external auditors are statutorily appointed.
- The internal audit function should be independent of the finance function and should be adequately resourced.
- Internal auditors carry out work in much the same way as external auditors but the scope of what they do is much wider.
- If external audit wish to use internal audit they should consider the independence and competence of the internal audit function.
- ISA 610 sets out the process whereby external auditors can consider using the work of internal auditors.
- Internal audit can be outsourced to external audit providers.

POINTS TO NOTE

- The nature of internal audit has changed over the years and it is now much more proactive in company processes and procedures.
- The Institute of Internal Auditors sets out competencies and standards for internal auditors.

CASE STUDY

Shark Estate Agents Ltd is a company offering estate agency services to the public through a network of branches in the Midlands. The company has some 270 staff in all.

The board consists of six people, a part-time chairman, a chief executive, two other full time executives and two representatives of the owners. The company is jointly owned by an American bank and a city property group. The company have an internal audit department consisting of Legge who is a young chartered certified accountant and Foot who is an accounting technician. They also have a secretary, Mavis. They report their activities monthly in detail to the board and to the audit committees of the American bank and the city property group.

Discussion

- What work would the internal audit department do?
- In what ways may the external auditors place reliance on their work?
- Draw up a checklist for the external auditor to use to assess the internal auditors as potentially being capable of producing work on which the external auditors may rely.

STUDENT SELF-TESTING QUESTIONS

Questions with answers apparent from the text

a) Why might an external audit rely on the work of an internal auditor?

b) In what way may they co-operate?

c) How may the external auditor assess the internal auditor and his work?

d) What factors influence the extent of reliance in a particular area?

e) How might the co-operation be planned and controlled?

f) What implications does all this have for the external auditor's working papers?

EXAMINATION QUESTIONS

1 Internal auditors often assist management in performing internal review assignments covering, for example, human resources, procurement (purchasing), marketing and treasury activities. Such reviews involve:

(i) the identification of risks

(ii) the identification of control systems and procedures implemented to manage those risks

(iii) tests of controls to ensure that internal controls are operating effectively

(iv) an evaluation of the overall effectiveness of the design and operation of controls in managing the risks identified

You are the internal auditor for a private company, Cleanco. Cleanco provides cleaning services to shops and offices and has a reputation for high-quality work. You have been asked to review the human resources, procurement and marketing functions within the company.

Cleanco employs about 500 cleaning staff, all of whom are on the payroll and most of whom work part-time. Cleanco does not employ subcontractors. Cleanco has a high turnover of staff.

The company buys its computers, office stationery and furniture, cleaning materials, equipment and work clothes for staff, from a variety of different suppliers. It processes its payroll in-house.

The company has recently decided to outsource its marketing to a large, aggressive, third party company that will advertise Cleanco's services by means of direct mail, sometimes by offering discounts; this company has been criticized in the past for breaching advertising regulations. There is growing price competition in Cleanco's market.

Cleanco is struggling to maintain its profitability and would like to expand its client base. Cleanco has three main functions:

(i) human resources

(ii) procurement

(iii) marketing

Required:

For each of the three main functions at Cleanco describe the:

(a) risks that you expect the company to face;

(b) controls you expect to be in place to manage the risks you have identified in (a), above;

(c) tests of control you should perform to check that the controls you have identified in (b) above are operating properly.

You may present your answer in tabular format, if you wish.

(ICAEW)

2 Reports produced by internal auditors are different from audit reports produced by external auditors performing audits under International Standards on Auditing. The reports are produced for different purposes and are directed at different users. They differ substantially in both form and content.

Internal audit reports often comprise the following:

(i) a cover page

(ii) executive summary

(iii) the main report contents

(iv) appendices

Required:

(a) List and briefly describe the general categories of information that you would expect to find in an internal audit report under each of the four headings above.

(b) Explain why the contents of external audit reports prepared under International Standards on Auditing and internal audit reports are different.

(c) Some reports produced by internal auditors are similar to the report to management (management letter) on internal controls and other matters that are produced by external auditors during the course of the audit. The steps taken by internal and external auditors in drafting, issuing and following up such reports are also similar.

Required:

Describe the common characteristics of the steps taken by internal and external auditors in producing reports to management. *(Note students may wish to read Chapter 28 before attempting this part of the question.)*
(ACCA)

SOURCES AND ADDITIONAL READING

CIPFA (2002) *Standard of Professional Practice on Auditing*. London: Chartered Institute of Public Finance and Accountancy.

CIPFA (2006) *Code of Practice for Internal Audit in Local Government*. London: Chartered Institute of Public Finance and Accountancy.

Financial Reporting Council (2016) *ISA 610 Using the Work of Internal Auditors*. London: Financial Reporting Council.

Institute of Internal Auditors (2016) *Code of Ethics*. London: Institute of Internal Auditors.

CHAPTER 20
ERRORS, FRAUDS
AND UNLAWFUL ACTS

Learning Objectives

After studying the material in this chapter you should be able to:

- explain what is meant by error or misstatement

- understand the implication for the auditor of materiality in connection with audit reporting of fraud and error

- the auditors' responsibilities in connection with bribery and corruption

- appreciate the importance of communication between members of the audit team

- understand who is responsible for the prevention and detection of fraud and error

- understand who auditors report to in particular circumstances

- explain the procedures in connection with the discovery of unlawful acts by the client or its staff

- understand the ethical rules on breaches of the principles of confidentiality

- discuss the auditor's options of resignation or continuance

INTRODUCTION

The Financial Reporting Council defines the role of the audit as:

'the independent examination of, and expression of opinion on, the financial statements of an enterprise by an appointed auditor in pursuance of that appointment and in compliance with any relevant statutory obligation.'

The emphasis is on the examination of the financial statements. However, the public, including much of the business community, tend to include in an auditor's duties, the detection, and possibly prevention, of fraud and error – part of something that is known as the 'Expectation Gap' (Chapter 1).

This section explores the relationship that an auditor has with the prevention, discovery and reporting of fraud and error.

Key ISAs here are:

- ISA 240 *'The auditor's responsibilities relating to fraud in an audit of financial statements'*
- ISA 315 *'Identifying and assessing risks of material misstatement through understanding the entity and its environment'*
- ISA 330 *'The auditor's responses to assessed risks'*

There is a difference known as the **Expectation Gap**, which we looked at in Chapter 1, between the public and the auditing profession in relation to an auditor's duty regarding errors and fraud.

To recap, the Expectation Gap is the difference between what the auditors actually do and what the public think they do. Research has shown that the public often think that auditors are responsible for detecting fraud. As students will know, this is not true, yet the myth persists. Responsibility for the prevention and detection of fraud and error lies with *management*, however, despite the expressed intention that it is not the auditor's job to detect fraud, it does behove the auditor to make every effort not to be fooled and to avoid the embarrassment of having a major fraud uncovered just months after signing an unmodified audit report.

The auditor's responsibility is to properly plan, perform and evaluate their audit work so as to have a reasonable expectation of detecting material misstatements in the financial statements, whether they are caused by fraud, other irregularities or errors.

ERRORS AND MISSTATEMENTS

Errors, within which for now we will include misstatements i.e. something described as one thing when it is, in reality something else, can, generally, be described as 'unintentional mistakes'. However, it is fairly obvious that misstatements can, in the case of fraud, be very intentional and designed to purposely mislead. One way a fraudster attempts to cover up their crime is by deliberately misstating entries in the accounting records.

Errors or misstatements can occur at any stage in business transaction processing and can take many forms, including the (mis) application of accounting principles such as including revenue costs in capital, simple mistakes in entering data such as entering 1234 as 1243, or describing a transaction incorrectly. Such errors are commonly divided into:

- mistakes of commission (doing something wrongly);
- mistakes of omission (leaving something out);
- errors in the interpretation of facts; and
- misstatements where some item or transaction is wrongly described or is false or misleading.

The existence of errors or misstatements may indicate to an auditor that the accounting records of the client are unreliable and thus are not satisfactory as a basis from which to prepare financial statements. The existence of a material number of errors may lead the auditor to conclude that proper accounting records, as required by Section 386, Companies Act 2006, have not been kept. This is a ground for qualification of the auditor's report under Section 498 (Chapter 26). For example, the financial position of the company may be unable to be disclosed with reasonable accuracy (Section 386(2) (b)) or all sums of money received are not entered in the accounting records (Section 386(3)(a)).

As we have seen in earlier chapters if the auditors wish to place reliance on internal controls, they should ascertain and evaluate those controls and perform compliance tests on their operation. If compliance tests indicate a material number of errors, then the auditors may be unable to place reliance on internal control to the extent that they would want to. If errors are of sufficient magnitude i.e. they are material, they may be sufficient to affect the truth and fairness of the view given by the financial statements. The effect of the total number of errors may not be material enough to affect the true and fair view, in which case the auditors are not concerned with them directly. However, if they show a pattern or some fault in the system they should include the details in the Management Letter (Chapter 27). The auditors will need to have very good evidence that the effect of the errors is not material before they decide to ignore them.

For audit purposes errors and misstatements can arise in four ways:

1   A mistake in gathering or processing data from which the financial statements are prepared.

2   An incorrect accounting estimate arising from an oversight or misinterpretation of facts.

3   A mistake in the application of accounting principles relating to measurement, recognition, classification, presentation or disclosure of transactions and balances.

4   Incorrect narrative in the description of an item in the financial statements or the omission of narrative which gives a false impression of the item.

When all the audit testing work is completed the auditor must assess the total level of errors and misstatements detected and form a judgement as to the adequacy of the accounting records and the truth and fairness, or otherwise, of the financial statements. Large, material errors have to be corrected and the system errors highlighted by the checking work would provide good points for the Management Letter.

The auditor is left with the decision as to whether or not, taking into account the level of errors and misstatements detected and the level of audit work carried out, the audit report can be signed without any form of qualification as to the quality of the accounting records.

FRAUD AND OTHER IRREGULARITIES

What constitutes fraud is now defined specifically in the Fraud Act 2006. This says:

(1)   *A person is guilty of fraud if he is in breach of any of the sections listed in subsection (2) (which provide for different ways of committing the offence).*

(2)   *The sections are—*
  (a)   section 2 (fraud by false representation);
  (b)   section 3 (fraud by failing to disclose information); and
  (c)   section 4 (fraud by abuse of position).

Fraud by false representation is fraud which involves the use of deception to obtain an unjust or illegal financial advantage. An example of this would be, say, a department store manager diverting cash takings into his own pocket and then falsifying sales and inventory records to cover up the theft.

Fraud by failing to disclose information and fraud by abuse of position cover circumstances where individuals fail to disclose relevant information with the intention to commit a fraud or abuse a position of trust which enables them to commit a fraud. An example of this kind of fraud might be the action of the directors of a company in falsifying financial information given to a bank in order to raise additional finance by hiding the fact that the company is not a going concern, thus keeping their jobs and salaries.

There is a difference between fraud and error. Errors should, hopefully, be detected either by the internal control procedures or the auditor's own procedures whereas fraud is a deliberate act and may well require specific procedures in order to detect it because the fraudster is taking deliberate steps to conceal their crime.

The auditors are primarily concerned about two types of fraud:

- misappropriation of assets and consequent misstatements arising from that, i.e. a cover up involving the alteration of the accounting records to disguise the theft; and
- misstatements arising from fraudulent financial reporting.

Characteristics of fraud

Misappropriation of assets is what most people immediately think of when fraud is mentioned. This can often be frauds committed by employees for relatively minor amounts which may not, in themselves, be material and which may not be detected by routine audit checking work. This could be simple frauds like short changing customers at a till or selling scrap for cash and pocketing it. However, it also encompasses management fraud where managers are in a position to disguise misappropriations in ways that are difficult to detect.

These types of fraud include:

- Embezzling receipts, e.g. misappropriating sales revenues or diverting receipts in respect of written-off accounts to personal bank accounts.
- Stealing physical assets or intellectual property, e.g. inventory theft, colluding with a competitor to disclose trade secrets in return for payment.
- Causing the business to pay for goods not received, e.g. payments to fictitious suppliers, kickbacks paid to purchasing managers in return for inflating prices, payment of fictitious employees.
- Using the business's assets for personal use, e.g. as collateral for a loan.

Fraudulent reporting frequently involves the **management override** of controls that otherwise might appear to be operating correctly.

Examples of this are:

- recording fictitious journal entries, especially close to the end of the accounting period, to manipulate operating results or other figures;
- inappropriately adjusting assumptions and changing judgements used to estimate account balances;
- omitting, advancing or delaying recognition in the financial statements of events or transactions which have occurred during the financial period;
- concealing or not disclosing facts that would affect the amounts recorded in the financial statements;
- engaging in complex transactions which are structured to misrepresent the financial position or financial performance of the business; and
- altering records and terms related to significant or unusual transactions.

Auditors should be aware that research indicates that fraudsters who commit the largest frauds are most likely to be:

- men
- in their mid-30s to mid-50s
- in a relatively senior position in the organization
- who have worked for the organization for a number of years
- who commit fraud over a period of years
- who commit multiple fraudulent transactions

These are quite often likely to be the very people the auditors come to for explanations, information and assurances. As fraudsters frequently tell lies, auditors must remain sceptical and evaluate everything they are told carefully in the light of their knowledge of the business and corroboratory evidence. An example of this can be seen in Figure 20.1.

Figure 20.1 The business manager and the trusting employer. Not everyone is who they seem.

An employee who developed a cocaine habit ended up stealing more than £70 000 from the engineering firm where she worked. Charlotte Fielding, 32, wrote 153 company cheques to pay her bills and also to buy clothes and other items.

The court heard how Fielding was the business manager of a small engineering company called Micro Tec at the Bersham Enterprise Centre near Wrexham. She admitted fraud between January 2007 and July 2008 in which she got away with £57 869 but she also asked for a further fraud involving £15 310 dating back to May 2006 to be taken into consideration.

Fielding was the business administrator and was so trusted that directors would provide her with blank signed cheques to pay the bills but she took advantage of the system and used some of the cheques to pay her own utility bills and other money went into her own account. Fielding was jailed for 14 months after admitting fraud. The judge said it was a gross breach of trust and Fielding had simply made out the cheques for her own benefit.

Source: Western Mail (2009)

Students will recall that ISA 200 'Overall objectives of the independent auditor and conduct of an audit in accordance with International Standards on Auditing' requires auditors to carry out their work with an attitude of professional scepticism. We looked at this in Chapter 9 and they should be wary of accepting assurances and explanations in the absence of convincing evidence.

Materiality of fraud and error

Materiality is discussed in Chapter 10 and should be fully understood.

A true and fair view may be given by financial statements of Huge plc with or without disclosure of a theft of, say, £50 000 where profits are £4.5m. On the other hand, a theft by an employee of £50 000 from Small Ltd, would have to be disclosed if the profits were reported as £45 000. The latter is material to the accounts and the former is not.

If the auditors know or suspect that an error or irregularity has occurred or exists, then they cannot apply a materiality consideration until they have sufficient evidence of the extent of the error or irregularity. Consequently, investigations may need to be made (by the auditor or by the client) into *all* errors and irregularities so that the auditor can have evidence of the materiality of the matter concerned.

BRIBERY AND CORRUPTION

The Bribery Act 2010 makes it illegal for organizations and their representatives to either take part in bribery or to seek to obtain bribes from a third party. An offence is committed whether the activity was carried out by the entity, its managers or staff or by third parties such as local agents acting on its behalf.

There is, however, a defence available for organizations and that is to ensure that they have comprehensive and adequate procedures in place to prohibit such activity, to attempt to prevent it happening and to identify perpetrators if it does. There is a self-reporting mechanism to the regulatory authority.

This presents some problems for auditors working in areas where bribery and construction has often been considered endemic. These include:

- extractive industries – oil and mining
- construction
- transport

The position of the auditors is no different in the case of bribery and corruption than it is in the case of fraud in general but the possibility of corrupt acts should form part of audit planning where the client operates in an industry where bribery is a real possibility. The difficulty arises where clients operate in countries where bribery and corruption are endemic and auditors should refer to Transparency International's annual Corruption Index to identify these areas. Unsurprisingly many of these countries are among the poorest in the world but countries such as India and China have well publicised problems with corruption within the public and private sectors.

The problems are not confined to businesses. Take for example a charity delivering aid to a poor country ravaged by war – the local official demands a bribe to enable the ship carrying much needed supplies to dock at the port. The local agent for the charity pays it – the charity is guilty of an offence under the Bribery Act.

Consequently, auditors must be alert not simply to large cash payments but also to items described as such things as 'Facilitation Payments', 'Consultancy or Advisory Fees', payments to overseas banks or to organizations where there is no ostensible commercial connection or sited in tax havens, cash discounts or refunds to overseas organizations, excessive loan repayments or simply excessive expenditure on entertaining overseas customers or foreign officials. It is important for auditors to inspect all the paperwork relative to any suspicious transactions and they should review transactions with local agents where the possibility of bribery and corruption is high.

Auditors should review the organizations systems and procedures with regard to bribery and corruption to ensure that they would be likely to present a sufficient defence under the Act should a case arise.

Should the audit work detect suspicious transactions these should be reported to the company which should self-report to the Serious Fraud Office. If the client fails to report the audit firms should consider reporting but should only do so after taking legal advice as the question may hang on the reliability of the evidence the auditor has that an offence under the act has actually taken place.

RESPONSIBILITY FOR PREVENTION AND DETECTION OF FRAUD AND ERROR

ISA 240 *The Auditor's Responsibility to Discover Fraud in an Audit of Financial Statements* places the responsibility squarely on the shoulders of management:

> *'The primary responsibility for the prevention and detection of fraud rests with both those charged with governance of the entity and with management. It is important that management, with the oversight of those charged with governance, place a strong emphasis on fraud prevention, which may reduce opportunities for fraud to take place, and fraud deterrence, which could persuade individuals not to commit fraud because of the likelihood of detection and punishment.'*

This responsibility arises out of a contractual duty of care by directors and managers and also because directors and other managers act in a stewardship capacity with regard to the property entrusted to them by the shareholders or other owners. How they exercise this duty of care is a matter for them, but in most cases their duty may be discharged by instituting and maintaining a strong system of internal control.

There are many ways the directors can discharge their duty toward prevention and detection of fraud and error. These include:

- complying with the UK Corporate Governance Code;
- developing a Code of Conduct, monitoring compliance and taking action against breaches;
- emphasizing a strong commitment to fraud prevention; this involves establishing a culture of honesty and ethical behaviour within the organization with clearly communicated policies on the corporate attitude to fraud and fraudsters; this is often known as **Tone at the Top**;
- establishing a strong control environment, monitoring its effectiveness and taking corrective action;
- establishing an internal audit function;
- establishing a compliance function, that is a separate department of the enterprise specifically charged with ensuring compliance with regulations of all sorts; and
- establishing an Audit Committee.

The auditor is not required to assist the directors in this task but guidelines suggest that an auditor should remind directors of their responsibilities in the Letter of Engagement and of the need to have a system of internal control as a deterrent to errors and irregularities. The engagement process (Chapter 8) should educate the client in the true nature of an audit and outline the auditor's duties towards irregularity and fraud.

The letter should leave the directors under no illusions that, whilst the auditors will endeavour to plan the audit so that they have a reasonable expectation of detecting material misstatements in the financial statements resulting from irregularities or fraud, the examination should not be relied upon to disclose all irregularities and frauds which may exist and that the primary responsibility for prevention and detection of fraud remains with them. Some clients may desire a special examination for irregularities and fraud outside the audit.

As we have seen, it is the responsibility of the auditors to obtain sufficient relevant reliable audit evidence to support their opinion that the systems are functioning properly. The attitude of professional scepticism required by ISA 200 recognizes the possibility that a material misstatement due to fraud could exist, notwithstanding the fact that in previous years the client may have been considered honest and trustworthy.

THE AUDIT APPROACH

Before preparing the audit plan, the auditors should carry out an audit risk assessment in order to appraise the risk of misstatements due to errors and fraud. Factors to take into account would include the situation facing the client (e.g. financial difficulties) or known problems with internal controls. The whole approach to the audit may be affected by the risks involved.

In the case of a new client the auditor must gain an understanding of the client and its environment, including its internal control, sufficient to identify and assess the risks of a material misstatement due to fraud or error. This, of course, could still mean the auditor has been misled by unscrupulous management but evidence of this preliminary review will help to justify the auditor's approach.

Auditors should also consider the circumvention of controls involving the possibility or likelihood of **collusion** between management and staff which would reduce the probability of the auditor being able to detect fraud through routine audit procedures. Deliberate collusion between members of upper management may induce auditors to accept evidence as persuasive when, in fact, it is false.

The auditor should assess the risks of a material misstatement due to fraud by considering several key factors, primarily:

- The nature of the business, its services and its products which may be susceptible to misappropriation. Organizations which involve cash takings (e.g. retailers) and easily portable and valuable assets (e.g. jewellers) are particularly at risk as also are organizations where assets are held in a fiduciary capacity (e.g. solicitors who hold clients' monies before handling them on to the appropriate persons). Also vulnerable are areas where payment is made on the basis of an opinion, i.e. the value of work certified in the construction industry or the value of extras to contract. This may involve corrupt practices such as bribery of a quantity surveyor. Evidence of cash payments of an unusual size may be indicative of corrupt practices however they are described in the accounts.
- Circumstances which may induce management to overstate profits (or understate losses), e.g. to retain the confidence of investors, bankers or creditors, to meet profit forecasts, to increase profit-related remuneration or to stave off the threat of insolvency proceedings, or where management have shares or share options.
- The known strength, quality and effectiveness of management.
- The internal control environment including the degree of management involvement and supervision, the degree of segregation of duties and where there is excessive authority vested in a senior manager.
- The ability of the management to override otherwise effective controls.
- The existence and effectiveness of internal audit.

This risk assessment is an ongoing, dynamic process and the risk assessment for each client must be kept under continual review, even though previous experience with the client has been that the management and staff are honest and trustworthy.

The auditor must retain the attitude of professional scepticism throughout the audit engagement, however this should not be taken too far; the auditor is allowed to accept evidence and representations as being honest in the absence of any indications to the contrary, otherwise nothing would ever be finalized! The auditor simply has to be alert to the possibility of fraud and to investigate suspicious or unusual transactions in the light of that possibility.

At the transaction level matters to consider include:

- the susceptibility of an area to irregularity, e.g. cash sales, portable and valuable inventory, exclusion of liabilities, cash payments;
- the possibility of collusion between members of staff – auditors should be alert to relationships between members of staff;
- the presence of unusual transactions;
- the existence of related party transactions;
- the materiality of transactions and the areas considered most vulnerable; and
- the complexity of transactions, e.g. financial futures, hedging operations, etc.

The information on the matters outlined above will come both from prior experience and the auditor's review of the business and control environment as part of the audit planning process (Chapter 10).

Process of discussion

ISA 240 is particularly insistent that the audit team actively discuss the audit amongst themselves as required by ISA 315 'Identifying and assessing risks of material misstatement through understanding the entity and its environment'. The purpose of this discussion is to consider the likelihood of fraud and the weaker areas of the organization's internal controls. This enables more experienced members of the team to share their experience as to the likelihood of fraud and how it might be perpetrated.

Regular discussions amongst the audit team enables them to consider management responses to areas identified as being susceptible to fraud and the audit procedures which might have to be introduced and how the results of any investigations might be shared amongst the team. It is a forum for discussion of the possibilities of certain types of fraud or indicators of fraud such as:

- changes in lifestyle by management of employees or unexplained changes in behaviour; and
- external or internal pressures on the organization which might be sufficiently strong as to encourage the possibility of manipulation of the financial statements.

It encourages an exchange of ideas amongst the team as to how such frauds could be carried out and how the audit team might detect them and enables a review of vulnerable areas such as cash management and inventory storage and management's oversight of them. Team members can share any indications of management override of controls, any reports of fraud or, indeed, any gossip or innuendo that fraud might be taking place.

The engagement partner should ensure that the team approaches the audit in a realistic frame of mind, i.e. one of healthy scepticism rather than deep suspicion, unless there are grounds, of course, to be suspicious!

AUDIT TESTS AND FRAUD

Tests designed specifically and uniquely to detect and establish the extent of fraud will be performed only when the auditor's suspicions are aroused; however, ISA 240 does require the auditor to undertake specific procedures with regard to fraud. These can be summarized as:

- Perform procedures which can identify the risks of a material misstatement due to fraud – this is part of the planning process – see Chapter 10 – and the auditor should consider fraud as part of the evaluation of the integrity of the management and the inherent risks surrounding the client's business.
- Ensure that all forms of audit testing are unpredictable to the client and serve to amass reliable evidence. Evidence from more than one source should be obtained where preliminary planning indicates that some figures may be susceptible to fraud. For example, if the audit team consider the possibility that revenue figures may have been

exaggerated through fictitious entries audit teams should carry out analytical review procedures whilst also looking for evidence that unusual journal entries have been put through the books or fictitious sales invoices have been created which have been reversed after the year end.

- Identify and assess the risks of fraud at both the individual transaction level and at the level of the financial statements as a whole. This involves making an assessment of the efficiency or otherwise of the internal control procedures relevant to those assessed risks.
- Decide on audit responses to the assessed risks including the assignment of experienced personnel and the development of a level of unpredictability in the audit testing.
- Design and perform procedures to address the risk of management override of controls.
- Consider whether any misstatements or apparent errors detected may be indicative of fraud.
- Ensure that all staff engaged on the assignment adopt the right degree of professional scepticism when evaluating their audit tests and dealing with management responses, despite any previous experience of the integrity of staff and management.
- Ensure that members of the audit team discuss the susceptibility of the client's financial statements to material misstatements due to fraud. This discussion should include the engagement partner and key members of the audit team but need not involve everyone. It is at the discretion of the audit partner how much of that discussion is disclosed to more junior members of the audit team.

Limitations on audit procedures

Auditors should recognize that there are limitations on the ability of an audit to detect fraud in particular because the primary objective of the auditor is to form an opinion on the financial statements not detect fraud. Auditing is based on testing samples of transactions and evaluating controls. Inherent in this approach is the possibility that not all errors or misstatements, whether due to fraud or not, will be detected even if the audit is properly planned and carried out.

Management, particularly senior management, have the capacity to hide fraud from the auditors and deliberately manipulate the accounting records. Where the misrepresentation involves the exercise of judgement, for example accounting estimates, it is difficult to decide whether these were caused by fraud or error.

Fraud may involve sophisticated and carefully organized schemes designed to conceal it including collusion, forgery or deliberate non-recording of transactions or intentional misrepresentations made to the auditor.

Action to be taken on discovery by an auditor of potential errors or fraud

Audit teams should consider materiality. If the matter is not material in the context of the accounts the auditors need take no further action in connection with their auditor's report but must inform the management, unless the management are themselves involved. Note however that some crimes, such as bribery are automatically material because they contravene a statute, in this case the Bribery Act 2010. Consequently, any instance of possible bribery and corruption must be reported to management and auditors will have to consider disclosure in the financial statements.

Unless the extent of the possible fraud is obvious at the outset audit teams should perform appropriate additional tests to discover the possible scale and extent of the fraud. Note that, when detected, fraudsters often lie to cover up the extent of their wrongdoing.

If it appears that irregularities or errors have occurred, and may be material, then auditors should consider the effects on the financial statements and ensure that these have been prepared with such adjustments and amendments (and disclosures) as may be required.

Note that if further investigations are required and the accounts cannot be delayed, then the auditor's report may have to be qualified for uncertainty (Chapter 26).

Where errors or irregularities have occurred auditors should ensure top management are aware of such events. If top management is involved, reports may have to be made to non-executive directors or regulators – probably via an Audit Committee.

Any significant weakness in the system of accounting and internal control which may give or have given rise to error or irregularity should be fully discussed with, and reported to, management.

REPORTING

To members (shareholders)

Errors and irregularities need not be reported to members as such but if financial statements or any part of them do not or may not give a true and fair view or conform to statute or if proper accounting records have not been kept, then the auditors have their statutory duties under Companies Act Section 386 to modify their auditor's report accordingly.

To top management

In the event of the auditors suspecting that lower level management may be involved in or condoning irregularities, then a report to the main board or the Audit Committee may be necessary. In companies with non-executive directors the auditors may well have a mechanism for reporting executive management irregularities by reporting to them in the first instance.

To management

All actual or potential irregularities discovered should be in the form of a Management Letter with recommendations for changes (Chapter 27).

To third parties

This is a very difficult area and the auditors have to proceed with caution, primarily because of the duty of client confidentiality they have. In certain cases, involving specific breaches of the law, i.e. money laundering or bribery, the auditors have a statutory duty to report to the relevant authority but in other cases their duty may not be so clear cut (Chapter 6).

Some audits under statutes or regulations other than the Companies Act give auditors more extensive duties towards internal control and irregularities. For example, the Financial Services and Markets Act 2000 requires the auditors of banks, building societies, insurance companies and similar bodies to report irregularities and breaches of regulations to the Financial Services Authority, particularly where the auditor's report may be being qualified or where solvency of the organization might be an issue.

Guidance on this matter is now given to auditors in the ISA 250B 'The auditor's right and duty to report to regulators in the financial sector', which is, in general, outside the scope of this book. This is a very sensitive matter but it does allow the auditor to report serious breach of statutory requirements to the regulatory body in order to protect the investing public, providing the auditor has gathered sufficient evidence and considers that any supposed breach of the regulations is reportable to the regulator.

The auditors should:

- take legal advice or advice from their professional body;
- disclose to third parties (e.g. the regulatory authorities) only matters where they have a clear public duty to disclose (e.g. if a serious crime is contemplated); and
- consider resignation.

ISA 240 considers resignation only if the circumstances are exceptional and make it impossible for the auditor to continue. Examples of this might be if the business fails to take the remedial action the auditor considers necessary in the case of a serious incidence of fraud or where the trust in the organization's management has been seriously undermined. Legal advice should be taken before this step is contemplated.

If the auditors do resign they must notify the Registrar of Companies accordingly and have to notify members (and creditors in the case of an unquoted company) of any circumstances surrounding their leaving office which the auditors feel should be brought to their attention by depositing a statement at the Registered Office. This will require very careful wording which should only be contemplated with legal advice.

SMALL COMPANIES

Auditors who are engaged to carry out audits of smaller companies or entities where owner/managers exercise a considerable degree of day-to-day control may have particular problems.

Clearly, as the senior management are more regularly involved in day-to-day matters of control the question of management override looms large. The danger to the auditor is that they are relying on that senior individual for a significant element of the internal control and any representations or explanations made by them may be considered to be unreliable if the auditor has any reasonable suspicions of fraudulent behaviour.

It is, of course, much easier for an owner/manager to conceal misappropriations from the business and staff working in small companies may be reluctant to reveal information where they work in such close proximity to their employer.

However, the auditor should only entertain such suspicions if there are reasonable grounds to do so and, whilst they should approach the audit with a degree of professional scepticism as they would any other client, they should not assume that a smaller company is any more prone to fraudulent behaviour than a larger one. Indeed, the proximity of an owner/manager to their staff may well discourage fraudulent behaviour by employees as it should be more probable that it would be detected.

Should the auditors encounter instances of fraudulent behaviour by owner/managers they should discuss it with them, if possible, in the first instance. Auditors are reminded that their duty is to the shareholders *collectively* so if there are other, non-management shareholders, the auditor's duty to report is the same as if the company were a larger one.

Should the situation become untenable the audit may have to resign and the resignation procedures under the Companies Act would have to be complied with.

UNLAWFUL ACTS OF CLIENTS AND THEIR STAFF

Introduction

This subject is a fascinating one for students who may see themselves in the role of detective. However, the reality of discovering or being involved in crimes committed by a client or members of the client's staff is usually very unpleasant or a cause for anguished inner conflict.

In practice, auditors must always act scrupulously and correctly and in accordance with the law. They should take legal advice if necessary and read the guidance provided by their professional body and by the Auditing Standards.

Current guidance is contained in:

- FRC Ethical Standards or the ethical standards of the Recognized Supervisory Body of which the individual auditor is a member (see Chapter 6)
- FRC Practice Note 12 – *Money laundering – Guidance for auditors on UK legislation*
- *Professional conduct in relation to defaults or unlawful acts* (ICAEW guidance for members in practice)
- ACCA Rulebook 2016 B1 *Professional duty of confidence in relation to defaults and unlawful acts of clients and others*
- ISA 240 *The auditor's responsibilities relating to fraud in an audit of financial statements*
- ISA 250A *Consideration of laws and regulations in an audit of financial statements* and ISA 250B *The auditor's right and duty to report to regulators in the financial sector*

The auditor's legal position

Auditors must not themselves commit a criminal offence and they would do so if they:

- advised a client to commit a criminal offence
- aided or conspired with a client in devising or executing a crime
- agreed with a client to conceal or destroy evidence or mislead the police with untrue statements

- knew a client has committed an arrestable offence and acted with intent to impede their arrest and prosecution; note that 'impede' does not include refusing to answer questions or refusing to produce documents without the client's consent, unless legally obliged to do so. this is because of the accountant's duty of confidentiality to their client
- knew the client has committed an offence and agreed to accept consideration (e.g. an excessive audit fee) for withholding information
- knew that the client had committed treason or terrorist offences and failed to report the offence to the proper authority
- had committed various activities, including the offence of 'tipping off' either deliberately or carelessly in connection with money laundering (see Chapter 6); note that, in this case, there is a legal requirement to disclose illegal acts to the authorities

Discovery of unlawful acts

If auditors discover an unlawful act, or if they are asked by the police or a regulatory authority to disclose information about a client 'to help with enquiries', they are in a difficult position.

Under normal circumstances they ought to first discuss any disclosure of information with the client – as they are bound by a duty of confidentiality. However, discussing possible disclosure with the client may not be appropriate and, indeed, it may well be a criminal offence to do so – particularly in respect of the 'tipping off' rules under the Money Laundering Regulations.

Consequently, the auditors must investigate the circumstances under which the disclosure is required and may make disclosures *without* consulting the client if it is justified:

(a) *by the law or legal process to the proper authorities*
'Proper authorities' are defined in the courts as those third parties who have a proper interest in receiving such information. Proper authorities include, but are not limited to:
  (a) the police
  (b) recognized professional bodies
  (c) the Serious Fraud Office and
  (d) HMRC
(b) *in the public interest*
Public interest includes matters of public concern, not public curiosity. Public concern may extend to the concerns of clients, government, financial institutions, employers, employees, investors, the business and financial community and others who rely upon the objectivity and integrity of the accounting profession to support the propriety and functioning of commerce.
  Examples of situations which may be regarded as being in the public interest include:
  - a criminal offence
  - a failure or likely failure to adhere to legal obligations
  - miscarriage of justice
  - health and safety matters which endanger or are likely to endanger members of the public and
  - damage or possible damage to the environment
  Disclosure depends on several issues including the gravity of the issue, the extent to which members of the public could be affected and the intention of the client to remedy the situation.
(c) *to protect the auditor's own interests*
In general, auditors should only disclose information which is adequate, relevant and necessary in order to protect their own interests – for example, to enable them to defend themselves in disciplinary proceedings.

Disclosure rules

When disclosing confidential information to the proper authorities, either proactively or due to a request, auditors should consider the following:

- advice from their own regulatory body;
- the employing organization's internal policies and procedures;

- the identity of the authority, agency or regulator and under what legal authority the disclosure is required or permitted;
- the form and manner of disclosure;
- who can be informed of the disclosure or request for disclosure; and
- what documentation should be kept in relation to the disclosure.

Auditors should keep detailed contemporaneous notes of meetings and telephone conversations relating to situations where they disclose confidential information to a third party, as well as a record of any consent given and discussions held or decisions taken concerning the disclosure of confidential information. They should maintain a schedule summarizing disclosures and to whom they were made, keep copies of relevant documentation and details of any legal or other advice obtained.

AUDIT ISSUES ARISING FROM NON-COMPLIANCE

Auditors should plan and perform their audit procedures and evaluate and report on the results, recognizing that non-compliance by the entity with law or regulations may materially affect the financial statements.

Some clients, in heavily regulated sectors such as banking, insurance or waste disposal, together with their auditors, should be particularly aware of the effect of non-compliance on both the organization being audited and of possible disclosures in the financial statements. Auditors also should recognize, however, that all businesses are now regulated generally in such areas as planning, health and safety, racial and sexual discrimination and many others and consider the effect of non-compliance on their client.

The effect of non-compliance can be fines, penalties or civil claims from third parties which will result in actual or contingent liabilities to be included in the financial statements. In addition, in very serious cases, directors may be held personally liable in criminal proceedings and face imprisonment.

Penalties may be material in amount and auditors need to gather sufficient appropriate evidence to evaluate the effect of such issues on the financial statements. Auditors will also have to consider the possibility of entities having to pay compensation, which may be wholly or partly insured, and the effect of this on the financial statements and the ability of the entity to continue trading in its present form.

The effect of non-compliance can be extremely serious and include the loss of licences or authorizations to continue in business. This may have implications for the financial statements in many ways, including the assumption of the going concern basis. For example, if a business running online gambling websites has its licence to operate withdrawn the very future of the business could be in jeopardy.

Directors' responsibilities

Under the general provisions of good corporate governance, and the specific provisions of the UK Corporate Governance Code (Chapter 2), it is the responsibility of directors to take steps to ensure that their entity complies with laws and regulations, to establish arrangements for preventing and detecting any non-compliance and to prepare financial statements which comply with all laws and regulations.

Directors may fulfil their responsibilities by:

- adopting the principles of good corporate governance (Chapter 2), including the involvement of non-executive directors
- instituting and operating appropriate systems of internal control, including an independent, properly resourced internal audit function which has compliance as one of its remits
- maintaining an up-to-date register of relevant laws and regulations and monitoring any changes to these
- developing an internal, business code of conduct to inform employees, ensure employees are properly trained and that sanctions exist against breaches of the code
- engaging legal advisers to assist in this area
- maintaining a register of complaints and breaches

Role of the auditors

The auditors cannot be expected to detect non-compliance hidden by collusive behaviour, forgery, override of controls or intentional misrepresentations by management. However, their audit procedures should be designed taking that possibility into account and should incorporate procedures to gather as much sufficient appropriate evidence as they can without relying too heavily on management or staff representations.

The auditors should obtain sufficient, appropriate audit evidence about compliance with those laws and regulations which relate directly to the preparation of, or the inclusion or disclosure of, specific items in the financial statements. Examples are the Companies Act 2006, other statutes and compliance with financial and accounting rules and the various taxation statutes.

The auditors should perform procedures to help identify possible or actual instances of non-compliance with those laws and regulations which provide a legal framework within which the entity conducts its business and which are central to the entity's ability to conduct its business and hence to its financial statements. This is part of the consideration of going concern issues (Chapter 23).

Procedures may include:

- obtaining a general understanding of the rules;
- inspection of any licences;
- obtaining confirmation from the regulatory authority that the entity is still entitled to carry on its business and has not committed any fundamental breach of regulations;
- enquiry of the directors on any non-compliance; and
- obtaining written assurance from the directors that they have given the auditors all information on non-compliance; audit staff should be alert for instances of actual or possible breaches which might affect the financial statements.

When actual or possible breaches are encountered the auditors should gather all possible information and evidence, evaluate it and fully document their evidence, reasoning, findings and conclusions.

The matters should be discussed with management, if appropriate, depending on the nature of the non-compliance or illegal act and the nature and extent of management's involvement in it.

After due consideration and taking legal advice the acts or omissions may be reported to relevant third parties.

One problem area is where illegal acts or non-compliances involve the directors of a subsidiary company who are not directors of any holding company. Auditors should be aware of their duty of confidentiality to their client, i.e. in this case the subsidiary, and should obtain permission from that client to disclose the facts of the case to the holding company. In practice this should not be difficult as, ultimately, the auditors will report to the holding company as shareholders, however, care must be taken in the interim not to breach client confidentiality.

Remember that auditors are appointed specifically to each company in a group as they will be signing an auditor's report in respect of each company – so the subsidiary company is just as much a client as the holding company which owns it.

However, if the board of directors of the subsidiary includes holding company directors who have not been informed of the illegal acts, they are entitled to know about them in their capacity as directors of the subsidiary – so the auditors could make their disclosure to the holding company board via that route.

The auditors, on discovering an unlawful act, must do nothing to assist in the offence or to prevent its disclosure and they must bring all offences of employees to the notice of the client.

If the offence has a material effect on the accounts which has not been properly disclosed, so that the non-disclosure means that the accounts do not show a true and fair view, they must insist on disclosure or qualify their report.

If the auditor is prevented by the client from discovering the full effect of the non-compliance or offence, so they are unable to judge its materiality, they should express a qualified opinion on the basis of an inability to obtain sufficient appropriate audit evidence (Chapter 26).

Should the auditors resign?

If the organization does not intend to take any form of remedial action once the offence has come to light, or the offence involves the most senior management of the company the auditor should consider resignation. This last point is important in that, if senior management are involved, the reliability of any management representations given by them to the auditors must be called into question and the auditor's position may well become untenable.

However, resignation is seen as a last resort. ISA 240 considers that, if possible, it is preferable for the auditors to remain in post and continue to fulfil their duties as auditors. Auditors are acting on behalf of the shareholders and it is their interests and the interests of other creditors which have to be considered.

If the directors refuse to release accounts, or the auditors are not given an opportunity to communicate their concerns to members they should consider resigning.

Remember that, if auditors resign, they must make a Statement of Circumstances, detailing the circumstances surrounding the resignation which can then become a public document.

They must also inform any incoming auditors, under the ethical code, of any professional reason why they may not take up the new appointment – and instances of illegal acts by directors just may be considered to be relevant. Remember that any disclosure of information to incoming auditors requires the permission of the client so, if this is not forthcoming, the outgoing auditors should inform the proposed new auditors of that fact. The incoming auditors should then decline to act.

The auditors should take legal advice and, probably, consult their professional body before acting.

In a liquidation the auditors can disclose any matter they wish to the liquidator who in fact becomes their client. Note that the ethical codes of the professional bodies prohibit an auditor from being appointed liquidator of the same company they have previously audited.

SUMMARY

- There is a difference in perception of the auditor's duties on errors and fraud between auditors and the public. This is known as the Expectation Gap-we looked at this in detail in Chapter 1.
- An auditor's primary duty is to give their opinion on the truth and fairness, etc. of financial statements, detection of frauds is secondary.
- The primary responsibility for the prevention and detection of fraud lies with management.
- Discovery of some errors and frauds may be a by-product of the audit.
- Discovery of the existence of and disclosure of errors and fraud may be essential to the true and fair view.
- Errors are unintentional misstatements in, or omissions of amounts or disclosures from, an entity's accounting records or financial statements. Fraud involves the use of deception to obtain an unjust or illegal financial advantage, intentional misstatements in or omissions of, amounts or disclosures from an entity's accounting records or financial statements as defined in the Fraud Act 2006.
- Materiality is an important concept in this area and the auditor must have evidence that a matter is not material before disregarding it for reporting purposes.
- Audit planning must take into account the risks of a material misstatement due to errors or irregularities.
- Audit teams should discuss amongst themselves the likelihood of fraud or error in the financial statements and should identify areas of activity which may be particularly vulnerable. Engagement partners should ensure that these discussions have taken place and disclose any concerns they have to appropriate members of the audit team.
- Auditors should report instances of fraud to those charged with governance. There may be situations where they should report to a regulator.

- Smaller companies are more difficult as they may not have the infrastructure to prevent frauds and owner/managers may tend to treat company assets as their own.
- Auditors may uncover criminal offences committed by a client or an employee of the client. This puts them in a difficult position. The auditor should act carefully and correctly and take legal advice.
- Auditors must not themselves commit criminal offences and should know the circumstances in which a criminal offence may be committed by not doing something.
- The auditor should not jeopardize a professional relationship by disclosing offences except in specified circumstances.
- The auditor should investigate the circumstances under which the information is required. They will not usually disclose confidential information to the police or other authority unless:
  - the client authorizes disclosure
  - the disclosure is compelled by process of law, e.g. a court order
  - disclosure is required in the auditor's own interest, e.g. in defending themselves against civil or criminal actions
  - the circumstances are such that the auditors have a public duty to disclose
  - disclosure is required in the circumstances envisaged by advice given on money laundering and disclosure to regulators in the financial sector
- Auditors have a responsibility to give an opinion on company accounts which they should not avoid by resignation.
- Directors have a responsibility to manage the company in a proper way and they should comply with the principles of corporate governance.
- Auditors must be aware, in their audit planning and procedures, of the possible impact of non-compliance with law and regulations on the financial statements.
- Firms of accountants must have procedures in place to recognize and report suspicions of money laundering activities.

POINTS TO NOTE

- Irregularities in the form of falsifying financial statements are a special risk in companies with going concern problems. The auditor must always be aware of temptations of management to dress or falsify their financial statements to present an untrue but desirable view of the results and position.
- Auditors have the right to require from management any information and explanations they may need. It is reasonable for auditors to ask management if any irregularities have occurred and, if any are discovered, for the full facts.
- If the auditors feel that they have not been given all the information and explanations that they need then the scope of the audit has been restricted and they could consider qualifying the report. In extreme cases they should resign and invoke the Companies Act rules on disclosure of the circumstances of their resignation.
- The auditor's duty when they discover an unlawful act or when they are made aware of an unlawful act while conducting the audit is not always clear.
- Regulatory authorities have mechanisms to detect non-compliance and it is not the role of the auditor to act on their behalf unless statutorily bound to do so, e.g. in connection with money laundering.
- Auditors may have a statutory duty in some circumstances to report to regulators and should do so in the form and manner provided and with the permission of their client.

CASE STUDY

Megachem plc is a multinational agri-business dealing in the import and export of agricultural produce, the manufacture and sale of fertilizers and pesticides and the sale of agricultural machinery worldwide.

During the audit, the auditors discover:

(a) There are several delivery notes for 'agricultural machinery' recording deliveries of crates of what are described as 'machinery parts' to several countries in the world where there are local conflicts. These delivery notes had been kept in a separate file in the CEO's office and marked 'confidential' and the auditors had been given it by the CEO's secretary, by accident, when requesting information about another, unrelated issue. No other documentation appears to exist in respect of the client's names recorded on the delivery notes and they do not appear in the receivables ledger.

(b) The company recorded the receipt of substantial bank transfers from accounts in Switzerland and Panama. These were recorded as 'consultancy fees' but there are no other records relating to these transactions and the actual client's name is not recorded.

(c) The firm appears to be employing consultants in various countries in the Balkans and the Far East as 'commissions' are being paid to them but it is unclear precisely what services these individuals provide. When asked, the Financial Director refused to divulge any information citing confidentiality.

(d) In addition to the sums received from Switzerland the company are making material payments to a numbered Swiss bank account. The Financial Director has told the auditors that these are commissions to government officials in various countries who obtain business for the company.

(e) Visits to one of the manufacturing plants reveal that workers appear to be handling what look like dangerous chemicals without proper protective gear. The factory manager says that the gear is provided but the workers refuse to wear it on the grounds that it makes them hot and impedes movement.

(f) There is an article on an environmental news website that a pipe at one of the company's plants is discharging chemicals into the adjacent river. The company says the effluent is treated and that they have a licence to do this but can't show it to the auditors as they claim they have lost it.

Discussion

– Discuss the implications of these discoveries for:

1. the auditors
2. the company
3. the financial statements

STUDENT SELF-TESTING QUESTIONS

Questions with answers apparent from the text

a) Define errors and frauds.

b) What are the auditor's duties towards errors?

c) What is the relevance of materiality to these matters?

d) Who is responsible for internal control in a company?

e) What should auditors do if they discover an irregularity in the form of (i) a material error or (ii) fraud?

f) To whom should auditors report such irregularities?

g) What options do auditors have if they detect a fraud by management?

h) When can auditors disclose unlawful acts to the police?

i) How does the auditor's professional duty of confidence affect disclosures to third parties?

j) What should auditors do if they discover an unlawful act?

k) What are the circumstances in which auditors can make disclosures without permission from their client?

l) What are the responsibilities of directors in connection with illegal acts?

EXAMINATION QUESTIONS

1   The audit of Binkle Ltd for the year ended 31 December 2X15 was completed on 2 February 2X16. Materiality was judged to be £150 000. As all tests yielded satisfactory results, the auditors, Blast & Pott, issued a clean opinion. In accordance with the quality control procedures operating in the firm, a partner reviewed the file in March 2X16 and concluded that the audit complied with all auditing standards and that sufficient, appropriate and reliable audit evidence was on file to support the opinion issued.

   On 14 May 2X16 the firm received an email from Nicholas Tasker, the Managing Director of Binkle Ltd, informing them that he had just received a postcard from the company's Financial Controller showing a nice picture of the beach in Burovia where he had absconded with the Marketing Assistant and £2.4m of the company's cash.

   Preliminary investigations carried out by the Managing Director indicated that the sum had been misappropriated over a period of five years. The Managing Director concluded his email by asking, rather pointedly, how was it possible for Blast & Pott to miss such a large fraud for such a long period of time and how they could justify the clean audit opinion issued a few months previously? He hinted darkly at possible legal action.

   Required:

   Prepare a draft memorandum addressing the concerns of the Managing Director of Binkle Ltd with specific reference to:

   (a) the respective responsibilities of the auditor and the directors with regard to the company's financial statements; and

   (b) the auditor's responsibilities in relation to fraud.

SOURCES AND ADDITIONAL READING

Association of Chartered Certified Accountants (2016) *B1 Professional Duty of Confidence in Relation to Defaults and Unlawful Acts of Clients and Others*. London: ACCA.

Financial Reporting Council (2016) *ISA 200 Overall Objectives of the Independent Auditor and the Conduct of an Audit in Accordance with International Standards on Auditing*. London: Financial Reporting Council.

Financial Reporting Council (2016) *ISA 240 The Auditor's Responsibilities Relating to Fraud in an Audit of Financial Statements*. London: Financial Reporting Council.

Financial Reporting Council (2016) *ISA 250B The Auditor's Right and Duty to Report to Regulators in the Financial Sector*. London: Financial Reporting Council.

Financial Reporting Council (2016) ISA *315 Identifying and Assessing Risks of Material Misstatement through Understanding the Entity and its Environment*. London: Financial Reporting Council.

Financial Reporting Council (2016) *SA 330 The Auditor's Responses to Assessed Risks*. London: Financial Reporting Council.

Financial Reporting Council (2011) *Practice Note 12 (Revised) – Money Laundering – Guidance for Auditors on UK Legislation*. London: Financial Reporting Council.

Financial Reporting Council (2009) *Auditor Scepticism: Raising the Bar*. London: Financial Reporting Council.

ICSA (2007) *Companies Act 2006 Handbook.* London: ICSA.

In Re: Kingston Cotton Mills Co. (1896).

Institute of Chartered Accountants in England and Wales (2014), *ICAEW Guidance for Members in Practice – Conduct in Relation to Defaults or Unlawful Acts*. London: ICAEW.

Jones, M (2011) *Creative Accounting, Fraud and International Accounting Scandals*. Chichester: Wiley.

Taylor, J (2010) *Forensic Accounting*. Harlow: Pearson.

TSO (2006) *Companies Act 2006*. London: The Stationery Office.

TSO (2006) *Fraud Act 2006*. London: The Stationery Office.

Western Mail (2009) *Woman jailed for £70,000 theft*. www.walesonline.co.uk 31 January.

Websites

www.oecd.org/corruption
www.Transparency.org/cpi2015#results

CHAPTER 21
RELATED PARTIES

Learning Objectives

After studying the material in this chapter you should be able to:

- identify related parties

- explain the disclosure requirements for related party transactions

- understand what is meant by a special purpose vehicle

- understand how to identify undisclosed related parties

- explain the approach to the audit of related parties

- understand the approach in respect to smaller entities

INTRODUCTION

ISA 550 *Related Parties* defines parties as being related if one has the ability to control or significantly influence the actions of the other or both are under common control.

These are all **related parties** as defined in Section 33 of FRS 102 issued by the Financial Reporting Council:

- parties that control or are controlled by the reporting entity or over which the entity has a significant influence either by itself or in conjunction with others
- parties under common control, e.g. subsidiaries of a common holding company
- joint ventures and associates (defined as being where the investor holds a participating interest and exercises significant influence) of the reporting entity
- one party has influence over the financial and operating policies of the other party to the extent that the other party might be inhibited from pursuing at all times its own separate interests
- the parties, in entering a transaction, are subject to influence from the same source to such an extent that one of the parties to the transaction has subordinated its own separate interest
- key management personnel (including directors and senior managers of the reporting entity) *and* close family members of those directors and managers
- any entity owned or controlled by key management personnel or their close family members
- pension schemes for the benefit of the employees of the reporting entity

However, ISA 550 goes on to say that the definition of a related party may not be self-evident and parties may be related or connected in ways different from those outlined above. It may be that management may not be aware of certain types of related party transaction or may be using **special purpose vehicles** for the purposes of accounts manipulation which they do not wish to disclose as related parties. Further related parties may operate as part of a complex web of inter-relationships and structures with a consequent increase in the complexity of related party transactions.

It may be that information systems do not identify related parties and it also may be that transactions take place outside normal terms and conditions, for example 'one-sided' transactions or swops. Auditors need to take steps to ensure that all related parties and transactions between them have been identified in the course of their work.

Transactions between related parties may not be at arm's length and disclosure of the existence of such transactions gives important information to users of the financial statements. Undisclosed related party transactions may significantly distort the results for the reporting period, e.g. the deliberate sale of a significant asset or part of the business to a connected party at an undervalue.

DISCLOSURE

Students should be familiar with the relevant accounting requirements dealing with related party transactions.

Both IFRS and FRS 102 can be complex but, broadly indicate that disclosure is required of all related party transactions, irrespective of whether a price is charged. FRS 102 does not require transactions between 100% owned subsidiaries to be disclosed.

Disclosure of related party transactions requires disclosure of:

- the amount of the transactions
- the amount of outstanding balances and:
  - their terms and conditions, including whether they are secured, and the nature of the consideration to be provided in settlement
  - details of any guarantees given or received
- provisions for uncollectible receivables related to the amount of outstanding balances
- the expense recognized during the period in respect of bad or doubtful debts due from related parties

If the client is controlled by a related party, details of ownership have to be disclosed.

Transactions involving related parties may include:

- purchases and sales of goods
- purchases and sales of property and assets
- agency arrangements
- leasing arrangements
- research and development transfers
- licence agreements
- finance (not including loans or overdrafts made by lenders in the ordinary course of business)
- guarantees or indemnities
- management contracts

Clearly, intergroup transactions eliminated on consolidation do not have to be disclosed. Note that it is common for groups to use 'captive' subsidiaries, particularly for insurance purposes, joint venture or consortium arrangements or partnerships as part of their normal trading, and transactions between the parties may or may not be at arm's length for bona fide reasons. These should be easily identified by the auditors.

The shining example in how to use and abuse related party transactions was revealed after the catastrophic failure of Enron in the USA. Revenue was fabricated and huge operating losses were hidden in what were related parties which were not required to be disclosed under the law as it stood at the time. Disclosure of these losses would have changed the face of the whole Enron situation and saved much grief and heartache, not to mention criminal convictions.

It is therefore of interest to the readers of the accounts that the nature and extent of related party transactions are disclosed in order to paint a complete picture of the nature and scale of the entity's operations.

Disclosure will include:

- the nature of the relationships between the parties
- the types of transactions
- elements of the transactions necessary for an understanding of the situation, including volumes, pricing policies and amounts outstanding

THE AUDITOR'S DUTIES TO RELATED PARTIES

The auditors are required to perform audit procedures designed to provide sufficient, appropriate evidence regarding the identification and disclosure by management of related parties and the effect of related party transactions that are material to the financial statements.

In accordance with ISA 240 *'The Auditor's Responsibilities Relating to Fraud in an Audit of Financial Statements'* the auditors need an understanding of related party transactions in order to evaluate the truth and fairness of the financial statements and also to evaluate the presence of any fraud risk factors, such as misrepresentation, collusion or concealment by management.

The ICAEW in their publication *'The Audit of Related Parties in Practice'* suggests a five-point plan:

1   Plan the work on the audit of related parties thoroughly. This requires auditors to plan and perform the audit with the objective of obtaining sufficient, appropriate audit evidence regarding the adequacy of disclosure of related party transactions and the nature and extent of the transactions. This will include discussions amongst the audit team as to the nature and extent of related party transactions.

2   When planning the audit, assess the risk that material *undisclosed* related party transactions may exist and the risk of a material misstatement.

3   Understand the internal controls which are used by the organization to identify related party transactions and to record them.

4   Design audit procedures to respond to identified risks.

5   On completion obtain confirmations that the directors have disclosed the identity of all related parties and the nature of the relationship.

We will look at the approach to this in detail.

DETAILED AUDIT PROCEDURES

As part of their procedure the auditors should:

- Review for completeness information provided by the directors identifying material transactions with those parties that have been related parties for any part of the financial period.
- Be alert for evidence of material related party transactions that are not included in the information provided by the directors. This requires the audit team to maintain an attitude of professional scepticism and to review the possibilities of related parties existing where none have been notified.
- Obtain sufficient, appropriate audit evidence that material identified related party transactions are properly recorded and disclosed in the financial statements.
- Obtain sufficient, appropriate audit evidence that disclosures in the financial statements relating to control of the entity are properly stated.
- Obtain written representations from the directors concerning the completeness of information provided regarding the related party and control disclosures in the financial statements.
- Consider the implications for their report if:
  - they are unable to obtain sufficient, appropriate audit evidence concerning related parties and transactions with such parties or
  - the disclosure of related party transactions or the controlling party of the entity in the financial statements is not adequate

The auditors should review information supplied identifying the names of known related parties and carry out the following procedures:

- Review previous year's working papers to identify known related parties.
- Review the entity's procedures for identifying related parties including ethical codes, policies and guidelines. This may also include obtaining details of any reports made to such things as whistle blowing hot lines.
- Review internal audit reports.
- Enquire of related parties details of significant transactions.
- Where related parties have been identified computer-based audit techniques should be able to identify and detail all the transactions. Auditors would then be able to evaluate the significance of these and ensure the required disclosures are made.
- Enquire of any individuals who may be in a position to know of or carry out significant related party transactions outside the normal course of business. Enquire also of in-house lawyers or ethics officers where these exist in larger entities.
- Enquire if directors and senior managers have relationships or connections with other entities.
- Obtain details of principal shareholders from share registers.
- Review minutes of directors, managers and shareholder's meetings.
- Review register of directors' interests in statutory records and the Annual Return.
- Review tax returns and information supplied to regulatory agencies.

The auditors then need to review the nature and extent of related party transactions based on information supplied and be alert for other material related party transactions.

The auditors will consider the adequacy of internal controls over the authorization and recording of related party transactions.

Auditors need to be alert to transactions which appear unusual in the circumstances and which might indicate a related party, in particular by reviewing:

- large or unusual transactions especially around the period end
- loans received and made
- third-party confirmations such as the bank letter for indications of guarantees
- sales or transfers of assets
- significant contracts signed during the period
- investment transactions, e.g. an investment in a joint venture
- details of and transactions with pension and other trusts
- returns to tax authorities, companies house, the stock exchange, HMRC, regulatory agencies and others
- any declarations made by directors in respect of conflicts of interest
- correspondence with lawyers

Identifying undisclosed related parties

During the course of the assignment, audit staff should be constantly alert to matters which may reveal an undisclosed related party. Such instances may include:

- abnormal terms of trade, e.g. unusual prices, payment periods or discounts
- unexpected contract terms
- unusual loan arrangements with directors or their families e.g. continual 'rollover' of loan or inadequate documentation
- transactions lacking commercial logic
- cash outflows not properly documented
- loans to employees on favourable terms
- complex equity transactions including corporate restructuring or acquisitions
- transactions with offshore entities in areas with weak reporting regimes or transactions with associates or partnerships ostensibly controlled by a third party
- transactions where substance differs from form, e.g. sales with a commitment to repurchase
- transactions processed in an unusual manner
- management charges from group companies without any real commercial justification
- leasing of premises or management services supplied to another organization without consideration passing
- circular arrangements involving leases
- transactions under contracts where the contractual terms change before expiry
- high volumes of business with certain customers or suppliers as opposed to others
- unrecorded transactions such as receipt or provision of management services at no charge; this may require a degree of substantive testing of transactions and balances

In addition to these types of rather suspicious transaction there may be some which it could be difficult for the auditor to broach with the directors such as:

- the company purchasing vessels, e.g. motor boats where there is a mixture of business and private use
- builders who carry out work at the homes of directors
- loans or collateral for loans to directors or employees

This type of thing is more prevalent in smaller entities but auditors should be alert for it.

CONTROL OF THE ENTITY

The auditors need to obtain sufficient, appropriate evidence concerning disclosures in the financial statements about control of the related entity. In most cases this will not be a problem, but where an entity is controlled from overseas or by a consortium, care will be needed. If the ultimate controlling party is not known, then that fact should be disclosed.

Auditors should be alert for indicators, such as:

- An unusually high turnover of senior management or professional advisors may suggest unethical or fraudulent business practices that serve the related party's purposes.
- The use of business intermediaries for significant transactions, for which there appears to be no clear business justification. This may suggest that the related party could have an interest in such transactions because it controls such intermediaries for fraudulent purposes.
- Evidence of the related party's excessive participation in or preoccupation with the selection of accounting policies or the determination of significant estimates may suggest the possibility of fraudulent financial reporting.

These may be indicative of frauds involving fraudulent misstatements.

The auditors must obtain evidence that the recording and disclosure in financial statements is appropriate. They may need to enquire more closely into disclosed transactions and obtain additional third party confirmations.

The auditors should obtain written assurances from management, in the Letter of Representation (Chapter 24):

- That all related parties and transactions have been notified to the auditors.
- Where they have approved related party transactions that are material and involve the management.
- Full and proper disclosure has been made in the accounts in accordance with FRS 102.
- That related party transactions or arrangements that have been made do not involve any undisclosed side agreements.

SMALLER ORGANIZATIONS

Smaller organizations may not have the resources internally to identify related party transactions, nor may they necessarily be aware that they are so doing. However, the increased level of control by senior management should go some way towards compensating for the lack of formal structures.

Auditors should discuss with senior management the possibility of related party transactions and carry out audit work with a view to identifying any such instances. They should also carry out audit procedures outlined above in order to identify any undisclosed related parties and obtain appropriate written confirmations from management.

Examples of related party transactions may include renting premises at low or non-existent rent or cheap or interest free loans. Owner/managers may not consider these to be related party type transactions, particularly where relatives or friends are involved.

QUALIFIED AUDIT REPORTS

In a few cases the auditors may conclude that they have been able to gather insufficient evidence on this subject. This represents, effectively, a restriction of audit evidence and may require a qualified opinion or, in extreme cases, a disclaimer of opinion.

If the auditors conclude that the disclosure is not adequate, then they may issue a qualified opinion or even an adverse opinion if they consider the non disclosure may involve material misrepresentation. They may also consider giving, in their report, the information which should have been given in the financial statements.

SUMMARY

- A true and fair view requires the disclosure of related party transactions and of controlling parties.
- ISA 550 sets out the auditor's duties and FRS 102 Section 33 deals with disclosures. Disclosure can sometimes be complex so auditors need to understand the nature of the relationships between the parties.
- The auditors need to plan for procedures to deal with related party transactions disclosed to them and also to identify related party transactions which have remained unidentified. This can be difficult but the auditors need to demonstrate they have tried.
- The auditors need to assess the risk of inadequate disclosure and act accordingly.
- It may be difficult to identify related parties in smaller entities.
- Where transactions involve overseas entities auditors must be suspicious of all transactions involving those entities particularly if they have no obvious commercial purpose.
- The directors are primarily responsible for the disclosure of related party and ownership matters and the auditors should obtain written representations from them.

POINTS TO NOTE

- Related parties can be of many kinds – owners, directors, 'shadow' directors, key management and their families.
- Auditors need to be alert to the fact that using related parties has been a common feature of financial scandals over many years and be alert for unusual or out of pattern transactions.
- Some persons and entities are not considered to be related parties for these purposes. For example, regulatory bodies, banks, major customers or suppliers, despite the fact that they may have considerable influence over the conduct of the company's affairs.
- Pension funds and pension fund trustees are related parties.

CASE STUDY

Convoluted Ltd is a company dealing in rare metals internationally. It has 40 employees (25 in the UK). It is owned by Joe King Ltd, a company registered in the Cayman Islands and is known to deal with several other UK and overseas companies also owned by that company. The company has four directors who are all UK residents and who do not own any shares in the company.

The company has a pension scheme with employee and employer trustees and is heavily indebted to its bankers.

The auditors are Sew & Sew, who are newly appointed.

Discussion

- List some possible related parties of this company.
- From the auditor's point of view what risks are there that all the requirements of FRS 102 may not be met?
- Set out a section in the overall audit plan covering the requirements of ISA 550.
- List some possible substantive tests on the subject of related party transactions and ultimate control.

STUDENT SELF-TESTING QUESTIONS

Questions with answers apparent from the text

a) Why are related party transactions and ultimate ownership important to the true and fair view?

b) List the requirements of ISA 550.

c) What are the risks that auditors face in this area?

d) How might an auditor seek confirmation of directors' representations and assess their completeness?

e) What matters might give concern to the auditors in preparing the auditor's report?

EXAMINATION QUESTION

1 Puce Watermelon have recently been appointed auditors to Massive Holdings plc, a group of ten companies based in the North of England. Massive has subsidiary companies, all of which are wholly owned, which trade in various activities from machinery importers to car dealerships.

One of the auditors, whilst looking for biscuits one night whilst the auditors were working overtime, stumbles accidentally across the minutes of a directors' meeting which is not in the minute book.

One of the minutes refers to a partnership called Dragon, which Massive appears to have lent money to, although there is no record of this in the books. In turn Dragon appears to have granted Massive a very lucrative machinery importing contract on which Massive has reported a substantial profit. The other partners in Dragon appear to be the directors of Massive.

Massive has transferred shares into a company called Bluebottle Ltd. Bluebottle appears to be a joint venture between Massive and a company called Dragon 2, about which nothing is known, for a time share development in India.

The wife of the CEO is reported to own 15 per cent of one of the company's major suppliers of office equipment. Massive appears to have made a loss on a contract to supply agricultural machinery to a company based in Africa which hasn't paid. The loss appears to have been covered by a transaction with a partnership called Massive 1. The auditors have checked the transaction in the books of Massive and to all intents and purposes the African contract made a profit and the debt was cleared by discounted bills of exchange. It is unclear how this transaction has been funded by Massive 1 but there is reference to a loan from an unknown bank to Massive 1 secured by Massive itself. This does not appear in the books of Massive.

Required:

(i) Explain what actions the auditors should take in respect of these revelations.

(ii) How are they likely to affect the future conduct of the audit?

SOURCES AND ADDITIONAL READING

Financial Reporting Council (2015) *FRS 102 s. 33 Related Party Disclosures*. London: Financial Reporting Council.

Financial Reporting Council (2016) *ISA 240 The Auditor's Responsibilities Relating to Fraud in an Audit of Financial Statements*. London: Financial Reporting Council.

Financial Reporting Council (2016) *ISA 315 Identifying and Assessing Risks of Material Misstatement through Understanding the Entity and its Environment*. London: Financial Reporting Council.

Financial Reporting Council (2016) *ISA 550 Related Parties*. London: Financial Reporting Council.

Institute of Chartered Accountants in England and Wales (2010) *The Audit of Related Parties in Practice.* London: ICAEW.

Taylor, J. (2010) *Forensic Accounting.* Harlow: Pearson.

CHAPTER 22
USE OF SERVICE ORGANIZATIONS

Learning Objectives

After studying the material in this chapter you should be able to:

- understand the specific problems faced by auditors when functions are outsourced

- explain how outsourced activities affect the judgement of inherent and control risk

- understand how outsourcing affects the auditor's evidence gathering requirement

- explain how the decision to outsource affects the decision by the auditors as to whether or not proper accounting records have been maintained

- explain the difference between Type 1 and Type 2 reports from the contractor's auditors

- discuss the ethical issues where services are supplied by the audit firm

INTRODUCTION

Many businesses use outside specialist organizations to perform functions which would otherwise be performed in house. This process is known as **outsourcing.**

Functions outsourced can include:

- information processing and maintenance of financial records
- internal audit
- debt management and collection
- facilities management
- maintenance of safe custody of assets, such as investments
- initiation or execution of transactions on behalf of the client business

The use of **service organizations** can create problems for auditors and this chapter considers the issues. There is an ISA 402 *Audit considerations relating to an entity using a service organization.*

WHY DO FIRMS OUTSOURCE?

There are many advantages to outsourcing all or part of a function within an organization. The problems of employing personnel (e.g. employment legislation, health and safety, etc.) are passed on to others, it can be cheaper, if not, firms may well consider that they can use internal resources for more productive activities.

Outsourcing creates a certain level of independence from the commissioning organization, which can be beneficial, particularly in the case of outsourcing internal audit (see Chapter 19) and the outsource provider may have expertise which is not available in house. Service organizations can keep up to date on equipment and expertise more easily than the user enterprise in a fast-moving world. It reduces the time management have to spend on housekeeping functions.

However, there are also significant disadvantages not least cost – the provider wants to make a profit so the question of cost has to be carefully considered. The service level the client wants has to be specified from the outset – if the client wants additional services or enhanced productivity this will have to be paid for or might not be possible.

The client has to be sure that the quality of service is appropriate and that the standards of the service organization's internal controls are compatible with its own. In addition, the client has to be sure that issues such as confidentiality of data are properly understood and dealt with. Consequently, the client must have a comprehensive **Service Level Agreement** setting out the terms between the two parties, the services to be provided and the cost agreed in place which the auditors should inspect as it forms the basis of the contract between the parties

AUDIT PLANNING ISSUES

ISA 402 says:

> *'The objectives of the auditor, when the entity uses the services of a service organization, are:*
>
> (a) *To obtain an understanding of the nature and significance of the services provided by the service organization and their effect on the user entity's internal control relevant to the audit, sufficient to identify and assess the risks of material misstatement; and*
> (b) *To design and perform audit procedures responsive to those risks.'*

ISA 402 is, in effect, an extension of ISA 315 *'Identifying and assessing risks of material misstatement through understanding the entity and its environment'* and the auditor should, as always, obtain a thorough knowledge of the client's business in accordance with ISA 315 (Chapter 10). Reports prepared under ISA 402 also meet the requirements of the International Standard on Assurance Engagements 3402 '*Assurance reports on controls at a service organization*'.

The auditor, in planning the audit, should determine which activities are undertaken by service organizations which are relevant to the audit and the significance of the services provided, including the effect of them on the internal controls of the service user.

Likely areas for consideration include:

- maintenance of accounting records, including payroll
- internal audit provision
- other finance functions, e.g. tax, receivables management, credit control
- IT operations including systems support
- management of assets and resources i.e. facilities management
- undertaking or making arrangements for transactions as agent for the business

The latter item may include, for example, firms selling on the Internet which outsource the collection of sales proceeds to service organizations which deal with credit card processing.

Some outsourced functions will have little relevance to the audit – for example, office cleaning or maintenance functions where the service user simply pays a regular maintenance charge, but outsourced management of areas which might be material to the audit such as debt collection or payroll operations require the auditor to consider the impact of the use of the service organization on the audit.

Possible areas of concern include:

- risk of misstatement in the financial statements
- whether or not proper accounting records have been kept
- the independence, or otherwise, of the outsourcing organization from the client
- where the audit firm supplies any services, e.g. internal audit, there are ethical issues around independence and possible ethical threats to objectivity (Chapter 6)
- the risk of fraud or error based on information supplied by the contractor and the risk of bribery and corruption in contract allocation

Having assessed the risks, the auditors can plan their actions in relation to each relevant outsourced function.

Contractual terms and obligations

The auditor should obtain and document an understanding of the contracted terms which apply to relevant activities and the way the user (i.e. the client) monitors those activities so as to ensure that it meets its fiduciary and other legal responsibilities.

Relevant points here include:

- right of access, by the user and/or the auditor to records held by the outsourcing company
- whether the terms take proper account of statutory or regulatory body requirements; of particular importance is the Companies Act 2006 requirement for proper accounting records
- performance standards measuring the success or otherwise of the contractor in supplying the service to the agreed level
- the extent of reliance on controls operated by the service organization
- any indemnity offered to the user

The first point is especially important as lack of access to records may mean that the auditors have to consider qualifying their report on the grounds of, effectively, a limitation of audit evidence (see Chapter 26). The problem is that the systems of the service company belong to them and they may process information for more than just the one client, so there is a major confidentiality issue.

Auditors need some form of access or assurances from the service organization.

Inherent risk

The auditors should determine the effect of relevant activities on their assessment of inherent risk.

The first issue is the competence, integrity and going concern status of the outsourcing company. Items include the reputation of the service organization for competence and integrity and the existence of external supervision, e.g. of investment management by regulatory authorities. In addition, it is important to ascertain the extent to which indemnities offered by the outsourcer can be honoured.

The latter matter may be important, for example, if the accounting records were lost and the outsourcer could not honour its indemnity due to insolvency. This may then even affect the going concern status of the client.

Control risk

Issues here include:

- the extent of controls operated by user personnel in the providing company
- the extent of undertakings by the outsourcing company on controls
- user experience of errors and omissions
- the degree of monitoring by the user
- the extent of information on controls provided by the outsourcer
- the quality assurance in the service organization, e.g. ISO 9000 quality standard or internal audit

As always the auditors have to gather sufficient, appropriate evidence to ensure that the information obtained from the outsourcer is reliable. They have to assess the risks involved in respect of the impact of the use of an outsourcing organization on the reliability of their audit opinion.

If the outsourcing company is considered to represent a low risk to the audit opinion the procedures will be little different from what they might be if the audit work was being conducted in house. Risks may even be reduced if the outsourcing company can demonstrate a high level of internal control as part of its own procedures.

ACCOUNTING RECORDS

When any or all of the accounting records are outsourced, the auditor faces special problems.
These include whether or not:

- the requirements of Section 386, Companies Act 2006 have been met
- the requirements of any relevant regulatory bodies have been met
- all the information and explanations required by the auditor have been made available
- all information required in respect of internal controls of the processing organization is available
- the records generally accord with relevant law and regulations

AUDIT EVIDENCE

Various approaches are available to satisfy the auditor's needs and these include:

- inspecting records and documents held by the client as a basis of procedures in respect of reports produced by the service organization
- obtaining an undertaking by the service organization in order to form an opinion as to whether or not its control systems provide assurance regarding the reliability of financial information
- obtaining representations to confirm balances and transactions from the service organization
- analytical review of such records as are held by the audit client and of returns and reports received by the client from the service organization, i.e. comparing inputs from the client with outputs from the service organization

- inspecting records and documents held by the service organization
- reviewing information from the outsourcer and its auditors on the design and operation of internal controls operated by the outsourcer
- requesting the service organization's auditors or the user's internal audit function perform specified procedures

The latter approach is perhaps very powerful but its application depends on the service agreement between the service organization and the client.

REPORTS BY SERVICE ORGANIZATION'S AUDITORS

One possible piece of audit evidence is a report issued by the service organization's auditors. These may be issued to user auditors and are in two parts as either (1) a description of the service organization's accounting and internal control systems, prepared by the management of the service organization, and their operating effectiveness or (2) an opinion by the service organization auditor that:

- the description is accurate
- the systems' controls are in operation
- the accounting and internal control systems are suitably designed to achieve their stated objectives
- the accounting and internal control systems are operating effectively based on the results from tests of controls; in addition to the opinion on operating effectiveness the service organization auditor would identify the tests of control performed and related results

In the standard these are identified as Type 1 and Type 2 reports. The major difference between the two types is that a Type 2 report is more comprehensive. It covers a specified period and includes details provided by the service company's auditors of tests of controls they have carried out in order to evidence their opinion on the management's report. Whether the user entity's auditors require the following report is a matter of judgement:

- A Type 2 report, which should provide sufficient reliable evidence of the service company's controls throughout the period, but which will be likely to be costly.
- A Type 1 report which describes the services company's control objectives and controls and supported by an opinion from the service user's auditors but which does not relate specifically to any period.

The user auditors then have to assess the service company's report for sufficiency and reliability. They might do this by assessing the standing and reputation of the service organization's auditor, the scope of the work performed, the timing of the work performed and whether or not the report is sufficient and appropriate for its intended use.

A critical aspect of the report is the period covered. The user auditor must be content that the accounting records and the concomitant controls and systems were adequate for the *whole period* covered by the financial statements.

ETHICAL THREATS

There have been cases where audit firms also supply outsourced services to the client, in particular the internal audit function. Audit firms must be aware of the potential conflict of interest this gives them and the threats to auditor independence, in particular the self-review and familiarity threats (Chapter 6), in the case of Public Interest Entities (PIEs) such services are specifically prohibited in order to preserve auditor independence so it is good practice to provide these services on an arms length basis i.e. by a completely different team, or not at all.

Clearly there must be a deep and actual division between the team supplying the service and the audit team. They should not share staff and any perceived advantage to the audit of familiarity with client systems must be resisted as this will compromise audit independence. Audit teams must make their own assessment of audit risks independently of any involvement by other staff supplying internal audit services. Any decision to rely on the work of the internal audit team must be fully documented in the usual way and the decision justified as being taken objectively and at arm's length.

SUMMARY

- Outsourcing is a common way of dealing with many necessary functions.
- This can present problems for an auditor, especially if accounting functions are outsourced.
- Auditors need to obtain knowledge of all functions outsourced by the client.
- The auditors need to assess the risk of a material misstatement arising from the use of an outsourcing organization.
- The user auditor needs evidence that proper books of account have been kept and that the records form a reliable basis for the preparation of the financial statements.
- Various approaches are possible in assessing the records including the records and controls operated by the user, assessing the competence, integrity and going concern status of the outsourcer, assessing the reports by the outsourcer and its auditor, inspecting the records at the outsourcer.
- There may be an ethical issue where the audit firm provides the outsourced service, e.g. internal audit.

POINTS TO NOTE

- The user's auditors should be wary of accepting the certificates of the outsourcing company or its auditor without considerable enquiry.
- Ultimately the auditors need to be satisfied that the outsourced records meet statutory and other requirements, form a reliable basis for the preparation of the financial statements and are adequately controlled.
- Enquiry should be made of the standing and competence of the outsourcer and its auditors that the certificates cover all the relevant times and records and that testing was adequate.

CASE STUDY 1

Cuthbert Ltd outsources most of its accounting function to Speedy Accounting Services Ltd. They have found the relationship with Speedy very effective. However, recently it has come to Cuthbert's attention that the statements of account sent by Cuthbert's main supplier have not been successfully reconciled for six months. The accountant of Cuthbert has also heard a rumour that Speedy are in financial difficulties having lost clients recently. Speedy have sent a report by Bludger & Co, their auditors, on the suitability of design and operating effectiveness of the system by which Cuthbert's records are maintained.

Young & Foolisch, the auditors of Cuthbert, are engaged on the audit of Cuthbert for the year ended 31 December 2X16.

Discussion

- Why might Cuthbert Ltd outsource its accounting function?
- What risks does Cuthbert Ltd run as a result of the outsourcing and how might these risks impinge on the financial statements?
- What risks do Young & Foolisch face in the conduct of the audit?
- Draw up a checklist of matters that might concern Young & Foolisch on the issue.

CASE STUDY 2

Hippay plc, a listed company, has outsourced all their employee (including directors) remuneration to a service organization. Hippay writes bespoke and general application software for environmental recording and employs 97 people.

Discussion

– Discuss the business risks attached to this company both in general and in respect of the outsourcing.
– Discuss the problems occasioned to the auditors by the outsourcing and how they might be overcome.

STUDENT SELF-TESTING QUESTIONS

Questions with answers apparent from the text

a) Which ISA relates to service organizations?

b) Why do firms outsource?

c) What clauses in an outsourcing contract may be relevant to the auditor?

d) List risks which arise to a firm as a result of outsourcing.

e) What special risks arise from outsourcing accounting records?

f) List actions that auditors can take to amass audit evidence in the presence of an outsourced function.

g) What might be covered in a report to users by an outsourcer's auditor?

h) What actions should the client's auditors take in respect of such a report?

EXAMINATION QUESTIONS

1   You are the auditor of Petite Ltd, a small company. In order to reduce the company's administrative costs, the financial director proposes transferring all the receivables and payables ledger processing to a computer bureau.

   Batches of invoices will be sent weekly to the bureau which will process them and send them back together with a printed transaction report.

   The bureau will also produce a monthly list of balances and an aged debtors listing.

   The receivables and payables ledger programmes are the property of the bureau and Petite's auditors may not access them in any way.

   Required:

   (a)   What problems might this present to the auditor?
   (b)   How may the auditor overcome the problems you have listed in (a) above?

SOURCES AND ADDITIONAL READING

Financial Reporting Council (2016) *ISA 315 Identifying and Assessing Risks of Material Misstatement through Understanding the Entity and its Environment*. London: Financial Reporting Council.

Financial Reporting Council (2016) *ISA 402 Audit Considerations Relating to an Entity using a Service Organization*. London: Financial Reporting Council.

International Federation of Accountants (2011) *International Standard on Assurance Engagements (ISAE) 3402 Assurance Reports on Controls at a Service Organization*. New York: IFAC.

CHAPTER 23
SUBSEQUENT EVENTS AND GOING CONCERN

Learning Objectives

After studying the material in this chapter you should be able to:

- understand what is meant by a subsequent events review

- differentiate been adjusting events and non-adjusting events

- understand the audit work to be carried out in respect of subsequent events and going concern issues

- explain the role of the directors in connection with subsequent events and going concern

- understand the implications to the auditor's report of going concern issues

- explain the particular problems with smaller entities

INTRODUCTION

A **subsequent events** review and examination of the assumptions around the issue of going concern are two key matters for the auditor and they are important because:

- an examination of events since the date of the Statement of Financial Position can shed light on events during the accounting period; and
- a decision as to whether or not an entity is a going concern is crucial to accounts presentation.

In both cases auditors may have to exercise some degree of judgement, particularly in the case of going concern decisions, and will need to document carefully both the nature of any uncertainty they have and the rationale for the eventual decisions they make.

SUBSEQUENT EVENTS

ISA 560 *Subsequent events* states:

'*Financial statements may be affected by certain events that occur after the date of the financial statements.*
    Such financial reporting frameworks ordinarily identify two types of events:

    (a) *Those that provide evidence of conditions that existed at the date of the financial statements; and*
    (b) *Those that provide evidence of conditions that arose after the date of the financial statements. ISA (UK and Ire-land) 700 explains that the date of the auditor's report informs the reader that the auditor has considered the effect of events and transactions of which the auditor becomes aware and that occurred <u>up to that date</u>. (Author's underlining).*'

Systems-based auditing

If they are using a systems-based audit strategy during the course of their checking work, the auditors will have spent most of their time looking at events and transactions that occurred in the financial period being audited. Only a limited amount of their work will have involved them in looking beyond the year end. For example, such work as reviewing payments of receivables balances after the year end, tracing uncleared cheques and uncredited lodgements from the bank reconciliation or carrying out audit work on the client's cut-off procedures.

Risk-based auditing

If the auditors are using a risk-based auditing strategy their work will not have encompassed the same level of detailed checking work but, on the assumption that they will have carried out some level of substantive testing on the Statement of Financial Position, they may well have carried out some, if not all, of the above procedures.

The consideration of business risk will not have stopped at the year end, however, and events since the Statement of Financial Position date will have a direct bearing on the auditor's view of the financial statements. They will be interested in:

- events since the Statement of Financial Position date in any particular high-risk areas they have identified
- material transactions since the Statement of Financial Position date in key business risk areas or areas where fraud or manipulation of financial accounting is considered feasible or possible
- results since the Statement of Financial Position date, consisting of management information including cash forecasts, to assist a general overview and analytical review of the financial statements

Events since the date of the Statement of Financial Position

The auditors should consider the effect of subsequent events on the financial statements and on the Auditor's Report. During the period between the end of the financial period and the date the Auditor's Report is signed there may be events which shed new light on the financial statements.

Examples of these sorts of events are:

- notification of insolvency of a customer after the year end resulting in adjustment of the bad debt provision
- adjustments to inventory or work in progress valuations, for example, where finished goods inventory has proved to be unsaleable or where a dispute has arisen in respect of work done on a contract and the amounts receivable look in doubt
- significant changes to borrowings from banks or other lenders which shed new light on the financial structure of the business, for example, where the company's bankers refuse to renew overdraft facilities or provide a loan which the company needed in order to continue its operations at their current level
- an issue of new shares
- a change in the way the business is carried on, for example, a clothing retailer decides to close all its high street shops and concentrate on selling over the internet

However not all events happening after the period end date affect the financial statements although the auditor needs to be aware of them in order to decide whether they are relevant or not. Some of these events will mean that the accounts will have to be amended to take account of them; others may simply require a mention in a note to the accounts or in the Directors Report, some may be safely left until next year's accounts.

ADJUSTING AND NON-ADJUSTING EVENTS

These are defined in Financial Reporting Standard (FRS) 102:32 – *Events after the End of the Reporting Period*. From the list above, events such as:

- the insolvency of a major customer owing a debt which is material,
- material writing down the values of inventory and work in progress, or
- major problems with financing the business.

would be likely to mean that the accounts would be adjusted because they cast new light on something which *already existed* at the date of the Statement of Financial Position

These are **adjusting events.**

However, again from the list above, events such as:

- an issue of shares after the Statement of Financial Position date, or
- a change in the way business was conducted after the year end

would only require including in a note to the accounts or the Directors' Report – these are **non-adjusting events**. In other words, they do not give us any further information about something which existed within the accounting period – they are simply events.

This concept can be difficult to grasp sometimes. For example, a factory burns down a month after the financial period end. It could be argued that the factory existed at the period end and so this event relates to it. However, this would be an error because, at the date of the Statement of Financial Position, the factory was complete and in an unburned state so it has to be reflected at that value.

This is because, whilst non-adjusting events are informative and add to the general financial picture of the company, they don't relate to a condition which actually existed at the Statement of Financial Position date or which happened within the financial period.

Obviously these are only examples and there are many types of events which could happen about which a decision would have to be made.

If, after discussion with the auditors, the directors of the business decide not to amend the accounts when the auditors think they should, the auditors will have to consider the effect of this on their audit report and we will look at this later in the chapter.

AUDIT TESTS FOR A SUBSEQUENT EVENTS REVIEW

ISA 560 states:

'The auditor shall perform audit procedures designed to obtain sufficient appropriate audit evidence that all events occurring between the date of the financial statements and the date of the auditor's report that require adjustment of, or disclosure in, the financial statements have been identified. The auditor is not, however, expected to perform additional audit procedures on matters to which previously applied audit procedures have provided satisfactory conclusions.'

In order to satisfy themselves that all events after the year end have been appropriately dealt with and disclosed in the financial statements, the auditors should carry out certain audit tests.

These will include reviewing management's procedures for identifying subsequent events which might affect the financial statements in any way. One way to do this is by reading minutes of board meetings, shareholders or other committee meetings since the Statement of Financial Position date and enquiring about matters discussed at meetings where the minutes are not yet available. Clearly reviewing management accounts, cash flow forecasts or other information since the Statement of Financial Position date and enquiries to legal advisors about outstanding legal matters are obvious areas which may reveal the existence of significant events. Other areas for review might include matters which have already been dealt with but on the basis of preliminary or inconclusive information and whether any new borrowing or guarantee commitments have been entered into.

Auditors should make enquiries of senior management about matters which may not be the subject of formal minutes or of which members of staff have no knowledge such as:

- details of any proposed or actual major additions to assets
- whether any mergers or acquisitions are planned or any new issues of shares
- whether any assets have been appropriated (e.g. nationalized) or destroyed; any developments in areas of risk or where contingent liabilities have been identified
- whether any unusual accounting amendments have been made or are planned to be made, e.g. reversals of transactions recorded during the financial year
- whether there are any events which would call into question the appropriateness of the accounting policies used or accounting bases adopted, in particular that of going concern

One audit test which should invariably be carried out is to review transactions since the year end for large or unusual items such as sales of assets, issues of credit notes to many customers on the same date (used to reverse fake invoices entered before the period end), exceptional discounts allowed or received, commissions paid, etc.

Auditors should review transactions after the period end for any material or unusual items which may not have been disclosed in the financial statements. Their work on validating the values of assets and liabilities should cover most of the review work and inspection of minutes and discussions with directors should, except in the case of serious management misrepresentation, provide the auditors with the information they require.

The auditors may well require written representations in the form of a Letter of Representation from management (Chapter 24) in respect of the detail of such events and would certainly require confirmation, as a minimum, that all material events have been disclosed to them and that no details have been withheld.

Events after the date of signing the Auditor's Report

Note that there is no obligation on auditors to apply procedures to discover relevant subsequent events from the date of signing their report to the date of laying the financial statements before the company, e.g. at an AGM.

However, if the auditors become aware of such events they should discuss the matter with the directors, consider the implications for their report and take such actions as may seem necessary depending on the significance to the company, and thus to the financial statements, of the events.

If the financial statements are amended the auditors will need to consider the amendments and revise their report accordingly. This can be done by issuing a revised report with a separate date recording the fact that additional audit work has been performed in respect of the subsequent events only; for example, the wording would be:

'*(Date of auditor's report), except as to Note Y, which is as of (date of completion of audit procedures restricted to amendment described in Note Y).*'

If the financial statements have already been issued and management does not propose to recall or amend them the auditors are advised to seek legal advice as to what might be done to prevent reliance on their report which, of course, will not include any reference to the subsequent event and its effect on the financial statements.

GOING CONCERN

Introduction

ISA 570 '*Going concern*' states:

'*The auditor's responsibility is to obtain sufficient appropriate audit evidence about the appropriateness of management's use of the going concern assumption in the preparation and presentation of the financial statements and to conclude whether there is a material uncertainty about the entity's ability to continue as a going concern.*'

One of the fundamental accounting concepts is that the financial statements of a company are assumed to be prepared on a going concern basis and FRS 102 '*Events after the End of the Reporting Period*' requires management to make an assessment of the entity's ability to continue as a going concern – but what does this mean?

The assumption is that the business will carry on its activities in the same way for the **foreseeable future**. In other words, that:

- the management will be able to influence the way the business is run;
- that its products or services will continue to be bought by its customers;
- that suppliers will continue to supply it; and
- that it will have the cash to fund its operations.

The last point is probably the most important of all. Most businesses fail because they run out of cash and are unable to pay their bills.

The 'foreseeable future', for this purpose, is defined as being for a period of *one year from the date of approval of the financial statements*. Note that this is a longer period than the period specified in FRS 102 which is simply between the period end and the date the financial statements were authorized for issue.

INDICATORS OF PROBLEMS

Auditors should be alert to indicators which might show actual or potential going concern problems. The list below is not intended to be comprehensive but includes indicators that a material uncertainty exists.

Financial indicators

- net liability or net current liability position
- fixed-term borrowings approaching maturity without realistic prospects of renewal or repayment; or excessive reliance on short-term borrowings to finance long-term assets

- indications of withdrawal of financial support by creditors
- negative operating cash flows indicated by historical or prospective financial statements; adverse key financial ratios
- substantial operating losses or significant deterioration in the value of assets used to generate cash flows
- arrears or discontinuance of dividends
- inability to pay creditors on due dates
- inability to comply with the terms of loan agreements
- change from credit to cash-on-delivery transactions with suppliers
- inability to obtain financing for essential new product development or other essential investments

Operating indicators

- management intentions to liquidate the entity or to cease operations
- loss of key management without replacement
- loss of a major market, key customer(s), franchise, licence, or principal supplier(s)
- labour difficulties, loss of key member of staff
- shortages of important supplies
- emergence of a highly successful competitor

Other indicators

- noncompliance with capital or other statutory requirements
- pending legal or regulatory proceedings against the entity that may, if successful, result in claims that the entity is unlikely to be able to satisfy
- changes in law or regulation or government policy expected to adversely affect the entity
- uninsured or underinsured catastrophes when they occur

Any or all of these might mean than the company will no longer be able to carry on for the foreseeable future. Again, it is the responsibility of the management to come to this decision and draft the financial statements accordingly. It is the auditor's job to validate that assumption.

CONSEQUENCES OF GOING CONCERN

The adoption of the going concern basis in financial statements means amongst other things:

- Assets are expected to be used for many years into the future and depreciated accordingly. Abandonment of the going concern basis would mean that the enterprise might have to immediately sell its assets which may fetch only a small fraction of their book value.
- Liabilities are recognized and measured on the basis that they will be discharged in the normal course of business. The Statement of Financial Position shows payables due after 12 months and payables due in less than 12 months. Abandonment of the going concern basis would make them all payable immediately.

If financial statements are drawn up without the going concern basis, then:

- All assets would be valued at net realizable values. Most would have much lower values than going concern values.
- All liabilities would be shown at the amount due. In addition to liabilities already identified additional ones might have to be provided for as a result of the possible closure of all or part of the operation of the business such as:
  - redundancy pay
  - closure costs
  - losses on sales of assets
  - penalties and guarantees under contracts
  - claims from customers

DIRECTORS' DUTIES

The directors should consider carefully whether the going concern basis is appropriate.

To do this they must consider a number of factors. Bear in mind that the directors should know the business better than anyone so should be able to come to an informed decision. The problem is that directors tend to be inherently optimistic, so whilst the outcome may look bleak to the dispassionate observer, the company director may well retain an attitude of sunny optimism which causes them to downplay their opinions. Auditors must be careful to ensure that they come to their own conclusions which may differ from those of their client who may be unwilling to face the inevitable.

Note that for listed companies there are specific disclosures the directors have to make concerning their assessment of the validity of the Going Concern basis of preparing the Financial Statements and the auditors must satisfy themselves that the basis for the directors' disclosure in the accounts is valid. These include – per 1SA 570:

(a) *The directors' confirmation in the annual report that they have carried out a robust assessment of the principal risks facing the entity, including those that would threaten its business model, future performance, solvency or liquidity;*

(b) *The disclosures in the annual report that describe those risks and explain how they are being managed or mitigated;*

(c) *The directors' statement in the financial statements about whether they considered it appropriate to adopt the going concern basis of accounting in preparing them, and their identification of any material uncertainties to the entity's ability to continue to do so over a period of at least twelve months from the date of approval of the financial statements; and*

(d) *The director's explanation in the annual report as to how they have assessed the prospects of the entity, over what period they have done so and why they consider that period to be appropriate, and their statement as to whether they have a reasonable expectation that the entity will be able to continue in operation and meet its liabilities as they fall due over the period of their assessment, including any related disclosures drawing attention to any necessary qualifications or assumptions.*

The work carried out by the directors and reviewed by the auditors comprises three parts:

1 Firstly, the directors should consider the inherent risks in the business such as:

- The nature of the business. The future of a civil engineering contractor is inherently more uncertain than that of a food retailer.
- Smaller entities can be more vulnerable than larger ones, particularly to factors such as the loss of a major customer or a key member of staff.
- The riskiness of the company or its industry. A one-customer firm is more at risk than a firm with many customers; a highly geared company is more at risk than an all-equity one when interest rates are rising.
- External influences, for example, a change in legislation might increase costs to such an extent that the business becomes unviable.
- Directors should assess the entity's exposure to contingent liabilities. For example, where companies have frequent disputes the scope for contingent liabilities, which may result in legal proceedings giving rise to large outflows of cash in the future, is much higher than a company which does not have many disputes.

2 Secondly, they should review their operations and consider the validity of the assumptions which underlie:

- forecast financial statements
- budgets and strategic plans
- cash flow forecasts

  For example, an entity, particularly a medium and large entity, should prepare a sensitivity analysis in order to understand any critical assumptions on which any budgets and forecasts are prepared. 'Stress testing' is a concept which involves assessing the extent to which budgets and forecasts react to changes in variables such as changes in interest rates and exchange rates.

3 Thirdly, they need to review the financing of the business, both currently and for the foreseeable future to ensure:

- that sufficient finance is available to continue current operations in the same way for the foreseeable future without the need for major refinancing
- that finance is available for future plans or developments
- directors should take account of the timing of cash flows

For example, if the company has a large outflow of cash due to take place in the period, directors should assess how this outflow of cash can be matched with inflows of cash. This is particularly important if the company has a large tax liability to be settled or if loan repayments are falling due.

The auditors need to review and document these considerations to evidence that they have considered the going concern position.

THE AUDITOR'S PROCEDURES

The auditors, when forming an opinion as to whether financial statements give a true and fair view, should consider the entity's ability to continue as a going concern and any relevant disclosures in the financial statements. The auditors should review the management's processes (above) for establishing whether or not the entity is a going concern, over the same period the management has used, which has to be for more than 12 months after the date the accounts were approved. If the directors have carried out a review for less than 12 months, the auditors must ask them to extend it.

Note that it is not the job of the auditors to decide whether or not the entity is likely to be a going concern for the relevant period, it is the job of the management to do so and it is the job of the auditor to verify that they have done so adequately.

The auditors have to gather sufficient, appropriate evidence to satisfy themselves that the going concern basis is appropriate. This must be done in respect of all audits, no matter how viable the company appears to be. The auditors must be able to demonstrate that they have considered it so must document the decision. For example, it may be necessary to assess the adequacy of the length of time into the future that the directors have looked. This may depend on the nature of the business, e.g. a company engaged in long-term contracting may require an assessment over a longer period than, say, a caravan manufacturer.

This is particularly the case where a risk-based audit strategy is being adopted.

It is difficult to be comprehensive and auditors should adopt suitable procedures for each individual client in order to obtain the evidence they need but some possible procedures are:

- Assess the adequacy of the means by which the directors have satisfied themselves that the adoption of the going concern basis is appropriate.
- Examine all appropriate evidence, e.g. budgets, forecasts, minutes of meetings, etc. and assess the reliability of such budgets by reference to past performance.
- Assess the systems or other means by which the directors have identified warnings of future risks and uncertainties.
- Consider the adequacy of guarantees and indicators of support from holding companies where the entity is a member of a group.
- Reading the terms of debentures and loan agreements and determining whether any have been breached.
- Examine management accounts and other reports of recent activities.
- Contact legal advisors for information concerning claims or liabilities the company may have to face.
- Consider the sensitivity of budgets and cash flow forecasts to variable factors both within the control of the directors (e.g. capital expenditure) and outside their control (e.g. interest rates or debt collection).
- Review any obligations, undertakings or guarantees arranged with other entities for the giving or receiving of support. Other entities may mean lenders, suppliers, customers or other companies in the same group. A UK company may be viable in itself but may have given guarantees to other members of the group and when, say, the holding company in Australia fails, the UK company goes down with it.
- Verify the existence, adequacy and terms of borrowing facilities and supplier credit and consider their adequacy.

- Evaluate the entity's plans to deal with unfilled customer orders.
- Consider the value of assets given as security for borrowings.
- Review correspondence with bankers either existing or proposed, particularly where facilities are coming up for renewal.

In the case of smaller entities financing may be dependent on continued support from owner/managers. This can take the form of the owner/manager subordinating any claim to that of the bank or the giving of a personal guarantee. Where this is the case the auditors should see evidence of the subordination, which is usually a letter, and satisfy themselves as to the owner/manager's capacity for meeting any claims under that guarantee as this is usually a condition of continued support from the lender.

Auditors should appraise the key assumptions underlying the budgets, forecasts and other information used by the directors and assess the directors' plans for resolving any matters giving rise to concern (if any) about the appropriateness of the going concern basis. Such plans should be realistic, capable of resolving the doubts, and the directors should have firm intentions to put them into effect.

Finally, the auditors should review all the information they have and all the audit evidence available and consider whether they can accept the going concern basis. They should always have all their evidence and conclusions documented.

Auditors should communicate any concerns they may have to the Audit Committee setting out the basis for their concerns and the actions they propose to take if their concerns are not remedied.

IF EVENTS ARE IDENTIFIED

If events are identified which cast doubt on the appropriateness of the going concern basis the onus is on the management to demonstrate to the auditors that they have identified the problem and have plans to deal with it.

The auditors must:

- Review the plans and consider their adequacy. If the auditors consider the plans inadequate and that the company is likely to fail they must consider an **adverse opinion** in their auditor's report (Chapter 26) if the directors will not amend the financial statements to reflect the loss of the going concern assumption.
- Consider if a material uncertainty about the company's ability to continue as a going concern exists which might need to be brought to the attention of the shareholders.
- Seek written representations from management as to its plans and the expected outcome. This may not be sufficient, appropriate evidence of anything but the auditors need it. This must come from the top level of the company's management and be approved by the Board of Directors.
- If auditors are dealing with an actual or potentially insolvent subsidiary company they should look to the holding company for guarantees of continuing financial support – particularly where there is considerable inter-company indebtedness. The effect on the holding company of giving such support must be considered also.

Clearly, the auditors will need to carry out audit procedures in respect of these plans. They should consider how realistic they are, the reactions of lenders or bankers, the effect on customers and suppliers, the effect on key members of staff and the consequences of any breaches of the terms of any lending and whether this will render any plans invalid.

EFFECT ON AUDIT REPORTS

We will look at this in more detail in Chapter 26 but for the moment the auditor's reporting will be based on three possible scenarios:

1 The going concern basis is valid but a material uncertainty about the ability of the company to continue as a going concern exists.

   The auditor has to consider how well this is explained in the financial statements. If the nature of the uncertainty is fully and properly explained the auditors so the auditors consider that the management have made adequate disclosure in the financial statements the auditors must include a separate paragraph in their Auditor's Report headed 'Material Uncertainty Related to Going Concern.' This should highlight the note in the financial statements which discloses the reasons for the uncertainty. It also has to state that the uncertainty exists but that the Auditor's Report has not been modified or qualified in respect of it. We look at this in more detail in Chapter 26.

2   The auditors disagree with the directors' approach to the financial statements or the disclosures in the accounts. Either the company is clearly not a going concern and the directors are, effectively, trying to maintain an illusion that it is or there is a material uncertainty as to whether or not the company is a going concern but the directors have not disclosed this in the financial statements.

   This is likely to result in an adverse opinion in their Auditors Report, (i.e. that the financial statements do not show a true and fair view of the financial position of the company for the accounting period) if the auditors consider that the use of the going concern basis is inappropriate or if adequate disclosure of a material uncertainty has not been made. The auditors must explain the reason for their adverse opinion and will use that opportunity to explain the nature of the uncertainty to the shareholders.

3   Rarely, in the event of multiple material uncertainties the auditors may consider a disclaimer of opinion altogether. If the directors have not considered the possibilities of going concern for an insufficiently long period a disclaimer of opinion (i.e. a statement by the auditors that they will not express any kind of opinion on the truth and fairness of the financial statements) may also be appropriate.

Of course the auditors may agree with everything the directors have done and the financial statements may disclose everything properly, in which case the auditors will not need to modify or qualify their report at all but they will need to include reference to the disclosures made by the directors in their Auditors Report in a separate paragraph.

One thing to bear in mind is that any qualification of a set of financial statements in respect of going concern is a very serious step. Indeed, it may precipitate the very thing the company does not wish to happen if, as a result of the qualification, creditors or lenders take fright and financial support is withdrawn.

GOING CONCERN AND SMALL ORGANIZATIONS

Small organizations have more going concern uncertainty than larger ones as they are often vulnerable to cash flow problems, have a limited numbers of key customers, have few reserves to cope with significant bad debts and may face much larger competition, etc.

Lack of proper management information and limited financial expertise can compound these problems. This is where the auditors can be drawn in to acting as quasi financial directors if they are not careful. For example, consider a situation where a client requests advice in preparation of budgets and cash flows, the audit firm prepares them and then discusses them with the directors. Great care must be taken to ensure that any decisions taken are taken solely by the owner/managers and not by any member of the accounting firm who may later act as auditor.

Directors of small companies should consider taking advice to ensure that disclosures and accounting treatment of items within the financial statements conform to the relevant standards.

SUMMARY

- Post Statement of Financial Position events, events occurring in the period between the end of the financial year and the date the Auditor's Report is signed, have an effect on the financial statements.
- Authority for the treatment of post Statement of Financial Position events is found in ISA 560.
- Auditors should apply procedures to discover the existence of relevant subsequent events which occur from the date of the financial statements to the date of signing the auditor's report.

- Some events may require the amounts to be adjusted if they relate to events or conditions which existed at the Statement of Financial Position date. Other events may be of interest but don't cause any adjustment of the accounts.
- Going concern is a major issue.
- ISA 570 is relevant to this subject.
- The definition of going concern is the assumption that the business will carry on its activities in the same way for the foreseeable future.
- The foreseeable future is a period of twelve months from the date the financial statements are approved.
- Abandonment of the going concern basis means that assets will be valued at net realizable values and some additional liabilities might become payable, including redundancy pay and other costs arising from any closure.
- The directors have a duty to consider the going concern basis very carefully and make suitable enquiries.
- The auditors have a duty also to consider the going concern basis and review and seek audit evidence to validate the directors' conclusion and opinions. The evidence must support any disclosures made by the Directors in the Financial Statements.
- Auditors should discuss their findings with the Audit Committee.
- A major issue in many going concern basis doubts is borrowing facilities. If in doubt the auditors need to confirm these directly with the bank and form an opinion on the bank's attitude toward supporting the company.
- Smaller entities are more vulnerable than larger ones and often rely on support from owner/managers.
- There are numerous situations where going concern basis is an issue. Some of these are financial, some operational and some external to the entity.
- If it clearly is not a going concern then an adverse opinion is called for if the financial statements are prepared on a going concern basis.
- If the financial statements are not prepared on a going concern basis, there are adequate explanations of the circumstances and the auditor concurs then an unqualified opinion is appropriate with a specific disclosure in the Auditor's Report.
- The grey area is when there are doubts about going concern but the auditor still considers that the going concern basis gives a true and fair view. In such cases the notes to the accounts should give adequate explanations of the situation and the directors' assumptions. If they do so the auditors should include an explanatory paragraph in the opinion but not qualify their report. If the notes are inadequate, then the auditors should modify their report.
- The going concern basis is one of the issues requiring mention in the Directors' Report on compliance with the UK Corporate Governance Code.

POINTS TO NOTE

- Apart from reviewing the period from the Statement of Financial Position date to when the auditor's report is signed for significant events auditors should be aware of attempts to 'window dress' the accounts. This is in connection with the auditor's responsibilities under ISA 240 *The auditor's responsibilities relating to fraud in an audit of financial statements.*
- It is important to understand the difference between adjusting and non-adjusting events. The key to this is to ask whether the event relates to or sheds more light on something which was in existence at the date of the Statement of Financial Position and was not a single, one-off event which happened in the new financial period but which has no bearing on values or estimates which existed at that date.
- The going concern principle can be considered in relation to the enterprise as a whole or a part only. For example, if a branch was not a going concern, realizable value of assets would need to be substituted for book values and new liabilities may appear in respect of the branch.
- The probability that a going concern qualification of an auditor's report may bring about a receivership or liquidation is a very real problem to auditors who have doubts about a client's future. The auditors must maintain their objectivity and should give their opinion without fear of the consequences to the client.

- The UK Code on Corporate Governance requires the directors of listed companies to make statements on going concern in the annual report and accounts. The auditor is required to review the statements and obtain evidence to support their opinion that the statements made by the directors are valid – or not.

CASE STUDY 1

Slipp & Slide are conducting the final audit of Woodhood plc who are importers and dealers in timber and manufacturers of packing materials. The accounts show results which are comparable to those of the previous year. The auditors are puzzled by this as they know that the company is having difficulties and that creditors are pressing and the bank is making difficulties over the overdraft. The auditors are suspicious of the accounts and resolve to be especially vigilant in the audit of post Statement of Financial Position events. The company's year-end is 31 March 2X16 and they are doing the audit in mid-June 2X16. Two specific items have come to their attention:

(a)   In the sales office the auditors found some promotional literature offering special very low prices for obsolete stock in July.

(b)   In conversation with the purchasing manager the auditors discovered that the company had signed a barter deal with an exporter in China for the exchange of specialized wood products for some wood-working machinery of Westwood that is surplus to requirements. The contract was signed in February 2X16 for completion in the winter of 2X16/17.

Discussion

– List the procedures that the auditors should adopt post Statement of Financial Position events.

– What particular further facts should they elicit with regard to (a) and (b)?

– What might be the significance of these items for the accounts?

CASE STUDY 2

Pingo Manufacturing Ltd imports electronic components and assembles them in a factory to make consumer gadgets which appeal to a younger market. They have traded successfully for many years because of favourable market conditions and extended their factory in 2X10 with the aid of a very large bank loan because they anticipated a further increase in sales as they brought some new products to the market.

The company has always been short of working capital as it paid for the components before they were delivered, in order to help the cash flow of their overseas suppliers, some of which were in developing countries. They also have a substantial overdraft which frequently exceeds the facility.

Sadly, the expected increase in turnover never occurred because the market suddenly declined due to a credit squeeze and the fashion for buying fairly pointless gadgets came to a sudden slowdown.

The directors think they have enough core business selling television monitors and closed circuit TV cameras to see them through until the market turns up again, although they may have to reduce the scale of their operations.

Discussion

– What evidence would the directors have to produce to justify their opinion that the company is a going concern and how might the auditors validate the evidence?

STUDENT SELF-TESTING QUESTIONS

Questions with answers apparent from the text

a) What is the definition of an adjusting event?

b) After the year end, but before the Auditor's Report is signed, there is a big fire at Megablow plc and their biggest factory burns down throwing the future of the company into doubt. How should this be treated (i) in the accounts and (ii) by the auditors?

c) List general and specific procedures to be adopted to identify relevant subsequent events.

d) Summarize an auditor's duties in respect of events occurring between the date of the auditor's report and the laying of the financial statements before the company.

e) Define the going concern basis.

f) What is the period which has to be considered and when does it start from?

g) List the consequences to the financial statements of not adopting the going concern basis.

h) List the directors' duties in respect of going concern basis.

i) List the auditor's procedures.

j) List the possible auditor's reports.

k) State the UK Corporate Governance Code requirements on going concern basis.

EXAMINATION QUESTIONS

1 An unqualified audit report normally states that the financial statements to which the report refers give a true and fair view of the state of the company's affairs at the Statement of Financial Position date and of its profits for the year ended on that date.

Bearing in mind the above statement the directors of Midland Builders Ltd have drawn up accounts for the year ended 30 April 2X16 which do not reflect certain events which have occurred since the year end. They justify their action on the grounds that the books and records correctly reflect what was known at the year end. The following are the events which are not reflected in the draft financial statements (in all cases the figures are material).

 (i) At a meeting in May 2X16 the local planning authority rejected the company's plans to develop one of its freehold sites. The site was included in the company's assets at its cost of £500 000 but it is likely that the site will have to be sold and will realize no more than £350 000 because of its reduced development potential.

 (ii) Following the completion of a long-term contract in June 2X16 it has been possible to calculate the final profit on the contract. It appears that the profit accrued at 30 April 2X16 was underestimated by £220 000. This arose from a material error at 30 April 2X15 in estimating the amount of work still to be completed.

 (iii) A public company in which Midland Builders Ltd held shares as a long-term trade investment announced in June 2X16 that it was going into liquidation. The investment is shown in the Statement of Financial Position at its historical cost of £340 000 and a note of its stock market value at 30 April 2X16 of £346 000 is included in the notes to the accounts. It now appears likely that the investment will prove worthless.

Required:

  (a) Discuss generally the effect which facts and events relating to a period but becoming known or occurring after the end of an accounting period can have on the financial statements for the period in question. Comment on the directors' view that the books and records reflect what was known at the year end and that no further adjustments are required.

  (b) List FOUR detailed procedures which an auditor should adopt in order to detect post Statement of Financial Position events.

  (c) In respect of each of the three events described above, list the detailed work which the auditor should undertake and comment on the acceptability of the company's decision not to adjust its financial statements:
    (i) refusal of planning permission;
    (ii) completion of long-term contract;
    (iii) liquidation of trade investment.

(ACCA)

2   You are planning the external audit of Steady Eddy Ltd (Steady Eddy) whose principal activity is the provision of road haulage services. You have been provided with the following information in respect of the year ended 31 May 2X16.

The company made a loss for the year to 31 May 2X16. This is mainly due to the loss of a major customer to a competitor and exceptional costs incurred in relocating to new premises. In previous years the company has been profitable but has recently experienced reduced margins due to the high cost of fuel.

Despite its poor trading results, the company has managed to stay within its overdraft limit of £500 000. This was achieved by the managing director temporarily lending the company £200 000 and delaying payments to creditors. The overdraft facility is to be reviewed by the bank in September 2X16 after the audited financial statements are available.

The company has a loan instalment falling due in October 2X16 which it plans to repay with the proceeds from the recently vacated premises which are currently for sale.

The company has fallen behind with its payments to HM Revenue & Customs, but the directors have successfully negotiated a scheme for settling the arrears over a period of four months. A condition of this concession granted by HM Revenue & Customs is that the company pays all its future monthly tax liabilities on the due dates.

The finance director is optimistic about the future and his profit forecasts indicate a return to profitability for the year ending 31 May 2X17. The company has recently negotiated a substantial contract with a national supermarket chain, which will generate at least £2 million in annual revenue for the next three years. In order to service the contract, the company will need to enlarge its fleet of refrigerated trailers and the finance director is negotiating with leasing companies to fund the acquisitions.

Required:

(a)   Explain what is meant by the going concern concept and why the auditor should consider whether a company is a going concern.

(b)   Explain the circumstances particular to Steady Eddy which may indicate that it is not a going concern.

(c)   Identify the matters to which you would direct your attention during the subsequent events review, in the audit of Steady Eddy.

(ICAEW)

SOURCES AND ADDITIONAL READING

Financial Reporting Council (2015) *FRS 102 The Financial Reporting Standard Applicable in the UK and Republic of Ireland*. London: Financial Reporting Council.

Financial Reporting Council (2016) *ISA 560 Subsequent Events*. London: Financial Reporting Council.

Financial Reporting Council (2016) *ISA 570 Going Concern*. London: Financial Reporting Council.

Financial Reporting Council (2009) *Going Concern and Liquidity Risk: Guidance for Directors of UK Companies*. London: Financial Reporting Council.

Financial Reporting Council (2016) *Guidance on the Going Concern Basis of Accounting and Reporting on Solvency and Liquidity Risks Guidance for Directors of Companies that Do not Apply The UK Corporate Governance Code*. London: Financial Reporting Council.

CHAPTER 24 MANAGEMENT REPRESENTATIONS

Learning Objectives

After studying the material in this chapter you should be able to:

- understand the purpose of a Letter of Representation

- discuss its worth as audit evidence

- explain the contents of such a letter and the requirements needed for its approval by the directors

- understand what steps the auditors should take if the directors refuse to provide written assurances

INTRODUCTION

As usual there is an ISA, this time it is ISA 580 '*Written representations*' which states:

> '*The auditor shall request written representations from management with appropriate responsibilities for the financial statements and knowledge of the matters concerned.*' and
>
>   '*The auditor shall request management to provide a written representation that it has fulfilled its responsibility for the preparation of the financial statements in accordance with the applicable financial reporting framework, including where relevant their fair presentation, as set out in the terms of the audit engagement.*'

In Chapter 11 we looked at the ways in which the auditors gather evidence to come to a conclusion on the truth and fairness of the financial statements prepared by the directors. To recap, wherever possible the auditors should:

- generate their own evidence through compliance and substantive testing, attending inventory counts, physically verifying assets, etc.
- obtain third party evidence, e.g. receivables circularizations, suppliers statements, bank confirmation letters
- ask questions and raise points with management and staff on which they will receive verbal assurances and responses

The written representations take the form of a letter, called a Letter of Representation, written by the directors to the auditors which confirms, in writing, statements which the directors have made during the course of the audit about key aspects of the accounts.

CONTENTS OF A LETTER

The contents of the Letter of Representation *should not* include routine matters, for example, confirmation that all fixed assets exist and are the property of the company or that inventories are valued at the lower of cost and net realizable value as these are implicit in the assertions (Chapter 11).

The letter *should* include matters which are material to the financial statements and for which the auditors cannot obtain independent corroborative evidence and thus have to rely on the directors as the primary source.

The letter will contain assurances from the directors such as:

- acknowledgement of their responsibility for presentation of the financial statements in accordance with the appropriate financial reporting framework
- confirmation that management has provided the auditor with all relevant information and access as agreed in the terms of the audit engagement
- confirmation that all transactions have been recorded and are reflected in the financial statements
- acknowledgement of their responsibility for maintaining a system of internal control
- confirmation that there have been no material irregularities by management or staff
- confirmation that the financial statements are free from material errors or misstatements

The letter may include reference to a **threshold amount.** This is an amount required by ISA 450 '*Evaluation of misstatements identified during the audit*' which is the level above which errors or misstatements cannot be regarded as trivial and which must, therefore, be reported. Management are required to confirm that they consider the level of uncorrected errors to be immaterial.

The letter will also include reference to specific matters on which the auditors require confirmation of items included in the financial statements such as:

- whether the selection and application of accounting policies are appropriate
- whether matters such as the following, where relevant under the applicable financial reporting framework, have been recognized, measured, presented or disclosed in accordance with that framework:
  - plans or intentions that may affect the carrying value or classification of assets and liabilities
  - liabilities, both actual and contingent

- title to, or control over, assets, the liens or encumbrances on assets and assets pledged as collateral and
- aspects of laws, regulations and contractual agreements that may affect the financial statements, including noncompliance
- any subsequent events and their effect on the business
- the basis of valuation of assets where reference is made in the financial statements to asset values
- the basis of any provisions or estimates where corroboratory evidence is minimal and the directors are expressing an opinion or 'best guess'
- confirmations of compliance with regulatory authorities and of the terms of any contracts

During the course of the audit there may be certain items for which the auditor is unable to find sufficient, appropriate evidence and so require specific written assurances from the management. Examples of these might include a situation where, say, a provision has been made for a future loss on a major contract based on the opinion of the directors and for which there is no supporting documentation. Common examples much used in examination questions are a) where the directors state that a legal claim against the company has been settled and they anticipate no further claims for the issue involved or b) where the directors consider the value of goodwill or another major asset to be partially impaired and are writing down its value.

In all of these cases it may be difficult for the auditors to find conclusive corroborative evidence and so are requiring assurances from the directors or confirmation of the basis of their decisions.

RELIANCE ON LETTER OF REPRESENTATION

In these circumstances there may be limited evidence to substantiate the figures shown in the financial statements; consequently, the auditors are reliant on the word of the directors as a form of evidence. The auditors will request that the management provide them with a Letter of Representation to provide assurance as to the information given to them.

A written assurance is more reliable than a verbal assurance but it is important to realize that this is additional supporting evidence and is *not* a substitute for audit testing.

If a risk-based audit strategy is adopted this letter may assume a significance out of proportion to its value as evidence and it is important that auditors do not use it as a substitute for proper risk evaluation and audit testing.

One important point to note is that ISA 580 '*Written representations*' includes an appendix which contains references to all the other ISAs which *require* the auditors to obtain specific assurances from management. These are the paragraphs in other ISAs that require subject matter specific written representations. The list is, of course, not a substitute for considering the requirements and related application and other explanatory material in ISAs. It includes:

- ISA (UK) 240 (Revised June 2016), *The Auditor's Responsibilities Relating to Fraud in an Audit of Financial Statements* – paragraph 39
- ISA (UK) 250 (Revised June 2016), *Consideration of Laws and Regulations in an Audit of Financial Statements* – paragraph 16
- ISA (UK) 450 (Revised June 2016), *Evaluation of Misstatements Identified during the Audit* – paragraph 14
- ISA (UK) 501, *Audit Evidence-Specific Considerations for Selected Items* – paragraph 12
- ISA (UK) 540 (Revised June 2016), *Auditing Accounting Estimates, Including Fair Value Accounting Estimates, and Related Disclosures* – paragraph 22
- ISA (UK) 550, *Related Parties* – paragraph 26
- ISA (UK) 560, *Subsequent Events* – paragraph 9
- ISA (UK) 570 (Revised June 2016), *Going Concern* – paragraph 16(e)
- ISA (UK) 710, *Comparative Information—Corresponding Figures and Comparative Financial Statements* – paragraph 9
- ISA (UK) 720 (Revised June 2016), *The Auditor's Responsibilities Relating to Other Information* – paragraph 13(c)

Students would not be expected to memorize this list – just to be aware that in certain circumstances specific representations are required by specific ISAs and that most of this has been covered in previous chapters.

EXAMPLE OF A MANAGEMENT REPRESENTATION LETTER

This is an example of a Letter of Representation. It is indicative only and every letter should be written to reflect the circumstances of a particular client and a particular audit. In particular, the provisions of ISA 580 regarding specific disclosures shown above should be borne in mind. This sample letter is by way of an indicative example and is not a template for such communications.

WIBBLE plc
GRUB STREET
BIGTOWN
BG3 4 TT

Messrs Junge & Foolisch

Addit Road

Bigtown

BG1 5ER

6 April 2X16

(Note the date must be as near as possible to, but not after, the date of the Auditor's Report)

Dear Sirs

This representation letter is provided in connection with your audit of the financial statements of Wibble plc for the year ended 30 June, 2X16 for the purpose of expressing an opinion as to whether the financial statements give a true and fair view in accordance with Financial Reporting Standards.

We confirm to the best of our knowledge and belief, and after having made enquiries of other directors and officials of the company, the following representations made to you in connection with your audit of the financial statements for the year ended 30 June 2X16.

We confirm that, to the best of our knowledge and belief, having made such inquiries as we considered necessary for the purpose of appropriately informing ourselves:

Financial statements

1   We have fulfilled our responsibilities, as set out in the terms of the audit engagement dated [insert date], for the preparation of the financial statements in accordance with Financial Reporting Standards; in particular, the financial statements give a true and fair view in accordance therewith.

2   Significant assumptions used by us in making accounting estimates, including those measured at fair value, are reasonable.

3   Related party relationships and transactions have been appropriately accounted for and disclosed in accordance with the requirements of the Financial Reporting Standards.

4   All events subsequent to the date of the financial statements and for which Financial Reporting Standards require adjustment or disclosure have been adjusted or disclosed.

5   The effects of uncorrected misstatements are immaterial, both individually and in the aggregate, to the financial statements as a whole. A list of the uncorrected misstatements is attached to the representation letter.

We have provided you with:

1   Access to all information of which we are aware that is relevant to the preparation of the financial statements such as records, documentation and other matters.

2   Additional information that you have requested from us for the purpose of the audit.

3   Unrestricted access to persons within the entity from whom you determined it necessary to obtain audit evidence.

4   All transactions have been recorded in the accounting records and are reflected in the financial statements.

5   We have disclosed to you the results of our assessment of the risk that the financial statements may be materially misstated as a result of fraud.

6   We have disclosed to you all information in relation to fraud or suspected fraud that we are aware of and that affects the entity and involves:

- Management
- Employees who have significant roles in internal control or
- Others where the fraud could have a material effect on the financial statements

7   We have disclosed to you all information in relation to allegations of fraud, or suspected fraud, affecting the entity's financial statements communicated by employees, former employees, analysts, regulators or others.

8   We have disclosed to you all known instances of noncompliance or suspected noncompliance with laws and regulations whose effects should be considered when preparing financial statements.

9   We have disclosed to you the identity of the entity's related parties and all the related party relationships and transactions of which we are aware.

In respect of specific matters:

1   The legal claim against us by Hugo Faster plc has been settled out of court by a payment of £250 000. No further claims have been received.

2   We confirm that the factory premises at Smalltown were properly valued by Messrs G Estimate & Co Chartered Surveyors and Valuers who are qualified to undertake this work. Their valuation of those premises on an open market existing use basis was £1.75 million which has been properly reflected in the accounts.

3   The loan and overdraft facilities were renewed by the bank on 2 August 2X16 with no adjustments to the terms and conditions of the loans.

4   The fire at the offices in Grub Street is not expected to cause any detriment to the trading capability of the business.

Signed on behalf of Wibble plc

_____   _____
Chief Executive Officer   Financial director
Minuted by the board at their meeting on 6 November 2X16

The letter should be:

- signed by the chief executive and/or financial director
- approved and minuted at a board meeting at which, ideally, the auditor would be present

In certain circumstances auditors might want separate written representations from particular directors or managers in respect of specific issues. For example, they may require confirmation that the minutes of meetings are complete from the person responsible for them.

REFUSAL TO CO-OPERATE

If there is a refusal by management to cooperate then the auditors should consider if they have obtained all the information and explanations they require in respect of all audit issues. If they have sufficient, appropriate evidence they may be able to dispense with a letter. However, they should consider the effect of the management's refusal to supply such a letter in their estimate of audit risk and on their future relationship with the client.

If they do not have sufficient, appropriate evidence and require the letter to support their audit opinion they may have to consider a qualification of the auditor's report on the grounds of restriction of audit evidence.

If the auditors have doubt about the competence, ethical values, diligence or integrity of the management they should consider withdrawing from the engagement. They may continue of course, even in the face of such doubts, but should evaluate any representations received from the management accordingly and in the light of reliable evidence obtained elsewhere.

SUMMARY

- A Letter of Representation is a letter from the management to the auditor confirming, in writing, opinions conveyed to the auditor orally.
- It is obtained on the occasion of each audit.
- ISA 580 'Written representations' governs this subject.
- The letter should contain only matters which are material and for which the auditor cannot obtain corroborating evidence.
- The letter should contain the directors' acknowledgement for their responsibilities under the Companies Act 2006 and under the Letter of Engagement, for preparing financial statements which give a true and fair view.
- It should also confirm that the management have made available to the auditor any information they may require and have not restricted the scope of their audit in any way.
- The letter should confirm that all the transactions are entered in the records and are included in the financial statements. It should also confirm that the effects of any uncorrected errors or misstatements are immaterial.
- It should contain representations concerning the management's risk assessments as to the likelihood of fraud including fraud by the management.
- The principal items will be matters of which management alone have knowledge and matters of judgement and opinion.
- Ideally the representation letter should be dated the same day as the directors formally approve the accounts.

POINTS TO NOTE

- The Letter of Representation is a form of audit evidence but not, of course, the only form or even a very reliable form. Thus, the auditor cannot rely on the Letter of Representation to save carrying out audit work.
- The letter is used only on the restricted number of matters discussed in this chapter.
- It is advisable for the auditors to ascertain that the persons responsible for the letter should fully understand what it is that they are being asked to confirm and why.

CASE STUDY

Runne & Hyde are auditors of the Zombrit Group plc. The accounts for the year ending 31 March 2X16 are being subjected to the final review. The following matters have been noted by the audit manager:

(a) The company has engaged in a number of long-term contracts in the Far East. During the last few years a minority of these have sustained losses. Work in progress at 31 March 2X16 includes a substantial amount of these contracts. Some are valued at cost and some include attributable profit. One contract has been valued with a provision for ultimate loss.

(b) The group has set up a subsidiary in Africa to manufacture motor parts for sale in that country. The group have lent this subsidiary material amounts but so far production difficulties, political problems and difficulties in finding adequate markets have plagued the project. All assets acquired by the subsidiary have been valued at cost.

(Continued)

(c) The group has a property in Milton Keynes which they used as the regional headquarters. This office has been closed and the staff transferred, with considerable opposition, to London. The property has been let to another company on a two-year lease and has been treated in the accounts as an investment property.

(d) The company has a project to manufacture and sell a range of video conferencing equipment as a package. Production should commence in 2X17. All expenditure so far has been treated as development costs as although prototype packs have been assembled they are not yet in production.

Discussion

– Identify the matters connected with these items which the auditor may include in a Letter of Representation.

STUDENT SELF-TESTING QUESTIONS

Questions with answers apparent from the text

a) Why should a Letter of Representation be obtained?

b) What kind of matter should be included in a Letter of Representation?

c) What should the auditor do if the client refuses to give one?

EXAMINATION QUESTIONS

1 Explain the purpose of a management representation letter.
2 You are the manager in charge of the audit of Crighton-Ward, a public limited liability company which manufactures specialist cars and other motor vehicles for use in films. Audited turnover is £140 million with profit before tax of £75 million. All audit work up to, but not including, the obtaining of management representations has been completed. A review of the audit file has disclosed the following outstanding points:

Lion's Roar
The company is facing a potential legal claim from the Lion's Roar company in respect of a defective vehicle that was supplied for one of their films. Lion's Roar maintains that the vehicle was not built strongly enough whilst the directors of Crighton-Ward argue that the specification was not sufficiently detailed. Dropping a vehicle 50 metres into a river and expecting it to continue to remain in working condition would be unusual, but this is what Lion's Roar expected. Solicitors are unable to determine liability at the present time. A claim for £4 million being the cost of a replacement vehicle and lost production time has been received by Crighton-Ward from Lion's Roar. The director's opinion is that the claim is not justified.

Depreciation
Depreciation of specialist production equipment has been included in the financial statements at the amount of 10 per cent per annum based on reducing balance. However, the treatment is consistent with prior accounting periods (which received an unmodified auditor's report) and other companies in the same industry and sales of old equipment show negligible profit or loss on sale. The audit senior, who is new to the audit, feels that depreciation is being undercharged in the financial statements.

Required:

For each of the above matters:
(i) discuss whether or not a paragraph is required in the representation letter and
(ii) *if appropriate*, draft the paragraph for inclusion in the representation letter.

3   A suggested format for the Letter of Representation has been sent by the auditors to the directors of Crighton-Ward. The directors have stated that they will not sign the Letter of Representation this year on the grounds that they believe the additional evidence that it provides is not required by the auditor.

Required:

Discuss the actions the auditor may take as a result of the decision made by the directors not to sign the Letter of Representation.
(ACCA)

SOURCES AND ADDITIONAL READING

Financial Reporting Council (2016) *ISA 450 Evaluation of Misstatements Identified during the Audit*. London: Financial Reporting Council.

Financial Reporting Council (2016) *ISA 580 Written Representations*. London: Financial Reporting Council.

CHAPTER 25
THE FINAL REVIEW
STAGE OF THE AUDIT

Learning Objectives

After studying the material in this chapter you should be able to:

- explain the process for auditing opening balances and comparative figures

- understand the importance of the final review process

- explain the audit procedures for carrying out a final review

- understand the process for evaluating the significance of uncorrected errors or mistakes

- understand the process for reviewing compliance with the UK Corporate Governance Code

- understand the importance of documentation

INTRODUCTION

At the end of the detailed work of the audit, auditors should make an overall review of the financial statements before preparing their report. The review should be sufficiently detailed to enable the auditors, using the conclusions drawn from the audit evidence obtained during the course of their audit work, to develop a reasonable basis for their audit opinion on the financial statements.

The auditors need to determine if the financial statements, as a whole, tell a consistent and logical story about the financial results of the organization for the reporting period.

The final review assists in this determination. The review of the financial statements should be carried out by a suitably experienced audit manager. The ultimate review should be carried out by the audit partner who has responsibility for the audit opinion.

OPENING BALANCES AND COMPARATIVE FIGURES

As part of the completion processes for the financial statements for a given accounting period the auditor must ensure that:

- the opening balances from the previous accounting period have been properly brought forward and incorporated into the financial records; and
- that comparative figures are shown for each item in the current financial statements.

Clearly, the bringing forward of the opening balances is a management responsibility but auditors should confirm them in order to ensure any last minute changes made in the previous period have been incorporated in the current year's records where this is appropriate.

In addition, accounting policies should be consistently applied and this process should form part of the final review process.

There are two ISAs involved – ISA 510 *Initial audit engagements – opening balances* and ISA 710 *Comparative information – corresponding figures and comparative financial statements*. There are similarities between the two ISAs so their requirements are broadly similar and the work required to verify the opening position and any comparative figures is, broadly, the same.

Companies Act requirements

The Companies Act, 2006, states that corresponding amounts are required to be disclosed in respect of every item in a company's Statement of Financial Position and Statement of Comprehensive Income for the financial year immediately preceding that to which the Statement of Financial Position and Statement of Comprehensive Income relates.

Corresponding amounts for the previous accounting periods are commonly known as the **comparative figures** and current practice is to print one narrative and two sets of figures as:

	2X16	2X15
	£'000s	£'000s
Tangible assets	£ 6180	£ 6420

FRS 102 *The Financial Reporting Standard applicable in the UK and Republic of Ireland* states:

'*...an entity shall present comparative information in respect of the preceding period for all amounts presented in the current period's financial statements.*'

Where the corresponding amount is not comparable, i.e. not able to be compared with the amount shown in the previous years' accounts, the previous year's figure should be adjusted and particulars of the adjustment and the reasons for it, shown in the notes.

Students should be aware of the reporting requirements of UK GAAP in respect of:

● acquisitions;
● discontinued operations;
● prior period adjustments; and
● comparative information.

These will cause the current year's figures not to be comparable with those of the previous period. There are many and various accounting requirements to deal with this position which are outside the scope of this book but with which students will be familiar from their accounting studies.

THE AUDITOR'S INTEREST

The auditors must ensure that there is nothing contained in the opening balances which might constitute a material misstatement which might affect the financial statements for the current period and that the accounting policies applied in the financial statements for the preceding period have been consistently applied during the current accounting period or, if they have been changed, that the appropriate adjustments to the comparative figures have been made.

The auditors are interested in the preceding year's figures because these figures form the opening position from which the present year's figures are derived. For example, the opening inventory is a component of the cost of sales figure. Thus the auditors must be assured that the opening figures have been properly brought forward. Clearly accounting policies must be applied consistently from year to year so corresponding amounts must be shown and the auditors must seek evidence that they are properly shown.

The auditors are not required to express any opinion on the corresponding figures, as such, but they are responsible for seeing that they:

● are the amounts which appeared in the preceding period's accounts, or
● have been restated to achieve consistency or comparability, or
● have been restated due to a change in accounting policy or a correction of a fundamental error.

Opening balances

The auditor will have to consider the position in cases where the opening balances were previously audited by someone else or where the opening balances were based on a set of accounts which had not been audited.

The auditors must satisfy themselves that the opening balances do not include any material misstatements which might affect the financial statements for the current period. Consequently, they should read any available financial statements for the previous period in an attempt to discover any hint of a material misstatement in the opening balances, including the relevant disclosures.

Comparative information

The relevant ISA is ISA 710 'Comparative information – corresponding figures and comparative financial statements'.

The auditor's report for the current accounting period does not, generally, give any assurance concerning any prior period except that there is an overriding requirement that the financial statements presented to shareholders are not misleading. Consequently, where the auditor's report on the financial statements for the previous period was modified or qualified in any way the auditor must decide whether or not that qualification and the issue that gave rise to it has any effect on the financial statements for the current year. If the matter is resolved no further consideration is necessary but if it is not, it may affect the auditor's report for the current financial period as well.

Where the comparative figures were audited by another auditor the current auditor must state that in an 'Other Matters' paragraph in their auditor's report and include details of the type of opinion given, including details of any modification to their report and its date. An example of such wording would be:

'The financial statements of ABC Company for the year ended December 31, 2X15, were audited by another auditor who expressed an unmodified opinion on those statements on March 31, 2X16.'

Clearly, where the report for the previous financial period was modified the current auditor's report should bring that fact to the shareholders' attention where the matter remains unresolved. Ideally all should be explained in the detailed financial statements but this does not absolve the auditors from explaining to the shareholders what happened in the previous accounting period and what effect, if any, any events from the previous period have on the current one. This may, of course, mean that any qualification from a previous period is repeated in the current period where the issue remains outstanding. An example of this might be an accounting policy which does not comply with UK GAAP but which the directors insist on using for some reason.

Audit procedures

Both ISA 510 and ISA 710 require that the auditors obtain sufficient appropriate evidence as to the opening figure brought forward into the current period and that the comparative figures from the previous accounting period are properly stated.

If the auditors were also the auditors of the preceding financial statements (a continuing auditor) and issued an unqualified report, then they should:

- consider whether the audit of the current period has revealed any matters casting doubt on the previous year's figures
- satisfy themselves that the balances have been properly brought forward and incorporated in the accounting records
- satisfy themselves that the preceding period's figures have been properly and consistently classified and disclosed as comparative figures
- satisfy themselves that consistent accounting policies have been applied

When the preceding period's financial statements were audited by another firm (known as 'predecessor auditors') the auditors will have to perform additional work.

This might involve:

- consultations with the client's management
- consulting with the predecessor auditors and reviewing their working papers and relevant management letters or obtaining assurances from them as to the opening balances; note that assurances received from predecessor auditors do not absolve the current auditors from satisfying themselves as to the sufficiency and appropriateness of audit evidence in respect of the comparative figures shown in the financial statements
- reviewing the client's records, working papers and accounting and control procedures for the preceding period, particularly as they affect the opening position
- considering whether work on the present year's financial statements also provides evidence regarding opening balances
- if necessary, the auditors should carry out substantive testing in respect of these balances on a sample basis; this might include substantive testing of opening receivables and payables balances and reviewing inventory count details for the previous period based on the audit experiences of a count for the current period

Normally, the actions outlined will enable the auditor to give an unqualified report at least in respect of use of the previous year's figures. If, however, some material matter cannot be adequately evidenced they will have to consider the implications for their auditor's report (see Chapter 26).

This may result in an 'except for' qualification on the grounds of, effectively, a limitation of audit evidence, i.e. that they were unable to assemble sufficient appropriate evidence to validate the comparative figures and the opening position. This is likely to be quite rare; however, care has to be taken that last minute audit adjustments from the preceding year have been incorporated into the current year's figures.

UNCORRECTED ERRORS OR MISSTATEMENTS

ISA 450 '*Evaluation of misstatements identified during the audit*' requires auditors to consider the cumulative and individual effects of uncorrected errors. The auditors should record the errors or mistakes they have uncovered during the course of their audit work, unless they are clearly trivial. Routinely they would ask management to correct or amend the results for the most material errors and in most cases management do so.

As the audit progresses the auditors will reassess their planned materiality and performance materiality levels in the light of the amount of errors they uncover.

Misstatements which go uncorrected, however, may have implications for the audit. Clearly if they are material they may compel the auditors to consider a modification of their auditor's report (Chapter 26). However, if they are merely an accumulation of errors which have reached a threshold amount so are clearly not trivial the auditors must consider:

- their materiality level in connection with their audit planning (Chapter 10)
- whether the accumulation of errors requires them to reassess the audit work they have carried out
- whether any of the uncorrected errors or misstatements affect the results for prior periods

The auditors must communicate the details of uncorrected errors to the management as part of the Management Letter (Chapter 27) and request that a list of uncorrected errors be included in the Letter of Representation (Chapter 24).

These errors can be:

- simple accounting or processing errors, i.e. mistakes of fact
- errors of judgement by the directors in, say, deciding on the level of a provision
- projected errors based on the level of errors based on the error rate found in audit sampling (Chapter 12)

The evaluation of what is considered material must include consideration of both qualitative and quantitative issues. The level of uncorrected errors may, for example, be lower than the level of materiality for the financial statements as a whole and would, presumably, remain uncorrected. Individually material items would be subject to audit report considerations but misstatements which fall in between trivial and material also need to be considered for mostly qualitative reasons including:

- Do the misstatements affect compliance with regulatory requirements, debt covenants or other contractual requirements?
- Do they relate to the incorrect selection or application of an accounting policy that has an immaterial effect on the current period's financial statements but is likely to have a material effect on future periods' financial statements?
- Are they masking a change in earnings or other trends, especially in the context of general economic and industry conditions?
- Will the uncorrected errors affect ratios used to evaluate the entity's financial position, results of operations or cash flows?
- Do they affect segment information presented in the financial statements?
- Do uncorrected errors have the effect of increasing management compensation, for example, by ensuring that the requirements for the award of bonuses or other incentives are satisfied?
- Do they relate to items involving particular parties, for example, whether external parties to the transaction are related to members of the entity's management?
- Do they represent or affect the presentation of information not specifically required by the applicable financial reporting framework but which, in the judgement of the auditor, is important to the users' understanding of the financial position, financial performance or cash flows of the entity or other information that will be communicated in documents containing the audited financial statements? For example, information to be included in a 'Management Discussion and Analysis' or an 'Operating and Financial Review' that may reasonably be expected to influence the economic decisions of the users of the financial statements.

All these points must be considered and the auditor must document that consideration and obtain the appropriated assurances from management.

FINAL ACCOUNTS REVIEW

The auditors need to ensure that:

- The financial statements use acceptable accounting policies, which have been applied consistently and are appropriate to the business.
- The results of operations (Statement of Comprehensive Income), state of affairs (Statement of Financial Position) and all other information included in the financial statements are compatible with each other and with the auditor's knowledge of the enterprise and the evidence gathered during the course of the audit work.
- There is adequate disclosure of all appropriate matters and the information contained in the financial statements is suitably classified and presented, for example, short-term loans should not be included in long-term finance liabilities.
- There is compliance with statutory requirements, for example, the Companies Act 2006.
- There is compliance with other relevant regulations, for example, the UK Corporate Governance Code.
- There is compliance with relevant financial reporting standards, most auditors will use checklists to:
  - facilitate the review – to ensure nothing is missed inadvertently and
  - to evidence the fact a final review has been carried out.
- All the information, both financial and nonfinancial included in the annual report is consistent and there are no anomalies or misstatements. The auditors must include this review as part of their final procedures.

PROCEDURES

The following set of procedures should be adopted for the final review.

Accounting policies

Review all accounting policies and, in particular, consider if they:

- are in accordance with UK Generally Accepted Accounting Practice (UK GAAP) and comply with the fundamental accounting concepts – going concern, accruals, consistency and prudence
- are acceptable to the particular circumstances
- are commonly adopted in the particular industry
- are consistently applied over the years
- are consistently applied throughout the enterprise
- comply with all relevant accounting standards
- where they have been changed that the appropriate adjustments have been made to the current and comparative figures
- conform to the substance over form convention – management may well have an interest in using accounting rules to help them disclose, or not disclose, information in as favourable a light as possible

Auditors need to balance the need to tell the true story (true and fair) to the shareholders against the need to overrule an accounting standard so the substance of transactions are disclosed and not merely their form (see Chapter 2).

The results for the period:

- Consider whether the accounts are consistent with the auditor's knowledge of the underlying circumstances of the business and the information, explanations and conclusions reached on the audit.
- Review the information in the accounts to determine if there are any abnormalities or inconsistencies. Background knowledge of the company is clearly essential for this.
- Consider the effect of uncorrected errors or mistakes. There may be a number or errors or mistakes which remain uncorrected. These must be evaluated to see if they are of sufficient seriousness to warrant a modification of the auditor's report.
- Carry out analytical review procedures (Chapter 12) on the financial statements including comparisons with previous periods, current year budgets and forecasts, etc. For example, gross profit ratios or liquidity ratios should be consistent with previous financial periods. Suitable benchmark data could also be used if possible.

The intention is that the results of analytical review should confirm the financial 'story' told by the accounts and the auditor's knowledge of any events during the financial year which may have affected the figures. For example, the company may have had to discount prices in the face of competition to maintain market share and this could be reflected in a reduced gross profit margin.

- Consider whether individual amounts shown in the accounts are compatible with each other and with comparative figures and whether they are consistent with previously reported management information, e.g. accounts, budgets, etc.

The auditors must read the whole of the annual report and accounts and check for consistency of reporting and that there are no anomalous or incorrect statements, e.g. if in the Chairman's Report it states that Revenues have increased by 5 per cent that this is reflected in the Statement of Comprehensive Income and is not a selective statement designed to present a better picture than is really the case. It may be necessary to rewrite such statements to ensure consistency of information.

Audit evidence

The procedures auditors should carry out in order to gather sufficient appropriate evidence require them to review the audit planning to ensure that it was properly carried out and that audit procedures were designed to produce sufficient, appropriate evidence to support the audit opinion.

They need to review all audit working papers to ensure that all audit procedures set out in the audit programme were carried out as required and that the results of those audit procedures were reviewed and the conclusions reached based on the audit checking work done are valid. They should review any points arising from the audit work and confirm whether or not they have been settled satisfactorily with management.

Clearly the auditors have to consider whether or not the going concern basis is appropriate based on the evidence gathered (Chapter 23) and they should also consider whether all necessary representations required from management have been received and properly minuted (Chapter 24) and whether they comprise sufficient, appropriate audit evidence to support the audit opinion where no corroborative evidence is available.

As part of the review the auditors will ensure all confirmations and evidence required from third parties (bank letters, solicitors' letters, etc.) have been received and constitute sufficient reliable evidence. They must review the outcome of the subsequent events review and ensure all outstanding issues have been cleared (Chapter 23).

Overall it is the role of the audit partner to decide if the amount of audit work carried out and the evidence gathered as a result of that work is sufficient to support the audit opinion. The partner should also consider whether any issues arising from the audit might warrant a second partner or **hot review** before signing the auditor's report. The file might be scheduled for a **cold review** after the audit is signed off so all checklists must be dated and signed and all documents filed correctly.

With regard to presentation and disclosure of the financial statements the auditors will:

- Consider if any conclusion that a reader might draw from a reading of the accounts would be justified and is consistent with the circumstances of the enterprise.
- Consider if the review has indicated that there are new factors which might alter the policies used or the presentation of the accounts and special attention needs to be paid to any going concern issues.
- Consider if all matters of importance have been disclosed by way of note if not by inclusion in the financial statements.
- Consider the form of the auditor's report and whether or not any qualification is required.

AUDITORS' DUTIES IN RESPECT OF COMPLIANCE WITH THE UK CORPORATE GOVERNANCE CODE

Here we will look specifically at the auditor's duties in considering whether or not the company has complied with the provisions of the UK Corporate Governance Code.

The requirements of the Code which are, broadly, relevant to the auditors can be summarized as follows.

Requirement for UK listed companies	Auditor requirements
Principles of good governance The directors have to disclose in a narrative statement in the Annual Report how they have applied the principles of good corporate governance.	Read only.
Statement of compliance with code provisions The directors must include in the annual report a statement as to whether or not they have complied throughout the period with the UK Corporate Governance Code provisions and if not, why not?	Review certain specific matters, especially the internal control report – and read the rest.
Directors' remuneration Inclusion in the Annual Report of a statement of directors' remuneration including details of the remuneration, pension contributions and benefits, etc. for each named director.	Audit and include in the audit report as if this was in the financial statements.
Going concern The directors must include in the annual report a statement that the business is a going concern with supporting assumptions or qualifications as necessary.	Review (see Chapter 23).

We will look at more detailed compliance provisions later in this book.

The auditor's duties are covered by ISA 720 Section A:

'The auditor's responsibilities relating to other information in documents containing audited financial information' and ISA 720 Section B – *'The auditor's statutory reporting responsibility in relation to Directors' Reports'*.

We will look at these in more detail in Chapter 26 but for now the requirements can be summarized as follows:

- The 'read only' requirement for other information.
- Any apparent inconsistencies or any apparent misstatements in the corporate governance statements should be resolved and the directors should amend the inconsistency.

If this does not happen then the auditors should:

- if the financial statements are incorrect, modify their report (Chapter 26)
- if the financial statements are correct and the other information is incorrect or inadequate, make a statement in the auditor's report. This statement is however not a qualification
- in extreme circumstances the auditors can withhold their report or resign from the engagement if possible

The auditors should obtain sufficient appropriate evidence to support any statements made in reports or summaries which are ancillary to the financial statements and the disclosures required by statute. These might take the form of:

- management reports
- financial summaries
- corporate governance statements
- operating reviews and other nonstatutory information

The auditors will apply the knowledge they have gained from their audit of the management information systems and the financial accounts themselves but additional information is often required. Appropriate evidence can be gained by the following procedures:

- reviewing the minutes of the meetings of the board and of relevant board committees (audit, nomination, remuneration, risk management, etc.)

- reviewing relevant supporting documents prepared for the board or board committees
- making enquiries of the directors and the company secretary
- attending meetings of the audit committee (or other committee) when the annual report and accounts and statements of compliance are considered and approved for submission to the board
- the auditors may ask for a Letter of Representation of any written or oral representations made in the course of the review (See Chapter 24)

If the auditors are not satisfied with the directors' compliance statement, they will include an explanatory comment in their Auditor's Report (See Chapter 26).

Directors' report on internal controls

Listed companies have to include, in their financial statements, a narrative report from the directors which:

- identifies the organization's business objectives
- identifies and assesses risks which threaten achievement of those objectives
- reports on the design and operation of controls to manage those risks
- reports on the process of monitoring and reviewing those controls to ensure they are operating correctly

We have covered the detail of risk identification and management and the whole system of internal controls earlier in this book – what we are concerned about now is simply the report the directors make.

ISA 720 requires the auditors only to read the report and comment on any inconsistencies *except that* part of the duties of the directors is to carry out a review of the internal controls and to report to the shareholders they have done so. The auditors have to verify that the directors have, in fact, carried out such a review.

The work the auditors carry out is to:

- enquire of the directors as to the process they use to carry out the review
- review the evidence gathered by the directors which they are going to use to support their statement to the shareholders and assess whether or not it is sufficient and appropriate
- match what the directors are saying with the evidence from other audit procedures and the auditor's own view of the internal control environment

If the auditors are not satisfied with the directors' disclosure, they will include an explanatory comment in their Auditor's Report (See Chapter 26).

DIRECTORS' REMUNERATION DISCLOSURE

The requirements of the Stock Exchange Listing Agreement go well beyond the requirements of the Companies Act insofar as the Listing Agreement requires full disclosure to be made of all amounts paid to or for the benefit of *named* directors. This includes salary, bonuses, pension contributions and benefits.

The auditor has to audit the required disclosure and should include this in their normal audit work and the Auditor's Report will include an opinion on the directors' remuneration statement.

For more detail on this see Chapter 26.

The final review is the last chance the auditors have to ensure that the financial statements really do present a true and fair view and that they have sufficient appropriate reliable evidence to support that opinion. Areas where audit work might have been skimped in order to reduce costs or simply through faith in the client may prove to be the audit firms' undoing if something goes wrong or if they become subject to an inspection by the regulators.

Some FRC compliance reports on audits of public interest are released. Poor reports can affect a firm's reputation and could impinge on its ability to retain or gain clients so it behoves auditors to get it right.

SUMMARY

- The final review is the last chance the auditors have to consider any issues arising from the audit before their report is signed.
- Preceding financial statements have a bearing on the current year's statements because they are the opening figures to the current year's financial statements, consistency of accounting policies is required and they are comparative figures.
- The Companies Act 2006 has requirements for comparative figures to be shown.
- The auditors have a duty towards these figures.
- Problems arise if the previous year's audit was performed by another firm or if the previous year's audit report was qualified.
- The review should be carried out and evidenced on the file.
- The final review should be carried out by the audit partner responsible for signing the auditor's report.
- The final review may reveal:
  - that all is well
  - that further audit evidence may be required in some areas
  - that amendment to the accounts may be desirable; the client should be requested to make any such amendment
  - that a modified or qualified audit report may be required
- The overall review of the financial statements is designed to confirm:
  - that the accounting policies used are appropriate and have been consistently applied
  - that the results etc. are consistent and conform to the auditor's knowledge of the enterprise
  - that disclosure and compliance with statutory and other regulations is complete
  - that the proposed audit opinion is appropriate

POINTS TO NOTE

- The final review is particularly important as the shareholders are not the only users of the financial statements and consideration has to be given to overall disclosure.
- The detail is still important but emphasis must be on the view given by the accounts which must be true in detail and fair in totality.
- The auditors, as ever, need to be aware of the requirements of the relevant reporting standards as to the disclosure in the accounts of comparative figures and ensure they are correctly disclosed.
- The comparative figures in respect of the Statement of Comprehensive Income should include in the continuing category only the results of those operations included in the current period's continuing operations. The auditors should verify that correct comparatives of continuing, discontinued and acquisition operations are shown.
- To some extent the auditing standards are not specific but use terms like 'the auditors should consider the implications for their report'. In essence the auditors will normally check only that the comparatives agree with previous year's accounts and consistent policies have been applied. The auditors must also bear in mind disclosures, acquisitions, prior year adjustments, etc.
- Problems arise when there are report qualifications in the previous year's audit report when the previous year's accounts were audited by predecessor auditors or were not audited, when the auditors come across material misstatements in the previous year's accounts or if the opening balances cannot be substantiated.

CASE STUDY

Angela Goodbody is a partner in Huppe & Downe and has come to the audit of E-musica Ltd to carry out a hot review of the audit which is in progress for the year ended 31 March 2X16.

E-musica have their own record label for dance and rap music, they sell musical equipment and control three recording studios.

She has noted comments on the audit file to the effect that:

(a) Inventory of CDs is valued at the lower of cost and net realizable value. Cost includes production overheads based on a global labour hour rate based on output in 2X15. Unsold stocks of CDs from before 31 March 2X15 are written down to £1.
(b) Advances to bands are written off as they are paid.
(c) Equipment is written off on the straight line basis over ten years.
(d) The freehold property is amortized over 30 years.

She has also noted that:

(a) The directors' report is optimistic about the current year and future year's success in selling dance and rap music despite the revival in live artists in which E-musica has no representation. They do not consider themselves a niche label, insisting that dance music is still mainstream.
(b) Inventories appear in the financial statements simply as 'Inventories £120 000'.
(c) The company rents out a leasehold property it owns but has no use for. The notes to the accounts say 'Gross rental income £4900.'
(d) No mention is made of the entry into liquidation on 13.3 2X16 of a wholesale music distributor who owed E-musica £142 000 on 13.3.2X16 and £71 000 on 31.3.2015. Angela knows of the liquidation as her boss is the liquidator.
(e) No mention is made of an action against a group for breach of copyright. The action was commenced on 31.3.2X15 and already uncharged legal fees of about £10 000 have been incurred.
(f) The list of directors shows 14 names and the remuneration breakdown only 13.
(g) The directors' report shows that Joe Gigli, a director, has 1000 shares in the company. She happened to note that the dividend paid to him indicated a shareholding substantially greater than that.

Discussion

– What should Angela do about these matters?

STUDENT SELF-TESTING QUESTIONS

Questions with answers apparent from the text

a) What is the auditor's interest in comparative figures?
b) What aspects of the comparative figures is the auditor responsible for?
c) What should the auditors do about previous accounts if they audited them and gave a clean report?
d) What additional work should be performed if the previous accounts were audited by another firm?
e) What paragraphs would appear in an auditor's report if there was an uncertainty in the opening balances on fixed assets?
f) What actions may be required as a result of a final review?
g) Distinguish analytical review from overall review of financial statements.

h) Why is it necessary to carry out a final review?

i) At what other stages of the audit are analytical procedures performed?

j) Distinguish between a hot review and a cold review.

k) Who would carry out a hot review and when?

l) List the necessary procedures which would take place at a final review.

EXAMINATION QUESTIONS

Your firm is the external auditor of Octavia Ltd (Octavia). The team conducting the audit for the year ended 31 December 2X16 has recently returned to the office following completion of the audit fieldwork. You are conducting your final review procedures. The audit file contains the following relevant information:

(i) Historically, Octavia's core business has been the manufacture of cast iron railings for supply to the construction industry. Over recent years Octavia has also developed a growing customer base for the manufacture of specialist cast metal products, an area where the company has established a recognized niche market.

In its core business, Octavia has seen its revenues decline by 30 per cent and its gross profit margins worsen over the last five years. These effects have been caused by increasing competition from overseas competitors who have lower operating costs. This has resulted in trading losses for Octavia in recent years, including the year ended 31 December 2X16.

Octavia underwent a major factory reorganization during the year to enable it to diversify its activities away from its core business and concentrate on its specialist cast metal business. This reorganization, which was completed in November 2X16, was partly funded by a large bank loan. The profit and cash-flow forecasts prepared by the company to support the application for bank finance indicated a return to profitability for the year ending 31 December 2X17.

(ii) During the year one of Octavia's major customers went into liquidation. Octavia has presented a claim to the customer's liquidator both for recovery of the outstanding debt and for the return of product which was supplied to the customer on a sale or return basis. Octavia has negotiated a sale of the returned product to another of its customers, dependent upon the successful recovery from the liquidator of the product in question. Initial indications from the liquidator are that 50 per cent of the outstanding debt is likely to be recovered by Octavia. The liquidator is also pursuing the recovery of the sale or return product on Octavia's behalf.

Octavia has included the receipt of this proportion of the debt, and the sale of the returned product to its alternative customer, within its cash-flow forecast.

(iii) Shortly before 31 December 2X16 the company's solicitors notified the company of an action being brought by a former employee who suffered a serious injury from an accident which occurred whilst operating heavy machinery in Octavia's factory. The former employee claims that the company did not have the necessary health and safety procedures in place to ensure that such an accident could not occur. The former employee is pressing for at least £750 000 in damages, an amount which is material to the financial statements of the company.

The directors of Octavia are adamant that the accident occurred due to the employee's own negligence and they maintain that their health and safety procedures are of an excellent standard. Octavia has to date had an exemplary accident record and previous health and safety inspections have raised no material issues. Octavia's solicitors have told the directors that the case is unlikely to come to court for at least 18 months. The company's insurance policy provides an element of cover for such situations. For these reasons the directors have not provided for the claim in the financial statements. However, a reference to the action has been made in the notes to the financial statements.

Required:

(a) Briefly set out the reasons why work performed by audit staff during an audit is reviewed by other more senior staff or the engagement partner.

(b) Identify the matters to which you would direct your attention during the subsequent events review in the audit of Octavia.

(c) Comment on the treatment in the financial statements of the matter referred to in (iii) above and indicate, with reasons, what kind of audit report modification, if any, may be appropriate. *(Students may wish to read Chapter 26 before tackling this part of the question.)*

(ICAEW)

SOURCES AND ADDITIONAL READING

Financial Reporting Council (2015) *FRS 102 The Financial Reporting Standard Applicable in the UK and Republic of Ireland*. London: Financial Reporting Council.

Financial Reporting Council (2016) *ISA 450 Evaluation of Misstatements Identified during the Audit*. London: Financial Reporting Council.

Financial Reporting Council (2016) *ISA 510 Initial Audit Engagements – Opening Balances*. London: Financial Reporting Council.

Financial Reporting Council (2016) *ISA 710 Comparative Information – Corresponding Figures and Comparative Financial Statements*. London: Financial Reporting Council.

CHAPTER 26
AUDITOR'S REPORTS TO SHAREHOLDERS

Learning Objectives

After studying the material in this chapter you should be able to:

- explain the form and content of the auditor's report

- understand the purpose of the Bannerman wording

- explain what is meant by a modified audit report

- explain how modified audit reports are worded

- understand the possible effect of a modified audit report on the entity

- understand the purpose of an emphasis of matter report

- explain the consequences of issuing an audit report knowing it to be false

INTRODUCTION

As we have seen from earlier chapters the auditor's primary task is to report to the shareholders on the truth and fairness of the financial statements prepared by the directors. At the end of the audit, when they have examined the organization, its records and its financial statements, the auditors produce a report addressed to the shareholders, in which they express their opinion of the truth and fairness, or otherwise, of the financial statements.

For the purposes of shareholder reporting it is reasonable for the auditor to assume that users of the financial statements are reasonably financially literate, in particular:

- that they have a reasonable knowledge of business and economic activities and accounting and have a willingness to study the information in the financial statements with reasonable diligence
- that they understand that the financial statements are prepared, presented and audited to levels of materiality i.e. that any errors or misstatements do not have a significant effect on the numbers or presentation
- that they recognize the uncertainties inherent in the measurement of amounts based on the use of estimates, judgement and the consideration of future events and
- that they are capable of making reasonable economic decisions on the basis of the information in the financial statements

As the auditor's report accompanies the audited financial statements, the users of the auditor's report are considered to be the same as the intended users of the financial statements.

REPORT ON THE DIRECTORS' RESPONSIBILITIES FOR THE FINANCIAL STATEMENTS

The director's responsibilities for the preparation of the financial statements must be clearly understood by a reader. These must be spelled out, in the case of listed companies often in a separate report, but a statement is also included as part of the Auditor's Report, as we will see later.

The reasons for this are:

- the readers of the accounts can have a clear understanding of what the directors are responsible for
- it also helps remind the directors of their responsibilities

Here is an example of some wording. Note that it includes references not only to the directors' responsibility for producing accounts but also responsibilities for:

- consideration of the company's ability to continue as a going concern – Chapter 23
- the directors' responsibilities to take reasonable steps to prevent fraud and other irregularities – Chapter 20

This wording is necessarily brief and is purely shown as an illustrative example. Interested readers will be able to find many real life examples from company websites for listed companies and other organizations.

EXAMPLE

Directors' responsibilities for the financial statements for a nonlisted company preparing its accounts under UK Generally Accepted Accounting Practice:

'The directors are responsible for preparing the Directors' Report and the financial statements in accordance with applicable law and regulations.

(Continued)

Company law requires the directors to prepare financial statements for each financial year.

Under that law the directors have elected to prepare the financial statements in accordance with United Kingdom Generally Accepted Accounting Practice (United Kingdom Accounting Standards and applicable law). Under company law the directors must not approve the financial statements unless they are satisfied that they give a true and fair view of the state of affairs of the company and of the profit or loss of the company for that period. In preparing these financial statements, the directors are required to:

- *select suitable accounting policies and then apply them consistently;*
- *make judgements and accounting estimates that are reasonable and prudent;*
- *state whether applicable UK Accounting Standards have been followed, subject to any material departures disclosed and explained in the financial statements;*
- *prepare the financial statements on the going concern basis unless it is inappropriate to presume that the company will continue in business.*

The directors are responsible for keeping adequate accounting records that are sufficient to show and explain the company's transactions and disclose with reasonable accuracy at any time the financial position of the company and enable them to ensure that the financial statements comply with the Companies Act 2006. They are also responsible for safeguarding the assets of the company and hence for take reasonable steps for the prevention and detection of fraud and other irregularities.'

AUDITOR'S RESPONSIBILITIES

The auditor's primary responsibilities are:

- To audit the financial statements. The auditors will give a **'true and fair'** report on these if they are of the opinion that they are free of material error or misstatement. There is an alternative form of words, more usually used in the case of public bodies such as Local Authorities and this is to state that the financial statements *'present fairly'* the financial position of the entity. Whichever form of words is to be used the principles are the same.
- To include in their opinion the compliance by the company with the provisions of the **Companies Act 2006** with regard to:
  - the maintenance of proper books and records and confirmation
  - the compliance of the financial statements with the underlying records
  - disclosure of directors' remuneration, and
  - whether or not they have received all the information and explanations they required.

The auditor's report negatively on these, i.e. they report only if they have anything to comment on regarding any of these issues:

- If it is a listed company – to review the company's compliance with the relevant parts of the UK Corporate Governance Code. Again, the auditors will report negatively on this – i.e. they will only report if the company has *not complied* with the provisions of the Code.
- To read the rest of the Annual Report, which they are not auditing, in order to ensure that it is consistent with the audited parts and does not give a misleading impression. The auditors, again, will report negatively, i.e. only if it is not consistent with the financial accounts.

BANNERMAN WORDING

In Chapter 29 we look at the question of the liability of auditors to third parties, that is to persons other than the shareholders to whom they report. This position is, broadly, regulated by common law and auditors rested for years under the protection of the decision in *Caparo Industries v Dickman and Touche Ross & Co (1990)* which, broadly, only made auditors liable to third parties of which they were actually aware at the time they signed the auditor's report.

The case of *Royal Bank of Scotland v Bannerman Johnstone Maclay (Scottish Court of Session) (2002)* has, however, led to cause for concern insofar as the audit profession appeared to have forgotten one third party who might have an investment in their client and of which they should be only too well aware, namely the bank. Since the Caparo judgment banks and other lenders have sought ways to establish that a direct relationship exists between themselves and their customers' auditors so as to entitle them to place reliance on audit reports and financial statements prepared for statutory purposes.

Lenders to an entity often use the audited accounts as an aid to lending decisions and the decision in Bannerman, although not binding in the UK, has led to the insertion in audit reports of a form of disclaimer. Following the decision in the Bannerman case, the Institute of Chartered Accountants in England & Wales (ICAEW) issued a technical release (Audit 01/03) which recommended that its members incorporate a disclaimer to third parties in their standard audit reports.

The wording of the disclaimer is as follows:

'This report is made solely to the company's members, as a body, in accordance with Chapter 3 of Part 16 of the Companies Act 2006. Our audit work has been undertaken so that we might state to the company's members those matters we are required to state to them in an auditor's report and for no other purpose. To the fullest extent permitted by law, we do not accept or assume responsibility to anyone other than the company and the company's members as a body, for our audit work, for this report, or for the opinions we have formed.'

The Association of Chartered Certified Accountants (ACCA) however took a different view. They felt that a disclaimer was not a proportionate response to the Bannerman decision as, essentially, there was nothing new within it which distinguished it from the law as established by Caparo.

They argued that, since Caparo, it has always been the case that professional advisers can assume a duty of care exists provided that proximity to a third party is established. Bannerman highlighted that proximity can exist even where the adviser has no actual knowledge (as opposed to constructive knowledge) that the third party intends to rely on the advice (although this aspect was not fully argued through by the court). The ACCA's argument is that the incorporation of a disclaimer as a standard feature of the audit report could have the effect of devaluing that report and could also cause problems for third parties and regulators and the inclusion of such blanket disclaimers and limitations on an audit report would not help encourage trust between the audit profession and investors.

The reason why auditors are being found negligent is primarily a failure to carry out their audit work in compliance with the ISAs. If the work was carried out with reasonable skill and care to a good professional standard the question of negligence could not arise.

The **Bannerman wording** has been tested in the courts in the case of *Barclays Bank plc v Grant Thornton LLP [2015] EWHC 320 (Comm)*. Barclays Bank brought an action against audit firm Grant Thornton with non-statutory audit reports prepared by Grant Thornton for their client Van Essen Hotels ('VEH'). The audit firm had a contractual relationship i.e. an Engagement Letter with Van Essen Hotels and not with Barclays. In this case the judge made the following points:

- Barclays was a sophisticated commercial party, used to reading accounts and audit reports.
- The disclaimers were clear and obvious on the face of the reports and therefore Barclays ought reasonably to have been aware of their existence – Grant Thornton could not anticipate that any competent banker would fail to read the first two paragraphs of a two-page report.
- Barclays did not engage or pay Grant Thornton for the reports yet it had engaged them directly before, both in relation to the review of the VEH group's affairs and in connection with the production of statutory reports for the purposes of a financial assistance 'whitewash'. In each of those engagements, Grant Thornton had limited its liability to Barclays. If the disclaimers in the non-statutory reports were struck down, Barclays would be in a better position than if it had entered into a direct engagement and paid for the relevant services since any such engagement would have contained a limitation of liability.
- Barclays could have taken steps to protect its own position by obtaining its own report via a direct engagement with Grant Thornton but it had chosen not to do so.

Accordingly, in the face of the express disclaimer, it was not enough to say that both Barclays and Grant Thornton expected Barclays to rely on the terms of the report for the purposes of the facility agreement. The reports told Barclays expressly that it relied on the reports at its own risk.

As a consequence of this decision audit firms appear to be able to rely on this disclaimer in the normal course of events but each case must be considered separately – it is not a blanket disclaimer.

The FRC, in their bulletin *Compendium of illustrative auditor's reports on United Kingdom private sector financial statements for periods commencing on or after 17 June 2016* issued in October 2016, which includes pro forma audit report wording, does not suggest any wording for a disclaimer of liability to third parties.

It may be appropriate for auditors to issue specific disclaimers where they are aware of a third party's interest in the accounts. For example, they may be made aware that a lender may rely on the audited accounts when considering an application for borrowings by the company. In this case it may be appropriate for there to be a specific disclaimer in the report to shareholders for this purpose and for the auditor to undertake a separate assurance assignment on behalf of the bank evidenced by a separate letter of engagement.

THE AUDITOR'S OPINION

The accounts presented to the shareholders at the AGM must include an **Auditor's Report**. Section 495 states:

(1) *A company's auditor must make a report to the company's members on all annual accounts of the company of which copies are during his tenure of office-*
   (a) *in the case of a private company, to be sent out to members …*
   (b) *in the case of a public company to be laid before the company in general meeting …*

(2) *The auditor's report must include-*
   (a) *an introduction identifying the annual accounts that are the subject of the audit and the financial reporting framework that has been applied in their preparation,*
   (b) *a description of the scope of the audit identifying the auditing standards in accordance with which the audit was conducted.*

(3) *The report must state whether in the auditor's opinion the annual accounts-*
   (a) *give a true and fair view-*
      (i) *in the case of an individual balance sheet, of the state of affairs of the company as at the end of the financial year,*
      (ii) *in the case of an individual profit and loss account, of the profit or loss of the company for the financial year,*
      (iii) *in the case of group accounts, of the state of affairs as at the end of the financial year, and the profit or loss for the financial year, of the undertakings included in the consolidation as a whole, so far as concerns members of the company.*
   (b) *have been properly prepared in accordance with the relevant financial reporting framework, and*
   (c) *have been properly prepared in accordance with the requirements of this Act.*

(4) *The auditor's report-*
   (a) *must be unqualified or qualified, and*
   (b) *must include reference to any matters to which the auditor wishes to draw attention by way of emphasis without qualifying the report.*

In addition to this Section 496 says:

'The auditor must state in his report on the company's annual accounts whether in his opinion the information given in the directors' report for the financial year for which the accounts are prepared is consistent with those accounts.'

Auditors, in their report, do not say that the financial statements *do* show a true and fair view; they can only say that *in their opinion* the financial statements show a true and fair view.

The reader or user of the financial statements will know from their knowledge of the auditing profession whether or not to rely on the auditor's opinion. If the auditors are known to be independent, honest and competent, then their opinion will be relied upon. This may seem an obvious statement but since the collapse of mega firm Arthur Andersen ('AA') after the huge frauds at Enron and WorldCom were exposed, both of which were AA clients, and the financial crash of 2007/8 involving banks and other financial institutions, the reputation of the audit profession as a whole and of individual firms in particular has become a serious issue for audit partners or directors and they are assiduous is ensuring that their firm and the profession remains free of any scandal or taint which might cause investors to doubt their integrity.

Thus ethical issues (Chapter 6) and quality control of audit work (Chapter 7) have, possibly, assumed a much greater significance than previously.

True and fair

The expression 'true and fair' is central to auditing and yet it is an abstraction whose meaning is far from clear.

As we will see, the Companies Act, 2006 states that every company Statement of Financial Position and Statement of Comprehensive Income must give a 'true and fair' view of the state of affairs and of the profit or loss of the company respectively, however, unhelpfully, it does not attempt to define what a 'true and fair view' might be.

Perhaps we can define what 'true and fair' might mean by explaining what it does *not* mean. It does *not* mean 'correct in all respects' or 'free of all errors' or 'absolutely right'.

Truth, for accountants, is not absolute – it is not as a scientist would measure it, i.e. a truth which is fixed and never changes.

'True', in this case, means true in accordance with the facts that pertain at the time, either at the accounting period end or at the time the Auditor's Report was signed. For example, the Statement of Financial Position records assets and liabilities at values which were considered to be true at the period end date. The day after the year end the values of those balances, or some of them, change.

The concept of truth also carries with it an understanding that the financial statements are prepared under those fundamental accounting concepts, such as the accruals basis, the historical cost convention, etc. which are implicit but not stated in the preparation of accounts as well as under all the accounting standards and rules which govern all the disclosures and presentation of the words and numbers.

'Fair' is an even more nebulous concept to grasp. Just as 'truth' carries with it the implication that the accounts have been prepared under generally understood accounting concepts and rules, so 'fair' implies that those rules have been applied impartially, objectively and with a view to presenting the facts of the financial situation of the company to readers of the accounts in as balanced, reasonable and unbiased way as is possible.

Whatever the meaning might be the starting point is that a 'true and fair view' requires compliance with the legislation and with all the applicable accounting standards. However, there is an *override* (called, rather obviously, the true and fair override) which we looked at in Chapter 4. If the auditors consider that compliance with any particular standard may result in a true and fair view *not* being shown by the financial statements they may ignore it, *but* they have to explain and justify why they have done so. As might be imagined, this is quite rare.

Basis of opinion

Having gathered all the necessary audit evidence and reviewed events since the Statement of Financial Position date the auditors are now in a position to come to an opinion on the financial statements.

There are several ISAs relating to the auditor's report. These are:

- *ISA 700 'Forming an Opinion and Reporting on Financial Statement's* which deals with an auditor's report which is unqualified or unmodified. This ISA states:

  The objectives of the auditor are:
  - *To form an opinion on the financial statements based on an evaluation of the conclusions drawn from the audit evidence obtained; and*
  - *To express clearly that opinion through a written report.*

- ISA 701 *Communicating Key Audit Matters in the Independent Auditor's Report* which deals with the requirement of the auditor to detail those matters which were of most significance in the audit of the financial statements. These are matters which required significant auditor attention during the audit and might include such issues as areas of significant risk, areas which are susceptible to **material uncertainty** or material areas where a significant amount of management and auditor judgement had to be exercised.

- ISA 705 *'Modifications to the opinion in the independent auditor's report'* which deals with modifications or qualifications to the auditor's opinion about a set of financial statements. If the auditor's opinion is that the accounts *do not* give a true and fair view, or that something has prevented them from forming an opinion on all or part of the financial statements, the client will receive a **modified audit report.**

- ISA 706 *Emphasis of matter paragraphs and other matter paragraphs in the Independent Auditor's Report* which deals with matters which may of relevance in terms of a reader's understanding of the financial statements but are not so significant as to be described as a Key Audit Matters under ISA 701.

- ISA 570 *Going Concern which* deals with the fundamental accounting concept of the financial statements being prepared on a going concern basis i.e. that the company or entity will be able to continue in substantially the same way for the foreseeable future, i.e. the next twelve months or so. We looked at this in Chapter 23.

We will deal with each of these in turn with particular reference to Key Audit Matters under ISA 701 and the forms of modified audit report which we will look at later, but first we will look in more detail at the contents of an unmodified auditor's report in particular:

- the form and content of an unmodified report; and
- when a modified audit report is appropriate and what form the wording would take.

GOING CONCERN

We looked at the concept of Going Concern in Chapter 23 so it's not necessary to repeat the key points here except that the directors' approach to going concern issues is a key aspect of audit reporting and auditors have to have addressed the issues in order to be able to report. It is a specific requirement of the Auditor's Report format that going concern issues are mentioned, in particular the question of the disclosures made by the directors in the financial statements.

KEY AUDIT MATTERS

This section applies to listed companies and public sector bodies but is included here for completeness as audit firms can include such a section in their Auditor's Report if they feel it is appropriate. For example, if a large unlisted entity has a significant number of shareholders who take no part in the running of the business this kind of section might be of relevance to them.

These matters may be technically complex accounting issues such as the carrying value of goodwill, bases of revenue recognition in certain industries such as telecoms or IT contracts, estimates of fair value of reserves for extraction companies and suchlike difficult issues. Whilst readers of the report can be assumed to be reasonably financially literate it is important that the issues are set out in a form and using language which can be understood by a reader of the financial statements so the use of jargon and unexplained acronyms should be avoided wherever possible.

ISA 701 requires the auditor to describe each key audit matter, include a reference to related financial statement disclosures (if any) and address why the matter was considered to be one of most significant in the audit.

The auditors must then go on to explain what they did, in terms of audit procedures, to address the issue: how they were able to gather sufficient appropriate audit evidence to satisfy themselves that, although the matter was a key audit matter and inevitably therefore there was some measure of uncertainty about it (e.g. it included estimates or significant assumptions made by management), they were able to eventually satisfy themselves that the reporting was acceptable. They have to explain why the matter was not one which contained such a level of uncertainty as to require the Auditor's Report to be modified.

While the amount of detail is a matter of professional judgement, the ISA notes that this might include:

- aspects of the auditor's approach that were most relevant to the matter or specific to the assessed risk for example the auditor's approach to assessed risk
- a brief overview of any audit procedures that were performed and an indication of the outcome of those procedures
- key observations with respect to the issue in question and how the auditors came to the conclusions that they did concerning the matter in question

One difficult area here is in connection with going concern. (Chapter 23). Where conditions exist which cause the auditors to have doubts about the ability of the company to continue as a going concern but there is no specific material uncertainty i.e. nothing which is specific enough to require a disclosure under the Going Concern section of the Auditor's Report, the auditors should disclose the situation as a Key Audit Matter. Examples of such matters are significant operating losses, doubts about borrowings or loans, etc.

The auditors have to decide whether the issues they have around going concern represent a material uncertainty and thus have to be separately disclosed or are not quite specific enough, but nonetheless serious, so are disclosed as a Key Audit Matter.

BASIS OF OPINION

As we have seen it is the auditor's responsibility to gather sufficient, reliable, appropriate evidence to support their opinion on the financial statements as a whole. They plan the audit, gather the evidence, make judgements about the judgements that management have made, review errors or misstatements uncovered by the audit process and generally come to conclusion as to whether or not the financial statements present a true and fair view of the financial position of the entity at the end of the reporting period.

In arriving at their opinion the auditors have to come to a conclusion as to whether they have received reasonable assurance about whether the financial statements are free from any material misstatement, whether due to fraud or error. In coming to that conclusion they must decide:

- whether sufficient appropriate evidence has been gathered to support their opinion (Chapter 11)
- whether any uncorrected misstatements are material
- whether the financial statements have been prepared in all material respects with the appropriate financial framework be that UK GAAP or IFRS (Chapter 4)
- whether all significant accounting policies have been properly disclosed and are in accordance with the framework and appropriate to the entity being reported on; bear in mind, for example, that public sector bodies such as Local Authorities have some different reporting rules to companies so accounting policies may differ
- where management have made accounting estimates that these are reasonable (Chapter 16)
- that the financial statements include all disclosures necessary for a proper understanding of them by a user and that any terminology used is appropriate including the disclosure of the financial reporting framework used
- that the information in the financial statements is comparable with that of previous periods, is relevant, reliable and understandable; this requires the auditor to ensure that the information included in the financial statements is complete and classified appropriately and that nothing has been included which might detract from or obscure a proper understanding of the accounts

Once all this is considered the auditor should look at the financial statements as a whole to consider whether the presentation of them in terms of their structure and content represents disclosure of the underlying transactions and events in a fair way.

WHEN IS AN UNMODIFIED REPORT APPROPRIATE?

The opinion given in the report is the summary of all the auditor's work and planning.

It means that the auditors agree that the financial statements are:

- in accordance with the books and records of the entity
- that those books and records include all the transactions for the accounting period
- that the financial statements comply with the appropriate financial reporting framework
- that the transactions have been properly disclosed in accordance with that framework and are free from material errors or misstatements
- that the Statement of Financial Position is a fair reflection of the assets and liabilities of the entity at a particular point in time
- that all the assumptions used in preparing the financial statements are reasonable and that all estimates used are fair and capable of explanation
- that the auditors have been able to obtain sufficient reliable evidence in respect of all aspects of the financial statements
- that the going concern basis on which the financial statements have been prepared is valid and appropriate and that the auditors have been able to satisfy themselves that this is so
- that there are no events which might affect the presentation of the financial statements that the auditors are not aware of
- if there are any errors or misstatements, they are not material

In other words, the audit has been completed satisfactorily and the auditors have been able to gather all the evidence they need to support their unqualified opinion.

It is not sufficient for the auditors to give an unmodified opinion solely because the financial statements have been prepared in accordance with the appropriate financial reporting framework. This is not about the directors preparing accounts in such a way as to comply with the appropriate technical reporting standards – it is about the auditors being able to say that the financial statements represent a true and fair view of what happened financially to the entity during the accounting period. It is less about technical compliance with accounting rules and more about truth and fairness.

CONTENTS OF AN AUDITOR'S REPORT

The auditor's report to the shareholders is a detailed document which should leave the reader in no doubt as to the way in which the audit has been carried out and the reasoning behind the opinion that has been reached.

Note that the company's annual report and accounts often contain, in addition to the financial statements and the auditor's report, some additional statements such as:

- financial review;
- environmental and social review;
- statement of principal risks and uncertainties;
- corporate governance report; and
- director's remuneration report.

The auditors *don't* have to report on these and will specifically exclude them from their report. Auditors do, however, have to ensure that there are no material misstatements or inconsistencies between the other information shown in the **annual report** and the financial statements. Auditors thus have to read and consider all the other pages in the annual report and ensure that statements made in those pages are consistent with the financial statements. If they are not and the directors refuse to amend them the auditors could modify their audit report to draw attention to the matter if they feel the issue is materially misleading.

Figure 26.1 sets out what an unqualified report contains together with a form of words which indicates what a finished audit report might look like. The report must contain all the elements prescribed in ISA 700 and in the order listed in the ISA. Each section has to have a header as described in the ISA. Note that this is the minimum requirement for an auditors' report and other sections such as Key Audit Matters may well be inserted if the auditors feel it appropriate.

FIGURE 26.1 Contents of the auditors' report

	SAMPLE WORDING
A clear heading including the word 'independent'	'Independent auditors' report'
It should be addressed to the shareholders	'to the members of XYZ Limited'
It should set out what is comprised in the financial statements, i.e. what has been audited	We have audited the financial statements of (name of entity) for the year ended 31ˢᵗ December 2X16. . . which comprise the Statement of Comprehensive Income, the Statement of Financial Position, [*the Cash Flow Statement, the Statement of Total Recognized Gains and Losses, the Reconciliation of Movements in Shareholders' Funds etc. if applicable*] and the related notes.
Explain the basis on which the accounts have been prepared	The financial reporting framework that has been applied in their preparation is applicable law and United Kingdom Accounting Standards (United Kingdom Generally Accepted Accounting Practice).
The responsibilities of the directors should be set out	As explained more fully in the Directors' Responsibilities Statement on page . . . the directors are responsible for the preparation of the financial statements and for being satisfied that they give a true and fair view.
It sets out the responsibilities of the auditors	Our responsibility is to audit and express an opinion on the financial statements in accordance with applicable law and International Standards on Auditing (UK and Ireland). Those standards require us to comply with the Financial Reporting Council's ethical standards for auditors. *Author's note. The auditors might include a disclaimer here (known as the Bannerman wording (see above)) to the effect that they are only reporting to the shareholders and accept no responsibility towards any third party.*
It sets out the scope of the audit. It also sets out the level of evidence required, i.e. enough to give 'reasonable assurance'	An audit involves obtaining evidence about the amounts and disclosures in the financial statements sufficient to give reasonable assurance that the financial statements are free from material misstatement, whether caused by fraud or error. This includes an assessment of: • whether the accounting policies are appropriate to the company's circumstances and have been consistently applied and adequately disclosed. • the reasonableness of significant accounting estimates made by the directors. • the overall presentation of the financial statements.
In includes a statement about the auditors' duties regarding the other information in the annual report and accounts which is not comprised in the statutory financial accounts	In addition we read all the financial and non-financial information in the (annual report and accounts) to identify material inconsistencies with the audited financial statements. If we become aware of any apparent material misstatements or inconsistencies we consider the implications for our report.
It gives the auditors' opinion (in this case an unqualified one) on the financial statements	In our opinion the financial statements: • give a true and fair view of the state of the company's affairs as at . . . and of its profit (or loss) for the year then ended. • have been properly prepared in accordance with United Kingdom Generally Accepted Accounting Practice and • have been prepared in accordance with the requirements of the Companies Act 2006.

(Continues)

FIGURE 26.1 Contents of the auditors' report (Continued)

	SAMPLE WORDING
It also gives an opinion on the consistency of the information in the Directors' Report with the financial statements	In our opinion the information given in the Directors' Report for the financial year for which the financial statements are prepared is consistent with the financial statements.
The Auditors are also required by the Companies Act to confirm that the company has kept adequate accounting records and that the auditors have had full access to them. This is done by means of a negative report, i.e. 'we have nothing to report about . . .'	We have nothing to report in respect of the following matters where the Companies Act 2006 requires us to report to you if, in our opinion: • adequate accounting records have not been kept, or returns adequate for our audit have not been received from branches not visited by us, or • the financial statements are not in agreement with the accounting records and returns, or • certain disclosures of directors' remuneration specified by law are not made, or • we have not received all the information and explanations we require for our audit.
It must be signed by the auditor personally and give the name of the audit partner signing. It must give the address of the auditor's office and be dated	*John Smith (Senior statutory auditor)* *Date* *for and on behalf of Tickett & Run, LLP, Statutory Auditor* *[Address]*

Figure 26.2 is an example of an audit report. Note the order in which the relevant paragraphs appear is in accordance with ISA 700. This example includes additional reporting such as the Bannerman Wording and Key Audit Matters for illustration.

FIGURE 26.2 Independent Auditor's Report to the Members of XYZ Limited

Opinion
We have audited the financial statements of XYZ Limited for the year ended 31 December 2X16 which comprise the Statement of Comprehensive Income, Statement of Financial Position, Statement of Changes in Equity, Statement of Cash Flows and notes to the financial statements, including a summary of significant accounting policies and other explanatory information. The financial reporting framework that has been applied in their preparation is applicable law and United Kingdom Accounting Standards, including Financial Reporting Standard 102 *The Financial Reporting Standard Applicable in the UK and Republic of Ireland* (United Kingdom Generally Accepted Accounting Practice).

In our opinion, the financial statements:

● give a true and fair view of the state of the company's affairs as at 31 December 2X16 and of the profit for the accounting period then ended;

● have been properly prepared in accordance with United Kingdom Generally Accepted Accounting Practice;

● have been prepared in accordance with the requirements of the Companies Act 2006.

Basis for opinion
We conducted our audit in accordance with International Standards on Auditing (UK) (ISAs (UK)) and applicable law. Our responsibilities under those standards are further described in the Auditor's Responsibilities for the Audit of the Financial Statements section of our report. We are independent of the company in accordance with the ethical requirements that are relevant to our audit of the financial statements in the UK, including the Financial Reporting Council's Ethical Standard, and we have fulfilled our other ethical responsibilities in accordance with these requirements.
    We believe that the audit evidence we have obtained is sufficient and appropriate to provide a basis for our opinion.

Disclaimer of Opinion
This report is made solely to the company's members, as a body, in accordance with Chapter 3 of Part 16 of the Companies Act 2006. Our audit work has been undertaken so that we might state to the company's members those

matters we are required to state to them in an Auditor's Report and for no other purpose. To the fullest extent permitted by law, we do not accept or assume responsibility to anyone other than the company and the company's members as a body, for our audit work, for this report, or for the opinions we have formed.

Conclusions relating to going concern

We have nothing to report in respect of the following matters in relation to which the ISAs (UK) require us to report to you where:

- the directors' use of the going concern basis of accounting in the preparation of the financial statements is not appropriate; or

- the directors have not disclosed in the financial statements any identified material uncertainties that may cast significant doubt about the company's ability to continue to adopt the going concern basis of accounting for a period of at least twelve months from the date when the financial statements are authorized for issue.

Key Audit Matters *(Mandatory for listed companies but can be included if appropriate)*

Key Audit Matters are those matters that, in our professional judgement were of most significance in our audit of the financial statements of the current period. These matters were addressed in the context of our audit of the financial statements as a whole, and in forming our opinion thereon, and we do not provide a separate opinion on these matters.

[*In this section the auditors should set out any matters which were of most significance in the audit of the financial statements. These might include such issues as*

- *areas of significant risk,*
- *areas which are susceptible to material uncertainty or*
- *material areas where a significant amount of management and auditor judgement had to be exercised*

The auditors should make reference to why this is a Key Audit Matter, what audit work they have performed in connection with it,its significance to an understanding of the financial statements and why the auditors came to the conclusions they did in connection with the matters in question.

Other information

The directors are responsible for the other information. The other information comprises the information included in the annual report, other than the financial statements and our auditor's report thereon. Our opinion on the financial statements does not cover the other information and, except to the extent otherwise explicitly stated in our report, we do not express any form of assurance thereon.

In connection with our audit of the financial statements, our responsibility is to read the other information and, in doing so, consider whether the other information is materially inconsistent with the financial statements or our knowledge obtained in the course of the audit or otherwise appears to be materially misstated. If we identify such material inconsistencies or apparent material misstatements, we are required to determine whether there is a material misstatement in the financial statements or a material misstatement of the other information. If, based on the work we have performed, we conclude that there is a material misstatement of this other information, we are required to report that fact.

We have nothing to report in this regard.

Responsibilities of Management and those charged with governance for the Financial Statements

As explained more fully in the Directors' Responsibilities Statement [set out on page ...], the directors are responsible for the preparation and fair presentation of the financial statements and for being satisfied that they give a true and fair view, and for such internal control as the directors determine is necessary to enable the preparation of financial statements that are free from material misstatement, whether due to fraud or error.

In preparing the financial statements, the directors are responsible for assessing the company's ability to continue as a going concern, disclosing, as applicable, matters related to going concern and using the going concern basis of accounting unless the directors either intend to liquidate the company or to cease operations, or have no realistic alternative but to do so.

Auditor's responsibilities for the audit of the financial statements

Our objectives are to obtain reasonable assurance about whether the financial statements as a whole are free from material misstatement, whether due to fraud or error, and to issue an auditor's report that includes our opinion. Reasonable assurance is a high level of assurance, but is not a guarantee that an audit conducted in accordance with ISAs (UK) will always detect a material misstatement when it exists. Misstatements can arise from fraud or error and are considered material if, individually or in the aggregate, they could reasonably be expected to influence the economic decisions of users taken on the basis of these financial statements.

(Continues)

FIGURE 26.2 (Continued)

As part of an audit in accordance with ISAs (UK), we exercise professional judgement and maintain professional scepticism throughout the audit. We also:

- Identify and assess the risks of material misstatement of the financial statements, whether due to fraud or error, design and perform audit procedures responsive to those risks, and obtain audit evidence that is sufficient and appropriate to provide a basis for our opinion. The risk of not detecting a material misstatement resulting from fraud is higher than for one resulting from error, as fraud may involve collusion, forgery, intentional omissions, misrepresentations, or the override of internal control.

- Obtain an understanding of internal control relevant to the audit in order to design audit procedures that are appropriate in the circumstances, but not for the purpose of expressing an opinion on the effectiveness of the company's internal control.

- Evaluate the appropriateness of accounting policies used and the reasonableness of accounting estimates and related disclosures made by the directors

- Conclude on the appropriateness of the directors' use of the going concern basis of accounting and, based on the audit evidence obtained, whether a material uncertainty exists related to events or conditions that may cast significant doubt on the company's ability to continue as a going concern. If we conclude that a material uncertainty exists we are required to draw attention in our auditor's report to the related disclosures in the financial statements or, if such disclosures are inadequate, to modify our opinion. Our conclusions are based on the audit evidence obtained up to the date of our auditor's report. However, future events or conditions may cause the company to cease to continue as a going concern.

- Evaluate the overall presentation, structure and content of the financial statements, including the disclosures, and whether the financial statements represent the underlying transactions and events in a manner that achieves fair presentation.

- Obtain sufficient appropriate audit evidence regarding the financial information of the entities or business activities within the company to express an opinion on the financial statements. We are responsible for the direction, supervision and performance of the audit. We remain solely responsible for our audit opinion.

We communicate with those charged with governance regarding, among other matters, the planned scope and timing of the audit and significant audit findings, including any significant deficiencies in internal control that we identify during our audit.

Opinions on other matters prescribed by the Companies Act 2006
In our opinion, based on the work undertaken in the course of the audit:

- the information given in the strategic report and the directors' report for the financial year for which the financial statements are prepared is consistent with the financial statements; and

- the strategic report and the directors' report have been prepared in accordance with applicable legal requirements.

Matters on which we are required to report by exception
In the light of the knowledge and understanding of the company and its environment obtained in the course of the audit, we have not identified material misstatements in the strategic report or the directors' report.

We have nothing to report in respect of the following matters in relation to which the Companies Act 2006 requires us to report to you if, in our opinion:

- adequate accounting records have not been kept by the company, or returns adequate for our audit have not been received from branches not visited by us; or

- the company financial statements are not in agreement with the accounting records and returns; or

- certain disclosures of directors' remuneration specified by law are not made; or

- we have not received all the information and explanations we require for our audit.

[*Signature*]

John Smith (Senior Statutory Auditor)

For and on behalf of ABC LLP, Statutory Auditor

[*Address*]

[*Date the report was signed*]

ADDITIONAL REPORTING FOR LISTED COMPANIES

There are some additional reporting requirements for listed companies in addition to those included in the example Auditor's Report shown above.

This can make these reports extremely long so in the case of listed entities several sections of the Auditor's Report may be hived off into subsidiary reports and merely referred to in the main report. An example of this would be the 'Auditor's responsibilities for the audit of the financial statements' which is often shown separately.

In addition to the main sections included above there are some additional requirements as follows:

1   Statement of communication with those charged with governance

There should be a separate note concerning the nature of the communications with those charged with governance i.e. in most cases the directors through the medium of an Audit Committee. Below is some sample wording (Figure 26.3).

2   The Directors' Remuneration Report

Under the Companies Act 2006 in Section 420 the directors of listed companies must prepare a Directors' Remuneration Report for each financial year of a company. The auditors must, in their Auditor's Report:

● report to the company's members on the auditable part of the directors' remuneration report; and

● state whether in the auditor's opinion that part of the directors' remuneration report has been properly prepared in accordance with this Act.

FIGURE 26.3 **Communication with those charged with governance**

We provide those charged with governance with a statement that we have complied with relevant ethical requirements regarding independence and we communicate with them all relationships and other matters that may reasonably be thought to bear on our independence, and, where applicable, related safeguards.

From the matters communicated with those charged with governance, we determine those matters that are of most significance in the audit of the financial statements of the current period and are therefore Key Audit Matters. We have described these matters in this report. In extremely rare circumstances law or regulation precludes public disclosure about the matter or we determine that a matter should not be communicated in the auditor's report because the adverse consequences of doing so would reasonably be expected to outweigh the public interest benefits of such communication.

The Companies Act 2006 also requires the auditors of a listed company to form an opinion as to whether the auditable part of the company's directors' remuneration report is in agreement with the underlying accounting records. If the auditor is of the opinion that the auditable part of the report is not in agreement with the accounting records the auditor is required to state that fact in the auditor's report. Further if the information forming the auditable part of the directors' remuneration report has not been properly prepared the auditor is required to include in the auditor's report, so far as the auditor is reasonably able to do so, a statement giving the required information.

The auditable part of the report is set out in Part 3 Schedule 8 of The Large and Medium Sized Companies and Groups (Accounts and Reports) Regulations 2008, a statutory instrument clarifying aspects of the form and content of company accounts. Part 3 outlines the auditable part of the Directors' Remuneration report which is basically the total amount of each director's emoluments and compensation in the relevant financial year including bonuses, benefits and compensation for loss of office.

Additional reporting requirements for PIEs

For audits of financial statements of public interest entities (PIEs), the auditor's report also has to:

(a)   state by whom or through which body the auditors were appointed;

(b)   indicate the date of the appointment and the period of total uninterrupted engagement including previous renewals and reappointments of the firm;

(c)   explain to what extent the audit was considered capable of detecting irregularities, including fraud;

(d)   confirm that the audit opinion is consistent with the additional report to the Audit Committee;

(e)   declare that the non-audit services prohibited by the FRC's Ethical Standard were not provided and that the firm remained independent of the entity in conducting the audit; and

(f)   indicate any services, in addition to the audit, which were provided by the firm to the entity and any controlled undertakings which have not been disclosed in the annual report or financial statements.

The FRC has included, in ISA 700, an example of an audit report for the consolidated financial statements, i.e. those of a holding company and its subsidiaries collectively, of a listed entity. Students can access this from the FRC website.

MODIFIED AUDIT REPORTS

In cases where:

- the auditors consider the financial statements to be materially misstated, i.e. they are not free from material error or misstatement, or
- the auditors have had problems gathering the evidence they need.

then the auditors may have to issue a form of modified or **qualified auditor's report**.

It is important that students understand that auditors *do not* have the power to insist that the financial statements are amended for any errors or omissions that have been found during the course of the audit. The financial statements are the responsibility of the directors and the auditors have no authority to overrule them when it comes to the content.

What the auditors can do is use their auditor's report to tell the shareholders of the company what they have discovered and to express their opinion on the truth and fairness of the financial statements.

Going Concern

As we saw in Chapter 23 the use of Going Concern is a fundamental accounting concept and is key to the proper presentation of the financial statements. If the audited entity is definitely not a going concern all aspects of the financial statements must be changed to, effectively, show the results on a 'break up' basis.

However, there may be situations where there is a material uncertainty as to whether the entity can continue as a going concern or not. This doubt is not sufficient to change the going concern assumption on which the accounts have been prepared but it is sufficient to make the auditors doubt whether or not it can continue to survive in its present form for the foreseeable future.

If a material uncertainty exists, the directors must make a full disclosure of it in the financial statements. If they do so and the auditors are happy with what they have disclosed the auditors will make reference to that disclosure in a paragraph to the Auditor's Report headed '*Material uncertainty related to going concern*'. This will obviously substitute for the paragraph headed '*Conclusions relating to going concern*'.

In this paragraph the auditors will refer to the disclosures made by the directors and comment that a material uncertainty exists. They will also state that they have not modified their audit report. This is because the directors have disclosed the uncertainty so the shareholders are fully informed of the situation.

An example of suitable wording is shown in Figure 26.4.

FIGURE 26.4 Material uncertainty related to going concern

We draw attention to Note 23 of the Financial Statements. This states that the company has incurred net losses of £2.4m during the year ended 31 December 2X16. At that date the company's current liabilities exceeded its total assets by £1.1m. As stated in Note 23 these conditions together with certain other matters set out in that note indicate that a material uncertainty exists which may cast doubt on the company's ability to continue as a going concern. We have not modified our Auditors' Opinion in respect of this matter.

If the directors had not made any disclosures but the auditors had established that a material uncertainty existed, then they would have to modify their report and give an adverse opinion (See below).

The problem lies where there is a middle ground i.e. that the auditors feel that there is uncertainty as to the future of the entity but there is not specific material uncertainty and no disclosure by the directors. In this case they can disclose the position as a Key Audit Matter (see below) with a full explanation so that the shareholders are aware of the situation. Again the auditors would not modify their report.

Key Audit Matters

As we saw above ISA 701 required disclosure of Key Audit Matters, i.e. those which were of most significance in the audit of the financial statements. These are matters which have been communicated to the directors and, no doubt, discussed at length during the audit.

The important point here is that something disclosed as a Key Audit Matter has, essentially been resolved and is not therefore something which would form the basis of a modified report. An example of a KAM disclosure is shown below (Figure 26.5).

FIGURE 26.5 **KAMs and modified audit reports**

Example – alternative scenarios

The directors of a building company have several major contracts in progress and, under the accounting rules, an estimate of the possibility of a loss on any of the contracts has to considered and, if necessary, provided for in order to reduce the value of Inventory Work in Progress to Estimated Realisable Value. The amounts involved are material.

Scenario one – the auditors review the estimates made by the directors, review the available evidence and consider that the estimates for future losses are reasonable in the circumstances. This is a KAM, would be reported as such with details of the issue involved, the audit work carried out, and the conclusion.

Scenario two – the directors don't make any provision claiming all the contracts will make a profit, the auditors review the available evidence and come to a different conclusion, i.e. that several of the contracts are likely to make losses which should be provided for and the figures are material. The directors disagree and refuse to amend the financial statements. In this case the figures are material so the auditors must issue a modified audit report and not report the details as a KAM.

The same issue cannot be both a KAM and the cause of a modified report.

Effect of a modified audit report

Auditors generally feel that modifying their report is a last resort.

In practice they will discuss these issues with the client's management at some length in order to avoid having to issue a modified report. In most cases the directors are prepared to adjust the financial statements for any material errors and omissions which the auditors have brought to their attention as they are keen for the accounts to be as accurate as possible.

They will also be aware that a modified report can have serious consequences for the company as it could:

- affect the shareholder's confidence in the company and its management
- discourage potential investors
- affect the willingness of lenders to continue offering a facility to the company
- affect the company's creditworthiness with its suppliers

However, if the auditors feel that a modified opinion is appropriate they must be able to justify the basis for the qualification and fully explain this in the audit report. The auditors must use their professional judgement to decide how serious the issues involved are. This will then influence precisely which form of qualification will be included in the audit report.

What they have to decide is how seriously the issue, or issues, affects the truth and fairness of the financial statements. If the issue is so significant that the accounts presented by the directors clearly do not show a true and fair view, then the issue is said to be '**pervasive**'.

If, however, the issue is not detrimental to the accounts as a whole, but affects only part of them it is said to be 'material but not pervasive'. Clearly any issue which has such an effect on the accounts will be material, but in this case only part of the accounts is affected and the rest will be 'true and fair'.

Under ISA 705 '*Modifications to the opinion in the independent auditor's report*' the auditor's report is considered to be modified in the following situations:

- a partially qualified opinion relating to a material issue
- a disclaimer of opinion, where the auditor refuses to express an opinion on the financial statements
- an adverse opinion where the auditor considers that the financial statements contain material errors or misstatements of such significance that the auditors are of the opinion that the financial statements do not present a true and fair view; this, of course, puts them in dispute with the directors who, presumably, have presented the auditors with financial statements which they consider to be true and fair but which the auditors do not

Figure 26.6 summarizes the position which students should familiarize themselves with. Let us look at these in more detail.

FIGURE 26.6 Audit report modification

Audit issue	Material and pervasive	Material but not pervasive
Financial statements are materially misstated	Adverse opinion	Qualified opinion – 'Except for'
Inability to obtain sufficient appropriate audit evidence	Disclaimer of opinion	Qualified opinion – 'Except for'

Qualified 'except for' opinion

The issue is material but not to the extent that the financial statements no longer give a true and fair view. In this case the issue is not so pervasive or material so as to require the auditors to disclaim an opinion or to give an adverse opinion but does require the auditor to draw the attention of readers of the accounts to the issue which they have been unable to resolve.

An 'except for' opinion is used when there is:

- a minor limitation of audit scope, i.e. the auditors have been prevented from obtaining the evidence they need in one area of the financial statements; and
- a disagreement about one particular aspect of the financial statements which is material but not to the extent that it invalidates the whole of the accounts.

Note however that the auditors may have more than one issue which, individually, might result in an 'except for' qualification. If this is the case they must consider whether, *collectively*, the issues become pervasive enough for the auditors either to decline to express an opinion or to issue an adverse opinion. In this case they must consider the questions raised in their final accounts review, particularly the question of uncorrected misstatements which we looked at in Chapter 25.

Disclaimer of opinion

The auditor's work has been limited either by the management or by lack of opportunity so they were not able to gather all the evidence they require. In order to issue a disclaimer, the auditors must have been unable to gather sufficient, appropriate evidence in order to support their opinion, either of the financial statements as a whole or of such a material or fundamental part of the financial statements, that to issue any other opinion would be unsupportable.

Adverse opinion

The issue is so material, involving significant uncertainties or lack of disclosure that it affects the truth and fairness of the financial statements as a whole.

Note that the auditors must make all reasonable efforts to find the evidence they need before issuing a modified report. This will include discussing the situation with directors and staff and seeking all alternative means to gather evidence suitable for their purposes. A modified audit report is very much a last resort.

There are numerous examples, many in ISA 705 itself, of where auditors might consider various forms of modification appropriate so it is impossible to list them all. Figure 26.7 contains some examples as guidance for students.

FIGURE 26.7 Illustrations of situations where modified audit reports may be appropriate

Wording of report	Example of situation where it might apply
'Except for' – significant uncertainty – issues are material but not pervasive	• Inadequate provision for doubtful debts. • Disagreement over the value of some part of inventories, e.g. obsolete inventories still valued at cost instead of scrap value. • Poor disclosure in the accounts of going concern problems.
'Except for' – inability to obtain sufficient, reliable evidence	• Limited evidence available for cash purchases. • Some cash sales records lost due to accidental flooding. • Cash flow statements only prepared for nine months after the year end so full consideration of going concern issues not possible.
Disclaimer of opinion – lack of sufficient, reliable evidence	• Appointed as auditors after year end and unable to attend inventory count where inventories are material item. • Records lost due to natural disaster outside entity's control. • Records taken by government agency and not returned. • Directors deny access to information regarding significant claims against the company. • No cash flow forecasts or cash budgets prepared so the going concern situation cannot be considered.
Adverse opinion	• Failure to comply with Companies Act 2006, accounting standards or UK GAAP without an acceptable reason. • Significant uncertainties regarding the existence, ownership valuation or recording of assets and liabilities to a material extent, e.g. failure to provide for material losses on long-term contracts. • Significant concern about the company's ability to continue as a going concern and the accounts have been prepared on a going concern basis.

SAMPLE WORDING OF MODIFIED AUDIT REPORTS

The wording of auditor's reports must be as clear and precise as possible ensuring that the reader is in no doubt as to why a qualification has been necessary. Whatever the basis of their qualification the auditors should always:

- explain the facts of the disagreement;
- detail the implications to the financial statements, and
- where possible quantify the financial effect.

For simplicity, and because students will not be asked to write an auditor's report, we have confined the examples shown below to the significant areas where auditors might issue a modified report, including going concern issues. We have included some sample wording to illustrate how a modified audit report might be drafted based on the examples in ISA 705 *Modifications to the Opinion in the Independent Auditor's Report*.

For simplicity we have only included one example of each type of modification so students can see how auditors express these qualifications formally.

In each of the reports below we have extracted the wording from some sample auditor's reports to illustrate the different forms of qualification. Key words and phrases are shown in bold italic to make them clearer.

Here are four examples of wording of auditor's reports in the following situations.

- Example A: 'Except for' report arising from a disagreement which is material but not pervasive.
- Example B: 'Except for' report arising from an inability to obtain sufficient reliable evidence which is material but not pervasive.
- Example C: Disagreement – inability to obtain sufficient reliable evidence which is pervasive.
- Example D: Adverse opinion – a fundamental disagreement which is pervasive.

In the interests of space and to avoid needless repetition the wording shown below is an *extract* from a full report and students should refer to the complete report shown above and substitute the following wording as appropriate. Key words have been underlined for clarity.

Example A: 'Except for' report arising from a disagreement which is material but not pervasive.

In this case the company has not made a bad debt provision which the auditors feel should be made.

Independent auditor's report to the members of XYZ Ltd (extract)

Qualified opinion

In our opinion, except for the effects of the matter described in the Basis for Qualified Opinion paragraph, the financial statements:

- give a true and fair view of the state of the company's affairs as at … and of its profit [loss] for the year then ended;
- have been properly prepared in accordance with United Kingdom Generally Accepted Accounting Practice; and
- have been prepared in accordance with the requirements of the Companies Act, 2006.

Basis for qualified opinion on financial statements

Included in the receivables shown on the statement of financial position is an amount of £Y due from a company which has ceased trading. XYZ Limited has no security for this debt. In our opinion the company is unlikely to receive any payment and full provision of £Y should have been made. Accordingly, receivables should be reduced by £Y, the deferred tax liability should be reduced by £X and profit for the year and retained earnings should be reduced by £Z.

Opinion on other matter prescribed by the Companies Act 2006

In our opinion the information given in the Directors' Report for the financial year for which the financial statements are prepared is consistent with the financial statements.

Matters on which we are required to report by exception

We have nothing to report in respect of the following matters where the Companies Act 2006 requires us to report to you if, in our opinion:

- adequate accounting records have not been kept, or returns adequate for our audit have not been received from branches not visited by us; or
- the financial statements are not in agreement with the accounting records and returns; or
- certain disclosures of directors' remuneration specified by law are not made; or
- we have not received all the information and explanations we require for our audit.

[Signature]   *Address*

John Smith (Senior statutory auditor)   *Date*

for and on behalf of Tickett & Run, Statutory Auditor

Example B: 'Except for' report arising from an inability to obtain sufficient reliable evidence which is material but not pervasive.

In this case the auditors were appointed after the inventory count and were thus not able to attend.

Independent auditor's report to the members of XYZ Ltd (extract)

Qualified opinion

In our opinion, except for the possible effects of the matter described in the Basis for Qualified Opinion paragraph, the financial statements:

- give a true and fair view of the state of the company's affairs as at [date] and of its profit [loss] for the year then ended;
- have been properly prepared in accordance with United Kingdom Generally Accepted Accounting Practice; and
- have been prepared in accordance with the requirements of the Companies Act 2006.

Basis for qualified opinion on financial statements

With respect to inventory having a carrying amount of £X the audit evidence available to us was limited because we did not observe the counting of the physical inventory as at [date], since that date was prior to our appointment as auditor of the company. Owing to the nature of the company's records, we were unable to obtain sufficient appropriate audit evidence regarding the inventory quantities by using other audit procedures.

Opinion on other matter prescribed by the Companies Act 2006

In our opinion the information given in the Directors' Report for the financial year for which the financial statements are prepared is consistent with the financial statements.

Matters on which we are required to report by exception

In respect solely of the limitation on our work relating to inventory, described above:

- we have not obtained all the information and explanations that we considered necessary for the purpose of our audit and
- we were unable to determine whether adequate accounting records had been kept.

We have nothing to report in respect of the following matters where the Companies Act 2006 requires us to report to you if, in our opinion:

- returns adequate for our audit have not been received from branches not visited by us; or
- the financial statements are not in agreement with the accounting records and returns; or
- certain disclosures of directors' remuneration specified by law are not made.

[Signature]   *Address*
John Smith (Senior statutory auditor)   *Date*
for and on behalf of Tickett & Run, Statutory Auditor

Example C: Disagreement – inability to obtain sufficient reliable evidence which is pervasive.

In this case the auditors were faced with two situations in which they were unable to obtain sufficient, reliable evidence, firstly the non-attendance at inventory count and secondly a problem with receivables.

Independent auditor's report to the members of XYZ Ltd (extract)

Disclaimer of opinion on financial statements

Because of the significance of the matter described in the Basis for Disclaimer of Opinion on Financial Statements paragraph we have not been able to obtain sufficient appropriate audit evidence to provide a basis for an audit opinion. Accordingly, we do not express an opinion on the financial statements.

Basis for disclaimer of opinion on financial statements

The audit evidence available to us was limited because we were unable to observe the counting of physical inventory having a carrying amount of £X and send confirmation letters to trade receivables having a carrying amount of £Y due to limitations placed on the scope of our work by the directors of the company. As a result of this we have been unable to obtain sufficient appropriate audit evidence concerning both stock and trade receivables.

Opinion on other matter prescribed by the Companies Act 2006

Notwithstanding our disclaimer of an opinion on the financial statements, in our opinion the information given in the Directors' Report for the financial year for which the financial statements are prepared is consistent with the financial statements.

Matters on which we are required to report by exception

Arising from the limitation of our work referred to above:

- we have not obtained all the information and explanations that we considered necessary for the purpose of our audit; and
- we were unable to determine whether adequate accounting records have been kept.

We have nothing to report in respect of the following matters where the Companies Act 2006 requires us to report to you if, in our opinion:

- returns adequate for our audit have not been received from branches not visited by us; or
- the financial statements are not in agreement with the accounting records and returns; or
- certain disclosures of directors' remuneration specified by law are not made.

[Signature]   *Address*
John Smith (Senior statutory auditor)   *Date*
for and on behalf of Tickett & Run, Statutory Auditor

Example D: Adverse opinion – a fundamental disagreement which is pervasive.

In this case there is a fundamental disagreement concerning a provision for losses on long term work in progress which is considered to be pervasive.

Independent auditor's report to the members of XYZ Ltd (extract)

Adverse opinion on financial statements

In our opinion, because of the significance of the matter referred to in the Basis for Adverse Opinion paragraph, the financial statements:

- do not give a true and fair view of the state of the company's affairs as at [date] and of its profit [loss] for the year then ended; and
- have not been properly prepared in accordance with United Kingdom Generally Accepted Accounting Practice.

In all other respects, in our opinion the financial statements have been prepared in accordance with the requirements of the Companies Act 2006.

Basis for adverse opinion on financial statements

As more fully explained in note [x] to the financial statements no provision has been made for losses expected to arise on certain long-term contracts currently in progress, as the directors consider that such losses should be offset against amounts recoverable on other long-term contracts. In our opinion, provision should be made for foreseeable losses on individual contracts as required by *Financial Reporting Standard 102*. If losses had been so recognized the effect would have been to reduce the carrying amount of contract work in progress by £X, the deferred tax liability by £Y and the profit for the year and retained earnings at [date] by £Z.

Opinion on other matter prescribed by the Companies Act 2006

Notwithstanding our adverse opinion on the financial statements, in our opinion the information given in the Directors' Report for the financial year for which the financial statements are prepared is consistent with the financial statements.

Matters on which we are required to report by exception

We have nothing to report in respect of the following matters where the Companies Act 2006 requires us to report to you if, in our opinion:

- adequate accounting records have not been kept, or returns adequate for our audit have not been received from branches not visited by us; or
- the financial statements are not in agreement with the accounting records and returns; or
- certain disclosures of directors' remuneration specified by law are not made; or
- we have not received all the information and explanations we require for our audit.

[Signature]   Address
John Smith (Senior statutory auditor)   Date
for and on behalf of Tickett & Run, Statutory Auditor

LISTED COMPANIES – SPECIAL PROVISIONS

There are particular situations which apply only to companies listed on the London Stock Exchange. Listed companies are expected to comply with the UK Corporate Governance Code and are, indeed, generally required to set an example. In addition to that compliance there are additional disclosure requirements for listed companies which are included in the Stock Exchange Listing Rules.

Readers should appreciate the need for additional disclosure in the interests of the corporate governance principles of accountability and transparency, (Chapter 2). Auditors are expected to be familiar with these disclosure requirements and, as part of their finalization of the audit, check that all the required disclosures have been made.

Clearly, therefore, failure to make the appropriate disclosures will require comment by the auditor in their report. Omitting to make a disclosure required by the Stock Exchange does not mean the financial statements are not true and fair, nor that they don't comply in all material respects with the Companies Act 2006 so students should realize that these are by way of additional reports by the auditors and do not constitute a modification of the auditor's report.

Note the reference later to the *comply or explain* basis of disclosure – that is companies are expected to comply or explain why they have not – so auditors only report issues of noncompliance with the Rules.

Here are some examples of possible reports:

- The auditors are required to comment on the disclosures made in the Directors' Remuneration Report. They will include in their auditor's report a reference to this, so that the second paragraph of their opinion is modified to read:

'The financial statements and the part of the Directors' Remuneration Report to be audited have been properly prepared in accordance with the Companies Act 2006.'

- All companies whose shares are listed are required to comply with the UK Corporate Governance Code (Chapter 2), or explain in the financial statements why they haven't complied. This is the *comply or explain* basis of disclosure.

  If, in the opinion of the auditors, the company hasn't complied, and furthermore has not given any reason for the noncompliance in the financial statements, the auditors will comment on the noncompliance and nondisclosure in their auditor's report. Note that in these cases the auditors only report negatively; that is, they only comment if some provision has *not* been complied with. If they make no comment, then the reader should assume all is well.

EXAMPLE

Assuming only that the Listing Rules have not been complied with, the auditor will add, immediately after the opinion section in their auditor's report.

Other matter
The Listing Rules of the London Stock Exchange require us to report any instances when the company has not complied with certain of the disclosure requirements set out in the Rules. In this connection we report that in our opinion, the company has not complied with the requirements of paragraph 9.8.8 (3) of those Rules because the Board's Report on Directors' Remuneration does not disclose the right of Jane Doe to receive a commission based on the Toytown contract achieving its target profits in 2X16.

- As part of the Listing Rules the directors are also required to review the internal control environment and include a statement on their review as part of the accounts.

If the review reveals some noncompliance, again, the auditors do not qualify their report but include a statement after the opinion section.

EXAMPLE

Other matter

We have reviewed the Board's description of its process for reviewing the effectiveness of internal control set out on page 17 of the Annual Report. In our opinion the Board's comments concerning their review of typhoon risk management do not appropriately reflect our understanding of the process undertaken by the Board because only 50 per cent of the Pacific locations were included.

EMPHASIS OF MATTER REPORTS

There is another situation which the auditors may have to consider and that is where they wish to draw the attention of the shareholders to a significant item in the financial statements. The reason for this is that there may be some situations which arise where the outcome is far from clear but where the company has taken all steps it reasonably can to provide for any costs, if appropriate, and to draw the attention of readers of the accounts to it, usually in a note to the accounts.

Key Audit Matters and Emphasis of Matter reports

As we have seen, prominence in audit reports is given to matters which the auditors consider to be of special significance in coming to the conclusions they have about the truth and fairness of the financial statements.

As a consequence, those issues will not constitute an Emphasis of Matter as the same item cannot be both.

So there may be an issue that is not a Key Audit Matter, perhaps because it did not require significant auditor attention, but which, in the auditor's judgement is fundamental to users' understanding of the financial statements (e.g. a subsequent event). If the auditors consider it necessary to draw a reader of the financial statements attention to such a point disclosure is included in an Emphasis of Matter paragraph in the Auditor's Report.

It is important to understand that the auditors are *not* qualifying their report but *are* drawing attention to the disclosure.

An example of this kind of situation might be the outcome of exceptional legal proceedings where there are claims and counter claims on both sides and the question of liability cannot easily be settled. Other examples might be:

- a significant subsequent event that occurs between the date of the financial statements and the date of the auditor's report
- early application (where permitted) of a new accounting standard that has a material effect on the financial statements
- a major catastrophe that has had, or continues to have, a significant effect on the entity's financial position

Here is an example of emphasis of matter wording based on a legal issue which is material but of which the outcome is uncertain and no amount of audit work will help:

Independent auditor's report to the members of XYZ Ltd (extract)

Opinion on financial statements

In our opinion the financial statements:

- give a true and fair view of the state of the company's affairs as at [date] and of its profit [loss] for the year then ended;

- have been properly prepared in accordance with United Kingdom Generally Accepted Accounting Practice; and
- have been prepared in accordance with the requirements of the Companies Act 2006.

Emphasis of matter – possible outcome of a lawsuit

In forming our opinion on the financial statements, which is not qualified, we have considered the adequacy of the disclosures made in Note [x] to the financial statements concerning the possible outcome of a lawsuit, alleging infringement of certain patent rights and claiming royalties and punitive damages, where the company is the defendant. The company has filed a counter action, and preliminary hearings and discovery proceedings on both actions are in progress. The ultimate outcome of the matter cannot presently be determined, and no provision for any liability that may result has been made in the financial statements.

Opinion on other matter prescribed by the Companies Act 2006 etc.

AUDIT REPORTING – SPECIAL CIRCUMSTANCES

There are three sets of circumstances relating to audit reports which we cover in other chapters:

- Auditing of opening balances and comparatives – see Chapter 25
- Groups of companies – see Chapter 28
- Assurance or non-audit assignments – see Chapter 30

AUDITOR'S LIABILITY IN RESPECT OF AUDIT REPORTS

The Companies Act 2006 brought in a new offence which affects auditors signing audit reports.

Under Section 507 it is an offence:

- knowingly or recklessly to cause an audit report made under s 495 to include *'any matter that is misleading, false or deceptive in any material particular'*
- knowingly or recklessly cause a report to omit a statement that is required under certain sections of the Act. These are:
  - Section 498(2)(b) – statement that company's accounts do not agree with accounting records and returns
  - Section 498(3) – statement that necessary information and explanations not obtained or
  - Section 498(5) – statement that directors wrongly took advantage of exemption from the obligation to prepare group accounts

We look at this in more detail in Chapter 29 – Auditor's Liability – but auditors need to be aware that signing the auditor's report is the culmination of a proper process which must have been performed in a competent, professional manner in accordance with the relevant ISAs. The implications of any shortcuts or risks which have been taken must be properly considered before the audit report is finalized and signed.

The offence is punishable by a fine – and no doubt disciplinary proceedings will follow.

SUMMARY

- Auditors should summarize their findings and discuss them with management to identify any alterations to the accounts.
- Key Audit Matters should be reported separately as they have a significant bearing on the audit process.
- Going concern is a key issue and detailed reporting is required.

- If all is well the auditors can sign an unmodified report.
- Audit reports now, generally, include a disclaimer, known as Bannerman wording, to the effect that the auditors consider that they have a responsibility only to the shareholders.
- If the auditors are unable to obtain sufficient, reliable evidence they must either issue an 'except for' opinion or a disclaimer of opinion depending on how limited their work has been and how material that limitation is to the accounts.
- If they disagree with the accounting treatment or disclosures, they can issue either an 'except for' opinion or an adverse opinion if the disagreement is material and so pervasive that it casts doubt on the integrity of the financial statements as a whole.
- If there is doubt about a significant event the auditors might want to draw the shareholder's attention to it by including an emphasis of matter paragraph in their report.
- It is an offence for auditors to sign an auditor's report knowingly or recklessly which includes a misleading opinion.

POINTS TO NOTE

- Readers must understand the terminology used in these reports and when each type of report is appropriate. It is a common failing to advise use of the wrong type of report in the wrong situation or to adopt the wrong form of wording.
- Practitioners should avoid taking a 'hard line' when reporting. Recommending an adverse opinion for a material disagreement which is far from pervasive would be incorrect practice and could lead to disputes with the client.

CASE STUDY

Hamm & Jamm LLP have just completed the audit of Gofaster Motors Ltd for the year ended 31 December 2X16. They asked one of the audit staff to draft the audit report and he produced this:

REPORT OF THE AUDITORS TO GOFASTER MOTORS LTD

Basis of opinion

We conducted our audit in accordance with auditing standards. An audit includes examination, on a test basis, of evidence relevant to the amounts and disclosures in the financial statements. It also includes an assessment of all the estimates and judgements made by the directors in the preparation of the financial statements, and of whether the accounting policies are appropriate to the company's circumstances, consistently applied and adequately disclosed.

We planned and performed our audit so as to obtain as much information and explanation as possible given the time available for the audit. We confirm that the financial statements are free from material misstatement, whether caused by fraud or other irregularity or error. The directors however are wholly responsible for the accuracy of the financial statements and no liability for errors can be accepted by the auditor. In forming our opinion, we also evaluated the overall adequacy of the presentation of information in the company's annual report.

Hamm & Jamm
Auditors

Discussion

Identify and explain the errors in the above extract.

(ACCA)

STUDENT SELF-TESTING QUESTIONS

Based on answers apparent from the text

a) List the main contents of an auditor's report.

b) Why are there paragraphs concerning directors in the auditor's report?

c) How do the auditors sign their report?

d) What does 'pervasive' mean?

e) What is a Key Audit Matter?

f) If auditor scope is restricted partially what form of report might be made?

g) Explain what the principle is behind the inclusion of the Bannerman wording.

h) Under what circumstances would the auditors state that the financial statements do not present a true and fair view?

i) What is an emphasis of matter report used for?

j) How does the auditor report noncompliance with the requirements of the Stock Exchange listing rules?

EXAMINATION QUESTIONS

1 Described below are situations which have arisen in three external audit clients of your firm. The year end in each case is 31 March 2X16.

Maris Ltd

A fire in the accounts office in April 2X16 destroyed the company's records of the physical inventory count undertaken at the year end. This was the only record of the inventory as the company does not maintain continuous inventory records. There were no reasonable alternative audit procedures that could be undertaken to verify the amount of inventory at the year end. The company has included an estimated inventory figure of £1.2 million in the financial statements for the year ended 31 March 2X16.

The total assets of Maris Ltd at 31 March 2X16 are £5.9 million and the profit before tax for the year ended 31 March 2X16 is £1.5 million.

Piper plc

The company builds and operates cable networks and during the year ended 31 March 2X16 the company incurred costs of £3.2 million in respect of repairs and maintenance to its networks. These costs have been capitalized and included in noncurrent assets. The directors refuse to make any adjustments in respect of this matter.

The total assets of Piper plc at 31 March 2X16 are £1250 million and the profit before tax for the year ended 31 March 2X16 is £152.6 million.

Tima Ltd

The directors have included a note to the financial statements for the year ended 31 March 2X16 explaining the status of litigation against the company for an alleged breach of environmental regulations. The note specifies that, in the opinion of the company's legal advisers, the future settlement of this litigation could possibly result in significant additional liabilities but it is not possible to quantify the effects, if any, of the resolution of this matter.

Required:

(a) In each of the circumstances outlined above, reach a conclusion on whether or not you would modify each audit report. Give reasons for your conclusions and outline the potential effect, if any, on each audit report.

(b) Explain the concept of reasonable assurance in the context of an external audit. *(ICAEW)*

2 **(a)** Explain why quality control may be difficult to implement in a smaller audit firm and illustrate how such difficulties may be overcome.

(b) Kite Associates is an association of small accounting practices. One of the benefits of membership is improved quality control through a peer review system. Whilst reviewing a sample of auditor's reports issued by Tickitt & Run, a firm only recently admitted to Kite Associates, you come across the following qualified opinion on the financial statements of Lammergeier Group Ltd:

Qualified opinion arising from disagreement about accounting treatment relating to the non-adoption of the relevant section 7 of FRS 102.

'The management has not prepared a group cash flow statement and its associated notes. In the opinion of the management it is not practical to prepare a group cash flow statement due to the complexity involved. In our opinion the reasons for the departure from FRS102 are sound and acceptable and adequate disclosure has been made concerning the departure from FRS102. The departure in our opinion does not impact on the truth and fairness of the financial statements.

In our opinion, except for the non-preparation of the group cash flow statement and associated notes, the financial statements give a true and fair view of the financial position of the Company as at 31 December 2X16 and of the profit of the group for the year then ended, and have been properly prepared in accordance with ...'

Your review of the prior year auditor's report has revealed that the 2X15 year-end audit opinion was identical.

Required:
Critically appraise the appropriateness of the audit opinion given by Tickitt & Run on the financial statements of Lammergeier Group for the years ended 31 December 2X16 and 2X15.

(ACCA)

SOURCES AND ADDITIONAL READING

Association of Chartered Certified Accountants (2008) *Technical Factsheet 84 The Use of Disclaimers in Audit Reports*. London: ACCA.

Audit Quality Forum (2007) *Fundamentals – Auditor Reporting Fatal Flaw Review*. London: ICAEW.

Barclays Bank Plc v Grant Thornton UK LLP [2015] EWHC 320 (Comm) (18 February 2015).

Caparo Industries v Dickman and Touche Ross & Co (1990).

Financial Reporting Council (2016) *ISA 700 The Auditor's Report On Financial Statements*. London: Financial Reporting Council.

Financial Reporting Council (2016) *ISA 705 Modifications to the Opinion in the Independent Auditor's Report*. London: Financial Reporting Council.

Financial Reporting Council (2016) *Compendium of Illustrative Auditor's Reports on United Kingdom Private Sector Financial Statements for Periods Ended on or after 17 June 2016 (Revised)*. London: Financial Reporting Council.

Institute of Chartered Accountants in England and Wales (2008) *Audit 01/03 (Revised) The Audit Report and Auditors' Duty of Care to Third Parties*. London: ICAEW.

Institute of Chartered Accountants in England and Wales (2010) *Revised Bannerman Clarification Language*. London: ICAEW.

Royal Bank of Scotland v Bannerman Johnstone Maclay (Scottish Court of Session) (2002).

CHAPTER 27
AUDITOR'S REPORTS TO DIRECTORS AND MANAGEMENT

Learning Objectives

After studying the material in this chapter you should be able to:

- understand the nature of what has to be communicated to those charged with governance

- appreciate the matters auditors may have to consider in addition to systems weaknesses

- explain the form and content of a Management Letter

- understand the timing implications for reporting

- discuss the need for a response by management

- explain the implications of the use of such letters in respect of third parties

- draft a suitable Management Letter given the circumstances

INTRODUCTION

There are two ISAs concerned with the auditor's communication with directors or **those charged with governance**. These are ISA 260 '*Communication with those charged with governance*' and ISA 265 *Communicating deficiencies in internal control to those charged with governance and management*' and they set out recommendations as to which matters and in what form the auditors should communicate audit matters to persons who it describes as 'those charged with governance'. Auditors also have to consider communicating details of uncorrected misstatements to those charged with governance under ISA 450 '*Evaluation of misstatements identified during the audit*' (Chapter 25).

For this purpose, '*those charged with governance*' can be defined as the governing body of the entity; in companies this will be the board of directors and members of the Audit Committee where there is one, for example, or in a public sector body it might be a Board of Trustees.

COMMUNICATION WITH THOSE CHARGED WITH GOVERNANCE

ISA 260 sets out a framework for communication between auditors and those charged with governance to enable them to build a constructive working relationship without impairing the auditor's independence and objectivity. The objective of the auditors here is to:

- communicate clearly with those charged with governance the responsibilities of the auditors in relation to the financial statement audit, and to provide an overview of the planned scope and timing of the audit;
- communicate clearly that the audit process does not relieve management of its responsibility to prepare accounts which show a true and fair view of the entity's financial position;
- obtain from those charged with governance information relevant to the audit;
- provide those charged with governance with timely observations arising from the audit that are significant and relevant to their responsibility to oversee the financial reporting process; and
- promote effective two-way communication between the auditors and those charged with governance.

In most cases the auditors will communicate directly with the main governing body, e.g. the board of directors but where the auditors deal with a sub-committee of the board, for example an Audit Committee, the auditors should consider whether or not to communicate with the main board as well.

The auditors have to ensure that their independence is not compromised and should ensure that those charged with governance have a clear understanding of the auditor's role and what the auditors need to do to ensure their ethical position is not compromised. For example, the auditors may turn down offers of corporate hospitality on the grounds that it is excessive; it is important that the client fully understands the auditor's reasons for doing so and does not interpret the refusal as an unfriendly gesture.

The auditors should communicate significant findings during the audit such as views about significant aspects of the organization's accounting practices, including accounting policies, accounting estimates and financial statement disclosures. It should report issues discussed with management, where those charged with governance are not involved in day-to-day management e.g. **non-executive directors** including mention of any significant difficulties, if any, encountered during the audit and detail the written representations the auditors are requesting from the directors or management (Chapter 25).

In addition, there may be various planning and practical issues to discuss and communicate, without revealing the audit strategy, such as:

- the appropriate person to act as a channel of communication
- the auditors estimate of any assessed risks which have influenced the planning of the audit
- the extent to which the auditors will use the work of internal audit and how the external and internal auditors can best work together in a constructive and complementary manner

- the entity's objectives, strategies and the related business risks that may result in material misstatements
- matters those charged with governance consider warrant particular attention during the audit and any areas where they request additional procedures to be undertaken
- the attitudes, awareness and actions of those charged with governance concerning:
  - the systems of internal control and how management oversee its effectiveness and
  - the detection or possibility of fraud
- any problems which might arise in response to changes in accounting standards, corporate governance practices, exchange listing rules and related matters
- the responses to previous communications with the auditors
- problems encountered during the audit such as delays in preparing financial information, shortened time scales, restrictions imposed by management
- management's estimate of the going concerns status of the organization
- any material errors or misstatements uncovered during the audit which require correcting or which, if not, may lead to the auditors modifying their report

ISA 260 requires the auditors to report to those charged with governance the general approach and overall scope of the audit, including details of any limitations and the form of the reports they expect to make, i.e. any problems which may cause them to modify their audit report. (Chapter 26).

The auditors should inform the directors of the selection of, or any changes to, significant accounting policies and practices that have or could have a material effect on the entity's financial statements. They should specify the potential effect on the financial statements of any material risks and exposures, such as pending litigation, that are required to be disclosed in the financial statements. Importantly the auditors should raise material uncertainties related to events and conditions that may cast doubt on the company's ability to continue as a going concern.

These relevant matters should be communicated to the management of the enterprise promptly enough to enable them to take appropriate action.

During the course of the audit and, as it nears a conclusion, the communication with management will intensify. Auditors will want to inform management of the detailed findings of their audit work, in particular those which relate to the financial statements and the auditor's report, such as:

- expected modifications to the auditor's report (see Chapter 26)
- any audit adjustments that have or could have a material effect on the financial statements
- unadjusted misstatements in the financial statements which were determined to be immaterial both individually and in aggregate, i.e. they were below the 'threshold amount' and are thus classed as trivial
- notes of any disagreements with management about matters which could be significant to the financial statements or the auditor's report, including whether or not the matter has been resolved

In general, most communication should be in writing, including email, as this serves as a documentary record of the points raised. Auditors must ensure they have a permanent record of any communication with management which has a significant bearing on the conduct or findings of the audit so if discussions are had by email these should be printed out or stored electronically with the audit papers and not just left on the email server where they may eventually be wiped.

It may be that matters will be discussed at a series of meetings, in which case it is important that these be properly minuted and the minutes agreed as a true record. This too provides a form of audit evidence. Matters should be discussed as promptly as possible rather than being left to the end of the audit when there may be a great deal to finalize and time to deal with outstanding issues might not be so readily available.

For example, care has to be taken where the body being communicated with is the board of a subsidiary company and the holding company is audited by a different firm. Matters raised with the subsidiary company board are confidential to that entity so permission will have to be granted for the subsidiary company auditors to communicate with the main board and to disclose the contents of that communication to the other auditors. This permission should not, under normal circumstances, be withheld (Chapter 28).

Communication of these matters requires disclosure to *all* members of that board so it would include non-executive directors. The reason for this is related to the practice of good Corporate Governance (Chapter 2) and is designed to ensure that the non-executive directors, particularly, are kept fully informed of audit findings and audit issues. In this way the executive directors cannot hide significant matters from the non-executives.

The auditors must consider whether the two-way communications during the course of the audit between themselves and the management have been adequate for an effective audit.

SIGNIFICANT DEFICIENCIES IN INTERNAL CONTROL

ISA 265 states:

'The objective of the auditor is to communicate appropriately to those charged with governance any management deficiencies in internal control that the auditor has identified during the audit and that, in the auditor's professional judgement, are of sufficient importance to merit their respective attentions.'

We looked at the principles of internal control in Chapter 9. 'Deficiencies' simply means that a control or a system of controls is inadequate, inefficient or is missing. The deficiency in the controls or that lack of controls is such that a material error or misstatement may go undetected with the possibility of it affecting the financial statements if it goes undetected. The auditor has to decide whether or not the inadequacies in the internal control systems are sufficiently serious as to constitute a **significant deficiency** and which, consequently, should be reported to management.

The auditors should explain to those charged with governance those matters which relate to the accounting systems and the systems of internal controls; in particular:

- any significant deficiencies in accounting and internal controls
- their views on the qualitative aspects of the entity's accounting policies and financial reporting, matters specifically required by other auditing standards to be communicated

Frequently these may be matters of which the management is unaware, in which case the auditors should discuss the matter fully with management at the appropriate level. It may be however that management is aware of the problem but that there is no readily available solution to it. This should not prevent the auditors from making a formal report but the responses of management to the identified deficiencies should also be noted.

These matters are routinely dealt with through the formal reporting mechanism of the Management Letter.

THE MANAGEMENT LETTER

These letters are variously known as a:

- Management Letter
- Letter of Weakness
- Internal Control Memorandum
- Letter of Recommendation
- Constructive Service Letter

Their object is the same – to inform the company of problem areas within the internal control environment, including specific control procedure problems.

We will call it a Management Letter as this is a frequently used term.

During their audit work the auditors may well uncover significant deficiencies in the accounting systems, incidences of poor accounting practice or other matters which should be reported to the client. Matters which might constitute significant deficiencies include:

- The likelihood of the significant deficiencies the auditors have identified leading to material misstatements in the financial statements in the future.
- The susceptibility of assets to loss or fraud.
- The subjectivity and complexity of determining estimated amounts, such as fair value accounting estimates or provisions.
- The size of the problem, i.e. some idea of the amounts of money involved or the volumes of transactions involved in the systems where the deficiencies have been identified.
- The importance of the controls to the financial reporting process, for example:
  - management controls to monitor the transaction volumes and the operations of the systems
  - controls over the prevention and detection of fraud
  - controls over the selection and application of significant accounting policies
  - controls over significant transactions with related parties
  - controls over significant transactions outside the entity's normal course of business
  - controls over the period-end financial reporting process (such as controls over nonrecurring journal entries)
  - the cause and frequency of the errors or misstatements detected as a result of the deficiencies in the controls
  - the interaction of the deficiency with other deficiencies in internal controls

Apart from the more routine transaction processing errors or omissions, or significant weaknesses arising as a result of inadequate internal control procedures such as those explained in Chapter 9, there are some significant forms of deficiency in the organization's operations which the auditor may well have to consider, such as:

- Indications that significant transactions in which management is financially interested are not being appropriately scrutinized by those charged with governance, i.e. executive directors' or senior management's involvement in business contracts or related parties which has not been brought to the attention of the non-executive directors.
- Identification of management fraud, whether or not material, that was not prevented by the entity's internal control, possibly due to **management override** or deliberate concealment. This could be either fraud against the company perpetrated by management, e.g. 'fiddling' expenses or deliberate misrepresentation of the financial statements to show an improved position.
- Management's failure to implement appropriate remedial action on significant deficiencies communicated to them from previous audits.
- Absence or ineffective risk assessment processes within the organization, where such processes would ordinarily be expected to have been established, or evidence of an ineffective response to identified significant risks, e.g. lack of risk assessment processes, poor security or inadequate insurance cover.
- Misstatements detected by the auditor's procedures that were not prevented, detected and corrected, by the entity's own internal controls.
- Restatement of previously issued financial statements to reflect the correction of a material misstatement due to error or fraud.
- Evidence of management's inability to oversee the preparation of the financial statements.

Auditors communicate significant deficiencies to management by means of a form of Management Letter. They have to consider several things including the appropriate level of management to send it to or to include in the communication circularization and the experience and involvement of those charged with governance. For example, an Audit Committee may have limited managerial or financial expertise so the significance of the deficiencies may well have to be explained in some detail so that they, in turn, can communicate their views to the main board.

The nature and complexity of the organization is important, for example communication of significant deficiencies to a large organization may well differ from the process of communication in an owner/managed business. The auditor must explain the fact that the auditor's own procedures will not be guaranteed to detect material errors or misstatements the entities own controls have also failed to detect – Detection Risk (Chapter 10).

Auditors must also bear in mind any legal or regulatory requirements relevant to the reporting of significant deficiencies – for example, in the financial services industry, deficiencies may have to be reported to a regulator.

The object of the Management Letter is to assist the directors and managers in improving the accounting systems and the internal control environment and to highlight any instances which may be of relevance to future audits. It is not a substitute for a qualified audit report – it is an ancillary document designed to benefit the client by recommending suitable improvements. This will also, hopefully, have the added benefit of making the auditor's life easier in future years!

Purposes

The purposes of the Management Letter are:

- to enable the auditors to give their comments on the accounting records, systems and controls
- to enable the auditors to bring to the attention of management areas of systems weakness that might lead to material errors or misstatements
- to enable the auditor to communicate matters that may have an impact on future audits
- to enable the management to put right matters that may otherwise have led to an audit report qualification
- to enable the auditor to point out areas where management could be more efficient or more effective or where economies could be made or resources used more effectively

Note that in some audit engagements there is a specific requirement to make a management report on internal control and the control environment. These include:

- audits of local authorities;
- stock exchange firms;
- housing associations; and
- organizations in the financial services sector.

The detail is outside the scope of this book but the principles shown here apply to such letters or reports.

Remember that what is being reported on, generally, doesn't affect the audit opinion; in most cases the auditors are simply suggesting systems improvements or pointing out weaknesses in systems, which may exist but which haven't prevented them giving an unqualified report.

If the auditors have had to qualify their report, particularly on the grounds of an inability to obtain sufficient, reliable audit evidence, the matters which forced them to do so would clearly have to be included in the Management Letter as they would be of great significance.

Timing

If it is to be effective the management should receive the Management Letter as soon after the completion of the audit work as possible. As the Management Letter is a natural by-product of the audit its production should be incorporated in the audit plan. It should be sent as soon as possible after the end of the audit procedures from which the report arises.

Where the audit is spread over several visits then it may be appropriate to send a report after each visit. Frequently two reports are sent – one after the interim and one after the final.

Where procedures need to be improved before the period end (e.g. on inventory control or identification of doubtful debts or undisclosed liabilities) then the report must be sent as soon as the weaknesses are identified by the auditor.

Procedures

There is a procedure for agreeing and sending Management Letters. What the auditors should *never* do is send a letter to the board or to the Audit Committee which they haven't discussed beforehand with the appropriate directors or senior managers.

The procedure is:

1   As weaknesses or breakdowns are identified they should be discussed in detail with the operating staff involved and/or with more senior management. It is vital that the auditors have their facts right!

2   The letter should then be written and discussed informally with the board or the Audit Committee prior to being formally submitted.

3   The letter should then be sent.

4   An acknowledgement should be obtained from management stating what they propose to do about the weaknesses.

5   The weaknesses should be followed up on the next visit.

It is usual to address the letter to the board or the Audit Committee who may then choose to refer it to the board for action. Alternatively, with the agreement of the board, it may be sent to the management of the appropriate section, branch, division, region, etc.

In some cases, separate letters are prepared for the board and for line management. This situation might arise where the auditors have a point to make, which is not material or unduly significant in the context of the company as a whole, but is relevant to one particular department or division. The auditors might consider making a separate report to the senior management of that department or division without including the points in the main letter addressed to the main board.

Care must be taken with this however for two reasons:

● The directors are entitled to know of any points the auditors make to their line managers, however limited they may be, and might not take kindly to not being informed.

● The matter may not be significant to the organization as a whole, as far as the auditors are aware, but may have greater significance to management in the context of operational issues with which the auditor has no concern or is unaware.

It is therefore wise for the auditors to inform the directors of these points on an advisory basis.

Contents

The Management Letter will include:

● A statement that the accounting and internal control systems were audited only to the extent that was necessary to provide evidence for audit purposes and not necessarily for management purposes or to provide any assurance for management.

● A statement that only the significant deficiencies that have come to the auditor's attention are reported and there may be others. A note that, had the auditor performed more extensive procedures, more deficiencies may have come to light.

● A list of any significant deficiencies in the structure of accounting systems or internal control procedures which have been uncovered during the audit and details of any controls which are ill-designed, inadequate or not functioning fully.

● A list of deficiencies in operation of the records or controls. In principle good records and controls may have been designed but they may be being bypassed or not always carried out by staff.

● Unsuitable accounting policies and practices – if material this would have to be discussed in the context of the auditor's report but that would not prevent it also being included in the Management Letter.

● Details of any noncompliance with accounting standards or legislation, which should have already been discussed with management in the context of the auditor's report.

● Explanations of the risks arising from each deficiency. The company should be advised of the implications of any significant deficiencies in the system and the possible consequences which may flow from not dealing with them.

● Comments on inefficiencies or waste in the systems which the auditors feel it appropriate to make.

- Recommendations for improvement. In some cases, the required changes may be complex and the auditors should not delay their report if suggestions cannot be made quickly. Also improvements, such as improvements to the computer system, may require research and, in such cases, the auditors would not be able to recommend specific action.

Format

There is no set format or layout for these letters. Sometimes they are prepared as a letter, others prepare them as a table in a columnar format showing:

- the deficiency;
- the implications for the company; and
- the corrective action needed.

Whatever format is chosen the report should be clear, constructive and concise. The Management Letter format includes, as a minimum:

- an opening paragraph explaining the purpose of the report
- a statement that it is for the use of the organization and possibly its holding company if it is a member of a group only and not for any other purpose
- a note that it contains only those matters which came to the auditor's attention and cannot be a comprehensive list of all significant deficiencies which may exist in the systems
- if required, the report may be tiered by having major weaknesses separated from minor weaknesses
- a request that the management should reply to each point made

RESPONSE BY MANAGEMENT

It is essential that the auditors should obtain a response from the client on each point in the Management Letter. The auditors should expect:

- an acknowledgement of receipt;
- a note of the actions to be taken; and
- in some important cases, the directors' discussions should be recorded in the minutes of directors' meetings.

THE REPORT AND THIRD PARTIES

The auditors should not disclose the report to any third party without permission from the client, unless there is a legal responsibility to disclose as in the case of money laundering or insider dealing, or the auditors can claim a public interest defence. In these cases, the auditors should seek legal advice before any such disclosure is made.

It may be that the client discloses the report to others (e.g. the bank, regulatory bodies). The auditors should include a disclaimer paragraph stating that the report has been produced for the private use of their client only and/or requesting that it not be shown to third parties without permission from the auditors.

As the report may be critical of individuals, care should be taken that all its contents are factually accurate and that there are no gratuitously derogatory remarks.

EXAMPLE OF A MANAGEMENT LETTER

Note: There are other layouts but this is a common one. This example is of a report sent to the company with a covering letter addressed to the directors; others may include material issues in the body of the letter.

Example

Private and Confidential

The Directors
Bodgitt Ltd
Upper Street
Downtown
DT1 2OK

20 June 2X16

Dear Sirs

Matters arising from the Audit for the year ended 31 March 2X16

In common with our normal practice we enclose details of matters which have arisen during the course of our audit for the year ended 31 March 2X16 which we feel are significant enough to bring to your attention.

Our responsibilities as auditors are set out in the Companies Act 2006 and require us to form an opinion on the truth and fairness of the financial statements presented to us by the directors. In addition, we are required to form an opinion as to whether proper accounting records have been maintained for the accounting period.

This report has been prepared exclusively for the sole use of the directors of Bodgitt Ltd. None of its content may be disclosed to third parties without our written consent and we accept no liabilities to third parties in connection with this letter.

The matters recorded in this letter are those which have come to our attention during the course of the audit. They are not intended to be a comprehensive statement of all significant deficiencies which exist or all improvements which could be made to the financial systems.

We should be pleased to discuss these matters further with you at a suitable time. In any event we should be grateful if you would kindly acknowledge receipt of this letter and comment on the points contained within it.

Yours faithfully
Jungg & Foolish
Chartered Accountants

Matters arising from the Audit for the year ended 31 March 2X16

The following points (please see tables on pages XX – XX) arose from the audit for the year ended 31 March 2X16.

Note that this is not a comprehensive statement of all significant deficiencies which may exist or of all improvements which could be made. We set out below those matters which we consider to be of fundamental importance.

Significant deficiency	Implication	Recommendation
Internal control – general points		
Budgeting		
At the moment we understand that you prepare an annual budget prior to the commencement of the financial year and submit it to the bank to support the application for the renewal of your overdraft.	As the budget does not appear to be used other than to support the finance application an opportunity is being lost to improve management's control of the business.	A budgetary control system be introduced comprising a monthly budget and management accounts and an explanation of significant variances.
Budgeting is a useful management tool and it would greatly assist the management of your business if the budget was used to monitor the progress of the business.	It is preferable for management to respond positively at the time problems or opportunities appear rather than have to rely on historical data which may be several months old by the time management see it.	The budget should be produced in a timely manner each month and presented to the board for discussion.
Management reporting		
We note that you have no system of monthly management reporting. It would assist the management of your business if you were to receive accurate monthly management accounts	The company is losing the opportunity to act quickly when comparison of actual results against forecast indicates a problem might be developing.	Any estimates or assumptions which have been used in the production of monthly management accounts should be disclosed to the board.
These could be compared with the monthly budgets to monitor the performance of the business.	Similarly, if management reporting indicates a potential benefit or opportunity the quicker this can be exploited the better the opportunity for management to maximize profits and cash flow.	The monthly accounts should include, amongst other things (i) the contribution made by different product lines and (ii) a cash flow statement
	It is important that managers monitor cash flows to avoid any cash shortages developing which may hinder the operations of the business.	
Internal control – accounting system		
The computer software currently being used is obsolete. You are using Version 3. The latest issue is Version 8.	Use of outdated software is a missed opportunity to enhance the speed, accuracy and flexibility of financial reporting.	The computer software should be upgraded to Version 8.

(Continued)

Significant deficiency	Implication	Recommendation
Internal control – general points		
Budgeting		
Whilst it continues to support the basic accounting system, that is the day books and ledgers, it has no facility for inventory control nor has it any facility for recording costing information.	The additional features provided by the upgraded software will improve managers' control of business activities and provide the information on which they could base business decisions.	The cost of doing this will be likely to be out-weighed by increased efficiencies in the sys-tem and the abolition of some of the current paper-based systems. For example, improved inventory control might serve to reduce current inventory levels and free up cash for use in the business.
Internal control – detail points *(Important points arising from the audit of the internal controls should be included here. We have shown a few as examples)*		
Payroll		
There is no evidence of review of the payroll. There is no independent evidence of authorization of recruitment of new staff. At present the starters form is signed by the wages clerk.	The payroll may contain unauthorized or fic-titious employees or payments at incorrect or unauthorized rates. Fictitious employees might be introduced to the payroll. Employees might not receive all the docu-mentation they are entitled to under the legislation which would cause the company to be in breach of legal requirements.	The payroll should be reviewed and signed by the production manager each week. New starter forms should be authorized by the production manager.
Receivables		
An aged receivables analysis is only produced quarterly. Slow-paying customers are often not identified until well after their terms of trade have expired.	Poor credit control means that slow-paying customers are not identified quickly and steps taken to collect sums due. This means that the working capital require-ment is greater than it otherwise could be. As this is presently financed by over-draft facilities the company is currently incurring excess interest cost because of slow-paying customers.	Aged debtor reports should be prepared monthly. The acquisition of new computer software should enable this to be done automatically. All customers should be reminded of the terms of trade and credit control procedures intro-duced to collect overdue debts.

This is a final report but reports could be prepared after the interim audit as well if sufficient credible audit points are unearthed during the checking work.

Note that auditors should resist the temptation to include all weaknesses discovered however minor. Only weaknesses which may lead to material errors or misstatements or areas where significant improvements may be made for the benefit of the client should be included as inclusion of trivial or insignificant points devalues the authority of the letter.

SUMMARY

- The auditors are required to communicate details of the scope and function of their audit and the findings from their audit work to those charged with governance.
- The auditors should confirm that management is still responsible for preparing true and fair financial statements.
- They communicate the scope, etc. of the audit formally using the Letter of Engagement. There are informal communications during the course of the audit. Reports of findings pertinent to significant deficiencies in financial systems are communicated formally by means of the Management Letter.
- The Management Letter has several purposes which include constructive advice to the client on economies or more efficient use of resources, comments on accounting, records, systems and controls with significant deficiencies and recommendations for improvement.
- Management Letters can be sent after the interim or final audit or both.
- Auditors must consider the level of management and the expertise they have for the purpose of communicating significant deficiencies.
- The contents should include an explanation as to the purpose of the letter, a third party disclaimer and details of the deficiencies and recommendations for improvement.
- Management should make a formal response to each of the points contained in the letter.

POINTS TO NOTE

- Clearly distinguish the auditor's report and a report to management.
- The audit plan should include the preparation of the Management Letter and a review of actions taken (if any) on previous letters.
- In some cases, the deficiencies are not material enough to merit a full scale letter so the auditors should choose not to send a report and communicate any minor weaknesses informally.
- A notable misapprehension is that the Management Letter can absolve the auditors from blame and hence a legal responsibility to pay for any losses which flow from deficiencies in internal control. If a significant deficiency is discovered by the auditors and they are unable to satisfy themselves that, to a material extent:
  - losses have not occurred;
  - the records can be relied upon, then they must qualify their report.

CASE STUDY

Dunbar Manufacturing PLC is a multi-product manufacturing company with four factories around the country. The auditors, Flossy & Co LLP, have completed the interim audit for the year ending 31 December 2X16 in September 2X16 and are considering their report to management.

The matters they have discovered include:

(a) Each factory has a separate bank account. Sometimes the individual accounts are overdrawn but the bank has agreed to set-off for interest calculation. At times there is a net credit balance.

(b) The factory at Tipton shares the policy of straight line depreciation for its plant but unlike the others does not keep a plant register.

(c) The factory in Oldham buys large quantities of scrap copper from scrap merchants, paying by cash. Each purchase is approved in writing by the plant works manager but there is no regular check of the cash balance kept to make these purchases.

(d) The inventory of finished goods at Wigan is valued at total absorption cost using budgeted direct wages for overheads purposes. The other factories use a more sophisticated system of departmental overhead recovery based on machine hours.

(e) In all the factories some of the manual workers, classed as casual employees, are paid in cash. Their wages packets are simply given to the foremen to hand out with no formalities.

(f) The factories each use a computerized sales ledger system with complex analytical facilities. One facility, to analyze sales on a month to month and year by year basis for each customer, is not used.

Discussion

– How should these matters be treated in reports to management?

– Draft such reports.

STUDENT SELF-TESTING QUESTIONS

Questions with answers apparent from the text

a) How do auditors communicate with management?

b) When should these Management Letters be sent?

c) Apart from weaknesses in systems what other matters need to be communicated to management?

d) List the contents of a Management Letter.

EXAMINATION QUESTIONS

1 Stopwatch PLC is an independent television production company. It specializes in the production of 30-minute long children's programmes in series of 10 to 15 episodes each.

Stopwatch PLC's main customers are the major television networks within the UK. The company's creative team present an idea for a television programme to the network and, if successful, the programme is then commissioned. A production budget, including an agreed profit margin for Stopwatch PLC, is agreed with the network before production commences. Stopwatch PLC's production team is then responsible for making the programme within these agreed budget limits. If the production goes over budget, Stopwatch PLC is responsible for meeting the additional cost of completing the programme concerned.

The following significant points have been identified during your audit of the company:

(a) Production budgets

On 6 out of the 22 commissions received by Stopwatch PLC during the year, the company has not adhered to its own internal control procedures which call for the weekly comparison of budget to actual spend. As a result, large overruns against budget in time and cost have occurred on these productions.

(b) Freelance staff

The company employs a large number of writers, directors and presenters in the making of its programmes. Under Inland Revenue guidelines, depending upon the length of their individual contract and the nature of their role, some must be paid after deduction of income tax and National Insurance whereas others are treated as freelance and can be paid without such deductions being made. Any such sums deducted must be paid over to the Inland Revenue monthly.

Due to staff changes within the company's human resources department during the year, a number of individuals for whom income tax and National Insurance should have been deducted, were found to have been treated as freelance and paid without the appropriate deductions being made.

(c) Audio-visual equipment

On four separate occasions during the year, equipment was found to have been ordered for the company by individual production staff without proper authorization and in contravention of company policy which calls for three quotes for all capital expenditure.

Required:

(a) Set out, in a manner suitable for inclusion in a report to management, the possible consequences arising from the weaknesses identified above, and your recommendations to remedy these weaknesses.

(b) Outline the points to be included in the covering letter accompanying the above report to management and explain why they should be included.

(ICAEW)

SOURCES AND ADDITIONAL READING

Chartered Institute of Internal Auditors (2007) *Communication Skills*. London: Chartered Institute of Internal Auditors.

Financial Reporting Council (2016) *ISA 260 Communication with Those Charged with Governance*. London: Financial Reporting Council.

Financial Reporting Council (2016) *ISA 265 Communicating Deficiencies in Internal Control to Those Charged with Governance and Management*. London: Financial Reporting Council.

Financial Reporting Council (2016) *ISA 450 Evaluation of Misstatements Identified during the Audit*. London: Financial Reporting Council.

CHAPTER 28
GROUP ACCOUNTS

Learning Objectives

After studying the material in this chapter you should be able to:

- understand the composition of a group of companies

- understand the responsibilities of the principal auditors

- understand the considerations to be taken into account before accepting appointment as principal auditor

- explain the nature of the communications between principal and component auditors

- understand the component auditor's assignment

- explain the key requirements for the audit of group components

- understand the role and function of a support letter

- explain the implications of transnational audits

- discuss the effect of globalization on the audit profession

INTRODUCTION

A group of companies comprises a holding company and its subsidiaries, some of which may be wholly owned but all of which are controlled by the holding company. In addition, there may also be related entities such as associated companies, where the holding company does not have overall control but can exercise a significant influence over its affairs, together with other related parties such as partnerships and joint ventures.

Parties are related when one party has direct or indirect control over the other party; or the parties are subject to common control from the same source; or one party has significant influence over the financial and operating policies of the other or the parties, in entering a transaction, are subject to influence from the same source to such an extent that one of the parties to the transaction has subordinated its own separate interest. We look at this in more detail in Chapter 21.

It is worth pointing out at this stage that the issues surrounding related parties have assumed particular significance following the Enron affair, when related parties were used to conceal the extent of huge losses which would otherwise have had a detrimental effect on the reported results of Enron itself.

Most listed companies are groups but many private companies are also groups. UK company legislation (and most other legal regimes) requires a financial statement to be prepared for the group as a whole as well as for the individual companies comprising the group.

Accounting for groups in the UK is governed by:

- The Companies Act 2006
- FRS 102 – *Section 9 Consolidated and Separate Financial Statements*
- FRS 102 – *Section 33 Related party Disclosures*

Internationally the relevant standards are:

- IFRS 3 *Business Combinations*
- IFRS 8 *Operating Segments*
- IFRS 10 *Consolidated Financial Statements*
- IFRS 11 *Joint Arrangements*
- IFRS 12 *Disclosure of interests in Other Entities*
- IAS 24 *Related Party Disclosures*
- IAS 27 *Separate Financial Statements*
- IAS 28 *Investments in Associates and Joint Ventures*

The Companies Act, 2006 and the Financial Reporting Standards have numerous and detailed requirements on the presentation of a holding company's own Consolidated Income Statement and Statement of Financial Position. Students should make themselves aware of the various accounting disclosure requirements as it is outside the scope of this book to detail them except where they are relevant to specific audit considerations.

The relevant ISA is ISA 600 '*Special Considerations – Audits of Group Financial Statements (Including the Work of Component Auditors)*'.

A note on terminology: ISA 600 refers to subsidiary companies and other entities whose accounts are to be included in the consolidation as **components** and the auditors of those entities as **component auditors.** It follows therefore that we can refer to *component management* and *component materiality*, etc. for those items relevant to components as opposed to the holding company or the group as a whole. The auditors of the group who bear responsibility for the group audit report, are designated **principal auditors.**

AUDIT CONSIDERATIONS

The key considerations for the principal auditors are:

- the often complex and numerous adjustments required to consolidate the accounts of a holding company and its subsidiary and related entities
- specific accounting standards relating to group financial statements

- some components (i.e. subsidiaries) of the group may be audited by firms other than the principal auditors
- planning the audit of a group will be significantly more complex than for a single company

The important thing for the student to understand, and from which all the procedures logically follow, is that the auditors who sign the group audit report are responsible for *all* matters arising from the audit, even in respect of subsidiaries not audited by them. There are, therefore, some important considerations identified in ISA 600 before looking at the practicalities of the audit process. These are:

- whether or not to accept appointment as principal auditors
- if deciding to accept the appointment the principal auditor must then have a method for communicating with any component auditors about scope and timing of their audit work on the component and the process of reporting of any findings in a timely manner
- to obtain sufficient appropriate evidence regarding the financial information in the components, including those not audited by themselves, and the consolidation process itself to enable them to express an opinion on the consolidated financial statements

Accepting appointment

The same considerations which apply to accepting appointment as auditors of a single entity, which are set out in ISA 210 and ISA 220 (Chapter 8), apply to accepting an appointment as group auditors. Audit firms must consider such matters as:

- Their ethical position – is there any reason ethically which may compromise their objectivity and independence and so mean they may not accept the appointment?
- Do they have the resources to carry out the audit work required? This is particularly relevant where the group components are geographically widely spread or are situated overseas.

In addition to the normal considerations ISA 600 requires the auditors to consider whether they are able to obtain sufficient, reliable evidence about the consolidation process itself and the financial statements of all the components.

This may, on the surface, seem relatively straightforward but many multinational companies have subsidiaries in countries where the reporting regimes are considerably less onerous than that of the UK and where the standards of auditing are much lower than in the UK. Where companies have subsidiaries incorporated in offshore countries such as the Cayman Islands, the Netherlands Antilles or the British Virgin Islands, no doubt for sound commercial reasons, there may be no disclosures at all.

This can place the principal auditors in a difficult position where they are aware of these subsidiaries and of material transactions with them.

Where component auditors are involved it is important that the main group auditors are able to satisfy themselves that they will be in a position to properly assess the work of the component auditors. This will involve review visits and the obtaining of documentary evidence as to the quality and comprehensiveness of the audit work carried out by the component auditors. This is one of the reasons why large diverse multinationals are invariably audited by one of the 'Big 4' mega firms which, with branches everywhere, can claim to audit with a uniform standard wherever group components are situated.

If the group audit partner considers that it will not be possible to obtain sufficient reliable evidence because of restrictions placed on them by management or for logistical reasons they should refuse to accept or withdraw from the appointment. This may be the case, for example, where there are considerable numbers of offshore subsidiaries with no proper disclosure of financial information.

The main or group auditor should audit a significant proportion of the group financial statements. The reason for this is that the group auditor cannot reasonably be expected to understand the business of their client if they do not carry out a significant part of the audit.

PLANNING ISSUES

The principal auditor is responsible for the overall audit strategy and for the plan for auditing the consolidated accounts. Don't forget that each of the components, where these are a company, will also require an audit and will produce their own financial statements.

The audit of group accounts creates specific planning issues which the principal auditor should make themselves familiar with, in particular:

- Reviewing the respective size and location of all the operating units of the group.
- Group-wide controls, such as:
  - How often do group and component management meet?
  - How does the group manage the financial position of its components?
  - What are the group's risk assessment processes?
  - Are there group-wide HR policies and fraud prevention strategies?
  - Are there centralized systems, particularly the Management Information System (MIS)?
  - Is there an internal audit function and how effective is it? (Chapter 19)
- Group accounting issues, such as:
  - identification and eliminating of intra group transactions from the consolidation
  - identification of consolidation only adjustments i.e. adjustments to the financial statements which do not appear in the books of account
  - consistency of accounting policies

Risk assessments

The principal auditor has to determine, for the purposes of the consolidated financial statements, how much audit work is carried out on the financial information of the components, whether by a group audit team or a component auditor.

If the audit of a significant component of the group is to be performed by a component auditor the principal auditor should become involved in discussions with the component auditor about the aspects of the business which are significant to the group. This discussion should cover the susceptibility of the financial statements of the component to a material error or misstatement.

It should also involve a review of the risk assessments carried out by the component auditor of the risk of a material error or misstatement. If there is a significant risk identified by the principal auditor, they must consider the amount and type of audit work to be performed to minimize the risk.

If the component is not significant to the group, the principal auditor can perform a minimal amount of work consisting mostly of analytical review.

Materiality

Group materiality should be greater than materiality limits for the individual components. This is to reduce the risk of a material error or misstatement in the group accounts.

If one of the components is material to the group then the materiality limit applicable to it is its own component materiality but, in addition, if it is considered to pose a risk to the group accounts because of its nature or a particular set of circumstances particular audit attention should be paid to the areas of the component considered to pose material risk. This will require an audit of the particular classes or types of transactions which may pose a significant risk and specific audit procedures relating to the risk itself and the likelihood of a material misstatement.

Indicators of risk of a material misstatement at group level include:

- poor or inadequate corporate governance procedures (Chapter 2)
- weak group-wide controls and poor financial monitoring
- component management allowed wide discretion and not subject to detailed scrutiny from the holding company
- complex group structures with constant changes
- components operating in overseas jurisdictions with low levels of disclosure or inadequate audit and reporting regimes (e.g. tax havens)
- unusual transactions with related parties (Chapter 21)
- complex transactions passing through more than one component
- high-risk business activities or activities in high-risk geographical areas where government intervention may be involved e.g. involving the threat of nationalization or closure of a component without compensation
- differing year ends and accounting policies; accounting policies may differ where local financial reporting requirements differ from the international reporting standards being applied to the group accounts
- previous experience of incomplete or unauthorized consolidation adjustments
- tax planning involving use of known tax havens or corporate forms designed purely for tax purposes
- frequent changes of auditor
- difficulty in tracing or reconciling intra group transactions

COMPONENT AUDITORS

Principal auditors cannot simply rely on the work of other auditors without carrying out any evaluation of the standard of work and the ethical position of component auditors. This is because the principal auditor carries the ultimate responsibility for the consolidated financial statements and, if the component auditors have failed to detect an error or misstatement which is material to the group because of poor audit work, the principal auditor will carry responsibility for its inclusion in the group financial statements.

The principal auditor therefore has to ensure that there are no independence issues, either at subsidiary or group level (e.g. that no one in the subsidiary audit firm holds shares in the group), and obtain a written confirmation that this is so and that the subsidiary auditors are aware of any specific group issues such as identification of inter-group balances and transactions and related parties, etc.

Consequently, the principal auditors must satisfy themselves that:

- component auditors understand and comply with the relevant Ethical Code
- the component auditors are professionally competent
- the group auditor is able to become involved in the work of the component auditor
- the component auditor operates in a regulatory environment which oversees the competence and ethical behaviour of audit firms

Professional competence is not usually an issue. The chief considerations are often the size of the component auditor and the significance of the component to the group. The group auditors must consider whether the component auditor has suitably competent staff and that the work can be completed within the group audit timetable.

In particular, there are specific audit issues with which the principal auditor must be satisfied before they allow the component auditors to proceed. If they are not satisfied that the component auditors are competent to carry out the work, they should undertake it themselves.

Key issues which must be resolved with the component auditors are:

- quality control of audit work
- the risk of material misstatements in work audited by other auditors
- arrangements for review of completed work
- the timing and co-ordination of audit work

- the standardization of audit working papers
- standardization of information to be sent to group auditors

During the course of the group audit, before the reports are signed, the holding company auditors should carry out procedures designed to obtain sufficient, appropriate evidence that the work of the other auditor is adequate. This includes documentary evidence and the component auditor must supply all relevant documentary evidence to the main group auditor to enable them to come to a decision as to the standard of the work done.

COMMUNICATION

As we have seen in connection with audit planning (Chapter 10) the ISAs are particularly insistent that auditors communicate with each other. In a routine audit of a single entity the team should meet regularly and discuss key audit issues and the same principle applies here between principal and component auditors. In particular, there are issues which the principal auditor must communicate to the component auditor. Component auditors are required by ISA 600 to co-operate with the principal auditors.

From principal auditors to component auditors

The group auditors are responsible for the group audit so it is they who should set the tone and approach to the audit. They should determine the strategy, determine the group materiality levels and identify any key risk areas they would like component auditors to pay special attention to.

As an aid to this the group auditors will frequently supply packs of standardized audit materials to ensure that they receive information in a consistent format. These can be electronic or paper-based depending on circumstance.

The key points which the principal auditors must agree with the component auditors are:

- The work to be performed and the use to be made of that work, i.e. it is for the purposes of the group audit only and not for any other purpose.
- The form and content of the component auditor's communication with the group engagement team or principal auditors. Quite often this takes the form of a standard pack of instructions, procedures and requirements.
- Confirmation that the component auditor will cooperate with the group engagement team – this is, of course, mandatory under ISA 600 but, again where there are components in jurisdictions with limited disclosure, this may not be as readily forthcoming as might be hoped.
- Observance of the ethical requirements relevant to the group audit and, in particular, the independence requirements. The principal auditor must get assurances on this.
- The level of component materiality (and, if applicable, the materiality level or levels for particular classes of transactions, account balances or disclosures) and the threshold above which misstatements cannot be regarded as clearly trivial to the group financial statements.
- Significant risks of material misstatement of the group financial statements, due to fraud or error where these can be identified.
- A list of related parties prepared by group management and any other related parties of which the group audit team is aware. The component auditor should inform the principal auditors of details of any related parties not previously identified by group management or the group engagement team.

The principal auditors should also communicate practical audit planning matters such as:

- the timetable for completion
- dates of planned visits by group auditors to review files, etc.
- lists of contacts
- guidance on particular issues affecting the group accounts
- details of subsequent events reviews to be carried out
- information particularly required for statutory reporting purposes

From component auditors to group auditors

In addition to various acknowledgements and assurances shown above, the group auditors need confirmation of several matters from the component auditors.

These include:

- Confirmation that the component auditor has complied with ethical requirements that are relevant to the group audit, including independence and professional competence.
- Whether or not the component auditor is able to comply with the group engagement team's requirements and has done so.
- Clear identification of the financial information of the component on which the component auditor is reporting.
- Information on instances of noncompliance with laws or regulations that could give rise to a material misstatement of the group financial statements.
- A list of uncorrected misstatements of the financial information of the component which need not include misstatements that are below the threshold amount for clearly trivial misstatements set by the group engagement team.
- Indicators of any possible management bias.
- Significant deficiencies in internal control at the component level.
- Any other significant matters that the component auditor has or will communicate to those charged with governance of the component, including fraud or suspected fraud involving component management, employees who have significant roles in internal control at the component level or others where the fraud resulted in a material misstatement of the financial information of the component.
- Any other matters that may be relevant to the group audit, or that the component auditor wishes to draw to the attention of the group engagement team, including exceptions noted in the written representations that the component auditor requested from component management.
- The component auditor's overall findings, conclusions or opinion.

In addition to reporting on the component's financial statements and the results of their audit work component auditors must also supply information required for the consolidation, e.g. inter-group balances and information relevant to the group financial statements but not for the subsidiary's own.

If this information, or any other evidence required by the group auditors is not forthcoming and the component auditors, for some reason, refuse to release it the group auditor can have recourse to the FRC as regulator.

AUDITING INVESTMENTS IN SUBSIDIARIES AND OTHER UNDERTAKINGS

The auditors have to consider three aspects of the audit of investments in subsidiaries (components) and related organizations in the books of the holding company:

- Obtaining evidence of the existence and ownership of the investment as stated on the Statement of Financial Position of the holding company's own accounts. The audit procedures here will be similar to those carried out in relation to the audit of investments as described in Chapter 15.
- Ensuring that the client has accounted for the investments correctly. This is not particularly difficult in the case of 100 per cent owned subsidiaries, but can present problems where the subsidiary is not wholly owned. The extent of the shareholding can be determined by reference to the share register of the subsidiary and, from that, the relevant accounting policy can be determined through legal and regulatory requirements.
- The nature of the relationship with partnerships, joint ventures and related parties. The question of any 'significant' or 'controlling' influence needs to be established. This can be evidenced by such factors as the composition of the controlling boards of the organization, funding arrangements, contractual arrangements, the existence of guarantees and support arrangements, etc.

This latter point can be a difficult one where the holding company uses several **special purpose vehicles** for particular types of transaction. These are usually companies or joint ventures set up for one particular purpose and they are often incorporated in offshore jurisdictions. They may be used as tax shelters or have an opaquer purpose but auditors must be alert to the possibility of such entities.

Many of the major corporate frauds including Enron and Parmalat made extensive use of these special purpose entities or vehicles and the auditors must have had great difficulty in identifying them in the first place let alone finding out what they were for and what they contained. This is why the related party audit provisions in Chapter 21 are so important. We look at some of the issues involved in more detail below.

AUDITING THE CONSOLIDATION

There are several key issues relating to the preparation of consolidated accounts which the auditors must address specifically, in addition to their work on the holding company's own financial statements. The student should be familiar with the various financial accounting requirements for dealing with these issues. The key accounting standard is FRS 102 Section 9 *Consolidated and separate Financial Statements* and students should be aware of the significant accounting considerations in these standards.

Key audit and accounting issues include:

- *Co-terminous accounting periods* – all accounts consolidated should be made up to the same accounting reference date. Any difference in year ends should not exceed three months.
- *Accounting policies* – these should, as far as possible, be consistent across the group. Where it is not possible, say in the case of overseas subsidiaries which adopt a different accounting regime, consolidation adjustments may be required in order to effect the required consistency of presentation. If this is not possible departures from group accounting policies have to be disclosed, where these are material, giving reasons for the inconsistency and an explanation of the sums involved.
- *Consolidation adjustments* – auditors should verify all consolidation adjustments, whether arising from acquisitions or as a result of inter-group trading. This includes adjustments arising from issues such as inconsistent accounting policies, elimination of unrealized inter-group profits, elimination of inter-group balances, etc. This is an area which should be reviewed by an experienced member of the audit team to ensure that the consolidation is not being used to distort the presentation of the financial accounts.
- *Loss-making subsidiaries* – directors need to consider the value of any investment in a loss-making subsidiary both in the Statement of Financial Position of the parent company and in the consolidation. This may require a write down in the carrying value of the investment in the holding company Statement of Financial Position and any goodwill arising on consolidation. In addition, the holding company will be undoubtedly guaranteeing the financial position of the subsidiary by means of a **support letter**. We will look at these in more detail later.
- *Acquisitions and disposals of interests in subsidiary or related companies or parties* – there are accounting rules and requirements which arise when the composition of the group changes and auditors must be aware of the nature of the change and the effect on both the group and the holding company's financial position. This will include the effect of any changes on such matters as going concern considerations (Chapter 23).
- *Any restrictions on paying dividends* – auditors have to ensure the parent company has sufficient distributable reserves to pay any distribution. Consideration has to be given to the availability of profits from subsidiary companies, especially where these are overseas companies.
- *Subsequent events* – as detailed in Chapter 23 auditors have to consider events between the Statement of Financial Position date and the date on which the financial statements are signed. This applies to the group as a whole and appropriate disclosures may have to be made where subsidiaries have been acquired or disposed of in that period.

MODIFIED AUDITOR'S REPORTS

The holding company auditor has to consider any significant findings of the subsidiary auditors in the context of the group as a whole. Items may be material at a subsidiary company level but not at the group level.

An audit qualification, for example, at the subsidiary company level need only be repeated at group level if the point in issue is material in the context of the consolidated accounts.

For example, depending on the materiality of the issue involved, an adverse opinion in the subsidiary's auditor's report *('these accounts do not present etc.')* may only result in an 'except for' qualification in the group report, as issues in the subsidiary may not be sufficient to invalidate the accounts of the entire group. This, of course, as with so many things in auditing, is a matter of professional judgement.

If the issue is material at both the subsidiary and the group level the holding company auditors should modify their report accordingly. If the subsidiary is not audited by the group auditors, it is not necessary to state this in the holding company auditor's report when reporting the modification.

Any discussions concerning the group auditor's report must, of course, be fully documented.

OVERSEAS SUBSIDIARIES

Auditors need to be aware of the problems of auditing subsidiaries based in countries other than that of the holding company.

The auditors need to consider whether there will be any difference in scope between the local audit and what the equivalent audit in the holding company's country would comprise. If the local auditor does not carry out sufficient work additional testing work should be requested.

Where international accounting standards have not been adopted in the overseas country the holding company directors should request additional work be carried out by the local directors to bring them in line with the IAS or the local auditors should be employed to do so. Accounting policies may differ from country to country and the principal auditors should be aware of the impact of any differences.

If the group auditors have significant doubts about the standard and quality of either the financial information produced by the subsidiary or the audit of that information, or indeed both, then, if the subsidiary is material to the group accounts, they may have to consider issuing a modified opinion.

There may well be language problems both in the presentation of the accounts and in liaising with the local auditors.

The effect of foreign currency translations has to be considered and the impact on the group results considered, particularly where the local currency is devaluing year on year against the parent country currency. For example, if the local currency exchange rate weakens substantially, an asset may appear to be declining in value when, in reality, its value has been maintained or has increased in local currency terms.

JOINT AUDITS

In some circumstances, the most common being where the auditors of a newly acquired subsidiary are required to work alongside the parent company auditors, two firms will act jointly as auditors, i.e. the auditor's report will be signed jointly. Note this is not the same situation as a parent company auditor liaising with the local auditor of a subsidiary – in that case they are not joint auditors.

This requires both firms to agree on:

- the audit approach to be adopted
- timing and staffing
- division of work
- sharing of audit working papers and who keeps what

Where two firms are to act jointly, issues of client and industry experience are as relevant as the size of each firm and the availability of staff. Geographical and language factors, in the case of overseas audits, are also relevant.

There needs to be a genuine spirit of co-operation between the two firms so that all discussions are documented and shared with all audit staff and there is free exchange of information both during and after the audit.

Both firms need to agree the audit opinion and the content of any Management Letter (Chapter 27).

There are both advantages and disadvantages to joint audits, particularly when the client company is a very large one with a wide geographical spread.

Advantages include:

- Wide geographical coverage.
- Close co-operation between the firms.
- Wider range of expertise and resources.
- More efficient audit processes including the accumulated knowledge and experience of subsidiary auditors following acquisition.
- Added assurance to client as report is signed by both firms.

However, there are disadvantages, principally:

- Joint liability means taking responsibility for the work of the other firm.
- It is likely to cost more.
- It requires a high standard of supervision and control to ensure that nothing 'falls through the cracks'.
- It may be difficult to agree a joint approach.

SUPPORT LETTERS TO SUBSIDIARIES

As stated above, it happens from time to time that a subsidiary makes losses and loses value. Perhaps, for operational reasons, the group deliberately runs a subsidiary at a loss or it may simply be as a result of poor trading.

Consequently, it may be that the subsidiary, taken on its own, ceases to be a going concern. If this were the case the group accounts would have to recognize this; however, the group will not allow its subsidiary to go under and so undertakes to continue to support it.

This means that the subsidiary is therefore a going concern and no audit reporting problem arises. However, the auditors need to evidence this and so they require what is known as a **support letter** (or 'comfort' letter) from the holding company directors.

This commonly states:

- that the holding company will continue to support its subsidiary financially so that external creditors will be able to be paid in full
- the holding company will not demand repayment of any inter-company loans or balances until all other creditors have been paid in full

The principal auditor cannot simply accept this letter at face value, nor can the auditor of the subsidiary concerned. If a going concern qualification is to be avoided in the subsidiary's auditor's report the auditor of the subsidiary must be assured that the supporting company is able to fulfil its obligations to the subsidiary. The principal auditor should evaluate the effect that the giving of such a letter of support may have on the financial statements of the supporting company and the group.

TRANSNATIONAL AUDITS

A **transnational audit** is an audit of financial statements which may be relied upon in more than one country or jurisdiction, for example for the purpose of lending or regulation. With increasing globalization this problem is becoming more prevalent for audit firms.

Globalization, in principle, treats the world as being the market place and the source of material and resources. Businesses are not confined within national boundaries and operate in a range of countries and jurisdictions. Goods, services and individuals move across international borders. This inevitably results in international companies operating and reporting in jurisdictions with a wide range of legal and financial requirements.

Clearly there are likely to be some significant differences in the area of company law and possibly the regulation of the audit profession between countries. This may mean that regulation and oversight of auditors may take different forms and be of varying quality so may lead to inconsistencies in audit practice and quality between countries.

Corporate governance requirements vary greatly between countries. This affects not only directors but also auditors who may be required to report on corporate governance in addition to their financial audit responsibilities. Where corporate governance standards are weak such matters as poor oversight of the directors or lack of internal audit may increase the possibility of inadequate internal controls.

There may be differences in auditing and financial reporting standards but, with increasing harmonization of standards and increasing adoption of standards internationally this is less of a problem than it might first appear.

For example, all EU countries have to agree to adopt the ISAs, albeit tailored for local conditions, so the essentials of auditing standards may well be common between countries even if there are some differences of detail. However, the adoption of ISAs is not universal so this can result in audit work being performed at varying levels of effectiveness depending on location.

Financial reporting standards do differ markedly between some jurisdictions, for example between UK GAAP and US GAAP and this may result, in the case of an international group, in some complex consolidation adjustments which may increase the risks of a material misstatement.

Globalization and audit firms

The consequence of globalization is that the auditors themselves must be able to audit such entities and this has inevitably led to the rise of global audit firms and the concentration of major transnational audits into their hands. In this case the so called 'Big 4' have a huge proportion of transnational clients.

As a counter to the 'Big 4' there has been seen a rise of affiliations among smaller audit firms to give them the international reach to audit clients operating in different countries and to create an international presence. These can include international co-operatives of smaller firms which retain their own identity in their home country but which cooperate and send each other business.

There are advantages to large international companies of using one international audit firm, including:

- consistency of standards of work;
- global facilities and capacity for advice; and
- expertise in multiple jurisdictions.

The disadvantages of using a global audit firm are those of restriction of choice and high cost.

As the world of international business grows and even relatively small companies are trading across boundaries the trend towards increased mergers and affiliations of audit firms is likely to continue. This may be particularly true of firms in developed countries and firms with practices in less developed areas where US and European companies are expanding their operations. The incidence of transnational audits is increasing.

SUMMARY

- Holding (parent) companies have, as their principal asset, investments in and loan and current accounts with subsidiaries and related undertakings.
- The principal group auditor is responsible for the opinion on the consolidated accounts. They have to consider the effect of any modified reports in subsidiary companies.
- Before accepting appointment as group auditors the firm must consider the usual ethical and practical issues and evaluate the potential client.
- Where not all the group is audited by one firm, arrangements must be made for the principal company auditors to review the work of the auditors of the components (subsidiaries) to ensure that the standard of audit work is satisfactory.
- The principal auditors must familiarize themselves with the activities and components of the group.

- There are particular problems associated with auditing overseas components including consideration of local accounting and auditing standards and foreign currency issues.
- Where a component makes losses the auditors have to consider the carrying value of the investment.
- They will require a support letter where a subsidiary is not a going concern.
- It is important that principal and component auditors communicate to ensure a free flow of information.
- Group auditors are responsible for planning the group audit.
- Group auditors must evaluate the work done by component auditors, in particular the risk of an error or material misstatement going undetected.
- Joint auditors present logistical problems centred on planning and sharing information.
- Problems arise where components are incorporated in jurisdictions with lower standards of disclosure than the principal auditors need. Auditing standards in some countries may be low or non-existent. Group auditors may well have to attempt to carry out the work themselves but this may be difficult in some countries with secrecy rules or they should issue a modified opinion where the component is material to the group.
- Transnational audits mean that the financial statements may be relied on in more than one jurisdiction. This presents issues in respect of differing auditing standards and reporting rules which audit firms need to be aware of.
- The subsequent events review must include the group as a whole.

POINTS TO NOTE

- The accounting rules relating to groups are complex but students of auditing need to know them.
- The group auditors must be confident that the work of component auditors is of the same standard as theirs and that audit risk has been fully considered.
- Communication between auditors is very important and component auditors must be fully aware of what the group auditors require of them.
- Globalization is bringing increased problems with transnational audits and the audit of overseas entities generally. This has encouraged the rise of global audit firms who can deal with reporting in different jurisdictions.

CASE STUDY

Bangi Chemicals Ltd make chemicals for the defence industry. They had no subsidiary companies but in mid 2X16, they acquired 60 per cent of the share capital of an American company for £6m paid partly in cash and partly in shares in Bangi. The net assets of the American company, Chemola Inc., were about £4.8m at the time of purchase. Since then the company has made a loss of £1.5m, but is expected to break-even next year and make a large profit after that. The auditors of Chemola are based in the USA and it is proposed that they will continue to carry out the audit as auditors Cherry & Blossom LLP have no representation in the USA.

Discussion

– Draw up a list of audit procedures that Cherry & Blossom LLP, the auditors of Bangi, should carry out in connection with Chemola. The audit of Chemola is carried out by an American firm. Cherry & Blossom LLP is engaged on the audit of Bangi's 2X16 accounts.

– How should the matters connected with Chemola appear in Bangi's own accounts? Bangi advanced £1.2m as a temporary loan to Chemola to cover a cash flow shortage and, in addition, has a trading balance of Dr £600 000 at 31.12. 2X16.

– What matters should Cherry & Blossom LLP consider when reviewing the group accounts?

– What actions should they take with regard to the audit by the American firm of the accounts of Chemola?

– Identify the risks and the risk areas that Cherry & Blossom LLP should worry about.

STUDENT SELF-TESTING QUESTIONS

Questions with answers apparent from the text

a) What considerations as to the value of investments on a holding company Statement of Financial Position are relevant to the audit?

b) List the auditor's duties regroup accounts.

c) How should a principal auditor evaluate the work of a component auditor?

d) What is a 'comfort letter' and how is it used?

e) How do auditors deal with a difference in auditing standards between principal and component auditors?

f) Why is it difficult to form an opinion when consolidated accounts include associated companies?

g) What is a transnational audit?

h) Why do transnational audits pose problems for audit firms?

EXAMINATION QUESTIONS

1 (a) Explain the role of 'support letters' (also called 'comfort letters') as evidence in the audit of financial statements.

(b) You are an audit manager in Wilde & Free, a firm of Chartered Certified Accountants, and currently assigned to the audit of Capri Group. The consolidated financial statements of Capri Group are prepared in accordance with the accounting standards and interpretations issued by the International Accounting Standards Board (IASB).

The draft financial statements for the year ended 30 June 2X16 show profit before taxation of £62 million (2X15 – £55 million) and total assets £325 million (2X15 – £298 million).

One of the Group's principal subsidiaries, Capri (Overseas), is audited by another firm, Bangit & Go. You have just received Bangit & Go's draft auditor's report as follows:

Basis of audit opinion (extract)
'As set out in notes 4 and 5, expenditure on finance leases has not been reflected in the Statement of Financial Position but included in operating expenses and no provision has been made for deferred taxation. This is in accordance with local taxation regulations.

Opinion
In our opinion the financial statements give a true and fair view of the financial position of the company as of 30 June 2X16 and of the results of its operations and its cash flows for the year then ended in accordance with . . .'

The draft financial statements of Capri (Overseas) for the year ended 30 June 2X16 show profit before taxation of £19 million (2X15 – £17 million) and total assets £65 million (2015 – £66 million). The relevant notes (in full) are as follows:

(1) Leased assets
     During the year the company has incurred expenditure on leasing agreements that give rights approximating to ownership of fixed assets with a fair value of £790 000. All lease payments are charged to the income statement as incurred.
(2) Taxation
     This includes current taxes on profit and other taxes such as taxes on capital. No provision is required to be made for deferred taxation and it is impracticable to quantify the financial effect of unrecognized deferred tax liabilities.

Required:
Comment on the matters you should consider before expressing an opinion on the consolidated financial statements of the Capri Group.
(ACCA)

SOURCES AND ADDITIONAL READING

Financial Reporting Council (2009) *FRS 102 The Financial Reporting Standard Applicable in the UK and Republic of Ireland*. London: Financial Reporting Council.

Financial Reporting Council (2016) *ISA 600 Special Considerations – Audits of Group Financial Statements (Including the Work of Component Auditors)*. London: Financial Reporting Council.

Jones, M. (2011) *Creative Accounting, Fraud and International Accounting Scandals*. Chichester: Wiley.

Shaxson, N. (2011) *Treasure Islands: Tax Havens and the Men who Stole the World*. London: Bodley Head.

Wood, F. (2005) *Business Accounting 2*. London: Prentice-Hall.

CHAPTER 29
AUDITOR'S LIABILITY

Learning Objectives

After studying the material in this chapter you should be able to:

- understand the auditor's duties under the Companies Act 2006 regarding audit reports

- understand the requirements of contract law to perform work with reasonable skill and care

- discuss the question of auditor's liability to third parties for negligence

- understand what is meant by 'proximity'

- explain how audit firms can minimize their liability to third parties

INTRODUCTION

Students should already have appreciated that the law has relevance for auditors, in particular the Companies Act, 2006 and its effect on auditors which has been detailed in Chapters 2 and 3. However, other branches of the law also affect auditors, in particular what happens when things go wrong.

Auditors perform audits and sign audit reports which, as we know, contain the auditor's opinion on the truth and fairness of financial statements. Auditors are reputed to be independent, competent and honest so, if the auditors certify that a set of financial statements show a true and fair view, readers of those financial statements will have faith in them because they have faith in the auditors. This is why maintenance of the independence and credibility of the audit profession is so important.

Because their work is relied upon by others, auditors clearly have a responsibility to do their work honestly and carefully. The judge in the *London & General Bank case (1895)* summed it up when he said, about an auditor:

> '*He must be honest – that is, he must not certify what he does not believe to be true, and he must take reasonable care and skill before he believes that what he certifies is true.*'

This set a standard for the performance level of audit work – auditors are not meant to be all seeing and all knowing, they must simply exercise 'reasonable care and skill' in carrying out their work. This is known as their 'duty of care' to the people to whom they report.

However, what 'reasonable care and skill' actually means depends on the circumstances of each case and it is very difficult to generalize. Where auditors fail to exercise sufficient care and skill in carrying out their audit work fraud or a material error may go undiscovered at the time of the audit, so they certify the accounts without qualification having failed to discover that the financial statements do not show a true and fair view because they contain a material misstatement which the auditors have failed to detect.

Because of that somebody who claims to or actually does rely on the work of the auditor may lose money. This loss of money flows directly from the failure of the auditors to do their job properly.

If those who have lost money are to somehow claim it back one question needs to be addressed and this has been left to the Courts to decide in a series of landmark cases which have, so far, set the boundary on the auditor's liability to third parties and to their clients. The question is: to whom does the auditor owe a duty of care – just to the shareholders or to the world at large?

We will return to that question later.

CRIMINAL LAW

Auditors are subject to a code of ethics and are generally held to be honest and trustworthy individuals. However, there are cases where professionally qualified individuals either become embroiled in, or worse, actually institute criminal acts so it is worthwhile having a working knowledge of the main aspects of the criminal law as it affects auditors and accountants.

There are some specific offences which are criminal offences under various statutes. It is not necessary to detail all of the legislation but the nature of the offences is listed here.

Companies Act offences

It is an offence (under the Companies Act 2006) to:

- Accept an appointment as an auditor when disqualified to do so or to continue as an auditor after becoming ineligible.
- Conspire with others to carry on a company with intent to defraud.
- Knowingly or recklessly to cause an audit report to include 'any matter that is misleading, false or deceptive in any material particular'.

- Knowingly or recklessly cause an audit report to omit a statement that is required under certain sections of the Act. These are:
  - Section 498(2)(b) – statement that company's accounts do not agree with accounting records and returns
  - Section 498 (3) – statement that necessary information and explanations not obtained or
  - Section 498(5) – statement that directors wrongly took advantage of exemption from obligation to prepare group accounts

The last two offences, concerning 'knowingly or recklessly' issuing a false audit report, are new under CA 2006 (Section 507). They can be committed by a director, member, employee or agent of an audit firm if such person is an accountant who would be eligible to be the auditor of the company and, on conviction, offences are punishable by a fine.

The audit profession was concerned that negligence or honest mistakes could come to be penalized as a criminal offence. The problem lies in the definition of 'recklessly'. The government said:

'the auditor would have to know that failure to act carried unreasonable risks and consciously decide to go ahead despite that. The real point is that it is a long way above negligence. One cannot be reckless inadvertently, a degree of consciousness has to be shown.'

This opens up several issues.

If negligence is proved because the auditor failed to carry out proper professional procedures, i.e. decided at the planning stage of the audit deliberately not to carry them out, this will almost certainly be negligent but is it reckless?

Courts may choose to look at the situation in this way:

- If the decision was taken as the result of a faulty risk assessment, and the auditors honestly believed the procedures weren't necessary, they may be guilty of negligent auditing, assuming they weren't being deliberately misled by the directors, perhaps because they failed to carry out proper procedures under the relevant ISAs.
- However, if they decided not to carry out audit procedures simply to save money by reducing audit time, perhaps based on some very superficial reasoning about the trustworthiness of their client, they may not only be negligent but also reckless.

Clearly it will require some prosecutions before the attitude of the courts becomes clear. Consequently, audit documentation will become even more significant, in terms of justifying decisions taken at the audit planning stage.

In addition to these Companies Act offences we saw, in Chapter 20, the auditor's responsibilities concerning fraud and in Chapter 6 the ethical rules with respect to money laundering and insider trading. Whilst these are of interest, of much more importance is the auditor's duties under what is known as common law concerning negligence.

CIVIL LIABILITY UNDER THE COMMON LAW

The most complex area for auditors is the civil law and this brings us back to the earlier questions relating to duty of care and negligence. Common law is law made by cases or precedents as opposed to statute law which is law set out in statutes passed by Parliament.

Duty of care

Duty of care is the obligation to exercise a level of care, as is reasonable in all the circumstances, in carrying out professional work. In the case of an audit for example, auditors have a duty to use their training and professional expertise to minimize the risk of material errors or misstatements going undetected and so being included in the financial statements with the result that these are misleading. This would require auditors to exercise the level of skill care and competence expected of a suitably qualified professional in the circumstances.

Note that this duty of care does not require any form of superhuman effort, nor does it require any particular foresight other than a reasonable consideration of the possible consequences of actions carried out. The duty of care is, therefore, based upon the relationship of the parties, the negligent act or omission and the reasonable probability of foreseeing any loss.

Only a negligent act will be regarded as having breached a duty of care.

Negligence

What is negligence? The broad principle was stated in 1932 in the case of *Donaghue v Stevenson* by Lord Atkin who said:

> *'you must take reasonable care to avoid acts or omissions which you can reasonably foresee might injure your neighbour'.*

This 'neighbour' principal has caused no little trouble in legal circles when considering the culpability of auditors for negligence as we will see later, but as a statement of general principles it is a sound one – auditors must use reasonable skill and care to avoid doing something, such as issuing an incorrect auditor's report, which might cause loss to their client *or someone reasonably close to them*. We have put this last point in italics to highlight it as it is this question of what lawyers call **proximity** which has caused all the trouble.

For an allegation of negligence to succeed the claimant must prove:

- the defendant had a duty of care to the claimant
- there was a breach of the duty of care which caused harm or damage
- that damage must have been foreseeable
- there must be proximity between the parties
- it is fair, just and reasonable for the court to impose a liability on the auditors

We will look at two situations under civil law where auditors can be sued for negligence:

- under contract law where a contractual relationship exists between two parties, in this case shareholders and auditors
- to a third party where a duty of care exists but is not contractual

One of the key issues we will be looking at in this chapter is quite how far that duty to a third party extends. Clearly auditors owe a duty of care to the shareholders, but what about other readers of the accounts such as lenders, suppliers or potential investors?

DUTY OF CARE

We have established (Chapter 8) that the Letter of Engagement, duly signed by the auditors and the client, represents the basis of a contract between them. Because there is a contract the auditors can be sued for a breach of it if they provide a negligently prepared audit report which results in loss to the client.

The reason for this is that the existence of the contract creates a duty of care between the auditors and the shareholders to whom they report. Although the Letter of Engagement is signed by the directors, they are signing it on behalf of the company, which is owned by the shareholders, so the duty of care is owed to the company, not to the directors. If the auditors fail to carry out their duties to a reasonable standard, they can be liable.

As we have already seen the auditors are only bound to exercise 'reasonable skill and care' in carrying out their activities. Quite what this means has often been left to the courts to decide.

This has been reflected in the ethical codes of various accounting bodies. For example, the ACCA requires their members to carry out their work with:

> *'due skill, care diligence and expedition with proper regard to the technical and professional standards expected of them as members.'*

The ICAEW expects their members to display what they call 'professional competence' and their ethical rules state:

> 'The principle of professional competence and due care imposes the following obligations on professional accountants:
>
> (a) To maintain professional knowledge and skill at the level required to ensure that clients or employers receive competent professional service; and
>
> (b) To act diligently in accordance with applicable technical and professional standards when providing professional services.'

The courts have also given guidance as to what is considered to be 'reasonable skill and care' in various judgements.

Re London & General Bank (No 2) (1895)

We have already noted, above, part of the wording of the judgment in the London & General Bank case but here is another point the judge made:

> '[The auditor's] business is to ascertain and state the true financial position of the company at the time of the audit and his duty is confined to that. But then comes the question: How is he to ascertain such position? The answer is by examining the books of the company.
>
> But he does not discharge his duty by doing this without enquiry and without taking the trouble to see that the books and records of the company show the company's true position. He must take reasonable care to ascertain that they do. Unless he does this his duty will be worse than an idle farce.'

Re Kingston Cotton Mill No 2 (1896)

This is a classic case which the auditing profession has relied on implicitly almost since the judgment was given by Mr Justice Lopes in 1896. The judgment contained two significant phrases which students should be aware of. One of them, the reference to the auditor being a 'watchdog not a bloodhound' we have already met in Chapter 20:

> 'It is the duty of an auditor to bring to bear on the work he has to perform that skill, care, and caution which a reasonably competent, careful, and cautious auditor would use.
>
> An auditor is not bound to be a detective, or, as was said, to approach his work with suspicion, or with a foregone conclusion that there is something wrong. He is a watchdog, but not a bloodhound.
>
> Auditors must not be made liable for not tracking out ingenious and carefully laid schemes of fraud, when there is nothing to arouse their suspicion ... So to hold would make the position of an auditor intolerable.'

This judgment set the tone for the audit profession for over a century – auditors were to be passive checkers rather than be proactive detectives in searching out errors, misstatements and frauds.

However, this statement may no longer have the force it once did in the light of ISA 240 'The auditor's responsibilities relating to fraud in an audit of financial statements'. Auditors have now to recognize at least the possibility that fraud may exist and, consequently, adopt an attitude of professional scepticism in their approach to audit work. They have to recognize that schemes of fraud may involve complex misrepresentations and carry out their work accordingly.

This ISA may well be interpreted by the courts as placing on auditors a rather greater element of awareness, if not actual sleuthing, than the previous decisions admitted. Auditors still do not have to actively seek out fraud, but they have to be alert watchdogs!

Re Thomas Gerrard & Son (1968)

For many years the managing director of the company falsified the inventory figures in the accounts in order to conceal losses and to enable dividends to be paid. To do this he included non-existent inventory and he also altered invoices, which were discovered by the auditors but not followed up or investigated.

The auditors relied on inventory certificates given to them by the managing director, a person who they trusted. They contended that it was not part of the auditor's role to count inventory, merely to verify the figures, and that they were entitled to rely on the assurances given by a responsible official of the company. This was supported by the decision in the Kingston Cotton Mill case where the judge stated that an auditor: '*is justified in believing tried servants of the company in whom confidence is placed by the company*'.

However, in this case the court held that the discovery of the altered invoices had put the auditors on enquiry and they should have investigated the matter.

They were no longer able to trust the assurances given to them and should have made enquiries, if necessary from suppliers, to verify the assurances given. Once the auditor's suspicions were aroused they had to investigate the matter fully. If they had done so the fraud would have been revealed. They were thus guilty of negligent auditing.

This is particularly relevant where auditors are obtaining information from officials of the company without a concomitant amount of corroborative checking work. If they have reason to doubt or are suspicious of any transactions, they must follow it up. This is supported by the content of ISA 240 which requires auditors to follow up on queries and anomalies and goes to the heart of the attitude of professional scepticism required.

LIABILITY FOR NEGLIGENCE

This is the most contentious area of auditor's liability and has given the courts and the audit profession, no end of trouble over the years.

The problem is as follows. Clearly as we have seen above, auditors can be liable to the shareholders for failing to carry out their audit with reasonable skill and care should they suffer loss as a result. However, parties other than shareholders use audited financial statements – for example:

- lenders
- employees
- regulators
- tax authorities
- suppliers
- customers
- potential investors

Indeed, a whole range of third parties some of whom the auditors might be generally aware of and others of which they have no specific knowledge at all. Are they liable to everyone?

To be liable in negligence there are five conditions to be fulfilled which we set out above but are worth repeating here if the subtleties of the law are to be understood clearly. They are:

- The defendant had a duty of care to the claimant.
- There was a breach of the duty of care which caused harm or damage.
- That damage must have been foreseeable.
- There must be proximity between the parties.
- It is fair, just and reasonable for the court to impose a liability on the auditors.

In these negligence cases much hangs on whether a duty of care is owed at all because if the auditors did not owe a duty of care they cannot breach it and so cannot be liable for damages for negligence. In most cases the facts of the case are clear, losses have been established and so has the apparent negligence of the auditors.

Clearly if they have not been negligent, i.e. they have carried out a proper audit in accordance with all the precepts of the ISAs and done all their work as a reasonably competent, cautious and careful auditor would do, but they have been lied to by a conspiracy of directors then they have no case to answer as they have not been negligent; but where they have failed in their duty as auditors the failure is often all too apparent.

The question at law then hinges on the question of 'proximity', i.e. did the auditors know about the third party and is that party sufficiently proximate to create a duty of care?

A review of the key cases in this area will give some guidance on how the legal arguments have progressed and of the present position.

Candler v Crane Christmas & Co. (1951)

In *Candler v Crane Christmas (1951)*, Candler sued the accountants (Crane Christmas) of a company as he had relied on the accounts they had prepared for the purposes of making a decision to invest money in that company. The accounts turned out to have been negligently prepared.

The courts ruled that, although the accountants had acted negligently, they did not have a contract with Candler and therefore did not owe him a duty of care. This ruling was taken by the accountancy profession as meaning that no duty of care was owed to third parties.

Hedley Byrne v Heller and Partners (1964)

This was a case concerning banks but it sent shockwaves through the auditing profession. The plaintiff (Hedley Byrne) lost money when a bank reference was negligently produced – the bank indicated that their client was a good credit risk when this was not the case.

The court ruled that, in principle, although there was no contract between Hedley Byrne and the bank, it was liable to pay damages because of its negligence.

In that case Lord Morris said:

> 'I consider that it follows and that it should now be regarded as settled that if someone possessed of a special skill undertakes, quite irrespective of contract, to apply that skill for the assistance of another person who relies upon such skill, a duty of care will arise ..... Furthermore, if in a sphere in which a person is so placed that others could reasonably rely upon his judgment or his skill or upon his ability to make careful inquiry, a person takes it upon himself to give information or advice to, or allows his information or advice to be passed on to, another person who, as he knows or should know, will place reliance upon it, then a duty of care will arise.'

The key point was that the judgment held that if a third party could show that it relied on the work of another, e.g. an auditor, which turned out to be wrong it could claim damages. However, the judgment was restricted to parties where the identity was known, unknown parties still couldn't claim.

JEB Fasteners v Marks Bloom (1981)

The audited accounts of the company did not show a true and fair view of the state of affairs and the auditors were held to be negligent in stating that they did. At the time it was accepted that the auditors were aware of the plaintiffs' interest in the company but not that they were contemplating a takeover bid.

The courts held in favour of the auditors as the plaintiffs had not suffered a loss and would have bought the share capital at the agreed price whatever the accounts had said. The duty of care issue was therefore irrelevant and was not considered by the court. What makes this case important however is that the courts stated that a duty of care *will* exist where the auditors:

- knew or reasonably should have foreseen, at the time that the accounts were audited, that a person might rely on those accounts for a particular purpose; and
- that, in all the circumstances, it would be reasonable for such reliance to be placed on those accounts for that particular purpose.

This case raised the possibility that an auditor might owe a duty of care to a third party who reads the accounts and then makes an investment or some other decision after relying on those accounts.

Effectively, after this decision, the auditor might owe a duty of care to an unknown person.

Caparo Industries v Dickman (1990)

This is the case which, at present, sets out the current position for the liability of auditors to third parties and it is this case with which students should be familiar.

Caparo had alleged that it had based its decision to make a successful takeover bid of Fidelity plc on the strength of the latter's 1984 accounts which were audited by Touche Ross. Before the takeover bid Caparo had been a minority shareholder in Fidelity plc.

The accounts significantly overstated the true position of Fidelity and so, subsequent to the eventual take-over, Caparo sued the auditors. The plaintiff argued that a duty of care was owed to them by the auditors. The Court of Appeal originally found for Caparo in 1989, however, on appeal the House of Lords overturned the decision and found in favour of Dickman (the Touche Ross partner).

The judgment against Caparo was clear that, in the circumstances of this case, the auditor did not owe a duty of care to *potential* investors.

It held that the auditor's duty of care was owed to the shareholders as a body and not to individual share-holders for purposes such as to assist them in making investment decisions.

In his judgment, Lord Bridge referred to the salient features of earlier cases, stating that, for a duty of care to arise in respect of the advice or information given, the person who it is alleged owes that duty of care must be fully aware:

- of the identity of any third party who purports to rely on the adviser's advice;
- of the nature of the transaction contemplated by the third party;
- that the advice or information given would be passed to the third party, directly or indirectly; and
- that it was very likely that the third party intended to rely on that advice or information in deciding whether or not to engage in the transaction.

In these circumstances, the judge considered that, subject to the effect of any disclaimer of responsibility, the person giving advice or information would be expected to be aware that the third party would rely on the advice or information given in deciding whether or not to engage in the transaction being contemplated.

This would create a duty of care and the auditors would be liable for any negligent misstatements.

This is the current situation as far as UK civil law is concerned, however, there is another decision which is relevant to a full appreciation of the legal position.

Royal Bank of Scotland v Bannerman Johnstone Maclay (Scottish Court of Session) (2002)

The defendants were auditors of a company which, in 1998, went into receivership with debts of around £13 million owing to Royal Bank of Scotland (RBS). RBS claimed that, due to a fraud, the accounts of previous years had misstated the true financial position of the company and the defendants had been negligent in not detecting it. RBS was the company's main banker/lender and, over a period of time, had also exercised options to subscribe for a majority of the company's shares. A requirement of the lending agreement was that monthly management accounts and audited accounts were to be sent to the bank as soon as was practicable.

The court held in favour of RBS on the basis that, broadly following the guidelines set by Lord Bridge in Caparo, the auditors knew the identity of the third party, the use to which the information would be put and that the bank intended to rely on it for the known purpose.

The court dismissed the defence's arguments that, for a duty of care to exist, there must be an express assumption of responsibility to the third party by the auditor. Significantly the judge commented that, having become aware of the details of the requirements of the lending agreement, the auditors could have disclaimed responsibility to the bank.

This is where the question of proximity arises. In the Bannerman case the auditors were only too well aware that the bank would be likely to use the financial reports and to rely on the auditor's report for fiscal purposes, they knew who the bank was and the relationships between themselves the bank and their client – in other words there was a proximate relationship. The auditors tried to claim that they had no actual knowledge of the use the bank would make of the audit report, merely inferred or constructive knowledge but the court dismissed this argument.

Whilst Bannerman may not widen the general principles of Caparo – audit firms are still not liable to any potential investor they know nothing about – it clearly, in the author's opinion, widens the duty of care of the auditors to include lenders to the company where it is reasonable to assume they may place reliance on the audited financial statements for a known purpose, e.g. continuing to lend to the company.

Although the decision of the Scottish Court of Session is not binding on other national courts, it does raise new questions about the duty of care to third parties. This has prompted audit firms to include disclaimers, known as the Bannerman wording, in their Auditor's Reports. (See Chapter 26).

This has now been tested in the case of *Barclays Bank plc v Grant Thornton LLP [2015] EWHC 320 (Comm)*. In this case Grant Thornton were auditors to Van Essen Hotels Ltd and were tasked with preparing non statutory audit reports. Grant Thornton knew that these were being looked at by Barclays bank to monitor the financial health of the group. When the Van Esssen group went into liquidation it was discovered that the financial director of Van Essen had falsified the figures to look as if the hotel chain was meeting its banking covenants when it was not. Barclays sued to recover some of their losses alleging that Grant Thornton owed it a duty of care.

The court dismissed Barclays claim granting summary judgment to Grant Thornton on the basis that Barclays would have no realistic prospect of success and there was no good reason why the action should go to trial. The judge stated that it was clear from the wording used in the reports that Grant Thornton anticipated they would be forwarded to Barclays and in the absence of the 'Bannerman' disclaimer clause it was arguable that a duty would exist between Grant Thornton and Barclays. So, the key question was whether the Bannerman disclaimer was reasonable. The judge decided that it was because Barclays was a sophisticated commercial party, used to reading accounts and audit reports and the disclaimers were clear and obvious on the face of the reports. Therefore, Barclays ought reasonably to have been aware of their existence – Grant Thornton could not anticipate that any competent banker would fail to read the first two paragraphs of a two-page report. The judge pointed out that Barclays could have taken steps to protect its own position by obtaining its own report via a direct engagement with Grant Thornton but it had chosen not to do so.

Accordingly, in the face of the express disclaimer, the reports told Barclays expressly that it relied on the reports at its own risk.

The Bannerman wording now appears to have been tried and tested in the courts however it should be pointed out that a case may be brought by a less sophisticated party than a bank and one who is relying on the financial expertise of an auditor in which case the court may well take the view that the clause is unfair and strike it out. However, for the time being these clauses are effective in limiting the liability of auditors.

Other cases

It is useful to examine the circumstances of other cases so students can understand the limitations of these decisions which are the cornerstone of the audit profession's understanding of its legal position.

ADT Ltd v BDO Binder Hamlyn (1996)

Assurances had been given to ADT by the auditors of Britannia Security Group ('Britannia'), BDO Binder Hamlyn (BBH). ADT asked them if they stood by their audit opinion and they replied that they did. This created a relationship between ADT and BBH who knew that ADT were looking to buy Britannia. After ADT had bought Britannia they discovered that its assets were overstated by £65m.

The court held that by confirming its audit opinion to ADT, BBH had created a contractual relationship and were liable for damages and costs totalling £105m.

Peach Publishing Co v Slater & Co (1997)

In this case the auditor gave an oral assurance as to the reliability of some unaudited management accounts which the purchaser relied on when buying a business. The judge said that an accountant does not automatically assume liability and that, in any case, the purchaser should have made his own checks rather than try and obtain some form of warranty where none was intended.

This case does, however, highlight the dangers of third parties trying to obtain some form of assurance from the auditors and care has to be taken in statements made to them, especially where there may be a possibility of that third party placing a reliance on the assurance given.

The general principle of liability to a third party, where the auditors know that the audit is going to be relied on as some form of assurance, is reflected internationally.

International decisions

In the USA the decision in *Ultramares Corporation v Touche (1931)* was that the auditors could be liable if they *knew* that the audit was for the primary benefit of the plaintiff, e.g. that the audited accounts were to be relied on by the plaintiff (a bank) which was to lend money to the client but not in general circumstances. As the judge put it that would expose the auditors to:

'liability in an indeterminate amount for an indeterminate time to an indeterminate class.'

This decision has been followed in another leading case *Credit Alliance v Arthur Andersen & Co (1985)* and was strengthened by the ruling that the auditors had to have performed some form of linking act such as sending a copy of the accounts to the plaintiff.

The Australian case of *Mutual Life v Citizens Assurance Co Ltd v Evatt (1971)*, involving negligent financial advice given by an insurance agent and the Canadian case of *Haig v Bamford (1977)* both held that:

- no duty of care is owed to a stranger;
- the liability to third parties cannot arise in the absence of knowledge that the third party is going to rely on the information given; and
- the person giving the advice must be doing so in their professional capacity and not as a citizen.

Clearly, therefore, the consensus is that auditors might be liable to third parties where they are aware of the third party and they could reasonably foresee that the third party might rely on the information contained in the audited accounts.

MINIMIZING RISK TO AUDIT FIRMS

Although all audit firms are required to carry professional indemnity assurance to protect partners from loss they are very reluctant to accept claims, not solely for financial reasons but also to preserve their reputation.

Auditors and accountants can minimize their potential liability for professional negligence in several ways:

- By not being negligent, i.e. by having a functioning quality control system (Chapter 7).
- Ensuring that the audit procedures in accordance with IAS 315 *Identifying and assessing the risks of material misstatement through understanding the entity and its environment* are carried out properly.
- Carrying out audit work in accordance with the International Standards on Auditing.
- Agreeing the duties and responsibilities in an Engagement Letter. This should specify the specific tasks to be undertaken and exclude specifically those that are not to be undertaken. It should also define the responsibilities to be undertaken by the client and specify any limitations on the work to be carried out. The Engagement Letter should also set out the purpose for which the report has been prepared and that the client may not use it for any other purpose.
- Defining in their audit report the precise work undertaken, the work not undertaken, and any limitations to the work. This is so that any third party will have knowledge of the responsibility accepted by the auditor for the work done. The revised audit report wording (Chapter 26) greatly assists this.
- By identifying the authorized recipients of reports in the Engagement Letter and in the auditor's report and by limiting or excluding liability by a term in the Engagement Letter or, to third parties, by a disclaimer in the auditor's report. This requires any auditor's report to state the purpose of the report and that it may not be relied on for any other purpose (the Bannerman wording, see Chapter 26).

- By operating as a limited liability partnership (see below).
- By making an agreement with the directors and approved by the shareholders as to the extent of any damages which may be claimed – a liability limitation agreement (see below).
- Finally the RSBs require that all auditors must carry Professional Indemnity Insurance (PII) – just in case!

LIMITED LIABILITY PARTNERSHIPS (LLPs)

Many audit firms have established themselves as Limited Liability Partnerships (LLPs) following the provisions in the Companies Act 2006.

The key features of an LLP include:

- It is a corporate body, i.e. a separate legal entity distinct from its members. The LLP can own and hold property, employ people and enter into contractual obligations. Debts incurred are the debts of the LLP not of the individual partners.
- An LLP does not have any restrictions on its activities.
- An LLP has members but does not have directors or shareholders, nor does it have share capital. Two of the members are classed as 'designated members' and are responsible for corporate legal matters such as signing the accounts, appointing auditors, filing returns, etc. at Companies House.
- The members of an LLP have limited liability. The LLP is liable for all its debts to the full extent of its assets. Individual members are only liable to the extent of their investment in the LLP. Individual members can be made liable for negligent advice, but any claim against them will not affect other members. This is the major change from the old partnership structure where liability was **joint and several**, i.e. all the partners in the partnership were individually and collectively liable for the liabilities of the partnership.
- An LLP has complete flexibility as to the internal structure which it wishes to adopt: there are no requirements for board or general meetings or decision-making by resolution. An LLP does not have a memorandum or articles of association.
- As the members have limited liability, the protection of those dealing with an LLP requires that the LLP maintains accounting records, prepares and delivers audited annual accounts to the Registrar of Companies and submits an Annual Return in a similar manner to companies. However, the exemptions available to companies, for example, with respect to the delivery of abbreviated accounts and exemption from audit, also apply to LLPs.

Broadly therefore, the partners of an auditing firm are afforded the protection of a corporate structure with its limited liability, but the price they have to pay is the loss of financial anonymity. They must prepare and publish accounts which will reveal such previously closely guarded secrets as the profits shared between the partners.

Where big audit firms audit huge clients, operating across boundaries, the potential for a disastrous claim against the firm is increased. The destruction of Arthur Andersen, post-Enron, showed how vulnerable even a mega-firm could be to catastrophic loss of clients following adverse publicity. The adoption of the LLP structure is a way for partners to preserve their personal assets at the expense of some disclosure and regulation.

LIMITING AUDITOR'S LIABILITY

Until recently auditors were not able to limit their exposure to claims for negligence. As we have seen they can adopt a form of corporate structure – the Limited Liability Partnership – and they have to have in place Professional Indemnity Insurance, but these are defensive measures designed to avoid the audit firm being wiped out by claims.

Under Sections 534–538, Companies Act 2006 shareholders of both public and private companies can, by ordinary resolution, agree to limit the liability of their auditors in respect of any negligence, breach of duty, default or breach of trust occurring during the course of an audit. This is called a **Liability Limitation Agreement (LLA)**.

There are, however, some provisos in the legislation:

- No agreement can reduce the auditor's liability to less than what is considered to be 'fair and reasonable' in the circumstances, taking into account the auditor's responsibilities, their contractual obligations and the professional standards expected of them.
- Shareholder approval can be gained either before or after the company enters into an LLA and private companies can agree to waive the requirement for approval.
- Any LLA made with the auditors has to be disclosed in the accounts or the Directors' Report.
- The LLA is only operative for one financial year and should be renewed annually.
- The shareholders have the right, by means of an ordinary resolution, to terminate the LLA in respect of any act or omission subsequent to the date set by that resolution – i.e. the LLA can be terminated by the shareholders.

The limit on auditor's liability need not be a sum of money or some sort of formula (e.g. a multiple of the audit fee) but could be, for example, a percentage of any loss suffered by the company, taking into account the level of the auditor's responsibility for such loss. When considering what is 'fair and reasonable' no account should be taken of events arising after the loss or damage has occurred, or any matters affecting the possibility of recovering the loss from anybody or individual considered liable in respect of it.

This last point was to alleviate the concern that the auditors may be the only people with any money after the loss or damage has occurred, because of their liability insurance, and the risk that the courts may find it expedient to make the auditors liable for all of the compensation when, for example, the directors might be equally culpable.

THE FUTURE

The profession has concerns that:

- increased caution by auditors will increase audit costs as they undertake more work in order to reduce risks
- the threat of criminal proceedings may make auditors even more risk averse than they are at present so that they will be more inclined to qualify audit reports

These worries may be unfounded. Auditors who carry out their work properly should not be guilty of negligence and cannot therefore be guilty of an offence under the Act. In fact, if the government's view is sustained that 'recklessly' is some way beyond 'negligently', it requires auditors to have been incredibly lax in carrying out their audit – in which case some might say they deserve to be prosecuted!

Alternatively, it requires them to deliberately issue a false report which would probably be likely only where additional criminal circumstances were present, such as corruption, blackmail or threatening behaviour.

However, this may not stop some firms of auditors using these provisions as an excuse to increase audit fees and to increase the level of written representations from directors and senior managers as some form of protection.

SUMMARY

- The criminal law makes possible prosecutions against auditors who act dishonestly or recklessly or connive at dishonesty.
- Auditors can also be found guilty of offences in connection with money laundering and insider trading.
- Civil liability can arise under common law where the auditors are sued to recover losses caused by their negligence in breach of contract.

- Liability can only arise if:
  - the auditor can be shown to be negligent
  - loss has been suffered
  - the negligence is the direct cause of the loss
- In certain circumstances, civil liability can arise to third parties. This can arise where third parties use audited information and suffer loss as a consequence because that information was negligently prepared. As the law presently stands the auditor has to be aware of the possibility.
- The Caparo decision is still the leading precedent in the UK.
- The Bannerman wording has now been tested in court and has been upheld as being fair and reasonable in the circumstances.
- Auditors can limit their liability by incorporating as a limited liability partnership or by agreeing a limitation of liability with shareholders.

POINTS TO NOTE

- The tests of liability in court are proximity, foreseeability and reasonableness.
- The section on minimizing auditor's liabilities is very important. All auditors have to have insurance cover under Professional Indemnity policies but may also operate as LLPs and come to an agreement with shareholders to minimize any claims.
- Cases of professional negligence concerning auditors very rarely come before the courts as such cases are mostly settled out of court to avoid incurring huge legal fees, if for no other reason. The auditor takes the view that if more cases were allowed to come to the courts the issues of:
  - What is negligence?
  - To whom does the auditor have a legal responsibility?
  would become clearer.
- However, in individual cases, a court hearing would involve enormous costs in terms of legal fees, partner time and adverse publicity.
- Auditors are required to perform their work with reasonable skill and care. It now seems well established that this means that the auditor must apply the standards of a reasonable, competent, professional auditor. The professional auditor applies all the auditing standards and guidelines.
- Because auditors are required to carry Professional Indemnity Insurance there is a tendency to sue the auditor knowing that they will not have to pay but the insurer will.
- The effect of this is that the insurer will insist on reasonable skill and care on the part of the insured. In addition, the professional bodies act as regulators of the conduct of their members.
- There is an argument that use of the limited liability partnership structure has lowered auditing standards as audit partners no longer feel the potential risk of losing everything if they do not perform the audit to a high standard and that the risk of losing everything forced auditors to be more aggressive with management.

CASE STUDY 1

Fisch & Schipp are the auditors to AHM Publishing Co. Ltd, publishers of textbooks. They carried out the audit for the year ended 31 December 2X15 and signed an unqualified audit report. Shortly after the AGM, which was on 23 June 2X16, negotiations began for the sale of the company to Amalgamated Publishers plc who acquired the company in November 2X16.

The audit of AHM's accounts for the year ended 31 December 2X16 by Puce Watermelon in March 2X17 revealed that a printing bill for two of AHM's bestselling titles dated 30.11.2X15 had been disputed and thus not entered in the books. The matter was resolved in August 2X16 when AHM paid the £288 000 owing. The bill had not been accrued in the 2X15 accounts.

Amalgamated Publishers plc paid £1m for AHM whose reported profits net of management remuneration were: 2X13 £216 000, 2X14 £213 000, 2X15 £217 000.

Amalgamated sued Fisch & Schipp for damages.

Discussion

– Discuss in detail all the issues raised by this case.
– How might Fisch & Schipp defend themselves against this action?

CASE STUDY 2

Zong & Dansse, the auditors to Daffodil Ltd, gave an unqualified report on 14 January 2X16 on the accounts for the year ending 30 November 2X15. These accounts were seen by The Wednesfield Bank plc in February 2X16 and the bank lent £250 000 to Daffodil on short-term overdraft on 19 March 2X16. In March 2X17 the company went into liquidation still owing the bank £200 000. The company was hopelessly insolvent and the bank recovered nothing. It turned out that the accounts for the year ended 30 November 2X16 were defective in that several substantial payables were omitted from the accounts. Had these payables been included it would have been apparent that Daffodil was not a going concern in November 2X16.

Discussion

– Can the bank recover from Zong & Dansse?

STUDENT SELF-TESTING QUESTIONS

Questions with answers apparent from the text

a) How can an auditor be criminally liable under the Companies Act?

b) How can an auditor be liable under the law of Tort?

c) What conditions must be satisfied for an auditor to have to pay damages for a tort? How can an audit firm minimize its potential for paying damages?

d) Summarize the Caparo case.

EXAMINATION QUESTIONS

1 You are an audit partner with Tickett & Run and three months ago you signed off the audit of Blastypot plc, a large engineering group with several subsidiaries. The turnover of the group is £750m and it has reported a profit for the last financial year ended 31 March 2X16 of £22m.

You receive a call from group financial director Rod Sneers who tells you:

- Internal audit has uncovered a fraud in the materials purchasing department of Blastypot. The purchasing manager had secretly set up several companies and had used them to sell materials and services to Blastypot at inflated prices by routing supplies from approved suppliers to his companies and adding on a large margin before selling them on to Blastypot. The manager had been suspended and the company were investigating with a view to prosecution.

- The managing director of one of the subsidiary companies, Big Hole Ltd, an operator of gravel quarries, had admitted that he and the subsidiary's financial director had falsified the results of the subsidiary for the last two years in order to reach profit targets and be paid a large bonus. In fact, Big Hole plc, rather than being profitable, was on the verge of insolvency and will have to be supported by the holding company until it recovers. You recall that your audit team was only at Big Hole for about a week and concentrated on verifying aspects of the Statement of Financial Position and did little systems audit work. Rod says the directors are of the opinion that Tickett & Run were negligent in their audit of Big Hole.

You have just recovered from this call when Sophie, a friend, rings you. She is an audit partner at another firm, Bashit & Hope and she says that they have received a notice of claim from a former audit client, Pongo Ltd which had just sold out to Massive plc. Massive alleges that the inventory valuation of Pongo was overstated by £25m and they are looking to her firm, as auditors who signed off a clean audit report on Pongo two months before Massive bought the company, to refund the £25m. She is looking to you for some advice.

Required:

(a) Explain the auditor's responsibility to detect fraud and how you would respond to Rod Sneers in respect of this.

(b) What factors would you need to consider in respect of the possible claim against Ticket & Run and their audit of Big Hole Ltd? What will you need to demonstrate in order to overcome such a claim?

(c) What information would you need to confirm from Sophie before you can give her advice and what advice would you give her?

SOURCES AND ADDITIONAL READING

ACCA (2016) *ACCA Rulebook Section 3 Code of Ethics and Conduct*. London: ACCA.

Financial Reporting Council (2016) *ISA 240 The Auditor's Responsibilities Relating to Fraud in an Audit of Financial Statements*. London: Financial Reporting Council.

ICAEW (2011) *Code of Ethics Parts A, B and C*. London: Institute of Chartered Accountants in England and Wales.

Cases:

ADT Ltd v BDO Binder Hamlyn (1996) BC 808 315
Barclays Bank plc v Grant Thornton LLP [2015] EWHC 320 (Comm)
Candler v Crane Christmas & Co. (1951)2 KB 164
Caparo Industries v Dickman (1990)2 AC 605
Credit Alliance v Arthur Andersen & Co (1985)483 2d 11
Donaghue v Stevenson [1932] AC, 562,580
Haig v Bamford (1977) 1 SCR 466
Hedley Byrne v Heller and Partners (1964)AC 465
JEB Fasteners v Marks Bloom (1981)3 All ER 289
Re Kingston Cotton Mill No 2 (1896)2 Ch 279

Re London & General Bank (1895)2 Ch 673

Mutual Life v Citizens Assurance Co Ltd v Evatt (1971), AC 793

Peach Publishing Co v Slater & Co (a firm) (1997) EWCA Civ 769

Royal Bank of Scotland v Bannerman Johnstone Maclay (Scottish Court of Session) (2002)

Re Thomas Gerrard & Son (1968) Ch 455

Ultramares Corporation v Touche (1931)255 NY 170 174N E 441 1931 NY

Companies House (2010) *Limited Liability Partnership Incorporation and Names.* London: Companies House.

Hansard (2006) Standing Committee on Bills, Company Law Reform Bill Column 724, Ms V Baird, 14 July, 2006.

Shaxson, N. (2011) *Treasure Islands: Tax Havens and the Men who Stole the World.* London: Bodley Head.

TSO (2006) *Companies Act 2006.* London: The Stationery Office.

TSO (2008) *The Companies (Disclosure of Auditors Remuneration and Liability Limitation Agreements) Regulations, 2008.* London: The Stationery Office.

TSO (2006) *Fraud Act 2006.* London: The Stationery Office.

CHAPTER 30 REVIEW ENGAGEMENTS AND NON-AUDIT ASSURANCE ASSIGNMENTS

Learning Objectives

After studying the material in this chapter you should be able to:

- differentiate between review engagements and other non-audit assignments

- understand what is meant by forensic auditing

- understand the level of work to be undertaken in respect of each type of assignment

- differentiate between reasonable assurance and limited assurance

- be able to decide when positive or negative assurance reports are required

- understand the wording of the differing reports

- differentiate between prospective financial information, a forecast and a projection

- explain the process of modifying reports where required

INTRODUCTION

This chapter deals with assignments which involve the auditor's skills but not in an audit context. The key to the essential nature of these assurance assignments is the level of assurance required. For example, an assignment requiring a relatively high level of assurance, such as an audit, requires the auditor to carry out extensive evidence gathering procedures, as we have seen. However other assignments which require a lower level of assurance involve the reporting accountant in much less work and, accordingly, the report is different.

Some assignments do not involve the reporting accountant in giving any form of certificate other than confirmation of the work carried out.

Students should familiarize themselves with the different types of assignment and, more importantly, the level of assurance required.

In this chapter the details of each type of assignment are described relatively briefly as the intention is to inform readers of the types of assignment a reporting accountant is likely to be asked to become involved with. As every assignment of this nature is different it is impossible to be prescriptive about each one but an understanding of the key principles will lead the reporting accountant in the right direction.

We also look at the relatively new practice of forensic auditing although, as this is really a book on its own, we can only cover it superficially.

REVIEW ENGAGEMENTS

Accountants in practice perform many different assignments for their clients. This book is primarily about auditing-type assignments but frequently accountants are also asked to carry out work which is non-audit but which includes many of the aspects of audit work, such as planning, gathering of evidence and risk evaluations.

For example, accountants are often asked to carry out reviews of financial information, such as interim accounts or management accounts prepared in support of a finance application, or are asked to perform investigations based on their client's instructions and to report on the results. Accountants often prepare accounts or management information – perhaps for smaller clients – and do not wish to give any form of assurance or opinion on those figures.

These types of assignment are governed by International Standards on Review Engagements (ISREs) produced by the International Auditing and Assurance Standards Board (IAASB).

They fall into two basic types:

1   Those in which the accountants carry out some form of work and simply report to their client factually without giving any form of assurance or opinion.
2   Direct reporting engagements where accountants carry out work, which falls short of an audit, on which they will give some form of limited assurance or opinion.

The first type of assignment on which no assurance is given comprises:

- attest functions – witnessing something
- compilation assignments – assembling financial statements from information supplied
- agreed-upon procedures assignments – work performed on a basis agreed with the client

Attest functions

To attest to something is to bear witness or affirm it.

EXAMPLE

A trade association may require that all its members must annually review the procedures they perform in order to secure compliance with the quality control requirements of the association. The directors of A Ltd duly performed the review but the association need confirmation that the review has been performed.

To that end Simon & Sayse, Chartered Accountants, are engaged to assure the society that the review has been performed. They might do this by:

- Enquiry of the directors to understand the processes carried out by the company in carrying out its review to ascertain if it complies with the requirements for the review set out by the association.
- Reviewing documentation prepared by or for the directors to support their statement and assessing whether or not it provides sound support for that statement.
- Reporting to the association that the review has been carried out.

The accountants may well say that the review by the board was conducted in accordance with the association's recommendations but will not say anything about the internal processes adopted by the company to secure compliance with the association's quality control requirements. Their work and their report are simply to *attest* to the fact that the board carried out a review.

Compilation assignments

Accountants are often called upon to compile or prepare financial accounts or other statements from client records. This is most common for sole traders, small partnerships and unincorporated bodies, e.g. charities. There is an International Standard on Related Services (ISRS) 4410 *'Compilation Engagements'* which covers this area.

The following procedures should be adopted:

- Agree an Engagement Letter with the client making it clear that the engagement is *not* an audit and that management is responsible for the accuracy and completeness of the compiled financial statements.
- Plan the work so that it is properly carried out and documented.
- Gain an understanding of the business – this need not necessarily be as extensive as would be required for an audit.
- Prepare the financial statements under the normal accounting conventions. They should comply with relevant accounting standards such as UK GAAP or IFRSs. Ideally the financial statements should include a statement of any significant accounting policies.
- Where the management have had to make judgements and have received assistance from the accountants this should be explained and the accountants must take great care to ensure that the final decision on the matter is that of the management not the reporting accountants.
- It is usual to perform limited audit-type procedures including analytical review and enquiry of management. The accountants should then ascertain that the financial statements are in accordance with their understanding of the business.

- Request a Letter of Representation from the management (Chapter 24). This will include:
  - representations about any estimates made by the management
  - an assurance that all necessary information has been given to the accountants and
  - confirmation that the information is complete and reliable

Any relevant explanations given orally will also be included as confirmation.

It is important to ensure that the accountants receive some written acknowledgement from the client that the clients are solely responsible for the presentation and content of the financial statements and that they have provided all the information and explanations necessary to the accountants.

This is an example of the wording which might be used in connection with a compilation assignment:

'*On the basis of information supplied by management we have compiled, in accordance with the International Standard on Related Services (or other national standard as appropriate), applicable to compilation engagements, the financial statements of Tinyco as at 31 December 2X16.*

Management is responsible for these financial statements. We have not audited or reviewed these financial statements and accordingly express no opinion thereon'.

It should then be signed and dated.

In the event of the accountants finding that the financial statements contain a material misstatement or are otherwise misleading, they should discuss the matter and recommend amendment. If the management refuses to alter the accounts, the accountants should either resign or include an explanatory paragraph in their report.

Agreed-upon procedures engagements

An agreed-upon procedures engagement is one in which either:

- the party engaging the professional accountant, or
- the intended user.

determine the procedures to be performed and the professional accountant simply provides a report of factual findings as a result of undertaking those procedures.

It is not an assurance engagement and no opinion will be expressed.

You will note that, in normal reporting engagements, the accountants decide upon their own procedures and their engagement is about reporting the results of carrying out those procedures, not about what to do or how to do it, i.e. ends not means. In agreed-upon procedures engagements the procedures are determined by the client or the end user of the report (who may not necessarily be the same) and the accountants merely carry them out as instructed and report.

The underlying authority for such assignments is the International Standard on Related Services (ISRS) 4400 '*Engagements to Perform Agreed-upon Procedures Regarding Financial Information*'.

The process is as follows:

1   The auditor will agree the terms of the assignment in an Engagement Letter to include:
  - The nature of the engagement including the fact that the procedures performed will not constitute an audit nor a review and that accordingly no assurance will be expressed.
  - The stated purpose for the engagement.
  - Identification of the financial information to which the agreed-upon procedures will be applied.
  - The nature, timing and extent of the specific procedures to be applied.
  - The anticipated form of the report of factual findings.
  - Limitations on distribution of the report of factual findings. When such limitation would be in conflict with any legal requirements the accountants should not accept the engagement. It would include a statement that the distribution of the report of factual findings would be restricted to the specified parties who have agreed to the procedures to be performed.
2   The accountants should plan the work so that an effective engagement will be performed.
3   The accountants should document matters which are important in providing evidence to support the report of factual findings and evidence that the engagement was carried out in accordance with the ISRS and the terms of the engagement.

EXAMPLE

Agreed upon Procedures - Example - Report of Factual Findings in Connection with Accounts Payable.

REPORT OF FACTUAL FINDINGS

To (those who engaged the accountant)

We have performed the procedures agreed with you and enumerated below with respect to the accounts payable of Megablast Ltd as at 31.12 2X16, set forth in the accompanying schedules (not shown in this example). Our engagement was undertaken in accordance with the International Standard on Related Services 4410 *'Engagements to Perform Agreed-upon Procedures Regarding Financial Information'* (or refer to relevant national standards or practices) applicable to agreed-upon procedures engagements. The procedures were performed solely to assist you in evaluating the validity of the accounts payable and are summarized as follows:

1   We obtained and checked the addition of the trial balance of accounts payable as at 31.12.2X16, prepared by Megablast Ltd, and we compared the total to the balance in the related general ledger account.

2   We compared the attached list (not shown in this example) of major suppliers and the amounts owing at 31.12.2X16 to the related names and amounts in the trial balance.

3   We obtained suppliers' statements or requested suppliers to confirm balances owing at 31.12.2X16.

4   We compared such statements or confirmations to the amounts referred to in 2. For amounts which did not agree, we obtained reconciliations from Megablast Ltd. For reconciliations obtained, we identified and listed outstanding invoices, credit notes and outstanding cheques, each of which was greater than £XXX. We located and examined such invoices and credit notes subsequently received and cheques subsequently paid and we ascertained that they should in fact have been listed as outstanding on the reconciliations.

We report our findings below:

(a)   With respect to item 1 we found the addition to be correct and the total amount to be in agreement.
(b)   With respect to item 2 we found the amounts compared to be in agreement.
(c)   With respect to item 3 we found there were suppliers' statements for all such suppliers.
(d)   With respect to item 4 we found the amounts agreed, or with respect to amounts which did not agree, we found ABC Company had prepared reconciliations and that the credit notes, invoices and outstanding checks over £XXX were appropriately listed as reconciling items with the following exceptions:

(Detail the exceptions)

As the above procedures do not constitute either an audit or a review made in accordance with International Standards on Auditing or International Standards on Review Engagements (or relevant national standards or practices), we do not express any assurance on the accounts payable as of 31.12.2X16.

Had we performed additional procedures or had we performed an audit or review of the financial statements in accordance with International Standards on Auditing or International Standards on Review Engagements (or relevant national standards or practices), other matters might have come to our attention that would have been reported to you.

Our report is solely for the purpose set forth in the first paragraph of this report and for your information and is not to be used for any other purpose or to be distributed to any other parties. This report relates only to the accounts and items specified above and does not extend to any financial statements of ABC Company, taken as a whole.

Sweete & Lowe

Date

Address

4   The accountants should carry out the procedures agreed upon and use the evidence obtained as the basis for the report of factual findings. The procedures applied in an engagement to perform agreed-upon procedures may include the following:

- inquiry and analysis
- re-computation, comparison and other clerical accuracy checks
- observation
- inspection
- obtaining confirmations

5   The final report will be a simple recitation of the work carried out and will not give any form of assurance at all.

It may be that the accountants are asked to give some level of assurance. In that case the assignment becomes an assurance assignment and additional work has to be carried out by the reporting accountants. It is important that the accountants carry out sufficient work to support their report. Indeed, it may be that the assignment ceases to be an agreed upon procedures assignment and takes on some of the characteristics, if not all of them, of the next type of engagement.

DIRECT REPORTING ENGAGEMENTS

Direct reporting engagements are those where reporting accountants <u>are</u> required to give a special report on some aspects of a client's affairs.

This is not easy to define, because of the varied nature of such assignments, but a special report arises at the request of their client and in accordance with instructions received and any relevant statutory or contractual obligations.

They arise where accountants carry out an independent examination of financial or other information prepared by their client for use by a third party and when they report their findings and conclusions *by expressing an opinion* on the information. Special reports do *not* include:

- reports on audited financial statements
- reports on prospectuses or profit forecasts, which are dealt with separately

Nor do they include:

- comfort letters associated with published documents, circulars or valuations, or
- the preparation of financial statements, or information on which no opinion is expressed.

An example of a direct reporting engagement is a due diligence review into a target company on behalf of a possible acquirer (see below).

The approach to a direct reporting engagement is:

- agree a precise Letter of Engagement. It is important to ensure that all parties (the accounting firm, the persons requiring the special report, the person or enterprise which is responsible for the information being reported on) understand their responsibilities, the relationship between them and what is to be done
- plan, control and record the work done
- carry out the work in accordance with the Ethical Code
- obtain evidence – from documents and records, enquiries of management and others, including analytical review and enquiry of third parties
- draw conclusions
- report
- sign and date

Due diligence

Due diligence covers a wide range of matters, some of which may not require a professional opinion. In that case they may or may not be assurance assignments.

Due diligence is work, commissioned by a client, involving agreed inquiries into aspects of the accounts, organization or activities of another organization, usually one the client is attempting to acquire or invest heavily in. The assignment is evidenced by the usual Letter of Engagement which will set out the work to be done and when by.

The term 'due diligence' is most frequently associated with takeovers and mergers because when a company is taken over or two entities are merged all parties to the transaction need to be assured that what is purported to be actually is.

For example, Huge plc takes over Medium plc and needs to be assured that the assets of Medium plc are as stated. An accounting firm will be engaged to investigate and report on this aspect of the purported information. Note that, particularly in connection with acquisitions, due diligence can be carried out not only by accountants but also by actuaries, surveyors, lawyers and other professionals and sometimes by the staff of the taking-over company. Usually the takeover or merger is not completed until the due diligence is completed.

Where the accountants are asked to express an opinion, view or assurance, such an assignment should be classed as a direct reporting assignment where objectivity is required.

Each report is different and is tailored to the assignment as set out in the Letter of Engagement. The accountants must be sure that they have dealt with all the items included in the Engagement Letter.

If they are asked to express an opinion they must have gathered sufficient, appropriate evidence to support it. Reports usually contain a restriction on the purpose for which the report can be used and the persons to whom it can be circulated.

Due diligence reports are too varied to provide an example, however the report should, broadly, contain the following parts:

- title – 'Accountant's report to . . . on . . .'
- addressee
- a description of the subject matter of the engagement and time period
- responsibilities of all parties
- restricted nature of the report – who the report may or may not be shown to
- identification of standards used in the engagement, e.g. the International Standards on Assurance Engagements
- the criteria against which the subject matter was evaluated
- the conclusion and any reservations or qualifications to the conclusion; this will include the form of assurance appropriate to the assignment (see below)
- the date
- the name, description and address of the reporting accountant

Engagements to review financial statements

This is a form of engagement which is something less than an audit on which reporting accountants are required to give some form of assurance.

The reporting standard here is International Standards on Review Engagements (ISRE) 2400, '*Engagements to Review Financial Statements*'. There is also ISRE 2410, *Review of Interim Financial Information Performed by the Independent Auditor of the Entity*' which covers similar ground and which we will look at later.

This provides guidance for performing review engagements particularly where the review is performed by the entity's auditor and interim financial information is prepared in accordance with an applicable financial reporting framework; but can also be in connection with small companies where the accountants do not or cannot perform a full audit, which would involve compliance with all of the various ISAs, etc. and the issuing of an audit report which:

- seeks to give a **positive assurance** on the financial statements, i.e. includes a conclusion as to whether the accounts represent (or do not represent) a true and fair view, or
- which results in the auditors failing to express an opinion because of the lack of sufficient appropriate evidence.

The form of assurance that the auditors will give under the provisions of ISRE 2400 is called **negative assurance**.

NEGATIVE ASSURANCE

What this means is that the auditors will carry out a limited amount of testing work which will provide sufficient appropriate evidence to give an opinion to the effect that there is *no reason to believe that the financial statements are not true and fair.*

Note the difference in the approach to the wording of the auditor's reports from the opinion paragraph in Chapter 26.

The differences between an audit and this type of review engagement can be summarized thus: ISRE 2400 requires the auditor to:

- Comply with ethical requirements relevant to an audit of annual financial statements, i.e. gaining an understanding of the client and its activities and ensuring the firm is independent and able to conduct the review, as described in earlier chapters of this book.
- Formalize the terms of the engagement with the client in an Engagement Letter which should include provisions concerning:
    - the objective of the review
    - management's responsibility for the relevant financial statements
    - the scope of the review
    - the auditor's access to information
    - the form of report to be issued
    - the fact that the review cannot be relied on to detect fraud or error
    - the fact that an audit is not being performed
- Plan and perform the review with an attitude of professional scepticism recognizing that circumstances may exist that cause the financial information to be misstated.

Specific review procedures include gaining an understanding of the entity and its environment, including its internal control, as it relates to the preparation of financial information, sufficient to plan and conduct the engagement so as to be able to identify the types of potential material misstatement and consider the likelihood of their occurrence. This enables them to plan the audit work so that it will provide the auditor with a basis for reporting whether anything has come to their attention that causes them to believe that the financial information contains material misstatements.

The auditors should make inquiries primarily of persons responsible for financial and accounting matters. In particular, they should enquire about major matters affecting the company in the year (e.g. new finance, acquisitions, major capital expenditure) and any problems concerning impairment of assets, provisions required, specific disclosures, contingencies, commitments, post balance sheet events, related party transactions, etc.

In terms of checking processes, the review will consist mainly of analytical review procedures which will include comparing ratios against previous years, budgets and industry averages. As well as the generally accepted ratios (GP per cent, Liquidity Ratio, Inventory turn, etc.). These may also include such procedures as inspecting an aged list of receivables for anomalies and reviewing items that require particular management judgement.

Clearly if the Statement of Financial Position can be largely verified any profit or loss for the period must be reasonably accurate. Clearly however the review falls short of a full audit so the reporting accountants are generally confining their review to areas where errors or misstatements are most likely to occur (such as Inventory values, Receivables recovery and asset values), much of which can be done through analytical review.

FIGURE 30.1 Difference between positive and negative assurance

	Assurance engagements	Review or limited assurance engagements
Level of assurance	Reasonable	Limited
Opinion wording	Positive assurance – *'true and fair'*	Negative assurance – *no reason to believe, etc.*
Level of work undertaken	Tests of compliance and substantive tests of detail	Analytical procedures and enquiry of management
Evidence requirement	High – obtain and document evidence for all financial assertions	No evidence required
Report to	Members	Management

Other procedures will include:

- reading the minutes of directors, shareholders and management meetings and reviewing correspondence with lenders, legal advisors, etc.
- obtaining evidence that the financial information agrees or reconciles with the underlying accounting records; this will include control account and bank reconciliations, etc.
- inquiring whether management has identified all events up to the date of the review report that may require adjustment to or disclosure in the financial information
- inquiring whether management has changed its assessment of the entity's ability to continue as a going concern
- evaluating, individually and in total, whether uncorrected misstatements that have come to the auditor's attention are material to the interim financial information

The reviewing accountants should obtain written representations from management on significant issues. They must also read any other information that accompanies the financial statements to consider whether any such information is materially inconsistent with them.

They may then issue a written report in accordance with the relevant ISRE. They need only to prepare review documentation that is sufficient and appropriate to provide a basis for the reporting accountants' conclusion and to provide evidence that the review was performed in accordance with the ISRE and any applicable legal and regulatory requirements.

Superficially the list of tasks to be undertaken shown above looks remarkably like the reporting accountants are being tasked with performing an audit but careful reading reveals that, in fact, the accountants work is very much less than would be performed in a full audit.

It basically consists of analytical review and enquiry together with a review of the client's accounting efficiency and a reading of minutes and letters which might give an indication of unrecorded liabilities or significant issues affecting the accounts.

Because of this, as you will see, the wording of this type of report is significantly different to the wording of a Companies Act type audit report as detailed in Chapter 26. The ISRE refers to 'moderate assurance' as a way to describe the opinion paragraph which will give the opinion in the form of negative assurance.

EXAMPLE

Review report to . . .

We have reviewed the accompanying Statement of Financial Position of AB Limited at 31 December 2X16, and the related statements of income and cash flows for the year then ended. These financial statements are the responsibility of the company's management. Our responsibility is to issue a report on these financial statements based on our review.

We conducted our review in accordance with the International Standard on Review Engagements 2400 *Engagements to Review Historical Financial Statements*, (or other national standard) applicable to review engagements. This standard requires that we plan and perform the review to obtain moderate assurance as to whether the financial statements are free of material misstatement.

A review is limited primarily to enquiries of company personnel and analytical procedures applied to financial data and thus provides less assurance than an audit.

We have not performed an audit and, accordingly, we do not express an audit opinion.

Based on our review, nothing has come to our attention that causes us to believe that the accompanying financial statements do not give a true and fair view in accordance with International Accounting Standards.

Sweet & Lowe LLP

High Street

Anytown

10 March 2X16

Note the wording of the last paragraph which states the negative view that there is *no reason* to believe that the financial statements do *not* give a true and fair view and accord with International Accounting Standards.

Report qualification

If the accountants are not happy with the accounts they are reviewing, and the management refuse to alter them, it is, of course, possible for them to give a qualified report. The key wording in the text has been underlined for clarity.

The first two paragraphs would be the same and a third and fourth might be amended to:

'Management has informed us that no provision has been made for a possible bad debt. We consider that a provision of £x should be made and net income and shareholders' equity reduced by that amount.

Based on our review, <u>except for the effects of the overstatement of receivables described in the previous paragraph</u>, nothing has come to our attention that causes us to believe that the accompanying financial statements do not give a true and fair view in accordance with International Accounting Standards.'

In practice, it is unlikely that the directors would issue or publish a review report with a qualification and normally the suggestions of the reviewer would be taken up in the financial statements.

Interim financial information

Most listed companies issue interim accounts, at half yearly or quarterly intervals depending on the relevant Stock Exchange listing agreement.

There is generally no requirement that these be audited, however, it may be that management request a review of these accounts.

The work to be performed would be similar to that detailed above, as this is a review assignment, but the report will be slightly different.

We will look at the guidance given, as to the form of report, in ISRE 2410 *'Review of Interim Financial Information Performed by the Independent Auditor of the Entity'* (UK and Ireland) which has been adopted.

EXAMPLE

Report on Review of Interim Financial Information

To: (Appropriate addressee)

Introduction

We have reviewed the accompanying Statement of Financial Position of Megablast plc as at March 31, 2X16 and the related statements of income, changes in equity and cash flows for the three-month period then ended, and a summary of significant accounting policies and other explanatory notes.

   Management is responsible for the preparation and fair presentation of this interim financial information in accordance with [indicate applicable financial reporting framework, e.g. UK GAAP, IFRSs]. Our responsibility is to express a conclusion on this interim financial information based on our review.

Scope of review
We conducted our review in accordance with International Standard on Review Engagements 2410, *'Review of Interim Financial Information Performed by the Independent Auditor of the Entity'*.

   A review of interim financial information consists of making inquiries, primarily of persons responsible for financial and accounting matters, and applying analytical and other review procedures. A review is substantially less in scope than an audit conducted in accordance with International Standards on Auditing and consequently does not enable us to obtain assurance that we would become aware of all significant matters that might be identified in an audit. Accordingly, we do not express an audit opinion.

Conclusion
Based on our review, nothing has come to our attention that causes us to believe that the accompanying interim financial information does not give a true and fair view of (or 'does not present fairly, in all material respects') the financial position of the entity as at March 31, 2X16, and of its financial performance and its cash flows for the three-month period then ended in accordance with [applicable financial reporting framework].

   Reporting accountant

   Date

   Address

If the reporting accountants feel that their work has been restricted in any way they can qualify the report for limitation of audit evidence, or if the accounts don't comply with the appropriate reporting framework they can qualify on those grounds also.

This is the form of wording for such a qualification – the first part of the report is unchanged. The key wording in the text has been highlighted for clarity.

EXAMPLE

Example (extract)

Basis for Qualified Conclusion
As a result of a fire in a branch office on (date) that destroyed its sales records, we were unable to complete our review of receivables totalling £___ included in the interim financial information. The company is in the process of

reconstructing these records and is uncertain as to whether these records will support the amount shown above and the related allowance for uncollectible accounts.

Had we been able to complete our review of accounts receivable, matters might have come to our attention indicating that adjustments might be necessary to the interim financial information.

Qualified Conclusion

Except for the adjustments to the interim financial information that we might have become aware of had it not been *for the situation described above*, based on our review, nothing has come to our attention that causes us to believe that the accompanying interim financial information does not give a true and fair view of (or 'does not present fairly, in all material respects') the financial position of the entity as at March 31, 2X16, and of its financial performance and its cash flows for the three-month period then ended in accordance with [applicable financial reporting framework].

Reporting accountant

Date

Address

Clearly if the accountants feel that the interim accounts don't present a true and fair view they can issue an adverse report.

If, for any reason, the accountants cannot complete the review they should explain to management, in writing, why this is so. They would have to decide whether or not it is appropriate to issue a report.

If there is a material uncertainty in the financial statements, providing this is adequately disclosed in the accounts the auditors should include an emphasis of matter paragraph in much the same way as they would in a statutory auditor's report (Chapter 26).

PROSPECTIVE FINANCIAL INFORMATION

Prospective financial information is information based on assumptions about events which may, or may not, happen in the future and how the organization will perform in the light of those events.

It is, naturally, highly subjective as it takes the form of budgets, profit projections and assumptions about performance of various parts of the organization.

Students should be aware of the following definitions.

Prospective financial information – means financial information based on assumptions about events that may occur in the future and possible actions by an entity. It is highly subjective in nature and its preparation requires the exercise of considerable judgement. Prospective financial information can be in the form of a forecast, a projection or a combination of both, for example, a one-year forecast plus a five-year projection.

A forecast – means prospective financial information prepared on the basis of assumptions as to future events which management *expects* to take place and the actions management *expects* to take as of the date the information is prepared (best-estimate assumptions).

A projection – means prospective financial information prepared on the basis of:

- Hypothetical assumptions about future events and management actions which are not necessarily expected to take place but may do in certain circumstances (i.e. if *this* happens then we will do *that*). This is common when all or part of an entity is in a start-up phase or is considering a major change in the nature of its operations or
- A mixture of best-estimate and hypothetical assumptions. Such information illustrates the possible consequences as of the date the information is prepared if the events and actions were to occur (a 'what-if' scenario).

Prospective financial information can include financial statements, or one or more elements of financial statements, and may be prepared:

(a) As an internal management tool, for example, to assist in evaluating a possible capital investment or
(b) For distribution to third parties in, for example:
   - a prospectus to provide potential investors with information about future expectations
   - an annual report to provide information to shareholders, regulatory bodies and other interested parties
   - a document for the information of lenders which may include, for example, cash flow forecasts

The International Standard on Assurance Engagements (ISAE) 3400 '*The Examination of Prospective Financial Information*' sets out the approach. It applies to assumptions and forecasts in their entirety and does not apply, for example, to general narrative comments made by directors about future performance in the annual accounts.

Management is responsible for the preparation and presentation of the prospective financial information, including the identification and disclosure of the assumptions on which it is based. The accountants may be asked to examine and report on the prospective financial information to enhance its credibility whether it is intended for use by third parties or for internal purposes.

Letter of engagement

Before accepting an engagement to examine prospective financial information, the accountants would consider, amongst other things:

- the intended use of the information;
- whether the information will be for general or limited distribution;
- the nature of the assumptions, that is, whether they are best-estimate or hypothetical assumptions;
- the elements to be included in the information; and
- the period covered by the information.

The accountants should not accept, or should withdraw from, an engagement when the assumptions are clearly unrealistic or when the accountants believe that the prospective financial information will be inappropriate for its intended use.

The accountants and the client should agree on the terms of the engagement. It is in the interests of both the organization and the accountants that the accountants send an Engagement Letter to help in avoiding misunderstandings regarding the engagement.

The Engagement Letter should address the issue of who the recipient of the information is likely to be and will set out management's responsibilities for the assumptions and for providing the auditor with all relevant information and source data used in developing the assumptions.

Knowledge of the business

The accountants should obtain a sufficient level of knowledge of the business to be able to evaluate whether all significant assumptions required for the preparation of the prospective financial information have been identified. The accountants would also need to become familiar with the organization's process for preparing prospective financial information, for example, by considering the following:

- The internal controls over the system used to prepare prospective financial information and the expertise and experience of those persons preparing the prospective financial information.
- The nature of the documentation prepared by the entity supporting management's assumptions.
- The extent to which statistical, mathematical and computer-assisted techniques are used.

Key to the forecasts are the methods used to develop and apply the assumptions on which they have been based and reviewing accountants should carefully evaluate the assumptions used. One way to do this is to look at the accuracy of any prospective financial information prepared in prior periods and the reasons for significant variances. The accountants should consider the extent to which reliance on the entity's historical financial information is justified.

Period covered

The accountants should consider the period of time covered by the prospective financial information. Since assumptions become more speculative as the length of the period covered increases, the ability of management to make best-estimate assumptions decreases as the period lengthens.

The period should not extend beyond the time for which management has a reasonable basis for the assumptions. This might be as long as five years or more in the case of, say a construction company engaged in long-term projects, or as short as, say, two years in the case of an Internet retailer. Each case is different.

Approach

In an engagement to examine prospective financial information, the accountants should obtain sufficient, appropriate evidence as to whether management's best-estimate assumptions on which the prospective financial information is based are not unreasonable and, in the case of hypothetical assumptions, such assumptions are consistent with the purpose of the information. They need then to ensure that:

- The prospective financial information is properly prepared on the basis of the assumptions.
- The prospective financial information is properly presented and all material assumptions are adequately disclosed, including a clear indication as to whether they are best-estimate assumptions or hypothetical assumptions.
- The prospective financial information is prepared on a consistent basis with historical financial statements, using appropriate accounting principles.

When determining the nature, timing and extent of examination procedures, the accountants' considerations should include:

- The likelihood of material misstatement.
- The knowledge obtained during any previous engagements.
- Management's competence regarding the preparation of prospective financial information.
- The extent to which the prospective financial information is affected by the management's judgement.
- The adequacy and reliability of the underlying data.

Specifically, the accountants should assess the source and reliability of the evidence supporting management's best-estimate assumptions. Sufficient, appropriate evidence supporting such assumptions would be obtained from internal and external sources including consideration of the assumptions in the light of historical information and an evaluation of whether they are based on plans that are within the entity's capacity.

Following on from that they should consider whether, when hypothetical assumptions are used, all significant implications of such assumptions have been taken into consideration. For example, if sales are assumed to grow beyond the company's current plant capacity, the prospective financial information will need to include the necessary investment in the additional plant capacity or the costs of alternative means of meeting the anticipated sales, such as subcontracting production.

The reporting accountants would need to be satisfied that hypothetical assumptions used are consistent with the purpose of the prospective financial information and that there is no reason to believe they are clearly unrealistic. They would need to review areas that are particularly sensitive to variation and which will have a material effect on the results shown in the prospective financial information.

It will be necessary to obtain written representations from management regarding the intended use of the prospective financial information, the completeness of significant management assumptions and management's acceptance of its responsibility for the prospective financial information.

Disclosure

The reporting accountants should assess the presentation and disclosure of the prospective financial information, in addition to the specific requirements of any relevant statutes, regulations or professional standards. They will need to consider whether:

- The presentation of prospective financial information is informative and not misleading.
- The accounting policies are clearly disclosed in the notes to the prospective financial information.
- The assumptions are adequately disclosed in the notes to the prospective financial information. It needs to be clear whether assumptions represent management's best-estimates or are hypothetical and, when assumptions are made in areas that are material and are subject to a high degree of uncertainty, this uncertainty and the resulting sensitivity of results needs to be adequately disclosed.
- The date as of which the prospective financial information was prepared is disclosed. Management needs to confirm that the assumptions are appropriate as of this date, even though the underlying information may have been accumulated over a period of time.
- The basis of establishing points in a range is clearly indicated and the range is not selected in a biased or misleading manner when results shown in the prospective financial information are expressed in terms of a range.
- Any change in accounting policy since the most recent historical financial statements is disclosed, along with the reason for the change and its effect on the prospective financial information.

Reporting

The report by the accountants on an examination of prospective financial information should contain the following:

(a) Title
(b) Addressee
(c) Identification of the prospective financial information
(d) A reference to the ISAE or relevant national standards or practices applicable to the examination of prospective financial information
(e) A statement that management is responsible for the prospective financial information including the assumptions on which it is based
(f) When applicable, a reference to the purpose and/or restricted distribution of the prospective financial information
(g) A statement of *negative assurance* as to whether the assumptions provide a reasonable basis for the prospective financial information
(h) An opinion as to whether the prospective financial information is properly prepared on the basis of the assumptions and is presented in accordance with the relevant financial reporting framework
(i) Appropriate caveats concerning the achievability of the results indicated by the prospective financial information
(j) Date of the report which should be the date procedures have been completed
(k) Accountant's address and
(l) Signature.

Here is an example of an extract from an unmodified report on a forecast. We have underlined key words:

'We have examined the forecast in accordance with the International Standard on Assurance Engagements applicable to the examination of prospective financial information. Management is responsible for the forecast including the assumptions set out in Note X on which it is based.

Based on our examination of the evidence supporting the assumptions, <u>nothing has come to our attention which causes us to believe that these assumptions do not provide a reasonable basis for the forecast.</u>

Further, in our opinion the forecast is properly prepared on the basis of the assumptions and is presented in accordance with . . . (relevant financial reporting framework). Actual results are likely to be different from the forecast since anticipated events frequently do not occur as expected and the variation may be material.'

Here is an example of an extract from an unmodified report on a projection. Students should note the differences in wording between this report and the one above, which are significant.

'We have examined the projection in accordance with *International Standard on Assurance Engagements (ISAE) 3400, The Examination of Prospective Financial Information*. Management is responsible for the projection including the assumptions set out in Note X on which it is based.

This projection has been prepared for (describe purpose, i.e. the purpose for which the entity exists). As the entity is in a start-up phase the projection has been prepared using a set of assumptions that include hypothetical assumptions about future events and management's actions that are not necessarily expected to occur. Consequently, readers are cautioned that this projection may not be appropriate for purposes other than that described above.

Based on our examination of the evidence supporting the assumptions, nothing has come to our attention which causes us to believe that these assumptions do not provide a reasonable basis for the projection, assuming that (here the accountants would state or refer to the hypothetical assumptions).

Further, in our opinion the projection is properly prepared on the basis of the assumptions and is presented in accordance with . . . (relevant financial reporting framework).

Even if the events anticipated under the hypothetical assumptions described above occur, actual results are still likely to be different from the projection since other anticipated events frequently do not occur as expected and the variation may be material.'

If the reporting accountants believe that:

- the presentation and disclosure of the prospective financial information is not adequate, or
- the assumptions don't provide a reasonable basis for the prospective financial information, or
- they have been limited in some way in the scope of their procedures,

then they should express a qualified or adverse opinion in the report on the prospective financial information, or withdraw from the engagement as appropriate.

FORENSIC AUDITING

The term 'forensic auditing' is a bit of a misnomer because it is more normally called 'forensic accounting'. The audit profession has, quite rightly, pointed out that much of the work uses audit skills so they have adopted the word 'forensic' to lighten the word auditing and make it sound interesting.

The word 'forensic' relates to a public discussion or arguments appropriate to a court of law and this is mostly what a forensic audit is about. In many cases audit firms are required to carry out an investigation into a suspected fraud and will use their audit skills to uncover the miscreant or to find out what has happened, its extent and how it was allowed to persist.

Fraud investigations could include:

- asset misappropriation
- financial statement manipulation
- bribery and corruption allegations

The process of accepting and carrying out an investigation in outline is similar to that of an audit. There is insufficient space in this book to deal with the process of fraud investigation in any detail and interested students are referred to the author's book '*Forensic Accounting*' for a detailed explanation of how it should be done.

Forensic auditing is carried out in stages as follows:

1 Acceptance of the assignment requiring a Letter of Engagement
This will require the firm to consider its ethical position insofar as it must avoid the self review threat, i.e. if the firm is the auditor of the client in question it cannot use the audit team in the investigation, it must have staff trained in IT investigation, evidence preservation and the techniques of investigation.

2   Planning the work – this requires a consideration of what type of fraud is being investigated and what the client's objectives are. These are normally:

- to discover what happened
- how long it has been going on
- how much is involved and
- whodunit!

3   Gathering evidence – this is absolutely critical if the case is going to end in a prosecution and there are a huge number of traps for the unwary investigator. If documents are not properly preserved or the **chain of evidence** is broken the prosecution may well fail. There must be sufficient evidence to prosecute a case in court beyond reasonable doubt where criminal proceedings are contemplated. Lower levels of evidence are required for civil claims and for employment tribunals.

4   Reporting – a report will be made detailing the investigations and its findings. Normally the report will be made to the client's legal advisor in order to preserve client privilege. A forensic audit into possible criminal actions should always be carried out with legal advice.

5   Court proceedings – if the forensic investigation is to be presented at court the audit partner will be in the nature of an expert witness and may well have to be cross examined. Any report must be in a prescribed format and disclosed to the defence. Again legal advice is essential.

It must be stressed that this is a highly specialized area and is very different from routine auditing.

In addition to this type of investigation forensic auditing can also be carried out in connection with disputes and divorce proceedings where it may be necessary to trace assets or resolve damages and compensation claims. This work is outside the scope of this book.

ASSURANCE ENGAGEMENTS

Assurance engagements performed by reporting accountants are intended to enhance the credibility of information about a subject matter by evaluating whether the subject matter conforms in all material respects with suitable criteria, thereby improving the likelihood that the information will meet the needs of an intended user.

Note that this type of assignment is different from assignments such as reports on projections or on interim financial information such as those detailed above. The difference is that in assurance engagements, such as those described in this section, the reporting accountant is measuring the actual subject matter against some criteria. In the other types of assurance assignment, the reporting accountant is simply reporting whether or not the figures are in accordance with books and records or whether assumptions seem reasonable – there are no criteria against which they are being evaluated – the opinion is based on a judgement by the reporting accountant founded on a limited amount of investigation.

So the objective of an assurance engagement is for a reporting accountant to:

- evaluate or measure a subject matter
- that is the responsibility of another party
- against identified suitable criteria

and to express a conclusion that provides the intended user with a level of assurance about that subject matter.

The level of assurance provided by the professional accountant's conclusion conveys the degree of confidence that the intended user may place in the credibility of the subject matter. An audit is a specific form of assurance assignment and we can see all the components of an assurance assignment there, i.e.

- evaluate or measure a subject matter – *the financial accounts*
- that is the responsibility of another party – *the directors*
- against identified suitable criteria – *the Companies Act, 2006, UK GAAP, etc.*

and this illustrates the difference between an assurance assignment of this type and those detailed above.

Apart from audits such assignments can include:

- reports on internal controls
- value for money reviews
- performance development reviews
- environmental or corporate social responsibility audits
- risk evaluations
- compliance reviews

We look at some of these in Chapter 31.

Companies often want to report on these issues to shareholders or demonstrate assurances that they are complying with regulations or best practice and the reporting accountants' role is to add credibility to the statements made.

It is not practicable to look at every type of assurance engagement in detail. Instead the principles contained in this section should be applied to the specific engagement. We will, however, look at one or two types of review specifically as this offers guidance on the general approach.

Approach

The applicable reporting standard is the ISAE 3000 '*Assurance Engagements other than Audits or Reviews of Historical Financial Information*' produced by the IAASB.

This applies to all assurance engagements, other than audits, but not reviews of financial information or prospective financial information, which we looked at earlier, and which are covered by the various ISREs.

It doesn't cover any assignments where the reporting accountants are not giving assurances or opinions so it doesn't apply to attestation, compilation or agreed-upon procedures type of assignments, nor does it apply to consultancy work or assignments to prepare tax computations where no opinion or conclusion is expressed.

The standard distinguishes between:

- reasonable assurance engagements; and
- limited assurance engagements.

We will look at these in more detail later.

The standard requires the accountant to comply with the appropriate ethical code and to have implemented quality control procedures applicable to the individual engagement.

There are two key points:

1   The accountants should consider any request to change the assignment, before it is completed, from an assurance engagement to a non-assurance engagement, or from a reasonable assurance engagement to a limited assurance engagement and should not agree to any change without reasonable justification.
2   The accountants should plan and perform the engagement with an attitude of professional scepticism recognizing that circumstances may exist where information may be materially misstated. Students will recognize parallels in the wording with that of ISA 240 – '*The auditor's responsibilities relating to fraud in an audit of financial statements*'.

The key components of this type of a review are:

- The bodies involved in this type of assignment, namely:
  1   The reporting accountants (called 'the practitioner' in the ISAE).
  2   The responsible party (i.e. a company, a public body, etc.)
  3   The intended user (i.e. members of the public, a regulatory body, etc.).
- The subject matter, e.g. set of accounts, an environmental report, the operations of a department, etc.
- The suitable criteria – e.g. benchmark data, IASs, etc.
- The process of completing the engagement – in many ways very similar to the approach adopted when undertaking a statutory audit.
- The conclusion and report.

Students should refer to the section above where we used the audit to illustrate the process. However, the audit is simply one kind of assurance assignment and not all assurance assignments carry audit type reports so the student has to distinguish between them.

Assignment risk

Every assignment carries with it some element of risk. The risk is that the reporting accountants will give an incorrect conclusion in their report, i.e. that they will positively confirm that X information complies with Y criteria when it doesn't or alternatively that it doesn't comply when it does.

Students will recall that the main components of this which are analogous to audit risk, and which relate only to the reporting accountant, are:

- inherent risk
- control risk
- detection risk

Remember also however that there is another type of risk – business risk, which relates to the risks faced by the entity itself. We looked at this in Chapter 14.

Only those risks which relate to the assignment are relevant but the reporting accountants must not only satisfy themselves that they can reduce assignment risk to an acceptable level but also that the organization's risk management processes are sufficient to identify and manage business risk so that it will not adversely affect their report and its conclusion.

The process

The ISAE sets out the basis on which the reporting accountants should approach the assignment. Much of it is familiar territory as it basically follows the same steps as the planning and completion of a statutory audit assignment so there is no need to go into detail about each aspect of the approach.

Students should be familiar with each of the steps in the process. The reporting accountants should obtain an understanding of the subject matter and other engagement circumstances, sufficient to identify and assess the risks of the subject matter information being materially misstated and sufficient to design and perform further evidence-gathering procedures. The accountants should then plan the engagement so that it will be performed effectively. Examples of the main matters to be considered include:

- the terms of the engagement; these should be evidenced by an Engagement Letter
- the characteristics of the subject matter and the identified criteria
- the engagement process and possible sources of evidence
- the accountants' understanding of the entity and its environment, including the risks that the subject matter information may be materially misstated
- identification of intended users and their needs and consideration of materiality and the components of assurance engagement risk
- personnel and expertise requirements, including the nature and extent of any experts' involvement

The accountants should assess the appropriateness of the subject matter. The reasons for this are that accountants should not take on an assignment where the subject matter is outside their competence to such an extent that they cannot properly assess the assignment risk – i.e. the risk of giving an incorrect or inappropriate report. If the assignment is of specialized nature the accountants should decline it. Accountants should consider the risk of being unable to gather sufficient, appropriate evidence about the subject matter in order to validate their conclusions. The reporting accountant should assess the suitability of the criteria to evaluate or measure the subject matter.

Criteria can either be established or specifically developed. In many cases this may not be easy. Suitable benchmark criteria may be difficult to find whereas in the case of an assignment to evaluate compliance with regulations, etc. the criteria are usually much more precise. Clearly if suitable criteria cannot be found the assurance cannot be given.

There are some other key issues to consider:

- The reporting accountants should consider materiality and assurance engagement risk when planning and performing an assurance engagement. The accountants should reduce assurance engagement risk to an acceptably low level in the circumstances of the engagement. Assignment risk has the same components as audit risk.

- The accountants should consider the use of experts as appropriate. Remember that the reporting accountant remains responsible for identifying a suitably qualified and experienced expert and cannot delegate any responsibility for the report's conclusions to the expert. The accountants are responsible for the totality of their report.

- The accountants should obtain representations from the responsible party, as appropriate. Written confirmation of oral representations reduces the possibility of misunderstandings.

- The accountants should consider the effect on the subject matter information and on the assurance report of events up to the date of the assurance report – i.e. perform a subsequent events review.

- The accountants should document matters that are significant in providing evidence that supports the assurance report and that the engagement was performed in accordance with ISAEs.

- The accountants should conclude whether sufficient appropriate evidence has been obtained to support the conclusion expressed in the assurance report. In developing the conclusion, the reporting accountants must consider all relevant evidence obtained, regardless of whether it appears to corroborate or to contradict the subject matter information.

- The assurance report should be in writing and should contain a clear expression of the reporting accountants' conclusion about the subject matter information.

The report can either relate to:

- the responsible party's assertions about the subject matter, or
- the subject matter itself in a form similar to the assertions made by the responsible party.

Assurance report content

The assurance report should include the following basic elements:

(a) *A title.*
The report should have a title that clearly indicates the report is an independent assurance report. An appropriate title helps to identify the nature of the assurance report, and to distinguish it from reports issued by others such as those who do not have to comply with the same ethical requirements as the reporting accountants.

(b) *An addressee.*
An addressee identifies the party or parties to whom the assurance report is directed. Whenever practical the assurance report is addressed to all the intended users.

(c) *An identification and description of the subject matter.*

This includes, for example:

- The point in time or period of time to which the evaluation or measurement of the subject matter relates.
- Where applicable, the name of the entity or component of the entity to which the subject matter relates.
- An explanation of those characteristics of the subject matter or the subject matter information of which the intended users should be aware, and how such characteristics may influence the precision of the evaluation or measurement of the subject matter against the identified criteria, or the persuasiveness of available evidence.

For example:

- the degree to which the subject matter information is qualitative versus quantitative, objective versus subjective, or historical versus prospective
- changes in the subject matter or other engagement circumstances that affect the comparability of the subject matter information from one period to the next

(d) *Identification of the criteria.*

The assurance report identifies the criteria against which the subject matter is evaluated or measured so the intended users can understand the basis for the accountants' conclusion.

The assurance report may include the criteria, or simply refer to them if they are contained in an assertion prepared by the responsible party which is available to the intended users or, if they are otherwise available, from a readily accessible source. The users must be able to evaluate the benchmark criteria for themselves.

The accountants should consider whether it is relevant to the circumstances, to disclose:

● the source of the criteria

● measurement methods used when the criteria allow for choice between a number of methods

● any significant interpretations made in applying the criteria in the engagement circumstances and

● whether there have been any changes in the measurement methods used.

(e) *Where appropriate, a description of any significant inherent limitations associated with the evaluation or measurement of the subject matter against the criteria.*

While, in some cases, inherent limitations can be expected to be well understood by readers of an assurance report, in other cases it may be appropriate to make explicit reference in the assurance report.

For example, in an assurance report related to the effectiveness of internal control, it may be appropriate to note that the historic evaluation of effectiveness of controls is not necessarily relevant to future periods due to the risk that internal control may become inadequate because of changes in conditions, or that the degree of compliance with policies or procedures may deteriorate.

(f) *When the criteria used to evaluate or measure the subject matter are available only to specific intended users, or are relevant only to a specific purpose, a statement restricting the use of the assurance report to those intended users or that purpose.*

Whenever the assurance report is intended only for specific intended users or a specific purpose, the reporting accountants should consider stating this fact in the assurance report. The reason for this is that if the report is made available to parties who do not have access to the relevant criteria their understanding of the full implications of any conclusions or points made in the report may be flawed.

(g) *A statement to identify the responsible party and to describe the responsible parties and the accountant's respective responsibilities.*

This informs the intended users that the responsible party is responsible for the subject or the subject matter information and that the practitioner's role is to independently express a conclusion.

(h) *A statement that the engagement was performed in accordance with ISAEs.*

Where there is a subject matter-specific ISAE, that ISAE may require that the assurance report refers specifically to it.

(i) *A summary of the work performed.*

The summary will help the intended users understand the nature of the assurance conveyed by the assurance report.

(j) *The conclusion.*

Where the subject matter information is made up of a number of aspects, separate conclusions may be provided on each aspect.

While not all such conclusions need to relate to the same level of evidence-gathering procedures, each conclusion is expressed in the form that is appropriate to either a reasonable assurance or a limited assurance engagement.

Where appropriate, the conclusion should inform the intended users of the context in which the practitioner's conclusion is to be read: the practitioner's conclusion may, for example, include wording such as:

'This conclusion has been formed on the basis of, and is subject to the inherent limitations outlined elsewhere in this independent assurance report.'

This would be appropriate, for example, when the report includes an explanation of particular characteristics of the subject matter of which the intended users should be aware.

(k) *The assurance report date.*

This informs the intended users that the accountants have considered the effect on the subject matter information and on the assurance report of events that occurred up to that date but no further.

(l) *The name of the firm and a specific location.*

This, ordinarily, is the city where the practitioner maintains the office that has responsibility for the engagement. This informs the intended users of the individual or firm assuming responsibility for the engagement.

LEVELS OF ASSURANCE

It is possible to give 'reasonable assurance' or 'limited assurance'.

Reasonable assurance

'Reasonable assurance' is less than absolute assurance but more than limited assurance.

The objective of a reasonable assurance assignment is to reduce assignment risk to an acceptably low level so the reporting accountant can give a *positive* opinion.

Again if the analogy of the audit is used the reporting auditor gives a positive opinion – *'the financial statements present a true and fair view, etc.'* and can do this only within the bounds of an acceptable level of audit risk.

As with audit risk, reducing assurance engagement risk to zero is very rarely attainable, or cost beneficial, as a result of factors such as the following:

- the use of selective, sample, testing
- the inherent limitations of internal control
- the fact that much of the evidence available to the practitioner is persuasive rather than conclusive
- the use of judgement in gathering and evaluating evidence and forming conclusions based on that evidence
- in some cases, the characteristics of the subject matter

In a reasonable assurance engagement, the conclusion should be expressed in the *positive* form:

EXAMPLE

'In our opinion internal control is effective, in all material respects, based on XYZ criteria.'
or:
'In our opinion the responsible party's assertion that internal control is effective, in all material respects, based on XYZ criteria, is fairly stated.'

Remember that the conclusion can either relate to the subject matter itself or to the responsible party's assertions about the subject matter.

Clearly reasonable assurance can only be given if the subject matter is:

- the responsibility of a third party;
- in a form which is clearly identifiable and which can be subjected to evidence-gathering procedures; and
- the accountants are not aware of any circumstances where reasonable assurance, based on suitable criteria if such can be found, cannot be given.

Note however that, in some cases, the evidence-gathering procedures may be difficult or expensive. If the accountants, for example, are required to report on local procurement policies for a multinational company this might involve a lot of staff and a lot of overseas travel. Cost or other such difficulties should not be a barrier to giving reasonable assurance if that is what is required, but the client must be aware of this before the engagement commences.

Limited assurance

Limited assurance requirements will result in a *negative assurance* opinion and will be based on much more limited evidence gathering procedures.

The objective of a limited assurance assignment is to reduce assignment risk to an acceptable level so a negative expression of opinion can be given.

In a limited assurance engagement, the conclusion should be expressed in the *negative* form:

EXAMPLE

'Based on our work described in this report, nothing has come to our attention that causes us to believe that internal control is not effective, in all material respects, based on XYZ criteria.'
or:
'Based on our work described in this report, nothing has come to our attention that causes us to believe that the responsible party's assertion that internal control is effective, in all material respects, based on XYZ criteria, is not fairly stated.'

Qualified conclusions, adverse conclusions and disclaimers of conclusion

Where the accountants express a qualified conclusion, the assurance report should contain a clear description of all the reasons.

The reporting accountants should express a qualified conclusion when, in their opinion, the effect of the matter is or may be material or where there is a limitation on the scope of the accountant's work preventing the accountants from obtaining the sufficient, reliable evidence required to reduce assurance engagement risk to the appropriate level.

The accountants should express a qualified conclusion ('*except for*') or, in extreme cases a *disclaimer* of conclusion:

In those cases, where the reporting accountants' conclusion is worded in terms of the responsible party's assertion, and that assertion is not fairly stated in all material respects; or the practitioner's conclusion is worded directly in terms of the subject matter and the criteria, and the subject matter information, is materially misstated; the accountants should express a qualified *(except for)* or *adverse* opinion.

When it is discovered, after the engagement has been accepted, that the criteria are unsuitable or the subject matter is not appropriate for an assurance engagement. The practitioner should express:

- a qualified conclusion or adverse conclusion when the unsuitable criteria or inappropriate subject matter is likely to mislead the intended users, or
- a qualified conclusion or a disclaimer of conclusion in other cases.

The practitioner should express a qualified conclusion when the effect of a matter is not so material and pervasive as to require an adverse conclusion or a disclaimer of conclusion. A qualified conclusion is expressed as being '*except for*' the effects of the matter to which the qualification relates.

Both reasonable assurance and limited assurance engagements require the application of assurance skills and techniques and the gathering of sufficient, appropriate evidence as part of an iterative, systematic engagement process that includes obtaining an understanding of the subject matter and other engagement circumstances.

The nature, timing and extent of procedures for gathering sufficient appropriate evidence in a limited assurance engagement are, however, deliberately limited relative to a reasonable assurance engagement.

For some subject matters, there may be specific ISAEs to provide guidance on procedures for gathering sufficient appropriate evidence for a limited assurance engagement. In the absence of a specific ISAE, the procedures for gathering sufficient appropriate evidence will vary with the circumstances of the engagement, in particular the subject matter and the needs of the intended users and the engaging party, including relevant time and cost constraints.

The next chapter looks in detail at some specific types of non-audit assurance assignments.

SUMMARY

- All assignments must be evidenced with a Letter of Engagement.
- Accountants are often called upon to prepare (compile) financial statements without necessarily being asked to audit them, to perform attest functions, to review financial statements and to perform agreed upon procedures.
- The ethical standards and quality control procedures which apply to audit work also apply to this kind of engagement.
- The engagements are regulated by various international standards on reporting engagements. Engagements to perform agreed-upon procedures are governed by ISRS 4400 *'Engagements to Perform Agreed-upon Procedures Regarding Financial Information'*. Engagements to compile financial information are governed by ISRS 4410 *'Compilation Engagements'* and ISAE 3400 *'The Examination of Prospective Financial Information'* governs the accountants' review of forecasts and projections.
- Students do not have to be able to write reports for these types of engagements but should be familiar with the different types of assignment and on which ones they will give limited assurance and on which ones will give no assurance.
- Assurance assignments may give 'reasonable assurance' or 'limited assurance'.
- The reporting accountants must consider the level of assurance risk.
- They must gather sufficient, appropriate evidence to validate their conclusions.
- The report for an assurance engagement should identify the criteria used and the work done to validate or otherwise the subject matter against those criteria.
- Conclusions may be positively worded in the case of reasonable assurance or negatively worded in the case of limited assurance.

POINTS TO NOTE

- Care must be taken not to give any form of assurance on this type of assignment unless sufficient work has been done to support the assurance given.
- Care must be taken when signing certificates or confirmations required by third parties who have drafted the certificate, e.g. in confirmation of grant claims expenditure. Quite often this requires the accountant to give some form of confirmation or assurance. In this case reporting should be given in a separate document and the certificate not signed.
- Where accountants have compiled financial information they must do so to a professional standard but must ensure that any user of the information does not get the impression it has been audited in any way.
- Firms of accountants are commercial enterprises as well as professional practices. They continually seek new work and new areas of application of their expertise. The demand for various forms of assurance and attesting is increasing.
- Assurance engagements are governed internationally by the International Standard on Assurance Engagements 3000. An assurance engagement is one where a professional accountant is engaged to evaluate or measure a subject matter that is the responsibility of another party against identified suitable criteria and to express a conclusion that provides the intended user with a level of assurance about that subject matter.
- This includes attest and direct reporting engagements but excludes agreed-upon procedures and compilation engagements.
- Reporting accountants can be exposed to professional risk with these types of assignments and should always carry out work to a competent standard and consider the wording of any reports carefully.

CASE STUDY 1

Sweete & Lowe are the auditors of BigBoy plc and have been asked as a special-purpose audit engagement to express an opinion on the present liquidity of the company and, in particular, the ability of the company to repay some proposed loan finance. The report is required by the Unlikely Bank plc in connection with a large loan for new premises and equipment.

Discussion

- What work should the accountants do in connection with the assignment?
  Produce an accountants' report on the basis that:
  (a) All is well and there are no apparent difficulties in repaying the loan based on management's forecasts of the benefits of the new assets to the business.
  (b) Present liquidity is adequate but could be problematic if some debts are not recovered in full and the assumptions underlying the forecast of ability to repay the loan are very optimistic.

CASE STUDY 2

The directors of Dunbar Holdings are seeking to win an award for business excellence. As part of the award process, reporting accountants have to assess the business performance against a set of predetermined criteria set out in the award documentation. This covers such matters as HR policy, staff morale, financial solvency, customer satisfaction and compliance with environmental regulations.

The assessment has to be performed by independent reporting accountants who will give an assurance as to compliance with the award rules.

Accountancy firm Smashe & Grabbe LLP are to investigate and report.

During the course of their work they discover that staff morale in some parts of the business is very low after some compulsory redundancies. The business was recently fined for illegal dumping of toxic materials and one of their new products is attracting a lot of complaints because it doesn't work very well. However, Dunbar is a large company and these issues are only a relatively minor part of their operations which are generally good.

Discussion

– What type of assurance is being sought?

– How will the reporting accountants deal with the issues they have uncovered in the context of their report?

– How will the report be worded?

STUDENT SELF-TESTING QUESTIONS

Questions with answers apparent from the text

a) List the procedures that should be adopted in compiling financial statements.

b) State the objectives of an assurance engagement.

c) What is an attest function?

d) What is due diligence and when is it performed?

e) What is a direct reporting engagement – give an example.

f) How should a direct reporting engagement be carried out?

g) What is negative assurance and when is it appropriate?

h) What should an accountant do if the prospective financial information is based on unrealistic assumptions?

i) What should appear in a direct reporting engagement report?

j) What are the three criteria for assurance assignments?

k) What is the role of the responsible party?

l) To whom are the accountants reporting?

m) What approach will the accountants take?

n) What two forms of reporting are there?

o) What is the difference between them in terms of the accountants' approach to the assignment?

p) When should accountants give a limited conclusion and what form will it take?

EXAMINATION QUESTIONS

1 Imperiol, a limited liability company, manufactures and distributes electrical and telecommunications accessories, household durables (e.g. sink and shower units) and building systems (e.g. air-conditioning, solar heating, security systems). The company has undergone several business restructurings in recent years. Finance is to be sought from both a bank and a venture capitalist in order to implement the board's latest restructuring proposals.

You are a manager in Peach Wimblehouse LLP, a firm of Chartered Certified Accountants. You have been approached by Paulo Gandalf, the chief finance officer of Imperiol, to provide a report on the company's business plan for the year to 31 December 2X17.

From a brief telephone conversation with Paulo Gandalf you have ascertained that the proposed restructuring will involve discontinuing all operations except for building systems, where the greatest opportunity for increasing product innovation is believed to lie. Imperiol's strategy is to become the market leader in providing 'total building system solutions' using new fibre optic technology to link building systems. A major benefit of the restructuring is expected to be a lower ongoing cost base. As part of the restructuring it is likely that certain of the accounting functions, including internal audit, will be outsourced.

You have obtained a copy of Imperiol's Interim Report for the six months to 30 June 2X16 on which the company's auditors, Discorpio, provide a conclusion giving negative assurance. The following information has been extracted from the Interim Financial Report:

1   Chairman's statement

'The economic climate is less certain than it was a few months ago and performance has been affected by a severe decline in the electrical accessories market. Management's response will be to gain market share and reduce the cost base.'

2   Statement of Financial Position

	30 June 2X16 (unaudited)	31 December 2X15
	$m	$m
Intangible assets	83.5	72.6
Tangible noncurrent assets	69.6	63.8
Inventory	25.2	20.8
Receivables	59.9	50.2
Cash	8.3	23.8
Total assets	246.5	231.2
Issued capital	30.4	30.4
Reserves	6.0	9.1
Accumulated profits	89.1	89.0
	125.5	128.5
Interest bearing borrowings	65.4	45.7
Current liabilities	55.6	57.0
Total equity and liabilities	246.5	231.2

3   Continuing and discontinuing operations

	Six months to 30 June 2X16 (unaudited)	Year to 31 December 2X15
	$m	$m
Turnover		
Continuing operations		
Electrical and telecommunication accessories	55.3	118.9
Household durables	37.9	77.0
Building systems	53.7	94.9
Total continuing	146.9	290.8
Discontinued	–	65.3
Total turnover	146.9	356.1
Operating profit before interest and taxation – continuing operations	13.4	32.2

Required:

(a) Explain the matters Peach Wimblehouse should consider before accepting the engagement to report on Imperiol's prospective financial information.

(b) Describe the procedures that a professional accountant should undertake in order to provide a report on a profit forecast and forecast Statement of Financial Position for Imperiol for the year to 31 December 2X17. *(ACCA)*

SOURCES AND ADDITIONAL READING

Financial Reporting Council (2007) *ISRE 2410 Review of Interim Financial Information Performed by the Independent Auditor of the Entity (UK and Ireland)*. London: Financial Reporting Council.

International Auditing and Assurance Standards Board (2012) *ISRS 4400 Engagements to Perform Agreed-upon Procedures Regarding Financial Information*. New York: IAASB.

International Auditing and Assurance Standards Board (2002) *International Standard on Related Services 4410, Compilation Engagements*. New York: IAASB.

International Auditing and Assurance Standards Board (2012) *International Standards on Review Engagements 2400, Engagements to Review Historical Financial Statements*. New York: IAASB.

International Auditing and Assurance Standards Board (2013) *International Standard on Assurance Engagements (ISAE) 3000 (Revised), Assurance Engagements other than Audits or Reviews of Historical Financial Information*. New York: IAASB.

International Auditing and Assurance Standards Board (2005) *International Standard on Assurance Engagements (ISAE) 3400, The Examination of Prospective Financial Information*. New York: IAASB.

Taylor, J. (2010) *Forensic Accounting*. Harlow: Pearson.

CHAPTER 31
VALUE FOR MONEY, PERFORMANCE EVALUATION, ENVIRONMENTAL REPORTING AND CORPORATE SOCIAL RESPONSIBILITY REPORTING ASSIGNMENTS

Learning Objectives

After studying the material in this chapter you should be able to:

- understand the auditor's responsibility for a wide range of non-audit assurance assignments

- appreciate the criteria for deciding if the assignment is of the assurance type

- understand the principle of value for money (VFM) initiatives

- discuss the approach to performance evaluation and the use of key performance indicators (KPIs)

- explain the principles underlying environmental standards and what environmental auditing involves

- understand the principles of corporate social responsibility (CSR)

- discuss the need for wider reporting by companies

- explain the approach to social audits

INTRODUCTION

Following on from Chapter 30 we can look at some specific assurance-type assignments which are not immediately obvious as being within the type of work auditors normally carry out, but with which audit firms are becoming increasingly involved. Auditing is now a much wider profession than in previous years where it was, generally, confined to the audit of financial statements or the sorts of assignments described in Chapter 30, which are, again, primarily financial.

Nowadays audit skills can be applied to a wide range of nonfinancial assignments such as:

- value for money (VFM) reviews;
- performance evaluations;
- environmental reporting; and
- corporate social responsibility reporting.

These are substantially nonfinancial type assignments – even VFM reviews, as any judgements about costs of a service or activity have to be made in the light of decisions about quality of delivery. Assurance assignments can be many and varied but the reporting accountant should not lose sight of their training and should follow the principles laid down in previous chapters, including those relevant to carrying out financial audit work, in order to complete such assignments satisfactorily.

Accounting firms are actively engaged in this type of work and are becoming increasingly involved, particularly in the public sector, in evaluating the performance of an organization against agreed criteria or best practice.

VALUE FOR MONEY

Value for money auditing is an audit methodology in which auditors are either required to, or exercise discretionary power to, satisfy themselves, by examination of the accounts and otherwise, that the organization has made proper arrangements for securing *economy, efficiency and effectiveness* in the use of resources.

Auditors in the public sector, have a statutory duty to report on the public body's arrangements for establishing value for money in their operations. Public money raised through taxation has to be fully accounted for and the public are understandably anxious to ensure that it isn't being wasted,

However, it is also applicable, increasingly being used by commercial organizations and by organizations such as charities who may want to obtain best use of limited resources.

Economy, efficiency and effectiveness

These terms, known as the 'three Es', are fundamental to an understanding of VFM audit approaches and the concepts involved should be explored more deeply than these definitions.

- **Economy** is '*acquiring resources of appropriate quality and quantity at the lowest cost – the measure of input*'.

  The most important thing to note is that, while obtaining low prices is certainly important, it is not the only consideration when obtaining resources. Achieving true economy also entails a consideration of qualitative aspects, such as whether the resources purchased are fit for purpose. For example, it would clearly be uneconomical to buy very cheap but poorly made equipment which would require regular replacement.

- **Efficiency** is '*maximizing the useful output from the resources used, or minimizing the level of work in producing a given level of input*'.

  The main VFM consideration is whether the resources obtained are put to good use and whether the processes and working practices in use represent best practice.

- **Effectiveness** is '*ensuring that the output from any given activity is achieving the desired result*'.

VFM takes a 'process-driven' approach, considering whether economically obtained resources are put to efficient use to generate outputs, however, it must also consider whether these outputs are useful and whether they are actually achieving the objective.

Areas for review

Common areas VFM auditors will consider as being involved in value for money initiatives within an organization include:

- The systems of budgeting, controlling revenue and capital expenditure and income and for allocating scarce resources. A sound budget-setting and monitoring process is essential for identifying and correcting poor economy and efficiency – if this is not present, management will be unable to achieve its VFM goals.
- The quality and robustness of strategic and business planning and forecasting.
- The monitoring of tendering arrangements for large capital, service or supply contracts.
- Personnel management, including arrangements for deciding and reviewing staffing levels and for recruiting, training, rewarding and otherwise motivating employees.
- Arrangements concerned with the proper management of all the assets of the organization to ensure they are all contributing to the efficiency of operations. This might include the introduction of energy efficiency policies and the disposal of inefficient or high-maintenance equipment which does not pay its way.
- Arrangements designed to take advantage of economies of scale or skill, particularly in the purchasing of goods and services.
- The quality and accuracy of management and performance information.
- Clear understanding of responsibilities, authority and accountability throughout the organization's structure.
- Clear communication of policy objectives throughout the organization.
- Monitoring results against predetermined performance objectives and standards, to ensure that outstanding performance is encouraged and unacceptable performance corrected.
- The use of comparative data or benchmarking arrangements with suitable comparator organizations.
- Mechanisms for consulting with, and responding to, the needs of customers.

Approach

When reviewing VFM performance, investigating accountants should also consider a wider set of indicators or information, such as:

- Key performance indicators as selected by management or as determined by investigating accountants based on experience in comparable organizations.
- Investigations in obtaining a detailed knowledge of the audited body, i.e. systems reviews, flow charting, discussions with staff and line management.
- The existence of standards such as the ISO 9000 series Quality Management standards or Investors in People and the outcome of standard reviews.
- Analytical procedures – fluctuating or increasing levels of expenditure might highlight risk factors.
- Comparison with other bodies or similar parts of the same organization (e.g. other subsidiaries) to identify areas where performance appears to be weak.
- Discussions with management and staff.
- Board and other committee minutes – minutes of staff meetings might be more relevant.
- The effect on the organization or parts of the organization which has been through rapid change.
- Information from outside sources: market research, customer complaints, press, internet comment.

Auditors should be alert to:

- Structural weaknesses, for example:
  - no clearly defined corporate strategy for the longer term
  - poorly defined and badly communicated objectives
  - use of outmoded or top heavy business structures
  - failure to consider outsourcing opportunities or more efficient ways of achieving objectives
  - poorly trained or inexperienced management

- duplication of effort within the business structure
- poorly defined responsibility allocation
- Waste, for example:
  - errors (overpayments, failure to take discounts)
  - poor communications (ordering goods not required); inefficiencies (high wastage rates of material); poorly performing, old or obsolete technology
- Extravagance, for example:
  - overstaffing
  - high rates of pay for poor productivity
  - excessive specifications
  - excessive quantity of purchases/inventory
- Weak management information systems, for example:
  - large overspends against budget indicative of poor monitoring or bad budgeting
  - prestigious projects with little economic justification
  - poor prioritization of work leading to inefficient use of resources
  - lack of client consultation or market research
  - lack of key performance indicators

PERFORMANCE EVALUATIONS

For most organizations the primary consideration of performance is measured by the financial statements, e.g. the profit for the year, the return on capital, the cash flow generated – in short any one of a host of financial measures.

However, other measures can be employed to evaluate the performance of the organization as it affects other stakeholders, for example, customers, suppliers and staff.

Operational performance

As we have seen in the section above there are a range of measures to evaluate operational performance from the point of view of economy, efficiency and effectiveness.

This is particularly relevant in service-based organizations such as public sector bodies or charities where the criteria for measuring performance are not financial. Such measures as:

- hospital waiting lists
- school league tables
- train delays, etc. have all provided indicators of performance efficiency

Assessing operational performance

The organization should develop its own measures for assessing its performance against clearly defined targets or **Key Performance Indicators** (KPIs).

There are various methodologies organizations can adopt and it is outside the scope of this book to discuss them in detail.

From a reporting accountants' perspective there are three key considerations. Firstly, the applicability of the KPI – is it a reliable indicator? It may be that one indicator is not sufficient or that, of itself, it is not a true indicator of underlying performance. KPIs must be SMART that is:

- **S**pecific
- **M**easurable
- **A**chievable

- **R**ealistic
- **T**imely

Secondly, the reporting accountants need to assess the ability of the management information system to provide information in order to measure actual performance against it. The KPI may be a desirable measure but, in practice, it may be too costly or time-consuming to collect the data or it is susceptible to misrepresentation or distortion in order to paint a false picture.

Thirdly, the reporting accountants should evaluate the amount of sufficient, appropriate evidence they can obtain in order to give the assurance required. The report of investigating accountants can be used to give credibility to management assertions about performance and accountants have to be very careful that they follow the precepts of the reporting standards and carry out their work with a due level of scepticism and professionalism. Examples of the kind of assurance reporting accountants may be asked to do are shown in Chapter 30.

Among the problems reporting accountants might face in this area are:

- The KPIs might not be particularly precise or well expressed – they may be aspirational rather than specific, e.g. 'to increase market share by 5 per cent'. This may seem specific but is unclear – which market? 5 per cent increase on what? Measured by volume or currency? If the KPI is precisely defined, it can be measured.
- The underlying concepts in some areas of reporting are difficult to define. For example, the organization may wish to become 'greener' or to increase 'customer satisfaction' but how can these be measured in a meaningful and consistent way?
- It may be difficult to gather sufficient reliable evidence to give even a Negative Opinion (Chapter 30). Gathering information in support of KPIs can be expensive and time consuming so the organization may devote less resources to it than may be desirable. The evidence is unlikely to be as clear cut as evidence to validate financial transactions.

ENVIRONMENTAL REPORTING

This is a fast growing area of the accountant's work, but does often require some particular expertise.

All enterprises in the twenty-first century face a climate of rapid change and escalating regulatory requirements. Amongst the major changes occurring are environmental obligations both legal and moral (known as constructive obligations). In recent years there has been an exponential growth in the awareness of environmental issues which has resulted in increased pressures on business and other organizations to respond to very public issues including:

- climate change
- a need for waste management
- a need to avoid polluting the earth, water and air
- a need for recycling
- a need for a safe and clean environment

The importance of environmental matters has affected auditors in that environmental matters can constitute considerable risks to some audit clients and environmental matters can, in some circumstances, lead to the risk of material misstatement in financial statements.

The professional bodies consider that, as environmental considerations increase in importance, there will be a growth in the investigation of and reporting of environmental matters. This will probably mean more opportunities for professional firms in auditing environmental statements. There are two aspects to environmental considerations as they affect auditors:

- The effect of environmental issues on financial statements and the risk of a material misstatement.
- Environmental reporting as an assurance assignment.

Environmental issues and financial accounts

Material environmental matters can present major risks to some clients and can lead to possible misstatements in the financial statements. Auditors should incorporate consideration of these risks specifically in their planning processes. Clients particularly at risk include mining and extraction companies, chemical companies, airlines, waste management companies, water companies and utilities and construction companies, etc.

The auditors need to be aware of the possible impact that the organization's processes and operations may have on the environment, including the possible effects caused by pollution and contamination and the hazards to employees and the immediate environs of the premises from which the operations are conducted. Clearly responsibility for environmental matters, their recognition, measurement and disclosure, lies with the management.

The main possibilities for misstatement in financial statements include:

- Environmental legislation may have the effect of impairing asset values due to non compliance or obsolescence. Auditors need to be aware of the relevant accounting provisions e.g. FRS 102 Section 27 *'Impairment of Assets'* or the provisions of IAS 36 *'Impairment of Assets'*. Noncurrent assets must be written down to their recoverable amount, which is the lower of net realizable value and the value in use. If the organization is the proud owner of, say, contaminated land, the value may be nil as it is unsaleable, or the costs of decontaminating it may be prohibitive.
- Failure to comply with legal requirements may require accrual of remediation, compensation or legal costs.
- Fines, damages and legal costs may need to be accrued for violations including contingent liabilities for pending legal actions.
- Some companies (including waste management companies, chemical manufacturers, etc.) may incur environmental obligations as a direct result of their core operations, e.g. site restoration costs.
- Products may have to be redesigned or may no longer be capable of being sold.
- Constructive obligations may occur from publicly stated environmental policies. These may not be legal obligations but may be just as binding.
- Contingent liabilities may need to be disclosed in some circumstances.
- Initiatives to abate environmental damage may cost a great deal but may not enhance the value of fixed assets.
- Auditors also need to be aware of major customers or significant suppliers who might be affected by environmental matters and consider the effect on the company as part of the consideration of business risk (see Chapter 14).

The auditors are required by ISA 315 *'Identifying and assessing risks of material misstatement through understanding the entity and its environment'* to consider all aspects of the business, its operations and the environment in which it operates. These environmental concerns should, therefore, be taken into account when considering the risks to, and the factors which affect, the business and its operations.

Laws and regulations

The auditor has to be aware of the relevant laws and regulations which affect the organization.

It is the management's responsibility to ensure adherence to laws and regulations but as environmental matters connected with laws and regulations may cause misstatements in financial statements, or give rise to penalties and fines which may have to be provided for, the auditors also need to be aware of any potential for misstatement.

The auditor's approach here may be:

- to use their existing knowledge of the business
- enquire of management as to policies and procedures on environmental matters
- enquire of management as to environmental laws and regulations that may have a fundamental effect on the entity and its financial statements
- discuss with management the policies or procedures adopted for identifying, evaluating and accounting for litigation, claims and assessments

Environmental reporting assignments

Audit firms are increasingly becoming involved in separate environmental reporting assignments as part of an organization's demonstration of its wider sense of corporate responsibility.

This is, quite rightly, often the preserve of experts in environmental issues but the experience of auditors in evaluating evidence against benchmark criteria and in pulling together information to provide a coherent reporting framework is often seen as a key skill in an organization's environmental reporting framework.

An environmental audit is a method used to obtain accurate, comprehensive and meaningful information on the environmental impact of a company from which management decisions can be based.

The benefits of carrying out environmental audits include:

- ensuring compliance with legislation
- reducing waste costs
- reducing water and energy costs
- good public relations (if the results are published)

There is a lot of legislation in this area but some of the most important legal rules are contained in:

- Environmental Protection Act 1990
- Waste Management Licensing Regulations 2005 (as amended)
- Environmental Protection (Duty of Care) Regulations 2011

The relevant British Standard is ISO 14004 (2016), '*Environmental Management Systems – General Guidelines on Principles*' and the complementary auditing standard is ISO 19011 (2011) '*Guidelines for Auditing Management Systems*'. It is outside the scope of this book to do anything other than outline the basic principles, but students and others interested in this topic will find a wealth of information on the internet and through bodies such as the British Standards Group (BSI).

In addition to ISO 14001 there is an EC approved scheme called EMAS – the Eco-Management and Audit Scheme. This is a voluntary initiative designed to improve companies' environmental performance.

Its aim is to 'recognize and reward' those organizations that go beyond minimum legal compliance and continuously improve their environmental performance. In addition, it is a requirement of the scheme that participating organizations regularly produce a public environmental statement that reports on their environmental performance. EMAS, the accrediting body, claims that it is this voluntary publication of environmental information, whose accuracy and reliability has been independently checked by an environmental verifier, that gives EMAS and those organizations that participate enhanced credibility and recognition.

Environmental audit

Environmental audits can be undertaken for a variety of reasons. They can be specific to a particular subject, i.e. water use, or more general such as initial reviews. Audits are also undertaken to accredit companies to environmental management systems (EMS) such as those under ISO 14001 and EMAS.

There are several different approaches to environmental audit and review. Audits may be carried out as part of an organization's routine processes to increase efficiency, in connection with an acquisition or as part of a larger compliance review.

They are often performed 'in house' by experts employed by the organization and it may well be part of the internal audit function to collate and review these internal reports.

Other audits will be carried out by external experts, including external audit firms.

Apart from specific anti-pollution type legislation much of the compliance work carried out is at the behest of the organization, there is no statutory compulsion. Organizations do not have to accredit themselves to a particular standard or develop an environmental management system so all the work carried out by the auditors is on an assignment basis.

There are eight main types of environmental audit assignments.

Environmental review (environmental audit)

This is a general term usually referring to a basic audit that looks at a range of environmental factors. This type of audit provides valuable management information regarding the environmental situation on a site and can be used to signpost areas of concern or where further investigative work may be required.

An environmental review would normally involve looking at the site as a whole to determine impacts on the local environment, e.g. location of nearby rivers, location of any local housing, etc. External areas would then be examined looking at areas where waste was stored, location of drainage systems, etc. The internal areas are often broken down into manageable units such as office, canteen, process areas, etc. then, within each area, environmental issues such as storage, waste, lighting, heating, air emissions and water emissions are noted.

Waste audit

These audits are often linked with environmental reviews and usually form the first step in any waste minimization exercise. The audit is concerned with waste production and handling at a site. The first concern is to ensure that wastes are being handled and stored in a safe, environmentally acceptable manner at a reasonable cost. Once this is determined then quantities of wastes are noted along with their origin and reason for production. 'Hidden' wastes should also be considered such as waste raw materials, energy and water, and wasted time, etc.

It is also important that adequate records are kept as proof of good waste management.

Waste disposal site audits

These audits cover the transport and disposal of wastes by a disposal contractor. They are often undertaken as part of compliance with Duty of Care Regulations, to ensure a company's waste is being handled correctly. They are usually carried out internally and involve a questionnaire-type approach covering issues such as how waste is stored and general housekeeping on the site. Transport issues are usually covered but can be dealt with separately, especially if the company that owns the waste site is different from the company that transports the waste.

Water audit

These audits are similar to waste audits in that they are often linked with environmental reviews and usually form the first step in any water reduction exercise. The audit is concerned with water use on a site and waste-water production. Water usage on the site is examined and quantified where possible to determine the areas of greatest usage. Waste water is also quantified if possible and areas of greatest production identified.

The result of the audit is a water mass balance where a company can identify water going into a site and water leaving the site; any large discrepancies can be investigated as this may indicate leakage or another problem on the site. Another benefit of the audit is that once identified, areas of high water usage or wastage can be investigated and savings made.

Compliance audit

This type of audit is usually done 'in house' to assess compliance with environmental legislation or company procedures. This can be either one aspect of it, e.g. Duty of Care audit, or more generally, all environmental legislation. This type of audit is rarely carried out in isolation and will normally form part of a general environmental review or EMS audit.

Environmental management system (EMS) audit

These audits form a key element of the environmental management systems established under ISO 14001 and the EC's Eco-Management and Audit Scheme (EMAS). These audits can be carried out by either internal or external auditors and there are set criteria to which audits must comply. The audit will have to be verified by an accredited person who is independent of the site's auditors to receive certification. These audits should not be confused with environmental reviews which are also carried out as part of an EMS (see above).

Acquisition audit

This can be pre- or post-acquisition and concentrates on any potential claims or liabilities for environmental damage, or the costs of installing pollution control equipment, which may affect the viability of purchasing a new site.

Potential for contaminated land is of particular importance; often this type of audit will recommend a more detailed study to investigate any potential contamination. These audits usually require the use of an expert as they can involve the use of techniques such as borehole drilling and chemical analysis.

Due diligence audit

This type of audit is normally carried out on behalf of potential investors in a company for similar reasons to the acquisition audits. It is a particularly comprehensive audit and will usually involve a team of professional auditors visiting a site over a period of several days. A wide range of environmental and other factors such as health and safety and fire risk assessments are included, as well as comprehensive site history and legislative reviews.

Audit tools

Each of the types of audit mentioned above use similar techniques adapted to a particular situation. Audit teams, whether internal or external, usually develop their own structure and approach for a particular study. Tools comprise:

- Checklists – useful in providing pointers to the type of information being sought. Also can be used to check compliance with certain procedures, where 'yes or no' answers can be given.
- Questionnaires – these are useful for straightforward situations or when audits are repeated as part of an ongoing programme. It is best to include open questions to allow for a full response rather than be restricted to 'yes or no' answers.
- Interviews – these can be undertaken to determine staff awareness on site of particular environmental issues such as contents of the Environmental Policy, or awareness of spillage procedures. Interviews are often used as a tool for EMS auditing to determine effectiveness of staff training.
- Observation – watching how a process is carried out can provide a more realistic picture of the extent of compliance with a specific procedure than could be obtained simply by asking an individual how a process is performed. However, this should never be used in isolation as it may not provide enough detail or may lead to incorrect assumptions if further investigations are not made.
- Discussion – at the start of an audit it is usual that a meeting is held with key personnel on the site to inform them of the audit activities and what is required of them. Depending on the scale of the audit, review meetings can be held during, but certainly after, the audit to allow for clarification of any points raised.

Reporting

Whatever the outcome of an audit, it is vital that it is recorded and that a report is produced. This report can be as detailed or as brief as the company requires. Phase 1 acquisition audits are often a 'tick sheet' type approach whilst due diligence audit reports can run into several volumes!

What is generally required is a description of the site and type of business, a breakdown of issues covered, results and an action plan for the way forward. A concise executive summary or action plan is often produced separately, as it can be used as an additional management tool. The audit team leader is responsible for preparing the report.

There is no specific format for a report but it could include:

- objectives
- what was audited, including the organization/area and scope
- details of the audit client
- audit team details and qualifications
- dates and locations of the audit investigation
- audit criteria
- audit plan
- people contacted within the auditee organization

- the audit process
- problems encountered that may have an impact on the reliability of the results
- achievement of the audit objectives
- areas within the scope of the audit but not covered
- audit findings
- conclusions
- improvement recommendations
- follow-up plans and arrangements

The audit report should be prepared, reviewed, approved and distributed within a defined time from the end of the investigation. ISO 19011 states that the report should be the property of the audit client (note that it is not, unless they are one and the same, the property of the auditee). The report should, of course, remain confidential.

Two things should be borne in mind:

- The auditors should bring to bear on this type of work the same qualities of skill and judgement that they would if this were a statutory audit under the Companies Act and the same criteria regarding independence, integrity and confidentiality need to be applied.
- Where the auditors are asked to give an opinion, as opposed to simply reporting facts, they should bear in mind the requirements regarding assurance assignments set out in Chapter 30. In most cases, unless there are suitable, independent, defined criteria against which environmental performance can be measured auditors should refrain from giving an opinion and simply report facts and make recommendations.

CORPORATE SOCIAL RESPONSIBILITY REPORTING

Organizations are becoming conscious of their public profile and are being made aware of their responsibilities not only to their shareholders, customers and staff but also to the environment and to the communities in which they operate. Society does not consider it acceptable for modern business organizations to ignore their wider social obligations in pursuit of profits and shareholder value and it is now considered good business practice to formulate corporate strategies taking social and environmental issues into account. Most large companies now have some form of ethical statement which will include recognition of the need for moral and ethical behaviour, compliance with all laws and regulations and recognition of the impact of their activities on the world around them.

Issues such as:

- fair treatment of workers, particularly in developing countries
- environmental 'footprint'
- product safety
- 'dumping' of products not acceptable in developed countries to emerging economies

have garnered increased press attention and investors and fund managers have begun to take note of organizations' commitment to ethical and environmental trading.

Increasingly consumers have become aware of social and environmental issues and, for example, have organized boycotts of products of companies found to be exploiting child labour in developing countries.

Companies are increasingly under pressure to operate in an ethical, environmental and sustainable way. Increasingly audit firms are becoming involved in the evaluation of the operations of client organizations against environmental and social criteria as part of their commitment to a wider corporate social responsibility programme. In these the organization is endeavouring to demonstrate its commitment to environmentally and socially aware policies by attempting to measure them against some benchmark criteria and have that achievement audited.

This requires audit firms to look at operational aspects of their clients from a nonfinancial aspect and to identify suitable criteria against which their client can be assessed. This type of work is often the province of experts and it is beyond the scope of this book to give anything other than a general outline of the type of work carried out and how it is reported.

This is, however, an expanding area as audit firms are now being asked, as independent arbitrators, to measure the achievement of organizations against identified benchmarks and to report, not just to shareholders, but to the world at large as the organizations acknowledge their performance in these areas to a wider public. We have looked at environmental reporting, which is one aspect of such a programme; the other aspect of it is the organization's interaction with the community in which it operates, its social performance.

Social audits

There are several definitions of a social audit but all, more or less, say the same thing.

A social audit is a process whereby an organization can assess its social impact and ethical behaviour in relation to its aims and objectives and also those of its stakeholders and the wider community. It is a process which involves a review of the organization's ethical and moral behaviour against its own ethical code and against the values of the society in which it functions and which it tries to promote. For example, there may be a marked difference between an organization's ethical policy and how it actually conducts its business giving the impression that no real importance is attached to the policy and that it is a mere PR tool.

Social responsibility applies to a wider group of stakeholders than simply shareholders and the bank.

There are increasingly a much wider range of expectations on organizations, for example:

- employees – expect fair remuneration for their work, a healthy and safe workplace and to have their rights as employees respected
- customers – expect products and services to do what they are advertised as being able to do and to be reliable and safe
- suppliers – expect to be paid on time and to be treated fairly
- the local community – expect the organization to respect and support local efforts and not to pollute their environment
- regulators – expect compliance with laws and good practice
- the government – expects taxes to be paid and financial performance to be properly disclosed where required

Organizations commonly develop policies and procedures to encompass such expectations. Such policies might include:

- health and safety
- training
- environmental compliance
- sustainable purchasing
- employment policies and practice
- relationships with local communities
- charitable support

Auditors may be able to review actual performance against such policies in certain areas. Such a review would not involve financial considerations, rather it would involve the consideration of any goals the organization may have and how it measured its achievements against those objectives and would include such matters as:

- the development, monitoring, dissemination of and compliance with ethical and moral codes within the organization
- actual support for charitable and community causes
- human resources policies for recruitment, training, remuneration and retention of staff
- maintenance of ethical standards in areas where the organization may not be required to do so, e.g. the use of child labour in developing countries or the avoidance of pollution where anti-pollution legislation does not exist
- information and transparency in reporting
- observance of human rights and ethical treatment of animals

Advantages and disadvantages

Organizations which have carried out social audits have reported benefits from the audit process such as:

- Improved knowledge about the operations of the organization both internally and as they affect stakeholders, which leads to business process improvements.
- Enhanced reputation and credibility in the marketplace and improved customer relations.
- Improved staff relations and human resources policies which help motivate existing staff and improves the calibre of applicants for jobs.
- Improved strategic planning as goals are more clearly defined.

However, there are two significant drawbacks:

- The process requires honesty and acceptance from everyone in the organization from the board of directors down-ward. One of the features of social auditing is improved transparency and communication in the organization and managers must be prepared to accept and deal with any performance issues thrown up by the audit.
- It is costly and resource-intensive. It requires a considerable time commitment from staff and often requires the company to buy in outside expertise. The benefits of carrying out the social audit must be evaluated in terms of the costs of carrying it out.

Audit methodology

The first question is to consider whether auditors are suited for this type of assignment at all. They are, after all, mostly trained in finance and, generally, don't have any scientific training or familiarity with concepts in the 'environment industry'. However, auditors can provide a valuable service because:

- They are used to enquiry and reporting.
- They can evaluate systems used for environmental and social reporting.
- They may be quite good, with their attitude of professional scepticism, at sorting out aspirational, woolly or fictitious thinking from provable or demonstrable achievements even where standards or measurements may be ambiguous or less than clear cut.

Clearly, with such a wide remit, and as every organization is different, there are no standard tests which social auditors can carry out. One of the major problems is that, in many areas, there are no universal standards. Organizations such as the Global Reporting Initiative (GRI) have produced some standards and guidelines but these are not universal and are not as comprehensive as an auditor used to dealing with ISAs might wish.

The organization may be able to develop its own standards by using GRI type information and by bench-marking against organizations which have a proven track record in some of these forms of reporting such as BT and the Co-op. Each organization must develop its own methodology and its own form of reporting.

One approach is:

- Identify all the stakeholders, all those affected by the company's actions.
- Identify that some organizations may be higher risk than others, for example oil companies have been polluters, clothing manufacturers have been caught using child labour or refugees in their supply chain and neither of them may wish those things to become too public.
- From this a number of stakeholder groups are selected to be questioned in detail, either in person or through written questionnaires.
- The key questions that would be of interest to each stakeholder group are then identified, normally in consultation with members of that group.
- Attempts to insert market research questions that would be of interest to the organization, but not to the stake-holders, should be resisted.

Auditors can be involved in the selection and design process, advising the organization on the process. They can then 'audit' the results to ensure that the process has been carried out honestly and fairly. Conclusions and recommendations for improvement can be drawn and an action plan developed.

Note that this need not be an annual process. The organization might carry out a comprehensive review, or design a rolling programme, taking into account cost and resource availability. However, it should not be a 'one-off' exercise – it is part of a continuous improvement programme.

SUMMARY

- Nonfinancial audits are becoming increasingly relevant to audit firms and practitioners are able to move away from purely accounts-based work.
- VFM involves consideration of economy, efficiency and effectiveness issues.
- Environmental and social matters have become very important in daily life and, for some companies, can lead to misstatements in financial statements.
- Management are responsible for dealing with and reporting on environmental matters.
- There are many opportunities for environmental matters to lead to misstatements in financial statements.
- Auditors need to consider the impact of environmental matters on items in the financial statements.
- Environmental audits are increasingly being developed as part of social responsibility programmes and to lead to compliance and process improvements.
- Environmental and social audits are carried out internally with involvement of internal audit but increasingly with assistance from external audit firms.
- These are assurance assignments and, generally, are confined to reporting facts, no opinion being given.
- Social issues are increasingly important and organizations are increasingly reviewing their nonfinancial performance in ethical and stakeholder matters.
- Social audits include considerations of a wider group of stakeholders than the shareholders and lenders and will include employees, customers, suppliers and the local community.

POINTS TO NOTE

- The government in the UK, reinforced by the EU-based agencies, has introduced much legislation to assist in improving or conserving the environment and many agencies and regulatory bodies now have statutory powers to require companies to take action. How legislation will be affected by the UK's decision to leave the EU has yet to be determined.
- Environmental audits are not just an investigation into the interaction of a company with its environment and with legal requirements but rather an investigation into policies and systems and how well practices and procedures fulfil policies.
- Listed public companies include information on environmental matters in their annual reports.
- Auditors need to be very alert to environmental factors in audits.
- Some legislation imposes personal liabilities on directors and managers in the case of infringement of environmental legislation.
- The public now expects ever-rising standards of corporate behaviour and this will affect both auditing and the auditors. Companies are not seen as vehicles for making money but, in many respects, as agents of social change with a responsibility to a much wider set of stakeholders than simply the shareholders.
- Environmental auditing or verification as a set of procedures is not very different from the audit of financial statements except in the lack of independent, universally accepted standards.

CASE STUDY

Diggitup plc are a quoted company heavily engaged in the waste disposal industry and engaged also in some open cast mining in land reclamation projects. The company sees itself as performing an unpleasant duty which the rest of the public are unwilling to do for itself. The company has inevitably acquired a reputation for being environmentally unfriendly and has noticed that the share price has fallen despite good profits and excellent prospects.

They operate from their old freehold factory and offices on a site in a manufacturing estate in Wolverhampton which dates back to the nineteenth century.

Their plant is relatively old but is regularly maintained to a good standard. They have certification under ISO 9000 but not under ISO 14000. The auditors are Tickitt & Run who are aware that the company has asked for a loan from the bank to be secured on the freehold premises.

Discussion

– Suggest factors which may have caused the company's reputation and fall in share price.
– Suggest an action programme for improving the company's public image.
– What possible misstatements may occur in the financial statements as a result of environmental factors?
– How might the auditor approach the audit?
– Indicate some green policies the company may adopt.
– What environmental factors may affect the audit?
– How might Tickitt & Run incorporate environmental factors in their audit?

STUDENT SELF-TESTING QUESTIONS

Questions with answers apparent from the text

a) List some major considerations regarding environmental factors and the audit.

b) What are the major environmental standards?

c) How might environmental issues affect the audit opinion?

d) What internal control issues concern environmental matters?

e) What substantive procedures may an auditor adopt?

f) How are auditors involved in corporate social responsibility issues?

EXAMINATION QUESTIONS

The Chemicon Company produces a range of industrial fertilizers and insecticides for sale to agricultural businesses, farmers and the general public. The items, some of which are extremely toxic, are produced under controlled environmental conditions to avoid accidental spillages and contamination. This requires Chemicon to invest in air filtration systems and increases their use of water. Chemicon also conducts extensive research into new products, although details of current research projects are currently kept secret to avoid their competitors obtaining knowledge of those projects.

As part of its philanthropic obligations to society, Chemicon recently announced the free distribution of insecticides and fertilizers to farming projects in Africa which had been devastated by locust swarms. Chemicon is moving to new, organic-based products and is trying to reduce its dependence on artificial chemicals. This has meant some reductions in efficiency but is believed to be more beneficial in the longer term.

Chemicon's annual report meets statutory and governance requirements for reporting. However, there is little additional information on the company as the directors consider this to be expensive and of limited value.

Required:

(a) Discuss the benefits of the voluntary provision of information in annual reports to exceed the statutory and governance minimum guidelines.

(b) Explain the term corporate social responsibility.

(c) Discuss the information that Chemicon could include in any CRS report, describing performance indicators that could be used to ensure CRS objectives had been met.

SOURCES AND ADDITIONAL READING

CIPFA (2010) *Value for Money Toolkit.* London: Chartered Institute of Public Finance and Accountancy.

Department for Communities and Local Government (2007) *Delivering Value for Money in Local Government*. Wetherby: Communities and Local Government Publications.

Financial Reporting Council (2016) *ISA 315 Identifying and Assessing Risks of Material Misstatement through Understanding the Entity and its Environment*. London: Financial Reporting Council.

Parmenter, D. (2010) *Key Performance Indicators (KPI): Developing, Implementing, and Using Winning KPIs*. Chichester: Wiley.

Sheldon, C. (2001) *Effective EMS Auditing (Practical Environmental Management)*. London: British Standards Institution.

Simpson, J. and Taylor, J. (2013) *Corporate Governance Ethics and CSR*. London: Kogan Page.

CHAPTER 32
CURRENT ISSUES

Learning Objectives

After studying the material in this chapter you should be able to:

- discuss the key issues currently facing the audit profession including:

  - international adoption of auditing standards

  - the future of audit

  - 'Big 4' dominance

  - audit challenges

  - data analytics

  - cryptocurrencies and blockchain technologies

- consider increased opportunities for the profession with the rise of developing economies

INTRODUCTION

Auditing is a changing discipline and this chapter is about issues that are currently exercising the profession.

By definition 'current issues' frequently go out of date quite quickly so this chapter contains only brief indicators of the issues facing the profession at the time of writing. Having said that, some issues, such as auditor independence, have been around almost as long as the profession!

In practice it is important for students to read the professional press and student periodicals to ensure they keep up to date with current issues as these often form the basis of examination questions.

INTERNATIONAL ADOPTION OF AUDITING STANDARDS

In an increasing global business world, the need for reliable quality financial information is becoming increasingly important, particularly now that companies, particularly manufacturers are operating across borders. Consistent, high quality standards with international application are now available for local auditing bodies against which local regulators can measure audit quality. This should go some way to reassure them, in the wake of several corporate scandals including Toshiba and Olympus in Japan, Tesco in the UK and Satyam in India.

However, a paper issued by the Audit Quality Forum points out that there are risks in assuming that these standards will be applied consistently in all jurisdictions. There are problems of alignment with the underlying assumptions implicit in the standards – in some countries values and norms may not be fully aligned with those on which the standards are based. For example there may be an expectation that certain audit procedures are carried out regardless of assessed risk – because *'that's how we do it here'*.

There are differences in approach to the quality of economic governance – basically the legal and political environment and its attitude to matters such as property rights and corporate governance. In some countries rules-based systems may make it appear that auditing should be confined to simple box ticking for compliance and the role does not attract individuals with the right qualities. Political considerations and the willingness of countries to accede to demands to limit corporate disclosure can discourage questioning and enquiry, as, of course, can corrupt regimes and those dominated by one party politics.

The nature of business relationships differs vastly; in some countries business relationships may be complex and built on trust. Employment of family members and relationships with related parties may be beneficial for trading purposes but may present auditors with huge problems in complying with the standards. A complex web of relationships and loyalties may serve to obscure the truth and cultural traditions may make it difficult for auditors to question senior management.

The strength of legal system is important to auditing, in particular, property ownership rights or the right of the government to seize property may be an issue, as well as the ability of the legal system to act as a regulator for audit purposes.

Not all countries have the quality of accounting and audit staff in depth nor the ability to distinguish substance over form in the recording of transactions.

There are broad cultural differences between countries in management's ability to communicate at all levels in an organization and also in the ability of an auditor to challenge management decisions or actions. It may be difficult for members of an audit team to question senior management as any challenge to management may be interpreted as a criticism of their ability to do their job rather than as a process of audit review. Further some cultures have an expectation that financial and other matters should be kept secret and there is an unwillingness to adopt measures which might lead to greater transparency of reporting. This culture of respect for senior management and a culture of secrecy was a contributing factor in the Olympus and Toshiba scandals in Japan.

Auditing is an art, not a science and in some countries with poor education systems, lack of opportunity to develop financial expertise, or limitations on cross border experience, it may be difficult to recruit a sufficient number of auditors to the profession, particularly if there is a poor perception of what auditors actually do.

With increasing attempts to standardize audit practice, questions are being raised as to whether a single set of audit rules fits all types of entity.

THE FUTURE OF AUDIT

Users of financial information want more contextual information to be provided, to explain the process whereby the auditors reached their opinion and the challenges they faced and overcame along the way. Although auditor reporting is changing, there is some frustration that it is not changing further and more quickly. Users want more disclosure from companies, particularly of nonfinancial information, such as on sustainability, and forward-looking information. Users also want assurance that this information is being disclosed fairly and accurately which implies an extension to the audit role away from purely financial certification.

Generally, the auditing standards revisions are placing more emphasis on how well an audit is done, with heightened focus on risk, professional scepticism and audit quality but, although changes to standards have begun to enhance confidence in audit for larger companies, they have introduced additional complexity for smaller entity audits. In response, some countries have exempted the smallest companies from the obligation to have an audit. The idea that an audit is a single, universal service that is the same for all types of entity anywhere in the world is under serious question.

Auditing standards are often seen to be more applicable to the audit of large companies with lots of staff rather than medium-sized companies where the objective of an audit might be somewhat different. The question arises then as to whether rules should distinguish between listed companies, unlisted companies, large enterprises and small and medium enterprises. Their reporting requirements are not the same and accordingly their assurance needs are not the same either. There are benefits to having a standard approach to audit in principle that is shared across all types of entity everywhere in the world, but the question is whether this should be a framework approach rather than a prescriptive one.

This is a problem for regulatory bodies and standard setters. For example, if they do not demonstrate how auditing standards for larger entities can be applied to SME audits the relevance of audit standards to the vast majority of companies may be diluted and become increasingly irrelevant. The danger is that a two tier system will develop and consistency of approach will be lost.

Finance teams in small and medium sized entities generally need more assistance than those at larger companies. The quality of financial information they publish is greatly enhanced by help from the auditor but this may create tensions with the traditional, listed-company view that the auditor must be, and be seen to be, completely independent of the audited entity. Specialist investors who are familiar with the risks of investing in smaller entities also know that those are the companies that produce the most growth. Different countries need different criteria by which to evaluate the need for an audit of an entity.

AUDIT CHALLENGES

New challenges are being posed to auditors arising from the increased use of the Internet and other electronic forms of trading. Auditing practices have to remain flexible to accommodate new forms of corporate activity. The increased use of risk-based auditing methods means that the calibre and experience of audit staff has to be maintained. In addition, the requirement for technical computer skills is growing and the auditing profession is now heavily computerized, both in preparing audit working papers and in carrying out audit testing.

Consider the challenge posed to the auditor of a client who is an internet-based retailer, with computers and offices in the UK, distribution warehouses in Germany and France, finance department in the Cayman Islands and a head office in the USA which carries out all its activities electronically using paperless systems. Systems-based audit testing is not going to work! Audit processes and procedures cannot afford to lag behind the trading methods of the client.

This is particularly relevant at a time when reports indicate that fraud is on the increase. This is not only fraud resulting from external attack, hackers, etc., but internal 'high flyer' fraud, corruption and deliberate evasion of taxes by companies.

Research into new forms of auditing involving such arcane areas such as game theory are being talked about in academic circles as a way of designing audit procedures in such a way as to improve the chances of detecting fraudsters, but this is very much in its infancy at the moment.

Data analytics

Data analytics involves specialized interrogation software which is used by audit firms to examine large quantities of data from a client's system. In one form or another this type of audit procedure has been in use for many years but its use is increasing with the development of increasingly sophisticated software.

For the 'Big 4' audit firms these tools are a must as it is probably the only way to carry out any form of meaningful data analysis on the huge populations comprising their client's transaction databases. For second tier and smaller firms the cost of development of such software has to be carefully considered as to write bespoke software of this nature is an expensive proposition. The software not only has to handle different platforms but it must also be able to be used by nonspecialist audit teams so it has to be user friendly and fairly intuitive.

The ISAs are presently drafted on the basis that auditors cannot interrogate entire populations and, consequently, they are designed to identify and determine the validity of sample-based audit testing where the auditor must apply their skill and judgement to decide whether they have sufficient reliable evidence to substantiate an audit opinion based on less than 100 per cent sampling of transactions.

This is now, in many ways, no longer the case as data analytics enables auditors to examine entire populations. It may be that this will force some change on the way ISAs are written in the future but extensive use of data analytics is far from universal and the old tried and trusted audit techniques will continue to apply in most cases. However, audit firms must become increasingly aware of the availability of such software and revise their audit procedures to recognize the new and powerful tools they have been given.

Cryptocurrencies and blockchains

Cryptocurrencies, the leading name being Bitcoin, have come and, in some cases gone. In 2016 a successor to Bitcoin called Ether slumped after a hacker siphoned off some $50m of digital bits. Ether is a currency used by an organization called Ethereum which is a **blockchain** platform. This can be used to create 'smart' contracts or automated agreements and is, in essence a distributed platform enabling business contracts to be made electronically without currency issues or the use of a middleman agency such as a bank. In theory clear rules embedded in the software make the contracts safe and also protect them from any interventions by central authorities.

Briefly, blockchain is a crowd managed distributed secure database (Figure 32.1). What is does is to allow consumers and suppliers to connect directly, removing the need for a third party. Using cryptography to keep exchanges secure, blockchain provides a decentralized database, or 'digital ledger', of transactions that everyone on the network can see. This network is essentially a chain of computers that must all approve an exchange before it can be verified and recorded. The technology can work for almost every type of transaction involving value, including money, goods and property. Its potential uses are almost limitless: from collecting taxes to enabling migrants to send money back to family in countries where banking is difficult.

Blockchain could also help to reduce fraud because every transaction would be recorded and distributed on a public ledger for anyone to see.

FIGURE 32.1   How a blockchain works

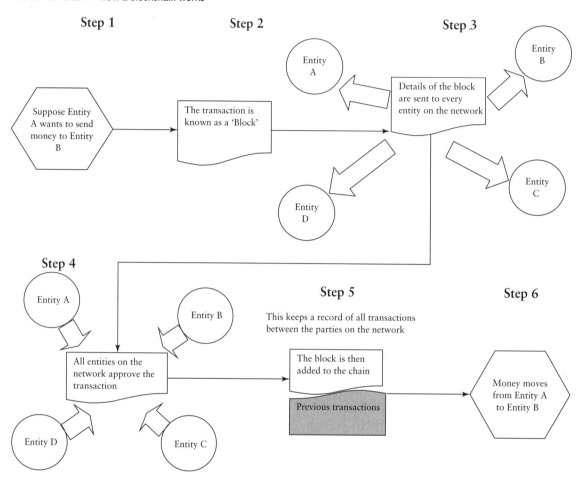

The use of cryptocurrencies and blockchain technology is in its infancy at the moment and problems with the software leading to the collapse of Bitcoin and problems with Ether are hampering its growth and development but it is likely to be the coming thing. Financial institutions see it as a way of making prompt settlements and to cut costs.

This will present problems to audit firms mainly in the area of technology. They will have to develop the skill and expertise to audit entities using blockchain approaches and this will require a very detailed approach to risk assessment.

How far this technology will go is so far unknown but it exists and is being used. Once secure systems are developed and use becomes increasingly common audit firms will have to have developed strategies and approaches to deal with it.

DOMINANCE OF THE 'BIG 4'

The costs of auditing and the international nature of many large clients have led to concentration amongst audit firms, particularly those below the 'Big 4'. Larger second rank firms are merging and are concerned about the domination of the 'Big 4' (PwC, Ernst, Deloitte and KPMG) in auditing FTSE 100 companies. They are trying to break the stranglehold of the big firms on this lucrative market. Some say that this dominance has led to increased audit costs and a cosy relationship between big company boards and the senior partners of major audit firms.

In addition, critics point out that the profession itself is dominated by big firm partners and that the 'Big 4' firms have a disproportionate influence over the profession both in the UK and internationally with IFAC. Opponents of self-regulation point out that where major audit firms dominate or influence the regulator and the standard setting bodies this cannot lead to a fair and unbiased system.

These arguments have rumbled on for many years but there is undoubtedly concern about the dominance of the 'Big 4', fuelled by firms just below their level, and prompting concern at government level.

The European Directive has brought in mandatory rotation of audit firms. Briefly, the rules require that larger listed entities must put their audit out to tender every ten years and change their auditor every twenty years. This is effective from 17 June 2016. This coupled with the restrictions on what auditors of so-called Public Interest Entities (PIEs) may not do by way of additional services delivered to clients, now restricted to 70 per cent of the audit fee, is causing some upheaval in the Big 4 firms.

Increasing audits are going out to tender and the Big 4 are having to create new and innovative ways of attracting audit clients as some long standing audit clients say goodbye. This has created some turmoil in the audit market but only in a relative small corner of it as, ultimately, there are few firms who can handle these enormous clients and inevitably the market will, in essence, remain apportioned between the four big firms. However, it does remain to be seen how it is sliced between them and whether one dominant player will emerge having captured clients on a larger scale than having lost them.

Firms below the 'Big 4' say this now gives them an opportunity to bid for a slice of a very lucrative audit market. It should be pointed out, however, that many of the UK's top companies already use firms below the 'Big 4' for consultancy and tax advice but it may be that they will now stand a much greater chance of picking up prestigious audit clients. It may be that the future for non-Big 4 firms lies in increasing specialization and focussing on niche markets where they can achieve greater market penetration than they otherwise would.

Role of the auditor

One of the senior partners of a 'Big 4' firm has suggested that the audit profession should question its role and responsibilities and how these have changed. This is in response to the increasing expectation that companies have a wider remit to stakeholders than simply making profits for the shareholders.

The firm is encouraging its largest clients to increase disclosure on matters such as risk management. As we have seen from Chapter 31 there is a drive for increased attention to nonshareholder stakeholders and the development of increased disclosure under the banner of corporate social responsibility, but change across the whole business spectrum and regulation on this type of disclosure is unlikely to happen any time soon.

NEW OPPORTUNITIES, NEW PROBLEMS

Apart from the new opportunities in the area of CSR already mentioned and the increasing technical demands on individual auditors, new opportunities are arising in the developing world. As described in Chapter 31, new opportunities for nonfinancial assurance work have developed. These include environmental and social auditing, value for money auditing and performance reporting.

Overseas investors in fast developing countries have expressed doubts about the quality of financial information being presented to them. Companies involved in joint ventures or partnerships are finding it increasingly difficult to rely on the results without inserting their own financial resources in an effort to ensure the probity of the information. This means that audit firms based in countries with a higher level of regulation are able to sell services into these countries. In addition, there are training and development opportunities for training the vast numbers of auditors and accountants required to service these new economies.

SUMMARY

- Auditing is a dynamic discipline and change is now rapid.
- Auditors may have to consider their role in the light of new expectations.
- The audit profession has to stay abreast of new forms of trading, particularly internet-based operations, cryptocurrencies and blockchain technologies and work out how to audit them.
- New opportunities have arisen in the fields of CSR and also in the developing world.

POINTS TO NOTE

- Auditing is a surprisingly dynamic discipline. Students are advised to keep up to date by reading the professional press, and the business pages of the newspapers can help as can reading annual reports and accounts, either in manually signed format or electronic format.
- The question of auditor independence is a difficult one due to the conflicting professional and commercial instincts of auditors. Regulators want more independence (namely, that auditors do not do other work) and auditors want more work other than auditing. The use of business risk assessment methods is now becoming central to audit work.
- Computers and the internet are changing the face of auditing and presenting extremely difficult problems for the audit profession.
- The present structure of the audit profession may be forced to change as pressure mounts for an end to self-regulation. The audit itself may change and become more fluid and dynamic as corporate structures change and new forms of reporting become available. The one-off annual audit seems quite antiquated and may no longer carry the force it once did.

CASE STUDY

Megablast Inc. trades internationally as a manufacturer and distributor of electrical goods ranging from consumer goods (TVs, washing machines, etc.), to electrical equipment and electronic components. Its shares are currently listed on the New York Stock Exchange and it is subject to the Sarbanes-Oxley legislation and lots of other listing rules.

The CEO, Lindsey Lovely, has been considering moving the operation to London and transferring the business to a new holding company listed on the UK Stock Exchange. There are many tax and accounting issues but the main one Lindsey is concerned about is the regulatory regime in America.

The auditors, international accounting firm Blockitt & Hope approve of the move to London and are helping Lindsey with the decision.

Discussion

– Why would Blockitt & Hope be so keen to see Megablast relocate?
– What benefits would it bring to Megablast to do so?
– What ethical issues are involved?

STUDENT SELF-TESTING QUESTIONS

Questions with answers apparent from the text

a) List some influences for change in auditing.

b) Where do new audit regulations come from?

c) List advantages and disadvantages of auditors taking other work from audit clients.

d) What approach to regulation has been taken by the USA?

e) How does it differ from the UK approach?

f) How can the audit profession benefit from the developing world?

EXAMINATION QUESTIONS

1 Here are some points based on extracts from recent articles in the accounting press:

- The UK's reporting regulator wants greater power to sanction and discipline audit firms.
- The Financial Reporting Council is pushing for 'a wider range of sanctions to address shortcomings in audit quality'.
- The regulator is suggesting licensing auditors of large 'public interest' companies.
- The role of the auditor needs to be reconsidered in the modern business world as the growth of corporate governance has raised expectations of increased disclosure and transparency and auditors should encourage clients to go beyond statutory disclosure.

Required:

(a) Briefly explain how the auditing profession is currently regulated.

(b) Why do you think a financial or economic crisis raises questions over the role of audit?

(c) Some of the demand for increased regulation has come from audit firms themselves, particularly medium-sized firms that find it difficult to secure audit contracts for public limited companies (PLCs) given the predominance of the 'Big 4' firms. One medium-sized firm has written to the House of Lords inquiry asking for a cap on the number of big audit contracts any one firm can have.
Do you think that this is necessary and what impact do you think this would have on audit quality?

(d) Set out the arguments for and against giving the FRC a greater role in regulating audit firms.

(LMU)

SOURCES AND ADDITIONAL READING

ACCA (2010) *Accountancy Futures: Reshaping the Audit for the New Global Economy*. London: Association of Chartered Certified Accountants.

ACCA (2010) *Accountancy Futures: Restating the Value of Audit*. London: Association of Chartered Certified Accountants.

Audit Quality Forum (2006) *Making Global Auditing Standards Local*. London: ICAEW.

Audit Quality Forum (2008) *Stakeholder Expectations of Audit*. London: ICAEW.

Economia (2016) *How Mandatory Audit Rotation is Impacting Firms*. London: ICAEW.

Grant Thornton and ACCA (2016) *The Future of Audit*. London: Grant Thornton.

Hinks, G. (2011) 'Audit must change', www.accountancyage.com/aa/news/2025716/audit-change-barnier

Sancto, J. (Accountancy Magazine) (2010) The future of audit, *Accountancy Magazine*, ICAEW.

Appendix 1

INTERNATIONAL STANDARDS ON AUDITING (UK and IRELAND) CURRENT STANDARDS

ISA 200	*Overall objectives of the independent auditor and the conduct of an audit in accordance with International Standards of Auditing*
	This standard sets out the overall objective of the independent auditor. It makes clear the purpose of the objectives in each of the other ISAs and explains that the auditor should use these objectives when planning and performing audits.
	It requires the auditor to ensure that they achieve the objectives of all ISAs applicable to the audit–it is not concerned solely with the final result.
	It also includes material explaining some of the fundamental concepts related to an audit, such as: ethical requirements relating to an audit; professional scepticism; professional judgement; limitations of an audit; sufficient appropriate evidence and audit risk; and responsibilities of management.
ISA 210	*Agreeing the terms of audit engagements*
	The standard requires the auditor to establish that 'the preconditions for an audit are present'. This includes:
	• the use of an acceptable financial reporting framework;
	• agreement by management of the premise on which an audit is conducted.
	This standard includes specific reference to determining whether the financial reporting framework to be applied is acceptable. Without a suitable accounting framework management do not have an acceptable basis for preparation of the financial statements and the auditor will not have a suitable basis for auditing the financial statements.
	The letter must include an acknowledgement by management or those charged with governance that they understand their responsibilities in connection with the preparation of the financial statements:
	• in accordance with the relevant reporting framework; and
	• free from material errors or misstatements.
	It also clarifies the requirement for the management to provide the auditors with all necessary information and explanations.
ISA 220	*Quality control for an audit of financial statements*
	This standard sets out the basis on which an audit firm should ensure that it has within it suitable quality control procedures, including a system of hot and cold reviews, to ensure compliance with ethical standards and sufficiently robust audit processes.
ISA 230	*Audit documentation*
	Sets out the requirements for documenting audit evidence including the need to evidence the work done and the review of it by a competent person.
	Audit documentation provides:
	• evidence of the auditor's basis for a conclusion about the achievement of the overall objectives of the auditor; and
	• evidence that the audit was planned and performed in accordance with ISAs and applicable legal and regulatory requirements.
	Audit documentation serves a number of additional purposes, assisting the engagement team to plan and perform the audit and assisting members of the engagement team responsible for supervision to direct and supervise the audit work and to discharge their review responsibilities enabling the engagement team to be accountable for its work. It also retains a record of matters of continuing significance to future audits and enables the conduct of quality control reviews and inspections.

ISA 240	*The auditor's responsibilities relating to fraud in an audit of financial statements* This requires the auditors to be alert to the possibility of fraud, particularly in the planning phase, and to adopt an attitude of *professional scepticism* in their audit approach. The possibility of management override of internal controls should be seen as a significant risk.
ISA 250A	*Consideration of laws and regulations in an audit of financial statements* The requirements in this ISA are designed to assist the auditor in identifying a material misstatement of the financial statements due to non-compliance with laws and regulations.
ISA 250B	*The Auditor's Statutory Right and Duty to Report to Regulators of Public Interest Entities and Regulators of Other Entities in the Financial Sector* This ISA deals with the circumstances in which the auditor of an entity subject to statutory regulation (a "regulated entity") is required to report direct to a regulator information which comes to the auditor's attention in the course of the work undertaken in the auditor's capacity as auditor of the regulated entity.
ISA 260	*Communication with those charged with governance* This ISA is designed to guide the auditor in the communication process with those charged with governance e.g. the directors. It is designed to foster good working relationships, communicate audit issues and to facilitate the flow of information from the company. Requirements include: • explaining why significant accounting practices, that are acceptable according to financial reporting requirements, are not appropriate to the circumstances of the entity • documenting matters communicated orally • communication of difficulties encountered during the audit
ISA 265	*Communicating deficiencies in internal control to those charged with governance and management* What were once known as 'material weaknesses' are reclassified as 'significant deficiencies'. The aim is to define a threshold of significance for when deficiencies in internal control should be communicated. The auditor has to determine whether individually or in combination any identified deficiencies in the financial systems or in the preparation of the accounts constitute a 'significant deficiency'. All such 'significant deficiencies' have to be communicated to those charged with governance in writing.
ISA 300	*Planning an audit of financial statements* The ISA sets out the requirements for all audits to be properly planned and for the planning process to be thoroughly documented. Planning an audit involves establishing the overall audit strategy for the engagement and developing an audit plan. Planning helps the auditor to devote appropriate attention to important areas of the audit and to make the best use of resources.
ISA 315	*Identifying and assessing the risks of material misstatement through understanding the entity and its environment* This ISA deals with the auditor's responsibility to identify and assess the risks of material misstatement in the financial statements, through understanding the entity and its environment, including the entity's risk assessment processes, the information system, control activities and monitoring of controls. This is one of the key ISAs as it outlines risk areas in some detail and makes recommendations to the auditor as to key areas of risk which need to be evaluated. This also includes evaluating the risks of management override of controls. ISA 315 also includes the Assertions which are implicit in a set of financial statements prepared under a suitable accounting framework.

ISA 320	*Materiality in planning and performing an audit* The focus of ISA 320 is the consideration of not only the size of an item but its nature and the circumstances of the entity. The standard explains that misstatements, including omissions, are considered to be material if they, individually or in aggregate, could reasonably be expected to influence the economic decisions of users. Judgements about materiality are made in light of surrounding circumstances, and are affected by the size and nature of a misstatement, or a combination of both. Thus an item may be material by virtue of its nature rather than simply its size. The standard includes the definition of the concept of *'performance materiality.'* This states that the auditor should set materiality for the financial statements as a whole however, in addition the auditor should establish an amount set at less than materiality when designing the nature, timing and extent of further audit procedures. The aim of this is to reduce the risk that misstatements in aggregate exceed the total for materiality for the financial statements as a whole. The standard clarifies that the determination of materiality requires the exercise of professional judgement. Both materiality and performance materiality levels may be revised if circumstances change during the course of the audit work.
ISA 330	*The auditor's response to assessed risks* This ISA deals with the auditor's responsibility to design and implement responses to the risks of a material misstatement identified and assessed by the auditor in accordance with ISA 315 in an audit of financial statements. The objective of the auditor is to obtain sufficient appropriate audit evidence regarding the assessed risks of material misstatement, through designing and implementing appropriate responses to those risks.
ISA 402	*Audit considerations relating to an entity using a service organization* This deals with a situation where the auditor intends to use a service auditor's report as audit evidence. If the auditor intends to use a report from a service auditor, they should perform procedures to ensure they are satisfied with the competence and independence of the service auditor and that the service auditor's report provides sufficient appropriate evidence about the effectiveness of controls.
ISA 450	*Evaluation of misstatements identified during the audit* All misstatements must be communicated to management on a timely basis, unless they are clearly trivial. Management should be asked to correct all misstatements identified during the audit. The auditor should obtain an understanding of management's reasons for refusing to adjust any of the misstatements. Prior to evaluating the significance of uncorrected misstatements the auditor should reassess materiality to confirm whether it remains appropriate to the financial statements. Then the auditor must assess whether uncorrected misstatements are, individually or in aggregate, material. To do this they should consider the size and nature of the misstatements, both in relation to the financial statements as a whole and to particular classes of transaction, account balances and disclosures. The auditor should obtain a written representation from management and those charged with governance that they believe the effect of the uncorrected misstatements is immaterial, individually and in aggregate. Note that ISA 320 also deals with materiality but the two are not necessarily the same as initial decisions about materiality may have been revised during the audit process.

ISA 500	Audit evidence
	The objective of the auditor is to design and perform audit procedures in such a way as to enable the auditor to obtain sufficient appropriate audit evidence to be able to draw reasonable conclusions on which to base the auditor's opinion.
	Most of the auditor's work in forming the auditor's opinion consists of obtaining and evaluating audit evidence. Audit procedures to obtain audit evidence can include inspection, observation, confirmation, recalculation, reperformance and analytical procedures, often in some combination, in addition to inquiry. Although inquiry may provide important audit evidence, and may even produce evidence of a misstatement, inquiry alone ordinarily does not provide sufficient audit evidence of the absence of a material misstatement nor of the operating effectiveness of controls.
ISA 501	Audit evidence-specific considerations for selected items
	The specific objective of the auditor is to obtain sufficient appropriate audit evidence regarding the:
	(a) existence and condition of inventory–requiring the auditor to attend the inventory count;
	(b) completeness of litigation and claims involving the entity; and
	(c) presentation and disclosure of segment information in accordance with the applicable financial reporting framework.
ISA 505	External confirmations
	Auditors are encouraged to obtain external confirmations as good audit evidence. When using external confirmations, the auditor should maintain control over external confirmation requests. If management refuses to allow the auditor to send a confirmation request the auditor should inquire as to management's reason, evaluate the implications, and, where possible, perform alternative procedures.
	The auditor must evaluate the reliability of confirmations received and when a response is not received the auditor shall perform alternative procedures. Negative confirmations provide less persuasive evidence therefore they should, generally, not be performed as the sole substantive procedure.
ISA 510	Initial audit engagements–opening balances
	In conducting an initial audit engagement, the objective of the auditor with respect to opening balances is to obtain sufficient appropriate audit evidence about whether:
	(a) opening balances contain misstatements that materially affect the current period's financial statements; and
	(b) appropriate accounting policies reflected in the opening balances have been consistently applied in the current period's financial statements, or any changes are appropriately accounted for and adequately presented and disclosed in accordance with the applicable financial reporting framework.
ISA 520	Analytical procedures
	This standard deals with the auditor's use of analytical procedures as substantive procedures ('substantive analytical procedures'). It also deals with the auditor's responsibility to perform analytical procedures near the end of the audit that assist the auditor when forming an overall conclusion on the financial statements. ISA 315 deals with the use of analytical procedures as risk assessment procedures. ISA 330 includes requirements and guidance regarding the nature, timing and extent of audit procedures in response to assessed risks; these audit procedures may include substantive analytical procedures.
ISA 530	Audit sampling
	This standard applies when the auditor has decided to use audit sampling in performing audit procedures. It deals with the auditor's use of statistical and non-statistical sampling when designing and selecting the audit sample, performing tests of controls and tests of details, and evaluating the results from the sample. Auditors should consider whether any deviations or misstatements identified in the samples are an anomaly or represent systemic failure.

ISA 540	*Auditing accounting estimates, including fair value accounting estimates, and related disclosures*
	The standard introduces the requirement for professional scepticism when auditing accounting estimates, including an assessment of management bias.
	It also places a greater emphasis on obtaining an understanding of the client's estimation process–and related controls–when performing risk assessment procedures in accordance with ISA 315.
	The revised standard clarifies the procedures that an auditor should perform in response to the assessment of material misstatement.
ISA 550	*Related parties*
	This standard on Auditing deals with the auditor's responsibilities relating to related party relationships and transactions in an audit of financial statements. Specifically, it expands on how ISA 315, ISA 330 and ISA 240 are to be applied in relation to risks of material misstatement associated with related party relationships and transactions.
	Auditors are required to focus on:
	• identification of previously unidentified related parties or those not disclosed by management
	• significant related party transactions outside the normal course of business
	• assertions that related party transactions are at arm's length
	Discussions on related parties must be included in any audit team discussions on fraud.
ISA 560	*Subsequent events*
	The standard on deals with the auditor's responsibilities relating to subsequent events in an audit of financial statements.
	Financial statements may be affected by certain events that occur after the date of the financial statements. Many financial reporting frameworks specifically refer to such events. Such financial reporting frameworks ordinarily identify two types of events:
	• those that provide evidence of conditions that existed at the date of the financial statements
	• those that provide evidence of conditions that arose after the date of the financial statements
	ISA (UK and Ireland) 700 explains that the date of the auditor's report informs the reader that the auditor has considered the effect of events and transactions of which the auditor becomes aware and that occurred up to that date.
ISA 570	*Going concern*
	This standard deals with the auditor's responsibilities in the audit of financial statements relating to management's use of the going concern assumption in the preparation of the financial statements.
	Under the going concern assumption, an entity is viewed as continuing in business for the foreseeable future. General purpose financial statements are prepared on a going concern basis, unless management either intends to liquidate the entity or to cease operations, or has no realistic alternative but to do so.
	The auditor's responsibility is to obtain sufficient appropriate audit evidence about the appropriateness of management's use of the going concern assumption in the preparation and presentation of the financial statements and to conclude whether there is a material uncertainty about the entity's ability to continue as a going concern.
	The auditor must evaluate whether management's plans are feasible.

ISA 580	*Written representations*
	The main emphasis of the standard is that, whilst written representations provide necessary audit evidence, they support other forms of evidence and do not on their own provide sufficient appropriate audit evidence. In addition to this clarification the standard also requires the auditor to obtain the following written representations about management's responsibilities:
	• that they have fulfilled their responsibility for the preparation of the financial statements
	• that they have provided the auditor with all relevant information and access to records, as agreed in the engagement terms
	• that all transactions have been recorded and reflected in the financial statements
	The standard clearly states that if the auditor concludes that there is sufficient doubt about the integrity of management, thus rendering the written representations unreliable, or if management does not provide the written representations requested then the auditor shall disclaim an opinion on the financial statements in accordance with ISA 705.
ISA 600	*Special considerations–audits of group financial statements (including the work of component auditors)*
	This ISA deals with special considerations that apply to group audits, in particular those that involve the work of component auditors (auditors of subsidiaries or similar entities which are not the principal or group auditor).
	In accordance with ISA 220 the group engagement partner is required to be satisfied that those performing the group audit engagement, including component auditors, collectively have the appropriate competence and capabilities. The group engagement partner is also responsible for the direction, supervision and performance of the group audit engagement in total.
	This ISA, adapted as necessary in the circumstances, also applies when an auditor involves other auditors in the audit of financial statements that are not group financial statements. For example, an audit firm may involve another auditor to observe the inventory count or inspect physical fixed assets at a remote location.
ISA 610	*Using the work of internal auditors*
	This deals with the external auditor's responsibilities relating to the work of internal auditors when the external auditor has determined, in accordance with ISA 315 that the internal audit function is likely to be relevant to the audit. The ISA provides guidance on instances when individual internal auditors provide direct assistance to the external auditor in carrying out audit procedures.
	The objectives of the internal audit function are determined by management and, where applicable, those charged with governance. While the objectives of the internal audit function and the external auditor are different, some of the ways in which the internal audit function and the external auditor achieve their respective objectives may be similar.
	Irrespective of the degree of autonomy and objectivity of the internal audit function, such function is not independent of the entity as is required of the external auditor when expressing an opinion on financial statements. The external auditor has sole responsibility for the audit opinion expressed, and that responsibility is not reduced by the external auditor's use of the work of the internal auditors.
ISA 620	*Using the work of an auditor's expert*
	The revised standard focuses on the use of an auditor's expert. The consideration of the use of management's experts is referred to in ISA 500.
	The procedures for evaluating the experts work have also been clarified, namely the auditor must consider: the consistency of the findings with other evidence; the significant assumptions made; and the use and accuracy of source data.
	The auditor has sole responsibility for the audit opinion expressed, and that responsibility is not reduced by the auditor's use of the work of an auditor's expert.

ISA 700	*Forming an opinion and reporting on financial statements*
	The standard provides guidance on the form and content of the auditor's report issued as a result of an audit performed by an independent auditor of the financial statements.
	The auditor's report on the financial statements must contain a clear written expression of opinion on the financial statements taken as a whole, based on the auditor evaluating the conclusions drawn from the audit evidence obtained, including evaluating whether:
	(a) sufficient appropriate audit evidence as to whether the financial statements as a whole are free from material misstatement, whether due to fraud or error has been obtained;
	(b) uncorrected misstatements are material, individually or in aggregate. This evaluation shall include consideration of the qualitative aspects of the entity's accounting practices, including indicators of possible bias in management's judgements;
	(c) in respect of a true and fair framework, the financial statements, including the related notes, give a true and fair view; and
	(d) in respect of all frameworks the financial statements have been prepared in all material respects in accordance with the framework, including the requirements of applicable law.
ISA 701	*Communicating Key Audit Matters in the Independent Auditor's Report*
	This standard deals with the requirement of the auditor to detail those matters which were of most significance in the audit of the financial statements. These are matters which required significant auditor attention during the audit and might include such issues as areas of significant risk, areas which are susceptible to material uncertainty or material areas where a significant amount of management and auditor judgement had to be exercised.
ISA 705	*Modifications to the opinion in the Independent Auditor's Report*
	The revision discusses the form and content of the audit report when a modification is considered necessary.
	The auditor should express an appropriately modified opinion when:
	• they conclude that, on the basis of evidence obtained, the financial statements as a whole are not free from material misstatement; and
	• they are unable to obtain sufficient appropriate evidence to conclude that the financial statements as a whole are free from material misstatement.
	When the auditor expects to modify their opinion they should communicate to those charged with governance, explain the circumstances behind the decision and the proposed wording of the modification.
ISA 706	*Emphasis of matter paragraphs and other matter paragraphs in the Independent Auditor's Report*
	This standard deals with those additional communications in the auditor's reports that do not affect the wording of the audit opinion, namely the 'Emphasis of matter' and 'Other matter' paragraphs and which are not otherwise disclosed as Key Audit Matters under ISA 701.
	The standard clarifies the purpose of these paragraphs:
	• 'emphasis of matter' paragraph: this is required to refer to a matter appropriately presented or disclosed in the financial statements that, in the auditor's judgement, is fundamental to the users' understanding of the financial statements but which is not determined to be a Key Audit Matter; and
	• 'other matter' paragraph: this is required to refer to a matter not presented or disclosed in the financial statements that, in the auditor's judgement, is relevant to the users' understanding of the audit, the auditor's responsibilities or the audit report.
	Once again, if the auditor expects to include such additional matters in their audit report they must communicate the fact, and an example wording, to those charged with governance.

ISA 710	*Comparative information–corresponding figures and comparative financial statements* This standard on auditing deals with the auditor's responsibilities relating to comparative information in an audit of financial statements. When the financial statements of the prior period have been audited by a predecessor auditor or were not audited, the requirements and guidance in ISA 510 regarding opening balances also applies. The auditor shall determine whether the financial statements include the comparative information required by the applicable financial reporting framework and whether such information is appropriately classified. For this purpose, the auditor shall evaluate whether: (a)　the comparative information agrees with the amounts and other disclosures presented in the prior period or, when appropriate, have been restated; and (b)　the accounting policies reflected in the comparative information are consistent with those applied in the current period or, if there have been changes in accounting policies, whether those changes have been properly accounted for and adequately presented and disclosed.
ISA 720	*The auditor's responsibilities relating to other information* This standard deals with the auditor's responsibilities relating to other information in documents containing audited financial statements and the auditor's report thereon. In the absence of any separate requirement in the particular circumstances of the engagement, the auditor's opinion does not cover other information and the auditor has no specific responsibility for determining whether or not other information is properly stated. However, the auditor reads the other information because the credibility of the audited financial statements may be undermined by material inconsistencies between the audited financial statements and other information.

There are two additional ISAs which are not considered as part of this book as they apply to very specific situations. These are:

ISA 800 *Special Considerations—Audits of Financial
Statements Prepared in Accordance with
Special Purpose Frameworks*

and

ISA 805 *Special Considerations—Audits of Single
Financial Statements and Specific Elements,
Accounts or Items of a Financial Statement.*

They do not deviate from the general application of ISAs but apply them to very specific circumstances.

Appendix 2

AUDITING PRACTICE NOTES ISSUED BY THE FINANCIAL REPORTING COUNCIL

PN 10 (Revised)	Audit of Financial Statements of Public Sector Bodies in the United Kingdom (Now issued by the Public Audit Forum)
PN 11	The Audit of Charities in the United Kingdom (Revised) *March 2012*
PN 12 (Revised)	Money laundering – Guidance for auditors on UK legislation *September 2010*
PN 14	The Audit of Housing Associations in the United Kingdom (Revised) *January 2014*
PN 15	The Audit of Occupational Pension Schemes in the United Kingdom (Revised) *January 2011*
PN 19	The Audit of Banks and Building Societies in the United Kingdom (Revised) *March 2011*
PN 21	The Audit of Investment Businesses in the United Kingdom (Revised) *December 2007* *(Paragraphs 180-263 and Appendices 1.1 and 2 are superseded by Client Asset Assurance Statement)*
PN 22	The Auditors' Consideration of FRS 17 'Retirement Benefits' – Defined Benefit Schemes *April 2002*
PN 23 (Revised)	Special Considerations in Auditing Financial Instruments – *July 2013*
PN 24	The Audit of Friendly Societies in the United Kingdom (Revised) *July 2011*
PN 25	Attendance at Stocktaking – *February 2011*
PN 26 (Revised)	Guidance on Smaller Entity Audit Documentation – *December 2009*

Note: *For some of these there are Northern Ireland equivalents not shown.*

Appendix 3

KEY ACCOUNTING RATIOS FOR ANALYTICAL REVIEW

PROFIT RATIOS

Gross profit ratio

$$\frac{\text{Gross profit} \times 100}{\text{Turnover}}$$

This is one of the most useful ratios as it represents the profit made by the organization from selling its goods and services excluding indirect costs. If the organization's pricing structure and type of customer base remain consistent this margin should remain reasonably constant whatever the level of activity, i.e. if sales double the cost of sales should also rise proportionally so the margin will remain the same despite the increase in activity. It includes the levels of turnover and inventory. Significant fluctuations in this ratio may indicate areas where additional audit work could be required.

Net profit margin

$$\frac{\text{Profit before interest and tax} \times 100}{\text{Turnover}}$$

This represents the profit on business activities after taking account of expenses. The points made above concerning the gross profit margin apply equally to this ratio.

ASSET AND LIABILITY RATIOS

These show aspects of the Statement of Financial Position assets and liabilities and can highlight changes in operational practice, such as worsening credit control, as well as providing indicators or audit areas warranting investigation. Key ratios are:

Current ratio

$$\frac{\text{Current assets}}{\text{Current liabilities}}$$

The current ratio measures the ability of the organization to meet its immediate liabilities. It is a ratio of liquidity and a ratio greater than 1 indicates that liabilities can be covered through realization of current assets. This ratio must be reviewed in relation to those ratios related to other elements of current assets and liabilities.

Quick ratio

$$\frac{\text{Current assets} - \text{Inventories}}{\text{Current liabilities}}$$

This ratio is another liquidity ratio but this excludes Inventories. The logic behind this is that, in a crisis, receivables and cash are more liquid than inventories which have to be sold and the cash collected before liabilities can be met. It measures the ability of the organization to meet its current liabilities out of liquid resources.

Inventory turnover

$$\frac{\text{Cost of goods sold}}{\text{Average inventory}}$$

This represents the number of times the inventory is turned over in the period. This is important as money tied up in inventory is not able to be used for anything else so, broadly, the more frequently it is turned over (into receivables and cash) the better.

Inventory days

$$\frac{\text{Closing inventory} \times 365}{\text{Cost of sales}}$$

This represents the inventory turnover ratio expressed as days. The formula can also be written as:

$$\frac{365}{\text{Inventory turnover}}$$

In commercial terms this ratio is relevant because days in inventory represents money tied up but also increases the risks of obsolescence, damage and storage costs.

Receivables days

$$\frac{\text{Trade receivables} \times 365}{\text{Credit sales}}$$

This ratio records the number of days it takes the organization, on average, to collect its trade debts.

Payables days

$$\frac{\text{Trade payables} \times 365}{\text{Cost of sales}}$$

This represents the number of days the organization takes to pay its trade payables. A reduction in this ratio, without a concomitant reduction in cash balances or receivables days (see above), may indicate that debits to trade payables represent non-cash transfers such as the write off of expenses from the Statement of Comprehensive Income to the Statement of Financial Position. In any case it would require investigation.

FINANCING RATIOS

These relate to the financing of the business. Key ratios are:

Debt/Equity (Leverage or Gearing) ratio

$$\frac{\text{Total debt}}{\text{Total equity}}$$

This ratio represents the proportion of the business funded by debt compared with shareholder's equity. There are many variations on this ratio which tend to centre around the definition of debt so one basis should be adopted and used consistently. It can include all liabilities including trade payables and overdrafts. This ratio should be reviewed in conjunction with any increases in trade payables.

Return on capital employed

$$\frac{\text{Profit before interest and tax} \times 100}{\text{Total assets} - \text{current liabilities}}$$

This shows the return earned by the business on the amount of capital employed in it. It should reflect the risk profile of the business, i.e. the greater the risks in the business the higher the return expected.

Glossary

Abbreviated accounts   A short form of accounts containing less than full disclosure which the Companies Act, 2006 permits small and medium sized companies and groups (as defined) to file at Companies House. The form and content of these accounts are set out in the Act.

Absorption costing   Basis of allocating overhead costs to products. Indirect costs are allocated to products based on an overhead absorption rate calculated from the total of overheads divided by a suitable unit of allocation, e.g. labour hours. The amount of labour hours involved in production of a product will thus attract a proportion of overhead.

Accountability   A principle of corporate governance which requires a board of directors, or those charged with governance, to take responsibility for actions with the obligation to report on the outcome of those actions.

Accounting records   The records of initial accounting entries and supporting records, such as cheques and records of electronic fund transfers; invoices; contracts; the general and subsidiary ledgers, journal entries and other adjustments to the financial statements that are not reflected in formal journal entries; and records such as work sheets and spreadsheets supporting cost allocations, computations, reconciliations and disclosures.

Accounting reference date   Date at which an accounting period for which statutory accounts have to be prepared and audited ends.

Accounting Standards Board   Body responsible for issuing accounting standards with the aim of establishing and improving standards of financial accounting and reporting, for the benefit of users, preparers, and auditors of financial information. This role is now taken by the Financial Reporting Council.

Accrual   An amount set aside for a specific liability, i.e. where the expenditure has been incurred in the period but for which no invoice has been received. The liability can normally be estimated with a reasonable degree of certainty and represents a known liability.

Adjusting events   Events which happened after the period end but which shed new light or provide new evidence on something which already existed at the date of the Statement of Financial Position.

Adverse opinion   Audit opinion in which the auditors state that the financial statements do not present a true and fair view of the financial position of the entity.

Agency theory   The principle whereby assets or productive resources owned by one party are managed by another. The theory holds that managers (agents) will tend to act in their own interests.

Analytical review procedures   Evaluations of financial information through analysis of plausible relationships among both financial and non-financial data. Analytical procedures also encompass such investigation as is necessary of identified fluctuations or relationships that are inconsistent with other relevant information or that differ from expected values by a significant amount.

Annual General Meeting (AGM)   Annual meeting of the shareholders at which the shareholders are called upon to approve the financial statements, elect directors and approve the appointment of auditors.

Annual report (and accounts)   The totality of the report sent to the shareholders including non-financial reports and publicity, etc. in addition to audited financial statements.

Assertions   Implicit statements made by management in preparing financial statements which state that the financial statements do not contain any material error or misstatements with regard to assets and transactions. It is the auditor's role to gather sufficient reliable evidence to confirm that the assertions are valid.

Associated company   Company which has at least 20 per cent of its shares owned by another company or over which another company has an influence amounting to some element of control.

Audit committee   Committee comprising non-executive directors which is responsible for liaising with internal and external auditors and communicating any relevant audit matters to the board of directors.

Audit planning memorandum   Document recording the audit planning process. It should be signed off by the audit partner after discussion with the audit team.

Audit programme   Checklist of detailed audit procedures to be carried out.

Auditor's report   Report made by the auditors on a set of annual financial statements prepared by the directors of an entity to be presented to the shareholders at the annual general meeting. The auditors are required to certify whether or not, in their opinion, the financial statements show a true and fair view of the company's financial position and if not, why not. The format of the report is set out in ISA 700 and the Companies Act, 2006.

Audit risk   The risk the auditors may sign an incorrect audit report by stating that a set of financial statements are true and fair when they are not.

Bannerman wording   Disclaimer introduced into Auditors' reports concerning the liability of auditors to third parties. Follows the decision in *Royal Bank of Scotland v Bannerman Johnstone Maclay (Scottish Court of Session) (2002)*.

Blockchain   A crowd managed secure encrypted database which enables the processing of transactions across a network which everyone connected to it can see. The netwok involves a chain of computers all of which must approve the transactions before it can move on. Transactions form a 'block' which moves along the 'chain' of computers.

Block sampling   Sampling technique which tests a majority of transactions for a single period, e.g. for one week or one month of the whole accounting period on the basis that this is likely to be representative of the entire period. This is not recommended as it does not test transactions throughout the whole period and thus cannot be a representative sample.

Business risk   The risks to the business arising from its everyday activities, the business environment in which it operates and the capabilities of its management. This is not the same as audit risk.

Cadbury Report   Report prepared by Sir Adrian Cadbury in 1992 entitled *The Financial Aspects of Corporate Governance* which forms the basis for the UK Corporate Governance Code.

CAVEBOP   Acronym for the audit of tangible and intangible assets comprising Cost, Authorization, Valuation, Existence, Beneficial ownership, Presentation.

Chain of evidence   Record of identification of evidence for use in criminal proceedings such that the use of the evidence can be traced throughout the course of the investigation and there is no question that it could have been tampered with in any way.

Cold review   A review primarily designed to ensure that the firm's policies and procedures have been complied with including reviewing auditor independence from the client and the quality of decision making in connection with audit issues.

Collusion   Situation where two or more individuals conspire together to circumvent internal controls with an intent to defraud the organization or misrepresent the financial statements.

Companies Act 2006   The basis for company law in the UK. It regulates the activities of companies, directors and auditors and sets out their respective duties and responsibilities.

Companies House   The main functions of Companies House are to:

- incorporate and dissolve limited companies
- examine and store company information delivered under the Companies Act and related legislation and
- make this information available to the public.

Comparative figures   Amounts for the previous accounting period shown as corresponding amounts to the amounts for the current financial accounting period.

Compliance testing   Testing of internal controls on a sample basis to confirm that the control is working effectively. These are tests of the control and individual transactions are not relevant for this purpose, merely as evidence of the functioning of the control.

Comply or explain   The provisions of the UK Corporate Governance Code and of UK GAAP have no statutory force. However reporting entities, particularly those whose shares are listed on the UK Stock Exchange, are expected to comply with their various provisions. If they are unable or unwilling to comply they should state the basis for noncompliance and their reasons in the financial statements. Any inadequate explanation for non-compliance is likely to result in the auditors reporting the non-compliance in their Auditors' Report.

Component (also component auditor, component materiality, etc.)   A subsidiary or related entity of a group of companies whose financial statements will be included in the consolidated financial statements.
Matters relating to components, e.g. component auditors.

Computer assisted audit techniques (CAATs)   Audit techniques involving computer software used to extract and analyse data.

Conceptual framework   Requirements based on a series of fundamental principles rather than detailed rules or regulations.

Conflict of interest   Can arise when auditors have a personal or professional involvement with a client which compromises their ability to behave impartially or where they are asked to act for both sides in a dispute.

Contingent liabilities   Liabilities which will only crystallize, i.e. become payable depending on the outcome of another event outside the organization's control, e.g. costs dependent upon the outcome of a court case.

Continuous inventory   Inventories are counted by the client on a continuing basis. Sample counts are made such that the whole of the inventory is counted at least once in a financial period. There is no formal inventory count where activity ceases for the duration of the count.

Control environment   The attitude and culture of the organization towards risk assessment and internal control.

Control objectives   The purpose for which internal controls are in place, e.g. to ensure goods are only sold to creditworthy suppliers, which is the control objective, companies institute credit control procedures.

Control procedures   Control procedures are the policies and processes implemented by management and staff to ensure that material errors are detected and that management's objectives are achieved.

Corporate governance   The processes of supervision and control intended to ensure that the company's management acts in accordance with the interests of shareholders. This includes the considerations of actions of directors, the composition of boards and the need for a sound internal control environment.

COSO   Formal system of internal control linking all components of internal control, the control environment, the risk management processes, the information system, control activities and the monitoring of controls into a formalized system. A process known as control and risk self assessment is often used to implement the COSO process.

CRSA   Control and risk self assessment - formalized approach to implementing the COSO principles requiring participation of parties connected to the risk assessment and internal control processes and a formal acknowledgement by managers that they have reviewed and monitored internal controls and risks.

Cryptocurrency   a means of exchange involving tokens denominated in specific sizes which is entirely internet based. One example of this is Bitcoin.

Cut-off   Audit procedures carried out at the period end designed to establish that the whole of a transaction has been recorded in the correct accounting period - the assertion of completeness. This is usually the case with inventories where tests are carried out to ensure that a payable exists for all items of inventory not paid for, thus ensuring that an asset and its associated liability are both included in the records.

Data analytics   The use of software to enable auditors to review, analyse and manipulate large volumes of data.

Detection risk   The risk that the auditors' own procedures will not detect a material error or misstatement.

Directional testing   Testing a population through an accounting system both from the accounting records to a sample of source documents (known as vouching) and from a sample of source documents to the accounting records.

Directors' report   A statutory report which must be included in the annual financial statements and which must contain, as a minimum, such matters as:

- the names of the persons who, at any time of the financial year, were directors of the company
- the principal activities of the company
- a business review

They must acknowledge their responsibility for preparing the accounts and confirm that they believe the company to be a going concern for the foreseeable future.

Disclaimer of opinion   Audit report wherein the auditors refuse to express an opinion on the truth and fairness of an entity's financial statements.

Dummy data (sometimes known as 'test decks')   Fictitious data used to test computer controls.

Duty of care   The obligation to exercise a level of care, as is reasonable in all the circumstances, in carrying out professional work in order to avoid loss to the party for whom the work is being performed.

Engagement partner   The partner or other person in the firm who is responsible for the audit engagement and its performance, and for the auditor's report that is issued on behalf of the firm, and who, where required, has the appropriate authority from a professional, legal or regulatory body.

Entity   A general term embracing all types of business, enterprise or undertaking including companies, charities, local authorities, government agencies, etc. Some are profit oriented and some are not.

Expectation gap   The difference between what auditors actually do and what the general public think they do. This includes a misunderstanding that auditors check all transactions and that their role is to find fraud.

Focus   The emphasis placed by management on the success of the enterprise.

Foreseeable future   A period of one year from the date of approval of the financial statements.

Fiduciary capacity   One, such as an agent of a principal, who stands in a special relation of trust, confidence or responsibility to others, in this case the shareholders. Directors are on trust to preserve the assets of the company and to make their best endeavours to trade for the benefit of the shareholders. They are in a *fiduciary relationship*.

FIFO   Basis of valuing inventory whereby inventory items issued out of stock are assumed to be the oldest first. Inventory items are valued at purchase cost such that the oldest items carry the lowest cost.

Financial Reporting Council   The UK's independent regulator responsible for promoting high quality corporate governance and reporting. It sets standards for corporate reporting and actuarial practice and monitors and enforces accounting and auditing standards. It also oversees the regulatory activities of the professional accountancy bodies and operates independent disciplinary arrangements for public interest cases involving accountants and actuaries.

Financial Services Authority   The regulator of the financial services industry in the UK. Its objectives are maintaining market confidence; promoting public understanding of the financial system; contributing to the protection and enhancement of the stability of the UK financial system; securing the appropriate degree of protection for consumers; and fighting financial crime.

Financial statements   Financial information presented in accordance with a relevant financial reporting framework usually comprising a Statement of Comprehensive Income and a Statement of Financial Position together with the associated notes. It may also include any additional information as required by the relevant standards such as information in respect of directors' remuneration or cash flows.

GAAP or UK Generally Accepted Accounting Practice (UK GAAP)   A summary of the best practice in respect of the form and content of financial reports. It provides recommendations as to accounting treatment and acceptable alternatives and regulates the form and presentation of financial reports in the UK. UK GAAP has no statutory basis but is observed on a 'comply or explain' basis (see above).

Going concern   The assumption that the entity will continue in operational existence for the foreseeable future. This is defined as a period of twelve months from the date of the financial statements (note *not* the period end).

Gross profit ratio (or gross profit margin)   Ratio showing gross profit or operating profit as a percentage of sales revenue.

Group accounts   Financial statements comprising the accounts of a holding company and its subsidiaries and other related entities.

Hot review   Review undertaken during the course of audit work, by a partner not connected with the audit, to ensure that all quality control procedures are being complied with and to review the basis of judgements, decisions made and the appropriateness of the draft audit opinion.

HMRC   HM Revenue and Customs - the UK taxation authority.

IDEA (interactive data extraction and analysis)   Modern form of audit interrogation software used by auditors to extract data from client's systems and sort and interrogate it. Replacing CAATs as the computer audit technique of choice.

Impairment   Reduction in the value of an asset due to damage, loss of market value or other reasons.

Imprest system   Method of controlling petty cash expenditure whereby the amount spent in the previous period is refunded so that the cash float remains at a constant amount. For example, if the cash float is £100 and £57.65 is spent in period 1 the amount of £57.65 is refunded to petty cash to bring the float back up to £100. The expenditure should be supported by authorized petty cash vouchers.

Independence   A fundamental principle of audit ethics. The auditor must be, and be seen to be, independent from their client at all times.

Inherent risk   Risks of a material error or misstatement arising from the nature of the organization, its culture or activities.

Integrity   Integrity requires not only honesty but a broad range of related qualities such as fairness, candour, courage, intellectual honesty and confidentiality. Integrity requires that the auditor is not affected, and is not seen to be affected, by conflicts of interest.

Interim audit   An audit visit made during the course of the accounting period in which audit testing of systems is carried out.

Internal audit   An audit function designed to improve and enhance corporate governance, risk management and internal control issues within the organization. Its scope is wider than that of external audit. It may be carried out by employees or may be outsourced. Internal audit is mandatory in the public sector.

Internal control   The process designed, implemented and maintained by directors, management and other personnel to provide reasonable assurance about the achievement of an entity's objectives with regard to reliability of financial reporting, effectiveness and efficiency of operations, and compliance with applicable laws and regulations. The term 'controls' refers to any aspects of one or more of the components of internal control.

Internal controls   The detailed controls within an accounting system which are designed to minimize the risk of a material error or misstatement going undetected. These primarily consist of segregation and authorization controls, arithmetic checks, physical controls over access to information and supervisory management overview.

Internal control questionnaire (ICQ)   A standardized checklist used for establishing the existence or otherwise of basic internal controls. These require 'Yes' answers to control questions.

Internal control evaluation questionnaire (ICEQ)   Questionnaire designed to establish the possibility of controls failing or being circumvented. This requires some experience and creativity and requires 'No' answers to questions.

International Auditing and Assurance Standards Board (IAASB)   Part of IFAC. Its role is to promote the harmonization of auditing standards by producing generic standards which can be adopted by local bodies and adapted for use in individual countries without losing sight of the essential requirements.

International Federation of Accountants (IFAC)   The global organization for the accountancy profession comprising most of the world's major accountancy bodies. Its role is to protect the public interest by:

- developing high-quality international standards
- promoting strong ethical values
- encouraging quality practice and
- supporting the development of all sectors of the profession around the world.

International Standards on Auditing   Statements issued by the Financial Reporting Council in the UK and Ireland regulating the conduct of an audit. They set out the audit objectives and define the scope of audit work and the methodologies to be adopted by the auditors to ensure that those objectives are achieved.

Joint and several   All partners in a partnership are jointly liable for all the liabilities of the partnership whether created through the actions of one individual partner or some or all of them.

Key fields approach   Approach to risk analysis in a computerized environment which analyses which operators can enter data into particular areas of the management information system. This identifies areas of vulnerability due to a lack of segregation of duties and highlights the danger of collusion.

Key performance indicators (KPIs)   Targets or objectives used to assess or measure performance against strategic goals or benchmarks.

Letter of engagement   Letter setting out the terms of the audit assignment addressed to the management by the auditor and countersigned by them. It sets out the respective responsibilities of each party and forms the basis of the contract between them.

Letter of representation   Letter prepared by the auditors for the management to sign. It reminds management of their responsibilities for the preparation of the financial statements and also contains a written confirmation of any representations made by the directors to the auditors.

Liability limitation agreement   Agreement made under Sections 534–538 CA 2006 whereby the shareholders approve a limit to the amount which could be claimed from the accounting firm in respect of a claim for negligence.

Management information system (MIS)   The information system used by the organization to produce financial and related information. It includes the financial accounting system together with costing and budgeting systems and often an executive reporting system to provide summarized financial and other information.

Management letter Letter to management detailing systems weaknesses and other matters revealed by the auditors in the course of their audit work.

Management override Situation where directors or managers override or bypass internal control procedures. This is a common problem in smaller entities but is also connected to management fraud where transactions are not processed through the normal routine accounting systems.

Materiality An item is material if its omission from or misstatement in a set of financial statements would change the economic decision of a user of those financial statements.

Material uncertainty Significant uncertainty relating to an event or condition that may cast significant doubt on the entity's ability to continue as a going concern.

Modified audit report Also known as a qualified report this is an auditors' report which contains a qualification or restriction of the 'true and fair' opinion, declines to express an opinion or disagrees with the directors' view that the financial statements are true and fair.

Monetary unit sampling (MUS) A sampling method which uses the cumulative value of transactions to establish the sampling interval.

Negative assurance Level of assurance less than positive assurance wherein reporting accountants state that there is no evidence to believe information is not true.

Non-adjusting events Events which happened after the period end but which do not affect the results of the accounting period. They may however require a note in the accounts.

Non-executive directors (NEDs) Directors of a company which do not have executive or management responsibility for the day-to-day running of the organization. They are there simply in their capacity as directors to provide advice and experience to the board.

Objectivity A state of mind that excludes bias, prejudice and compromise and that gives fair and impartial consideration to all matters that are relevant to the task in hand, disregarding those that are not.

Outsourcing Contracting out of services or functions which otherwise would be performed by organization employees, to third party suppliers.

Parallel simulations The auditor models the client's software on their own hardware and runs data through it to compare with the results from client processed data.

Pay as you earn (PAYE) A system of collection of tax from individuals by direct deduction from gross pay. This is collected by employers and remitted to HMRC without the individual taxpayer becoming involved.

Performance materiality A level of materiality set lower than the overall materiality level designed to ensure that the level of detected errors plus the possibility of undetected errors does not exceed materiality.

Permanent file File recording basic information about the client which does not change from year to year including constitution, board composition, activities, etc.

Pervasive An issue which is so material that it affects the truth and fairness of the financial statements as a whole.

Probity not merely the strict legal definition of compliance with laws and regulations but incorporates ideals of honesty, truthfulness and ethical behaviour in compliance with some form of moral code.

Population The volume of transactions or data set from which a sample is taken for testing.

Positive assurance Opinion given by an auditor in a report which makes a positive statement concerning the matters reported on. An auditor's report is a positive opinion report.

Postulate   A statement or assertion taken as self evident and not requiring proof. Used as a basis for discussion.

Principal auditors   Auditors of the holding company and other components of a group of companies and responsible for signing the audit report on the consolidated accounts.

Professional scepticism   An attitude that includes a questioning mind, being alert to conditions which may indicate possible mis-statement due to error or fraud, and a critical assessment of evidence.

Proper accounting records   Accounting records which are sufficient to show the financial position of the entity at any time. Minimum records to be kept are specified in the Companies Act 2006.

Prospective financial information   means financial information based on assumptions about events that may occur in the future and possible actions by an entity. It is highly subjec-tive in nature and its preparation requires the exercise of considerable judgment. Prospective financial information can be in the form of a forecast, a projection or a combination of both, for example, a one-year forecast plus a five-year projection.

Provision   A liability which exists but for which the amount or its timing is uncertain.

Proximity   A legal term defining the closeness of a relationship where one party might be rely-ing on another not to be negligent in carrying out their duties. Without a proximate relation-ship audit firms may not be liable to another party for negligent misstatements.

Public interest   Matters of public concern, not public curiosity where public has its ordinary meaning. Thus reporting acts or omissions by the organization which may affect the public in the immediate area or at large are an exemption from the normal duty of confidentiality.

Public interest entity (PIE)   Fundamentally listed companies, banks and insurance com-panies and entities in the public sector which are so designated because of their size and significance.

Qualified auditor's report   *See* Modified audit report.

Reasonable assurance   This is a high but not absolute level of assurance. It represents a level of assurance based on the gathering of sufficient reliable evidence that the statement an auditor makes as to the matter being reported on has a much greater probability of being true than not true. Such probability is not stated but could be as high as 95 per cent. It is something less than 100 per cent.

Reciprocal population   Generally the 'other side' of the double entry from the item being tested. For example the reciprocal population for receivables (debit) is sales (credits). Testing for under or overstatement of one item may lead to an under or overstatement of another.

Recognized supervisory bodies (RSBs)   A body established in the UK which maintains and enforces rules as to the eligibility of persons seeking appointments as statutory auditors and the conduct of audit work, rules which are binding on such persons because they are mem-bers of these supervisory bodies or subject to its control.

Registrar of Companies   The official who embodies Companies House. The main functions of Companies House are to:

- incorporate and dissolve limited companies
- examine and store company information delivered under the Companies Act and related legislation and
- make this information available to the public.

Regularity   Requirement of public sector financing that money is only spent for the pur-pose for which it was allocated or budgeted.

Related parties   Parties are related when one party has direct or indirect control over the other party; or the parties are subject to com-mon control from the same source; or one party has significant influence over the financial and operating policies of the other or the parties, in entering a transaction, are subject to influence from the same source to such an extent that one of the parties to the transaction has subordi-nated its own separate interest.

Residual risk   The level of risk which the organization is prepared to accept. This should be risks which have a low impact on the organization and/or a low probability of occurring.

Risk assessment   A review of the probability of events turning out other than in the way anticipated or planned for, due to events which could have been foreseen with proper planning and review.

Sampling risk   The risk that the level of errors in a sample used for audit testing is not representative of the population as a whole.

Sarbanes–Oxley (Sarbox)   The Sarbanes–Oxley Act (or 'Public Company Accounting Reform and Investor Protection Act') 2002 sets standards for all US public company boards, management and public accounting firms. It is the statutory basis for corporate governance for all US public companies or UK subsidiaries of US public companies.

Service Level Agreement   An agreement between a provider of services and a client setting out the nature, timing and quality of service to be provided in return for a chargeable fee.

Service organization   A third-party organization (or segment of a third-party organization) that provides services to user organizations which are part of those entities' information systems and are relevant to financial reporting.

Significant deficiency   Deficiency (control weakness) or combination of deficiencies in internal control that, in the auditor's professional judgement, is of sufficient importance to merit the attention of those charged with governance.

SOAPSPAM   Acronym recording the types of internal control, i.e. Segregation of duties, Organization, Authorization, Personnel, Supervision, Physical, Arithmetical, Management.

Special purpose vehicle   A legal entity (usually a limited company of some type or, sometimes, a limited partnership) created to fulfil narrow, specific or temporary objectives. These are often used in connection with fraudulent accounts manipulation to create fictitious transactions or to hide losses.

Stratified sampling   The population is stratified into layers by transaction size. The largest transactions receive the greater amount of audit testing as these are most likely to be material.

Stakeholders   Groups or individuals having an interest in the activities or financial performance of an entity.

Statement of comprehensive income   Formerly known as the profit and loss account. Recording the profit or loss made by an entity based on its activities within a financial accounting period.

Statement of financial position   Formerly known as the balance sheet - records assets and liabilities of an entity at the end of a financial period.

Statutory audit   An audit as required by the Companies Act 2006 of a company whose results are above the statutory audit threshold.

Statutory auditor   Individual accredited by a recognized supervisory body to carry out audits under the Companies Act 2006.

Statutory audit threshold   The Companies Act 2006 established the size and level of activity above which a company must have a statutory audit. Currently the limits for smaller companies are - Turnover of £6.5m, Net assets of £3.26m and employing more than 50 people. If a company fulfils two out of three of these criteria it must have an audit.

Statutory books   Records required to be kept by the Companies Act 2006 including a register of shareholders, a register of directors, minutes of meetings, etc.

Subsequent events   Events after the date of the financial statements.

Subsidiary company   Company which has more than 50 per cent of its shares owned by another company or over which another company has control.

Substance over form   An accounting and auditing principle which concentrates on the nature of each type of transaction or activity rather than how it is described. The principle encourages the auditor to look past any superficial description of a transaction or series of transactions in an effort to see what they actually are rather than what they appear to be.

Substantive testing   Detailed testing of transactions and balances. In contrast to compliance testing the individual transaction is what is being tested.

Sufficient, appropriate   Usually used in connection with the gathering of audit evidence. Sufficiency is the measure of the quantity of audit evidence and appropriateness is the measure of its quality in respect of the matter being evidenced.

Support letter   Letter given by a holding company to an insolvent subsidiary which the holding company is financing declaring that it will subordinate recovery of its debt to that of third party creditors.

Systems-based auditing approach   An audit strategy whereby the auditor tests the internal controls within a client's system in order to ascertain whether or not reliance can be placed upon them.

Systems control audit review files (SCARF)   Audit files embedded in software processing routines providing continuous or on demand audit information.

TARA   Strategic approach to risk management - transfer, accept, reduce, avoid.

Teeming and lading   Form of fraud whereby receipts from customers are misappropriated and receipts from other customers are used to cover the theft. Usually detected when receipts from customers banked intact are shown as split between different accounts in the receivables ledger.

Theory of rational expectations   Auditing theory which holds that the value of the auditor's report derives from the expert nature of the auditor as an independent professional and as society's expectations of an audit change so must the role and function of the auditor.

Those charged with governance   Term used in ISAs to denote the person(s) with responsibility for overseeing the strategic direction of the entity and obligations related to the accountability of the entity. This includes overseeing the financial reporting process. For some entities in some jurisdictions, those charged with governance may include management personnel, for example, executive members of a governance board of a private or public sector entity, or an owner/manager.

Threshold amount   Level above which errors or misstatements cannot be regarded as trivial. Relates to materiality and performance materiality.

Tipping off   Offence under the Money Laundering Regulations 2007 whereby an individual or organization engaged in transferring or concealing the proceeds of crime is deliberately or inadvertently informed that a suspicious transactions report has been made to the Serious & Organized Crime Agency.

Tolerable misstatement   The maximum level of error in the population that auditors are willing to accept and still conclude that their audit objectives have been achieved. Analogous to performance materiality.

Tone at the Top   Management's leadership and commitment towards openness, honesty, integrity, and ethical behaviour. It is a most important component of the control environment.

Top down approach   Process of auditing using risk evaluations to assess the risk of a material error or misstatement going undetected. The process involves ascertaining the general or overall risk framework and then establishing organization specific risks which derive from the more general risks. This involves discussing issues with senior management.

Transnational audit   A transnational audit is an audit of financial statements which may be relied upon in more than one country or jurisdiction, for example for the purpose of lending or regulation.

Transparency Principle underpinning good corporate governance. It encompasses ideas of openness and willingness to communicate and as such encourages disclosures in excess of statutory minimum requirements.

True and fair Financial statements should be prepared in such a way that anyone reading them would gain an impression of the entity's financial performance. Generally, financial statements prepared under UK GAAP will show a true and fair view but as there may be matters of judgement involving the 'true and fair override' the terms should have their literal meaning as well as their technical one. True and fair does not mean 'accurate in all respects' or 'correct in every detail'.

True and fair override A situation which calls for a departure from the provisions of UK GAAP in order to show a true and fair view which more properly reflects the substance of transactions. Such departures must be properly disclosed and explained.

UK Corporate Governance Code A code of practice which is mandatory for all companies whose shares are listed on the UK Stock Exchange. It sets out good practice for directors in the areas of leadership, remuneration, performance monitoring and relationships with shareholders.

Walkthrough test A test designed to check whether a system has been properly documented. The auditor will trace three or four sample transactions through the accounting system to ensure that it has been documented correctly and that what has been recorded reflects actual activity.

VAT (value added tax) A sales tax which is charged on taxable supplies and is recoverable by entities in the supply chain. It is basically paid by the end user.

Value for money A public sector initiative designed to maximize the benefit from public spending by examining the economy, efficiency and effectiveness of processes and activities.

Vouching Testing entries in the accounting records with original or source documents, e.g. testing entries in a purchase journal or day book with purchase invoices.

Index